Thought and Knowledge:
An Introduction to Critical Thinking

Third Edition

Thought and Knowledge:
An Introduction to Critical Thinking

Third Edition

Diane F. Halpern
California State University
San Bernardino

LEA **LAWRENCE ERLBAUM ASSOCIATES, PUBLISHERS**
1996   Mahwah, New Jersey

Lawrence Erlbaum Associates
10 Industrial Avenue
Mahwah, New Jersey 07430

Cover design by Robert Perine

Library of Congress Cataloging-in-Publication Data

Halpern, Diane F.
      Thought and knowledge : an introduction to critical thinking / Diane
   F. Halpern. — 3rd ed.
      p.   cm.
      Includes bibliographical references and index.
      ISBN 0-8058-1493-0 (hard : alk. paper). — ISBN 0-8058-1494-9 (pbk. :
   alk. paper)
      1. Critical thinking. I. Title.
   BF441.H25 1995
   153—dc20   95-18970
                                                                 CIP

Books published by Lawrence Erlbaum Associates are printed on acid-free
paper, and their bindings are chosen for strength and durability.

Printed in the United States of America
10 9 8 7 6 5

To Sheldon, my husband, and
Evan and Jaye, my children,
for their support, encouragement, and love

Contents

Preface

Perhaps you have seen the advertisement that appears in many magazines and goes something like this: "The World's Greatest Literature Is Now Available on Audio Cassette." Like most Californians, in fact, most other large-city-dwellers and many rural and suburban folks, too, I have a very long commute to work. Although I love to read, I also enjoy listening to good books on tape as I crawl through "rush" hour traffic with a million other grumpy commuters. So, it is not surprising that I continued to read the smaller print below this large headline. Someone had selected the "100 GREATEST BOOKS OF ALL TIME" and made them available for purchase on audio cassettes. "Sounds good," I thought. But wait, it wasn't the original books that had been recorded onto tape, but a highly abridged version of these books. In fact, every one of "THE WORLD'S GREATEST BOOKS" was abridged so that actual listening time was less than 30 minutes per book! The advertisement ended by assuring readers/listeners that the audio company executives would never tell if we wanted to pretend that this fast-found wisdom reflected a doctorate in literature. In other words, after only 50 hours of fast-forward listening, I could fake a deep knowledge of fine literature.

I wondered who would purchase this microset of "literature for your listening pleasure." A few pages later in the same magazine, I found an advertisement for a series of "books" selected from the most important knowledge ever written on succeeding in business. Every one of these critically acclaimed (whatever that means) business books had been reduced to eight pages, for the "busy professional."

As I pondered this super-fast-track route to superficial knowledge, I began to look more closely at the other messages that bombard us everyday on billboards, television, and in our mailboxes.

I received an amazing offer in the mail. I "won" the right to purchase a beautiful "flawless CZ diamond simulant." Comparable items were priced at $3,559. The $19 purchase offer was certainly a substantial bargain.

With this bargain-of-a-lifetime still in my hand, I turned on the television.

Numerous celebrities were touting the many benefits of consulting with a psychic. In fact, television viewers were invited to phone their "own private psychic" for help with their personal and professional decisions. Apparently, many do. The psychic business must be booming because I also received an advertisement for a session with a private psychic over the Internet.

I know that most readers are thinking that these "silly" examples don't apply to them. Yet, statistics show that many of you start every day by consulting your horoscope, believe that bad (or good) things happen in threes, and can cite at least one instance in which you believe that you were psychic. At the same time that we are offered the thinnest veneer of knowledge, "genuine fake diamonds," and advice from paid strangers who have no training, the world in which we live is becoming increasingly complex. Computer monitors that can deliver massive quantities of information are almost as ubiquitous as television screens in middle-class households, news from the most remote regions in the world can be seen as it is happening, fluctuations in the Japanese yen or the Mexican peso affect prices in neighborhood supermarkets, and higher education is more important than ever before in determining the type of job at which we can work and the kind of life we will live. Simple answers, the appearance of knowledge, quick and slick fixes, and cunning scams seem to increase along with the increasingly rapid rate of change in what we need to know and be able to do to function and thrive in this age of information and technology.

There is one constant in the maelstrom of change—the ability to acquire knowledge and use it to think clearly about a myriad of complex issues is more important than ever before. How else can we decide if the "CZ diamond simulant" is a good buy at $19? (A "CZ diamond simulant" is a fancy term for a worthless piece of glass.) How can anyone believe that a "personal" psychic can help him find true love, make medical decisions, and guide his financial investments? There are so many important decisions and problems that everyone faces. How can an average person interpret the mixed and emotional research on the benefits of certain diets, the risk involved with radon exposure or electromagnetic fields, the costs and benefits of expensive medical screening tests (like mammograms), or think intelligently about the question of whether AIDS is really a major health threat or, as some have suggested, a government plot to kill off certain segments of the population?

As you are pondering these heavy issues, you can cheer up because there is good news. There is clear evidence that has held up over decades of replications showing that adults can improve how they think (e.g., Astin, 1977; Kitchner & King, 1981; Trent & Medsker, 1968). Ample evidence for this conclusion is provided throughout this book. For example, King (1991) and her colleagues have shown that adults can and do move from earlier stages of thinking in which they believe that everyone's opinions are equally valid and truth is relative to a more advanced stage of thinking in which they are able to make reasoned judgments about evidence and the nature of knowledge. Reflective judgment, the highest stage in this development sequence, is developed most effectively by educational experiences that are designed to foster intellectual growth. The purpose of the third edition of *Thought and Knowledge: An Introduction to Critical Thinking* is to provide knowledge about ways to improve the process of thinking and experiences in which to apply and hone critical thinking skills, while encouraging readers to value good thinking and make it a habit. And, not incidentially, I also want readers to enjoy the learning and thinking process.

I have lofty goals for every reader of this book. I want you to change in substantial and meaningful ways so that you think better after you have read this book and worked through the problems in the accompanying workbook. I want you to use the skills of critical thinking in all sorts of settings and in ways that will benefit you and others. If every reader changes how she or he thinks, just a little, then the cumulative effect will be greater than all of us. Just think what we can achieve.

If we all take even a small step toward better thinking, we can really shake things up.

ACKNOWLEDGMENTS

I have been fortunate in having the benefit of the opinions and thoughts of some of the finest minds in psychology. First and foremost, I thank all of the marvelous students who have used the first two editions of this book. Their questions and comments have shaped the third edition in several ways by pointing out those sections that needed to be clarified, suggesting where I should cut material, and convincing me of the need to write a separate exercise book so that the skills can be practiced with many different sorts of problems.

Several psychologists have given freely of their time and expertise to help make the third edition as clear and as accurate as possible. I sincerely thank Dale Berger at Claremont Graduate School, Steve Ceci at Cornell University, Carole Wade at Dominican College at San Rafael, and Linda Coodley at Napa Valley College for their helpful comments on sections of this edition. Larry Wagner at Claremont Graduate School patiently read and commented on every chapter, and numerous faculty from colleges all over the world have written and phoned me with their thoughts and comments over the 12 years since the first edition was published. My sincere thanks to all of you.

I also express my gratitude and admiration to the renowned San Diego artist and my good friend, Robert Perine, who created the cover for this book. His new interpretation of Rodin's famous statue "The Thinker" shows how the artist expresses his critical and creative thoughts in a nonverbal medium. I hope that you, the reader, find pleasure in this fine drawing.

ACKNOWLEDGMENTS FOR THE FIRST EDITION

Many people have assisted in the preparation of this book. Mr. Jack Burton, Vice President, Lawrence Erlbaum Associates, Inc., has guided me through the publication process with tact and wisdom. In the process, he has become an admired and respected friend. Dr. George Mandler at the University of California, San Diego, has read and reread the manuscript, offering expert advice and practical good sense. His wise counsel has been very much appreciated. My dear "aunt," Dr. Katherine D. Newman, now retired from the English Department at West Chester State College, has not only commented on the manuscript, offering helpful suggestions and corrections, but has also served as a life-long role model. She has influenced greatly the course of my life. Dr. Susan Nummedal at California State University, Long Beach, has afforded me the benefit of her expertise with helpful suggestions on the manuscript and has given me support and encouragement with this project. It is deeply appreciated. Dr. Dorothy Piontkowski at San Francisco State University provided several useful insights, especially on chapter 3, "The Relationship Between Thought and Language." I would also like to thank an "anonymous philosopher" for comments on the reasoning chapter. Ms. Sandi Guideman, production editor, deserves special thanks for all of her help in "pulling the book together" and contributing to its format.

The people most responsible for this text are my husband, Sheldon, and my children, Evan and Joan. Sheldon has read and commented on the entire manuscript, suffered through low points in the writing, encouraged me throughout this project and in almost every endeavor in my life. Evan and Joan have helped in numerous ways, but mostly by just being there and taking pride in my accomplishments. Thanks to all of you.

ACKNOWLEDGMENTS FOR THE SECOND EDITION

This book has benefitted greatly from the thoughtful comments of many wonderful colleagues. My sincere appreciation goes to Dr. Richard Block of Montana State

University, Dr. Gregory Kimble of Duke University, Dr. David Riefer of California State University, San Bernardino, and Dr. Robert Sternberg of Yale University. Their suggestions and insights have been invaluable. Thanks to all of you for sharing your time and thoughts with me and with the readers.

TO THE READER AND INSTRUCTOR

Be sure to get the workbook that accompanies this text. It is called *Thinking Critically About Critical Thinking.* It is filled with active learning exercises that provide the opportunity to apply the thinking skills that are presented in every chapter. A wide variety of everyday examples are used as a way of promoting transfer to real-world settings. It also has chapter objectives, opportunities for reflection, guidelines for writing papers, thoughtful questions, and more. It's sort of a workout program for your mind. Although I can't guarantee "brains of steel," your thinking and your understanding and knowledge of how you think should improve if you work your way through the exercise book.

There is also an Instructor's Manual with answers that is available to teachers who use this as a class text.

Diane F. Halpern

1

Thinking: An Introduction

Contents

Many people would sooner die than think. In fact they do.

—Bertrand Russell (quoted in Macmillan Publishers, 1989)

"Think about it!" How many times have you heard this phrase or said it yourself? Look around you. Watch a student solving a calculus problem, or a programmer "debugging" a computer program, or a politician arguing that the Strategic Defense Initiative will not work. Watch a child absorbed in a fairy tale, or an architect designing a skyscraper, or a senior citizen planning to live on a fixed income. What are they doing that makes their faces appear so serious, so quizzical—so much like the original interpretation of Rodin's famous statue, "The Thinker," which appears on the cover of this book? They are all "lost in thought," yet lost seems like a strange word to describe the process of thinking—maybe "finding knowledge in thought" would be a more appropriate phrase.

THE NEED FOR CRITICAL THINKING SKILLS

Although the ability to think critically has always been important, it is imperative for the citizens of the 21st century. For the first time in the history of the human race, we have the ability to destroy all life on earth. The decisions that we make as individuals and as a society regarding the economy, conservation of natural resources, and the development of nuclear weapons will affect future generations of all people around the world. We are also called upon to make decisions on a wide range of important local and personal topics. For example, in a recent election, voters had to decide if they favored or opposed an increase in property taxes, the construction of a canal that would divert water from one part of the state to another, mandatory AIDS testing for

GRIN AND BEAR IT   by Lichty & Wagner

"Fifty cents for my thoughts?"

criminals, and a rent control ordinance, in addition to deciding which candidate they preferred for diverse political offices including governor, state treasurer, county commissioner, and trustee of the local library system. Consumers need to decide if the nitrates in their hot dogs are carcinogens, if the public school system is providing an adequate education, and whether health plans that allow you to choose your physician are preferable to plans that do not allow this flexibility. Because every citizen is required to make countless important decisions, it may seem obvious that, as a society, we should be concerned with the way these decisions are made. Surprisingly, it is only within the last 10 to 15 years that educators, politicians, and the general public have begun to address this topic in a serious manner.

Most recently, the (U.S.) National Education Goals Panel recognized the need to ensure that college graduates have the knowledge and skills to enhance and sustain a strong global economy and to participate in the democratic process so that we can all enjoy a world of peace with adequate resources. One of the goals that they set for college graduates in the coming decade is: "The proportion of college graduates who demonstrate an advanced ability to think critically, communicate effectively, and solve problems will increase substantially" (National Education Goals Panel, 1991, p. 237).

Numerous national reports have shown that instruction designed to improve the thinking process is desperately needed. The United States has been described as a "nation at risk" because we are failing to provide students with the most essential component of education—instruction that fosters the development of the ability to think (National Commission on Excellence in Education, 1983). Steen (1987) summarized the results of an international study on mathematical reasoning with this ominous warning, "Indeed, as the 'back-to-basics' movement has flourished in the last 15 years, the ability of U.S. students to think (rather than to memorize) has declined accordingly" (p. 251). The Education Commission of the States reached a similar sobering conclusion in its 1982 report: "The pattern is clear: the percentage of students achieving higher order skills is declining" (cited in Baron & Sternberg, 1987, p. x).

International studies repeatedly paint a gloomy picture of the current status of critical thinking. Izawa and Hayden (1993) summarized the results from an international comparison in which the best students from the United States scored lower than the worst Japanese students in mathematical problem solving; abysmal results were also obtained for reading skills and knowledge of history. Neubert and Binko (1992), using data from a different study, concluded that only 39% of 17-year-olds can find, summarize, and explain information. And, in what may be the most horrifying tale ever told by the prolific science fiction writer, Isaac Asimov, he reported (1989) on the true state of scientific understanding and knowledge by Americans. In a telephone survey conducted by the Public Opinion Laboratory at Northern Illinois University, he noted, the researchers found that 20% of the more than 200 adults surveyed believe that the sun revolves around the earth. Why, asked Asimov, over 400 years since the scientific community agreed on the fundamental scientific fact that the earth revolves around the sun, are the vast majority of adults still unaware of a basic fact that is "taught" in grammar school science?

The depressingly long list of findings and reports by prestigious panels that conclude that many adults do not have adequate thinking and learning skills shows that it is time to stop issuing reports and time to start acting in ways that promote these skills.

The poor state of critical thinking is not restricted to the United States. Numerous other countries have recognized that the world community is growing smaller and the need for a citizenry that can think critically is imperative in every country. Such was the conclusion of a panel of experts on higher education that met in Mexico. They agreed that "the job of the university today is to turn out students who can think in a rapidly changing world" (De Lopez, 1992, p. B4).

If the conclusions of national and international study groups don't convince you of the need for critical thinking instruction, consider this: Most people will finish their formal education between the ages of 18 and 22. Today's young adults are expected to have the longest average life span in the history of the world, with most living into their 70s and many living into their 80s and 90s. We can only guess what life will be like in the years 2050 or 2060 or beyond, years that many of you who are reading this book will live through. One likely guess is that many of today's young adults will be working at jobs that currently don't exist and dealing with technologies that dwarf the imagination of present-day science fiction writers. What do they need to learn during their first two decades of life that will prepare them for their remaining 50+ years?

A forward-looking education must be built on the twin foundations of knowing how to learn and knowing how to think clearly about the rapidly proliferating information with which we will all have to contend. I have an inexpensive modem attached to my home computer that I can use to access virtually all of the research articles in a major university library, the contents of dozens of daily newspapers, airline flight schedules, several encyclopedia services, the Dow Jones Index, a pharmaceutical reference guide, college catalogues for thousands of colleges, government publications, movie reviews, and much more. All of this information is available in the comfort of my own home with only a few minutes of "search time" on the computer. The problem has become knowing what to do with the deluge of data. The information has to be selected, interpreted, digested, learned, and applied, or it is of no more use on my desk than it is on a library shelf. If we cannot think intelligently about the myriad issues that confront us, then we are in danger of having all of the answers, but still not knowing what they mean.

With this same modem, I can communicate almost instantly with people in all corners of the globe, and I can "talk" simultaneously with multinational groups via electronic bulletin boards and interest groups. Information can be sent at speeds that are faster than eye movements, but whether this and other new technologies are a boon or burden to humanity depends entirely on the presence of critical thinkers at both ends of these ultra-high-speed communication highways.

Despite what may seem to many to be an obvious need in higher education, it is only in recent years that educators have been concerned with designing educational programs to improve the thinking process. It's difficult to imagine any area where the ability to think clearly is not needed. Yet, few of us have ever received explicit instructions in how to improve the way we think. Traditionally, our schools have required students to learn, remember, make decisions, analyze arguments, and solve problems without ever teaching them how. There has been a tacit assumption that adult students already know "how to think." Research has shown, however, this assumption is not warranted. Psychologists have found that only 25% of first-year college students possess the skills needed for logical abstract thought—the type of thought needed to answer "what would happen if …" questions and to comprehend abstract concepts (McKinnon & Renner, 1971). The situation is succinctly summed up by Brock, formerly the Republican Party chairman and currently an international consultant, who, after reading a recent report on the low level of learning and thinking skills of college graduates, exclaimed, "It ought to terrify everybody" (quoted in Frammolino, 1993, p. A41).

Thought and Knowledge

This is a book about thought and knowledge and the relationship between these two constructs. It's about thinking in ways that allow us to use previous knowledge to create new knowledge. Everything we know, and everything everyone else knows—that is, all existing knowledge—was created by someone. When we learn Euclidean geometry, we are learning about knowledge created by the great mathematician, Euclid. Similarly, other eminent inventions and insights such as the wheel, shoes, video games, toilet paper, $E = mc^2$, and the "discovery" of America, all represent knowledge created by people. Knowledge is not something static that gets transferred from one person to another like pouring water from one vessel to another. It is dynamic. Of course, it's silly to think that we should all start from "scratch" and begin by re-creating the wheel. We build on the knowledge created by others to create new knowledge.

We also create knowledge every time we learn a new concept. The newly acquired information is used to construct our own internal knowledge structures. (*Knowledge structures* is a somewhat technical term used by cognitive psychologists to stand for all of the interrelated concepts that each of us has about different subjects.) Knowledge is a "state of understanding" that exists only in the mind of the individual knower (King, 1994, p. 16). It is something that we can share with others via communication. We use our existing knowledge when we receive new information in order to make sense of the new information; thus the acquisition of knowledge is an active mental process. Each individual builds "extensive knowledge structures" that connect new ideas to what is known so that knowledge is always personal and somewhat idiosyncratic. These knowledge structures or *schemata* are our personal internal representations about the nature of the world. When we recombine them in new ways with other schemata, we are creating new knowledge. This idea was expressed more eloquently by Resnick (1985) when she said: "Knowledge is no longer viewed as a reflection of what has been given from the outside; it is a personal construction in which the individual imposes meaning by relating bits of knowledge and experience to some organizing schemata" (p. 130).

A Working Definition of Critical Thinking

Although many psychologists and others have proposed several definitions for the term *critical thinking*, these definitions tend to be similar in content. Here is a simple definition that captures the main concepts: **critical thinking** is the use of those cognitive skills or strategies that increase the probability of a desirable outcome. It is used to describe thinking that is purposeful, reasoned, and goal directed—the kind of thinking involved in solving problems, formulating inferences, calculating likelihoods, and making decisions when the thinker is using skills that are thoughtful and effective for the particular context and type of thinking task. Other definitions include the notions that critical thinking is the formation of logical inferences (Simon & Kaplan, 1989), the development of cohesive and logical reasoning patterns (Stahl & Stahl, 1991), and careful and deliberate determination of whether to accept, reject, or suspend judgment (Moore & Parker, 1994). All of these definitions capture the idea of a mental activity that will be useful for a particular cognitive task.

The "critical" part of critical thinking denotes an evaluation component. Sometimes the word *critical* is used to convey something negative, as when we say, "She was critical of the movie." But, evaluation can and should be a constructive reflection of positive and negative attributes. When we think critically, we are evaluating the outcomes of our thought processes—how good a decision is or how well a problem has been solved. Critical thinking also involves evaluating the thinking process—the reasoning that went into the conclusion we've arrived at or the kinds of factors considered in making a decision. Critical thinking is sometimes called **directed thinking** because it focuses on obtaining a desired outcome. Daydreams, night dreams, and other sorts of thinking that are not engaged in for a specific purpose are not subsumed under the critical thinking category. Neither is the type of thinking that underlies our daily routinized habits, which, although goal directed, involve very little conscious evaluation, such as getting up in the morning, brushing our teeth, or taking our usual route to school and work. These are examples of **nondirected** or **automatic thinking**.

The focus of this book is on the development and improvement of those skills that characterize clear, precise, purposeful thinking. It is a practical book, based primarily on applications of cognitive psychology to memory, reasoning, problem solving, creativity, language, and decision making. Despite the fact that some critics have claimed that critical thinking is just a fad that will surely go out of style, it has a very long history in psychology and education. John Dewey, the pioneering American educator identified "learning to think" as the primary purpose of education in 1933. Besides, it is difficult for me to consider that the need to think well is a "passing fancy" that will soon be out of style, much like Rubik's cube, "big hair," and bell-bottom trousers.

Although psychology has been concerned with the way people think for much of its 100+ years of existence as an academic discipline, cognitive psychology, the branch of psychology that is concerned with thought and knowledge, has virtually dominated scientific psychology for the past 20 years. Cognitive psychologists have been concerned with learning about the skills and strategies used in problem solving, reasoning, and decision making and the way these abilities relate to intelligence. All of this interest in human thinking processes has given birth to a new area of psychology that has come to be known as **cognitive process instruction**. Its goal is to utilize the knowledge we have accumulated about human thinking processes and mechanisms in ways that can help people improve how they think. For example, by examining correct and incorrect responses in a variety of situations, psychologists have found that most people's spontaneous and intuitive approaches to problems are frequently wrong. Furthermore, they can often predict when an incorrect response will be made either because of the nature of the problem or because of biases that a problem solver may bring to the problem. This knowledge is already being put to use to solve a host of applied problems that range from providing military personnel with map-reading skills to designing "user-friendly" (easy to use) computer programs.

Changing How People Think: Should It Be Done?

We know that the average American, because of changes in the economy at home and abroad, will change work seven or eight times in a lifetime … If that is true, it is clear that we need an agenda as a people for lifetime learning.

— U.S. President Bill Clinton ("Clinton's Message," 1994, p. 6A)

The whole idea of influencing the way people think may seem somewhat scary. It suggests terms like *mind control* and *propaganda*, or perhaps even a "Big Brother," like the one in Orwell's chilling novel 1984, who knew what you were thinking. In reality, though, critical thinking is an antidote to the kind of mind control Orwell was worried about. Learning the skills of clear thinking can help everyone recognize propaganda and thus not fall prey to it, analyze unstated assumptions in arguments, realize when there is deliberate deception, consider the credibility of an information source, and think a problem or a decision through in the best way possible.

When I discuss the topic of critical thinking with students and other people I come in contact with, I am sometimes told that there is no such thing as critical thinking because different viewpoints are "all a matter of opinion" and that everyone has a right to his or her own opinion. They argue that a "better way to think" does not exist. I certainly agree that we all have the "right" to our own opinion, but some "opinions" are better than others. If, for example, you believe that heavy alcohol consumption is good for pregnant women, you had better be able to back up this belief with sound reasoning. (There isn't any.) (More precise definitions of the terms *opinion* and *belief* are presented in chapter 5.) The opposite belief, that pregnant women should drink very little, if at all, can be supported with carefully controlled laboratory studies that document the deleterious effect of alcohol on a developing fetus. Similarly, everyone has the right to believe in phenomena such as astrology and extrasensory perception, but there is no sound evidence to support these beliefs. All beliefs are not equally good.

Let's consider some examples of the need to think critically in a variety of contexts. A good place to start is with commercials. Sponsors pay substantial sums for the opportunity to persuade customers to purchase their products. An advertising campaign is rated as successful if more of the product is sold after the advertisement, and the additional sales more than cover the cost of the advertisement. One of my favorite examples is cigarette advertisements. As you undoubtedly know, every cigarette advertisement in the United States must carry a message like this one: "Warning: The U.S. Surgeon General has determined that cigarette smoking is dangerous to your health." It would seem that this message would conjure up visions of hacking coughs, stained teeth, and lung cancer, and thus reduce the effectiveness of any cigarette advertisement. To counter the surgeon general's warning, many cigarette advertisements show smokers in natural outdoor surroundings with crystal lakes, clear blue skies, and tall, green, pine trees. One cigarette advertisement reads, "Come to where the clean is." Another classic cigarette ad reads, "Alive with pleasure"—an attempt to counteract the association of smoking with premature death.

Have you ever stopped to consider the association of cigarette smoking and the beauty of an outdoor scene? Does cigarette smoking seem healthier when it is associated with beautiful people in beautiful settings? One brand of cigarettes is called Malibu. The advertisements depict the soft white sand and foamy blue ocean at Malibu Beach in California, which is probably the ultimate setting for "beautiful people." The beautiful setting that is brought to mind by the name of this brand of cigarettes is designed to counteract images of sickly people gasping under oxygen tents—a more probable associate of cigarette use.

Another example of the need for critical thinking comes from a conversation I once had with a cab driver. Our conversation got around to the way laundry products are advertised. He told me that he never paid any attention to advertisements and that they had no effect on his decision about which product to buy. He went on to say that he always buys the blue liquid detergent that is good at getting out "ring around the collar." Do you see the inconsistency in his statements? Although he believed that he was not allowing the advertising claims to influence him, in fact, they were directly determining his buying habits. I doubt if many people worried about "ring around the collar," "waxy yellow buildup" on their kitchen floor, "fresh-smelling carpets," or "soft elbows" before commercials told us that we were remiss and socially undesirable unless we attended to these details. The unstated assumption in these commercials is that the "problems" they raise (dark lines on the inside neck portion of shirts, or floors that aren't as clear as new ones) are important ones that can be remedied if you purchase the advertised products. The cab driver, for example, accepted the problem of "ring around the collar" as a valid concern and then purchased the advertised product without any conscious awareness of the ways his thoughts and behaviors had been influenced.

In a recent political campaign, one candidate told voters he was opposed to waste, fraud, pollution, crime, and overpaid bureaucrats. This speech was followed with loud cheering and applause. What's wrong with his speech? He never really said anything. I've never heard any candidate claim to be *for* waste, fraud, pollution, crime, or overpaid bureaucrats. Voters should have asked him to be more explicit about his goals, how he would accomplish them, and where the money would come from to finance his plans.

The following problem was posed to 9-year-olds in the United States: "Jason bought three boxes of pencils. What else do you need to know to find out how many pencils he bought?" (Solorzano, 1985). Only 35% of the youngsters realized that the missing information was how many pencils were in each box. Here is a problem that was presented to a large sample of 13-year-olds: "An army bus holds 36 soldiers. If 1,128 soldiers are being bussed to their training site, how many busses are needed?" (Chance, 1986, p. 26). Most of the students tested had no trouble carrying out the computations. The problem came in using the answer in a meaningful way. Many rounded the answer they received to the nearest whole number and concluded that 31 busses were needed. Others gave a decimal answer (31.33) or showed the remainder from their long division. The problem was not one of basic computational skills, but of thinking about the kind of answer that the problem required and using a strategy that was different from one that was taught in school, namely rounding "up" to the next highest whole number rather than rounding to the nearest whole number. Perhaps simple examples like this one provide the most convincing answer to the question of whether critical thinking should be taught. America's most precious commodity is thinking, educated adults. We must make this the goal of education.

EMPIRICAL EVIDENCE THAT THINKING CAN BE IMPROVED

Everyone agrees that students learn in college, but whether they learn to think is more con- troversial.

—Wilbert J. McKeachie (1992, p. 3)

If you've been thinking critically about the idea of improving how you think, then you've probably begun to wonder if there is any evidence that thinking can be improved. Although there has been some debate about whether it is possible to produce long-lasting enhancement in the ability to think effectively (Block, 1985; Bruer, 1993; Glaser, 1984; Halpern & Nummedal, 1995; Norris, 1992), we now have a consid- erable body of evidence that thinking skills courses have positive effects that are transferable to a wide variety of situations. Numerous qualitatively different forms of outcome evaluations for thinking courses have been conducted. Taken together, they provide substantial evidence for the conclusion that it is possible to use education to improve the ability to think critically, especially when instruction is specifically de- signed to encourage the transfer of these skills to different situations and different domains of knowledge. In fact, it is difficult to identify any aspect of critical thinking that could not be taught and learned. We learn mathematics in the belief that mathe- matical skills can be used in real-world contexts where they are needed; similarly, we learn writing and speaking skills in the belief that learners will use these skills when they write or speak in any context.

Here is a brief summary of some of the findings that support the conclusion that critical thinking skills can be learned in educational settings and later used in a variety of contexts:

1. A formal evaluation of a nationwide thinking skills program in Venezuela showed that students who had participated in classes designed for instruction in thinking skills showed greater gains in orally presented arguments and in answering open–ended essay questions than did a comparable control group (Herrnstein, Nickerson, de Sanchez, & Swets, 1986). This study is particularly notable because the oral arguments and writing samples were graded blind; that is, the graders did not know if the students they were assessing had received the thinking skills instruction or were in the control group. Results from this project show that the targeted thinking skills were transferred and used appropriately with novel topics.

2. Self-reports by college students show that the overwhelming majority believe that they have made substantial gains in their ability to think critically after completing a thinking skills course (e.g., Block, 1985). Students rate themselves higher on numerous self-report scales including the willingness to suspend judgment, ability to evaluate conflicting claims, use of likelihood and uncertainty, and utilization of numerous problem-solving heuristics such as working backward from the goal, eliminating useless information, and evaluating the credibility of an information source. Of course, believing that you have improved in the ability to think critically is not the same as actually demonstrating improvements in critical thinking, but at least student self-assessments are in agreement with other sorts of data.

3. There is also research showing that college students who take a course in critical thinking show substantial gains in standardized tests of intelligence (M. F. Rubinstein, 1980). Although there is ample reason to be skeptical about any claim that intelligence can be enhanced by a single course, this is an additional source of evidence that critical thinking courses can have positive effects.

4. Other researchers have documented the gains in adult cognitive development that was enhanced with a college-level critical thinking course (Fox, Marsh, & Crandall, 1983). Cognitive development was assessed with the measures that were devised by the famous developmental psychologist, Jean Piaget, which have become standards for marking cognitive growth. This is an impressive improvement in light of the finding that only 25% to 50% of first-year college students possess the skills needed for abstract logical thought when this ability is assessed with Piagetian measures (McKinnon & Renner, 1971).

5. A theoretically advanced means of assessing changes in thinking ability is to study how a body of knowledge is represented mentally. Although the theoretical rationale for this technique is beyond the scope of this book, the findings of these sorts of studies are easily comprehended. Schoenfeld and Hermann (1982), for example, found that when college students were taught general thinking skills, they demonstrated substantial improvement in problem solving relative to students who received more traditional instruction. In addition, these students organized their mental representation of the content matter in ways that were more similar to an expert's mental representation than a control group did.

6. Using a skills approach, Facione (1991) found that college students who received coursework in critical thinking scored significantly higher on a multiple-choice test of thinking skills than comparable students who had not taken such a course. Improvements on a different multiple-choice test were also documented with graduate-level college students by Lehman, Lempert, and Nisbett (1988). They concluded that training with general "rules" of thinking is generalized to other contexts. Similar conclusions were obtained from studies reported by Fong, Krantz, and Nisbett (1986) and Fong and Nisbett (1991), who summarized their studies this way: A series of studies show that thinking "can be improved by methods such as formal instruction" (p. 44).

7. In a strong test of whether adult students can learn thinking skills that they will use, Lehman and Nisbett (1990) examined the spontaneous transfer of thinking skills in an out-of-the-classroom, real-world environment. They phoned students at home several months after the completion of their coursework and posed questions under the guise of a household survey. For example, former students were asked to comment on the winning streak that a rookie ball player was enjoying. The former students recognized that a common statistical principle was at work in this example. Results were supportive of the idea that the students had learned and spontaneously used the thinking skills that had been taught in their college classes when the questions were asked in an ecologically valid setting (their own homes), with novel topics, several months after the semester had ended.

8. There are numerous other successful reports in a recent book edited by Nisbett (1993), which contains 16 chapters that show that rules of logic, statistics, causal deduction, and cost-benefit analysis can be taught in ways that will generalize to a variety of settings. Another collection of studies that document the positive effects of critical thinking instruction can be found in Bruer (1993). A similar conclusion about the positive effects of courses designed to promote critical thinking was reached in another independent review of the literature (Chance, 1986).

All of the diverse findings point to the same conclusion: College students can be taught to think more critically when they receive instruction that is designed for this purpose. Ideally, different subsets of the skills of critical thinking would be reinforced and practiced in every college classroom, so that students learn to recognize and transfer skills across contexts. The assessment studies that used comparison groups, however, suggest that gains are most pronounced when instruction is specifically designed for the promotion of critical thinking. Critical thinking does not automatically result as a by-product of standard instruction in a content area. A systematic educational effort to improve thinking is needed to obtain these positive effects (Baron, 1990). Critical thinking instruction needs to overtly and self-consciously focus on the improvement of thinking, and the learning experience has to include multiple examples across domains in order to maximize transfer.

Transfer of Training

Why Johnny can't read was one of the central questions raised about American education in the 1970s. Why Johnny can't think replaced it in the 1980s.

—A. L. Brown and J. C. Campione (1990, p. 108)

All of these studies that attest to the effectiveness of critical thinking instruction are studies of the generalizability or transfer of critical thinking skills. The real goal of any instruction to improve thinking is **transfer of training**. What I mean by transfer is use of critical thinking skills in a wide variety of contexts. The whole enterprise would be of little value if these skills were only used in the classroom or only on problems that are very similar to those presented in class. Ideally, critical thinking skills should be used to recognize and resist unrealistic campaign promises, circular reasoning, faulty probability estimates, weak arguments by analogy, or language designed to mislead whenever and wherever they are encountered. Critical thinkers should be better able to solve (or offer reasonable solutions to) real-world problems, whether it's the problem of nuclear war or how to set up a new video recorder. These skills should also be long lasting and useful for the many decades of critical thinking that most of us face.

Admittedly, these are lofty goals, but they are important ones. The best way to promote the kind of transfer I'm advocating is with the conscious and deliberate use of the skills that you learn in a wide variety of contexts. Students can actively enhance transfer by looking for instances that call for critical thinking skills and using them.

The problems and review exercises that are provided in the workbook that accompanies this text are designed to maximize transfer. A variety of different types of problems are presented about different topics. By working through these problems, you will increase the likelihood that you will recall and use the thinking skills that are presented in the text, in real life, when you really need them. There are many variables that affect how likely you are to transfer a thinking skill from one area of study to another, but we do know that transfer can and does occur (Klaczynski, 1993). Be sure to be on the lookout for other instances when these thinking skills are needed, and be sure to use them!

Exotic Learning

A sucker is born every minute.

—P. T. Barnum (cited in J. Bartlett, 1980, p. 460)

There are no quick and easy crash programs that will make you a competent thinker overnight despite some unscrupulous claims that you can think better instantly without really trying. One article in a supermarket checkout-line type "newspaper" claimed that pregnant women could make their as yet unborn children more intelligent by listening to fine music and reading classical literature during their pregnancy. Other ludicrous schemes for better thinking include breathing into paper bags and listening to subliminal tapes. A large-scale study by the National Academy of Sciences concluded that there is no scientific evidence to support the claim that biofeedback, "neurolinguistic programming," subliminal learning, or other commercial "super learning" techniques can improve your thinking (Gillette, 1987; Hostetler, 1988). In a second major study, the National Research Council (1994) found that there is no evidence to support claims that sleep learning is possible, even though most of us believe that it sure would be nice. A trip through most so-called "health food stores" will reveal a wide variety of products and pseudomedicines that claim or suggest that they can improve your memory, enhance your thinking, or do whatever else is desirable (e.g., make you thin, sexy, strong, and smart), although there is absolutely no valid evidence that any of these products can bring about their promised effects.

THINKING ABOUT THINKING

There are many different ways to conceptualize the thinking process. From the perspective of a neuropsychologist or biologist, thinking is the activation of groups of neurons. Other researchers have concentrated their studies on the medium of thought, that is the conscious and unconscious use of symbols, images, and words. Another approach is to conceptualize thinking as the flow and transformation of information through a series of stages. As I think about using the brain to study the way the brain works, I am reminded about a joke I once heard: A comedian commented that he never eats tongue, a common food in many cultures, because he wonders if the tongue he is eating is tasting him while he is tasting it. Similarly, I wonder if we can use the brain to reveal its own mysteries? I think that questions like these are best left for comedians and philosophers to ponder.

Thinking as a Biological Process

The brain exists in order to construct representations of the world.

—Philip Johnson-Laird (quoted in Restak, 1988, p. 235)

Researchers from many fields have spent their lifetimes trying to understand what people do when they think. Brain researchers are interested in understanding how the brain and other parts of the nervous system work. Every time you have a thought, feel an emotion, or receive information through your senses, your nervous system is involved. If you could examine your own brain, you would no doubt be surprised to find that it looks like a giant mushy walnut with the consistency of a soft-boiled egg. There is nothing in its appearance to even suggest that it is the foundation of human thought. Brain researchers study the brain in their attempt to unravel the mystery of the human mind.

The capacity of the human brain is awesome. "If each of the brain's 10 to 15 billion neurons is capable of only two states, on or off, the capacity of the brain would be 2^{10} billionth power. To write out this number at the rate of one digit per second would take ninety years" ("Footnotes," 1987, p. A2). Even if these figures are off by a few billion or so, it is clear that we each have some undeveloped potential. The human brain has remained essentially unchanged since the dawn of modern history, yet during that time humans have used this amazing mass to develop advanced technologies that include the ability to visit distant planets and have more than doubled the average expected life span. What has changed is "the information that is going into the brain and the processing it receives" (Machado, cited in Walsh, 1981, p. 640). It is the ability to learn and to think that has changed the world.

Although brain researchers have discovered fascinating links between the physiology and anatomy of the brain and intellectual skills, there is still much to learn. As a discipline, brain research is still in its infancy. Thus far, biologists have discovered that factors like malnutrition, lead poisoning, and some drugs can impair the capacity for higher level thought. Current science fiction notions about brain transplants, pills to make us smarter, or miracle foods that prolong neural life remain in the realm of late-night movies and Saturday afternoon matinees.

Thinking as Imagery and Silent Speech

Thinking is the talking of the soul with itself.

—Author Unknown
(Found in a Fortune Cookie)

Psychologists at the beginning of the century believed that thinking was composed of mental images. Later, other psychologists hypothesized that thinking was simply a form of "silent speech," much like talking to yourself without vocalization. In order to test these hypotheses, psychologists would ask subjects to describe what they did when responding to certain questions. Let's try some examples. As you answer each of the following questions, try to be aware of what you did when you "thought about it."

1. How many windows are in your living room?
2. What does your mother look like?
3. What letter comes after N in the alphabet?
4. Name a word that rhymes with *shoe*.
5. How much is 2 + 3?
6. Can you define critical thinking?

As you answered these questions, were you aware of the use of images and/or words? Most people find that when they are asked to describe some concrete object, like the number of windows in their living room or their mother, they are aware of picturelike images. In fact, it seems almost impossible to answer these questions without generating an internal representation or utilizing **imagery** in some way. Can you describe your mother or anyone else without creating an image? Questions like 3 or 4, which involve the order of letters in the alphabet and the sounds of words, usually require an individual to recite the items silently. (Did you sing "l-m-n-o-p" to yourself in order to answer Question 3?) When answering questions like 5 and 6, people are often unable to say how they arrived at an answer. (By the way, if your answer to Question 6 was "no," you should go back and reread the beginning sections in this chapter.) Most people feel that the answers just seemed to "pop into their heads" without their being conscious of the "medium" or "stuff" of thought.

Currently, research psychologists are debating whether the "true" medium of thought involves imagery, or sentence-like propositions, or both. For most people, the question is moot, as almost everyone reports that, at least under some circumstances, they are aware of both mental images and "silent speech" during the thought process. Most of the time, however, we have little or no conscious awareness of what happens when we think.

Sometimes, thinking can be improved if we "work at" generating an image or using speech-like thought. Albert Einstein often credited his ability to solve difficult problems

THE FAMILY CIRCUS.   **By Bil Keane**

12-2

Copyright 1982
The Register and Tribune
Syndicate, Inc.

"Thinking is when the picture is in your head
with the sound turned off."

to his extensive use of imagery. The most famous use of imagery was recorded by the chemist Kekulé. He knew that if he could understand the structure of a benzene molecule he would have hit upon one of the most important discoveries in organic chemistry. Kekulé knew that most chemical molecules are long strands of atoms, and that the structure of a benzene molecule had to be different. In order to solve this problem, Kekulé practiced generating visual images that might help him to find the right one. His hard work was rewarded when the historic answer came to him this way:

> Again the atoms were gamboling before my eyes ... My mental eye ... could now distinguish larger structures ... all twining and twisting in a snakelike motion. But look! What was that! One of the snakes had seized hold of its own tail, and the form whirled mockingly before my eyes. As if by a sudden flash of lightning I awoke. (Kekulé, quoted in Rothenberg, 1979, pp. 395–396).

The image of a snake biting its own tail led Kekulé to the discovery that the benzene molecule was structured as a closed ring and not like strands of the other molecules. Thus, he was able to use visual imagery to direct his thoughts about a complex topic.

Words also serve to direct and stimulate thought. Although it may be obvious that thoughts are usually communicated with language, it is also true that language helps to generate thoughts. The generative role of language can be seen in an experiment by Glucksberg and Weisberg (1966). They used a classic problem in the psychology literature that was originally devised by Duncker (1945). In this problem, subjects are required to attach a candle to a wall so that it could be lit. They are given a candle, a box of matches, and some thumbtacks. Stop now and think how you would go about solving this problem if you were given only these materials (see Fig. 1.1). Don't go on until you've thought about it.

The best solution is to dump the matches from their box, tack the box to the wall, and set the candle in the box. Most subjects have difficulty with this task because they fail to think of the box as part of the solution—they see it only as a "box of matches." Glucksberg and Weisberg (1966) had people solve this problem under one of two conditions. The items were either labeled (*box, tacks, candle,* or *matches*) or they were not labeled. Subjects in the labeled condition solved the problem in about 1 minute, whereas those in the unlabeled condition took an average of 9 minutes. The labels directed attention to the relevant items and changed how the subjects in the first group solved this problem.

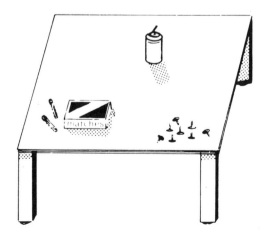

FIG. 1.1. Using only the materials shown in this figure, how would you attach the candle to the wall so that it can be burned?

Let's consider a somewhat different example of the way language directs thought. There is a popular riddle that goes something like this:

> A young boy and his father went for a Sunday drive. A drunken driver swerved in front of their car, killing the father on impact. The young boy was rushed to the nearest hospital where the chief of neurosurgery was summoned to perform an operation. Upon seeing the boy, the chief of neurosurgery cried out, "I can't operate on him, he's my son!" How is this possible?

When I've posed this riddle to students, they have sometimes replied: "The chief of neurosurgery is the boy's stepfather"; "The real father didn't die"; or "It's impossible." Have you guessed the correct answer? The answer is that the chief of neurosurgery is the boy's mother. The reason for the difficulty is that in our society, when we hear terms like "chief of neurosurgery" we tend to consider only males. The words we use can determine the kinds of thoughts we think. (This concept is developed more fully in chapter 3.)

Have you ever listened to two professionals in the same field discussing their work? Most professionals have highly developed specialized terms to communicate their thoughts. Often, these specialized terms also serve to guide the way the professionals think:

> How did the surgeon acquire his knowledge of the structure of the human body? … It has taken hundreds of dissections to build up the detailed and accurate picture of the structure of the human body that enables the surgeon to know where to cut. A highly specialized sublanguage has evolved for the sole purpose of describing this structure. The surgeon had to learn this jargon of anatomy before the anatomical facts could be effectively transmitted to him. Thus, underlying the "effective action" of the surgeon is an "effective language." Learning this anatomical language was a prerequisite to the transmission of the factual information that is needed here for effective action. (Bross, 1973, p. 217)

As this author pointed out, technical jargon not only facilitates communication among professionals, it is an inherent part of the development of ideas in a specialized discipline. As you see, later, I stress the learning of specialized terms in every chapter in this book because the terms carry much of the meaning that is being conveyed.

The use of jargon can serve as an efficient shorthand for communication among professionals. Specialized terms, however, can also serve as a barrier that keeps laypersons from understanding. Have you ever gone to a physician and found you were unable to communicate with her because you didn't understand the technical terms she used? A physician with a clear understanding of the problem should be able to communicate the nature of your problem in plain language. Beware of anyone who scatters terms indiscriminately or uses them as labels for simple phenomena.

A friend of mine once went to an allergy specialist who, after extensive tests, announced that my friend had "chronic rhinitis." Although my friend found this diagnosis alarming, with further questioning, she learned this means "runny nose"—a diagnosis she could have made by herself.

Preferred Modes of Thought

Even though most people report that they are aware of the use of imagery and silent speech, at least some of the time, there is good evidence that individuals have **preferred modes of thought**. That is, some people seem to think more fluently or easily with one of these types of internal representation than the other. Suppose that I were giving you

Driving Directions:

1. Take Embarcadero Road exit from the Bayshore Freeway.
2. Make a right at the exit (South) and continue straight for approximately 2 miles.
3. When you cross El Camino Real the street name changes to Galvez Street. Continue on Galvez to the next large street, which is Campus Drive.
4. Make a left on Campus Drive. (This is a curvy street. Follow it around as it curves to the right.)
5. Make a right onto Mayfield Avenue.
6. Take the first right, which is Lagunita Drive.
7. Park in the second lot on the left.

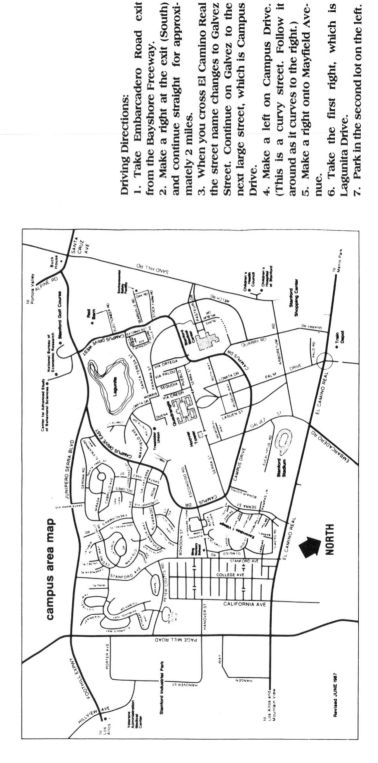

FIG. 1.2.   Preferred modes of thought. Consider the map and the verbal driving directions presented above. If you had to choose between these two information formats, which would you prefer?

directions to a building on a college campus. Consider the two types of directions shown in Fig. 1.2. Do you prefer the map, which conveys information in a spatial array, or the verbal directions (e.g., "Take the second left after you pass Lake Avenue")? There also seem to be individual differences in preferred sensory modes. Some students report that they comprehend difficult material best when they read it; others prefer to listen to difficult material.

There is more than just anecdotal evidence in support of the notion that people have preferred modes of thought. Gardner (1983) provided considerable evidence for the concept of "multiple intelligences." There is abundant evidence that some people prefer to think "spatially" whereas other prefer a verbal mode of thought (Clarkson-Smith & Halpern, 1983; Halpern, 1992). For example, college students with low verbal ability performed much higher on their tests when they were instructed with a knowledge map, which is a spatial representation of information, than when they were instructed in the usual manner that relies more heavily on verbal skills (Patterson, Dansereau, & Wiegmann, 1993). There are also some tasks that are particularly well suited for a particular thinking mode. Imagery, for example, is usually a better strategy when dealing with spatial problems like those commonly encountered in geometry, the building trades, and architecture. Deliberately switching from one mode to another is often a critical thinking strategy. I return to this notion several times throughout this book. I suggest that you write out in words the procedures and solutions to mathematics and science problems and use imagery and spatial techniques when comprehending complex prose. Comprehension and problem solving can often be enhanced with the deliberate use of different thinking modes. Even if you are particularly proficient with one mode, it is good to develop less preferred modes as well.

Thinking as Human Information Processing

A currently popular approach to understanding human thought utilizes computers to model the ways humans think. One approach that psychologists and others concerned with computer models of thought (engineers, linguists, medical personnel) have taken is to program a computer so that the processes and strategies it uses in solving a problem are similar to those used by humans. Thus, programs are written that can simulate or imitate human thought. This approach is called **computer simulation.** One problem with this approach is that we need to have very good ideas about the ways humans think in order to tell a computer to do it the same way.

One way of finding out how people think is to ask them to say out loud everything that they consciously thought about as they solved a problem. In this way, experimenters collect **thinking aloud protocols,** which are verbatim records of what the subject says he is doing while working on a problem. We have already tried something like this earlier in the chapter, using very simple questions. Let's try it with a more complex problem. As you work through this problem, say out loud every thought you have while working on the problem. It's important that you try to say all of your thoughts out loud. Your false starts, mistakes, repetitions, and so on, are all valuable in understanding how you think.

Here's the problem: Your friend has invited you to a birthday party. She has a square cake that she wants to share equally among the seven guests and herself. Using only three cuts with a knife, how would you cut the cake into eight equal slices?

Stop now, and recite out loud how you would go about solving this problem. If you have a tape recorder available, tape your think-aloud protocol so that you can analyze the thought processes you reveal in the protocol when you're finished. If you don't have a tape recorder, find a friend who is willing to take detailed notes of what you're saying. This gives you the added advantage of having someone with you to discuss your thinking process.

It's important to stop here and say out loud what you're thinking as you go about trying to solve this problem. If you go on reading before you've tried to think aloud, you don't get to eat any of the cake.

Most people find that they try several combinations of three slices before they hit upon the correct answer or give up. Imagery is often useful as you try to think about solutions to this problem because of the spatial nature of the problem. (The correct answer involves slicing the cake into quarters with two cuts, then placing the cake on its edge and slicing through the middle of the cake.) After collecting data from many subjects, a computer can be programmed (given a set of instructions in a computer language) to "think" about similar problems the way people do. If the simulation is successful, then the computer would also make the same mistakes that people make. Now that you have gotten the idea of thinking aloud protocols, try it again with the next problem: "Given Jug A, which contains 9 quarts; Jug B, 42 quarts; and Jug C, 6 quarts, measure out exactly 21 quarts" (Hayes, 1982, p. 65).

Stop now, and verbalize aloud how you go about solving this problem. Be sure to say everything that you're thinking, even if it doesn't seem relevant. As before, you'll find the process more interesting if you can tape your responses so that you can review them later. Don't go on until you've tried to solve this problem.

Compare your protocol with the one presented here. Did you try the same problem-solving strategy used by the 37-year-old lawyer who answered this way?

> OK, I want to, uh, see what is the highest number that will go into 21, of those 3 numbers. A, B, and C ... 42 is too high, uh, 9 will go into 21 twice ... and leaves a remainder of, uh, 3 ... that doesn't work, uh ... I, uh, will then take 6; 6 will go into 21, 3 times ... that's no good; it leaves a remainder of 3 ... If I make it twice, that's 12; that will leave a remainder of 9 quarts and I can use A. That's 9 quarts, so I've got two of the Cs, the 6 quarts, and one of the As. That's 9 quarts.

Sometimes these attempts to describe the thinking process are written out instead of being said aloud, and then subjected to **thought protocol analysis.** In thought protocol analysis, the protocol is broken down into segments so that each segment can be analyzed separately. Sometimes psychologists have theories about the processes involved and try to confirm or disconfirm them with the protocol. Other times, the purpose of the analysis is exploratory.

Thought protocols have proven to be useful in both understanding thinking processes and improving them. Thomas Good, an authority on research in mathematical education, has found that mathematics students learn best when teachers actively work with them and model out loud the problem-solving process. It seems that when teachers think out loud they provide "a structure and a way of thinking about the information ... so [students] can better understand relationships" (Cordes, 1983, p. 7). One way to improve thinking is to analyze the thought protocols of experts and then model your own thinking processes after them. This modeling technique has been found to be a useful aid in developing the thinking processes of novices. It is also useful to examine these records of your thinking in order to identify problems such as the failure to consider certain types of information or other slips. When people practice thinking aloud, they learn to work systematically, without jumping ahead and guessing. The process of verbalizing thoughts encourages thinkers to evaluate their strategies and strengthens communication skills (Narode, Heiman, Lochhead, & Slomianko,

1987). This technique is also useful in content area courses because it helps students attend to their own mental representations of the content area (Pestel, 1993).

Artificial Intelligence

The term **artificial intelligence** (AI) is sometimes used to refer to the way computers solve problems when there has been no attempt to simulate or mimic human behavior. In AI, the programmed instructions to the computer may be very different from the way humans solve the same problem.

Have you ever played chess with a computer? Many computer programs are designed to simulate the moves that humans make. Other chess programs take advantage of the vast "memory" of the computer and have it evaluate the consequences of several different possible moves. Several chess programs can consider between 5,000 and 50,000 possible combinations of moves (Berliner, 1977). Several years ago, it was predicted that world chess championships would eventually all be won by computers. This has not happened. Our best human chess players can still beat the computers with regularity—a fact that makes most of us human beings very happy.

Can Computers Think?

The answer to the question of whether or not computers can think is tied to the way we choose to define thinking. If thinking is defined as a human activity that is dependent on the neural structure of the brain, then, by definition, computers would not qualify. Suppose we don't rule out a priori the notion that computers can think. How would you go about answering this question? The late A. M. Turing (1950) suggested a test for deciding if a computer can think. Appropriately, it is called **Turing's test**. Suppose that you are sitting alone in a room with a typewriter keyboard. You can type in any question you want, and the typed message will go to two different rooms. In one of these rooms there is a person; in the other there is a computer. Each will send its answer back to you, again via typewriter keyboard. You can ask any question that you want except, "Are you a computer or a human?" According to Turing's test, if you cannot tell from the messages you receive which is the person and which is the computer, then it has been demonstrated that computers can think. What do you think about Turing's test?

Most people find that they are unwilling to conclude that a computer can think just because they couldn't distinguish the computer's answer from a human's answer. After all, is mimicking thought the same as thinking? If a magician can fool you into believing that he has created a rabbit from thin air, it doesn't mean that he really has. Suppose I designed a robot that would come to your front door every day and take your dog for a walk. The end result would be the same as if a person had walked the dog, but would you be willing to conclude that the robot had exercised its muscles? Just because the end product is the same, it doesn't follow that the process was the same.

On the other hand, consider the following line of reasoning. The most famous mathematical treatise of the 20th century, *Principia Mathematica*, was written in 1927 by Whitehead and Russell. All of us would agree that these outstanding mathematicians were exceptional thinkers. More recently, the information that was known prior to Whitehead and Russell's mathematical discoveries was fed into a computer that rapidly proceeded to derive most of the same theorems that these famous mathematicians had derived. When this intellectual feat was accomplished by humans, it was hailed as extraordinary thinking. Are we then also obliged to label the same feat in the same way when it is done by a computer? Whitehead and Russell's contribution is impressive because they had to select relevant information and ignore other information in order to devise their mathematical treatise. Part of their genius was recognizing which information was relevant. Even more important, the human geniuses were able to recognize which mathematical problems they should try to solve. From an entire universe of possible mathematical problems, they picked the ones that were likely to yield to their investigations and were worth solving. The computer was given all of the needed information and the problem to solve, making the computer-generated solutions much less creative and impressive than the task accomplished by these brilliant mathematicians.

Of course, computers and humans differ in many basic ways. Their underlying hardware—neural patterns for humans, electronic circuits for computers—are different. And, of course, humans reproduce themselves, whereas computers rely on humans for their production. It could be argued that computers don't really think because they rely on programs to tell them what to do; however, a similar argument could be made for humans because they rely upon their experiences, genetic programs, and input from other humans to tell them what to do. In any case, premonitions of a world ruled by computers like Hal in the movie *2001: A Space Odyssey* still remain in the realm of science fiction.

The Brain-as-a-Computer Model

Unfortunately, critical thinking sometimes has a pejorative connotation. This is especially true in common media depictions of the good thinker as someone who is cold and calculating. The quintessential "brain-as-a-computer model" of thinking is the pointy-eared Mr. Spock of "Star Trek" fame. As you probably know, Mr. Spock is a fictitious character from the popular television series and movies about space travel in the distant future. Spock, as he is most commonly called, is only half human, a fact that is revealed by his pointy ears. The other half of his bispecies heritage is Vulcan, a species of being whose thinking is totally rational. In fact, he is so reasoned that he is unable to understand the mushy and sentimental emotions that seem to plague mere humans—emotions like love and hate that have no rational counterpart. The media depiction of this popular fictitious character shows that rational thought is cold and incompatible with human feelings.

Other times, the media depict the "good thinker" or good student as the "nerd." The good thinker is rarely the attractive beauty queen or the athletic stud who "gets the girl." More typically, this character is ridiculed for wearing thick glasses, sniffing or wiping a perpetually runny nose, and expressing a predilection for plaid clothing. This negative message about thinking is a common theme in movies made for the huge teen market. In many ways, the idea that thinking reflectively or following a reasoned plan of action instead of an emotional one is made to appear "uncool." The impulsive and dashing bubbleheads who are portrayed as the heroes in this genre of immensely profitable movies are as ludicrous a stereotype as the nerdy good thinker. It is important that we all work to correct these negative stereotypes and make critical thinking a desirable goal.

The negative image of thinking is not just restricted to teen movies. After every televised presidential debate, a small army of "spin masters" come on the air to tell the American public what the candidates just said. Their task is to put a positive "spin" on their preferred candidate (e.g., He provided a clear vision for America ... blah, blah, blah) and a negative spin on the opponent (e.g., He was perspiring and did not smile enough...blah, blah, blah). In one retelling of what the candidates just said, a prominent spin master faulted the opposition candidate for providing too much information and for hesitating before answering complex questions! It seems to be the expected format that candidates will provide quotable snippets that are completely unrelated to reasoned responses about immensely important issues (e.g., I knew John Kennedy and you're no John Kennedy; Read my lips!) and short answers that reduce complex issues to one-liners.

Critical thinking has been unfairly portrayed as cold and unemotional. This portrayal is untrue. The desirable goal of a problem or decision is often based on values, feelings, and predilections. In addition, one frequently recommended skill in improving an outcome is to try to "see" the issue from the perspective of other individuals. This sort of perspective taking should increase empathy rather than decrease it. In addition, critical thinking, because of its roots in psychology, takes into account the intimate connection between thinking and feeling. Most psychotherapies involve the use of cognitive processes—thinking, communicating, and understanding—as a way to alter emotional responses. Empathy, imagination, and value setting are all part of critical thinking.

INTELLIGENCE AND THINKING SKILLS

If we want to improve America's schools, we will have to apply in the classroom what we know about humans as intelligent, learning, thinking cultures.

—Bruer (1993, p. 1)

One of the most frequently asked questions concerning thinking skills instruction is whether learning to be a critical thinker will make someone more intelligent. The answer to this important question depends on how intelligence is defined.

The Nature of Intelligence

Solving problems is the specific achievement of intelligence.

—George Polya

Intelligence is one of the most controversial topics in psychology. It is a basic topic in thinking because intelligence is the "stuff" of thought. You can conceptualize intelligence as the raw material from which thoughts are made. It is difficult to imagine a context in which intelligence isn't manifested or needed. The term intelligence is used commonly in everyday language. Most people believe that they are at least about average or above average in intelligence (Brim, 1966). (Despite Garrison Keillor's assurances to the contrary, you should realize that this is mathematically absurd because most people can't be above average.)

Psychologists continue to debate exactly what the term intelligence should mean (Herrnstein & Murray, 1994; Perkins, Lochhead, & Bishop, 1987). Think for a minute about your own definition of intelligence. A dictionary won't be much help, because dictionaries define difficult multifaceted concepts like intelligence with a few simple words. When Robert Sternberg (1982), a psychologist known for his research on understanding the concept of intelligence, asked people to list the characteristics of an intelligent person, the following answers were frequently given: "reasons logically and well," "reads widely," "keeps an open mind," and "reads with high comprehension." Most people share these intuitive notions of intelligence.

Sternberg's (1981) own definition of intelligence is concerned with the way people approach novel tasks. He believed that little can be learned about intelligence by watching someone perform well-learned tasks. For example, if you are already proficient at long-division, then analyzing your performance on long-division problems won't reveal much about your intelligence. If, however, you are unfamiliar with long division problems, then examining the way you go about solving them and the kinds of answers you formulate will reveal a great deal about your intelligence. Thus, the ability to handle novel tasks and situations is a key element in Sternberg's definition. Sternberg said: "It is not merely the ability to learn and reason with new concepts but the ability to learn and reason with new kinds of concepts. ... intelligence is in large part the ability to acquire and reason with new conceptual systems" (p. 4).

The notion of intelligence as learning and thinking was articulated early in this century by the famous Russian psychologist, Lev Vygotsky. He offered an alternative to the static view of human learning and intelligence as "fixed quantities" that could be observed and assessed in laboratory settings. According to Vygotsky, intelligence is best indexed by the way in which people learn rather than in the level of learning they have achieved at some point in time. This emphasis is not surprising in light of Vygotsky's work with disadvantaged populations in the aftermath of the Russian revolutionary war.

Intelligence is also conceptualized as "practical," that is, it serves a purpose in real-world activities (Sternberg & Wagner, 1986). A person who has "practical intelligence" has the know-how to succeed at a task. This involves knowing how to spend your time and effort in order to achieve a goal. The student who is practically intelligent, for example, will know which subjects to study, when to visit a professor during office hours, what to say when coming late to class, how to write a good paper, and so forth. In real-life situations, the goal is often hard to define and there are many possible paths to obtain it. If you want to graduate from college with good grades, it probably would not be a good use of your time to type each lecture verbatim from a tape recorder, but it probably would be a good use of your time to review your notes after every class and summarize them in your own words. A student high in practical intelligence knows these things, and is more likely to graduate with good grades than a student who does not.

The definitions of intelligence that we've considered so far include the "person-on-the-street's" notion of intelligence, which includes traits like common sense and open-mindedness, the notion that the ability to master new kinds of tasks constitutes intelligence, and the idea that knowing what needs to be done to attain a goal is a kind of intelligence that is practically important. Another definition of intelligence was offered by E.G. Boring (1932) many years ago: "[I]ntelligence is what the tests test" (p. 35). The "tests" he was referring to are, of course, intelligence tests. The way psychologists have measured intelligence has had a direct effect on the way they have come to think about intelligence.

The Measurement of Intelligence

As you can imagine, the measurement of intelligence has proven to be a difficult task. The underlying idea is that intelligence exists, and because it exists, it exists in some quantity (in each individual), and because it exists in some quantity, it can be measured. The only difficulty with this line of reasoning is: How?

There is an obvious need to be able to quantify or measure intelligence. Historically, intelligence tests were designed for a very practical reason. In the early part of this century, the French government realized the need to know which children should get regular classroom instruction and which should get remedial or accelerated instruction. Alfred Binet and Theodore Simon were given the job of designing a test that could be used to place children in the appropriate educational setting. Modern day intelligence tests are still used for this purpose.

Binet and Simon soon realized that the type of question that an intelligent 4-year-old can answer correctly is very different from the type of question that an intelligent 8-year-old can answer correctly. Thus, they devised a test with items that varied in difficulty for each age level.

Sample Test Items

The tests designed in France by Binet and Simon have been revised many times. The most popular revision was undertaken by Lewis Terman, a psychologist at Stanford University. Terman's revision of the earlier intelligence test is commonly referred to as the Stanford–Binet. Another popular battery of intelligence tests was written by David Wechsler. He authored two separate tests, the Wechsler Intelligence Scale for Children (WISC) and Wechsler Adult Intelligence Scale (WAIS) designed for adults over 15 years of age. Wechsler's intelligence tests yield three IQ scores—one based on Verbal test items, one based on Performance test items, and one based on all of the test items, called Full Scale IQ. Following are some test items written to be similar to the ones found in the WAIS (Jensen, 1980):

Verbal Test Items

1. At what temperature does water freeze?
2. Who wrote *The Republic*?
3. Why is gold worth more than copper?
4. How many inches are there in 3½ feet?
5. If six men can finish a job in 3 days, how many men would be needed to finish it in 1 day?
6. In what way are sperm and ovum alike?
7. Repeat a series of digits after the test administrator recites them. For example, a test taker would hear "8175621" and then repeat the digits either in the same order they were given or in reverse order.
8. Explain the meaning of strange.
9. Explain the meaning of adumbrate.

Performance Test Items

Test takers are asked to:

10. Translate the numerals 1 to 9 into code symbols (e.g., 1 = [, 2 = }, 3 = #, etc.).
11. Tell what is missing from familiar objects or scenes (e.g., a clock without hands).
12. Use wooden cubes painted red and white to duplicate a design shown on cards.
13. Arrange a series of cartoons into a logical sequence.
14. Assemble jigsaw puzzles.

The actual test items vary in difficulty and are presented in increasing difficulty within each type of test. The IQ score that an individual receives is determined by calculating how many questions she or he answered correctly relative to the average person in the standardization group.

As you can see from these items, intelligence is measured with a variety of questions. The general knowledge verbal questions tap information that most people would be expected to learn as a member of our society. For most of us, answering questions about the temperature at which water freezes involves only memory retrieval. Some of the more difficult ones, like "Who wrote *The Republic*?" would obviously favor those with a good academic background. Abstract reasoning about the nature of supply-and-demand is needed to answer the question "Why is gold worth more than copper?" The ability to use numbers as well as the knowledge that there are 12 inches in 1 foot is needed to answer the fourth question. Question 5 is a typical mathematical word problem. The answer to Question 6 is difficult because the differences between sperm and ovum may be more salient than their similarities. Of course, you also need to know what these terms mean. Repeating a series of digits forward or backward requires good memory skills. If you practice the memory aids (mnemonics) discussed in the memory chapter, you can go off the top of the scale on this question. The eighth and ninth questions are standard vocabulary questions.

The performance items are more difficult to categorize. Because most of the tests are timed, speed is an important factor in determining performance IQ. Changing numerals to code symbols involves a careful balance of speed and accuracy in order to finish as many numeral to code transformations as possible with few errors. Question 11 tests knowledge of common objects. The ability to duplicate designs is a spatial ability. Arranging a series of cartoons in a logical sequence requires the test taker to generate hypotheses about the actions depicted. It's necessary to be able to see a whole object from its parts, a spatial ability, to put jigsaw puzzles together. Intelligence tests assume that the test taker is motivated to perform well (which is often not true) and that the test taker has had the sorts of experiences that are assumed to be "normative," another assumption that is often unwarranted. The notion of intelligence that is embedded in testing is that intelligence is a fixed quantity. Not surprisingly, intelligence testing yields lower scores for minority groups and any low-income population because these groups have not had the same learning experiences that are assumed by the writers of the IQ tests. Readers are probably aware of the recent, acrimonious controversies surrounding some of these issues, many of them generated by the publication of a massive book entitled *The Bell Curve* (Herrnstein & Murray, 1994). The authors argued that intelligence is largely inherited, that it is measured fairly by standard intelligence tests, that it remains fairly constant from childhood into old age, and that it is affected only marginally by education. I disagree with all of these points (Halpern, in press).

Learning to Be Intelligent

Cognitive science enables us to go beyond intelligence tests and understand how the human mind solves problems.

—Robert Sternberg (1992, p. 53)

Thus far, we have considered several different notions of what it means to be intelligent and some of the problems in determining how intelligent someone is. Because this text is concerned with thinking and helping you to learn how to improve your thinking, it seems reasonable to return to the question posed at the beginning of this section: "Will learning to be a critical thinker make you more intelligent?" An increasing number of psychologists are answering this question with a "yes."

One contemporary view of intelligence is that it is not a single unitary construct. Rather, it is made up of component parts. Sternberg (1985) had a three-component theory of intelligence, which he called a **Triarchic Theory of Intelligence.** (Triarchic means three parts.) According to this view, intelligence is comprised of (a) **metacomponents**, which are used to plan, evaluate, and monitor how we are thinking; (b) **knowledge acquisition components,** which include the ability to utilize information we have in memory as well as the information provided in the environment; and (c) **performance components,** which are the thinking skills we use throughout this book. All of these components can be learned, developed, and improved. These three components determine the degree to which an individual can deal with novelty. Whenever you are faced with an unfamiliar task (e.g., fitting in at a new job, solving a calculus problem, caring for a newborn), the efficiency, accuracy, and speed with which you perform the task will depend on how well you plan and monitor your progress, how well you acquire the information needed, and the ability to select and apply an appropriate thinking skill or strategy. There will always be some people who are more intelligent than others. There are individual differences and limits on how well each of us can think and reason. But we all also have some amount of undeveloped potential and can make substantial gains in these areas. Even though we cannot all be Einstein, we can all learn to think more intelligently.

Sternberg is not alone in his belief that intelligence is comprised of skills that can be enhanced with training (A. A. deGroot, 1983; Nickerson, 1986; Perkins, 1986). Sadler and Whimbey (1985), pioneers in the area of thinking skills improvement, echoed these sentiments when they defined intelligence as "a complex of skills" (p. 44). The same basic idea can be seen in deGroot's definition of intelligence as a mental program consisting of heuristics and in Nickerson's (1987) advice to teachers that they teach for tactics. Skills, strategies, heuristics, tactics are all different words for the same idea—learnable components of intelligent thought. One of my favorite definitions of critical thinking was published over 35 years ago (1960) and comes very close to this contemporary notion of intelligence as learnable skills: "Critical thinking then is the process of evaluation or categorization in terms of some previously accepted standards … this seems to involve attitude plus knowledge of facts plus some thinking skills" (Russell, cited in d'Angelo, 1971, p. 6). In short, Russell's equation is:

Attitude + Knowledge + Thinking Skills = Intelligent Thinking

A CRITICAL THINKING ATTITUDE AND DISPOSITION

All our dignity lies in thought.

—Blaise Pascal (1623–1662)

No one can become a better thinker just by reading a book. An essential component of critical thinking is developing the attitude and disposition of a critical thinker. Good thinkers are motivated and willing to exert the conscious effort needed to work in a planful manner, to check for accuracy, to gather information, and to persist when the solution is not obvious or requires several steps.

Performance–Competence Distinction

Very often there is an important distinction between what people can do and what they actually do. This is called the **performance–competence distinction.** It is of no value to learn a variety of critical thinking skills if you never use them. Developing a **critical thinking attitude** is at least as important as developing thinking skills. Sears and

Parsons (1991) described critical thinking as an ethic in order to emphasize the importance of attitude to good thinking. Many errors occur not because people can't think critically, but because they don't. One of the major differences between good and poor thinkers, and correspondingly between good and poor students, is their attitude. A critical thinker will exhibit the following dispositions or attitudes:

1. Willingness to Plan. I've watched thousands of students (literally) take exams. There are always some students who begin to write as soon as the exam hits their desk. They just plow ahead and begin writing before they begin thinking. Not surprisingly, the results are a disoriented jumble that often bears little relation to the questions being asked. When asked a question in class, they will often answer with the first idea that comes to mind. These students need to learn to check their impulsivity and plan their response. (I talk more about how to plan in the next section.) They should be outlining or diagramming the structure of a response before they begin to write. Planning, the invisible first step in critical thinking, is essential. With repeated practice, anyone can develop the **habit of planning**.

2. Flexibility. In a classic old book, Rokeach (1960) talked about rigidity and dogmatism as the characteristics of a "closed mind." A person with a closed mind responds negatively to new ideas by stating, "That's the way I've always done it." Another common retort that shows the unwillingness to consider new ideas is the well-worn phrase, "If it ain't broke, don't fix it." This sort of close-minded response cuts off consideration of new ideas. By contrast, an attitude of flexibility is marked by a willingness to consider new options, try things a new way, reconsider old problems. An open-minded person is willing to suspend judgment, gather more information, and attempt to clarify difficult issues. This does not mean that all opinions are equally good or that judgment should take a backseat to openness. It does mean that a critical thinker is willing to think in new ways, review evidence, and stick with a task until it is completed.

You may be disappointed if you fail, but you are doomed if you don't try.

—Beverly Sills

3. Persistence. Baron (1987), in an excellent essay on the significance of attitudes, emphasized the importance of persistence to academic success. Closely related to persistence is the willingness to start or engage in a thoughtful task. Some people look at a seemingly difficult task and opt not to even begin the thinking process. They're defeated at the start. Others will start working on a task and stop before it's completed. Good thinking is hard work that requires diligent persistence. It can make you as tired as any physical labor, but can be much more rewarding. In a comparison of students who were unsuccessful in mathematics with those who were, researchers found that much of the difference in success rates was directly attributable to differences in attitudes. The unsuccessful students believed that if a problem could not be solved in less that 10 minutes, then they would not be able to solve it. By contrast, the successful students persisted in working on difficult problems (Schoenfeld, 1985).

4. Willingness to Self-Correct. We all make mistakes. Instead of becoming defensive about errors, good thinkers can acknowledge them and learn from them. They utilize feedback and try to figure out what went wrong and to recognize the factors that led to the error. They recognize ineffective strategies and abandon them in order to improve the thinking process.

5. Being Mindful. Psychologists call this disposition *metacognition or metacognitive monitoring.* It is the tendency to monitor one's comprehension and progress toward a goal. Critical thinkers develop the habit of self-conscious concern for and evaluation of the thinking process. Because this topic is of major importance, it is discussed in more detail in the next section.

6. Consensus-Seeking. Committee and group structures are most often the norm in the world of work. A critical thinker will need to be disposed to ways in which consensus can be achieved. Consensus seekers will need high-level communication skills, but they will also need to find ways to compromise and to achieve agreement. Without this disposition, even the most brilliant thinkers will find that they cannot convert thoughts to actions.

A major difficulty in developing an attitude of critical thinking is that many people don't realize when they're acting impulsively or thinking rigidly. McTighe (1986) described the problem this way: "Students seemed satisfied with their initial interpretation of what they had read and seemed genuinely puzzled at requests to explain or defend their points of view. Few students could provide more than superficial responses to such tasks, and even the better responses showed little evidence of well-developed problem solving strategies or critical thinking skills" (p. 7).

An early study of thinking attitudes (Bloom & Broder, 1950) examined individual differences in the thinking processes of college students. Although this study is an old one, many of their conclusions remain valid today. College students were tested on a series of reasoning problems. They were required to think out loud so that their thinking processes could be monitored. Here is a sample item. (Assume that these statements are true):

Any action that impedes the war effort of the United States should be made illegal. All strikes impede the war effort of the United States.

Conclusions: (pick one)

A. All strikes should be made illegal.
B. Some restrictions should be placed on the right to strike, but it would be unwise to make them all illegal.
C. Some strikes should be made illegal.
D. Unjustifiable strikes should be made illegal.
E. None of the foregoing conclusions follows.

Don't worry if you're having difficulty answering this question. Reasoning problems like this one are discussed in detail in chapter 4. (The correct answer is A.)

Bloom and Broder (1950) compared the kinds of answers given by poor thinkers to those who answered correctly and found several important differences. The students who performed poorly utilized "one-shot" thinking instead of the extended sequential thinking processes of the good thinkers. The poor thinkers were willing to allow gaps in their knowledge to exist. There were basic differences in the *attitude* of the good and poor thinkers. The poor thinkers rushed through the instructions or skipped them altogether. They were passive rather than active in their approach to the problems. When the problems were difficult, they utilized only a few clues to answer the questions or guessed at an answer. They failed to break down complex problems into their constituent parts. In short, they failed to plan, responded impulsively and rigidly, and never realized that improvement was needed.

The researchers developed a remedial course to improve these students' perform-ance. Students were given experts' think-aloud protocols for model solutions. They were taught how the correct answer was obtained, not merely what the correct answer was. The researchers reported significant success with this program.

The most important message that I want to convey is that you need to adopt and value the attitude and disposition of a critical thinker.

Metacognition

Ultimately, it is not we who define thinking, it is thinking that defines us.

—quote from Carey, Foltz, and Allan (1983)

Metacognition refers to what we know about what we know, or, in more formal language, our knowledge about knowledge. It seems that most people have little awareness of the nature or even the existence of the thinking processes that underlie their judgments, beliefs, inferences, and conclusions about complex issues (Nisbett & Wilson, 1977).

There are many experimental examples of how little we know about the variables that influence our thinking. I'll demonstrate this point with one of my favorites. Researchers (Wilson & Nisbett, 1978) asked consumers in a large bargain store to select which of four pairs of nylon pantyhose they preferred. The stockings were hung on a rack above the researcher's table. The consumers examined the weave, the heel, and the toe. Very few had difficulty making a choice. The stocking in the left-most position was preferred by 12% of the consumers; the one to its right by 17%; the next one to the right by 31%; and the right-most stocking by 40%. This indicates that there were clear preferences among the shoppers. This is especially interesting in light of the fact that the four stockings were identical. Position alone accounted for the consumer prefer-ences, yet none of the consumers indicated that position influenced his or her decision. People are simply not aware of the variables that affect how they think.

Being Mindful

In order to develop basic thinking skills, it is necessary to direct your attention to the processes and products of your own thoughts. You need to become consciously aware of the way you think and to develop the habit of examining the end products of your thought processes—the solution you've arrived at, the decision you've made, the inference that you believe to be true, or the judgment you've formulated. In short, you need to become mindful or aware of how and what you are thinking (Langer, 1989). Metacognitive monitoring of your thinking process includes deciding which problems are worth working on, allocating time and effort to different problems and parts of problems, and keeping track of whether you are making progress toward the goal. **Being mindful** requires a self-conscious concern for and evaluation of the thinking process.

Consider what happens when a student in mathematics or the sciences learns to rely on formulas that she does not understand and therefore uses mindlessly. She may be able to substitute numbers for the algebraic symbols, then work through the appropri-ate arithmetic and arrive at the correct answer without ever understanding the princi-ples involved or the meaning or importance of the answer.

Students in the sciences and in mathematics are taught a technical jargon. Too often, they believe that scattering these terms in a discussion is evidence that they understand the concepts, when in fact their understanding of the phenomena involved is shallow and consists mainly of the ability to label events.

Griffiths (1976) raised an interesting question when he asked: "Physics teaching: Does it hinder intellectual development?"(p. 81). Griffiths answered this question by noting that the way physics is currently taught, with vocabulary drills and reliance on formulas, prevents students from learning how to reason or think critically about the issues. In studying how students think about physics problems, Griffiths found that, "In many instances, when a conflict was apparent between the predicted results and the experimental evidence, a technical term was imposed to explain the discrepancy" (p. 84). Here is one of his student's responses to a classic problem involving an inclined plane: "You have to calculate it. You must set all forces to zero, then sum all the forces acting on the body equal to zero, then solve it for what it really means" (p. 84). You don't need to know anything about physics to realize that this student is in trouble. He has acquired a meaningless vocabulary and has not acquired the ability to think in a cogent way. More troublesome than the student's lack of knowledge in this case is the fact that he doesn't know that he doesn't know. He has not developed the ability to monitor his knowledge and recognize the difference between scattering terms and understanding concepts. He has no awareness or self-monitoring process for his own knowledge.

Consider the following example: Working alone, Stacy can mow her front lawn in 2 hours, whereas it takes her sister Carole 4 hours. How long will it take them to mow the lawn if they work together? Many students routinely apply the well-known formula for finding an average. They add 2 + 4 and divide by 2, concluding that it will take them an average of 3 hours if they work together. Few students stop to realize that this is an unreasonable answer, because it implies that it will take them longer if they work together than it would if Stacy were working alone! Why are students misled into thinking that this is the correct answer? I believe that they have been overly trained to rely on rote applications of formulas. They have not learned to stop and think about the kind of answer they should expect (e.g., a number less than 2); nor have they learned the skills of working through a problem. They have never learned the importance of being mindful. (In case you've been working on this problem and want to check your answer, the correct answer is 1 hour and 20 minutes.)

Another way that thinking may be discouraged in educational settings is in the kinds of examinations that are used to assess learning. Too often, learning is measured solely with fill-in-the-blank, true–false, and multiple-choice questions that are concerned only with recitations of previously presented material. It is possible for students to be able to place the correct word in the correct blank without understanding very much about the topic.

Perhaps one of the most poignant examples of the way that education has not fostered thinking skills was recounted by Carpenter (1981). She presented college students with a novel problem devised by the Swiss psychologist Jean Piaget. Students were given a small container of water, a large, heavy wooden block, and a small, light wooden block. Their task was to determine if either or both blocks would float and to explain their results. They found that the large, heavy block floated whereas the small, light one did not. When faced with the task of explaining the results, the college students assumed that they ought to know the answer and tried to remember formulas and terms. The college students who had taken several science courses brought in the terms *center of gravity, specific gravity,* and *surface tension.* They were unwilling to test the situation or to explore the materials that were provided. In general, they were unable to generate testable hypotheses. This may be symptomatic of the discomfort many college students feel with science and mathematics courses. (The correct answer concerns the relationship between weight and area.)

The college students' approach to the problem can be sharply contrasted to the one used by sixth-grade children when they were presented with the same task. The sixth-graders manipulated the materials and revised their hypotheses as they tested the relevant variables of size and weight. Unburdened with technical jargon or the expectancy that this problem could be solved best with a formula, the 6th graders were more likely to generate testable hypotheses and to manipulate the materials in order to solve the problem than their college counterparts!

A FRAMEWORK FOR THINKING

Thinking ... is continuous, a series of informed improvisations more like those of a jazz musician than the playing of a classical musician performing a set piece of music from a score.

—Restak (1988, p. 233)

Unfortunately, there is no simple "how to" formula that can be used in every situation that calls for critical thought. You already know about the importance of planning, but knowing that it's important to plan is of little value if you don't know how to plan. Consider the following advice about wilderness survival (Vancouver Community Business Directory, 1987):

Wilderness Survival
Things you must *not* do:
Wear brand new boots
Leave an open fire unattended
Panic. If you meet trouble, stop and think.

I'm sure that the first two recommendations are excellent, but I'm less sure about the value of telling someone to think without any instructions about how to go about it. Presented next is a general, all-purpose framework or guide that can be used to direct the thinking process. It's not a surefire guarantee to good thinking (there are none), but it is a way of getting started and ensuring that the **executive processes** needed in thinking—planning, monitoring, and evaluating—are being used in a reflective manner. You can probably guess why these are called executive processes. They function like the "boss" in a busy office by directing the flow of work and deciding where to put the available resources. The framework is a series of questions, some of which may be repeated several times during the thinking process, that are general enough to be useful in a wide variety of applications, including reasoning from premises, analyzing arguments, testing hypotheses, solving problems, estimating probabilities, making decisions, and thinking creatively. Although the framework will remain the same for all of these thinking tasks, the actual skills used will vary somewhat with the nature of the task. The proposed framework is an adaptation of the problem-solving procedures originally proposed by the brilliant mathematician and scholar George Polya in 1945. Polya's model is presented in chapter 9.

As you progress through each of the following chapters in this book, you will gain experience in applying this framework in different contexts and different knowledge domains. The thinking skills you acquire as you work through this book will transfer to other contexts if you acquire the habit of using the framework. The purpose of presenting the framework now is to provide an introduction and overview of what's to come. It's an easy-to-use guide that, through repeated practice, should become automatic. The following questions are used to guide the thought process:

1. What Is the Goal?

Critical thinking was defined earlier in this chapter as the use of those cognitive skills or strategies that increase the probability of a desirable outcome. This term is used to describe thinking that is purposeful, reasoned, and goal-directed. The first step in improving thinking is to be clear about the goal or goals. Real-life problems are messy. Sometimes there are multiple goals, and sometimes we return to this question several times, as our understanding of the goal often changes after we've worked on it for a while. A clearly articulated goal provides direction to the thinking process. In the course of thinking about real-world problems, you may need to change direction, but it's still important to provide some focus. After all, if you don't know where you're going, you can never be sure if you've arrived.

There is a large variety of possible goals. Goals can include deciding among a set of possible alternative solutions, generating a solution where there is none, synthesizing information, evaluating the validity of evidence, determining the probable cause of some event, considering the credibility of an information source, and quantifying uncertainty.

Are you making a decision about whether or not to have a heart transplant or what flavor ice cream to select from the corner store? Impulsive thinking about ice cream flavors is not a bad thing; impulsive thinking about life and death decisions is. Not everything we do in life requires critical thought. The way you identify the goal should help you plan the time and effort required by the situation.

2. What Is Known?

This is the starting point for directed thinking. Although this may seem fairly straightforward now, when we actually use this framework on real problems, you'll find that you may have to return to the "knowns" several times. Some information will be known with certainty; other information may be only probably true or partially known. This step also includes recognizing gaps in what's known and the need for further information gathering.

3. Which Thinking Skill or Skills Will Get You to Your Goal?

Once you have some idea of where you are (the knowns or givens) and where you're going (the goal or purpose), you're better able to plan goal-directed thinking processes. Knowing how to get from where you are to where you want to be is the power of critical thinking. These are the thinking skills or strategies that have been alluded to throughout this chapter. Just as there are many different possible goals, there are many different strategies for attaining them. Let's consider the "thinking is like a map" analogy a little further because it can help to clarify some abstract concepts by making them more concrete. Suppose you are about to go on a trip to visit two old friends. One has become a Buddhist monk and lives high on a mountain top in the Himalayas. The other has become a surfing champion and is living on the beautiful island of Hawaii. You'd have to use a different method of travel to reach each destination, one time scaling a mountain, the other deciding between a plane or boat. Similarly, you'll have to use different thinking skills with different types of thought problems.

This step involves generating and selecting the appropriate strategy to reach the goal. If you've given any thought to how you will reach a Himalayan mountaintop

(I'm assuming that this is a novel thought for most of you), you'll start to generate several options. You'll probably have to cross an ocean, which means deciding between a plane or boat of some sort, and then travel by train and/or car, and then travel by foot and/or animal (which one?). Of course, you'll probably need a guide. And what are the vaccination requirements for someone traveling to Tibet? Oh yes, will you need a visa? I think you've gotten the idea by now that traveling to a Himalayan mountain top is a lot like other quests for knowledge. It will take time and careful planning. By contrast, your trip to visit your surfer friend will be easier and cheaper. Some problems are like that.

4. Have You Reached Your Goal?

I've taught statistics for nearly 10 years now. I must have asked students if they've checked their work as often as I've said my name. A concern with accuracy is probably the biggest predictor of success. Does your solution make sense? Did you get to your mountaintop in Tibet or are you on an anthill in Iowa? Was your goal the right one or should it really have been "where shall I travel this summer?" If it really should have been the latter goal, then you can forget Tibet and consider Paris or Japan or the rugged beauty of Newfoundland. What have you learned on the way that you can use again?

A Skills Approach

Critical thinking skills are those strategies for finding ways to reach a goal. Of course, dividing the thinking process, which is fluid and continuous, into discrete skills is somewhat artificial, but it is necessary to break the massive topic of critical thinking into manageable pieces. Although I have divided the topic of critical thinking into several chapters, each of which focuses on a different type of problem (e.g., reasoning, analyzing arguments, testing hypotheses, making decisions, estimating likelihoods), these problems are not easily separable in real life. You will often need to estimate likelihoods when making a decision or generate possible solutions in a reasoning task. The division is necessary for teaching and learning and is not meant to imply that critical thinking can be cut into neat packages.

The use of skills is a convenient way of learning about good thinking, even if it seems to simplify the complexities in thinking. The actual skills and ways to evaluate and generate them are presented in the subsequent chapters. This is what critical thinking instruction is all about.

Critical thinking instruction is predicated on two assumptions: (a) that there are clearly identifiable and definable thinking skills that students can be taught to recognize and apply appropriately, and (b) if recognized and applied, students will be more effective thinkers. Intellectual skills, like physical skills, require specific instruction, practice in a variety of contexts, feedback, and time to develop. So, please get comfortable, prepare for some hard work, and enjoy this book.

CHAPTER SUMMARY

1. It is imperative that citizens of the 20th and 21st centuries think critically, yet recent tests have shown that only 25% of first-year college students have the skills needed for logical thought. The need for critical thinking skills has been identified as a national and international priority.

2. Critical thinking can be defined as the use of those cognitive skills or strategies that increase the probability of a desirable outcome. It is used to describe thinking that is purposeful, reasoned, and goal directed.

3. There is considerable empirical evidence from a variety of sources that cognitive skills can be learned in specific courses designed to teach them and that these skills transfer to real-world settings when they are practiced in multiple contexts.

4. Although it is possible to view thinking as a biological process, this perspective will not be helpful in devising ways to improve thinking.

5. People report that thinking sometimes seems to rely on visual imagery and sentence-like propositions. There are individual differences and task differences in the use of these modes of thought.

6. Thought process protocols are used to understand and improve human thought. In computer simulation, they are used to write computer programs that mimic human thought.

7. Many contemporary psychologists conceptualize intelligence as made up of component parts, which include knowledge acquisition and utilization, executive processes, and skills. These components can all be improved and developed with instruction and practice.

8. Developing a critical thinking attitude and disposition is at least as important as developing the skills of critical thinking. The skills are useless if they are not used. The attitude of a critical thinker must be cultivated and valued.

9. Researchers have found many differences between good and poor thinkers. The poor thinkers had a poorer attitude toward the reasoning problems that they were asked to solve. They were more likely to skip the instructions, work hastily, and guess at the answer. With remedial instruction, they showed considerable improvement.

10. Metacognition refers to people's knowledge of their own thought processes. We often have little conscious awareness of how we think. Self-monitoring your own thought processes is one way to improve how you think.

11. A general all-purpose framework for thinking was presented. It consists of four questions that should be asked whenever you're faced with a critical thinking task. It will serve as a guide for the thinking process.

12. Remember, you are what (and how) you think! Have fun with this book.

TERMS TO KNOW

You should be able to define the following terms and concepts. A good way to review and check your comprehension is to cover up the definition, then try to define each term, then uncover the definition and compare your answer with the brief one that is provided. (Your answer is expected to be more complete than the one presented in this review.) Your goal is not to memorize the terms; instead you should be sure that your definition captured the meaning of the term. Be sure to cover the definition because it is easy to believe you know it when the answer is in front of you but hard to fool yourself when you have to generate your own answer. If you find that you're having difficulty with any term, be sure to reread the section in which it is discussed.

Schemata. Internal representations of knowledge. The way we organize our knowledge about the world.

Critical Thinking. The use of those cognitive skills or strategies that increase the probability of a desirable outcome. It is purposeful, reasonable, and goal directed. Also known as directed thinking. Compare with nondirected thinking.

Nondirected Thinking. Daydreams, night dreams, and other sorts of thinking that are not engaged in for a specific purpose or do not involve the use of critical thinking skills. Compare with directed (or critical) thinking.

Cognitive Process Instruction. Instruction based on cognitive theories and research that is designed to help people improve how they think.

Transfer of Training. The spontaneous use of skills that are learned in one context in a different context.

Imagery. The use of an internal picture-like representation while thinking.

Preferred Modes of Thought. Individual preferences for different types of internal representations.

Human Information Processing (HIP). A model of human thinking that uses the flow of information through a computer as an analogy of human thought.

Critical Thinking Attitude. The willingness to plan, flexibility in thinking, persistence, willingness to self-correct, mindful attention to the thought process, and the seeking of consensus. It is not possible to be a critical thinker without this sort of attitude.

Habit of Planning. The repeated and automatic use of plans.

Metacognition. Our knowledge about our memory and thought process. Colloquially, what we know about what we know.

Being Mindful. The conscious and deliberate use of critical thinking skills.

Executive Processes. The oversight or planning and monitoring processes in thinking.

SUGGESTED READINGS

There are many fine books that can serve as an introduction to critical thinking and the psychology of thinking. I highly recommend *Rules for Reasoning*, an edited book by Richard Nisbett (1993). It is a large collection of articles that Nisbett has written with numerous colleagues. He and his coauthors showed that people use abstract rules in reasoning and that these rules can be easily learned. You may also want to check out the Special Issue of the journal *Teaching of Psychology* (1995) entitled "Psychologists Teach Critical Thinking" which I coedited with Susan G. Nummedal. It is divided into sections that include a theoretical overview, teaching and learning strategies that are useful across the curriculum, and suggestions for the enhancement of critical thought. Not too surprisingly, I also like another new book that I edited (Halpern, 1994), *Changing College Classrooms: New Teaching and Learning Strategies for an Increasingly Complex World*. Although the chapters address a variety of topics (e.g., using new technologies, diversity in higher education), you can probably guess that there is a lengthy section on critical thinking.

If you are looking for a good place to start reading, you could try Cassel and Congleton's (1993) *Critical Thinking: An Annotated Bibliography*. As its name implies, it is a listing of some of the recent literature on critical thinking along with brief abstracts. It contains 930 entries arranged by categories including definitions, research, theory, and testing. Another good choice is Stroup and Allen's (1992) collection of short articles entitled, *Critical Thinking: A Collection of Readings* which is filled with suggestions for developing and using critical thinking. The articles in this volume are reprinted from previously published sources.

If you're interested in the use of visual imagery to improve how you think, you'll enjoy Arnheim's (1971) *Visual Thinking* and McKim's (1980) *Thinking Visually: A Strategy Manual for Problem Solving*. Among the older classic "thinking books" is Flesch's (1951) *The Art of Clear Thinking*. Every chapter in this clever book begins with quotable quotes from the famous and not so famous. A large and somewhat rambling book that reflects on the nature of thought is *The Act of Creation* by Koestler (1964). A good, nonscientific introduction to thinking is *The Mind's Best Work* by Perkins (1981). It's an interesting book filled with strange illustrations and thoughtful questions. It is good food for thought.

If you're interested in the way education has responded to psychology's views of thinking, you'll find the collection of articles in *Problem Solving and Education: Issues in Teaching and Research*, edited by Tuma and Reif (1980), *Cognitive Process Instruction: Research on Teaching Thinking Skills*, edited by Lochhead and Clement (1979), and *Thinking and Learning Skills* (Vol. 1), edited by Segal, Chipman, and Glaser (1985) to be informative. A special issue of the journal *The Long Term View* (1994) tackles the question, "Has American education forsaken critical thinking?" It presents commentaries by multiple experts from different fields. By the way, their short answer is "Yes."

The psychological literature on intelligence is enormous. One of the major controversies is addressed in a book edited by J. Rubinstein and Slife (1982): *Taking Sides: Clashing Views on Controversial Psychological Issues*. "Is intelligence inherited?" is one of the issues they consider. An article written by Jensen answers this question with a "Yes," and an article written by Whimbey answers "No." Jensen expanded his position in his 1981 book, *Straight Talk About Mental Tests*, and in a more technical book written in 1980, *Bias in Mental Testing*. Advanced readers who want to understand some of the recent controversies concerning intelligence may want to tackle *The Bell Curve* by Herrnstein and Murray (1994). But beware, it should also be accompanied by the many critiques of their thesis, such as a special issue of *Skeptic* magazine (1995). If you are interested in an ambitious attempt to improve intelligence be sure to consult Sternberg's (1986) skills development book, *Intelligence Applied*. This book reflects Sternberg's work as a consultant to the Venezuela intelligence enhancement project that was described earlier.

There have also been a slew of new books that are devoted to improving critical thinking in kindergarten through high school. Collins and Mangieri (1992) have edited a collection of articles that are relevant for this age group. Two books that seem geared for the upper elementary school grades are Langrehr's (1990) *Sharing Thinking Strategies* and Little and Greenberg's (1991) *Problem Solving, Critical Thinking, and Communication Skills*. A terrific collection of readings and thinking exercises for elementary school children can be found in Swartz and Parks' (1994) *Infusing Critical and Creative Thinking Into Elementary Instruction*. *ThinkAbility* is a computerized thinking skills program designed for students in fourth through ninth grades. It uses a game format to keep students motivated. It is no coincidence that the author of this program, Meirovitz (1995), is a game "expert." Meirovitz invented the well known game, "MasterMind" which was a best seller for many years. It will be interesting to see how other new technologies are adapted to help students improve how they think.

2

Memory: The Acquisition, Retention, and Retrieval of Knowledge

Contents

Many years ago I read a story about a beautiful young woman who, because of a terrible fear of growing old, made an interesting deal with the Devil. She agreed to sell her soul to him. In return, he promised that she would spend her old age in complete happiness. The Devil kept his promise. When the woman grew old, she became totally senile. Her old age was spent in the memories of her youth, visiting with friends who had long since died, totally oblivious of life around her. The memory of this story has stayed with me for a long time. I wonder if she would have made this deal if she had known that her happiness would be bought with senility and would consist of a life among her memories. I would like to be able to tell you who wrote this story and give you the title, so that you can read it for yourself, but I can't. I've forgotten where I read it. While I believe that I can remember accurately many of the details of the story, I can't remember where I read it or who wrote it.

MEMORY AS THE MEDIATOR OF COGNITIVE PROCESSES

How wonderful, how very wonderful the operations of time, and the changes of the human mind! … If any one faculty of our nature may be called more *wonderful than the rest, I do think it is memory.*

—Austen (quoted in Powell, 1985, p. 403)

Ulric Neisser (1982), a cognitive psychologist, once asked, "What do we use the past for?" (p. 13). This may seem like a strange question, but a good way to begin our quest to understand memory is by examining its function. According to Neisser, we use the past to define ourselves. If you are a fan of the soap operas, you'll recognize this as one of the favorite themes. Soap opera plots often involve memory loss (amnesia) in one of the protagonists. The usual sequence of events consists of a sudden blow to the head of a leading man or woman followed by a peculiar loss of memory in which the identity of family members is forgotten. Although this is rare in real life, it does point out the essential role of memory. It tells you who you are, where you're from, and where you're going.

Try to imagine what life would be like if you had no memory. For most of us, this is a frightening thought. A loss of memory is a kind of death. If we had no memory for our past, the people we are would no longer exist, even if our bodies continued to function. Our memories are our most valuable possession. I don't know anyone who would sell the memories he or she has accumulated over a lifetime, no matter how much money was offered. Life without memory is unfathomable.

All intelligent systems (e.g., humans, computers, dogs, cockroaches) have the ability to learn and remember. These abilities play a crucial role in all of our lives. Most important, they are inevitable consequences of living. For humans, the ability to learn and remember well often determines the quality of life, economic status, and sometimes even survival. Because the ability to think clearly depends, in large part, on how well we can utilize past experiences, memory is a central topic in developing thinking skills. In this chapter, we consider current views of how memory works, why forgetting occurs, and ways to improve memory.

All thinking skills are inextricably tied to the ability to remember. As you proceed through the chapters in this book, you will repeatedly find evidence of the pervasive influences of memory on how and what we think. Consider, for example, the perception of risk. Psychologists have found that hazards that are unusually memorable such as a recent disaster or a sensationalized depiction in a film or televised newscasts (e.g., stories about teenagers who kill their parents and knife-wielding wives who mutilate their husbands) distort people's perception of risk. Most people rate dramatic causes of death such as earthquake or shark attack as many times more likely than they actually are, whereas less memorable causes of death are routinely underestimated (Lichtenstein, Slovic, Fischoff, Layman, & Combs, 1978).

The distortion in perceived risk is due to the sorts of events that people can think of when they make judgments about risk. Public opinion polls show that crime is the number one concern for most Americans. But, is there really a crime wave, or just the perception of a rapid increase in the rate of crime? The Center for Media and Public Affairs found that the three major television networks in the United States showed more than twice as many crime stories in 1993 than in 1992—even though the crime rate had not changed ("The Nightly Crime News," 1994). Why are television news shows increasing their coverage of crime? In part, a few violent crimes dominated the news, but it is also possible that the major networks are trying to compete with the tabloid-type shows that feature violent crime.

A related media-made impression of a crime wave can arise from reporting increases without ever stating the actual number of crimes. For example, although the killing of tourists in Florida has gone up 300% in 2 years, it helps to mention the number that have been killed: The number has increased from three deaths to eight deaths—hardly a crime wave! It is not surprising then that people would conclude that there has been a rapid rise in the rate of crime—after all, this is what is shown and reported on news shows, and what we are likely to recall when deciding about the risk of crime.

Another example of the centrality of memory to the thinking process can be seen in decision making by juries. The jury process is at the heart of the U.S. legal system. It is one of our most cherished rights as citizens. A group of strangers is cloistered in a small room for the sole purpose of evaluating evidence pertaining to the guilt or innocence of an accused. The synthesis, analysis, and weighing of evidence that is often contradictory is a complex cognitive process that, like all cognitive processes, depends on what is remembered. In a simulated study of how juries reach decisions, Reyes, Thompson, and Bower (1980) varied the vividness (and, therefore, the memorability) of the evidence provided during a mock trial. In half of the cases, the prosecution presented the more vivid information; in the other half, the defense presented the more vivid information. Judgments of guilt paralleled the differential recall of the prosecution and defense arguments. When the information favoring the defendant was more vivid, he or she was more likely to be acquitted (found not guilty), and when the information favoring the plaintiff was more vivid, the defendant was more likely to be found guilty. The "jurors" based their decision about guilt or innocence on the information available to them from their memories of the trial. The vivid information was more memorable, more available, and therefore was more likely to be utilized in the jury deliberations. The influence of the availability of information in decision making is considered again in chapter 8.

The Time Line

The relationship among learning, retaining, and recalling involves the passage of time. Let's clarify this with an example. It is reasonable to expect that during a college career, students will take many, many exams. When you finish reading this section of the book, you should be able to answer a question like: "What is the relationship among learning, retaining, and recalling?" If you write the correct answer on an exam, your professor will infer that sometime before the exam you learned the relevant material, you retained it (kept it in memory), and you were able to recall it when it was needed (on the exam). Learning and retaining are always inferred from recall. No one can ever observe you learning or retaining. These activities are inferred from some behavior such as writing the correct answer in response to a question. A friend can watch you while you move your eyes across the lines of print that appear in a book propped up in front of you, but she can't see you learn. In the example presented here, writing the correct answer on an exam is the behavior that allows the inference that learning and retention have occurred. Learning and retention are **hypothetical constructs,** terms that have been made up to help psychologists study and understand the mind and, thus, they have been called *convenient fictions.* Learning and retention are like perception, motivation, thirst, sex drives, hallucinations, and many other terms in that they have no external physical reality. They are known only by inference, and they are helpful in understanding the processes of the mind.

Learning and retention are usually inferred together. If I asked you what notable event occurred in Lillehammer, Norway, in 1994, and you answered correctly, then I would infer that you learned, retained, and recalled that Lillehammer was the site of the 1994 Winter Olympics. If you are unable to answer this question, then either: (a) you never learned the fact in question; (b) you learned it, but forgot it; or (c) you could recall it in some other situation, but not this one.

The relationship between learning and memory is a temporal one (time based) and is depicted on the time line in Fig. 2.1. Something happens at Time 1 that we call learning or the acquisition of information. Following Time 1 is an interval that can be as short as a few thousandths of a second or as long as a lifetime. Retention of information during this time interval is attributed to memory, but indexed by retrieval. At Time 2 (sometime after Time 1), the individual exhibits some behavior, like correctly answering an exam question, that allows us to infer that the material was both learned and remembered.

Varieties of Memory

Thought and memory are closely related, for thought relies heavily on the experiences of life.

—Norman (1988, p. 115)

The goal of good remembering is to learn information that may be useful in the future and to learn it in a way that makes it easy and likely to be recalled when it is needed.

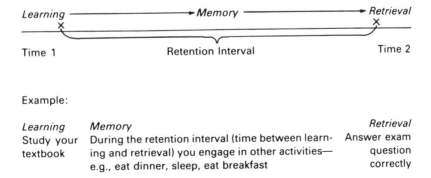

FIG. 2.1. A time line depicting the relationship among learning, memory, and retrieval.

By gaining some insight into the way memory works, you should be able to use this knowledge to improve the ability to remember.

In the first chapter, I provided a working definition for critical thinking. A key idea is that thinking, in general, is the manipulation or transformation of some internal representation (E. Hunt, 1989). Our internal representations are manipulated or transformed in symbolic ways so that the knowledge we have can be used to solve problems and make decisions. Notice that I use the term *knowledge* whenever I refer to an internal representation. Information exists in the world. When we learn it, that is incorporate it into our existing mental structures, it becomes meaningful—it becomes knowledge. When we think, we use our knowledge to accomplish some goal. When we think in deliberate ways that increase the probability of obtaining that goal, we are engaging in critical thinking.

Memory is not a single process. It is a series of processes or systems, each of which has its own operating principles. Psychologists do not agree about the number of separate processes that comprise memory because there are many dimensions to memory and many different ways to conceptualize the remembering processes. I like to think of it as different ways to cut the "memory pizza." (I was a pizza waitress when I was in college, and I frequently tried to cut the pizza in novel ways. I'm not sure why I recalled this experience as I searched for an analogy for memory, but this is what I remembered. I hope that this is a useful way to understand this discussion. At least, it should provide food for thought.)

For example, memory operates differently when you learn a motor skill like skiing than it does when you study for a history test. Therefore, you would not use the same methods to learn to ski as you would to learn about an event in history. Similarly, what you do during the retention interval and at recall is different. The length of the retention interval also governs what and how you learn and recall. If you had to remember the date of the Civil War for only 5 seconds, you would engage in different remembering activities during the retention interval than if you had to remember it for 5 months. What you already know about skiing or history is also an important determinant of the way in which you go about adding to that knowledge. Similarly, the complexity of the information and the context in which you learn and remember also play a role in the selection of the best strategies for learning and remembering. Intuitively, we all know about some of these differences, but an improved understanding of the operating principles of memory should help to use it more efficiently.

Perhaps another analogy would be useful at this point because the concept of memory systems is so abstract. Think about the many interrelated components in an automobile engine. If you understand that pumping too much gas into a stalled car can flood the engine, then you can avoid this problem. Similarly, if you understand that the battery can lose its charge if you run the heater, lights, and radio for a long time when the motor is off, you can also use this knowledge to avoid the problem of a dead battery. The many systems of memory also have operating rules, and if you acquire, retain, and recall information with these rules in mind, you should be a better driver of your own memory system.

Here are some of the distinctions that have been made to differentiate among memory systems:

Episodic memory is the memory we have for events in which we can recall our own participation (Tulving, 1972). Examples of episodic memory include remembering where you spent your 17th birthday, recalling the plot from a movie you saw last week, and remembering the day you got engaged. This sort of memory is fairly easy to acquire because it seems to happen without much effort on your part.

Semantic memory is the memory that we have for facts like the multiplication table and word meanings. You probably cannot remember where and when you learned that 7 x 9 = 63 or the definition of "chauvinist pig," but these are parts of your memory system. You probably can recall all of the trouble you had learning the multiplication tables. Both episodic and semantic memory contain knowledge that you can easily talk about. For this reason, these two systems are part of a larger grouping in memory that is called **declarative memory.**

Motor memory, as you might expect, pertains to remembering motor skills. Let's suppose that you are an excellent outfielder in baseball. You can get your hand to the place where the ball is going and send it sailing in the right direction within fractions of a second. This is certainly an impressive skill, but it is very difficult to verbalize exactly how you do it. You are able to call upon your knowledge when it is needed, but can't say exactly what it is that you do. If you wanted to teach me to be a great outfielder (lots of luck), you could not just tell me what you do. It would be of little use for you to describe your activities; "I catch the ball instead of missing it, then throw it where it is most needed, instead of somewhere else." On the other hand, if you wanted to teach me the multiplication tables, you could do that in words.

Procedural memory, or remembering how to do something, shares some features with motor memory. The difference is that the procedure does not necessarily have to involve motor skills. For example, if you are as old as I am (unlikely), then you once learned how to use a slide rule. (For those of you who grew up in the age of cheap and efficient calculators, a slide rule is a device that looks like a ruler and can be used to perform mathematical calculations.) This is a kind of "knowing how" that is often differentiated from declarative tasks that involve "knowing that."

Another way of dividing memory depends on how hard you have to "work" in order to remember. This distinction is between automatic and effortful memory. How many movies have you seen in the last 2 months? Even avid moviegoers can almost always answer this question (Hasher & Zacks, 1984). Frequency information is one type of learning and remembering that occurs fairly automatically, that is with little conscious awareness or practice. For this reason, it is often called **automatic memory**. By contrast, suppose that you need to remember a series of dates for a history exam. Unfortunately, this sort of information will require that you work at remembering—most probably you would repeat the dates until you could recite them without looking. This is an example of **effortful memory.**

Recognizing yet another dimension of memory, **implicit memory** is memory that we are unaware of, even at recall (Roediger, 1990). For example, suppose that your family always spoke Italian in the home when you were a child, and now that you are an adult, you cannot seem to remember a single word of Italian. Yet, if you took a class in Italian, you would find that the words that you thought you didn't know come back to you so that you are soon speaking Italian once again. This is a kind of implicit memory because you had no conscious awareness of the fact that you knew some Italian, yet you found that you did. On the other hand, memories for which you have conscious memory are called **explicit memories.**

Other, totally different ways of "slicing the memory pizza" depend on the length of the retention interval. If the retention interval is up to 1 or 2 minutes, then the best ways to ensure recall will be different than when the interval is longer (up to an entire lifetime). Simple rehearsal, such as repeating a phone number that needs to be remembered long enough to dial it, will work well for short retention intervals. If you needed to learn your new phone number so that you can recall it months or years from now, you could not spend the retention interval repeating your phone number. You need to engage in activities that are appropriate for long-term retention.

Memory can also be categorized by the type of recall task that will be performed. If you only have to recognize the correct response, you will need less effort at acquisition than if you have to actually generate the response with few cues. Students frequently tell me that they study differently when they are expecting a multiple-choice test (recognition) than an essay test (recall with few cues). If recall will be accomplished with the aid of cues or hints to help you remember, this sort of memory task is called *priming*. Recall can also seem to be spontaneous; that is, you don't know what caused you to remember something at some particular time such as thinking of a childhood friend when walking down the street. I don't know why I remembered my years as a pizza waitress when I was thinking about ways to explain the abstract concept of memory. It came to me spontaneously. Several different ways of conceptualizing the multiple processes of memory, or, as I have been calling it, cutting the memory pizza, are shown in Fig. 2.2.

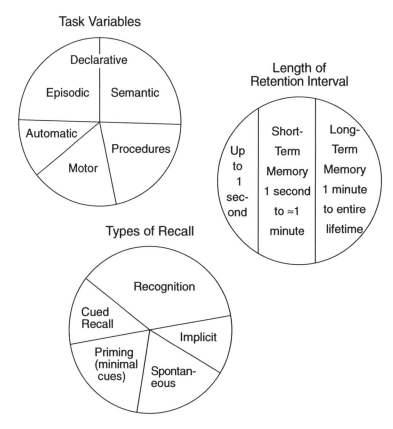

FIG. 2.2. Varieties of memory. There are many different ways to conceptualize the types of memory processes. I suggested that you think of it as ways to cut up a pizza—in this case a memory pizza. Each of these "pieces" or categories of memory has its own set of operating principles. This means that each piece or type of memory is best for certain types of memories (e.g., personal memories, knowledge of how to play football, names of cities) for different retention intervals, and is susceptible to different factors that cause forgetting.

As you can see, there are many ways to categorize the multiple processes of memory. What you need to remember from this discussion is that you will have to consider what you need to remember and when and why you will need it, and what you already know about the topic when you engage in activities that promote remembering. But, whatever the nature of the memory task, a consistent theme throughout this book is that the knowledge we retain in that amazing organ that perches on top of our spines directs the mental processes that we call thinking. A strong base of knowledge and good thinking skills operate together in the critical thinker (Champagne, 1992). However, it is important to bear in mind that although an excellent memory may direct and influence thinking, the two are separate constructs. One of the saddest sights in college is the student whose memory is an encyclopedic compendium of unintegrated factoids. Just as great thinking skills with a head that contains no knowledge is worthless, so is information without the thinking skills, unless you aspire to be a game-show contestant! Thought and knowledge—sounds to me like a great title for a book.

ACQUISITION

In 1935, *Time Magazine* featured the predictions of Ralph S. Willard, a Hollywood chemist who claimed to be able to freeze monkeys and resuscitate them. Willard suggested that this process could be used with prisoners because it was cheaper than jail, the unemployed, who could be kept frozen until the economy produced more jobs, and even the depressed, who could remain in the freezer until a cure was found. By the way, it is clear that "Willard was a humbug" who disappeared into science fiction history. (S. B. Harris, 1993, p. 55)

Unless you already knew this, you have just acquired new information. You can answer questions that you couldn't answer a few moments ago. You are a changed person, and you will never be the same again. The knowledge you have embedded in memory pertaining to *Time Magazine*, cryogenics (freezing people), and strange ideas from the 1930s is altered. So it is with all new information that causes you to change what you know and how you think.

You may have heard the term *information explosion*, which refers to the tremendous increase in the amount of information we have to deal with in contemporary society—information that has to be acquired, retained, and retrieved if we are to function in an increasingly complex world. Consider, for example, the documentation that soldiers have to master in order to learn and perform maintenance on military tanks. There are more than 40,000 pages of instructions, and the tools required for maintenance could fill a large truck (Brooks, Simutis, & O'Neil, 1985). The soldiers who are responsible for the tanks need to know how to learn and recall large amounts of technical information in order to perform well at this highly complex task. As more of us log on to electronic networks, we are privy to staggering quantities of information. We need to know how to search selectively and how to navigate through a sea of databases, bulletin boards, discussion groups, and "buying opportunities."

We are surrounded every moment by more information than we could possibly acquire. Stop some friends some time during the day and ask them to close their eyes. Ask them questions about the room they're in (e.g., which pots are on the stove, if they're in the kitchen), or the book they're reading, (e.g., whether there are headings on the page they're reading or what is shown on the book cover), or the person they're with (e.g., does a friend part her hair on the side or down the middle). You'll be surprised how much of this potentially available information is not known. We are selective about the nature of the information we acquire.

Strategies That Promote Learning

There is no substitute for the serene pleasure that learning can bring.

—Izawa (1993, p. 43)

Although there are many different kinds of memory processes and contexts, several general rules have emerged that can promote the learning of new information. There is an old saying that goes something like this: "The head remembers what it does." Embarrassingly, I once again have to admit that I don't remember where I first heard it, but I do recall the message: What you do at acquisition is an important determinant of what you will remember. Simply put, if you engage in activities that promote learning, you will improve your memory.

Pay Attention

One of the primary determinants of what we know is what we attend to. Think back to the last time you were at a large, noisy party with people standing around in small groups talking to each other. Imagine that you're standing with two acquaintances discussing the weather. There are several small groups of people standing nearby who are also carrying on conversations. If someone near you, but not talking to you, mentions your name or something of interest (e.g., "Did you hear the latest news about Debbie and Stanley ... ?"), this will attract your attention. If, however, the same person standing at the same distance from you, speaking in the same voice, is discussing tree blight, you probably would never notice, unless you have a special interest in tree blight. Think about what will happen to the conversation you've been having about the weather. If your answer is "Not much," you're correct. When you switched your attention to the more interesting conversation, you lost most of the meaning of the original conversation. If, at this point, the person who has been talking to you suddenly stops and asks, "What do you think about it?" you'd have to give an embarrassed explanation, because you would have no knowledge of her conversation.

The phenomenon described here is called the *cocktail party effect.* Most people can think of an episode where they've experienced this effect. It demonstrates several basic properties of attention:

1. If you don't pay attention, you won't acquire information. Let's consider the scenario a little more closely. When you were attending to the weather conversation, you knew very little or nothing about the other conversations around you. When you switched your attention to the more interesting conversation, you could not say what was happening in the weather conversation. Thus, attention will be a major concept in what gets remembered, because it determines what gets into the human information system.

2. There are limitations on your ability to process information. All of the conversations going on around you are not processed.

3. There are individual differences in what is attended to. If you had no interest in "the latest news about Debbie and Stanley," but found the weather fascinating, then you would not have switched your attention and could have responded with more than a sheepish grin to the question, "What do you think about it?"

If you're interested in knowing more about memory so that you can improve your own, then you'll have to pay attention to attention. Many people complain that they forget the names of people soon after they've been introduced. It is likely that they never paid attention to the name at the time of introduction. If information is not acquired, then it can never be remembered. When meeting someone, it is a good idea to repeat the person's name aloud to be certain that you've heard it correctly and to be certain that you've paid attention. You need to develop the habit of monitoring your attention. If your eyes are moving across a text, but your mind is somewhere else, you need to be consciously aware of the fact that you're not attending, so that you can redirect your effort to the material to be learned. It's been said that a good politician remembers names. This is also true of successful salespeople, teachers, waiters, and waitresses. Even if you'll never be a politician, salesperson, teacher, or waiter or waitress, it is a good social skill that is well worth the effort.

In case you're unimpressed with the rule that unless you attend to something you won't know it, let's try a demonstration. Most people will admit that they like money, have worked hard to earn it, and have spent it countless times. In Fig. 2.3 there are several drawings of a penny. Only one is correct. If you're like most people, you won't be able to recognize the correct penny because you never attended to its details. Although you've dealt with pennies numerous times (if you are a resident of the United States), you learned only enough of the details to tell it apart from other coins. You probably never acquired a detailed memory of pennies. To find the "correct" answer, check it with a real penny, but be certain that you attend to all of the details carefully. If you're still dubious, try drawing a telephone dial from memory. Few people find that they know which numbers and letters go together, yet we've all dialed telephones thousands of times. The moral is simple: Without attention there will be little memory.

The need to pay attention in school should be obvious. John Holt (1964), a respected educator and author of the book *How Children Fail*, believes that many children fail in school because they don't pay attention. Think about how your mind sometimes seems to wander when reading textbooks or during lectures. Most students are not even aware when they're not paying attention. It should be obvious by now that in order to develop better memory skills, you will also have to develop attentional skills.

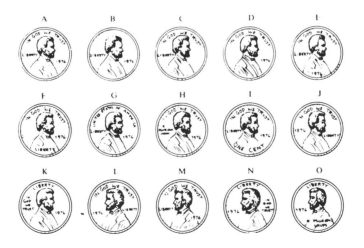

FIG. 2.3. Fifteen drawings of a U.S. penny. Which one is correct? (From Nickerson and Adams, 1979).

Monitor Meaning

Comprehension and memory are closely related concepts because memory is enhanced when the material is meaningful, and meaningful information is retained more easily than material that is low in meaning. If you are learning in a classroom setting, from a textbook, or some similar setting where the information is complex prose and you need to be able to recall it some time later, you need to monitor how much and what you are understanding. Stop at the end of each section, and state or write in your own words, without looking at the text, what you just read. If you cannot meaningfully summarize each section just after reading it, then you will not be able to summarize it at some later date. You need to be aware of what you are learning, and take action if you have "lost it." This is a concrete way to check on your attention. If you finished a section in a text and have no idea what you just read, you need to go back and attend to the content. Additional suggestions for monitoring meaning are given later in this chapter in the section on metamemory and in the next chapter where questioning strategies are presented. Stop now, and say aloud or write out in two or three sentences what this section on memory is conveying.

To demonstrate the powerful influence of meaning on memory, look at A, B, and C in Fig. 2.4 for a few seconds, then cover the figures and reproduce them from memory. Try this now.

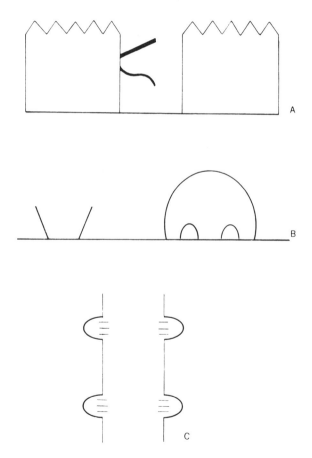

FIG. 2.4. A demonstration of the effect of meaningfulness on memory. Look at these figures for a few seconds, then cover them and reproduce them from memory. (Figures A and B are adapted from Osgood, 1953. Figure C is adapted from Hanson, 1958).

You probably remembered some parts of the figures shown in Fig. 2.4, but didn't remember them perfectly. Suppose I now tell you that Fig. 2.4A is a soldier walking his dog behind a picket fence (Do you see the dog's tail and the end of the soldier's rifle?), and that Fig. 2.4B is a washerwoman scrubbing the floor (Do you see her water bucket and the bottoms of her shoes?). If you recognized Fig. 2.4C as a bear behind a tree, then you drew it more accurately than if it seemed more like abstract art. Making the figures meaningful will enhance how well they are remembered. You can test this with friends by telling them what the figures are, uncovering them briefly, and then comparing how much your friends remembered to your own drawings.

Your elementary school teachers recognized the role that meaning plays in memory when they told you to "read for meaning." We can add meaning to information by elaborating on it. For example, when you are learning something, try to relate it to something that you already know. Put the topic in context or make your own summarization of the information. The idea is to exert the effort and spend the time needed to relate new material to something that is already known so that you won't remember it as an isolated bit of information.

In a clever demonstration of the principle that anything that improves comprehension will improve memory, two psychologists (J. D. Bransford & Johnson, 1972) presented college students with the following passage to read. Read it for yourself and then see how much you can remember:

> The procedure is actually quite simple. First you arrange things into different groups depending on their makeup. Of course, one pile may be sufficient depending on how much there is to do. If you have to go somewhere else due to lack of facilities that is the next step, otherwise you are pretty well set. It is important not to overdo any particular endeavor. That is, it is better to do too few things at once than too many. In the short run this may not seem important, but complications from doing too many can easily arise. A mistake can be expensive as well. The manipulation of the appropriate mechanisms should be self-explanatory, and we need not dwell on it here. At first the whole procedure will seem complicated. Soon, however, it will become just another facet of life. It is difficult to foresee any end to the necessity for this task in the immediate future, but then one never can tell. (p. 722)

You probably did not remember very much of this passage. I also doubt that you found it very understandable.

I'd like you to read the passage again, this time keeping the title "Washing Clothes" in mind. It should seem much more memorable because the title provided a context or a framework for understanding the passage. When information is provided before a person reads a text or learns about a topic, the reader is better able to assimilate the incoming information. The **advance organizers**—the preliminary information—act as a guide or framework that helps the learner to anticipate information and to relate it to other topics. This is the rationale behind the outlines that appear at the beginning of each chapter in this book and the reason why each chapter in the accompanying workbook begins with a series of questions that requires you to think about the topics in the chapter you are about to read.

We seldom remember anything verbatim, that is in the exact words that were spoken or read. Most of our memory is for **gist** or interpretation of the meaning of the message. If a student ever answered an examination question with the exact words I had spoken in class or the student had read from the text, I'd be worried. I'd think that the student probably didn't understand the material and hadn't learned it in a meaningful way.

Distribute Learning

In plain English, this strategy means, "Don't cram." You will learn material in a way that is more resistant to forgetting if you space out the learning sessions. This seems to hold true whether you are learning a motor skill, like how to return the ball with a strong backhand in tennis, the derivation of chemistry formulas, or how to use a new piece of equipment. Spread out the study sessions for maximal benefit. If you can allocate only 5 hours to studying for an exam, spread it out over 3 or 4 days, instead of spending the entire time at one sitting. Of course, study periods also need to be long enough to allow for integration of the information you're reading. The ideal study period depends on many factors including the difficulty of the material, your own attentional capacities, and how much has to be learned.

Get Organized

"Clean up your room!" I don't think that there is a person alive who hasn't heard (or spoken) these words. The idea that "you'll never be able to find anything in this mess" may also apply to how you store information in memory. Although the similarity between memory and a messy room is obviously a gross oversimplification, organization does make it easier both to find a pair of socks that match and retrieve information from memory.

I'd like to demonstrate this point with two lists of words. Read one list, at a rate of approximately one word per second, cover the list and write down as many of the words as you can remember, then repeat this process with the second list.

Girl
Heart
Robin
Purple
Finger
Flute
Blue
Organ
Man
Hawk
Green
Lung
Eagle
Child
Piano

Stop now, cover the preceding list, and write down as many words from this list as you can remember.

Now read the next list, cover it, and then write down as many of the words that you can remember from this list:

Green
Blue
Purple
Man
Girl
Child

Piano
Flute
Organ
Heart
Lung
Finger
Eagle
Hawk
Robin

Stop now, cover the preceding list, and write down as many words from this list as you can remember.

Undoubtedly, you recalled correctly more words from the second list than from the first. You may not have realized that the lists were identical except for the order in which the words were presented. You might expect that you did better the second time because you already had a chance to practice the words once. This is true. The additional time spent studying the words can partially account for the improvement in recall. But, most of the improvement on the second list came from the organization provided by presenting words in categories. Research has shown that when lists of words are presented in categories, recall of material is two to three times better than when the same list of words is randomly presented (Bower & Clark, 1969). When words are presented in random order, as in the first list, recall is improved when subjects have enough time to generate their own categories (Bousfield, 1953).

You can apply this memory principle by organizing material that you need to learn. If you are learning a classification system for a biology course or the properties of metals for a course in science, study one group or category at a time. See how the groups relate and note similarities and differences within and between categories. Impose a structure or organization on the material to be learned. Interrelate the items so that they become coherent. I present several strategies for organizing complex prose passages in the next chapter. Organizational strategies are as important in the recall of prose passages as they are in the recall of lists.

Generate Multiple Cues for Retrieval

I've seen it happen many times. A good student, who worked hard, finds that he can't remember an answer on a exam, and then soon after turning in his paper, the answer seems to pop into his head. Or, similarly, as soon as he hears the answer, he realizes that he "knew" it, but couldn't remember it when it was needed. These are frustrating experiences that can have dire consequences if you can't recall, for example, the CPR (cardiopulmonary resuscitation) you learned in high school or the emergency procedures for those times when you run low on air in the middle of a deep sea dive. Knowledge that you can't recall when it is needed is called **inert knowledge.** Psychologists know a great deal about forgetting, including some ways to make information that you "know" available when you need it. We know that what you do when you are learning something will have a strong effect on whether you are able to recall it when it is needed.

When you recall something, it is in response to some cue. For example, "name some strategies that promote recall." In this example, the terms "strategies to promote recall" are the cues for what is to be remembered. You would not answer with a statement like "Pee Wee Herman is a great actor," although this might be your answer to the question, "Name a great actor." When you learn something, you need to learn it along with the cues that are likely to be present at recall. Ask questions about causes and consequences of the material you are learning. How does the newly acquired information relate to other concepts? What I am describing is the principle of **encoding specificity,** the idea that material is most likely to be recalled when you are presented with the same cues that were available when you learned it.

Suppose you meet Svetlana at a conference of physicists. You learn about her work in theoretical physics and some information about her life, such as the fact that she is the sister of Pavel, an old friend of yours from grade school. Several years pass and you run into Svetlana again at Pavel's wedding. You are likely to remember her if you encoded the information about her brother at the same time you were learning about her work as a physicist. You are more likely to recall Svetlana, or anyone or anything else, if you have the same cues available at recall as you had at learning.

You can use the principle of encoding specificity to improve your memory by generating a rich variety of cues whenever you learn. A "deep" understanding will help to prevent the problem of inert knowledge. By asking why, when, and how questions and developing interconnected knowledge structures in which you relate what is learned to what you already know, you will be able to respond to a greater variety of retrieval cues (The Cognition and Technology Group at Vanderbilt, 1993). Learning that encourages a "deep" or extensive knowledge will help to make the information spontaneously available in those situations when you need it (Van Haneghan, Barron, Young, Williams, Vye, & Bransford, 1992). Be sure to concentrate on cues that you are most likely to encounter when you have to remember something. You can also use external memory aids as cues to recall, a topic I discuss later in this chapter.

Overlearn

When can you stop studying? Well, if this question is applied to a specific example, like studying for a literature exam, then the best answer is when you know the material perfectly over several different sessions. Consider what happens when a child learns her multiplication tables. At some point, she gets through the entire pack of dreaded flash cards (remember them?) without an error. If she stopped learning there, you would find that the next time she went through the deck of flash cards, a few errors would "creep" in. She needs to overlearn, that is go through the pack of cards without errors many times, with sessions spaced out over time, to ensure good recall when these arithmetic facts are needed.

Be Aware of Noncognitive Factors

There is a wide variety of factors that can affect your ability to learn that has little to do with cognition; but you do need to be able to recognize them so that you can find ways to eliminate them. Suppose that you are trying to learn something (anything), but are exhausted from lack of sleep or from excessive exercise (say, the marathon you just ran); your ability to attend, encode, and retain information will suffer. Your ability to learn can also be adversely affected by drugs (prescription and nonprescription varieties), an extremely anxious or depressed emotional state ("I'll never learn this, then I will flunk out, then everyone will know I am dumb, then I will have to sell hamburgers for the rest of my life," etc.), a lack of time for learning, a poor background in the subject area, and many more factors. Of course, all of these examples will depress your ability to learn. I hate to sound like your mother, but take care of yourself, eat right, exercise, get enough sleep, and get help with physical and emotional problems. There is little point in working on the thinking skills that are presented throughout this book if you are going to be spending much of your life strung out on drugs or too anxious to learn.

RETENTION

The art of remembering is the art of thinking ... our conscious effort should not be so much to impress *or* retain *(knowledge) as to* connect *it with something already there.*

—William James (1890)

The term *retention* is sometimes used synonymously with memory. Unfortunately, this term suggests that memory is like a vast storage tank or library where memories are stored and something like miniature pictures of events are retrieved when we need to recall an event. This notion of memory is wrong.

The Constructive Nature of Memory

Many of the popular notions people hold about memory are wrong. For example, in a story by the famous mystery writer Agatha Christie, the witness to a crime had her memory of it "covered over" by a series of events that followed the crime so that she was unable to remember what happened. As the years passed and the witness grew old, the distracting and confusing information was forgotten until only the "true" memory remained. The notion of how our memory works makes for great fiction, but is a wrong account of what psychologists have learned about memory.

Prior Knowledge

Your ability to learn and remember new material depends on what you already know. You certainly wouldn't take an advanced course in nuclear physics if you never had a basic course in physics. However, you probably never realized that prior knowledge, the information you already know, influences how you think and how you remember new information in almost any context. You can read a passage about a familiar topic more quickly than you can read a passage of (objectively) comparable difficulty regarding an unfamiliar topic because your prior knowledge about a known topic facilitates comprehension. Later in this book, I consider the differences between novices and experts in how they solve problems. The expert is better able to comprehend a problem and to remember important aspects of the problem because of her prior knowledge of the field.

Stereotypes and Prejudice

Stereotyping is a category based cognitive response to another person.

—Fiske (1993, p. 623)

An interesting experimental demonstration of the idea that prior knowledge influences what people will remember was conducted by two psychologists, Snyder and Uranowitz (1978). Two groups of college students served as subjects. Students in both groups read the same story about a woman named Betty. The story contained information about her life. Among the information presented was the fact that she occasionally dated men. Up to this point, everything was the same for the students in both groups. After reading the story, one group of students was told that Betty had become a lesbian, whereas the other group of students was told that she was leading a heterosexual lifestyle. The question of interest was whether this would influence what they remembered about Betty's life story. One week later, all of the students returned to the laboratory to answer questions about the story they had read. They were asked many questions, but the critical question was;

In high school, Betty:

(a) occasionally dated men
(b) never went out with men
(c) went steady
(d) no information provided

Can you guess the results of this experiment? The group of students who were told that Betty is now a lesbian were much more likely to "remember" (b) as the correct answer than the group of students who were told that Betty is a heterosexual. The students who had been told that Betty is a lesbian believed that they remembered something that hadn't occurred. Their prejudices and beliefs about lesbians caused them to remember events that never transpired.

In an experiment designed to determine how sex role stereotypes influence memory (Halpern, 1985), high school students were given dull, boring stories to read about the life of a main character who was either a male ("David") or a female ("Linda"). The events described in the story were those commonly engaged in by both women and men. Female high school students who read stories with Linda as the protagonist remembered the story better than other female students who read the same story with David as the protagonist, whereas male high school students remembered the story better when David was the protagonist. It seems that the high school students were able to identify with the main character when his or her sex was the same as their own, and this resulted in better memory for the details of the story. In addition, errors in memory were biased toward conformity with sex role stereotypes.

Our beliefs about lesbians, women, men, and other groups, especially racial and ethnic groups, exert strong influences on what we will remember about members of these groups. People may honestly believe that they are recalling something that, in fact, never occurred because their beliefs about what must have happened bias how they recall the events.

Experiments like the ones just described have important implications for understanding the nature of prejudice. Let's return to the earlier example and suppose that Betty was a real person whom you knew while growing up. There may be many things that you can remember about Betty. You now learn that she is a lesbian. Suppose further that you have a stereotype of lesbians as women who drive trucks, crush beer cans with one hand, and hate all men. Because this stereotype, like most, contains very little truth about any hypothetical "average" lesbian, you would be forced either to change your stereotype or to change what you remember about Betty. It seems that it is our specific memories that change, whereas, the more abstract memory information underlying our stereotypes resists change. You might selectively remember information like the fact that she always liked to play basketball and forget other information about Betty that is inconsistent with your stereotype, like the fact that she also liked to cook and plant flowers. Allport (1954), in a classic book on prejudice wrote, "It is possible for a stereotype to grow in defiance of *all* evidence...." (pp. 189–190). This is an important point that I want to reiterate. Our beliefs are not easily changed; instead, we tend to change our memory for what we saw and heard so that the memory is made consistent with the beliefs. Most often, memory is altered without conscious awareness that the information is being recalled in a way that does not match the event. This is why stereotypes are so resistant to change and the need to understand how we think and remember is so important. The critical need to understand and reduce stereotyping and prejudice was concisely summarized by Fiske (1993), "Without stereotypes there would be less need to hate, exclude, exterminate" (p. 621).

Inference and Distortion

Memory is malleable. Our memory depends on how we encoded or interpreted events, not the events themselves. What we remember changes over time. When our knowledge and experience change, our memories also change (F. C. Bartlett, 1932). There are additions made to memories so that we remember events that never occurred and deletions made so that we forget other events that did. Often, people cannot distinguish between their own thoughts and their perceptions (Johnson & Raye, 1981). Have you ever wondered, "Did she really say that or did I think she said that?" At your next high school or college reunion get together with friends to remember old times. You may be surprised to find that the same events are remembered differently by each of you, and each will have memories that others don't have. Furthermore, each of several people who shared a common event and remembered it differently will be highly confident that his or her memory is highly accurate. Overconfidence about our ability to remember is another pervasive psychological trait.

Eyewitness Testimony

Seeing is believing, or so they say. Nowhere is this adage held as strongly as in our legal system. Very often eyewitness testimony is the determining factor between a conviction and an acquittal. Defendants with credible, plausible alibis have been convicted by an eyewitness identification. Should we be placing so much faith in the accounts given by eyewitnesses?

If we use the theoretical framework provided earlier, then recall of the event depends on acquisition, retention, and retrieval. Information can never be recalled correctly unless it was attended to at the time it occurred. This would not seem to be a problem if we're interested in memory for a crime, because it would seem to demand our attention. In fact, witnesses and victims fail to notice many important details because of a narrowing of attention that occurs under stress. If there is a gun or other weapon used during the crime, then the victim focuses on the weapon. Other details that are needed for correct identification, like whether the assailant had a mustache, may go unnoticed (E. F. Loftus, 1979).

There are many alterations of the memory of the event that occur during the retention interval, which in this case is the time between the crime and the recollection of it at trial. Discussions of the crime after it occurred can be incorporated into memory so that the individual may honestly believe that she is recalling the crime, whereas what is really being recalled is a discussion of the crime.

A notorious example of the fallibility of human memory was seen in a highly publicized case involving a Catholic priest who was positively identified as an armed robber by several different witnesses. The trial ended abruptly when a much younger and taller man confessed, offering details of the crime that could only have been known by the real robber, because they were never publicized. The witnesses had not lied. Each honestly believed that he or she remembered seeing the priest as the robber. It is important to realize that although memory can sometimes be astonishingly accurate, it can also be astonishingly wrong.

Real and False Memories

An explosive controversy involving memory has shaken public confidence in many accounts of memories that were not recalled for long periods of time and then suddenly emerged, often during psychotherapy sessions. These memories usually involve traumatic events such as witnessing a murder or experiencing sexual or other physical abuse. Some psychologists believe that these memories are quite accurate and that they were not available for recall because they were repressed as a protective mechanism for the individual who could not deal with the trauma. Other psychologists believe that although some of these memories may be accurate accounts of real events, many are likely to be "false" memories for events that either did not occur or were very different from the way they were remembered (E. F. Loftus, 1993).

Memories can be accurate or inaccurate. In some cases, there is corroborating evidence showing that the memory is "true" (e.g., physical evidence of abuse), and in other instances, there is evidence that these "memories" were "suggested" by therapists and others, and thus, never occurred. But, in many cases, there is no scientific or other way to detect the differences among a highly accurate memory, an altered memory that is partly accurate and partly inaccurate, and a completely false memory. There have been many highly publicized cases involving prominent figures where some horrible deed was alleged to have happened. Unfortunately, some innocent people have been accused of horrible crimes. One such case involved Cardinal Bernardin, a respected Catholic leader, who was accused of abusing a young man who remembered the abuse for the first time many years after it allegedly occurred. The young man later decided that he didn't really remember such abuse. On the other hand, memories of abuse and other tragic events are sometimes accurate. The evidence must be considered on a case-by-case basis, which is how our legal system works.

RETRIEVAL

What is your mother's maiden name? Unless you happened to be sitting here thinking about your mother's name, the name seemed to "pop" into your mind. The answer must have been stored in some way that allowed it to be retrieved with a simple question. In fact, it seems almost impossible not to remember your mother's maiden name, when you are asked this question. Now try this one: What are the names of Diana's and Charles' children? (Yes, the Diana and the Charles, princess and prince of Wales.) You probably are having trouble with this question, even though you probably heard their names and read them several times. Forgetting can be a frustrating experience for everyone. How can we understand the retrieval process when it works so well sometimes and so poorly other times?

Forgetting

Happiness lies in good health and a bad memory.

—Ingrid Bergman (quoted in M. U. Smith, 1992, p. A1)

One of the major theories of forgetting is that events interfere with each other in memory. This is called the **interference theory of forgetting.** Suppose that you are studying French and Spanish in college. You'd probably find that you sometimes get them confused because what you've learned about one language "interferes" with what you've learned about the other. In general, the more similar two events are (or in this case languages), the more interference there will be. Knowing this, can you think of a way to reduce interference and improve memory? In the example just given, one way would be to take the courses in different semesters to minimize the interference, or at least one course early in the morning and the other in the evening. By keeping the French and Spanish courses as separate as possible, you can reduce some of the interference.

Thinking and Forgetting

By definition, we can't recall what we have forgotten. Often, we will have partial information about the forgotten material, such as the frustrating, "I know that I know the answer, but I can't remember it now." Psychologists call this experience "tip of the tongue" because of the maddening way the information seems to be right on the tip of the tongue, but can't quite be recalled. Other times, we simply do not know what we have forgotten. Researchers have found that most often people treat the absence of information as though it is evidence that there is none. Let me explain with an example. Should you marry your significant other? Suppose that you can think of ("thinking of" is the same as recalling) two reasons why you should and none why you shouldn't. Because you cannot recall any reasons that run counter to this decision, you rely on what can be recalled to guide your decision. The problem, of course, is that we cannot know what we have forgotten. But, it is possible to spend some time and effort considering what sort of evidence might have been forgotten and overlooked. Did you forget to consider that she picks her nose and this really bothers you, or that he is a sloppy housekeeper, a trait that is driving you "crazy?" The need to generate information so that it can be evaluated is discussed in several places throughout this book. For now, think of it as a forgetting problem that can be lessened, but not eliminated, with conscious effort to consider what might have been forgotten. Because we cannot recall any reasons why we may be making the wrong decision, people tend to be overconfident about the quality of their decisions. A second reason for the overconfidence that we have in our thinking and remembering processes is that we can only act on one decision (e.g., marry or not), and we can never know if another decision would have been better.

Recall Errors

It is clear that we store knowledge (or generate it) in highly organized ways. Sometimes, the errors we make can provide clues to how it is organized. Has your father or mother ever called you by your sibling's name? Most people respond, "Yes." But, few people report that their father or mother called them by the name of the family dog. Intuitively, this would be insulting (unless they really love the dog) because it suggests some underlying facts about how your parent thinks about you. Similarly, if your boyfriend or girlfriend called you by the name of a former significant other, this is also perceived as insulting because it suggests that he or she was thinking about the former boyfriend or girlfriend or that information about you and the former love are stored together in memory.

I can think of several examples where these "slips of the tongue" have revealed some telltale signs about the way people store information in memory. In one embarrassing example, a university administrator kept mixing up the names of two minority deans. This painful mix-up showed how he had stored information about them in memory and tended to think about them as "minority deans" instead of some other grouping or as individuals.

Stop now, and answer the two questions in the following box. After you write in the answer for each question, rate how confident you are that your answer is correct. Use the numbers 1 to 7 to rate your confidence with 1 = not at all confident, 7 = completely confident, and 4 = middle level of confidence.

1. How many animals of each kind did Moses take on the ark?

_____ Confidence rating (1–7) _____

2. In the biblical story, what was Joshua swallowed by?

_____ Confidence rating (1–7) _____

Look over your confidence ratings and compare with them with the ratings of other students. If you responded like most people, you were very confident and very wrong. Did you respond with the "2" to the first question? If you did, you were wrong because Moses didn't have an ark; you were thinking about Noah. What about the second question? Were you confident that the answer is a "whale?" If so, you were wrong again because it wasn't Joshua who was swallowed by a whale. Demonstrations like this one show how memory works. When you read about animals on an ark, you activated your knowledge for the biblical ark story and never noticed that Moses was named in the question. The same thing happened with your knowledge of the biblical whale story. Reflect on what this shows us about human memory—the way it is organized and used and the way we can be completely confident and completely wrong. Try this demonstration with your family and friends and then explain to them what you have learned about remembering.

Retrieval Cues

As you recall (I hope, I hope) a strategy for good learning is to generate multiple cues when you are learning new information that should be useful at recall. Let's consider how these cues operate at recall. Have you ever heard a song on the radio and then thought about the time you first heard it? ("They're playing our song.") Where did these memories come from? Something in the environment acted as a retrieval cue so that the memory was brought into conscious awareness.

Let's try a demonstration of the powerful effect retrieval cues can have on memory. Following is a list of words I'd like you to read through. Go through the list once at a rate of approximately one word per second, or have someone read them aloud to you. See how many words you can remember:

Winter
Green
Foot
Pencil
Sweater
Jupiter
Chicago
Bible
French
Violin
Lunch
Russia

Collie
Spaghetti
Melrose Place
Newsweek

Stop now; cover the preceding list and see how many of the list items you can recall in any order. Be sure to try this exercise before you go on. Don't look back at the list when you are finished. If you didn't remember all 16 words, I'd like you to think about the items you forgot. What happened to them? Are they permanently lost or could you remember them with the proper retrieval cues?

Here is a list of cues. See how many of the "forgotten" words you can recall.

A season of the year
A color
A part of the body
A writing instrument
An article of clothing
A planet
A name of a city
A type of book
A language
A musical instrument
A meal
A country
A breed of dog
A food
A television show
A magazine

Certainly you can remember many more of the items on the list with the appropriate retrieval cues, and this improvement can't be attributed simply to guessing. Generating your own cues while you are trying to learn something in order to facilitate recall is one good way to improve memory when the cues that you use at learning are those that are likely to be available at recall. The cues act like "hooks" in memory so that information is more accessible and can be more readily remembered.

Many of the strategies to improve memory "work" by providing retrieval cues. Have you ever had the frustrating experience of struggling to recall the name of your best friend or your favorite author and then remembered it *after* you embarrassed yourself by forgetting such obvious information? As discussed in the section on generating multiple cues at the time of learning (encoding cues), the fact that you may have the knowledge needed in a situation does not guarantee that access to that knowledge will occur. Retrieval cues help us to locate relevant information that is stored in memory; they allow us to use what we know. The ability to access stored knowledge is an "important hallmark of intelligence" (J. D. Bransford, Sherwood, Vye, & Rieser, 1986).

WORKING MEMORY

A common theme among researchers who study memory is that memory has a limited capacity; that is, we cannot remember everything that we would like. Nor can we keep too many different "pieces" of information in an active form in memory so that we can use them all simultaneously. If I asked you to recite the alphabet backwards while solving calculus problems, you would object because there is simply not enough "space" or "effort" or whatever term you want to use to execute these two tasks simultaneously, although either one alone can be performed. The cognitive resources that are used to execute mental operations and to remember the outcomes of these processes are available only in a limited supply. The "place" where conscious thought occurs is called **working memory** because it is the hypothetical space where we perform the work of thinking. One goal of an efficient system is to make the work of thinking easier, or, metaphorically, to reduce the amount of space or effort needed in working memory.

Baddeley (1986, 1992) proposed a view of working memory that includes a "central executive" or "boss" that directs the activities we engage in while thinking, and other systems that involve visual and verbal modes of thought. Often without awareness, we make decisions about how to spend the limited resources of working memory. One of these decisions is to use external aids. For example, instead of trying to remember my shopping list, I write it down. I know that it is not worth the mental effort of committing this list to memory. We also categorize information to reduce the load on memory. I could remember to buy "stuff" for the dog (dog food, biscuits, flea powder) and "stuff" for the kids' lunches (sandwich makings, apples, lunch bags), and so on. This would reduce the number of items that I would have to recall and make forgetting less likely.

Another way we manage our memory is by making decisions about what information we need to use and how much mental effort to "spend" on a particular task. For example, suppose that you had to make a decision concerning a complex issue. You could decide to omit technical information that is difficult to understand, and therefore uses a great deal of working memory. If you had to decide if there is danger from the nuclear waste dump that is next to your house, you might decide to deal with only a subset of the information to simplify the difficult task of understanding nuclear risk. Unfortunately, you could also reduce the mental work load by seeking simple explanations for complex issues such as crime (it's caused by unemployment), truancy (it's caused by bad parents), or economic downturns (it's caused by some minority group that is different from you). These simple purported causes for difficult problems help to reduce the amount of information that is used to reach a conclusion, but they are also a detriment to good thinking because complex problems do not have simple, single causes.

Chunking

As you can see, the strategies that we use to reduce the effort of thinking and remembering can lead to biases and errors. What is needed is an efficient way to reduce the demands on working memory that will not have a negative effect on what and how we think. Multiple studies of the ways that experts think have shown that one of the major differences between people with expertise in some field and those without the expertise is in the efficient way that the experts organize and recall information that is specific to their specialty. The experts are able to perceive large, meaningful patterns of information that reflect the highly organized nature of the information in their memories. They also know how to search for answers to problems using information available in the environment and knowledge that they have stored in memory. Experts keep the goal clearly in mind, and regulate their thinking process (Glaser, 1992). These highly compact memory "units" and efficient search strategies place fewer demands on working memory. Interestingly, these advantages are specific to the expert's specialization; they approach cognitive tasks in other domains much like the rest of us, a fact that suggests that the real advantage is not in a generally superior mind or memory, but in the highly developed knowledge structures and search procedures that correspond to one's area of expertise (Chi, Glaser, & Farr, 1988).

Meaningfulness and familiarity can account for some individual differences in the ability to utilize highly compact memory units. Have you ever wondered how a good poker or pinochle or chess player is able to remember which cards have been played or which moves have been made? In a classic study of chess players' memories for the positions of chess pieces on a board, A. D. de Groot (1966) found that chess masters could remember chess positions that actually occurred in a game after looking at the board for only 5 seconds. Novice chess players had much more difficulty in remembering where the chess pieces had been. Does this mean that really good chess players have extraordinary memories? To answer this question, de Groot placed the pieces randomly on the board and asked master and novice players to view the board for 5 seconds and then recall the positions of the pieces. In the random placement condition, both groups performed about the same. It seems that the master players remembered more than the novices only when the board positions were highly meaningful to the chess masters and consequently were remembered quite accurately.

It seems likely that good card players remember which cards have already been played because each hand is highly meaningful to them. For example, John Moss (1950, a pseudonym for the author of *How to Win at Poker*) described a series of possible hands that a player can be dealt along with several possible cards that could be drawn. It would be easy for him or another poker shark to remember a "four of diamonds in the hole with a four of hearts, six of diamonds and ace of spades exposed." He could remember this as a single familiar hand, whereas a novice player would have to remember four separate cards. For the good players, this hand would represent a single chunk in memory. Reducing a large number of items to a single item to be remembered is called **chunking**. (No, it is not a brand of Chinese food.) It is a subtle and ubiquitous memory process. It allows us to recall whole sentences instead of words and whole words instead of letters. As material becomes increasingly meaningful, we can reduce the number of items that need to be remembered. Master chess players and card players seem to have this memory advantage.

Look quickly at the following rows of letters and numbers, and then cover them and try to remember as many as you can:

IB MF BI TW AJ FK

816 44 93 62 51 69 41

If you had difficulty with this task, the reason may be that the information was not chunked or grouped into meaningful units. Suppose I reorganize the letters by changing the spacing but not their order. They now become IBM, FBI, TWA, and JFK. You should have no difficulty remembering all of the letters now. The amount of information hasn't changed, but the cognitive demand has. It is much easier to recall information that is chunked into meaningful units. Consider the row of numbers. Suppose I tell you that this series, if regrouped, is the sequence 9^2, 8^2, 7^2, and so forth. Again, by relating the input to what's known to make it meaningful, a difficult memory task can be made trivial.

The notion that meaning is important in memory is raised again, later in this chapter, when we consider strategies for improving memory.

METAMEMORY

If one has poor insights into the inner workings of their cognitive system, this should inhibit their performance on virtually all tasks, because it is hard to imagine a single cognitive task that does not require some level of metacognitive awareness for its successful completion.

—Ceci and Ruiz (1993, p. 175)

The term **metamemory** refers to one's personal knowledge of his or her own memory system. It seems that much of the difference between good and poor learners can be attributed to metamemory. D. Bransford (1979) summarized this:

> [E]ffective learners know themselves what they need to know and do in order to perform effectively; they are able to monitor their own levels of understanding and mastery. These active learners are therefore likely to ask questions of clarification and more efficiently plan their study activities. Such activities are quite different from passively accepting (yet momentarily actively processing) the particular information that a person or text presents. (p. 248)

In the next chapter, I build on this theme and emphasize the importance of asking questions as a metamemory strategy.

This quote from D. Bransford (1979) brings up the important concept of active learning. Very little, if anything, can be learned passively (American Psychological Association, 1992). You need to actively deal with material if you want to remember it. Good learners know when they understand the material and when they do not understand it; poor learners don't seem to notice the difference. Good learners know what they have to do to facilitate learning. These are the executive processes that keep the learner mindful of what and how much is being learned. For example, good learners may spontaneously link new information to information previously learned or think of possible applications for the new materials they are learning. As you read this paragraph, you may be applying this learning "device" by noting the similarity of this concept with one you learned in the section entitled organization, that imposing additional organization on material by activities like these will result in improved comprehension.

An interesting study has shown that students who are having academic problems in college approach their text assignments differently from good students (Whimbey, 1976). The less successful college students read difficult material straight through without seeming to notice when they didn't understand the material and without rereading the difficult sections. Good students know these strategies. Whimbey found that he could improve performance for the poorer students by teaching them how to organize the material and how to become aware of what they were understanding and what they weren't. Too often college students and others believe that they know some material because they've read or heard it. They're surprised to find that they can't answer basic questions about the material they supposedly knew.

Nelson and Narens (1990) provided a list of tasks that are used in experimental settings to assess metamemory. This list can easily be adapted as a way to enhance metamemory. For example, before you begin a learning task, carefully assess the ease with which you expect to achieve the learning, called **ease of learning judgments.** If you are a senior in college who has majored in sociology, you might decide that the material presented in an introductory psychology text would be easy for you to learn. Alternatively, you could decide that a course in Asian philosophy would be relatively difficult to learn. The reason for making ease of learning judgments is that they require you think about the to-be-learned material, considering what you already know about the topic, your ability in the area, and the learning context. These reflections will prepare you to allocate the necessary time and mental resources to accomplish the task.

While you are learning, consider how well you know the material—that is, make judgments of how well you are learning—**quality of learning judgments.** If you can determine that it is not going well, then you can redirect your learning activities and seek help. After learning, think about how well you know and understand what has just been learned—**feelings of knowing judgments.** Finally, when you are using the material in a response, make **degree of confidence judgments** about your answers. Taken together these four tasks will provide an ongoing monitor of learning and memory, and they can help with the selection of control procedures such as allocating more time and effort, trying another study mode, and stopping the learning session. These four metamemory tasks are summarized in Table 2.1.

MNEMONICS

In an episode of the popular children's television show, *Sesame Street,* Bert and Ernie, two lovable muppets, discussed an intriguing memory phenomenon. Bert noticed that Ernie had tied a piece of string around his finger to help him remember something. In fact, Ernie tied string around each of his eight fingers (apparently muppets have eight fingers) to be really sure that he didn't forget. After some prompting from Bert, Ernie recalled that the string was supposed to help him remember he should buy more string, as they had run out of string.

Although this story is humorous, it illustrates some fundamental assumptions and problems encountered by humans (and muppets) in dealing with their memory. The wide range of activities from tying a string around one's finger to the more elaborate

TABLE 2.1
Self-Reflective Tasks That Can Serve as a Guide for Monitoring the Process of Remembering

When	What	How
Before learning	Ease of learning judgments	Look over the material that is to be learned and judge the ease with which you will learn it. Consider what you already know about the topic, the reason why you are learning it, and your own abilities.
While learning	Quality of learning judgments	As you learn, monitor how well you are understanding the information or performing a motor skill. Can you summarize in your own words what is being learned? Are you generating multiple cues and using techniques that foster deep learning?
After learning	Feeling of knowing judgments	When the learning task is completed, reflect on how well you learned the material. Have you overlearned for maximal retention and used distributed practice? Will you be able to recall the material some time in the future?
At recall	Degree of confidence judgments	When you are recalling the information, consider how confident you are in your recall.

procedures presented later are called **mnemonic devices.** They are techniques for organizing and elaborating information so that it can be more easily remembered. Many students use mnemonic devices to prepare for exams and some of the techniques are so common that we usually don't think of them as mnemonics.

During the summers when I was in college, I worked as a waitress at a resort in the Catskill Mountains of New York. The resort had a nightclub with the usual array of singers, dancers, jugglers, and animal acts. (The kitchen help was not allowed to attend the nightclub, so, of course, we would sneak in as often as we could.) One particular act that amazed me was a memory act by Harry Lorayne. He went around the audience recalling people's names. His memory seemed limitless. I was also surprised at how much the audience enjoyed his performance and that an amazing memory would qualify as a nightclub act. Harry Lorayne later wrote two books on this topic (Lorayne, 1975; Lorayne & Lucas, 1974). The mnemonic principles he used are presented here along with several others.

Most mnemonics are based on a few simple memory principles. They all force you to pay attention to the items to be remembered, and they provide a meaningful context for unrelated items. The user is often required to organize the material and to use the mnemonic as an efficient retrieval cue. The use of mnemonics also requires metacognitive monitoring—keeping track of what you know. They are intentional strategies, ones that you can use when you decide that you want to remember something. Thus, from what you've already learned about memory earlier in this chapter, you can see that mnemonics are not mere theatrical tricks. They work because they represent applications of basic principles of memory.

We all employ memory aids everyday. The most common aids are **external memory aids,** such as the sticky notes that are popular, calendars in which we write appointments and other activities that we want to remember, timers to remind us to turn off the stove, and shopping lists. Mnemonics that are designed to help us retrieve information from memory are called **internal memory aids.** In this chapter, I present four basic types of internal memory aids—keywords and images, rhymes, method of places, and first letters. Each is discussed in turn followed by some guidelines for selecting the appropriate mnemonic for the type of material to be learned.

Keywords and Images

The following demonstration was presented as an anecdote by Donald Norman (1976). I have used it as a class demonstration many times, and students are always surprised at how well it works. The use of this mnemonic depends on first learning *keywords*, which serve as "hooks" for information that is learned later. In this case, the keywords are in the form of a simple poem to learn. Spend a minute or two learning this poem:

> One is a bun,
> Two is a shoe,
> Three is a tree,
> Four is a door,
> Five is a hive,
> Six are sticks,
> Seven is heaven,
> Eight is a gate,
> Nine is a line, and
> Ten is a hen.

Do you have this memorized? If not, go over the poem again.

Now, I'm going to present a list of words to be remembered. You have to form an image or association between the listed items and the items in the poem you just learned. For example, the first item on the list is ashtray. Image an ashtray with a bun in it, because the bun was the first item in the poem. You could imagine something like a large hamburger bun sitting in a dirty ashtray. Read the items on the list one at a time, allowing enough time to form an image:

1. ashtray
2. firewood
3. picture
4. cigarette
5. table
6. matchbook
7. glass
8. lamp
9. shoe
10. phonograph

Now, cover the list of words and answer the following questions:

What is number eight?
What number is cigarette?

If your experience was like the one Norman (1976) described or the ones my students report, then you've been surprised to find that the answers were easily available. In this case you learned a list of rhyming keywords and then used imagery to relate the words to be learned to the keywords. Research has shown that images are best when they're interacting (e.g., the bun is in the ashtray and not just next to it) and when they are vivid and detailed (the bun that I was imaging was a hamburger bun and the ashtray was glass; Bower, 1972). The deliberate use of both verbal and imagery modes of thought was introduced in the first chapter. We use this strategy again in the chapters on creativity and problem solving. Of course, you're probably thinking, "Why not just write the list down on paper?" If paper and pencil are allowable and available, this is certainly the best and cheapest mnemonic that you can find, but often we need to commit lists to memory. If you are an anatomy student, you have to learn long lists of the names of nerves, bones, and other organs. Chemists need to learn complex formulas, and it would not instill confidence in me if I found that my surgeon kept a written list of body parts above the operating table (but, it might not be a bad idea). There are many real-life instances when we need to learn long lists of material in as efficient a way as possible.

Images can also be used alone (without keywords). They are especially advantageous when you want to remember names and faces. This is the technique that Harry Lorayne (1975) used. Change the names you want to remember to a concrete noun; pick out a distinctive feature of the face and image the two as interacting. He suggested that you pay special attention to cheeks, lips, facial lines, forehead, nose, eyebrows, and eyes. For example, if you meet Ms. Silverstein and you notice that she has wide-set eyes, you could image a silver beer mug (stein) between her eyes. Mr. Dinter could be changed to dinner and an entire dinner could be imaged on his large forehead. Try this at the next party you attend. You'll find it fun, and you may surprise yourself with your new abilities.

A keyword mnemonic system has been developed especially for learning a second language (Atkinson, 1975). Suppose you are learning French and are faced with the following three vocabulary words with their English translations to learn:

French	English
homme	man
etoile	star
legume	vegetable

Students begin by generating their own keywords. The keyword should sound like the foreign vocabulary word. Thus, for the word *homme*, I'd generate "home," for *etoile*, I'd use "a towel," and for *legume*, I'd use "lagoon."

The second step makes use of imagery by linking an image of the keyword with the correct translation of the foreign word. I'd visualize a man entering a large home, a towel with a star painted on it, and vegetables floating in a lagoon. (It's best when the items are interacting.) When the foreign words *homme, etoile,* and *legume* are encountered, students would then automatically recall the images and retrieve the correct translations.

Atkinson (1975) claimed that as facility with the foreign language develops the need to remember the images diminishes and students can extract the intended meaning without the use of imagery. Students who are taught to use this method consistently recall more correct English translations (72% compared with 46%) than students who use the usual rote rehearsal method of repeating the words until they "stick." Furthermore, this method seems to work best when students generate their own keywords and images. The need for active participation in learning is a general rule. This is a mnemonic that is well worth using if you are studying a foreign language.

Rhymes

We also use rhymes to help us remember. For example, there are few people who haven't heard: "I before E, except after C"; or "Thirty days hath September, April, June, and November."

Answer this question quickly. What letter comes after N? Most people find that they need to sing that portion of the alphabet (l, m, n, o, p) to answer this question. Like rhymes, the rhythm established in songs helps to deter forgetting.

Rhymes are useful when order is important because mistakes in order will usually destroy the rhyme. Notice that the first keyword poem I presented relied on keywords, images, and rhymes (one is a bun, etc.). This is an especially easy mnemonic to use, probably because several mnemonic devices are employed in the same poem to guard against forgetting.

Methods of Places

Before I describe how "places" works as a mnemonic device, I'd like you to remember my back-to-school shopping list. Read the list through slowly once, then see how many items you can recall:

Pencils
Ruler
Notebook
Marking pens

Compass
Tape
Paper
Scissors
Sharpener
Reinforcements
Tablet
Glue

How many items on this list did you remember?

Now I'll show you how the **method of places** (or method of loci) could improve your recall for this list. Pick a familiar route, like the one from your house to school. Now imagine each of the items on this list placed somewhere along this route. The pencils could be very tall and form a fence around your front lawn, the ruler could be sitting across your car, the notebook could be the stop sign at your corner, and so on. Try this now with the back-to-school shopping list just presented. Once the images are formed, you should be able to remember every item by "mentally walking through" your route and noticing the items you've imaged along the way.

I once went to an introductory lesson for a very expensive memory improvement course. The method of places was the demonstration they used to convince potential students that the course was valuable. For months afterward, I received letters in the mail asking me if I "forgot" to send my money and to register for their course. The expensive (there are no cheap ones) memory improvement courses teach the same methods presented in this chapter. They have no magic secrets that are unavailable in the psychology literature.

The Greeks, who were famous for giving long speeches from memory, have left us with many tips on how to best use this method. For example, the same route can be used repeatedly for different lists, but we should be careful not to put more than one item at the same place (Ross & Laurence, 1968). They also suggested that the places should not be too much alike (e.g., don't use only stop signs along your route) and that they should not be too brightly lit (or there will be glare) nor too dimly lit (or the objects will be difficult to see). This is a good method to use when events need to be remembered in a particular order, because the route can be mentally traversed forward or backward.

Research with the elderly has shown that they can perform as well as much younger college students when they are taught and use this mnemonic. This is important because America is an aging society, and many elderly fear a loss of memory. If you are elderly, or if you know someone who is, many of the simple mnemonics presented in this chapter such as the method of places and use of visual imagery can be used as an aid to memory and thus, postpone or reduce cognitive aging effects. It is also particularly useful to assist the elderly with the use of external memory aids such as medication boxes that have an alarm to signal the time for the medication, calendars, and timers (D. C. Park, 1992). External aids have the advantage of helping those with failing (or poor) memory recall the tasks that are important. The internal mnemonics offer the benefit of helping the elderly retain their own cognitive abilities.

First Letters

First-letter mnemonics are probably most commonly used in preparing for tests. To use this technique, take the first letter of each term to be learned, insert vowels and other letters if necessary, and make a word. When you need to remember the list, you recall the word you formed and then use each letter as a retrieval cue for each item on the list. Many of us learned to remember the names of the Great Lakes as HOMES (Huron, Ontario, Michigan, Erie, and Superior). If you never learned this before, you'll never forget it again.

The first-letter mnemonic organizes unrelated terms into a single word. You already know how important good organization is for memory. I can remember using this technique when I was a college student. The class had been told to be prepared to answer a long essay question that was to be written during an in-class exam. There were six points that I wanted to make in the essay, and I wanted to be sure that I included all of them in order. I took the first letter of each of the points, made up a word using these letters, and used this word to help me remember all of the points for the exam. (It worked well.) This technique is also especially useful when you have to speak in front of people without notes. Select one word that can stand for each point you want to make and use the first letter of each word to form a single retrievable word. Even though good speeches may appear unrehearsed, good speakers practice with techniques like this one. It helps them to present their speech in a confident and professional manner.

A related mnemonic that doesn't fit clearly into any of the categories is the one used to recall the value of pi. I'm presenting it in this section because even though it doesn't involve first letters, it is a letter-based technique. Read the following sentence: May I have a drink, alcoholic of course. By counting the letters in each word, you can read off the digits for pi, which are 3.1415926. It is easier to remember a single meaningful sentence than it is to recall eight digits.

Mnemonic Principles

Mnemonic devices can be powerful aids for memory. They are also somewhat paradoxical because it seems that to remember better you need to remember more. The first-letter mnemonic requires that you remember the new word you created with the first letters as well as each of the words. The keyword systems require that you learn a keyword system, and the rhymes present you with a song or poem to be learned. They each necessitate work. Acquiring a good memory means working at it, but it is work that pays off in lifelong dividends. There are literally hundreds of studies that demonstrate that the deliberate use of mnemonics improves recall (McCormick & Levin, 1987).

Let's try to develop a mnemonic that could help you to remember the types of mnemonics. First, let's review what they are: keywords and images, rhymes, method of places, and (first) letters. Although you could use the method of places and image each of these terms along a route, or associate them with a keyword, or make up a poem, my choice for a list like this one is the first-letter mnemonic. Start by listing the first letter of each term: K, R, MP, L. You can modify the first-letter technique by using each letter to begin a word in a sentence, because incorporating these letters in a single word may be difficult. Try it. The sentence one of my students came up with is "Kind Round Men, Please Listen." Use imagery also to aid recall. Imagine a round (fat) man with a kind face and very big ears (for listening). Make your images detailed and vivid. (Can you see his round tummy and elephant-size ears?) If you're asked to recall the mnemonic devices, you can list each one, and by remembering the name of each, all of the information you've learned about them should also be easily retrieved.

Many people find it difficult to remember how to spell the word *mnemonics*. Another student suggested this one: *Memory Never Explains MONey and Ice Cream Sand-*

wiches? Be sure to think about this mnemonic. You should never have difficulty spelling this word correctly again.

External Memory Aids

External memory aids, which are sometimes called "cognitive prostheses" are also valuable in helping with the multitude of remembering tasks that we all encounter. If you have to remember to do something, a kind of remembering called **prospective memory** because it is memory for a future event, why not set an alarm, post a note, tie a string on your finger, or leave something in an obvious and unavoidable place (e.g., the wastebasket in front of the door).

Some people have acquired specialized and specific external memory aids. I was impressed with such a system when I was attending a ballet at the grand Bolshoi Theatre in Moscow. Like many cities with very cold weather, it is customary to check your coat when you arrive at the theater. In addition, many people also check bags with boots and large hats. The worker at the wardrobe has to be able to dispense hundreds of possessions very quickly when the ballet is over. In addition, the checker also rents binoculars and needs to remember who rented the binoculars so as to be certain that the binoculars are returned. I found that the checkers had devised a simple external mnemonic system. The coat hooks are numbered (into the hundreds at each station). When someone checks a bag with the coat, the checker uses a number that ends in 4 (14, 24, 34, etc.). Then when the claim ticket is presented at the end of the show, a 4 in the last digit means that the checker should look below for a package. If a person rents binoculars, then a chalk line is marked above the coat hook number. Then if a coat is retrieved and there is a chalk mark above the number, the checker knows that binoculars are to be returned. This simple system, which has probably developed over many years, helps to get a large number of people out of the wardrobe area and reduces the time spent in line. This last point is critical to Russians who can spend up to 2 hours a day in lines. If only such a system could be used to reduce the other lines as well.

Remembering Events

Most often we need to remember events rather than lists or related concepts. Much of the work done in the area of event memory has been conducted by psychologists trying to assist victims and witnesses of crime with recall of the criminal activity. We can borrow the mnemonic techniques that they use to improve memory.

The Cognitive Interview

"Information is the lifeblood of a criminal investigation" (Stewart, 1985). How can eyewitnesses to an event be helped to remember what happened so that they can provide law enforcement officers with the needed information? One way to improve the quantity and quality of what gets remembered is with the use of a memory aid for events known as the **cognitive interview** (Geiselman & Fisher, 1985). The cognitive interview is based on principles derived from cognitive psychology about how information is organized and the types of retrieval cues that can work to prime recall. It seems that the unflappable Sergeant Friday from the old television show *Dragnet* was wrong when he asked for, "just the facts, ma'am." The accuracy and completeness of recall is improved by elaboration, especially about objects and activities that occurred near the crime in time or space. Geiselman and Fisher (1985) found that recall for events can be enhanced by using the following strategies:

1. Start by recalling ordinary events that occurred before the target event (i.e., the crime). Visualize the circumstances. Think about the layout of the room, weather, traffic flow, or any other aspect of the scene. Think about your mood at the time.
2. Be as complete as possible in your recall. Don't edit your report or exclude something because you think that it might not be important.
3. Recall the event in both forward and backward order, or start from the middle and recall both forward and backward in time from some central incident.
4. Change your perspective. Try to recall the event as though you were some other person such as a spectator (real or imaginary) or you were the perpetrator of a crime.

There are additional techniques that can be useful for recall of specific types of information. If you are trying to remember the physical appearance of someone, does someone else you know come to mind? Why? In what ways are they similar? If you can't recall a name, recite the alphabet to see if a particular letter can "jog" your memory. Sometimes partial information like the number of syllables in a name can be recalled. If numbers are involved (e.g., a license plate), try to recall the number of digits or some physical characteristic of the digits like their size or color.

The techniques of the cognitive interview can be used anytime you need to remember an event. For example, suppose that there has been a recent rash of burglaries in your neighborhood. Suppose further that you hid a valuable piece of jewelry as a deterrent to theft, but later realize that you can't remember where you hid it. Or, more commonly, suppose you can't remember where you left your car keys. This can be a very frustrating type of forgetting. In this case you would try to retrace your steps and try to recall the last time you used them. Systematic and deliberate use of these techniques should be helpful in recall.

BIASES IN MEMORY

All of the mnemonics or strategies for remembering presented thus far in this chapter have been concerned with the *deliberate* use of memory strategies. Much of what we remember was acquired incidentally, that is without the use of a conscious, deliberate scheme. If you go to the movies, you can later recall the plot and actors as well the name of the theater you were sitting in, without deliberately creating images or using rhymes. It's fortunate that we don't always have to work at remembering.

Unfortunately, our memories are subject to certain biases. All items stored in memory are not equally likely to be recalled. One type of bias that was already discussed is the effect of stereotypes. Stereotypes alter memory in predictable ways. The influence of stereotypes is just one instance of a more general bias to remember more easily information that confirms our hypotheses than information that contradicts them (Beyth-Marom, Dekel, Gombo, & Shaked, 1985). We also know that there is a recall advantage to information that is well known, familiar, prominent (generally important or personal), recent, vivid, and dramatic. There is also the frustrating problem of inert knowledge, which occurs when we do not recall information at a time when it is needed. In addition, general knowledge about events is sometimes mistaken as memory for a specific event because people cannot tell the difference between events as they were experienced and events that they constructed from general knowledge

(Jacoby, Kelley, & Dywan, 1989). These biases in memory have profound effects on how people think. For this reason, I return to biases in memory several times throughout this book.

You can take advantage of these operating principles of memory in two ways. First, you could use them to improve memory by considering information that you want to remember and making it familiar and prominent, generating encoding cues, using organization, and elaborating. Second, and more important, you can be aware of the ways your memory is likely to be biased and deliberately attempt to debias your recollections.

APPLYING THE FRAMEWORK

A general framework for thinking was presented in chapter 1. Let's see how we can apply it to the topic of memory.

1. What Is the Goal?   At least three different types of thinking goals involve memory. The first is how to acquire (learn) something so that it can more readily be recalled at a later time. This is an **encoding** (or acquisition) **goal**. A second type is a **retrieval goal** in which the desired outcome is recall of some item that was previously stored. Finally, there is **a debiasing goal**. This involves examining your recall for evidence of bias so that you can recognize the possibility that a memory may not be veridical and correct for it.

The first step in applying the framework is to determine what the appropriate goal is for a given situation. Are you learning new material, trying to recall something accurately, or examining your recollections for possible bias?

2. What Is Known?   This is a question about where you're starting from. Is there a list of foreign vocabulary words sitting in front of you that you have to learn? Can you remember seeing your wallet this morning, but can't remember what you did with it after that? Can you remember most of the battles fought in Europe during the 19th century, but can't get the order straight? Different skills would be used in each of these situations. By paying careful attention to what is known or given, you can use this information as a guide for selecting the appropriate skill for each situation.

3. Which Thinking Skill or Skills Will Get You to Your Goal?   Several different strategies to improve memory were presented in this chapter. You have to select among them for one that is most likely to help you attain your goal. The selection is based on the nature of the goal, what is known, and how much effort you are willing to put into goal attainment. For example, if your goal is to remember the names of the people you meet during a business meeting or during the course of interviewing with many different people, you would select Harry Lorayne's imaging technique for associating names and faces. Similarly, if you were able to take notes during the interviews, you would review your notes. You could use the method of places for subject areas like history and social sciences where knowing the correct sequence of events is crucial to understanding them.

The following memory skills were presented in this chapter. Review each skill and be sure that you understand how to use each one:

- Monitoring your attention.

- Developing an awareness of the influence of stereotypes and other beliefs on what we remember.
- Making abstract information meaningful as an aid to comprehension and recall.
- Using advance organizers to anticipate new information.
- Organizing information so that it can be recalled more easily.
- Generating retrieval cues at both acquisition and retrieval.
- Monitoring how well you are learning.
- Using external memory aids.
- Employing keywords and images, rhymes, places, and first letters, as internal memory aids.
- Applying the cognitive interview techniques.
- Developing an awareness of biases in memory.

4. Have You Reached Your Goal?   Suppose that you selected the keyword mnemonic for foreign language learning to learn a list of technical terms in a course in physics. You go through the list, generate familiar English words that sound like the ones you're trying to learn, and so on. (You cleverly adapted the technique for use with words that may as well be from a foreign language as far as you're concerned.) The effort doesn't stop there. Go over the list "cold" (without your notes and with their definitions covered). Distribute your learning and overlearn. Do you know the words? If not, go through the technique as many times as needed to pass this quality assurance test. As mentioned in the first chapter, parts of this framework may have to be reiterated. You may need to select a different mnemonic if the first one isn't getting you to your goal. Try singing the words and their definitions. (Sure, your roommate will think you're strange. So what!) These steps call for careful monitoring of progress, persistence, and flexibility until you find a strategy that works.

CHAPTER SUMMARY

1. Memory was described as the mediator of cognitive processes because all of our thoughts depend on the ability to use what we have stored in memory.

2. There are many different varieties of memory, and what and how you learn and remember will depend on the type of information, what you already know, the length of the retention interval, and noncognitive factors like health and motivation.

3. There are many learning strategies that reflect the fact that all learning is not the same. Good learners will know what they have to do to learn and remember, and they will do it.

4. It is important to attend to information that you want to learn and to monitor how well you are learning.

5. Our memories are not perfect true "copies" of events that have occurred. Prior knowledge, subsequent knowledge, stereotypes, and meaningfulness of the material all influence what will be remembered.

6. Memory can be improved with appropriate retrieval cues and good organization.

7. Working memory is the term used for the "place" in which we consciously think. It has a seriously limited capacity that we can control by deciding which information to attend to and how much effort a particular task is worth.

8. Mnemonics improve recall because they utilize the basic memory principles of attention, organization, meaningfulness and chunking. The mnemonics presented

were keywords and images, rhymes, method of places, and first letters. (Remember: *Kind Round Men, Please Listen*).

9. Memory for events can be improved with the cognitive interview technique, which uses elaboration at recall to improve memory.

10. Our memories are biased in predictable ways. Examine recall for the possible influence of biases related to stereotypes, general knowledge, or for information characteristics such as being well known, familiar, prominent, recent, vivid, and/or dramatic.

TERMS TO KNOW

You should be able to define or describe the following terms and concepts. If you find that you're having difficulty with any term, be sure to reread the section in which it is discussed.

Hypothetical Constructs. Terms like learning, memory, and perception that are used as labels for the theoretical processes that underlie human thought and behavior.

Thinking. The manipulation or transformation of some internal representation.

Acquisition. Used to describe learning. Also known as encoding, or putting information into memory.

Retention Interval. The time interval between the acquisition of new information (learning) and its retrieval.

Retrieval. The act of recalling or remembering information that had been previously acquired (learned).

Episodic Memory. Memory for events in which we can remember our own participation.

Semantic Memory. Memory for facts like word meanings and the multiplication tables.

Declarative Memory. Knowledge that can be verbalized easily.

Motor Memory. Memory for the performance of motor skills like swimming or riding a bicycle.

Procedural Memory. Memory for accomplishing some task such as using a slide rule or operating equipment.

Automatic Memory. Remembering that seems effortless such as the memory for the frequency of events.

Effortful Memory. Remembering that requires the deliberate and conscious use of strategies such as memory for a series of dates.

Implicit Memory. Memory about which we have little conscious knowledge.

Explicit Memory. Memory that can be discussed and described. Compare with implicit memory.

Cocktail Party Effect. Information that is being attended to will be remembered, whereas information that is not being attended to will be forgotten or never learned. Phenomenon is named for the way people switch their attention among different simultaneous conversations at large parties.

Advance Organizers. Outlines or other summaries that are used before learning to assist with the process of acquisition.

Gist. The interpretation or meaning of a message.

Inert Knowledge. Knowledge that isn't recalled when it is needed.

Encoding Specificity. The cues that are available at learning (or encoding) will be useful if they are also available at retrieval.

Interference Theory of Forgetting. A theory of how we forget that attributes forgetting to "interference" or displacement of the to-be-remembered items by other material that has been previously or subsequently learned.

Working Memory. The "place" where knowledge is consciously manipulated or transformed. Thinking is constrained because working memory has a limited capacity.

Chunking. A memory process in which a number of related items are stored and retrieved as a unit in order to facilitate memory.

Metamemory. A person's knowledge about his or her own memory system; for example, knowing that you have to repeat a series of digits in order to maintain them in memory.

Ease of Learning Judgments. Individual estimates of how easy or difficult it will be to learn a skill or information. This type of judgment is made before the learning process.

Quality of Learning Judgments. Individual estimates of how well material is being learned. This type of judgment is made during the learning process.

Feelings of Knowing Judgments. Individual estimates of how well something is known. This type of judgment is made after the learning process.

Degree of Confidence Judgments. Individual estimates of whether a particular response is correct. This type of judgment is made at the time of retrieval.

Mnemonic Devices. Memory aids or techniques that are utilized to improve memory.

External Memory Aids. The deliberate use of lists, timers, calendars, and similar devices to remind an individual to do something.

Internal Memory Aids. Mnemonic devices or memory aids that rely on plans or strategies to make retrieval easier and more likely.

Keywords. A mnemonic device or memory aid in which a previously learned list of words or rhymes serve as associates or "hooks" for the to-be-remembered items.

Method of Places. (Also known as method of loci.) A mnemonic device or memory aid in which a familiar route is selected and the to-be-remembered items are imaged at intervals along the route. At recall, the individual "mentally traverses" the route to retrieve the items.

First-Letter Mnemonics. A mnemonic device or memory aid in which the first letters of each word to be learned are combined into a single word.

Prospective Memory. Remembering to do something at some time in the future.

Cognitive Interview. A technique for recalling events that uses principles of cognitive psychology to guide the retrieval process.

Encoding Goal. Recognizing that you want to learn something—use the strategies for promoting learning.

Retrieval Goal. Recognizing that you want to recall something—use the strategies for improving recall.

Debiasing Goal. A conscious attempt to recognize the ways in which memory can be biased and engaging in activities that are designed to minimize the bias such as continuing to search for additional information and reflecting on stereotypes.

SUGGESTED READINGS

There are many excellent books on memory. These books tend to divide into two types—those that are devoted to the scholarly study of memory and those that are written for the general public. One exception to this dichotomization is a highly recommended book on external memory aids called *The Psychology of Everyday Things* by Donald Norman (1988). This best-seller places the onus of remembering on the objects that we use. Norman believes that objects need to be designed so that they facilitate their own use and provide the remembering for us. For example, the whistling kettle reminds us to turn off the stove when the water is boiled, and the car that will not start unless the seat belt is fastened reminds us to "buckle up." Norman's book is written in a witty style with great pictures of good and poor designs of objects ranging from the knobs on various spigots to gas tanks in automobiles with "built-in-caps" so that users won't be able to leave the gas stations with their gasoline caps lying behind.

Three recent books written by Herrmann and his colleagues provide a contemporary overview of memory. Searleman and Herrmann (1994) wrote an easy-to-read text entitled *Memory From a Broader Perspective*. Herrmann's (1991) *Super Memory* shows the author's fascination with super memory abilities, and Herrmann, Weingartner, Searleman, and McEvoy (1992) have an edited collection entitled *Memory Improvement: Implications for Memory Theory*. This trio spans several memory-related topics and will satisfy most casual readers who want to gain a better understanding of how their memory operates. A somewhat more advanced collection of articles can be found in an edited book by Collins, Gatherole, Conway, and Morris (1994), *Theories of Memory*. This is a very large book with multiple chapters covering several fascinating topics including autobiographical memory, imagery, and implicit memory.

An emerging theme in memory research is to study everyday remembering—that is the kind of memory tasks that people typically engage in during the usual course of living such as remembering to stop at the store on the way home from school or remembering the name of the person who called 2 hours ago. Cohen (1989) has a book that covers these real-world topics, appropriately called *Memory in the Real World*. An edited collection entitled *Aspects of Memory: Vol. I. The Practical Aspects* by Gruneberg and Morris (1992) also covers a wide range of real-world memory topics. A collection of classic and contemporary articles on metamemory and its fraternal twin, metacognition, edited by Nelson (1992) is entitled *Metacognition: Core Readings*. Readers with a particular interest in the problems of memory in old age will want to consult Craik and Salthouse's (Eds., 1992) *The Handbook of Aging and Cognition*. The range of topics that are addressed in its 10 chapters are general enough to be of interest to readers who do not have a special interest in gerontology.

Some older books that I also recommend are *Memory: Surprising New Insights Into How We Remember and Why We Forget* by E. F. Loftus (1980), which is an interesting account of some of the more intriguing aspects of memory; but you should realize it is not intended for a college audience, and you may find her treatment of some of the topics to be too simplistic. E. F. Loftus (1979) is also the author of several other excellent texts in this area of memory. If your interest was piqued by the sections on eyewitness memory and false memories, then I suggest that you read *Eyewitness Testimony*, which is a pleasant meld of memory theory, research, and law, and a recent book on the controversies surrounding false memory that she wrote with Ketcham in 1994 entitled *The Myth of Repressed Memories and the Accusations of Sexual Abuse*. An updated review of the research findings related to eyewitness memory can be found in a chapter by Fruzzetti, Toland, Teller, and Loftus (1992) entitled "Memory and Eyewitness Testimony."

The mnemonist Harry Lorayne has written two books, which have also been popular with general audiences. They are *The Memory Book* by Lorayne and Lucas (1974) and *Remembering People* by Lorayne (1975). These are both "trade" books, which means that you are likely to find them in mall bookstores. Beyth-Marom, Dekel, Gombo, and Shaked (1985) provided numerous examples of the way memory can bias decisions in a book they wrote for Israeli teenagers to help them learn how to make sound judgments, *An Elementary Approach to Thinking Under Uncertainty.*

3

The Relationship Between Thought and Language

Contents

There is an old story about three umpires that goes something like this:

Three umpires were unwinding at a local pub after a very tough day. All three had endured abusive shouts like, "Kill the umpire" and had numerous offers for new pairs of eyeglasses. After a few mugs of brew, they began discussing how they decide to call balls and strikes. The first umpire, Jim, explained that it was really quite simple. "I simply call them as I see them."

Donnie, the second umpire, disagreed when he said, "I see them as I call them."

Neil, the third umpire, emphatically shook his head in disagreement with the other two. "You're both wrong," he said, slurring his words somewhat. "They don't even exist until I call them."

Neil had a good point. Whether a ball whizzing past home plate is a ball or strike depends on what the umpire labels it. The words he uses both interpret and define reality.

THOUGHT AND LANGUAGE

The development of mind, thought, and language is simply a nexus in which it is impossible to separate one from the other.

—Michael Studdert-Kennedy (quoted in Restak, 1988, p. 231)

How do you express your thoughts in words and sentences? How influenced are you by your particular language? You will have difficulty answering these questions because you use both so automatically and because you have no conscious awareness of the way your thoughts give rise to the words you use to express them. In fact, if you try to monitor your speaking process, you'll find yourself stuttering and interfering with the fluid speech that you normally create so easily. It's as though speech emerges automatically and preformed. Conscious attention directed at the process tends to interfere with it.

Psycholinguistics

Communication is primarily an exercise in thinking.

—Pitt and Leavenworth (1968, p. viii)

Psycholinguistics is the field of psychology that is concerned with how we acquire and use language. Language is a complex cognitive activity that all normal humans perform with skill and apparent ease. As speakers, we select the words we want to use and produce them in a (mostly) grammatically correct form. As listeners, we use the information in another's utterance in order to share the expressed thoughts. What do we know about the way speakers and listeners share thoughts through the medium of language?

Underlying Representation and Surface Structure

Language appears to be simply the clothing of naked thought.

—Miller (1972, p. 43)

The comprehension of language is a process in which the message is used to construct a representation of the information referred to in the message (Resnick, 1985). The sequence of sounds that we produce must correspond to our intended meaning if we are to communicate successfully. The "sender" and the "receiver" also must share a common knowledge of word meanings and grammar. Because language is always incomplete, the receiver must rely on prior knowledge, context, and other cues to comprehension in order to construct a correct representation.

Psychologists who are concerned with the way people use and understand language divide language into two structures or types of representations. The underlying representation of language refers to the meaning component of language—it's the

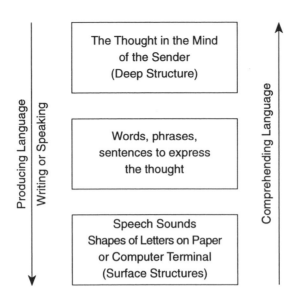

FIG. 3.1. The problem of comprehension. The sender has a thought that she wants to communicate to a receiver. The thought (deep structure) is private and known only to the sender. It is transformed by speech sounds or the shapes of letters (surface structure), which are used by the receiver to reconstruct the meaning expressed by the sender's words.

thought you want to convey. Surface structure refers to the sounds of the verbal expression that you use or its written form on paper, a computer monitor, or some other writing surface. Look carefully at Fig. 3.1 where this process is depicted.

As you can see, the thought in the mind of the sender is the underlying or deep structure. The thought is private and known only to the sender. The problem in producing language is deriving surface structure from the underlying representation in the sender's mind, whereas the problem in comprehending language is getting from the surface structure back to the speaker's (or writer's) underlying representation. Language is integral in these processes because it is the medium with which thoughts and emotions are most often expressed and interpreted (although other media such as dance, mime, and visual art are sometimes used to express thoughts and emotions).

A communication is "successful" when the underlying representation constructed by the receiver matches the underlying representation of the sender. The receiver's representation of the meaning is constructed over time because language is a sequential process with words uttered or read one after the other. All strategies for improving comprehension involve ways of building representations so that they will most nearly match the one intended by the sender. It is the representation of knowledge about the world, the "architecture of the cognitive system," that mediates comprehension (Bower & Cirilo, 1985). When language is ambiguous, the surface structure can have more than one meaning or underlying representation. Some examples of ambiguous sentences are:

- Visiting professors can be boring. (This can be interpreted to mean either that it is boring to visit the homes of professors or that it is boring when professors visit campus.)
- They are kissing fish. (This can be interpreted to mean either that they are a variety of fish called "kissing fish," or that they are a variety of fish who kiss, or that at least two people have their mouths in the fish bowl and are engaging in the somewhat kinky behavior of kissing fish.)

- He cooks carrots and peas in the same pot. (I won't explain the two possible interpretations, but you will need to read this one aloud.)

Each of these sentences is ambiguous because there is a single surface structure (the sound of the sentence) and at least two possible underlying representations or interpretations. Clear communications are unambiguous. With only a little effort, an ambiguous statement can be made clear so that it corresponds to only one underlying representation. For example, the first sentence can be made unambiguous with simple changes:

It is boring to visit professors.

or

Visiting professors are boring.

When there is a problem in the communication process, it is often difficult to know if the problem stems from the sender's thinking, the sender's use of language, the receiver's use of language, or the receiver's thinking. For example, consider a conversation that I had with a 5-year-old girl with whom I spent a very long afternoon. She asked me to buy her a hamburger, which I was glad to do. While standing in line to order her food, she let me know in a very loud voice that she wanted her hamburger "with no meat." Obviously puzzled, I thought perhaps she didn't understand that the brown patty on the roll, the "hamburger," was meat. I patiently tried to explain this concept to her. Adamantly, and even louder, she screamed that she wanted her hamburger without meat. Aha, I thought, she must want plain cheese on a bun—sort of a cheeseburger without the burger. But no, she rejected this possibility and began a full-scale tantrum at this point. What was the problem? Was the problem with language in that she did not know the meaning of the words *hamburger* or *meat*? Was the problem in her thinking, which was illogical? Was I the problem? Perhaps my background knowledge of what constitutes a hamburger did not match hers. In other words, did the problem stem from faulty thinking or faulty use of language, or possibly both? I never did find out what she had wanted. We beat a hasty exit from the restaurant with the other customers and the servers giving us very disapproving looks. By the way, I took a regular hamburger with us, which she happily ate in the car as I drove her home.

Implications and Inference

Communication depends as much on information that is implied as it does on the words that are explicitly stated. Comprehension of meaningful material will always require the listener or reader to make inferences by going beyond the words uttered. Consider this very simple three-sentence story:

Matt inherited a great deal of money. Bertha loves diamonds and furs. Bertha married Matt.

Although very little factual information was provided, it is a meaningful story. Readers infer that Bertha married Matt for his money and that she will use his money to buy diamonds and furs, although this interpretation need not be correct. All communication requires the receiver to fill in gaps between given bits of information in order to understand the intended meaning. This is why psychologists conceptualize the acquisition of knowledge as a process of construction that is built by integrating new information with what is already known by the receiver and the sender. Many decades ago, Bruner (1957) succinctly defined thinking as "going beyond the information given." Understanding language by making inferences is a prime example of this definition of thinking.

The Role of Inference in Advertisements

When you produce speech, the intended meaning is implied or suggested by the words you use, the context in which it is embedded, and verbal and nonverbal expressions. It is possible to say one thing while communicating something quite different. This technique is often used by advertisers who want to persuade you to buy their products, yet have legal restrictions on the kinds of statements they can make.

A television commercial for American Express Travelers Cheques goes something like this:

> "Oh, no, we've lost our travelers cheques! What will we do?" (Couple wrings their respective hands at this point, obviously looking distressed.)

> The voice of a distinguished actor comes on, "What kind were they?"

> Distressed couple responds, "American Express."

> The distinguished actor calmly reassures them, "Good thing you have American Express Travelers Cheques. You can get a refund at their conveniently located office across the street."

> The now-smiling couple walk off the screen to the tune of "Don't leave home without them."

Other travelers check companies have complained about this advertisement because it implies that people who lose other brands of travelers checks may not get a refund. Notice that although this is never stated, it is a reasonable inference from the information offered.

Perhaps you're familiar with a popular advertisement for Listerine, a brand of mouthwash. An apparently middle-class mother bundles her children in warm clothing while discussing colds and flu. She earnestly states how much she dislikes "scratchy sore throats" and "runny noses." To keep her family healthy, she sees that they eat right, get plenty of rest and exercise, and "gargle with Listerine." Of course, she never says that Listerine will prevent or cure colds. This would be a false claim because there is no evidence that it does. Yet, this information is implied. Studies with fictitious commercials have shown that viewers do infer from advertisements like this one that mouthwash will protect against colds (R. J. Harris, 1977).

Carefully selected words in advertisements are used to create an inference that something is true when it is not. Airlines and other businesses often boast:

> "Nobody beats our fares."

They expect that readers will infer that this means that they have the lowest fares. Of course, they never state that they have the lowest fares because that would be false. Nobody beats their fares because virtually all of the fares are the same. They could have said,"Our fares are the same as our competitors." But, if they said it that way, it would not mislead readers into believing that they have the lowest fares, and consumers would correctly conclude that it doesn't matter which airline they book with if cost is the sole determining factor. Always consider the distinction between the linguistic content of the message and the inference you draw from it.

When you start reading and listening critically to advertisements, you may be surprised to find appalling attempts to create impressions that can change beliefs. It is instructive to read the advertisements for supposed weight loss products (e.g., cellulite creams, sauna suits, herbal wraps, vitamins, magic formula pills). Even the ubiquitous "before and after" photos are designed to create the inference that you will lose "30 or more pounds in 2 weeks" eating anything you want and without "tedious" exercise.

Moreover, R. J. Harris (1977) found that people remember the implied meaning of a message, and not the actual statements that were made. If you have already read the chapter on the development of memory skills, this shouldn't be surprising to you. Meaningful information is more easily remembered than nonmeaningful information. People remember the meaning or gist of the message and not the actual words that were spoken. We rarely remember statements verbatim. Thus, our memory of events depends on the interpretations we give them when they occur.

Rules for Clear Communication

"When I use a word," Humpty Dumpty said, in a rather scornful tone, "it means just what I choose it to mean—neither more or less."

"The question is," said Alice, "whether you can make words mean so many different things."

"The question is," said Humpty Dumpty, "which is to be master—that's all."

—Lewis Carroll (*Through the Looking Glass*, 1872/1971, p. 190)

In order to communicate effectively, you need to know a great many things in addition to the thought being communicated and the words being used as the vehicle for the communication: What is the purpose of the communication? What are your listener's characteristics? That is, what are your listener's age and social status? How much does the listener know or want to know about the topic? The answers to all of these questions shape the nature of communications. We implicitly change the way we speak or write, depending on how we answer these questions, and we make these changes without realizing the extent to which the listener shapes our use of language. Communication is governed by rules that we all obey, although you may never have consciously considered them.

Rule 1: Tell Listeners What You Believe They Want to Know

Consider how you would answer a simple question like, "Where do you live?" If I met you in Europe and asked you this question, you would probably respond, "In the United States." If I asked you this question in New York, you would respond with the name of a state, "In Pennsylvania." If I asked you the same question on your college campus, you might respond, "In the dorms." If I asked you this question while we were in the dorms, you might respond, "In Wing D, Room 331." And, if I asked you this question in your dorm room, you would probably reply by giving the name of your home town. The same question could be asked each time, yet you would give a different answer that depended on the context in which the question is asked and what you thought I wanted to know. The level of information you choose to convey depends on the purpose of the communication.

Rule 2: Don't Tell Listeners What They Already Know

In the first chapter, I began by introducing the topic of thinking and the need for the development of critical thinking skills. You probably did not think that this was unusual. Suppose I started every chapter in this book the same way. You would not only think that this was unusual, you would also question my mental status.

When you present information to an audience, you balance the amount of new information that you present with the old or already known information. If you present too much new information at once, listeners will be lost and will not be able to extract the intended meaning; if you present too much old or known information, listeners will be bored. The relative proportion of old information to new information is known as the **given/new distinction** (Clark & Haviland, 1977).

The ratio of given or known information to new information is a determinant of the difficulty of a communication. If a passage (spoken or written) contains too much new material for a listener or reader, it will be difficult to comprehend. No one would take an advanced course in biochemistry without first obtaining the requisite background in biology and chemistry. The educational process, if successful, fosters the transformation of new information into the students' systems of known information.

Rule 3: Vary the Style of Your Communication, Depending on the Knowledge, Age, and Status of the Listeners

Suppose you are an expert computer programmer given the task of describing the operations of a computer center to a group of visitors. You would vary the way you convey the necessary information for each of the following: a group of politicians, a third grade class from an elementary school, your history professor, a close friend, or an expert programmer from another university.

Your communication would be more or less technical depending on what you believe your listener knows about the topic. You might tell the politicians about the high costs of maintaining a computer center, the third-grade class might simply be told about the general use of computers, you might explain to your history professor how computers can be used in research, your close friend might be told that you feel you're being underpaid, and the visiting programmer might be told about the capacity of the computers and the steps you've taken to prevent the spread of computer "viruses."

The readability of text (or ease with which spoken language is understood) depends, in large part, on the match between the text and the reader. The reason so many of us find income tax and legal documents so difficult is that they are written by and for accountants and lawyers—people with highly differentiated underlying representations of the topics referred to in these documents. The rest of us have to make many more inferences and a greater number of memory searches to understand the concepts because our underlying representations of these concepts are relatively sparse. This is why whenever we're engaged in communication, it is important to consider the characteristics of the reader or listener. This is a more formal way of saying that the beliefs, knowledge, and expectations of the intended audience for a communication should determine how much detail goes into a communication and which words are used. The difficulty of a text does not reside in the text itself, but in the reader–text interaction.

Rule 4: Tell the Truth

When we communicate with each other, it is assumed that the information being conveyed is truthful. This is an imperative for meaningful communication. Of course, sometimes people lie. How do you process information when you believe that the speaker is lying? All components of the communication are scrutinized. In general, the communication process breaks down when the listener suspects that the speaker is violating this rule. This loss of communication is eloquently described by Chang (1993) in her description of life during Mao's reign over Communist China, a time when no one dared to speak the truth: "The whole nation slid into doublespeak. Words became divorced from reality, responsibility, and people's real thoughts. Lies were told with ease because words had lost their meaning" (p. 298).

Rule 5: Use a Simple Straightforward Style

Mark Twain said this best when he said, "Eschew surplusage." Information is transmitted best when simple and precise language is used. Some people think that use of multisyllabic words and intricate sentence structures is a sign of intelligence. This is not true. It is a far more difficult task to express complex thoughts in simple language than to express simple thoughts in complex language. The transformation of our private thoughts into easily understood language is the benchmark of human cognition.

Rule 6: Utilize Manner and Context to Clarify Meaning

Meaning depends not only on the words that we use, but also on the context and the manner we use to convey it. Have you ever had the experience of having someone say, "I'll be happy to do that for you" in a manner that clearly showed that she was most unhappy?

Context is a critical aid for comprehension. "The food is on the table" can be an invitation to eat or a simple descriptive statement, depending on the context. Context is also used to decide which of two possible meanings is the intended meaning for ambiguous sentences. The intended meaning of "They are kissing fish" is usually straightforward when spoken in context. One way that context directs comprehension is by influencing the way we process incoming language.

Ekman (1992) spoke of "lying truthfully," that is, literally telling the truth but leaving the listener with the opposite impression. For example, he told about a man who had been unfaithful to his wife for years without getting caught! He had, on several occasions, taken money from her purse to buy flowers for the other women. Each time he did this, she noticed the missing money and innocently commented to him: "I could have sworn I had an extra $50 in my purse; I must have lost it." Finally, one day she suspects that her partner has been unfaithful to her because she finds matches from a local hotel in his coat when she takes it to the cleaners. When she confronts him about this, he "honestly lies," by retorting: "Right. I've been having a torrid affair during my lunch breaks; and do you remember those times you thought you had lost money? Well, you didn't. I've been stealing your money to buy my noon-time lovers gifts. And, let me see, what other ignominies have I omitted?" This man just made a complete confession, yet the intent was to mislead his wife by casting it in irony. Intonation matters!

Figure 3.2 is a visual demonstration of the context effect. You'll find that you have no difficulty reading any of the words in Fig. 3.2. Now look carefully at the letters that make up the words. The "H" in "the" is the same form as the "A" in "cat," yet you may not have noticed this unless I pointed it out to you. Similarly, the way we perceive the other "inky" letters depends on the rest of the letters that make up the word context. Context provides strong cues that guide the way we construct knowledge about the nature of the world.

Analogy and Metaphor

Midway between the unintelligible and the commonplace, it is metaphor which most pro-duces knowledge.

— Aristotle (Rhetoric III, 1410b)

TAE CAT
RED
SROT
EISH
DEBT

FIG. 3.2. Examples of the way context influences meaning. Notice, for example, that the "D"
in "RED" is identical to the "B" in "DEBT."
(Adapted from Rumelhart, D. E., McClelland, J.
L., & the PDP Research Group. (1986). Parallel
distributed processing. Cambridge, MA: The MIT
Press, p. 8).

One exception to the rule that the words used to convey a message should correspond
to their intended meaning is the use of analogy and metaphor. (The English grammatical distinction among analogy, metaphor, and simile is not being considered here
because it is irrelevant in this context.) If I tell you that "Myrtle is a hard-headed
woman," the literal translation is not the one intended. In this case, the receiver must
use his knowledge about the referent topic (hard surfaces) and "map" the relevant
knowledge onto his knowledge of Myrtle. Although you certainly have never met
Myrtle, and you may never have heard the expression "a hard-headed woman," you
can probably tell me that she is a stubborn, strong-willed person. You came to this
understanding by taking your knowledge of hard surfaces, selecting characteristics of
hard surfaces that might be relevant to a description of a person, and transferring that
knowledge to what you already know about Myrtle.

Using Analogies as an Aid to Understanding

Analogies are pervasive in human thought. Whenever we are faced with a novel
situation we seek to understand it by reference to a known familiar one. When we think
by analogy, we map the underlying structure of a known topic onto the target or
unknown topic. This mental process is known as *structure mapping* (Gentner & Gentner,
1983; Halpern, Hansen, & Riefer, 1990). Structure mapping assumes networklike
representations of concepts in memory in which underlying structural relationships
and surface attributes (physical characteristics) are coded along with each concept.
For example, when we read that an atom is like a miniature solar system, the
implication is that the solar system and the atom have similar relationships among
their component parts—smaller bodies revolving around a larger one in fixed path
patterns. Surface similarity (e.g., the sun is hot and large and contains burning gases)
is not implied.

All analogies and metaphors state that two concepts are alike in some way. Good
analogies have similar underlying structures even when the topics are highly dissimilar. They maintain much of their underlying structure in the transfer from base (known)
to target (unknown) domains whereas surface features are of minimal importance.
Poor analogies are ones in which only surface or superficial characteristics are similar.
If I said that Myrtle is like milk because they both start with the letter *m*, this would be
a very poor analogy. Whenever you encounter an analogy, you need to consider the
nature of the similarity relationship. Are the two concepts similar in their underlying

structure so that relevant information about one concept can be mapped onto the other concept, or is the similarity superficial or trivial?

Analogies are a useful tool in the comprehension and recall of scientific passages (Halpern, 1987a; Halpern et al., 1990). When students read technical passages that contained good analogies to familiar topics, they scored higher on tests of comprehension and recall than a control group of students that read the same passage without the analogy.

Using Analogies as Problem-Solving Aids

What do you do when you are faced with a problem that has no obvious solution? I address this question in more detail in the chapter on problem solving, but one strategy that is appropriate to consider here is the use of a solution that is borrowed from a problem with a similar structure, often from a very different domain of knowledge. The conditions under which people do and don't recognize and use analogous solutions for problems from very distant domains of knowledge has been the subject of much research (e.g., Vosniadou & Ortony, 1989). In order for this strategy to "work," the problem solver must recognize that the essential characteristics of the two problems are similar, despite the fact that the topics may be very different.

Consider, for example, the problem of bonding (gluing) two surfaces during dental surgery. All bonding substances require a dry surface for bonding, and the mouth is a wet environment. How can this problem be solved? The use of the small towels or "teeth driers" do not work well during oral surgery, which can involve profuse bleeding and the production of much saliva. Some creative dental surgeon looked for similar problems in other domains. He or she (I don't know the identity of this unsung critical thinker) studied the way barnacles attach themselves to piers and other surfaces in the ocean. The adaptive barnacle displaces the water (sort of moves it aside) from the small area to which it (she or he?) is attaching. This displacement of fluids has been modified for use in dentistry. If you're like most people, you will agree that any discovery that makes dental surgery quicker and more successful is a welcome advance. In this example, the problem solver considered the similarities in the two problems of bonding in wet environments and then adapted a solution from one domain (barnacles in the ocean) to a very different one (dental bonding). In this way, an analogy was used to solve a problem.

Using Analogies to Persuade

In the popular movie *Dead Poets Society*, the unlikely hero, Robin Williams, who plays a high school teacher of English, asks his class of young men, "What is the purpose of language?" After a short period of silence, a student yells out the obvious answer, "to communicate." Of course, this is not the correct answer in the movie. The hero-English-teacher-character responds that the purpose of language is to "woo women." An important point is made in this fictional exchange between student and teacher. The purpose of language is to persuade—to change how and what people think. We use language to persuade others to like or date us (as expressed in this movie), to alter or maintain political beliefs (e.g., capitalism is good), to convince someone to make a purchase (e.g., a particular brand of jeans), and any other topic that you can think of.

We frequently use analogies to persuade someone that X is analogous to Y, therefore what is true for X is also true for Y. A good example of this sort of "reasoning by analogy" was presented by Bransford, Arbitman-Smith, Stein, and Vye (1985). They told about a legal trial that was described in the book, *Till Death Us Do Part* (Bugliosi, 1978). Much of the evidence presented at the trial was circumstantial. The attorney for the defense argued that the evidence was like a chain, and like a chain, it was only as strong as its weakest link. He went on to argue that there were several weak links in the evidence; therefore, the jurors should not convict the accused. The prosecutor also used an analogy to make his point. He argued that the evidence was like a rope made of many independent strands. Several strands can be weak and break, and you will still have a strong rope. Similarly, even though some of the evidence was weak, there was still enough strong evidence to convict the accused. (The prosecutor won.)

Can you see how the use of analogies can guide how we think? In the trial example, different sorts of outcomes depend on which of the analogies you found more compelling. Let's consider another example. At a meeting of county administrators, several people who were receiving welfare argued that there should be welfare recipients on the county board. They argued that welfare recipients were in the best position to understand the problems of life on welfare and therefore should be part of the group that makes decisions about welfare. One of the board members said that was an absurd proposition. He argued that having welfare recipients on the county board was like putting residents of an "insane asylum" on the committee that makes the rules for the asylum. What do you think of this analogy? In what ways are people on welfare like the residents of an insane asylum? How are they different? Are they different in ways that make the board member's conclusions invalid? The insane are unable to think rationally, by definition. This is not true for the poor. I don't believe that this was a good analogy and would not have been persuaded by it. (In fact, I find it insulting.)

As a final example of the power of analogies to persuade, consider the following speech made by Bishop Desmond Tutu (1986), an eloquent leader in the political movement that ended apartheid in South Africa:

> Sometimes you get the notion that people try to inject into your heart that what you do is insignificant; it cannot make a difference. Let me disabuse you of that notion. When people see a colossal problem, they wonder whether they could do anything that makes a difference. They need to keep remembering what they are told about how you eat an elephant—one piece at a time. (p. 216)

Analogies are useful thinking strategies in many different contexts. The deliberate use of analogies as an aid to solving problems and enhancing creativity is discussed in greater detail in later chapters.

WORDS AND THEIR MEANINGS

Eight years after resigning as president, Richard Nixon denied lying *but acknowledged that he, like other politicians, had* dissembled."

—Paul Ekman (1992, p. 25)

Is alcoholism an illness or is it the lack of willpower by weak people who could stop drinking if they really wanted to? I have frequently been asked questions like this one, especially by students who are worried about or disgusted with a loved one who has a drinking problem. There are many aspects to this question. First, the answer to the question of whether alcoholism is an illness depends on how the term *illness* is defined, and more important, who gets to do the defining. Second, it is possible that alcoholism would fit a definition of illness and be controllable by the individual. The way this question is posed reveals many unstated assumptions by the asker of the question regarding the nature of illness and alcoholism.

Definitions and the Control of Thought

An amazing event occurred in 1973—millions of mentally ill people were suddenly cured! Well, not exactly suddenly cured. What happened in 1973 was that the American Psychiatric Association removed "homosexuality" from its list of official mental disorders, with the result that the millions of homosexuals were no longer considered by the psychiatric establishment as mentally ill. The American Psychiatric Association maintains the powerful position of deciding which categories of human behavior and emotion should be defined as a mental illness. This is an immense power because the human behaviors and emotions that are listed in the official "handbook" of mental disorders, the *Diagnostic and Statistical Manual* (American Psychiatric Association, 1994), determine whether an individual will receive medical funding for treatment, whether a judge will decide to commit an individual to a mental facility or to a prison, and whether people label themselves and others as "normal." Similarly, if alcoholism is an illness, then the alcoholic can expect medical treatment, and perhaps, even some sympathy for being stricken with this debilitating affliction. If alcoholism is a lifestyle choice, then the alcoholic can expect to be imprisoned (if drunk in public), abhorred, and will receive little in the way of treatment. The definition is not inherent in the actions or state of being an alcoholic. The definition is, instead, an agreement, among people and by "experts" as to what a term should mean.

For most of everyday transactions, definitions do not pose a problem. We do not normally have to decide what is meant by terms like *desk, book, house,* and so on, unless the particular desk, book, or house is so unusual that there might be doubt about how well it fits our notions of what these terms mean. Of course, we cannot define every term that we use—this would be a tedious and pointless exercise as we go "around in circles" using words to define other words until we end up where we started. However, the problem of definition can be critical when words are used as a means of persuasion.

Consider the disastrous situation that occurred when Americans were held against their will in Iran during Jimmy Carter's term as president of the United States. At first, the Americans were described as "detainees," but the term quickly changed to "interees." Soon, the Americans were being referred to as "prisoners" and then "hostages." Each time, the word used to describe their status escalated in its emotional impact. The label *detainees* suggests that there is nothing to worry about; *hostage* is a "fighting term" that will cost lives and means armed conflict is likely. Americans can be convinced that military action is needed to free hostages, but people are unlikely to be willing to kill or die for detainees. It is of little value to try to decide which of these terms is the most correct; the more important question is who gets to decide which term is used?

This is an important point because the words used to describe a situation become more warlike as a prelude to armed conflict. For example, in 1985, Philadelphia police dropped a bomb on the home and headquarters of a Black militant group called "MOVE." It destroyed two city blocks and left over 200 people homeless. How could this happen? According to Wagner-Pacifici, a professor at Swarthmore College, as the confrontation heated up, the words used to describe this group changed from more neutral terms like *zealots* to more inflammatory terms like *terrorists*. The language used to frame the problem was a major factor in the action taken by the police. She concluded that, "If you end up talking about an action you're going to take against a group in military terms, you begin to think and operate as if you are in a war" (quoted in "Footnotes," 1994, p. A8).

Let's take a simple concept, like death. When is a person dead? It is now possible to maintain an individual on machines that breathe for her and tubes that carry nutrients into the body and wastes out. Is such an individual dead? How do you know? We think very differently about an individual who is dead than one who is not. We bury the dead and not the living, but how can we know what to do if we cannot decide whether an individual is living or dead? New technologies and medical advances have made even simple concepts like death more complex. There are countless other examples in which the definition that we apply to a situation determines how we think and act.

The use of terms that are heavily laden with emotional impact often evoke strong images. If you have already read the chapter on memory, then you recall (I hope) that imagery helps to maintain a concept in memory, a factor that is related to its ability to evoke strong emotions. This fact is well known by propagandists who want to convince the masses to act in extreme ways. In Mein Kampf, Adolph Hitler used expressions like "racial brew," "purity of the blood," "poisoning of the blood," and "bastardization" in his successful attempt to convince millions of people to participate in the killing of millions of other people who differed from them in their religious beliefs. Hitler even offered the "final solution," which means that he found a way to solve a problem: His solution was to massacre an entire religious group. Hitler and his compatriots also used actual visual images to reinforce these emotions. Pictures of Jews were alternated with revolting pictures of sewer rats and roaches crawling over filth so that the images of Jewish faces and the vermin would become associated in people's minds. It is interesting to note that the Nazis studied American advertising in the 1920s to develop their persuasive techniques. If you are thinking that no contemporary person would fall prey to such blatant tactics designed to increase racism, you have not read the papers lately.

Stop now and consider the way in which you would define the term *crime*, if you had the power to write the definitions.

(Did you really stop and try to define what you think the word *crime* should mean?) Don't go on until you try this simple exercise.

According to Peck (1986), there was a famous inmate in a federal jail, a gangster named Louis Lepke. In the cell next to his was a young conscientious objector from Iowa, named Lowell Naeve. Mr. Naeve tried to explain what a conscientious objector was to Mr. Lepke. Lepke replied incredulously, "You mean they put you in here for *not* killing?" (p. 146). Lepke then laughed and laughed. Did your definition of crime include the crime of refusing to go to war? Is Mr. Naeve a criminal?

Definitions are not static "truths." Meanings change over time as a function of technological development, changing social mores, and a drift in the way words are used. However, it is not true that a word can mean anything that anyone wants it to. There is an advertisement in a large city newspaper for a plastic surgeon who "specializes in nose reduction, breast enlargement and reduction, liposuction, baggy eyes, weak chins, face lifts, and saddlebag thighs." Putting aside the obnoxious idea that every body part needs "fixing," this surgeon claims to be able to do it all. How then, can he claim to be a "specialist?" The word is being misused to convey the idea that he has great depth of knowledge and experience in *all* aspects of plastic surgery. If he can perform many types of plastic surgery, he is a generalist. By definition, he can't specialize in everything.

Similarly, I bristle at offers for "free gifts with purchase." This is a marketing scheme based on the idea that we all love gifts and bargains. A gift is free, or it is not a gift. Consider the great deal that I saw advertised for soap.

Buy three bars, get one free.

The cost of the four bars of soap was $1.00. How does this differ from buying soap at $.25 a bar? Do I really believe that the soap manufacturer has a "gift" for me? It is not "free" nor is it a "gift," if I have to pay money to receive it. Every brand of vitamins in the store near my home offers 30 "free" vitamins with the purchase of a bottle of 100 vitamins. (The free vitamins are packaged separately in a small bottle, thus adding to production costs and increasing waste and the cost of the vitamins.) Wouldn't it be more honest to state instead that the price shown is the cost for 130 vitamins? I promise to buy such a brand, if I ever find one that is honest in advertising its cost. Also, if I ever meet up with the advertising giant who devised this particular scheme to separate consumers from their money, I will have a "free gift" for her or him.

The Power of Labels and Categories

As I sat with friends drinking coffee at my kitchen table, someone yelled, "Kill it, kill it," as a very large bug darted across the floor. "Yuk, it's a cockroach." But upon further inspection, we found that it was not a cockroach, but a "cute little cricket." A friend scooped up the cricket in a paper cup and gently released it outdoors while my daughter ran after it trying to feed it lettuce and grass. Why was it disgusting and in need of immediate extermination when we believed it to be one type of bug—a cockroach—and cute and in need of saving when it turned out to be another—a cricket?

The process of categorization is essential in understanding the world and guiding our responses. When we see a bug, or a baby, or an old person, or a professor, we use our knowledge about the categories they belong to in order to make inferences about how they are likely to act. We know that a baby will share some essential features with all babies. It will sometimes cry for reasons that we cannot understand; it will need to have its diaper changed; it will slobber, and coo. Of course, every baby is unique, but, fortunately, we can use our knowledge of category membership to know something about every baby. This is fortunate because it reduces the load on memory and allows us to understand and predict what will happen when interacting with any baby. The process of categorization is an example of **cognitive economy**, which means that it is a process that reduces the mental work load and makes thinking less effortful. Instead of having to learn a set of new expectations for every stimulus with which we come in contact, we can use category membership to reduce the uncertainty in the situation.

Although categories are necessary in dealing with the large variety of objects in the world, they also can be the cause of serious errors. Not all members of a category are the same, and often a stimulus is miscategorized. Stereotypes result from several cognitive and noncognitive processes, but one clear reason that they persist is due to the effect of categorical thinking. Think about a racial or religious group that is different from your own. Describe the members of that group. You will find that general terms emerge that clearly do not apply to all group members, and may not even apply to any group members. When you think about members of your own race or religion, you will tend to think of them as much more individualized than members of other groups. As long as we classify individuals into racial and religious groups and label the members of these groups with certain attributes, stereotypical beliefs will be maintained.

Every year U.S. park rangers report that someone is seriously mauled by a bear in one or more of our national parks. Often, the injured person was trying to feed or even hug a large, wild bear. Why? Because many Americans have categorized bears along with dogs as friendly animals that we can play with. After all, the only bears that most of us know personally are Yogi Bear (a lovable and dim-witted cartoon character),

Smokey the Bear (the spokesbear for fire prevention, also a cartoon character), teddy bears (popular stuffed animals), and possibly the highly trained, humanlike bears that we see riding bicycles and playing ball in zoo and circus acts. These artificial situations lead many people to miscategorize bears as cuddly animals instead of dangerous ones.

Similarly, people decide what is natural or right based on their categorical systems. In Western countries, dead cow and chicken are acceptable foods. The Vietnamese traditionally consider dogs and monkeys to be food, yet many Westerners cringe at this "unnatural" food choice. Many Japanese find raw seafood to be a delicacy, and the French often enjoy eating snails and frogs' legs. (I have often wondered what happens to frog arms. Yes, this is a feeble attempt at a joke. Do I get points for just trying?) In times of severe famine, people have been known to eat old shoes, the bark of trees, and even other humans. The point of this stomach-turning paragraph is that what seems to be a natural category, like what is a food, often turns out to be culturally bound and arbitrary when it is inspected more closely. We use the same processes of categorical thinking when we determine which behaviors are natural for women and men and other groups, such as old people and the disabled, based on experiences in our own culture. Most of us are completely unaware of the extent to which culture influences our thinking by creating categories and determining what belongs in each category.

Prototypical Thinking

At the local baseball game, the final score was 9–8, yet no man on either team ever crossed home plate. How is this possible?

You should be able to solve this riddle fairly easily because it has the same structure and answer as a riddle that I posed in the first chapter. I repeat it here to make a point. We tend to think in terms of **prototypes** or best examples of a category. Give up? It was an all-women league. For those of you who could not solve this problem, it is probably because you automatically think of men when you think of baseball players, just as in the first chapter, many people did not think of a woman when the physician was described as a neurosurgeon. Even if you had heard the neurosurgeon puzzle before, did you recognize that the same principle was affecting your thinking when I changed the riddle so that it pertained to baseball players? Of course, you know that women play baseball, but this does not readily "come to mind."

Although I have never met you, I already know a great deal about what and how you think. Let me demonstrate this with an exercise devised by Decyk (1994). For each of the following categories, give a good example. In fact, give the first example that comes to mind:

1. a bird
2. a color
3. a triangle (a picture is okay)
4. a motor vehicle
5. a sentence
6. a hero
7. a heroic action
8. a game
9. a philosopher
10. a writer

Are you finished? Here is a list of your most likely answers:

1. For a bird you probably named robin or sparrow, or possibly eagle.
2. For a color you most likely said red or blue.
3. For your triangle you either drew or named an equilateral triangle.
4. For a motor vehicle you probably listed a car.
5. For an example of a sentence you probably wrote a short declarative sentence (e.g., The girl ran home.).
6. The hero you named is most likely one of the following men—Superman, Batman, or possibly a fireman.
7. The heroic action you named probably involved a single act by a man such as a rescue by a fireman.
8. Most likely you listed Monopoly as an example of a game, or some other board game.
9. For a philosopher you probably named Socrates or Aristotle.
10. Finally, for a writer you probably named Stephen King, but if you named someone else, it is very probably a White male author.

What is the point of this demonstration? People tend to think in terms of prototypes or "best examples" of a category. Our prototypes vary from culture to culture, but they are relatively standard within a culture. People living in Australia might name a "kiwi" as an example of a bird, a response that would be very unusual for Americans or Chinese. Thinking in terms of prototypes biases how and what we think. When we think about members of a category only the most typical exemplars (examples of a category) readily come to mind. Consider the implications of the finding that most people name only living White males as an example of a writer. It means that we carry a standardized "picture" or "definition" of those characteristics that writers share and these characteristics are restricted with regard to time, race, and sex. Of course, different answers would be expected from people from other countries or, possibly, other cultural groups within the same country. Most Russians would probably name Pushkin, or less probably, Tolstoy or Chekhov, if they were asked to give an example of a writer. But, regardless of what the particular prototype is, the reliance on the most typical member of a category limits thinking. Few people will name an older person or a child or a dog when asked to think of a hero, yet old people and children and even dogs (e.g., Lassie) can and do perform heroic acts. The most commonly named philosophers are dead, Greek men. With prototypes like this, few people will "think of" philosophy as a popular, contemporary profession that is open to all ages and races.

If you maintain a conscious awareness of the way prototypes restrict thinking, it is possible to reduce their effect (Decyk, 1994). Practice giving unusual answers to the category questions asked previously. With a little thought, you can think of ways to subdivide the categories and expand the possibilities that you can think of. For example, Monopoly is a board game. Name some other types of games (e.g., ball games, card games, jacks). Think about games played alone (e.g., solitaire) and games played with others (e.g., hangman). What about games from other countries, games from other times in history, and games played by children (e.g., pat-a-cake and peek-a-boo)? With very little effort, you can generate a wide variety of games that differ from your prototype. The deliberate use of giving unusual examples of categories is one way of making a wider array of information that is stored in memory more accessible, so that you can use the knowledge that you already have acquired when you need it.

LANGUAGE: TOOL OR MASTER OF THOUGHT?

Learn a new language and get a new soul.

—Czech proverb

We use language not only to convey our thoughts, but also to mold and shape them. Language and thought are inextricably related concepts that exert mutual influences on each other. Some psychologists believe that language, at least in part, influences thought. Examples of this concept were presented earlier in this chapter in the section on labeling and the way labels affect how we think. The hypothesis that the language we use affects how we think is called the Sapir–Whorf hypothesis of linguistic relativity, or more informally, the Sapir–Whorf hypothesis (Sapir, 1960; Whorf, 1956).

"How do I know what I mean until I see what I say?" (Miller, 1972, p. 43). In a humorous way, this question examines the relationship between thought and language. Although it seems clear to most people that our thoughts influence the language that we use, it is sometimes more difficult to understand the reciprocal nature of the relationship. Anthropologists and psychologists have studied whether people who speak different languages also think somewhat differently. Perhaps you have had the experience of translating a passage from one language to another and had difficulty conveying exactly the same meaning. Jokes are a good example of this. Ethnic jokes that are told in their native language frequently lose their humor when they are told in translation. Could this indicate that ways of thinking, as reflected in language, differ across cultures?

Some chilling implications of the Sapir–Whorf hypothesis appeared in George Orwell's classic book written in 1949 titled *1984*. In *1984*, he wrote about a repressive society that was able to control the thoughts of its citizenry by redefining some words and removing others from the language. By gaining control of the language, this futuristic society dictated which thoughts were possible and which were not.

The Orwellian example is an extreme interpretation of the Sapir–Whorf hypothesis that language absolutely determines thought. According to this view, if a term does not exist within a language, speakers do not have the corresponding thought. Do you believe that if the word love didn't exist in our language, then people wouldn't be able to feel this emotion? Most people would disagree with the strong form of the Sapir–Whorf hypothesis. Cross-cultural research that has examined the way different languages influence thought has not supported the strong version of the Sapir–Whorf hypothesis (Berlin & Kay, 1969; Rosch, 1977). A weaker version of the Sapir–Whorf hypothesis is that language influences, but does not determine thinking. As an example of this, consider the following terms carefully and decide if each evokes a somewhat different thought: senior citizen, old man, golden-ager. Did each term connote a different thought? Did you think about a different type of person with each word? Most people agree that they did. (See Fig. 3.3.)

The Direction and Misdirection of Thought

All words are pegs to hang ideas on.

—Henry Ward Beecher (1812–1887)

Given that language will influence what we think, it is only a short leap to suggest that language can be used in deliberate ways to shape thinking so that it conforms with a particular ideology or point of view. It also seems likely that if we understand how language is used to direct how we think, then an awareness of the ways in which this

Senior Citizen   Old Man   Golden Ager

FIG. 3.3.   The words we use influence how we think. Compare the different thoughts that are evoked by the terms "senior citizen," "old man," and "golden ager."

occurs should help us to resist the automatic type of thinking that goes along with an uncritical approach to communication.

Emotional Language and Name Calling

As described in the earlier section on labeling, the same event can be described in several different ways. Yet, the words we use to describe an event are not interchangeable in the meaning they convey. Language that is highly emotional has a different effect on readers and listeners than more mundane ways of conveying the intended meaning. This is the weaker version of the Sapir–Whorf hypothesis—although language may not *determine* thought, it directs, and sometimes misdirects, it. Consider the heated debate between those for and against abortion. The faction opposed to abortion realized that it is better to be for something than against something and therefore decided to call their stance "pro-life" rather than "anti-choice." On the other side, those who favored abortion certainly didn't want to be called "anti-life" and decided to label their stance "pro-choice." They hoped that people would think differently about a position that is "pro-choice" than they would about one that is "anti-life." Of course, the position hasn't changed—only its label or name has changed, but presumably the way the position is labeled influences how people think about it. One "pro-lifer" told a colleague that the best way to win a debate on this topic is to use frequently the words *kill* and *baby* in the same sentence (Kahane, 1992). The juxtaposition of these two words is sure to bring about an emotional response.

Another example of the deliberate choice of words to create a carefully planned impression concerns the "rewriting" of history. All history texts (indeed, everything) were written by someone with a particular point of view. Recently, the word *aggression* was taken out of Japanese history books that described World War II invasions. Do the same descriptions of an act seem "better" in some sense when they are not modified by the word *aggressive*? The contemporary Japanese historians who asked for this deletion apparently think so. Similarly, Russian historians are now using harsher terms to describe Stalin's role when he was the leader of the former Soviet Union. They now know and are free to say that Stalin slaughtered millions of innocent Russians whose "crime" was to disagree with his policies. Such people were officially labeled *enemies of the state*, a label that was meant to instill fear in the individual who received such a label and to convey to everyone else that disagreement with Stalin's official policies would be considered an act of treason. History is also being rewritten in nonverbal ways in the new capitalist Russia. A massive number of statues of Lenin and Stalin are now being sold as scrap metal with new statues of Peter the Great and other Romanovs (members of the former ruling family) now standing on the pedestals that held the bronze busts of Communist leaders for most of the 20th century. With the advent of advertising in the new capitalist Russia, images of the "Marlboro Man" puffing away on imported cigarettes are now more numerous than depictions of the formerly ubiquitous Lenin. It is clear that emotionally laden words and inspiring visual displays both reflect and influence how people think.

The lesson is clear: When you want to influence how people think, choose your words and images carefully. You also need to be aware of the ways in which other people attempt to manipulate your thoughts by the labels they use. The deliberate use of words designed to create a particular attitude or foster certain beliefs is called **semantic slanting.** The meaning (semantics) is slanted so that the listener's thoughts will be directed in some way. It's fairly easy to find examples of this around election time when issues and groups label themselves with favorable terms and others with negative terms (name calling). During a recent election, a group called "Citizens for Sane Laws" opposed a proposition, whereas another group called "Citizens for Better Government" favored it. The political advertisements continued to broadcast these group names and the message to vote "No on 10" or "Yes on 10" depending on who financed the advertisement. Very little meaningful information was ever given on the merits or problems of the proposition. Be wary of attempts to influence your thinking through the use of positive and negative labels, especially on the important issues that concern social and political policies.

Ambiguity, Vagueness, and Equivocation

The thinking process can also be misled when words are imprecise or misused. Words are **ambiguous** when they can have multiple meanings depending on context, and the appropriate meaning is unclear in a given context. The problem here, as in the sentences described earlier, is one of determining the intended meaning or underlying representation. A good example of this was provided by von Oech (1983). According to von Oech, J. Edgar Hoover, the former director of the FBI, was reviewing a typed copy of a letter he had dictated to his secretary. He didn't like the margin widths she had used for the letter and wrote, "Watch the borders" on the letter and asked her to retype the letter and send copies to top FBI agents. For the next 2 weeks, FBI agents were put on special alert along the Canadian and Mexican borders.

Another humorous example of ambiguity was provided by Fogelin (1987). Compare the following two sentences:

Mary had a little lamb; it followed her to school.
Mary had a little lamb; and then a little broccoli.

The word "had" is ambiguous. It is used to mean "owned" in the first sentence and "ate" in the second sentence. Its meaning is not clarified until the second half of each sentence. A clever example of ambiguity can be found in the title of a popular book by Phyllis Chesler (1972), *Women and Madness,* in which she meant madness to mean both anger and insanity. I also deliberately used ambiguity in the title of my recent edited book *Changing College Classrooms* (Halpern, 1994). The word changing could refer to the fact that college classrooms are changing or that we should engage in activities to change them. I meant the word in both senses; hence I made use of ambiguity. Often, a situation is ambiguous and you are not sure how to respond or which of several definitions is appropriate. Although this sort of ambiguity can lead to errors, not all ambiguity is negative. Sometimes, creative interpretations of the intended meaning and creative responses are the result of ambiguous situations.

Whereas ambiguous words have multiple meanings, vague words have imprecise meanings. **Vagueness** refers to a lack of precision in a communication. If your friend Valerie told you to bake a cake in a hot oven, you'd probably ask her how hot it should be. In this context, the word *hot* is too vague and needs to be specified further. Consider the "clarification" provided by Justice Brennan of the U.S. Supreme Court when he provided a working definition that would assist those in the legal process of determining the sort of punishment that is cruel and unusual. As you probably know, punishment that is cruel and unusual is prohibited by the U.S. Constitution. But, we have little guidance for determining what makes a punishment cruel and unusual. He offered, "a punishment is cruel and unusual … if it does not comport with human dignity." Such a definition will not help a judge or jury decide whether a particular punishment is cruel and unusual. Justice Brennan's comments are much too vague to be useful. It is not easier to determine which actions do not comport with human dignity than it is to decide if they are cruel and unusual. A communication is vague if it does not specify enough details for its intended purpose.

There is legislation in California that requires that warning notices be posted in all places where the public may come in contact with cancer-causing chemicals. The sign designed for gas stations is shown in Fig. 3.4.

As you can see, the new signs are too vague to be of value. There is no information about the level of risk, or the likelihood of developing cancer, or how long you would have to be exposed to these chemicals to reach some level of risk. This is a clear example of a deliberately unclear communication. The gasoline companies were opposed to this law and have registered their complaint by posting the required signs, but not providing the public with interpretable information.

Vagueness is sometimes a socially polite way of handling an unpleasant situation. If you ask someone about her divorce you may get a vague response like, "We were incompatible" rather than a more precise, but less acceptable, "The stinking rat cheated every chance he could get."

Equivocation occurs when the meaning of a word is changed in the course of the same discussion. Consider the following "line of reasoning" (Reasoning is considered more fully in the next chapter):

1. Man is the only rational animal.
2. No woman is a man.
3. Therefore, no woman is rational. (Damer, 1987)

The meaning of the word *man* changed from the first to the second sentence. In the first sentence, *man* stood for all of humanity—both female and male. In the second sentence, it was used as a gender-specific term, with women conveniently omitted. This is an example of equivocation.

> ## Warning
>
> Detectable amounts
> of chemicals known to
> the State of California
> to cause cancer, birth
> defects, or other
> reproductive harm may
> be found in and
> around this facility.

FIG. 3.4. An example of vagueness. California law requires that warning signs be posted in all places where consumers come in contact with cancer-causing chemicals. Signs like this one are being used at all gas stations. The information they convey is too vague to be meaningful.

Etymology and Reification

These two terms both concern word meanings. **Etymology** is the study of word origins. It's often interesting to learn how language evolved and developed. But, it is wrong to conclude that a word has a particular meaning or nuance based on the word from which it was derived. Consider, for example, the use of the word gay to refer to homosexual men. The word is commonly used today to denote pride and other positive attributes of male homosexuals. The origin of the word was quite different. The word gay was derived from a definition meaning "wanton and licentious." It would be wrong to conclude that gays are therefore wanton and licentious. Language is a living entity and word definitions evolve and change. Returning to a word's origins to find its contemporary meaning is like studying the writings of Karl Marx to understand how modern Communism is practiced in Cuba.

Reification is a somewhat more difficult concept to explain. Reification occurs when something abstract is given a name and then treated as though it were a concrete object. An example should help here. Consider the Freudian notion of the "ego." According to Freudian theory, it is that portion of the personality that deals with reality. It is an abstract concept that was developed by Freud. Sometimes, therapists forget that it is an abstract concept and start treating it as though it were tangible. If a physician suggested that you take vitamins or engage in exercise to strengthen your ego, you should run quickly from his office. The ego is not something that can be physically altered because it is an abstract concept, not a physical body part. Perhaps the most obvious case of reification involves the concept of intelligence, where intelligence tests yield "IQ" scores that are said to measure it, and then IQ is used as though it were the physical embodiment of intelligence.

Bureaucratese and Euphemism

Two language barriers to comprehension are bureaucratese and euphemism. **Bureaucratese** is the use of formal, stilted language that is unfamiliar to people who lack special training. The same information can be expressed better with simpler terms. Bureaucratese is different from the use of precise technical terms that may be needed in specialized disciplines; in bureaucratese the style and language hinder our understanding instead of aiding it. The legal profession is often guilty of bureaucratese. I once read a legal document that began with the term "Witnesseth." Of course, I questioned what meaning was being conveyed with the use of this term, which is standard on many legal forms. The answer was, "very little." It could have been deleted altogether or replaced with "Notice" or "Read this document," both of which would have been more meaningful than the obscure, "Witnesseth." Ditto for other obscure terms like "party of the first part" and "party of the second part," not to mention the archaic Latinisms that riddle the law (e.g., *ex parte* and *corpus delecti*).

Euphemism is the substitution of a desirable term for a less desirable or offensive one. The result is often a loss of communication. Euphemism is common in hospital and medical facilities where bodily functions need to be discussed. Hospital personnel may ask a patient if he has "voided his bladder." Many patients do not realize that this refers to urination. In fact, it has been shown that a majority of patients do not understand the language that is commonly used in their interactions with medical staff. Many do not understand words like *malignant, benign, terminal,* and *generic.* You can imagine a solemn physician telling a patient that she is "terminal," with the patient then brightly inquiring when she'll get better. It is easy to see how the use of euphemisms can lead to misunderstandings.

Euphemisms abound in advertisements of all sorts. Do "bathroom tissue" and "feminine hygiene products" seem more desirable and glamorous than toilet paper and menstrual pads? Euphemisms often obscure the intended meaning. Although polite speech is a necessary rule of society, euphemistic terms that are not commonly used interfere with the communication of ideas, and thus should be avoided.

Euphemisms are designed to change the affect or emotion that we feel when we confront topics that we may find repugnant. The idea is that feelings will be less negative if a phenomenon is given a more acceptable name. For example, many people have complained that "beauty pageants," like the "Miss America Pageant," are demeaning to its participants whose value is determined by their appearance—much like a horse or cow at an auction. Officials and sponsors of these pageants disagree. They argue that these pageants are opportunities for the contestants to demonstrate their talents and to win money and other prizes that can be used to finance an education or to launch a career. Those who believe that such displays are demeaning reply that the bathing suit competition, in which women march around in skimpy bathing suits and high-heel shoes, should not be a requirement for scholarship money for a college education. This argument has continued heatedly for years, mostly centering around the bathing suit competition. In recognition of the fact that a contestant's appearance when clad in scanty clothing probably is unrelated to her talent, academic potential, or scholarship, the officials of the Miss America Pageant decided to remedy this situation. They renamed the competition. Women still parade in scanty swimsuits and high heels, but now it is called "health and fitness in a swimsuit" (Leive, 1994). This is a strange euphemism for the portion of the competition that leads the contestants to resort to starvation diets and plastic surgery—neither of which promotes health and fitness.

Probably the biggest perpetuators of euphemisms are politicians. In response to public protests over tax increases, we now have "revenue enhancement" bills. With very little effort, you should be able to find other examples.

Framing With Leading Questions, Negation, and Marked Words

Framing occurs when a question is asked in a way that suggests what the correct response should be. The reader is "led" into assuming a particular perspective or point of view.

Consider the following problem: (Tversky & Kahneman, 1981):

Imagine that the U.S. is preparing for the outbreak of an unusual disease, which is expected to kill 600 people. Two alternative programs to combat the disease have been proposed. Assume that the exact scientific estimate of the consequences of the programs are as follows:

If Program A is adopted, 200 people will be saved.

If Program B is adopted, there is $\frac{1}{3}$ probability that 600 people will be saved, and $\frac{2}{3}$ probability that no people will be saved. (p. 453)

Which of the two programs would you favor?

Now consider the same problem, and select between the following two programs:

If Program C is adopted, 400 people will die.

If Program D is adopted there is $\frac{1}{3}$ probability that nobody will die, and $\frac{2}{3}$ probability that 600 people will die. (p. 453)

Which of these two programs would you favor?

When this problem was presented to college students, 72% of those given the first set of choices selected Program A, whereas 78% of those given the second set of choices selected Program D. Look closely at the choices. Programs A and C are effectively identical—they differ only in that A is described in terms of the numbers of lives saved, whereas C is described in terms of the number who will die. Programs B and D are also identical, differing only in the language used to describe the outcomes. It seems that most people are **risk averse,** which means that they prefer options that do not involve loss. When an alternative makes a potential loss prominent (e.g., focuses on the number that die), people will reject that alternative. It is clear that a loss is more negative than a comparable gain is positive.

The percentage of people who prefer each alternative differs significantly depending on the language used to describe each alternative and whether the focus is on gains or losses. This is an important result, showing that human judgments and preferences can be readily manipulated by changes in the way questions are asked or framed. If I tell you that a new medical treatment has a 50% success rate you will be more likely to endorse its use than if I tell you that it has a 50% failure rate. The only difference is whether the information was presented in a positive (success rate) frame or a negative (failure rate) frame (Halpern & Blackman, 1985; Halpern, Blackman, & Salzman, 1989).

Another example of the influence of language on thought comes from a study by Loftus (1975). Forty people were asked questions about their headaches. A key question was posed in one of two ways: "Do you get headaches frequently, and, if so, how often?" or "Do you get headaches occasionally, and, if so, how often?" (p. 561).

Can you anticipate the results of this study? The respondents who answered the first question reported an average of 2.2 headaches per week, whereas those who answered the second question reported an average of .7 headaches per week. It seems that if people are asked questions with the word frequently, they will believe they have experienced more headaches than if they are asked the same question with the word occasionally. Note that although this example does not seem to contain any deliberate attempts to mislead or direct respondents' answers, the changes in wording have accomplished exactly that end. Pay careful attention to the way that questions are posed. Always consider if slight changes in the language used would result in different responses.

Salespeople know that leading questions can be good for business. If I am showing you some household items, a good sales technique is to ask, "How many will you take?" The assumption here is that the sale is made, and it is only a matter of how many you will buy and not whether you will buy. Similarly, a car salesperson who is ready to "close the deal" will ask, "What color do you want?" This makes it clear that you have already decided that you will buy the car and the only decision left is that of color.

Advertisers and merchants like to price their wares in uneven amounts, like $19.99 and $24.95. Have you ever wondered why they don't simplify matters and price garments to the nearest dollar so that $19.99 would be labeled $20.00 and $24.95 would become $25.00? They believe that consumers will think that $19.99 is considerably less than $20.00. The frame or perspective being induced here is one of considering the price as "less than $20.00." Of course, the 1¢ difference is negligible, but it does seem to change how people think about the price.

Listeners can also be framed or misled with **negation.** Suppose you read that a prominent politician is not a drunk. Suppose further that this is absolutely true; she is not a drunk. Most people would infer that there was some question about her sobriety and the truth of the assertion. The pragmatic function of negation is to deny something that is plausible (D. W. Carroll, 1986). Thus, listeners will infer the plausibility of that which was denied. President Richard Nixon hadn't considered this psycholinguistic principle when he uttered the now famous words in response to his Watergate debacle, "I am not a crook." Most people took this to mean that it was plausible that he was a crook. Thus, the denial of some act often has the paradoxical result that people now believe it is more likely to be true than they would have if no denial had been made.

Contrast and Context

Are you making a good salary? How is your health? Is the new love in your life intelligent and kind? Do you approve of the current president? The way you are likely to answer all of these questions depends on what you are comparing them to and the context in which the comparison is being made. Contrast and context provide meaning to cognitive activities like judging and evaluating. In a classic study, Parducci (1968) asked subjects to decide how bad it is to "pocket the tip that the previous customers left for the waitress." Half the subjects were asked to judge this event along with the following mild infractions: stealing a loaf of bread from a store when you are starving; playing poker on Sunday; cheating at solitaire. The other half of the subjects were asked to judge the same event (pocketing the tip that the previous customers left for the waitress) along with the following infractions: spreading rumors that an acquaintance is a sexual pervert, putting your deformed child in the circus, murdering your mother without justification or provocation.

Taking a waitress' tip was judged to be a more serious offense when it was presented along with milder infractions than when it was presented among a list of serious infractions. The event (pocketing a tip) was exactly the same in each case, and the wording was identical. Changes in the context in which it was presented created changes in the way it was evaluated. Context is an important determinant of the meaning we assign to events.

Judgments and evaluations are always made relative to some frame of reference. Suppose that your friend has just moved into a small one-room apartment near campus. This apartment will seem like heaven, if he has moved from an even smaller one-room apartment that he shared with four people he did not like, and it will seem awful if he moved from a large swanky penthouse in the best part of the city. The object being evaluated (the apartment) and the evaluator are the same in both scenarios. The only change is the frame of reference that is being used. Contrast is a powerful determinant of the way in which we evaluate an alternative.

Dear Mother and Dad:

Since I left for college I have been remiss in writing and I am sorry for my thoughtlessness in not having written before. I will bring you up to date now, but before you read on, please sit down. You are not to read any further unless you are sitting down, okay?

Well, then, I am getting along pretty well now. The skull fracture and the concussion I got when I jumped out the window of my dormitory when it caught on fire shortly after my arrival here is pretty well healed now. I only spent two weeks in the hospital and now I can see almost normally and only get those sick headaches once a day. Fortunately, the fire in the dormitory, and my jump, was witnessed by an attendant at the gas station near the dorm, and he was the one who called the Fire Department and the ambulance. He also visited me in the hospital and since I had nowhere to live because of the burntout dormitory, he was kind enough to invite me to share his apartment with him. It's really a basement room, but it's kind of cute. He is a very fine boy and we have fallen deeply in love and are planning to get married. We haven't got the exact date yet, but it will be before my pregnancy begins to show.

Yes, Mother and Dad, I am pregnant. I know how much you are looking forward to being grandparents and I know you will welcome the baby and give it the same love and devotion and tender care you gave me when I was a child. The reason for the delay in our marriage is that my boyfriend has a minor infection which prevents us from passing our pre-marital blood tests and I carelessly caught it from him. I know that you will welcome him into our family with open arms. He is kind and, although not well educated, he is ambitious. Although he is of a different race and religion than ours, I know your often expressed tolerance will not permit you to be bothered by that.

Now that I have brought you up to date, I want to tell you that there was no dormitory fire, I did not have a concussion or skull fracture, I was not in the hospital, I am not pregnant, I am not engaged, I am not infected, and there is no boyfriend. However, I am getting a "D" in American History, and an "F" in Chemistry and I want you to see those marks in their proper perspective.

Your loving daughter,

Sharon

FIG. 3.5. This fictitious letter is a good example of the use of contrast to influence judgments of "how bad" different events are perceived. From Cialdini (1993). Reprinted by permission of HarperCollins College Publishers.

I recall reading a book, when I was a child, entitled *Cheaper by the Dozen* (Gilbreth, 1963). It was a (mostly) true story about a family with 12 children, hence the title, and their parents, who were psychologists. The father knew very well about the power of contrast effects. After he purchased a new home for his family, he took them out to see it for the first time. He drove around the city, stopping at various run-down houses in bad neighborhoods, while he pretended to be lost. Finally, he pulled up to the home he had purchased, which looked like a palace in comparison to the decaying shacks he had stopped at earlier. The family was delighted with their luxurious new home, which certainly seemed even better when compared to the others that they had just seen. This principle is used quite well in the letter that is reprinted from a delightful book by Cialdini (1993) and shown in Fig. 3.5.

Contrast can be used effectively in a wide range of situations. For example, Zimbardo and Leippe (1991) offered this advice when you want to borrow money from a friend or parent. They suggested that you first ask for a large sum that you are fairly certain will be refused. (Hey, can you loan me $75?) Follow this by asking for the smaller sum that you really need. (No, well, how about $25?) They found that you are more likely to receive the smaller amount when it follows a large request than when it is requested without the larger request being made first. Zimbardo and Leippe reported that charitable contributions are also more likely when the requestor asks for any amount—"even a penny will help." When solicitors for charities request "even a penny," people are more likely to give larger sums of money to the charity than to charitable appeals that do not emphasize that "even small amounts will help."

Barometers of Thought

I am writing this book during a 5-month stay in Moscow, Russia, where I am teaching critical thinking at Russia's premiere university, Moscow State University (in 1994). Everyone here is interested in knowing what Americans think about a wide range of topics including child care, the economy, and the dramatic change in Russian political philosophy. It is impossible to provide a straightforward answer to the question, "What do Americans think?" Not only is there the obvious problem that Americans are quite diverse in their thinking, there is also the problem of assessing what any individual thinks.

The kind of answers that people give to opinion questions depends on the way the questions are asked. Read the following two opinion polls, which gave very different indices of what the American people thought about the controversial U.S. policy in the former Yugoslavia (Brennan, 1993, p. A5):

Gallup Poll:

As you may know, the Bosnian Serbs rejected the United Nations peace plan and Serbian forces are continuing to attack Muslim towns. Some people are suggesting the United States conduct air strikes against Serbian military forces, while others say we should not get militarily involved. Do you favor or oppose U.S. air strikes?

The Results:

Favor: 36%
Oppose: 55%
Depends: 3%
No Opinion: 6%

ABC News Poll:

Specifically, would you support or oppose the United States along with its allies in Europe, carrying out air strikes against Bosnian Serb artillery positions and supply lines?

The Results:

Support: 65%
Oppose: 32%
No Opinion: 3%

What is the difference between these two opinion polls, which were taken on the same day, yet yielded very different results? In the Gallup poll, no mention was made of joining with our European allies, whereas in the ABC News poll, the action was described as working with our allies. Well, what did Americans *really* think about the American role in Bosnia-Herzegovina on this particular day in 1993? Like all difficult questions in life, the answer is, "It depends." In this case, it depends on how and what is asked. It is fairly easy to deliberately slant the results of an opinion poll by carefully selecting wording that will favor one position or another. Try this one for yourself:

Are you in favor of a national program that ensures good-quality, affordable day care for infants and young children whose parents work outside of the home?

YES   NO   NO OPINION

Are you in favor of programs that are paid for with your tax dollars that place infants and young children in child-care institutions for 9 to 10 hours each day?

YES   NO   NO OPINION

Can you see how it would be easy to present data to Congress and other decision-making bodies that either support or refute the idea that most Americans are in favor of or opposed to a program of national day care? Before you interpret the results from any poll or respond to one, consider very carefully the way in which the questions were posed. What sort of background information was given and what words were used?

COMPREHENSION: THE REASON FOR LANGUAGE

Language is the first medium of the rational mind.

—Ferguson (1981, p. 120)

A student once told me that although she really wanted to understand the material in her textbook, she found that the information went "in one eye and out the other." In other words, it "didn't stick" or seem to involve her brain at all. Although her "eyes" read every word, she was unable to understand or remember the material. We can all sympathize with her because we've all had this experience at one time or another. Comprehension failures often result from the language used to express an idea and not from the difficulty of the idea itself. Good teachers know how to communicate complex ideas so that they can be easily understood, while poor teachers could talk or write for days without conveying the ideas to their students.

Strategies for Comprehension

What can you do to enhance your ability to comprehend? There are a number of comprehension strategies or skills that are designed to help make information that is presented in natural (everyday) language more understandable. These strategies act as aids in discovering, retaining, and utilizing the information in speech and written prose. They all involve ways of building a meaningful representation that matches the one used by the sender (i.e., speaker or writer).

The process of comprehension may be best described with an analogy. Imagine that a friend has a large jungle gym (child's climbing toy) in his backyard, and that he is giving it to you as a present. Because it is too large to transfer in its assembled state, you need to take it apart in order to move it to your home. Once you get it home, you need to reassemble the toy. In order to do this, you have to identify which part is the base and then add component parts to it. When it is reassembled, it should look the same as it did in your friend's yard.

The same is true of comprehension. If your friend has a complex knowledge structure in his head, he would transfer the information to you via language. You would have to identify the main ideas (or base) in order to build your own mental representation. You would also have to understand the relationships among the parts of the information so that you can graft them onto the main ideas in the correct way. Comprehension is attained when your knowledge structure "looks the same as" the one your friend has in his head. In other words, you would both have the same underlying representation for the transferred information. All comprehension strategies are activities that aid in the transfer of underlying structures. They provide guides for identifying main ideas and determining the relevance of various components of the message. They assist the comprehender in discovering the underlying relationships among the constituent parts of the message.

What do you do when you comprehend a passage? Most people respond that they have no idea what they do to aid their understanding, yet they can say what they do when they study. As previously stated, any cognitive activity that aids comprehension will also aid memory, so any effective comprehension strategy is also a memory strategy.

Questioning and Explaining

Good thinkers are good questioners.

—Alison King (1994, p. 18)

There have been numerous demonstrations of the beneficial effects of posing questions to oneself and others as part of the learning process. Palincsar and Brown (1984), for example, found that when students were required to formulate relevant questions for their peers they were better able to comprehend new passages than a control group of students who never practiced posing questions. The best known technique for studying from text is based on the process of asking good questions about the material being read and then demonstrating comprehension by answering the questions. Several studies have shown that when students generate and answer their own questions about a text, comprehension and recall improves (Heiman & Slomianko, 1986).

One of the best known methods based on the combination of questioning and paraphrase is **SQ3R**, which stands for Survey, Question, Read, Recite, Review (A. Adams, Carnine, & Gersten, 1982). The first thing to do when you begin reading complex text is to Survey the chapter (or some other manageable unit of text). When you survey, you look at section headings and subheadings to gain an overview of what you will be reading about. This will allow you to anticipate related topics as you read. It also forms a skeletal framework for the mental representation you will be building that can be used to interpret and organize incoming information. Before you read each section (approximately one or two pages is usually a good length), turn the section heading into a Question. For example, the main heading for this section of text is "strategies for comprehension." A good question that you should be able to answer when you finish this section is, "What are some strategies for comprehension, and how do they work?" If you can't answer this question, with the book closed, when you finish this section, then you do not know the information presented. A good question for this subsection on "questioning and explaining" is, "How are questioning and explaining used to improve comprehension?"

The first of the 3 **R**'s is Read. Reading is the third step; it is not the first thing you do when learning from text. It is often useful to take notes at this time. In order for these notes to be beneficial, they need to be a **paraphrase** or restatement in *your own words* of the information. The Recite portion is the answering of the questions you previously posed. This needs to be done without reference to the book or your notes.

When succinct summaries are generated by the reader, they provide a check on the reader's comprehension. It is too easy to believe that you know the material when it is sitting in front of you, only to later discover that you really don't "own" it when away from the book or your notes. At this point, you need to monitor the quality of your response by assessing how well you can answer the questions. It's a good idea to recite the answer out loud or to write out an answer. Cognitive psychologists know that "one of the most demanding tests of people's comprehension of a text is to have them summarize it, distilling and abstracting it into a few sentences" (Bower & Clapper, 1989, p. 293). If you can't answer the questions, you need to go back and recycle. Reread the section, reconsider the questions you've posed, review the structure of the information. The final **R** is for *Review*. Go over the material again. Psychologists call this **overlearning**. Overlearning is an important part of the process of understanding and learning because it ensures that newly acquired information will be available when it is needed. Recall becomes increasingly automatic, accurate, and less effortful, with overlearning.

King (1989, 1992, 1994) conducted a series of studies that clearly demonstrate the value of **reciprocal peer questioning**, a technique in which learners learn to pose thoughtful questions, which they then take turns answering. She concluded that the ability to ask thoughtful questions is a skill that needs to be learned because most people tend to ask "low level" simple recall questions (e.g., What is the date of … ? Who did … ?) and not those that require a meaningful analysis of complex information, if they are not trained in the formulation of thoughtful questions. King (1994) devised a series of **generic questions** that can be used with modifications in almost any context. Look at the generic questions that are presented in Table 3.1. When learners completed these questions using information from a lecture or text, they showed better recall and comprehension than did control groups who were instructed to either study independently, engage in group discussions, generate summaries, or ask questions without training in how to ask good questions (King, 1989, 1992). More important, King found that when students become proficient at using higher level questioning, they spontaneously ask these questions in a variety of learning situations (King, 1994). These studies provide further support for the conclusion that I presented in the first chapter: Critical thinking skills transfer to novel contexts when instruction emphasizes the need to practice and use these skills in many contexts. Thus, there are very strong indications that you can improve your comprehension and memory by using the generic questions that appear in Table 3.1. Here are some examples applied to the information in this chapter:

1. How does context affect judgment?
2. Compare underlying structure with surface structure with regard to their role in the process of communication.
3. Explain how analogies can be useful in enhancing comprehension.
4. Why are prototypes important?
5. What is the difference between ambiguity and vagueness?
6. What is the meaning of the term "generic questions?"

Can you answer these questions?

Graphic Organizers

An oft-repeated theme in this book is to utilize both verbal and spatial-like strategies as thinking aids. **Graphic organizers** (sometimes called concept maps) are spatial arrays that require learners to attend explicitly to the underlying structure in a passage.

TABLE 3.1
Guiding Thought-Provoking Questioning

Generic Questions	Specific Thinking Skills Induced
What is a new example of ...?	Application
How could ... be used to ...?	Application
What would happen if ...?	Prediction/hypothesizing
What are the implications of ...?	Analysis/inference
What are the strengths and weaknesses of ...?	Analysis/inference
What is ... analogous to?	Identification and creation of analogies and metaphors
What do we already know about ...?	Activation of prior knowledge
How does ... affect ...?	Activation of relationship (cause–effect)
How does ... tie in with what we learned before?	Activation of prior knowledge
Explain why ...	Analysis
Explain how ...	Analysis
What is the meaning of ...?	Analysis
Why is ... important?	Analysis of significance
What is the difference between ... and ...?	Comparison–contrast
How are ... and ... similar?	Comparison–contrast
How does ... apply to everyday life?	Application—to the real world
What is the counterargument for ...?	Rebuttal argument
What is the best ... and why?	Evaluation and provision of evidence
What are some possible solutions to the problem of ...?	Synthesis of ideas
Compare ... and ... with regard to ...	Comparison–contrast
What do you think causes ...? Why?	Analysis of relationship (cause–effect)
Do you agree or disagree with this statement: ...? What evidence is there to support your answer?	Evaluation and provision of evidence
How do you think ... would see the issue of ...?	Taking other perspectives

Note. A list of generic questions provided by King (1994). These question stems can be used in almost any context. Research has shown that comprehension and memory are improved when students learn to ask and answer thoughtful questions based on these stems. More important, students use these generic questions in novel contexts, showing that transfer of critical thinking skills occurs when students understand that transfer is the goal of activities that improve thinking.

They can provide a picture of a learner's knowledge structures and show the way in which new information is incorporated into information that is already known. Mayer (1987) called the deliberate use of graphic organizers "structure training techniques" because they force the learner to focus on the structure of a text. There are several varieties of graphic organizers, but all of them use spatial representations to make efficient use of the information in a text.

Linear Arrays.   Sometimes, the best way to understand a topic is to represent the information in a **linear array**. This is useful when the information presented is fairly linear, or straight-line-like, in its structure. An example of this would be a very simple "line" of causal reasoning: The girl hit the boy. He started to cry. The teacher heard the boy's cry. She ran into the room. She punished the girl. The girl was sent to the principal's office. And so on.

This rather boring story is a straightforward sequence of events that followed each other in a strict temporal ordering. A simple linear representation would adequately capture all of the relevant information.

girl hit boy
boy cried
teacher arrived
teacher punished girl
girl to principal's office
▼ and so on

Another example when a modified linear array would be a good choice of representation is in representing any parts or processes that are aligned linearly in the physical world. Vaughan (1984) taught medical students how to utilize graphic organizers when learning from medical texts. The digestive system is aligned in a fairly linear manner beginning with the mouth and ending with the rectum. Students who read about the digestive system listed the parts of the digestive system in linear order and noted along with each part its purposes in the digestive process and its components. The resulting linear array is shown in Fig. 3.6. Vaughan reported that the medical students who learned to use graphic organizers like this one showed significant improvement in their comprehension of medical school texts.

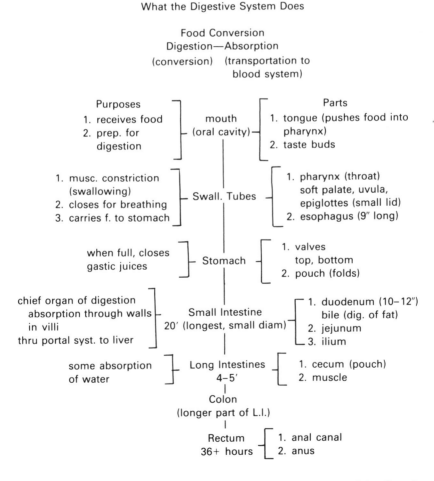

FIG. 3.6.   Modified linear array depicting the purposes and parts of the digestive system. A linear array is a good spatial arrangement for this information because, like the array, the digestive system is linear. Adapted from Vaughan (1984).

Time lines that are commonly used in history are useful in providing a visual picture of and appreciation for time spans and the co-occurrence of events. When the distance between events is proportional to the time between their occurrence, a much more accurate understanding of the importance of time as the key underlying dimension of history is possible than with any verbal description. This is another situation in which a linear array can foster comprehension.

Hierarchies

Most of the information we deal with is considerably more complex than simple linear chains. An alternative structural form for information is that of **hierarchies** or tree structures in which information is organized around class inclusion rules. Class inclusion rules are those rules in which something is a part of or a type of something else. Examples of class inclusion rules are the classification of toes as part of the foot and roses as a type of flower. Information of this sort can usually be categorized into levels with higher levels dividing into lower levels according to some rule. Biological classification systems are a good example of hierarchically organized information. Bower (1970) studied organizational factors in memory using hierarchically arranged information about minerals. Consider Fig. 3.7 which depicts this hierarchy. Bower found that when subjects organized information this way, they had significantly better recall than did a group of control subjects. Furthermore, he found that when a "node" or branch of the hierarchy was forgotten, subjects failed to recall the entire portion of the "tree" that was below it. I return to these results later in this book, in chapter 9 on problem solving. Hierarchies or tree diagrams are sometimes used as problem-solving aids.

Networks

The relationships among ideas in a communication are not usually based on simple class inclusion rules. Concepts can be related to each other in numerous other ways, and it is the depiction of the correct relationship among concepts that is central to all

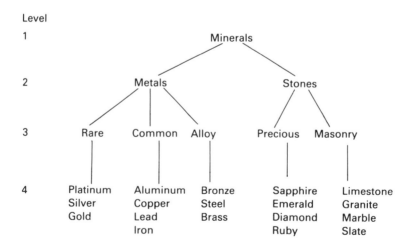

FIG. 3.7. Hierarchy of minerals. An example of a hierarchical graphic organizer. Hierarchies are particularly useful when the information is organized according to class inclusion rules. Adapted from Bower (1970).

graphic organizing techniques. **Networks** are graphic organizers in which several different types of relationships are made explicit. Much of the work in this area has been conducted by Dansereau and his colleagues and is presented in an edited book by Holley and Dansereau (1984) and in a chapter by Tinzmann, Jones, and Pierce (1992).

When students learn the technique of networking, they are taught to focus on and identify six different types of relationships or links among concepts (Holley, Dansereau, McDonald, Garland, & Collins, 1979). Two of these relationships are the class inclusion rules of hierarchies: X is a part of Y (e.g., France is a part of Europe), and X is a *type of* Y (e.g., mangoes are a type of fruit). The third relationship is called a *leads to link*. This type of relationship occurs whenever X leads to Y (e.g., stealing leads to jail). The other three relationships or links are *analogy* (X is like Y; e.g., a paw is like an arm), *characteristic* (X is a characteristic or feature of Y; e.g., brilliance is a characteristic of diamonds), and *evidence* (X is evidence that Y occurred; e.g., antibodies are evidence of infection). These six relationships are described more fully in Table 3.2.

TABLE 3.2
Six Types of Links Used in Networks

Type	Example	Structure	Key Words
Part of link	hand |p finger	*Hierarchy*—the lower node is part of the higher node	is a part of is a segment of is a portion of
Type of/ example of link	school |t private	*Hierarchy*—the lower node is an example of the higher node	is a type of is in the category is an example of is a kind of three procedures are
Leads to link	practice |l perfection	*Chain*—the object of the higher node leads to or results in the lower node	leads to results in causes is a tool of produces
Analogy link	school_a_factory	*Cluster*—the content of one node is analogous to the other node	is similar to is analogous to is like corresponds to
Characteristic link	sky_c_blue	*Cluster*—the content of one node is a trait of the other node	has is characterized by feature is property is trait is aspect is attribute is
Evidence link	broken_e_x-ray arm	*Cluster*—the content of one node is evidence for the other node	indicates is illustrated by is demonstrated by supports documents is proof of confirms

Note. This table is adapted from Holley et al. (1979). Notice how the "key words" suggest the type of link that is being described.

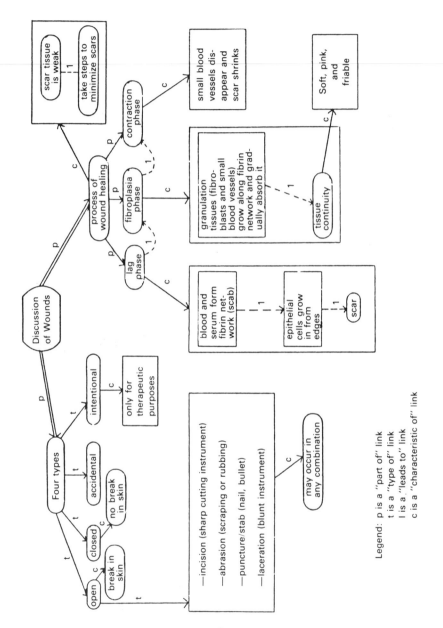

FIG. 3.8.   Example of a network of a chapter from a nursing text on wounds (Holley et al., 1979). The use of linking relationships force the learner to consider the way concepts are related.

As you can see from Table 3.2, networking requires students to consider the nature of the relationship among concepts in a text and then to categorize them into six different possible types. Once this is done the relationships are depicted in a network-like array with all of the relationships labeled. Eylon and Linn (1988) reported that errors in understanding often result from inappropriate links among concepts. When learners construct networks, they must consciously consider the relationships among concepts, a strategy that leads to greater comprehension.

An example of a completed network is shown in Fig. 3.8. The network shows the relationships among concepts in a nursing text on wounds. Look carefully at this figure. "Types of wounds" and the "process of healing" are *parts* of the discussion of wounds. "Open," "closed," "accidental," and "intentional" are *types* of wounds. In the process of healing, the "lag phase" *leads to* the "fibroplasia phase," which *leads to* the contraction phase. "Soft, pink, and friable" is *a characteristic of* tissue continuity. The other two types of relationships, analogy and evidence, are not used in this network.

Identification and use of these six types of relationships or links and their combination in a unified network requires considerable practice. This is an effortful strategy that, like some of the mnemonic techniques, pays off once it is well learned. Holley et al. (1979) found that when subjects were well trained with this technique, they performed significantly better on subsequent tests than control students who did not learn this technique, with the biggest improvement for students with low grade point averages. It seems that the students who were doing very well in school were already attending to the relationships among concepts; therefore, it was the poorer students who benefited most from explicit instruction and practice in identifying, labeling, and diagramming the relationships among concepts.

Matrices

When the material to be comprehended involves comparisons of several topics along a number of dimensions, a **matrix** is the representation of choice. (The word *matrices* is the plural of matrix.) Suppose, for example, that you are reading a passage about wars. The purpose of the passage is to compare and contrast various antecedent conditions of war and to consider their effect. Suppose further that the wars being considered are the Revolutionary War, World War I, World War II, the Korean Conflict, and the Vietnam Conflict. In order to understand the nature of these U. S. wars, you need to organize the information so that commonalities and distinctions will emerge. A suggested matrix for this information is shown in Table 3.3.

By filling in the empty cells in Table 3.3, selected categories of information can readily be compared and similarities and differences can easily be spotted. A coherent "pattern" of information about these wars can then be extracted. The framework can be applied to other wars involving other countries to determine, for example, if there are universal commonalities for all wars.

Similarly, matrices can be useful when a judgment has to be made about products or courses of action that differ along multiple dimensions. If you are familiar with the way in which the magazine *Consumer Reports* provides information about products to consumers, you will recognize that this is the technique that they use. For example, if you want to buy a refrigerator, you will find that *Consumer Reports* rates several different brands and models of refrigerators along many dimensions. The models would be listed in the left-hand column and the dimensions across the top, such as cost to operate, ease of opening the door, how well it maintains a set temperature, storage space built into the door, and the other features that differ among refrigerators. The ratings in each cell are pictorial (colored circles) that help to convert a large amount of

TABLE 3.3
Example of a Matrix Graphic Organizer

	War				
	Revolutionary War	World War I	World War II	Korean Conflict	Viet Nam Conflict
Major precipitating events					
U.S. justification for the war					
"Other side" justification for the war					
Number of lives lost—each side					
Major battles					
Resolution					
Types of weapons					
Relationship to later war, if any					

Note. Matrices are particularly good spatial arrays when the information involves several different topics (e.g., wars) that are being compared on several dimensions (e.g., characteristics of war).

information to a format that is comprehensible in a single glance. A similar technique was used by the RAND Corporation (1992) in their analysis of three different plans for financing health insurance. Look at this matrix, which is presented in Fig. 3.9.

As you can see in Fig. 3.9, the RAND Corporation listed five desirable goals for any health care plan. These are listed under "Goal." The three health care plans they compared are a 20% voluntary subsidy, a simple mandate or law that would require employers to provide health insurance, and a play-or-pay plan that would allow employers to shop for the best plan for their employees. The degree of shading in a square is an indication of how well the particular plan satisfies a goal. Which plan seems the best given their evaluation and the way they presented the data? It is easy to see that the third option meets three goals very well, one goal somewhat, and one goal not at all. Thus, it would seem that the third plan is the best overall, but this conclusion is only warranted if all of the goals are equal in importance. If the containment of government costs is much more important than any of the others, then the third plan is not a good one because it does not satisfy this goal. The relative importance of each goal depends on individual judgment that, ideally, is informed by knowledge of the issues.

Matrices can also be used to organize information so that it can be used more easily. Day, Rodin, and Stoltzfus (1990) investigated the effect of changing the representation of information on the ease with which it is used. A medication schedule that was given to a (real) patient is shown in Fig. 3.10. The list format shown on the left side of Fig. 3.10 is the way that the physician presented the medication schedule to the patient. The matrix format shown on the right provides the same information, but is clearly easier to use. Not surprisingly, Day, Rodin, and Stoltzfus found that both young and old subjects were more accurate in their understanding and memory of the medication schedule when it was provided in a matrix format.

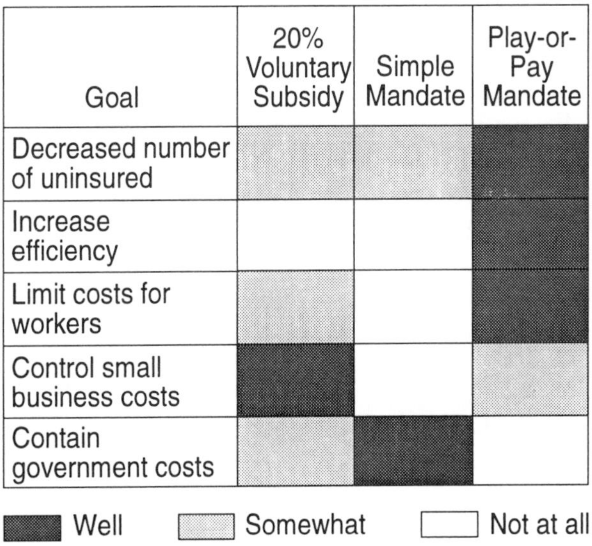

Goal	20% Voluntary Subsidy	Simple Mandate	Play-or-Pay Mandate
Decreased number of uninsured	Somewhat	Somewhat	Well
Increase efficiency	Not at all	Not at all	Well
Limit costs for workers	Somewhat	Not at all	Well
Control small business costs	Well	Not at all	Somewhat
Contain government costs	Somewhat	Well	Not at all

■ Well   ▦ Somewhat   □ Not at all

FIG. 3.9.   A shaded matrix that compares three possible health care plans on five "goals." The use of shading with a matrix allows for an easier comparison among the plans. Adapted from RAND (1992). Health care and the uninsured: Who will pay? RAND Research Review, XVI, pp.6–8.

LIST FORMAT

Inderal   - 1 tablet 3 times a day
Lanoxin   - 1 tablet every a.m.
Cafafate   - 1 tablet before meals
              and at bedtime
Zantac   - 1 tablet every 12 hours
              (twice a day)
Quinaglute - 1 tablet 4 times a day
Coumadin - 1 tablet a day

MATRIX FORMAT

	Breakfast	Lunch	Dinner	Bedtime
Inderal	✓	✓	✓	
Lanoxin	✓			
Cafafate	✓	✓	✓	✓
Zantac		✓		✓
Quinaglute	✓	✓	✓	✓
Coumadin				✓

FIG. 3.10.   Two representations of a medication schedule for an elderly patient. The list on the left is the format that was given to the patient. The matrix on the right was devised by Day, Rodin, & Stoltzfus (1990). Adapted from Day, R. S., Rodin, G. C., & Stoltzfus, E. R. (1990). Alternative representations for medication instructions: Effects on young and old adults. Paper presented at the 3rd Cognitive Aging Conference, Atlanta, GA.

Flow Charts

Sometimes the content of a passage is best described as a series of actions with the specific action to be taken dependent on some previous circumstance. A relevant example of this sort of passage is instructions for selecting the appropriate graphic organizer for a passage. In general, the "rules" generally fit the format: "If X is true, then do Y. If X is not true, then do Z." A good representation for these decisional rules is a flow chart. **Flow charts** are particularly useful when the passage contains explicit, logical, and sequential instructions. As you probably know, they are used by computer programmers when the programmers are planning the sequence of operations that a computer must perform in order to accomplish a task.

One of the benefits of using a flow chart is that it forces the learner to be very clear and explicit about the nature of decisions and the sequence of steps. A flow chart for selecting the appropriate strategy for comprehension is depicted in Fig. 3.11.

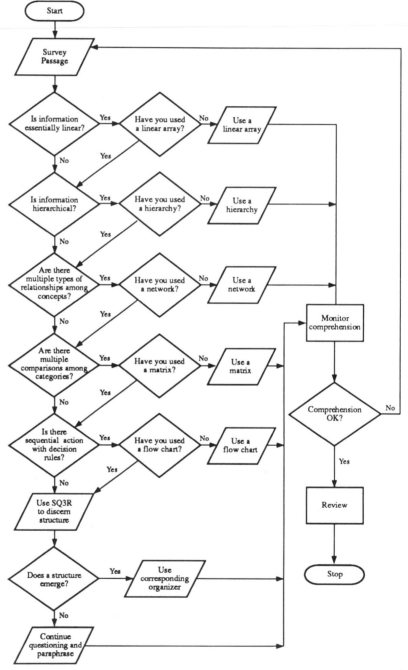

FIG. 3.11. Flow chart for deciding which graphic organizer is best suited for the comprehension of a specific text.

General Guidelines and Principles

In a recent study of "at risk students" (those identified as being at risk of failing and not completing their education), Pogrow (1992) concluded that these students have academic difficulties because "they do not understand 'understanding'" (p. 90). What he meant by this is that these students do not know what they need to do to ensure that information is acquired in a way that is meaningful and resistant to forgetting. Many ideas about learning and knowing are foreign to them such as: complex information will contain multiple interacting concepts; learners need to understand how concepts relate to one another; difficult material has to be questioned, explained, drawn, and discussed; and comprehension needs to be continually monitored. There is ample empirical evidence that more of these at-risk students could complete their education if they were taught how to improve their comprehension.

Techniques that promote understanding are critically important in our complex world. The ability to comprehend difficult material is empowering because it allows us to understand and act intelligently on a wide range of issues including the purchase of a new refrigerator, understanding how AIDS is transmitted, or deciding how to vote on a variety of health insurance initiatives. We all need a society in which citizens think and respond thoughtfully, if we are to prosper, or even survive, in a time of skyrocketing complexity.

All of the strategies for comprehension require learners to monitor their understanding of the information. They are all active cognitive strategies that facilitate the construction of meaningful representations. The graphic organizers offer ways to transform text into explicit spatial representations that display relationships among concepts. They all make abstract concepts more concrete. Like all good cognitive strategies, they require the learner to relate new information to prior knowledge in a way that makes knowledge retrieval (remembering) most efficient. And, like many of the other thinking skills presented in this book, they require effort and must be practiced in order to be useful. It is not enough to read about them. They have to be used in a variety of situations to ensure transfer.

Although most of this chapter has been concerned with the process of comprehension, that is going from surface structure to underlying structure, many of the principles can be used in language production or going from underlying structure to surface structure. The task of writing involves transforming your internalized meaning into words. Many people have difficulty with writing because they find that this is a difficult translation. Kellogg (1990) compared the quality of persuasive papers written by college students who either prepared an outline before they began their papers (a linear display) or used a clustering technique in which associated ideas were first generated from memory and then connected with lines that showed how the ideas were related. He found that the students who were required to outline before they wrote improved in their organization and writing style (writing is a mostly linear activity), and the students who used clustering produced a larger number of ideas than those who used outlines. I return to these results in chapter 10 on creativity, where I discuss the generation of ideas.

Graphic organizers, like clustering or flow charts, or matrices, can be terrific aids in the writing process. Suppose you were to write an essay about Acquired Immune Deficiency Syndrome (AIDS). You could begin the planning process by considering the kinds of links employed in networking (type of, part of, leads to, evidence for, characteristics of, and analogy). What "types of" people are most and least at risk? What is the "evidence for" AIDS (laboratory tests, symptoms)? What are the "characteristics of" at-risk groups or risky activities? Some people have called for quarantine, which is "analogous to" the way the way society has responded to other dread diseases. Once you have considered the information you want to present, the relationship among the facts can be depicted in a network. The network offers a nonlinear alternative to outlines when planning the writing process. Thus, by "running comprehension strategies backward," they can be used to produce language (spoken or written) instead of their more usual role in comprehending language.

APPLYING THE FRAMEWORK

1. What Is the Goal?   The thinking goal addressed in this chapter is how to enhance comprehension when the medium for communication is natural language. A more formal way of saying the same thing is that the goal is to create an accurate underlying representation (i.e., re-presentation of the underlying message) from the surface structure provided in speech and written text. The newly acquired knowledge will ideally be stored in memory in a way that will make it easily accessible when it is needed.

2. What Is Known?   This step requires determining where you are before selecting the appropriate thinking skill. Are you in a situation in which there are likely to be deliberate attempts to bias your thinking on an issue (e.g., consumer decisions, political rhetoric)? Do you have to learn from a text that contains information that you will soon be tested on? Is the information particularly complex? Do you already have good background knowledge? What is the structure of the information and the reason why you need or want to understand it? Will a graphic presentation help with comprehension? If so, does the material match a structure such as a linear array, hierarchy, matrix, network, or flow chart?

3. Which Thinking Skill or Skills Will Get You to Your Goal?   The skills presented in this chapter are those involved in comprehending language. As with every list of skills, users need to monitor their comprehension to determine what is and what isn't being understood. The process of skill use often requires trying a different skill if the one being used is not promoting understanding. The following comprehension skills were presented in this chapter. Review each skill and be sure that you understand when and how to use each one:

- Recognizing and defending against the inappropriate use of emotional language, labeling, name calling, ambiguity, vagueness, and arguments by etymology.
- Developing the ability to detect misuse of definitions, reification, euphemism, and bureaucratese.
- Understanding the use of framing with leading questions, and negation.
- Using analogies appropriately, which includes examining the nature of the similarity and its relationship to the conclusion.
- Employing questioning and explaining as a skill for text comprehension.
- Selecting and using graphic organizers (linear arrays, hierarchies, networks, matrices, flow charts).

4. Have You Reached Your Goal?   Have you been monitoring your understanding? Can you paraphrase a passage with the book closed? Did you systematically consider all of the ways that we can be misled with language that were presented in this chapter? Did you consider the reason for the communication and have you satisfied that reason?

CHAPTER SUMMARY

1. Psycholinguistics is the branch of psychology that is concerned with understanding how people produce and comprehend language.

2. Psychologists view language as comprising two components or levels: a meaning component (underlying representation) and a speech sound component (surface structure). The problem of comprehension is moving from a thought by the sender (underlying structure) through language and then reconstruction of the thought by the receiver.

3. Language is ambiguous when a single surface structure has two or more possible underlying representations.

4. Language and thought exert mutual influences on each other with our thoughts determining the language we use and, in turn, the language we use reshaping our thoughts.

5. Six rules of communication were presented. Every time we attempt to communicate with others, we utilize these rules to determine what information we will convey and how to express the information.

6. Language comprehension requires that the listener make many inferences. The kinds of inferences we make depend on context, manner, and the words selected to convey the message.

7. There are many ways that words can be used to deliberately mislead the listener. Several ways that the choice of words can influence thought were presented. The deliberate use of emotional and nonemotional words is designed to influence how you think about a topic.

8. Emotional words often evoke strong mental images. Because images are highly resistant to forgetting, they are readily available when the topic is mentioned.

9. Prototypes, or the most typical member of a category, are usually thought of first when we think about an example of a category. These prototypes bias what we think. This bias can be overcome with deliberate practice at generating examples that are not typical.

10. The way in which we judge or evaluate a situation depends on the context in which it is embedded and the way it contrasts with similar recent events. Our judgments are strongly determined by recent experiences.

11. Strategies to improve the comprehension of text were described. They all require learners to attend to the structure of the information and to make the relationships among concepts explicit.

TERMS TO KNOW

You should be able to define or describe the following terms and concepts. If you find that you're having difficulty with any term, be sure to reread the section in which it is discussed.

Psycholinguistics. The branch of psychology that is concerned with the acquisition, production, comprehension, and usage of language.

Underlying Representation. The meaning component of language. It's the thought that you want to convey with an utterance. Compare with surface structure.

Surface Structure. The sounds of an utterance or the outward appearance of a language expression. Compare with underlying representation.

Given/New Distinction. The ratio of known (given) information to new information in a communication. It is a primary determinant of the difficulty of a communication.

Cognitive Economy. Refers to any process that reduces the mental work load and makes thinking or remembering less effortful.

Prototypical Thinking. Using the most typical member in a category as a guide to making inferences about other members of that category.

Prototype. The best or most typical example of a category. For example, dog is the prototype for the category "animal."

Sapir–Whorf Hypothesis of Linguistic Relativity. The hypothesis that language, at least in part, determines or influences thought.

Semantic Slanting. The deliberate use of words designed to create a particular attitude or foster certain beliefs.

Ambiguous. An utterance is ambiguous when it can have more than one meaning or underlying representation.

Vagueness. A lack of precision in a communication. A communication is vague if it does not specify enough details for its intended purpose.

Equivocation. A change in the meaning of a word in the course of the same discussion.

Etymology. Reference to the origin of a word in order to determine its meaning.

Reification. Occurs when an abstract concept is given a name and then treated as though it were a concrete object.

Bureaucratese. The use of formal, stilted language that is often unfamiliar to people who lack special training.

Euphemism. The substitution of a desirable term for a less desirable or offensive one.

Framing. Occurs when a question is asked in a way that suggests what the correct response should be. The reader is "led" into assuming a particular perspective or point of view.

Risk Averse. A general preference for options that do not involve possible loss over options that involve possible gain.

Negation. The use of denial to imply that a fact is plausible.

SQ3R. A strategy for comprehension that requires the use of questioning and paraphrase. The letters stand for **S**urvey, **Q**uestion, **R**ead, **R**ecite, and **R**eview.

Paraphrase. Restating ideas in your own words.

Overlearning. Reviewing material after it is learned so that recall becomes automatic and less effortful.

Reciprocal Peer Questioning. The process of having learners pose thoughtful questions, which they take turns answering.

Generic Questions. Question "stems" that can be modified and applied to many different topics.

Graphic Organizers. The use of spatial displays to organize information. Also known as concept maps.

Linear Arrays. A graphic organizer in which information is presented in a list format.

Hierarchies. A type of graphic organizer that uses a tree structure. Most useful when information is organized according to class inclusion rules.

Networks. Graphic organizers in which types of relationships among concepts are depicted.

Matrix. A rectangular array that is useful when the information presented involves comparisons along several dimensions.

Flow Charts. A graphic organizer that depicts specific actions to be taken when these actions depend on previous circumstances.

SUGGESTED READINGS

An excellent and easy-to-read text in psycholinguistics is Clark and Clark's (1977) *Psychology and Language: An Introduction to Psycholinguistics*. Although it is now almost 20 years old, it is still highly recommended for anyone who wants to obtain an overview in this area of psychology. An even older book that is somewhat rambling and difficult to classify is R. Brown's (1958) *Words and Things*. It's provocative reading on the wide range of topics that concern language.

An interesting book that describes the interpersonal aspects of communication is Adler, Rosenfeld, and Towne's (1980) *Interplay: The Process of Interpersonal Communication*. It is easy reading.

The best collection of articles on the use of graphic organizers is Holley and Dansereau's (1984) edited volume *Spatial Learning Strategies*. In fact, theirs is the only edited collection that I know of on this subject. Holley et al.'s (1979) journal article titled "Evaluation of a Hierarchical Mapping Technique as an Aid to Prose Processing" describes the use of networks and presents empirical evidence for their effectiveness as an aid to comprehension. An excellent and more recent chapter on spatial strategies was written by Tinzmann et al. (1992). It appears in an edited book by Collins and Mangieri (1992) entitled *Teaching Thinking: An Agenda for the 21st Century*. Their book contains a practical set of chapters on a range of topics that concern instruction in critical thinking.

It seems that the importance of training students to ask good questions is an idea whose time has come to many researchers. S. Brown and Walter (1993) edited a book on this topic which is entitled, *Problem Posing: Reflections and Applications*. There is also an extensive research base on the use of generic questions that has been compiled by King (1994, 1995). See, for example, her recent book chapter (1994) entitled "Inquiry as a Tool in Critical Thinking."

Two outstanding books that a cover a broad range of topics, including the mutual effects of thought and language, are Pratkanis and Aronson's (1992) *Age of Propaganda: The Everyday Use and Abuse of Persuasion* and Gilovich's (1991) *How We Know What Isn't So*. Both are highly recommended.

4

Reasoning: Drawing Deductively Valid Conclusions

Contents

As far as Joan's opponent was concerned, the debate wasn't going well. It was clear from the sea of nodding heads and sounds of "uh huh" and "yeah" that Joan was scoring points and convincing the audience; whereas, he seemed to be losing support every time he spoke. He wasn't surprised; he had been warned. Joan had studied reasoning and now knew how to make people believe anything. Soon she would have everyone convinced that the war was justified and what was wrong was right. The way she's going, she could probably make people believe that day is night. It certainly wasn't fair, but what can you expect from someone who studied reasoning?

This fictional vignette was taken from a real-life incident. I was present at a debate where one debater accused the other of cheating by using reasoning. At the time, I thought that this was pretty funny because I had come to think of reasoning as an important critical thinking skill—the sort of skill that you would use to make valid conclusions when dealing with information that is complex and emotional. To the losing side of this debate, it was a trick. Trick, skill, or strategy, reasoning is the best way to decide whom and what to believe.

LOGICAL AND PSYCHOLOGICAL

The trick, of course, is to reason well. It isn't easy and it isn't automatic.

—Kahane (1980, p. 3)

Reasoning is often taken to be the hallmark of the human species. Colloquially, reasoning tells us "what follows what." When we reason, we use our knowledge about one or more related statements that we can reasonably believe are true to determine if another statement, the conclusion, is true. A **conclusion** is an inferential belief that is derived from other statements. The ability to reason well is a critical thinking skill that is crucial in science, mathematics, law, forecasting, diagnosing, and just about every other context you can imagine. In fact, I can't think of an academic or real-world context in which the ability to reason well is not of great importance.

Many definitions of the term *critical thinking* identify reasoning as central to the concept as seen in the definition that was derived from three rounds of rankings by school administrators in the United States. The procedure they used to come up with their preferred definition of critical thinking is called the **delphi technique,** which refers to a method for achieving agreement among experts in some field. In this case, definitions were circulated among all participants three times. They agreed that "critical thinking is … cohesive, logical reasoning patterns" (Stahl & Stahl, 1991, p. 84).

Pragmatism and Logic

When we reason logically, we are following a set of rules that specify how we "ought to" derive conclusions. **Logic** is the branch of philosophy that explicitly states the rules for deriving valid conclusions. The laws of logic provide the standard against which we assess the quality of someone's reasoning (Garnham & Oakhill, 1994). According to logic, a conclusion is **valid** if it necessarily follows from some statements that are accepted as facts. The factual statements are called **premises.** Conclusions that are not in accord with the rules of logic are **illogical.** Although we maintain that the ability for rational, logical thought is unique to humans, all too often we reach invalid or illogical conclusions. This fact led M. Hunt (1982) to award "A flunking grade in logic for the world's only logical animal" (p. 121).

Psychologists who study reasoning have been concerned with how people process information in reasoning tasks. The fact is that in our everyday thinking, the psychological processes quite often are not logical. In a classic article on the relation between logic and thinking, Henle (1962) noted that although everyday thought does not generally follow the formal rules of logic, people use their own imperfect rules. If we were not logical, at least some of the time, we wouldn't be able to understand each other, "follow one another's thinking, reach common decisions, and work together" (Henle, 1962, p. 374). To demonstrate this point, stop now and work on one of the problems Henle posed to her subjects in one of her studies:

> A group of women were discussing their household problems. Mrs. Shivers broke the ice by saying: "I'm so glad we're talking about these problems. It's so important to talk about things that are in our minds. We spend so much of our time in the kitchen that, of course, household problems are in our minds. So it is important to talk about them." (Does it follow that it is important to talk about them? Give your reasoning.) (p. 370)

Do not go on until you decide if it is valid to conclude that Mrs. Shivers is correct when she says that it is important to talk about household problems. Why did you answer as you did?

When Henle (1962) posed this problem to graduate students, she found that some arrived at the wrong answer (as defined by the rules of logic), whereas, others arrived at the right answer for the wrong reasons. Consider the following answer given by one of her subjects: "No. It is not important to talk about things that are on our minds unless they worry us, which is not the case" (p. 370). Where did this subject go wrong? Instead of deciding if the conclusion followed logically from the earlier statements, she added her own opinions about what sorts of things it is important to talk about. Thus, whereas the answer is incorrect as evaluated by the standard rules of logic, it is correct by the subject's own rules. Consider this answer: "Yes. It could be very important for the individual doing the talking and possibly to some of those listening, because it is important for people to 'get a load off their chest,' but not for any other reason, unless in the process one or the other learns something new and of value" (p. 370). This time, the subject gave the correct answer, but for the wrong reasons. This subject, like the first one, added her own beliefs to the problem instead of deriving her conclusions solely on the basis of the information presented. Henle termed this the **failure to accept the logical task**.

It seems that in everyday use of reasoning, we don't determine if a conclusion is valid solely on the basis of the statements we are given. Instead, we alter the statements we're given according to our beliefs and then decide if a conclusion follows from the altered statements. We function under a kind of **personal logic** in which we utilize our personal beliefs about the world to formulate conclusions about related issues.

Psychologists and philosophers have puzzled over the finding that for some everyday and formal reasoning tasks, most people seem to behave as though they are using the rules of logic, but for other reasoning tasks, there seems to be little evidence that the laws of logic are being followed. In other words, whether most of us appear logical or not depends on the type of reasoning problem that is being studied. Simon and Kaplan (1989) did not find this state of affairs surprising. They asserted that "intelligent behavior is adaptive and hence must take on strikingly different forms in different environments" (p. 38).

The word **pragmatic** refers to anything that is practical. In real life, people have a *reason for reasoning*, and sometimes the laws of logic are at odds with the setting, consequences, and commonly agreed upon reasons and rules for deriving conclusions. As Henle's (1962) subjects showed in the earlier example, in real life, we add our own beliefs and knowledge to the facts we are given when we determine if a conclusion is supported by the premises. In most everyday settings, this is a pragmatic or practical approach to reasoning problems. This point is made more clearly in later sections in this chapter.

Inductive and Deductive Reasoning

Actual thinking has its own logic; it is orderly, reasonable, reflective.

—Dewey (1933, p. 75)

A distinction is often made between inductive and deductive reasoning. (See chapter 6, Thinking as Hypothesis Testing, for a related discussion of this topic.) In **inductive reasoning** observations are collected that support or suggest a conclusion. For example, if every person you have ever seen has only one head, you would use this evidence

© King Features Syndicate, Courtesy KFS, INC.

to support the conclusion (or hypothesis) that everyone in the world has only one head. Of course, you can't be absolutely certain of this fact. It's always possible that someone you've never met has two heads. If you met just one person with two heads, your conclusion must be wrong. Thus, with inductive reasoning you can never *prove* that your conclusion or hypothesis is correct, but you can disprove it.

When we reason inductively, we collect facts and use them to provide support or disconfirmation for conclusions or hypotheses. It's how we discover what the world is like. Lopes (1982) described induction this way: "Scientists do it; lay people do it; even birds and beasts do it. But the process is mysterious and full of paradox ... induction cannot be justified on logical grounds" (p. 626). We reason inductively both informally in the course of everyday living, and formally in experimental research. For this reason, hypothesis testing is sometimes described as the process of inductive reasoning. When we reason inductively we generalize from our experiences to create beliefs or expectations. Sometimes inductive reasoning is described as reasoning "up" from particular instances or experiences in the world to a belief about the nature of the world.

In **deductive reasoning**, we begin with statements known or believed to be true, like "everyone has only one head," and then conclude or infer that LaTisha, a woman you've never met, will have only one head. This conclusion follows logically from the earlier statement. If we know that it is true that everyone has only one head, then it must also be true that any specific person will have only one head. This conclusion necessarily follows from the belief; if the belief is true, the conclusion must be true. Deductive reasoning is sometimes described as reasoning "down" from beliefs about the nature of the world to particular instances. Rips (1988) argued that deduction is a general-purpose mechanism for cognitive tasks. According to Rips, deduction "enables us to answer questions from information stored in memory, to plan actions according to goals, and to solve certain kinds of puzzles" (p. 117). The notion of reasoning up from observations and reasoning down from hypotheses is schematically shown in Fig. 4.1.

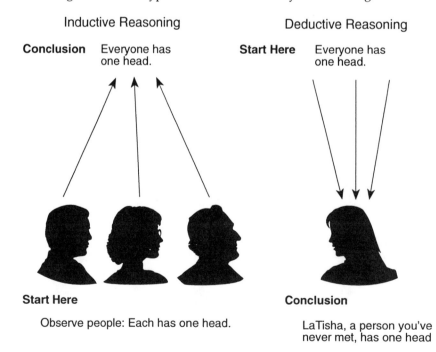

FIG. 4.1.   A pictorial distinction between deductive and inductive reasoning. In most real-world settings, we use both types of reasoning recursively.

Although it is common to make a distinction between inductive and deductive reasoning (Neubert & Binko, 1992), the distinction may not be a particularly useful description of how people reason in real life. In everyday contexts, we switch from inductive to deductive reasoning in the course of thinking. Our hypotheses and beliefs guide the observations we make, whereas our observations, in turn, modify our hypotheses and beliefs. Often, this process will involve a continuous interplay of inductive and deductive reasoning. Thinking in real-world contexts almost always involves the use of multiple types of thinking skills.

LINEAR ORDERING

Reasoning is simply a matter of getting your facts straight.

—B. F. Anderson (1980, p. 62)

Joel is stronger than Bill, but not as strong as Richard. Richard is stronger than Joel, but not as strong as Donald. Who is strongest and who is second strongest?

Although I'm sure that you've never met Joel, Donald, Richard, and Bill, I'm also sure you could answer this question. The premises or statements in this problem give information about the orderly relationship among the terms; hence, it is called a **linear ordering** or **linear syllogism**. Like all the deductive reasoning problems, the premises are used to derive valid conclusions—conclusions that must be true if the premises are true. In linear ordering problems, we're concerned with orderly relationships in which the relationships among the terms can be arranged in a straight-line array.

Linear Diagrams

How did you solve the problem about Joel, Donald, Richard, and Bill? Most people work line by line, ordering the people as specified in each line:

"Joel is stronger than Bill but not as strong as Richard" becomes:

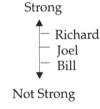

"Richard is stronger than Joel, but not as strong as Donald" adds Donald to the previous representation:

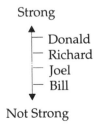

Thus, it is easy to "see" that Donald is strongest and Richard is second strongest. Research with linear syllogisms has shown that people rely, at least in part, on spatial imagery or some sort of spatial representation to answer the question.

Work through the following pairs of linear syllogisms. Try to decide if one member of each pair is easier to solve than the other:

1. a. Julio is smarter than Diana.
   Diana is smarter than Ellen.
   Who is smartest? Julio, Diana, Ellen, or don't know.

   or

   b. JoAnne is taller than Susan.
      Rebeccah is taller than JoAnne.
      Who is shortest? JoAnne, Susan, Rebeccah, or don't know.

2. a. Pat is not taller than Jim.
   Jim is shorter than Tiffany.
   Who is tallest? Pat, Jim, Tiffany, or don't know.

   or

   b. Les is worse than Moshe.
      Harold is worse than Moshe.
      Who is worst? Les, Moshe, Harold, don't know.

3. a. Stuart doesn't run faster than Louis.
   Louis doesn't run slower than Dena.
   Who is slowest? Stuart, Lois, Dena, or don't know.

   or

   b. Howard is fatter than Ace.
      Ace is thinner than Kyla.
      Who is thinnest? Howard, Ace, Kyla, or don't know.

As you worked through these problems, did some seem more difficult to you than others?

You probably found Problem 1a to be the easiest. Research has shown that when the second term in the first premise is the first term in the second premise (Diana in Problem 1a), and when the comparison terms are congruent (smarter, smarter, smartest), the linear ordering is fairly easy to solve. Problem 1b does not follow this simple form. The comparisons are between JoAnne and Susan and Rebeccah and Susan. In addition, the comparison terms are not congruent (taller, taller, shortest). The correct answer for 1A is Julio. The correct answer for 1b is Susan.

Problem 2a contains the negation term "not," which adds to the complexity of the problem. In addition, information is given in terms of both taller and shorter, which makes this a difficult problem. The correct answer is Tiffany. (Pat could be the same height or shorter than Jim.) You can represent this relationship graphically as:

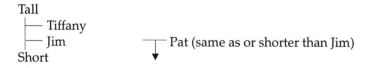

Although Problem 2b contains all congruent comparison terms (worse, worse, worst), some people find it tricky because we don't know if Les or Harold is worst. In addition, research has shown that it is more difficult to comprehend terms like "worse" than terms like "better" because "worse" denotes that all three are bad, whereas "better" is a more neutral term. (The correct answer is "don't know".) Problem 3a contains two negative terms as well as incongruent comparison terms (faster, slower, slowest). From the information given, we can't determine who is slowest. Problem 3b is somewhat easier because it doesn't contain negatives, but it does contain incongruent comparison terms (fatter, thinner, thinnest). The answer as to who is thinnest is Ace.

As you worked through these problems, you should have discovered some of the following psychological principles of linear orderings:

1. Orderings are easiest to solve when comparison terms are congruent (e.g., short, shorter, shortest).
2. Solutions will be facilitated if the second term in the first premise is the first term in the second premise (A is better than B; B is better than C).
3. Negations make the problem more difficult (e.g., A is not hairier than B).
4. Comparisons between adjacent terms (e.g., Julio and Diana in Problem 1a) are more difficult than comparisons between end terms (Julio and Ellen) (Potts, 1972).
5. When you are faced with a difficult syllogism of any sort, a good strategy for solving it is to draw a spatial array. With a linear syllogism, draw a linear array, so that the relationships among the terms can be inspected visually.
6. Comparison terms that limit the meaning of a sentence, like worse and dumber, are more difficult to process than more general and neutral terms like better and smarter. The adjectives that connote a bias (e.g., worse, dumber) are called **marked adjectives**, whereas the neutral adjectives are called **unmarked adjectives**.

These summary remarks can be used as an aid for clear communication of linearly ordered information. When you want someone to understand a linear ordering, use congruent terms, make the second term in the first premise the first term in the second premise, and avoid negations and marked adjectives. These few rules for communicating linear information show some basic cognitive principles. It is a general principle of cognitive psychology that negative information (no, not) is more difficult to process than positive information, in part because it seems to place additional demands on working memory (Matlin, 1994). There are many advantages to using diagrams when dealing with verbal information, including reducing the load on working memory and making relationships obvious and visible.

Confusing Truth and Validity

Knowing is only part of being educated, thinking and reasoning with what we know completes it.

—Schauble & Glaser (1990, p. 9)

Logically, the rules for deciding if a conclusion is valid are the same no matter what terms we use. In the first example in this section, I could provide the premise that Donald is stronger than Richard or I could substitute any name that I wanted (Igor is stronger than Yu-Chin) or any letter or symbol (C is stronger than A). The truth is not important in these examples, because the premises are treated as though they were true. This probably bothered some of you. Suppose I said:

Your sister is uglier than the witch in the Wizard of Oz.
You are uglier than your sister.
Therefore, you are uglier than the witch in the Wizard of Oz.

You'd probably protest this conclusion. You may not even have a sister, but given the premises, the conclusion is valid. Test it for yourself. But, that doesn't make it true. Chapter 5, Analyzing Arguments addresses the issue of determining the truth or believability of the premises. So far, we've only considered the question of validity: whether a conclusion must be true if the premises are true. People very often have trouble separating truth from validity. This is particularly difficult when the conclusion runs counter to cherished beliefs.

Although the rules of logic dictate that content is irrelevant to the conclusions we formulate, in most real-life situations, content does influence how we choose valid conclusions. It is possible to construct deductive reasoning problems so that the beliefs most people maintain conflict with logical conclusions. **Belief bias** occurs when an individual's beliefs interfere with her or his selection of the logical conclusion. This effect has been demonstrated many times. It was studied systematically by Morgan and Morton in 1944. Obviously, most Americans in 1944 had very strong beliefs about World War II, which clearly influenced their reasoning process. When presented with deductive reasoning problems, Americans were more likely to select conclusions that agreed with their belief biases than conclusions that ran counter to their belief biases.

It should come as no surprise to you that human reasoning becomes illogical when we are discussing emotional issues. This is true for people in every strata of society, even for Justices of the U.S. Supreme Court. When Justice William O. Douglas was new to the Supreme Court, Chief Justice Charles Evans Hughes gave him these words of advice, "You must remember one thing. At the constitutional level where we work, ninety percent of any decision is emotional. The rational part of us supplies the reasons for supporting our predilections" (M. Hunt, 1982, p. 129). Unfortunately, appellate legal proceedings are sometimes exercises in politics, with decisions changing as frequently as the political climate. Legal "reasoning" has sometimes served as a framework to persuade others that a conclusion is valid. If you understand how to formulate valid inferences, you'll be able to withstand and recognize its misuse by those who would use it to their advantage.

IF, THEN STATEMENTS

Reason, of course, is weak, when measured against its never-ending task. Weak, indeed, compared with the follies and passions of mankind, which, we must admit, almost entirely control our human destinies, in great things and small.

—Albert Einstein (1879–1955)

"If, then" statements, like the other examples of reasoning presented in this chapter, utilize premises that are known or believed to be true to determine if a conclusion validly follows. "If, then" statements are concerned with **contingency relationships**—some events are dependent or contingent on the occurrence of others. If the first part of the contingency relationship is true, then the second part must also be true. If, then statements are sometimes called **conditional logic** or **propositional logic**. Work through the four following if, then statements. Decide if the third statement is a valid conclusion:

1. If she is rich, she wears diamonds.
    She is rich.
    Therefore, she wears diamonds.
    Valid or Invalid?

2. If she is rich, she wears diamonds.
    She isn't wearing diamonds.
    Therefore, she isn't rich.
    Valid or Invalid?

3. If she is rich, she wears diamonds.
    She is wearing diamonds.
    Therefore, she is rich.
    Valid or Invalid?

4. If she is rich, she wears diamonds.
    She isn't rich.
    Therefore, she isn't wearing diamonds.
    Valid or Invalid?

In each of these problems, the first premise begins with the word "if"; the "then" is not explicitly stated, but can be inferred ("then she wears diamonds"). The first part of this premise (if she is rich) is called the **antecedent**; the second part (she wears diamonds) is called the **consequent**.

Tree Diagrams

Like the other types of deductive reasoning problems, conditional statements can be represented with a spatial display. **Tree diagrams**, diagrams in which the critical information is represented along "branches"—like a tree, are used in several chapters in this book, and can be used to determine validity with if, then deductive reasoning problems. Tree diagrams are very handy representational forms in many situations and it is well worth the trouble of learning to use them. We use tree diagrams in chapter 7 on understanding likelihood, chapter 9 on problem solving, and chapter 10 on creativity.

Tree diagrams are easy to begin. Every tree diagram begins with a "start" point. A start point is a dot on the paper that you label "start." Everyone finds the first step easy:

Start

The dots are formally called **nodes**, and branches (lines) come out from nodes. The branches represent everything that can happen when you are at that node. In "if, then" problems, there are two states that are possible from the start node. In this example, either she is rich or she is not rich. There are two possibilities, so there will be two branches coming from the start node. The antecedent is the first event on the "tree" with a second branch representing the consequent. The validity of the conclusion can be determined by examining the branches. Let's try this with the first problem.

"If she is rich" becomes:

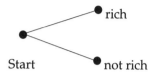

"She wears diamonds" is added as a second set of branches by showing that the "rich" node is always followed by "diamonds," but the "not rich" node may or may not be followed by "diamonds." We put both possibilities on the branches leading from "not rich" because we are not given any information about the relationship between being "not rich" and "wearing diamonds."

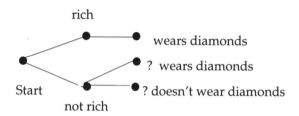

When we are told that "She is rich," circle the branch or branches that have this label and move along the branches from the "rich" node and conclude that she "wears diamonds." There is only one node in this diagram that represents the possibility that she is rich, and this node has only one branch attached to it—the branch that leads to "wears diamonds." Once you locate the "rich" node, the only possible consequent is "wears diamonds." Thus, the conclusion to Problem 1 is valid. The technical term for this problem is **affirming the antecedent**. In this case, the second premise affirms or indicates the antecedent is true; therefore, its consequent is true.

Problem 2 also contains a valid conclusion. The tree diagram is exactly the same as in the first problem because the same "if, then" statements are made. In determining the validity of the conclusion, we begin with "She isn't wearing diamonds," which is represented at only one node, so we trace this back to the "not rich" node. Because the second premise indicates that the consequent is not true, this sort of problem is technically called **denying the consequent**.

Many people are willing to conclude that Problem 3 is also valid when, in fact, it is not. Although it must be assumed to be true that if she is rich, she wears diamonds, it is also possible that poor people wear diamonds. I have found that intelligent college students have difficulty with this problem. Because the second premise states that the consequent has occurred, this sort of problem is called **affirming the consequent**. It is fallacious (i.e., wrong) to believe that because the consequent is true, the antecedent must also be true. "If," in these reasoning problems, doesn't mean "if and only if," which is how many people interpret it. Of course, she may be rich—it may even be more likely that she is rich—but we cannot conclude that she is rich just because she is wearing diamonds. You can see this on the tree diagram. There are two different nodes labeled "wears diamonds," one connected to the "rich" node and one connected to the "not rich" node. We cannot determine which must be true because either is possible.

The fallacy of affirming the consequent is one type of deductive reasoning error called **illicit conversion.** Illicit conversions, in "if, then" statements, occur when people believe that "If A, then B" also means "If B, then A."

Problem 4 is also invalid, although it is tempting to conclude that if she isn't rich, she isn't wearing diamonds. Can you guess the technical term for this sort of problem? It is called **denying the antecedent** because Premise 2 states that the antecedent is false. Again, by starting at the "not rich" node, you can see that it is connected to both "wears diamonds" and "doesn't wear diamonds," so either is possible.

A summary of these four kinds of reasoning, with examples of each, is shown in Table 4.1.

Several popular advertisements take advantage of people's tendencies to make invalid inferences from "if, then" statements. A highly successful yogurt commercial goes something like this:

> Some very old people from a remote section of the Russia are shown. We're told that it is common for people in this remote region to live to be 110 years old. We're also told that they eat a great deal of yogurt. The conclusion that the advertisers want people to make is that eating yogurt will make you live 110 years.

Implicitly, we're being told that if we eat yogurt, then we'll live to be 110 years old. Of course, it's possible to live to be 110 without ever tasting yogurt, and we have no reason to believe that yogurt added years to their lives. There is no basis for making a causal inference, that is for believing that eating yogurt can *cause* anyone to live a long time. These remote Russians engage in strenuous physical labor most of their lives and do not come into contact with many outsiders who carry potentially contagious diseases. Either of these facts, or countless others, including heredity, could account for their longevity. (It is also possible that the longevity claim is subject to question.) The advertisers are obviously hoping that the viewers will fall prey to the fallacy of affirming the consequent and say to themselves, "If I eat yogurt, I will live to a very old age."

TABLE 4.1
Four Kinds of Reasoning With If, Then Statements

	Antecedent	Consequent
Affirming	Affirming the Antecedent Valid Reasoning Example: If I am dieting, then I will lose weight. I am dieting. Therefore, I will lose weight.	Affirming the Consequent Invalid Reasoning Example: If Harry went to the supermarket, then the refrigerator is full. The refrigerator is full. Therefore, Harry went to the supermarket.
Denying	Denying the Antecedent Invalid Reasoning Example: If it is raining, then my hair is wet. It is not raining. Therefore, my hair is not wet.	Denying the Consequent Valid Reasoning Example: If Judy and Bruce are in love, then they are planning to marry. They are not planning to marry. Therefore, Judy and Bruce are not in love.

"If, Then" Reasoning in Everyday Contexts

"If, then" statements, like linear orderings, appear implicitly in standard prose. Of course, we seldom find them neatly labeled *premise* and *conclusion*. Yet, they are often the basis for many common arguments. The fallacies of denying the antecedent and affirming the consequent in everyday contexts are quite common.

There is currently an acrimonious debate over the issue of providing junior and senior high school students with contraceptive information. The pro side argues that if students are given this information, then they will act responsibly when engaging in intercourse. Formally, this becomes: If students receive contraceptive information, then they will engage in "protected" intercourse. The con side argues that students should not engage in intercourse (whether protected or not); therefore, they should not receive contraceptive information. This is an example of the fallacy of denying the antecedent. It does not follow that if they are not given contraceptive information, then they will not engage in intercourse.

A point that has been made repeatedly throughout this chapter is that people often do not reason according to the laws of formal logic without instruction in reasoning. In everyday (practical) reasoning, we use information that is not stated in the premises in order to decide if the conclusion follows from the premises. One sort of knowledge we rely on is our knowledge about the content of the premises. The following two sentences demonstrate this point (Braine, 1978):

> If Hitler had had the atomic bomb in 1940, he would have won the war.

> and

> If Hitler had had one more plane in 1940, he would have won the war. (p. 19)

Although logic dictates that people should be able to reason identically with both of these premises and should avoid the fallacies of affirming the consequent and denying the antecedent, in fact most people find it easier to reason correctly with the first sentence than the second. As with all of the forms of deductive reasoning that are covered in this chapter, the content of the premises and our own belief biases influence the way we determine what sorts of conclusions we are willing to accept as valid. When we interpret "if, then" statements in everyday contexts, we rely on our knowledge about the content to decide if a conclusion follows. According to the rules of formal logic, we should be able to reason in ways that are independent of content. We should all arrive at identical, logically correct conclusions, no matter what the content is. Of course, humans are not perfect logic machines. We do and should determine if the premises are true before deciding if a conclusion follows. (This point is emphasized in chapter 5.)

Negation

As seen in the previous section on linear reasoning, the use of negatives ("no," "not") in a reasoning problem makes it much more difficult to solve (Wason, 1969). These difficulties are apparent in the following examples, in which either the antecedent or consequent is negative:

> If the light is not green, I will go to Rome.
> It is not true that the light is not green.
> What, if anything, can you conclude?

If the letter is B, then the number is not 4.
The number is not 4.
What, if anything, can you conclude?

These are difficult to deal with because of the use of negation and its affirmation or denial. The first statement denies the negative antecedent (not [not green]). This is called a **double negation**. You can't assume anything about the consequent when the antecedent is denied, even when the antecedent itself is negative. Look at the second example. Most people incorrectly decide that it is correct to conclude from the second example that "The letter is B." You should recognize this as an example of affirming the consequent. If you are having difficulty answering these questions, draw the corresponding tree diagrams, and the answer will "appear."

I once heard a politician make a statement similar to these. He said, "It is not true that I do not favor the legislation." It took me a few seconds to realize that he implied that he favored the legislation. He could have meant that he was neutral with respect to the legislation, neither favoring nor opposing it, but in the context, I interpreted his statement to mean that he favored the legislation. This is an example in which I utilized context to clarify intended meaning. In order to communicate clearly, avoid negations whenever possible.

Confirmation Bias

Confirmation bias, the predilection to seek and utilize information that supports or confirms your hypotheses or premises, is a topic that has received a great deal of attention in recent years. It appears in several places in this text because it is seen in so many contexts. Like the fact that negation makes most thinking tasks more difficult, the tendency to seek confirming evidence seems to be a pervasive cognitive bias. (See chapters 6 and 8 for related discussions.)

Demonstrate this effect for yourself (Johnson-Laird & Wason, 1970): Four cards are lying face up on a table in front of you. Every card has a letter on one side and a number on the other. Your task is to decide if the following rule is true, "If a card has a vowel on one side, then it has an even number on the other side." Which card or cards do you need to turn over in order to find out whether the rule is true or false? You may turn over only the minimum number necessary to determine if this rule is true. Please stop now and examine the cards below to determine which ones you would want to turn over. Don't go on until you have decided which cards you would want to turn over.

Few people select the correct cards in this problem, which has become known as the **four-card selection task**. It is a widely studied task that is popular in the literature of cognitive psychology. Most people respond "A only" or "A and 4." The correct answer is "A and 7." Can you figure out why?

The best way to solve this reasoning problem is to draw a tree diagram that corresponds to the statement, "If a card has a vowel on one side, then it has an even number on the other side." It should look like this:

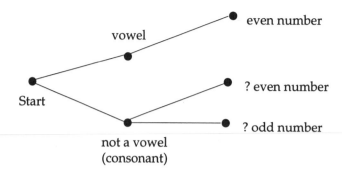

If A doesn't have an even number on the other side, the rule is false. Similarly, if 7 has a vowel on the other side, the rule is false. What about D and 4? *D* is a consonant. It doesn't matter if there is an even or odd number on the back because the rule says nothing about consonants. Because 4 is an even number, it doesn't matter if there is a vowel or consonant on the back. The reason that this is such a difficult problem is that people interpret the rule to also mean "If a card does not have a vowel on one side, then it does not have an even number on the other side" or, without negatives, "If a card has a consonant on one side, then it has an odd number on the other side." These alternate interpretations are incorrect. Do you recognize the error as denying the antecedent? This is a robust (strong) effect. It is an extremely difficult task because of the crucial role of disconfirmation. People fail to appreciate the importance of a falsification strategy. That is, we need to think of ways to show that a hypothesis may be false, instead of looking for evidence that would show that a hypothesis may be correct. This is exacerbated with the incorrect assumption that the converse of the rule is also true. The only correct way to solve this problem is to select only cards that can falsify the rule.

Part of the difficulty people have with this task may be related to the abstract nature of the problem. After all, there is very little we do in our everyday life that relates vowels and even numbers. Try out a more realistic and less abstract version of this task (adapted from Johnson-Laird, Legrenzi, & Legrenzi, 1972):

> In order to understand this task, you may need some background information (depending on your age). Many years ago, the United States Post Office had two different postage rates known as first-class and second-class mail. You could pay full postage, which was 5 cents, if you sealed your letter (first class), or you could pay a reduced, 3-cent rate, if you merely folded the flaps closed and didn't seal them (second class). (First-class mail had priority for delivery over second-class mail.)

> Suppose you are a postal employee watching letters as they move across a conveyor belt. The rule to be verified or disconfirmed is: "If a letter is sealed, then it has a 5-cent stamp on it." Four letters are shown in Fig. 4.2. Which ones would you have to turn over to decide if the rule is true?

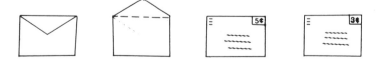

FIG. 4.2. Which of these letters would you turn over to decide if the following rule is true: "If a letter is sealed, then it has a 5¢ stamp on it?" (Adapted from Johnson-Laird, Legrenzi, and Legrenzi, 1972.)

Stop now and work on this problem. Don't go on until you've decided which letters (at a minimum) you would have to turn over to test this rule.

Did you notice that this is the same task that was posed earlier? The correct answer is the first sealed envelope and the last envelope (the one with the 3-cent stamp). This is an easier problem than the more abstract one because people find it easier to understand that a letter that is not sealed could also have a 5-cent stamp on it than it is to understand that if the letter is not a vowel it could also have an even number on the back. Your tree diagram should look like this:

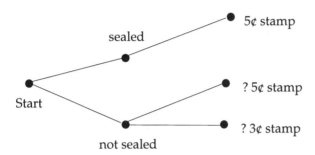

Johnson-Laird and Wason (1977) found that when the problem was presented in this realistic manner, 22 out of 24 subjects were able to solve the problem. Johnson-Laird and Wason concluded that our everyday experiences are relevant in determining how we reason.

Permission and Obligation Schemata

Many researchers have tried to understand why so many people have so much difficulty with the four-card selection task (I also find it very confusing), but have little difficulty when it is rephrased in the stamped-letter example. These are identical problems from the perspective of logic—the rules for reasoning are the same in the two problems.

Cheng and Holyoak (1985) explored the basic differences in how people think about these two problems. They postulated that when people use "if, then" reasoning for pragmatic purposes, they usually involve either the permission to do something, called **permission schema** (if something is true, then you have permission to do something else) or they involve an obligation or contractual arrangement, called **obligation schema** (if something is true, then you have an obligation to do something else). In real life, these are the two most common situations in which people use "if, then" reasoning. Instead of using the rules of formal logic, people tend to develop abstract general rules that work well in specific situations and help them to achieve their goals. Cheng and Holyoak found that the permission and obligation schemata work across domains. In other words, it does not matter if the topic concerns stamped letters, an agreement to perform a job, or permission to borrow the car. Here is an example of each:

- *If a passenger has been immunized against cholera, then he may enter the country.* (permission schema)
- *If you pay me $100,000, then I'll transfer ownership of this house to you.* (obligation schema)

When "if, then" statements involve permission or obligation, then people make few reasoning errors. Furthermore, when most people understand the rules of permission and obligation, the content of the statement doesn't matter—people apply the rules appropriately across domains.

Cheng and Holyoak (1985) also found that when they included a rationale for the rule, most of the people they asked to solve this problem had no difficulty with it. In the sealed-envelope problem, they added the following rationale for the rule, "The country's postal regulation requires that if a letter is sealed, then it must carry a 20-cent stamp" (p. 400). Thus, a rule that was extremely difficult to apply when it was presented in an abstract form was easily used by most people when it was used in a familiar context with an explanation.

If, and Only If

Certain contents seem to require that we understand them in a way that is inconsistent with the laws of logic. Suppose you are told: "If you mow the lawn, I'll give you five dollars" (Taplin & Staudenmeyer, 1973, p. 542). This statement invites the interpretation, "If you do not mow the lawn, I won't give you five dollars." In the everyday inference we make from language, this is a valid conclusion, although it is erroneous from the perspective of formal logic. In understanding statements of the "if p, then q" variety, the conclusions that we are willing to accept as valid depend very much on what p and q are. In this lawn-mowing example, the intended meaning is "if, and only if you mow the lawn, then I'll give you five dollars." In dealing with real-world "if, then" statements, you need to decide whether the intended message is "if p, then q" or "if, and only if p, then q."

Chained Conditionals

We can make things just a little more complicated (just what you were hoping for), by building on "if, then" statements and making them into longer chains. A **chained conditional** occurs when two "if, then" statements are linked so that the consequent of one statement is also the antecedent of the other statement. In skeleton form, or fill in the blank form, this becomes:

If A, then B. If B, then C.

As before, it doesn't matter what we use to fill in for A, B, and C. If she wants to be a physicist, then she will study calculus. If she is studying calculus, then she has a final exam on Wednesday. With this conditional chain, we can conclude that she has a final exam on Wednesday, if we learn that she wants to be a physicist.

Don't be tempted to assume that every time you have three terms, you have a chained conditional. Consider this example:

If she wants to be a physicist, then she will study calculus.
If she wants to be a physicist, then she will have an exam on Wednesday.

These are two conditional statements, but they do not have the chained structure because the consequent of one statement is not the antecedent of the other statement.

If, Then Reasoning in Legal Contexts

As I write this chapter, much of America is sitting glued to their television sets watching the evidence and the agony of an American star who is accused of killing his ex-wife and her friend. By the time you read this, this trial will probably be history, but there will always be similar crimes in which the key to the defense or prosecution hinges on "if, then" reasoning. In this particular case, the suspect has an excellent alibi from 11 p.m. and later on the night of the killing. In other words: If the murder occurred any time from 11 p.m. or later, the defendant is innocent.

The prosecution will attempt to show that the murder occurred prior to 11 p.m. Suppose that the prosecutors are successful in convincing the jury that the murder occurred at 10:30 p.m. What can we conclude about the guilt or innocence of the defendant?

To make it easier for you, I have drawn the tree diagram that corresponds to this real-life situation:

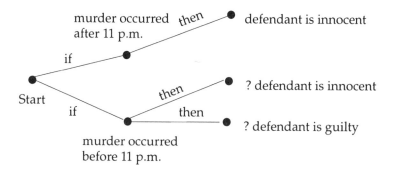

I hope that you determined that if the murder occurred at 10:30 p.m., we do not know if the defendant is guilty or innocent. Unless there is other evidence that "proves beyond a reasonable doubt" that the defendant committed these grisly murders, then the jury must acquit him. They cannot convict a man because of the error or denying the antecedent. If anyone tries to tell you that this critical thinking stuff is a "bunch of bunk" (or some more colorful phrase), then give him or her this example in which misunderstanding could lead to a wrongful conviction. Whom would you want on a jury that decides your guilt or innocence—people who think critically or those who rush to a hasty decision and are easily misled with persuasive techniques?

COMBINATORIAL REASONING

We recognize the gravity of the challenge to get our students to think, to think critically, and even to think scientifically. Certainly it is abundantly clear to me that science education fails if it doesn't tackle the matter of thinking.

—Munby (1982, p. 8)

One approach to enhancing reasoning skills is based on a model of intelligence that was proposed by the Swiss psychologist Jean Piaget. Piaget was primarily concerned with the way people acquire knowledge and the way cognitive processes change throughout childhood and early adulthood. According to Piaget, there are four broad developmental periods (each broken into stages). As people move from infancy into adolescence, their cognitive abilities mature in qualitatively distinct stages culminating with the ability to think in orderly, abstract ways. Piaget's examples of abstract thought involve thinking skills that are needed to understand scientific concepts. One of the

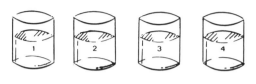

FIG. 4.3. Mixing colorless liquids.
How would you determine which
combinations of colorless liquids
are needed to obtain a yellow
color?

scientific reasoning skills that Piaget believed to be important is combinatorial reasoning. Here is a classic task that involves this skill:

> **Mixing Colorless Chemicals.** This task involves mixing chemicals until a yellow color is obtained. Suppose that you were given four bottles of odorless, colorless liquids. They appear to be identical except for being labeled 1, 2, 3, and 4. You are also given a fifth beaker labeled X, which is the "activating solution." The activating solution is always needed to obtain the yellow color, which results from a chemical reaction. How would you go about finding which of the chemicals in combination will yield the yellow color?

Some rules: The amount of each chemical is not important, nor is the order in which you combine them. It may help you in working on this problem to visualize the materials as presented in Fig. 4.3. Stop now and think about how you would approach this problem. Do not go on until you have written down all of the tests you would perform.

How did you approach this problem? Did you realize that you needed an organized plan or did you begin by randomly mixing the liquids? The best approach to this task is a very methodical one. It must include mixing each liquid separately with the activating solution (1 + X, 2 + X, 3 + X, 4 + X), then carefully mixing two liquids at a time with X (1 + 2 + X, 1 + 3 + X, 1 + 4 + X, 2 + 3 + X, 2 + 4 + X, 3 + 4 + X), then three at a time with X (1 + 2 + 3 + X, 1 + 2 + 4 + X, 1 + 3 + 4 + X, 2 + 3 + 4 + X), then all four at once (1+2+3+4+X), being careful to observe which combinations would yield the yellow color. Look over the way the chemicals were combined in a systematic manner so that no combinations would be missed or duplicated. This technique of systematic combinations will be needed to perform the reasoning tasks in the next section.

SYLLOGISTIC REASONING

Nothing intelligible ever puzzles me. Logic puzzles me.

—Lewis Carroll (1832–1898)

Syllogistic reasoning is a form of reasoning that involves deciding whether or not a conclusion can properly be inferred from two or more statements. One type of syllogistic reasoning is categorical reasoning. **Categorical reasoning** involves **quanti-**

fiers or terms that tell us how many. Quantifiers are terms like "all," "some," "none," and "no." The quantifiers indicate how many items belong in specified categories.

A **syllogism** usually consists of two statements that are called **premises** and a third statement called the conclusion. In categorical syllogisms, quantifiers are used in the premises and conclusion. The task is to determine if the conclusion follows logically from the premises.

The premises and conclusion of a syllogism are classified according to **mood**. (The word *mood* has a special meaning in this context that is unrelated to its more usual meaning about how someone feels.) There are four different moods, or combinations of positive and negative statements with the terms "all" or "some." The four moods are:

Mood	Abstract Example	Concrete Example
Universal Affirmative	All A are B.	All students are smart.
Particular Affirmative	Some A are B.	Some video games are fun.
Universal Negative	No A are B.	No smurfs are pink.
Particular Negative	Some A are not B.	Some Democrats are not liberals.

As you can see from this table, a statement is universal if it contains the terms "all" or "no"; it is particular if it contains the term "some"; it is negative if it contains "no" or "not"; and it is affirmative if it is not negative. Thus, it should be easy to classify the mood of any statement by searching out the key terms.

Several syllogisms are presented here. Each consists of two premises and a conclusion. Work through each syllogism and decide if the conclusion is valid (V) or invalid (I). In order to be valid, the conclusion must *always* be true given its premises. In other words, when you decide that a syllogism is valid, you are saying "if the premises are true, then the conclusion must be true." Another way of saying this is "Does the conclusion 'follow from' the premises?" *If you can think of one way that the conclusion could be false when the premises are true, then it is invalid.* Don't go on until you have worked through these syllogisms.

1. Premise 1:   All people on welfare are poor.
   Premise 2:   Some poor people are dishonest.
   Conclusion: Some people on welfare are dishonest.   V or I?

2. Premise 1:   No parents understand children.
   Premise 2:   Some teachers understand children.
   Conclusion: No parents are teachers.   V or I?

3. Premise 1:   Some lawyers are not smart.
   Premise 2:   Some smart people are rich.
   Conclusion: Some lawyers are rich.   V or I?

4. Premise 1:   All physics students are good in math.
   Premise 2:   Some coeds are physics students.
   Conclusion: Some coeds are good in math.   V or I?

5. Premise 1: All Americans need health insurance.
   Premise 2: Everyone who needs health insurance should vote for it.
   Conclusion: All Americans should vote for health insurance.   V or I?

According to the rules of logic, it should not matter if the syllogisms are presented in abstract terms of As and Bs (e.g., Some A are not B), nonsense terms like zev and creb (All zev are creb), or meaningful terms like lawyers and cool (No lawyers are cool). The logical rules for deciding if a conclusion can be validly inferred from the premises remain the same. We're really saying "All _____ are _____." It should make no difference how we fill in the blanks, any letters, nonsense or meaningful words, or even fancy pictures should be handled in the same way. However, from a psychological perspective, there are important content differences. One way to avoid the problem of having one's biases affect how we reason with quantifiers is to use circle diagrams which, like linear diagrams and tree diagrams, alleviate the limitations of short-term memory and make relationships obvious and visible.

Determining If a Conclusion Is Valid

How did you go about deciding if the conclusions were valid? There are two different types of strategies that can be used with syllogisms to determine if a conclusion follows from its premises. If you've been reading the chapters in order, then you know that a common approach to improving thinking is the deliberate use of both spatial and verbal strategies. The same two approaches apply here. First, I present a spatial method for testing conclusions, then I provide some verbal rules that can also be used. Either method will "work," but you'll probably find that you prefer one method over the other. I have been teaching this material to college students for many years and have found that individual students have very strong preferences for either circle diagrams or verbal rules.

Circle Diagrams for Determining Validity

One way of determining if a conclusion is true is with the use of circle diagrams that depict the relationships among the three terms (A, B, C, or whatever we used to fill in the blanks). The degree to which the circles overlap depicts the inclusion or exclusion of the categories.

There are several different methods of drawing diagrams to depict the relationships among the terms in a syllogism. One of these methods is known as *Venn diagrams*, named for a 19th-century English mathematician and logician who first introduced them. These are the same diagrams that you probably used in mathematics classes if you ever studied set theory. (This was a very popular way to teach the "new math," before it was abandoned and replaced with the "old math.") A second method of diagramming relationships is known as *Euler diagrams*. According to popular lore, this method was devised by Leonard Euler, an 18th-century Swiss mathematician, who was given the task of teaching the laws of syllogistic reasoning to a German princess. Because the princess was having difficulty understanding the task, Euler created a simple procedure that could be used to understand the relationships among the terms and to check on the validity of inferences. A third method is called the *ballantine method* because of its use of three overlapping circles. In all of these methods, circles are used to indicate category membership. The differences among these methods are not important here, and the general strategy of checking conclusions with circle drawings is referred to as **circle diagrams**. If you've learned a different method of circle diagrams in another context (e.g., a class on set theory or a logic class), then continue to use that method as long as it works well for you.

Look very carefully at Fig. 4.4. The four moods that statements in syllogisms can have are listed in the left-hand column of Fig. 4.4. Next to each statement are circle

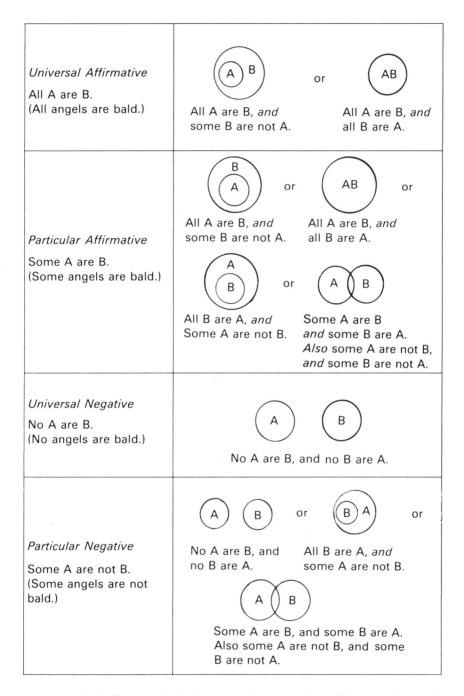

FIG. 4.4. Circle diagrams depicting correct interpretations of the premises used in syllogisms. Note that "all" can have two correct interpretations, "some" can have four correct interpretations, "no" has one correct interpretation, and "some–not" can have three correct interpretations.

diagrams that are correct depictions of the relationships in the statement. Stop now
and really look carefully at Fig. 4.4. One circle represents everything that is A, and a
second circle represents everything that is B. For the purposes of deductive reasoning,
it does not matter what A and B are. In the example in Figure 4.4, A is used to stand for
angels and B is used to stand for bald, but it could be anything. I could just as easily
have used A to stand for college students and B to stand for punk rockers.

Look at way the circles are combined so that they form a "picture" of what is being
said in words. Let's start in the middle of the figure, with universal negative, the easiest
example. When we say, "No A are B," this means that nothing that is in category A is
also in category B. This is depicted by drawing a circle labeled A and one labeled B that
do not touch or overlap in any way. There is only one way to draw this relationship.
Notice that when we say, "No A are B," we are also saying that "No B are A." Can you
see that from the circle diagram?

Consider now universal affirmative, "All A are B." Again we use two circles—one
labeled A and one labeled B. And again, we want to draw the two circles so that they
represent this relationship in which everything that is A is B. As you can see in Fig. 4.4,
there are two different ways of depicting this relationship because there are two
possible correct ways of understanding what it means. By drawing the A circle inside
the B circle, we are depicting the case where "All A are B," but there are some B that
are not A (some bald people are not angels). The second drawing shows the case where
"All A are B," and "All B are A" (all bald people are angels). Either of these two
interpretations could be true when we are told that "All A are B."

Don't be discouraged if this seems difficult to you. It will soon be easier as it becomes
more meaningful and you work your way through the examples. Look at the other
two possibilities in Fig. 4.4. There are three possible ways to depict particular negative
(Some A are not B) and four possible ways to depict particular affirmative (Some A are
B). Look at the ways that two circles can be combined. There are five different possible
ways to combine two circles, and each combination represents a different meaning!

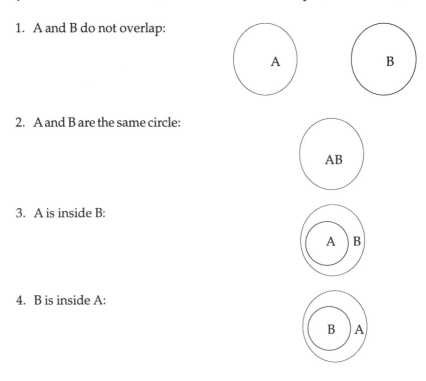

1. A and B do not overlap:

2. A and B are the same circle:

3. A is inside B:

4. B is inside A:

5. A and B partially overlap:

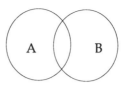

Let's draw circle diagrams to depict the relationships in Syllogism 1. The first two sentences are the premises. Write out each premise and next to each premise, draw the appropriate circle diagrams. For example, the first premise states, "All people on welfare are poor." In skeletal form, it is "All A are B" with A standing for "people on welfare" and B standing for "poor." You should recognize this as universal affirmative. Go to Fig. 4.4, look across from universal affirmative, and you will see that there are two possible ways to draw circles that correspond to this premise. You repeat this with the second premise: "Some poor people are dishonest." You already decided that A = people on welfare, and B = poor. The new term, dishonest, can be represented by C. The 2nd premise then becomes, Some B are C. This is an example of particular affirmative. Look across from particular affirmative on Fig. 4.4 and you will see that there are four possible ways to draw circles to represent this relationship. The only difference is that for Premise 2, we are using the letters B and C to stand for the categories. Thus, the first two premises will look like this:

A = people on welfare; B = poor; C = dishonest.

1. All people on welfare are poor.
      (All A are B.)

Premise 1a

A B

Premise 1b

AB

2. Some poor people are dishonest.
      (Some B are C.)

Premise 2a

C
B

Premise 2b

BC

Premise 2c

C
B

Premise 2d

B C

To determine if the conclusion is valid, we systematically combine each of the figures in the first premise with each of the figures in the second premise. If we find one combination that would not correspond to the conclusion, then we can stop and decide that the conclusion is invalid. If we make all possible combinations of figures from Premise 1 and figures from Premise 2, and they are all consistent with the conclusion, then the conclusion is valid. In other words, if all combinations of Premise 1 with

Premise 2 support the conclusion, then the conclusion is valid. The first few times you work on these, it may seem laborious, but you will soon "see" the answers and find ways to shortcut the process of working through all the combinations.

Here is the conclusion:

Some poor people on welfare are dishonest.

          (Some A are C).

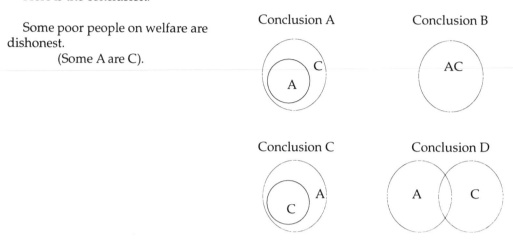

Premise 1 has two possible drawings and Premise 2 has four possible drawings. You can see that I labeled the two Premise 1 drawings 1a and 1b and the four Premise 2 drawings 2a, 2b, 2c, and 2d. In order to work systematically, you need to use the combinatorial reasoning rules that were presented in the last section. Start with 1a and combine it with 2a, then 1a and 2b, 1a and 2c, 1a and 2d. Then repeat the pattern by combining 1b with 2a, then 1b with 2b, then 1b with 2c, and finally 1b with 2d. Of course, you hope that you won't have to go through this entire procedure because you can stop as soon as you find one combination that violates the conclusion that Some A are C. Work along with me.

When I combine these two depictions, I will get a figure with A inside B and B inside C:

This combination shows a result that is consistent with the conclusion that Some A are C. Go on!

Premise 1a   +   Premise 2b

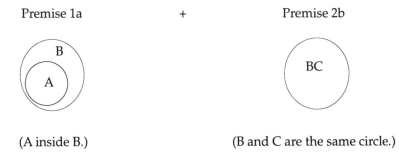

(A inside B.)   (B and C are the same circle.)

When I combine 1b and 2b, I get a depiction where A is inside the B/C circle:

This is consistent with the conclusion that Some A are C. Go on!

Premise 1a   +   Premise 2c

(A inside B.)   (C inside B.)

This gets a little tricky here, because *there are several different ways to combine 1a and 2c and we have to try all of them* until we run out of combinations or find one that is not consistent with the conclusion. Here we draw all ways that A can be inside B and C can be inside B.

A and C are the same circle inside B.

This is still consistent with Some A are C. Go on!
A and C partially overlap inside B.

This is still consistent with Some A are C. Go on!
A and C are two circles inside B.

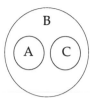

This does not agree with the conclusion that Some A are C.

Stop here! Given our two premises, it is invalid to conclude that: Some people on welfare are dishonest.

I know that this seems like a lot of work, but after you work a few problems, you can spot the combinations that will make a conclusion invalid, so you will not need to try every possible combination. Until then, work systematically through all combinations. A list of steps for checking the validity of conclusions with circle diagrams is shown in Table 4.2. Stop now and look over the steps. Refer back to them as we work through the rest of the syllogisms.

Let's try Syllogism 2.

TABLE 4.2
Steps for Determining the Validity of Conclusions Using Circle Diagrams

1. Write out each premise and the conclusion of the syllogism.

2. Next to each statement, draw all correct diagrams using the diagrams shown in Fig. 4.1.

3. Systematically combine all diagrams for Premise 1 with all diagrams for Premise 2. Try Premise 1a (the first diagram for Premise 1) with Premise 2a (the first diagram for Premise 2). Continue combining Premise 1a with all Premise 2 diagrams, then go on and combine all Premise 1b with all Premise 2 diagrams. Continue in this manner (Premise 1c with all Premise 2 diagrams, then Premise 1d with all Premise 2 diagrams) until

4. You find *one* diagram in which the conclusion is invalid or

5. You have tried all combinations of Premise 1 and Premise 2 diagrams.

Note. Sometimes there will be more than one way to combine diagrams from the two Premises. Be sure to try all combinations.

When trying out all combinations, remember that there are five possible ways to combine two circles: (a) A inside B, (b) B inside A, (c) A and B overlapping partially, (d) A and B with no overlap (two separate circles), and (e) A and B represented by one circle (A and B are the same circle). These five possibilities are shown below.

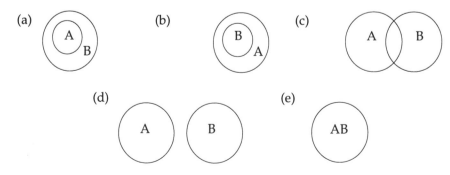

A = parents; B = understand children; C = teachers.

1. No parents understand children.
        (No A are B.)

Premise 1a

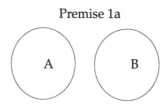

2. Some teachers understand children.
        (Some C are B.)

Premise 2a   Premise 2b

Premise 2c   Premise 2d

 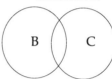

No parents are teachers.
    (No A are C.)

Conclusion A

The two circles that depict the first premise are only one figure because it is universal negative, and two separate circles are needed to depict this relationship. It is labeled 1a. The second premise is particular affirmative, which is depicted with four figures (2a, 2b, 2c, 2d). The conclusion is universal negative, so it is also depicted with one figure consisting of two separate circles. Now combine 1a + 2a, 1a + 2b, 1a + 2c, and 1a + 2d. You can stop as soon as you find one combination that is not consistent with the conclusion and decide that it is invalid, or try all combinations and then decide that it is valid.

Premise 1a   +   Premise 2a

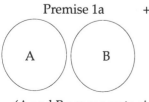 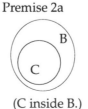

(A and B are separate circles.)   (C inside B.)

A and B are separate circles and C is inside B. Go on!

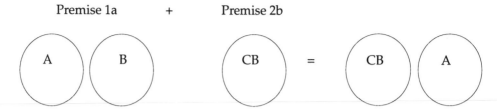

Premise 1a   +   Premise 2b

(A and B are separate circles.)   (C and B are the same circle.)

A and B are separate and C and B are the same. Go on!

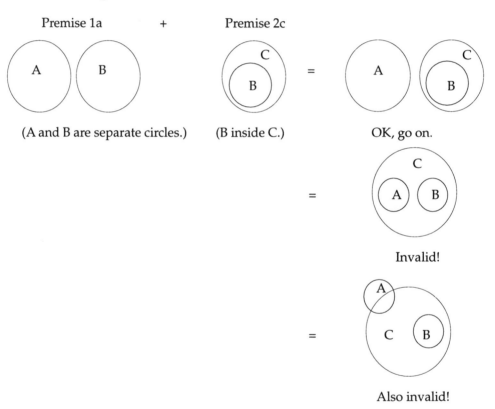

Premise 1a   +   Premise 2c

(A and B are separate circles.)   (B inside C.)   OK, go on.

Invalid!

Also invalid!

There are several ways to combine 1a and 2c, and we need to try all of the ways in which A and B are separate circles and B is inside C. If you can find one combination of 1a + 2c that violates the conclusion that No A are C, then you can stop the combination process and decide that the conclusion is invalid.

Stop here! It is possible to draw this combination in a way in which A and C are not separate. The conclusion is invalid! Based on the two premises that were given, we cannot conclude that: No parents are teachers.

Here are the next three syllogisms worked out for you. Work them yourself without looking at the examples, then compare your work to these examples.

A = lawyers, B = smart, C = rich

1. Some lawyers are not smart.
   (Some A are not B.)

Premise 1a

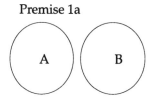

Premise 1b

Premise 1c

2. Some smart people are rich.
   (Some B are C.)

Premise 2a

Premise 2b

Premise 2c

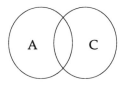

Premise 2d

Conclusion: Some lawyers are rich.
    (Some A are C.)

To test the validity of the conclusion, combine 1a + 2a, 1a + 2b, 1a + 2c, 1a + 2d, 1b + 2a, 1b + 2b, 1b + 2c, 1b + 2d, 1c + 2a, 1c+ 2b, 1c + 2c, and 1c + 2d

1a + 2a

(A and B are separate.)   +   (B inside C.)   Stop here! Invalid.

Based on the two premises given, it is invalid to conclude that: Some lawyers are rich.

Next problem:

A = physics students, B = good in math, C = coeds

1. All physics students are good in math.
   (All A are B.)

Premise 1a

Premise 1b

2. Some coeds are physics students.
   (Some C are A.)

Premise 2a

Premise 2b

Premise 2c

Premise 2d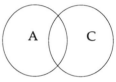

Some coeds are good in math.
      (Some C are B.)
It is not necessary to draw out the conclusion if you understand what you are doing.

1a + 2a = OK, go on.

1a + 2b = OK, go on.

1a + 2c = OK, go on.

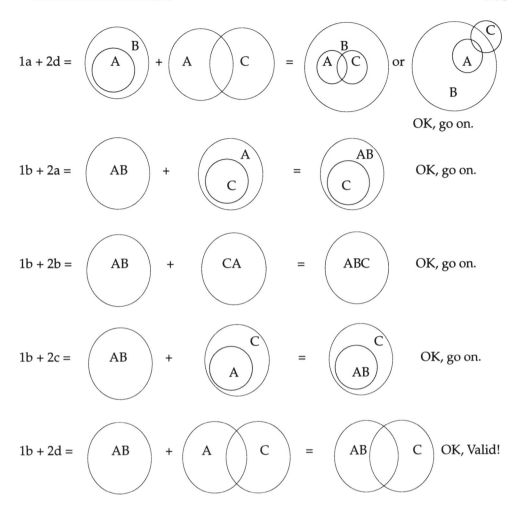

1a + 2d =   (A B) + (A C) = (A C B) or (A B, C)   OK, go on.

1b + 2a =   (AB) + (C A) = (C AB)   OK, go on.

1b + 2b =   (AB) + (CA) = (ABC)   OK, go on.

1b + 2c =   (AB) + (A C) = (AB C)   OK, go on.

1b + 2d =   (AB) + (A C) = (AB C)   OK, Valid!

Next problem:
1. All Americans need health insurance.
    (All A are B.)

    Premise 1a

    Premise 1b

2. Everyone who needs health insurance should vote for it.
    (All B are C.)

    Premise 2a

    Premise 2b

Conclusion: All Americans should vote for health insurance.
              (All A are C.)

1a + 2a = (diagram) + (diagram) = (diagram)   OK, go on.

1a + 2b = (diagram) + (diagram) = (diagram)   OK, go on.

1b + 2a = (diagram) + (diagram) = (diagram)   OK, go on.

1b + 2b = (diagram) + (diagram) = (diagram)   OK, valid!

Verbal Rules for Determining Validity

It's a peculiar thing about circle diagrams: Some people love working on them and others seem to hate them. The problem in working with them is trying all possible combinations of representations for both premises. People who prefer to think spatially seem to "see" the combinations with apparent ease, whereas those who prefer verbal modes of representation seem to have more difficulty with this. For those of you who have difficulty combining premises into circle relationships, take heart because there are verbal rules for determining if the conclusion of a syllogism is valid. These rules will work just as well as circle diagrams. Sternberg and Weil (1980) found that verbal and spatial strategies draw on different abilities and that the effectiveness of a given strategy depends on one's preferred mode of thought. There are five rules that can be used to determine the validity of a conclusion. In order to use these rules there are two additional terms that need to be learned.

There are three categories named in syllogisms, the A, B, and C, or whatever category names we substitute for them in more concrete examples. One of these categories is called the **middle term**. To determine which is the middle term, go to the conclusion. There are two categories in the conclusion; one is the subject of the sentence, the other is in the predicate. The category that is *not* mentioned in the conclusion is the middle term. It is called the middle term because it links the other two terms in the premises. Look back at Syllogism 1. The conclusion is "Some people on welfare are dishonest." "People on welfare" is the subject of this sentence, and "dishonest" is in the predicate. The middle term is "poor." The middle term is in both premises, but it is not in the conclusion.

The second term that you need to know is **distributed**. A term is distributed if the statement applies to every item in the category (Govier, 1985). Consider the four types

TABLE 4.3
Distributed and Undistributed Terms in the Four Moods of Syllogisms

All A are B.	A is distributed. (A is modified by "all.")
	B is undistributed. (B is undistributed because there may be some B that are not A.)
Some A are B.	Both A and B are undistributed.
No A are B.	Both A and B are distributed. (Both A and B are modified by "no.")
	(This is the same as saying that "No B are A.")
Some A are not B.	A is undistributed.
	B is distributed. (B is modified by "not.")

TABLE 4.4.
Rules for Determining Validity of Conclusion When Reasoning With Quantifiers

1. If the conclusion is negative, one premise must be negative, and conversely, if one premise is negative, the conclusion must be negative.

2. The middle term must be distributed in at least one premise.

3. Any term that is distributed in the conclusion must be distributed in at least one premise.

4. If both premises are particular, there are no valid conclusions.

5. If one premise is particular, the conclusion must be particular.

6. At least one premise must be affirmative. (There are no valid conclusions with two negative premises.)

of category relationships shown in Table 4.3. I've indicated next to each one which terms are distributed and which terms are undistributed. As you see in Table 4.3, categories that are modified by "all," "no," and "not" are distributed.

Look carefully at the statement "All A are B." B is undistributed in this statement because there may be some B that are not A, so the statement is not about every B. On the other hand, consider "No A are B." In this case, B is distributed because when we say "No A are B," we are also saying "No B are A." Thus, in the second case, the statement is about all B.

For a conclusion to be valid, the syllogism must pass all of the rules in Table 4.4. If it fails on any one of them, then it is invalid.

Let's apply these rules to the syllogisms we've already solved with circle diagrams.

Syllogism 1.
A = people on welfare, B = poor, C = dishonest

All people on welfare are poor. (All A are B.)
Some poor people are dishonest. (Some B are C.)
Some people on welfare are dishonest. (Some A are C.)

The middle term for this syllogism is B. It is the one mentioned in both premises and is missing from the conclusion. The first rule starts "if the conclusion is negative." Because the conclusion is positive, we can immediately go on to the second rule. The second rule states that the middle term must be distributed in at least one premise. Let's check this. The middle term is B (poor people). Is it modified by all or not in either premise? It is not distributed in either premise, so we can stop here. This conclusion is invalid! But, of course, you already knew that because you discovered that it was invalid when you completed the circle diagrams.

Let's try the verbal rules with the second syllogism.

Syllogism 2.
A = parents, B = understands children, C = teachers

No parents understand children. (No A are B.)
<u>Some teachers understand children. (Some C are B.)</u>
No parents are teachers. (No A are C.)

The first rule says that if the conclusion is negative, then one premise must be negative, and vice versa. The conclusion is negative and so is one premise, so we can check the next rule.

The second rule is that the middle term must be distributed in one premise. What is the middle term? It is B, the one not mentioned in the conclusion. It is distributed in the first premise, so we can move on.

The third rule is that any term distributed in the conclusion must be distributed in at least one premise. Both A and C are distributed in the conclusion. A is distributed in the first premise, but C is not distributed in a premise, so stop here. This conclusion is invalid!

Briefly, here are the answers to the remaining syllogisms.

Syllogism 3.
A = lawyers, B = smart, C = rich

Some lawyers are not smart. (Some A are not B.)
<u>Some smart people are rich. (Some B are C.)</u>
Some lawyers are rich. (Some A are C.)

fails #1: passes the first part because the conclusion is not negative; fails the second part because the first premise is negative and the conclusion is positive.
Invalid!

Syllogism 4.

All physics students are good in math. (All A are B.)
<u>Some coeds are physics students. (Some C are A.)</u>
Some coeds are good in math. (Some C are B.)

passes # 1: There are no negatives.
passes # 2: The middle term is A. A is distributed.
passes # 3: No term in the conclusion is distributed.
passes # 4: Both premises are not particular.
passes # 5: One premise is particular and the conclusion is particular.
passes # 6: At least 1 premise is affirmative.
Valid!

Syllogism 5.

All Americans need health insurance. (All A are B.)
<u>Everyone who needs health insurance should vote for it. (All B are C.)</u>
All Americans should vote for health insurance. (All A are C.)

passes # 1: There are no negatives.
passes # 2: The middle term is B. B is distributed.
passes # 3: A is distributed in the conclusion and the first premise.
passes # 4: Both premises are universal, not particular.
passes # 5: No premise is particular.
passes # 6: At least one premise is affirmative.
Valid!

Syllogisms in Everyday Contexts

Somewhere during the last section, you may have said to yourself, "Why bother!" It may seem that syllogisms are artificial stimuli created solely to make work for students and teachers. If you did have this thought, you were questioning the **ecological validity** of syllogisms. Ecological validity concerns the real-world validity or applications of a concept outside of the laboratory or classroom. In other words, do people use syllogistic reasoning in real-world contexts?

Syllogistic reasoning and the other types of reasoning like linear ordering and "if, then" statements are sometimes considered as a subset of problem solving. Often, when solving a problem, we begin with statements that we believe or know to be true (the premises) and then decide which conclusions we can logically infer from them.

Syllogisms also appear implicitly in normal English prose. Of course, in natural context, the premises and conclusions aren't labeled, but the underlying structure is much the same. They are especially easy to spot in legal and political arguments, and thus often appear on standardized tests for college, graduate, and law school admissions. Here is an example of syllogistic reasoning that may seem more like the kind of syllogism you'd find in everyday contexts:

> The death sentence should be declared unconstitutional. It is the cruelest form of punishment that is possible, and it is also very unusual. The constitution specifically protects us against cruel and unusual punishment.

Can you conclude from these statements that the death sentence is unconstitutional? Try to formulate these sentences into standard syllogism form (two premises and a conclusion). Use circle diagrams or the five rules to check on the validity of the conclusion. Stop now and work on this natural language syllogism.

Your syllogism should be similar to this:

Premise 1: The death sentence is cruel and unusual punishment.
Premise 2: Cruel and unusual punishment is unconstitutional.
Conclusion: The death sentence is unconstitutional.

If we put this in terms of A, B, and C, this roughly corresponds to:

A = the death sentence
B = cruel and unusual punishment
C = unconstitutional

This then becomes:

All A are B.
All B are C.
All A are C.

In its abstract form, this becomes a syllogism that can be tested with either circle diagrams or verbal rules that will determine if the conclusion validly follows from the premises. The point here is that syllogisms are often contained in everyday arguments. Often, we don't recognize them because they are not neatly labeled by premise and conclusion, but if you get in the habit of looking for them, you may be surprised how frequently they can be found.

Missing Quantifiers

If there is any equality now, it has been our struggle that put it there. Because they said "all" and meant "some." All means all.

—Beah Richards (in Beilensen & Jackson, 1992, p. 22)

When syllogisms are found in everyday use, the quantifiers are often missing. Sometimes this is done deliberately in the hope that you will infer one particular quantifier (e.g., assume "all" instead of the more truthful "some.") Here is an example of categorical reasoning used in a recent presidential campaign. A presidential candidate (in the U.S. primaries) was questioned about his well-publicized extramarital affairs. He responded this way: I have not been perfect in my private life, but we have had other great presidents who were also not perfect in their private lives.
Let's convert this to a categorical syllogism:

Premise 1: I am not perfect (in my private life).
Premise 2: <u>Some great presidents were not perfect (in their private lives).</u>
Conclusion: I will be a great president. (implied)

It its abstract form this becomes:

A = I (the speaker)
B = people who are not perfect
C = great presidents

or

All A are B.
<u>Some C are B.</u>
All A are (will be) C.

The conclusion he wanted listeners to draw is that he would also be a great president. Check the validity of this conclusion either with circle diagrams or the five rules. Is the implied conclusion valid? Note also his choice of words to describe his extramarital affairs (not perfect). This is the same reasoning that is being used in the Calvin and Hobbes cartoon shown on the following page.
In everyday language, the quantifiers may be somewhat different from those used here. "Every" and "each" may be used as substitutes for "all," and "many" and "few" may be used as substitutes for "some." It is a simple matter to change them to the quantifiers used here and then check the conclusion for its validity (Nickerson, 1986).
Here is an example (with some editing) that I recognized in a recent conversation: "People who go to rock concerts smoke dope. Jaye went to a rock concert. Therefore, Jaye smokes dope." The validity of this everyday syllogism depends on whether the

Calvin and Hobbes   by Bill Watterson

speaker believes that "All people who go to rock concerts smoke dope" or "Some people who go to rock concerts smoke dope." In understanding statements like these, it's important that you specify which missing quantifier is intended. If "some" is intended, then you quickly point out that it is not valid to conclude that Jaye was among those who smoke dope. If "all" is intended, then you can question whether it is the appropriate quantifier.

Changing Attitudes With Syllogisms

The basic organization of two premises and a conclusion is frequently used to change attitudes. When used in this fashion, the first premise is a belief premise, the second premise is an evaluation of that belief or a reaction to the belief premise, and the conclusion is the attitude (Shaver, 1981). The basic structure is like this:

Belief premise
Evaluation premise
Attitude Conclusion

Consider how this works in the following example (Shaver, 1981):

Preventing war saves lives.
Saving lives is good.
Therefore, preventing war is good.

Over time, attitude syllogisms become linked so that the
conclusion from one syllogism is used as the evaluation premise
of another:

Defense spending prevents war.
Preventing war is good.
Therefore, defense spending is good.

In these syllogisms, the middle term (remember what this means?) becomes the reason for the conclusion. In general, the greater the number of syllogisms with the same conclusion that we believe are true, the greater the support for the conclusion. If I wanted you to conclude that defense spending is good, I'd also tell you that:

Defense spending creates jobs.
Creating jobs is good.
Therefore, defense spending is good.

The quantifiers are implicit in these syllogisms, but the underlying organization is the same. It's a matter of determining if a conclusion follows from the premises.

Common Errors in Syllogistic Reasoning

At this point in the history of psychology, when it is claimed that machines can think, it seems strange to say that people cannot.

—Ceraso & Protivera (1971, p. 400)

Research has shown that some syllogisms are more difficult to solve than others. An analysis of the erroneous conclusions that people make has revealed that the errors fall into distinct types or categories. One category of errors that I consider here is illicit conversions.

Illicit Conversions

No, this is term has nothing to do with people who make you change religions when you don't want to. It has to do with changing the meaning of a premise. When most people read statements like, "All A are B," the representation they form in their mind is one in which it is also true that "All B are A," (Chapman & Chapman, 1959). As you should realize by now, "All A are B" is not the same as "All B are A." Transforming a premise into a nonequivalent form is a type of error known as an **illicit conversion**. In real-world terms, knowing that "all Republicans voted for this bill" is not the same as saying that everyone who voted for this bill was Republican. These are not equivalent statements.

Another common illicit conversion is the belief that "Some A are not B" also implies that "Some B are not A." The second statement is not equivalent to the first. Here are circle diagrams of these two statements. As you can see more clearly in their diagrams, they are not identical statements. To make this point clearer, consider the difference between "Some of the children are not immunized" and "Some of those immunized are not children. Note the difference between Premises 1b and 2b.

A = children, B = immunized

1. Some A are not B.
   Some children are not immunized.

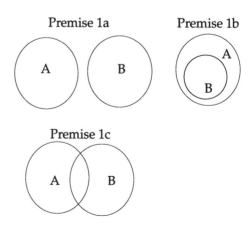

Premise 1a   Premise 1b

Premise 1c

2. Some B are not A.

   Some of those immunized
   are not children.

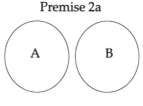 Premise 2a

 Premise 2b

Premise 2c

DISJUNCTIONS

Consider these two sets of premises:

Either Chuck is handsome, or else he is famous.
<u>Chuck is not famous.</u>
What can you conclude?

Either Chuck is handsome, or else he is not famous.
<u>Chuck is famous.</u>
What can you conclude?

The conclusions to both of these sets of premises is the same—Chuck is handsome. Most people find the second set of premises to be much more difficult to comprehend. Either or premises are also used in reasoning and are called *disjunctions*. These kinds of premises can easily be recast in an if, then format with a negative statement; for example, if Chuck is handsome, then he is not famous.

With either/or statements only one of the two (or more categories) is true. The easiest way to deal with them is to draw two symbolic representations of what could be true, then see if you can eliminate one of them. The remaining one is the answer.

Let's try this with the either/or statements just discussed. Either Chuck is handsome, or else he is famous.

Draw two circles, one representing each possible state, handsome and famous.

 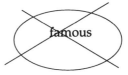

Now read the second sentence: Chuck is not famous. Cross out the circle labeled famous.

The remaining circle is "handsome." Therefore, he is handsome. Now, try this with the more difficult second example.

Either Chuck is handsome, or he is not famous.

Draw circles representing these two possible states.

Now read the second sentence: Chuck is famous. Because he can't be both famous and not famous at the same time, cross out the circle labeled "not famous."

What is left? The circle labeled "handsome." This is the correct answer.

Either/or statements are frequently used in advertising. This is one of my favorites:

> Our low prices are guaranteed. If you can find a lower advertised price anywhere, we'll either match it or you get the item free!

Quite a deal. I doubt that they'll choose to give me the item free. What then is the alternative? The advertisement could have said: "We'll match any advertised price." Does it seem like a better deal to know that they'll either match the price *or* give it to you free? The issue here, of course, is who gets to choose. If it were my choice, I'd get the item free, but I doubt that the buyer will be the one to decide.

PROBABILISTIC REASONING

The straight path of reason is narrow, the tempting byways are many and easier of access.

—Joseph Jastrow

In everyday reasoning, we don't view premises as "truths" that will necessarily require certain conclusions; instead, we think of premises as statements that either support or fail to support certain conclusions. Probabilistic reasoning occurs when we use the information we have to decide that a conclusion is probably true or probably not true. In everyday reasoning, we rely on notions of probability to assess the likelihood of a conclusion being true. Although probability is discussed in chapters 6 & 7, it is also a reasoning skill that should be considered in this context.

Suppose you learn that people who have untreated diabetes are frequently thirsty, urinate often, and have a sudden weight loss. You notice that you have these symptoms. Does it necessarily follow that you have diabetes? No, of course not, but these symptoms do make a diagnosis of diabetes more likely. In everyday contexts, much of our reasoning is probabilistic.

Consider this example presented by Polya (1957):

If we are approaching land, we see birds.
Now we see birds.
Therefore, it becomes more credible that we are approaching land. (p. 186)

In a shorthand format this becomes:

If A, then B.
B is true.
Therefore, A is more probable than it was before we knew that B is true.

Much of our everyday reasoning is of this sort, and although A is not guaranteed with probabilistic reasoning, it does become more probable after we've told the second premise. When viewed from the perspective of "if, then" reasoning, we would be committing the fallacy of affirming the consequent. But, in real life we need to consider many variables and goals. While seeing birds doesn't guarantee that land is near, I'd be getting happy if I saw birds while I was drifting and lost at sea.

Probabilistic reasoning is often a good strategy or "rule of thumb," especially because few things are known with absolute certainty in our probabilistic world. From the standpoint of formal logic, it is invalid to conclude that land is near. As long as you understand the nature of probabilities and the distinction between probabilistic and valid (must be true if the premises are true) reasoning, considering probabilities is a useful way of understanding and predicting events. When we reason in everyday contexts, we consider the strength and likelihood of the evidence that supports a conclusion and often decide if a conclusion is probable or improbable, not just merely valid or invalid. This point is explained more fully in chapter 7 on understanding probabilities.

As much of our reasoning is dependent on the rules of probability, McGuire (1981) coined the term **probabilogical** to describe the joint effects of these disciplines on the way we think. Accordingly, we place greater faith in conclusions when we believe that the premises are highly probable than when we believe that the premises are unlikely.

REASONING IN EVERYDAY CONTEXTS

Reasoning is the only ability that makes it possible for humans to rule the earth and ruin it.

—Scriven (1976, p. 2)

Syllogisms, linear orderings, disjunctions, and "if, then" statements are commonly found in everyday conversation. Of course, they are embedded in discourse and not labeled by premise or conclusion. They are sometimes used in ways that seem to be either deliberately misleading, or at least to capitalize on the common reasoning errors that most people make.

If you pay careful attention to bumper stickers, you'll probably be surprised to find that many are simple reasoning problems. Consider the bumper sticker I saw on a pick-up truck:

Off-road users are not abusers.

The off-road users that this bumper sticker refers to are dirt bike riders who enjoy racing through open land (unpaved areas). Many people are concerned that this sport is destroying our natural resources by tearing up the vegetation. This bumper sticker is designed to present the opposing view. Notice how this is accomplished. The term "all" is implied in the first premise, when in fact "some" is true. You should recognize this as a syllogism with missing quantifiers.

Another popular bumper sticker that relies on missing quantifiers to make the point is:

> If guns are outlawed,
> only outlaws will have guns.

This is a standard "if, then" statement. The implied conclusion is "don't outlaw guns."

Suppose someone responded to this bumper sticker by suggesting that if guns are outlawed approximately 80% of the crimes of violence and 90% of the petty crimes that are committed with a gun would probably be committed with a less dangerous weapon. How does an argument like this refute the "if, then" statement and its implied conclusion on the bumper sticker?

Here is a disjunctive argument that was common during the Vietnam War: America, love it or leave it! You may be surprised to learn that this was a slogan for those who went to fight in Vietnam. The implication was that anti-war protest meant that you didn't love America. In the next chapter, I return to the use of disjunctions and ask if there really are only two options when we are given two options.

Reasoning With Diagrams

Although it seems like a lot of work to get used to thinking with diagrams, they are useful in many situations where you have to check relationships and conceptualize inferences (Bauer & Johnson-Laird, 1993). The following discussion is loosely based on a discussion by Rubinstein and Pfeiffer (1980) that I have applied to the events surrounding the Los Angeles riots that occurred in 1992. In 1992, following an unpopular verdict in which Los Angeles police officers were acquitted of the crime of beating a suspect, an event that was captured on video, a massive, bloody riot occurred. In the painful trials that followed, the prosecution attempted to show that a particular defendant was at the scene of the riot. One piece of evidence was a footprint that was at the site. The strategy for the defense was to show that many people could have left that particular footprint, while the prosecution tried to show that few people other than the defendant could have left the footprint. Look at these two diagrams:

What the Defense Wants   What the Prosecution Wants

Everyone   Everyone

Defendant

People who   People who
could leave   could leave the
the footprint   footprint

An expert from the Nike shoe company was called to testify that the print was left by a Nike sneaker. The prosecution then showed that the defendant owned a pair of Nikes in the same size as the footprint. This shrinks the size of the circle, so that few people besides the defendant would fit:

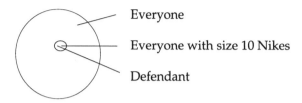

By contrast, the defense tried to widen the circle by showing that many people in that neighborhood wear Nike sneakers and that it was a popular shoe size. Each side, in turn, tried to widen and then narrow the circle in an attempt to persuade the jury that the defendant and few others could have left that footprint or many people could have left that footprint.

Similar strategies are used implicitly in many trials. Here is a quote from an article that appeared in the *Los Angeles Times* on October 18, 1989. It is a description of a trial for an accused child molester: "Telling an attentive jury in Los Angeles Superior Court that the totality of evidence 'draws the ring around R. B. and P. B. closer and tighter, to the extent that you should find them guilty.'" Here the idea of drawing smaller and smaller circles was used explicitly in the prosecution's arguments. Once you get used to using diagrams as a thinking aid, you will find that you will use them often.

APPLYING THE FRAMEWORK

1. What is the goal?   In deductive reasoning, the goal is to determine which conclusions are valid given premises or statements that we believe are true. When you identify your goal as a deductive reasoning task, you will use the reasoning skills presented in this chapter.

2. What is known?   In everyday prose, you will have to convert phrases and sentences into a reasoning format. You will have to determine what the premises are before you can decide whether they support a conclusion. Often quantifiers are missing and conclusions are left unstated. Sometimes you will have to consider context to decide if "if, then" really means "if, and only if, then." You will have to decide if you are reasoning with implied or explicit quantifiers, if there is a linear ordering, and whether an "if, then" statement is being made.

Perhaps, most important, you need to determine if you should be assuming that the premises are true. A conclusion is valid if it follows from the premises, but good reasoning from poor premises will not produce desirable outcomes.

3. Which thinking skill will get you to your goal?   The following skills to determine whether a conclusion is valid were presented in this chapter. Review each skill and be sure that you understand how and when to use each one:

- Discriminating between deductive and inductive reasoning.
- Identifying premises and conclusions.

- Using quantifiers in reasoning.
- Solving categorical syllogisms with circle diagrams.
- Solving categorical syllogisms with verbal rules.
- Understanding the difference between truth and validity.
- Recognizing when syllogisms are being used to change attitudes.
- Using linear diagrams to solve linear syllogisms.
- Watching for marked adjectives.
- Using the principles of linear orderings as an aid to clear communication.
- Reasoning with "if, then" statements.
- Using tree diagrams with "if, then" statements.
- Avoiding the fallacies of confirming the consequent and denying the antecedent.
- Using circles with either/or statements.
- Examining reasoning in everyday contexts for missing quantifiers.

4. Have you reached your goal?   This is an accuracy check on your work. When determining valid conclusions from categorical syllogisms, did you get the same answer with both the rules for syllogisms and the circle diagrams? Did you consider all combinations of representations when drawing your diagrams? Does your answer make sense?

CHAPTER SUMMARY

1. Deductive reasoning (the type of reasoning considered in this chapter) is the use of premises or statements that we accept as true to derive valid conclusions.

2. People don't approach reasoning problems according to the laws of formal logic. Instead of determining whether a conclusion logically follows from the premises as they are stated, there is a tendency to alter the premises according to one's own beliefs and then decide whether a conclusion follows from the altered statements.

3. Human reasoning is often biased by beliefs about emotional issues.

4. People often confuse truth with validity. Validity refers to the form of an argument and is unrelated to content. If a conclusion necessarily follows from the premises, then it is valid. The topic of truth and believability of premises is addressed in the next chapter.

5. In linear orderings, we use premises to establish conclusions about ordered relationships. A good strategy for solving linear orderings is to utilize a spatial representation with the items arranged in an ordered manner.

6. In "if, then" statements a conditional relationship is established. As in syllogisms and linear orderings, the premises that are given are used to determine valid conclusions.

7. "If" is frequently interpreted as "if and only if" in "if, then" statements. Although this conversion is an error according to the rules of formal logic, sometimes it is justified by the context in which it is embedded.

8. Confirmation bias is the predilection or tendency to seek and utilize information that supports or confirms the hypothesis or premise that is being considered. The four-card selection task is a demonstration of this robust bias.

9. Quantitative syllogisms indicate which terms belong in the categories that are specified. Statements in syllogisms can take one of four different moods: universal affirmative, particular affirmative, universal negative, and particular negative.

10. When syllogisms involve meaningful terms and categories, people often use their knowledge of the categories and their beliefs about the topics to determine which conclusions are valid.

11. Circle diagrams are useful aids for understanding relationships and checking inferences in syllogisms. The extent to which circles overlap depicts category inclusion and exclusion. An alternative to circle diagrams that many people prefer is to check conclusions for validity using the verbal rules of syllogisms.

12. The greatest difficulty in using circle diagrams is being certain that all combinations of the two premises have been represented.

13. Illicit conversions are common errors in syllogisms. The most frequent illicit conversion is to interpret "All A are B" as also meaning that, "All B are A."

14. Diagrams are useful reasoning tools in many situations. The logic of circle diagrams is frequently used in legal settings and other settings in which evidence is considered.

TERMS TO KNOW

Check your understanding of the concepts presented in this chapter by reviewing their definitions. If you find that you're having difficulty with any term, be sure to reread the section in which it is discussed.

Reasoning. Has two forms: deductive and inductive. When reasoning deductively, we use our knowledge of two or more premises to infer if a conclusion is valid. When reasoning inductively, we collect observations and formulate hypotheses based on them.

Conclusion. An inferential belief that is derived from premises.

Delphi Technique. A method for achieving agreement among experts in some field. With this method, comments from experts about an issue are circulated among the experts until agreement is reached.

Logic. A branch of philosophy that explicitly states the rules for deriving valid (correct) conclusions.

Valid. A conclusion is valid if it must be true if the premises are true.

Premises. Statements that allow the inference of logical conclusions.

Illogical. Reaching conclusions that are not in accord with the rules of logic.

Failure to Accept the Logical Task. In everyday reasoning we alter the statements we're given according to our personal beliefs and then decide if a conclusion follows from the altered statements. We reject the logical task of deciding if a conclusion follows from the statements as they are given.

Personal Logic. The informal rules that people use to determine validity.

Pragmatic. Anything that is practical. In this context, the consideration of context and purpose when engaging in real-world reasoning tasks.

Inductive Reasoning. Observations are collected that suggest or lead to the formulation of a conclusion or hypothesis.

Deductive Reasoning. Use of stated premises to formulate conclusions that can logically be inferred from them.

Linear Ordering. (Also known as linear syllogism) Reasoning that involves the inference of orderly relationships along a single dimension (e.g., size, position) among terms.

Linear Syllogism. See linear ordering.

Marked Adjectives. Adjectives that connote a bias when they appear in a question (e.g., poor, dumb, or small). When asked "How poor is he," it is presumed that the response will be toward the poor extreme and not toward the rich extreme.

Unmarked Adjectives. Adjectives that are neutral in that they don't connote a particular direction when they appear in a question (e.g., big, smart, tall). When asked "How big is he," the response could be a larger or a small number. Compare with marked adjective.

Belief Bias. The interference of one's personal beliefs with the ability to reason logically.

If, Then Statements. Statements of a contingency relationship such that if the antecedent is true, then the consequent must be true.

Contingency Relationships. Relationships that are expressed with "if, then" statements. The consequent is contingent or dependent on the antecedent.

Conditional Logic. Also known as propositional logic. Logical statements that are expressed in an "if, then" format.

Antecedent. In "if, then" statements, it is the information given in the "if" clause appealing to your reason.

Consequent. In "if, then" statements, it is the information given in the "then" clause.

Tree Diagrams. Diagrams in which the critical information is represented along the branches of a "tree."

Affirming the Antecedent. In "if, then" reasoning, the second premise asserts that the "if" part is true.

Denying the Consequent. In "if, then" reasoning, the second premise asserts that the "then" part is false.

Affirming the Consequent. In "if, then" reasoning, the second premise asserts that the "then" part is true.

Denying the Antecedent. In "if, then" reasoning, the second premise asserts that the "if" part is false.

Double Negation. The denial of a negative statement.

Probabilogical. Term coined to label the joint influences of probability and logic on the way we think.

Confirmation Bias. The predilection to seek and utilize information that supports or confirms one's hypothesis or premises while ignoring disconfirming information.

Four-Card Selection Task. A task that is often used to demonstrate confirmation biases. Subjects are required to indicate which of four cards they need to turn over in order to verify a rule about the contents of each side of the card. Overwhelmingly, subjects only select cards that will confirm the hypothesis that they are considering instead of seeking information that would disconfirm their hypothesis.

Permission Schema. Informal rules that people use when reasoning with "if, then" statements that pragmatically give permission.

Obligation Schema. Informal rules that people use when reasoning with "if, then" statements that pragmatically create an obligation.

Chained Conditional. Two "if, then" statements linked so that the consequent of one statement is also the antecedent of the other statement.

Syllogistic Reasoning. A form of reasoning that involves deciding whether or not a conclusion can be properly inferred from two or more statements.

Quantifiers. Terms like "all," "some," "none," and "no" that are used in syllogisms to indicate category membership.

Categorical Reasoning. A type of syllogistic reasoning in which the quantifiers "some," "all," "no," and "none" are used to indicate category membership.

Syllogism. Two or more premises that are used to derive a valid conclusion or conclusions.

Mood. Used to classify the premises and conclusions of a categorical syllogism. There are four moods that are dependent on the quantifiers used in the statements. The four moods are: universal affirmative (all A are B), particular affirmative (some A are B), universal negative (no A are B), and particular negative (some A are not B).

Universal Affirmative. The mood of statements in a categorical syllogism with the format, "All A are B."

Particular Affirmative. The mood of statements in a categorical syllogism with the format, "Some A are B."

Universal Negative. The mood of statements in a categorical syllogism with the format, "No A are not B."

Particular Negative. The mood of statements in a categorical syllogism with the format, "Some A are not B."

Circle Diagrams. A spatial strategy for determining the validity of a conclusion in a categorical syllogism. Circles are used to represent category membership.

Middle Term. In a categorical syllogism it is the term that is omitted from the conclusion and is mentioned in both premises.

Distributed. In a categorical syllogism a term is distributed when it is modified by "all," "no," or "not."

Ecological Validity. Concerns the real-world validity or applications of a concept outside of the laboratory.

Illicit Conversions. Transformations of the premises in a syllogism into non-equivalent forms (e.g., converting "All A are B" into "All B are A").

SUGGESTED READINGS

The literature on reasoning dates back, at least, to Aristotle's time, and probably earlier. Currently, reasoning texts are written either by philosophers or psychologists, and each field has a different perspective on the area. The philosophical approach tends to be more prescriptive or concerned with what reasoning should be, whereas the psychological approach tends to be more descriptive or concerned with the way people actually reason. There is, however, considerable overlap between these two disciplines.

Some recommended texts that assume a philosophical viewpoint are Kelley's (1988) *The Art of Reasoning*, Garnham and Oakhill's (1994) new text *Thinking and Reasoning*, Hitchcock's (1983) *Critical Thinking: A Guide to Evaluating Information*, Copi's (1986) *Informal Logic*, and Ruggiero's (1995) *Beyond Feelings: A Guide to Critical Thinking*. My favorite of all of the texts in this area is Govier's (1985) *A Practical Study of Argument*.

Among the texts with a psychology perspective, my favorite is Nickerson's (1986) *Reflections on Reasoning*. It's interesting reading, filled with thought-provoking examples and excellent questions. Other recommended books in psychology are Evans and Newstead's (1993) *Human Reasoning: The Psychology of Deduction*, Wason and Johnson-Laird's (1972) *Psychology of Reasoning*, and Johnson-Laird and Byrne's (1991) *Deduction*. An old classic text in psychology with a good basic section on reasoning is Bruner, Goodnow, and Austin's (1956) *A Study of Thinking*. Another addition to this area is an edited book by Sternberg and Smith (1988). If you are interested in reasoning errors, consult Evans (1989) *Bias in Human Reasoning*, where he demonstrated that people don't engage in the effortful process of reasoning when the conclusion fits well with their belief system.

If you are interested in the development of reasoning skills in children, you will want to consult Piper's (1985) article entitled "Syllogistic Reasoning in Varied Narrative Contexts: Aspects of Logical and Linguistic Development." He presented several interesting examples of reasoning from text.

A useful and clever guide to logical pitfalls is Thouless' (1932) *Straight and Crooked Thinking*. The back section of the book contains a wealth of everyday examples of faulty logic. It may help you win arguments. Despite the fact that it is an old book, you may find it filled with contemporary wisdom.

If you're looking for additional reasoning problems to practice and sharpen your skills, you'll enjoy Summers' (1968) *New Puzzles in Logical Deduction* and Summers' later book (1972) *Test Your Logic: 50 Puzzles in Deductive Reasoning*. Some of the material presented in Summers' books is similar to the topics covered in chapter 9, on Development of Problem-Solving Skills. This shouldn't be surprising to you because early in the chapter, reasoning was described as one kind of problem solving. Two edited volumes with good collections of articles on this topic are Wason and Johnson-Laird's (1968) *Thinking and Reasoning* and Johnson-Laird and Wason's (1977) *Thinking: Readings in Cognitive Science*.

5

Analyzing Arguments

Contents

Eat All Day and Still Lose Weight

Trade your old body for a new one now through an amazing scientific breakthrough. Doctors and medical technicians have made it possible for people like you and me to lose weight **quickly** and **permanently**. Tested at university labs, retested at clinics and major hospitals and acclaimed by doctors all over the world, finally there is something that helps you lose weight. If years of stubborn fat build up have been your problem, **NOW AT LAST THERE IS A WAY TO ELIMINATE FAT, A WAY TO LOSE WEIGHT FAST AND EASILY.** We call it XXXXXXX because it totally attacks excess fat and fluids that have plagued most people for years. ... Everyday you will feel stronger and full of pep and energy as the excess weight you have carried for so long is carved off your body. ... **DON'T LET THIS GOLDEN OPPORTUNITY AND CHANCE OF A LIFETIME PASS YOU BY.** Just fill out the coupon below and let it be the ticket to a slimmer you. So, what are you waiting for?

I hope that you weren't looking for a coupon for this marvelous weight loss product. The preceding paragraph was taken verbatim from a full-page advertisement in a popular fashion magazine. The only change that I made was to omit the name of this "miracle" diet. The name has a chemical sound to it. It's multisyllabic and ends with a number. The name sounds like a chemical formula. I had trouble selecting which advertisement I wanted to use here because there were so many that made numerous unsupported claims. Advertisements like this one can be found in most magazines and newspapers. I refer back to this advertisement later in this chapter when I talk about analyzing arguments and recognizing fallacies. Hold onto your money until you've read these sections.

THE ANATOMY OF AN ARGUMENT

Neither a closed mind nor an empty one is likely to produce much that would qualify as effective reasoning.

—Nickerson (1986, p. 1)

The technical meaning of the word **argument** is somewhat different from its everyday meaning. When we use the word *argument* in everyday language, it means a dispute or a quarrel. We say two people "are having an argument" when they disagree about something in a heated or emotional way. More technically, an argument consists of one or more statements that are used to provide support for a **conclusion**. The statements that provide the support for a conclusion are called the **reasons** or **premises** of the argument. The reasons or premises are presented in order to persuade the reader (or listener) that the conclusion is true or probably true. Let's consider an example. Suppose that I want to convince you to stay in college until graduation. Here are some reasons (premises) that I could give:

Premise 1: College graduates earn more money than college dropouts or people who have never attended college.
Premise 2: College graduates report that they are more satisfied with their lives than people who have not graduated from college.
Premise 3: College graduates are healthier and live longer than people who have not graduated from college.

Premise 4: College graduates have jobs that are more interesting and more responsible than people who have not graduated from college.

Conclusion: You should graduate from college.

Arguments are sometimes called "the giving of reasons." Harman (1986) called this process "a change in view" because the objective is to change an "old view" or belief into a "new view" or belief with reasoning.

Reasoning

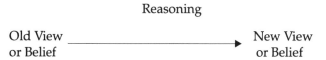

Old View ⟶ New View
or Belief   or Belief

Every argument will have one or more premises (or reasons) and one or more conclusions. Usually, there will be several premises for one conclusion, but other combinations (one premise for several conclusions and several premises for several conclusions) are possible. **If you cannot identify at least one premise** *and* **at least one conclusion, then it is not an argument.** Of course, in everyday, natural-language arguments, the premises and conclusions are not labeled. They are usually embedded in extended prose. The extended prose could be a paragraph, a section or chapter of a book, or even an entire book.

Here are some examples that are *not* arguments:

- I like my critical thinking course better than my chemistry course. (No reasons are given for this preference.)
- We drove up to the mountains, went skiing, then drove home. (This is just a descriptive list of activities linked together. There are no reasons or conclusions.)
- Buy your burgers at Burgerland. (No reasons given, but see the following section because reasons are often inferred from context in statements like this one.)
- We saw the Martians land. (This is a simple description.)
- Never trust anyone over 30. (This is an opinion without reasons.)
- Is dinner ready? (simple question)

It may seem that it should be fairly simple to determine whether or not a statement or set of statements contain an argument, but in everyday language most arguments are incomplete. Sometimes the premises aren't stated, but are inferred, and other times the conclusion is unstated. Sometimes arguments are deliberately disguised so that it may appear that the speakers are not supporting some conclusion, when they really are. Consider the popular automobile advertisement that goes something like this:

More people have bought LaBaroness automobiles than any other American car.

At first glance, this seems like a straightforward declarative sentence with no reasons and no conclusion. But, the advertisers expect consumers to convert this sentence into an argument. When you hear this sentence, you presumably start generating your own reasons for the popularity of LaBaroness. If more people are buying it, it must be best. And shouldn't you also buy the best? This is an example in which the listener supplies both the reasons and the conclusion. Statements very similar to this one can be found in advertisements for a diverse assortment of products including beer, beauty supplies, fitness clubs, and airlines. (The use of the comparative term "more" is discussed later in this chapter.)

If an advertiser wants to be sure that you supply the missing reasons and conclusion, the advertisement could be altered slightly so that it now reads:

More people have bought LaBaroness automobiles than any other American car. There must be some very good reasons.

Notice that a second sentence was added, but no reasons were given. It is expected that the second sentence will cue listeners (or readers) to start supplying their own reasons.

Premises

The premises are the reasons that support a conclusion. They are the "why" part of an argument. In everyday language, they can appear anywhere among a set of statements. Sometimes, the conclusion will be stated first followed by its premises. (Here is what I believe and the reasons for this belief are. …) Other times the conclusion may be presented last or embedded in the middle of a paragraph or other text with premises both before and after it. Premises are not always easy to recognize. There are certain key words, called **premise indicators** or **premise markers** that often signal that what comes after them is a premise. Although premise indicators aren't *always* followed by a premise, they often are, and for this reason, it is a good idea to check for these key words when identifying premises. These terms often indicate that what follows is a reason.

Premise Indicators

because
for
since (when it means because and not the passage of time)
if
given that (or being that)
as shown by
as indicated by
the reasons are
it may be inferred (or deduced) from
the evidence consists of
in the first place (suggests that a list of premises will follow)
secondly
seeing that
assuming that
it follows from
whereas

Here are some simple examples of the use of premise indicators:

You should graduate from college **because** you will earn more money with a college degree.
The need for the United States to send troops to Central America **is indicated by** the buildup of armed rebels in countries neighboring those with civil wars.
Seeing that the current policy of supplying organ transplants is benefiting the rich, a new program is needed.

Premises can be "matters of fact" or "matters of opinion" or both. Consider, for example, the following sentences:

All teenagers should be taught safe sex practices because of the risk of AIDS and other sexually transmitted diseases. (The reason is a matter of fact.)
All teenagers should be taught how to knit because this will provide them with an enjoyable hobby. (The reason is a matter of opinion.)

Conclusions

The conclusion is the purpose or the "what" of the argument. It is the belief or point of view that is supported or defended with the premises. Some authors have identified the conclusion as the most important part of an argument, but I think that this is misleading. Both the premises and the conclusion are important, and both are essential components of any argument.

It is usually easier to identify the conclusion of an argument than the other components. For this reason, it is a good idea to start with the conclusion when you are analyzing arguments. There are **conclusion indicators** or **conclusion markers** that indicate that what follows is probably a conclusion. As with premise indicators, they do not guarantee that a conclusion follows them.

Conclusion Indicators

therefore
hence
so
thus
consequently
then
shows that (we can see that)
accordingly
it follows that
we may infer (conclude) (deduce) that
in summary
as a result
for all these reasons
it is clear that

Some simple examples of the use of conclusion indicators are:

Based on all of the reasons just stated, we **can conclude that** the flow of illegal drugs must be stopped.
In summary, postal rates must be increased because we can no longer afford to run the postal system with a deficit.
We have had very little rain this season. **Consequently,** water will have to be rationed.

Has my use of the word *simple* to describe these examples made you feel uneasy? Have you begun to expect that things will soon get more complex? If so, you are right. Natural language is complex and so are natural-language arguments. (A natural language is a language that has evolved over time for the purpose of communication between people. Artificial languages are those languages that were created for special purposes, such as computer languages.) Although all arguments *must* contain at least one argument and one conclusion, most arguments consist of additional components. Three additional components are presented here. They are assumptions, qualifiers, and counterarguments.

Assumptions

An **assumption** is a statement for which no proof or evidence is offered. Although assumptions can be either stated or unstated (implied), they are most often unstated. Advertisements and political rhetoric are good places to look for examples of stated and unstated assumptions. Let's go back to the example of the advertisement for LaBaroness that was presented earlier in this chapter (I changed the name of the real car being advertised):

> More people have bought LaBaroness automobiles than any other American car.

The implied statement is that if more people bought the LaBaroness, it must be better (in some way) than its competitors. The unstated assumption is that when large numbers of consumers make a choice, it is a good choice. There is no justification for this assumption. The implied conclusion is that you should also be making this wise choice. The advertisement could easily be altered so that the assumption is made explicitly:

> More people have bought LaBaroness automobiles than any other American car. When so many people agree, it must be the right choice.

Notice that with the addition of the second sentence, the assumption is now stated explicitly. It is still an assumption because it is stated without any justification. If I had supplied some justification for this belief, then it would no longer be an assumption.
Suppose I alter these statements so that they now become:

> More people have bought LaBaroness automobiles than any other American car. Recent research by several well-known social psychologists and economists has shown that whenever a majority of people agree on something, they make the best choice.

Look carefully at the changes I just made. In this version, I provided a reason or justification for believing that whenever large numbers of people make a choice it is a good one. The research that I made up is phony, but suppose for now that it is true. The research findings become the premises or reasons for the conclusion that whenever large numbers of people make a choice, it will be a good one. In this context, it is no longer an assumption because there are now reasons supporting it. This new conclusion then becomes the premise for the unstated conclusion that you should also buy a LaBaroness. If you read the previous chapter on reasoning, this should not be a new idea for you. The idea that the conclusion from one set of statements can then become the premise for another set of statements was demonstrated in the previous chapter. In extended (longer) arguments, the conclusion from one set of statements will often become the premise in another set of statements.
The arguments that are used to build the main argument are called **subarguments**. The main argument in an extended passage is called the **main point**. The kinds of arguments that are often found in books, book chapters, and sometimes sections of

chapters proceed in stages with subarguments linked to provide support for a main point.

Here is another example of an unstated assumption. The following example was taken from a catalog that sells copper bracelets. I have altered it only slightly for this context:

> For hundreds of years people have worn copper bracelets to relieve pain from arthritis. This folklore belief has persisted and copper bracelets continue to be popular. These bracelets promote close contact between the copper and your wrist.

The writers of this advertisement expect that readers will assume that copper can help alleviate the pain of arthritis and that the "medical" effect is enhanced by the close contact with the wrist. Notice that this is never stated—it can't be because there is no evidence that shows that copper has any effect on arthritis. But, this advertisement for copper bracelets is clearly written to suggest that it works. (Many people believe that it does.) Furthermore, there is a suggested assumption that the popularity of copper bracelets is due to its medical effects. Maybe they have just become fashionable, or cheaper, or better advertised, or perhaps there are just more people with arthritis who are willing to believe anything that promises to relieve their pain. We discuss the need to consider missing information and alternative conclusions in a later section of this chapter.

Qualifiers

A **qualifier** is a constraint or restriction on the conclusion. It states the conditions under which the conclusion is supported. An example might be helpful:

> It is important that we have some indicators of what and how much students are learning in college. For this reason, a national college-level testing program is needed. But, if the national assessment is not related to the subjects taught in the college curriculum, then it will not be a valid measure of college-level learning.

Let's dissect this paragraph into its component parts:

The conclusion is: A national college-level testing program is needed.

A premise is: It is important that we have some indicators of what and how much students are learning in college. (This is the reason that supports the conclusion. It tells us why we should believe that the conclusion is true.)

An unstated assumption is: A national college-level testing program is a good way to indicate what students are learning.

A qualifier (or limiting condition) is: The conclusion is valid only when the assessment is related to what is taught in the curriculum.

As you can see from this example, a qualifier states the conditions under which the conclusion is valid. It sets limits or constraints on the conclusion.

Counterarguments

Critical thinking requires a sense of the complexity of human issues.

—Sears and Parsons (1991, p. 64)

Sometimes, an extended argument will state reasons that support a particular conclusion and reasons that refute the same conclusion. The set of statements that refute a particular conclusion is called a **counterargument**. Let's extend the previous argument so that it now also contains a counterargument:

> It is important that we have some indicators of what and how much students are learning in college. For this reason, a national college-level testing program is needed. But, if the national assessment is not related to the subjects taught in the college curriculum, then it will not be a valid measure of college-level learning. Of course, the results of a national assessment of college students could be misused in a way that would keep good students from entering graduate or professional school.

I hope that you're paying careful attention to the way the additions are altering the argument. As just presented, the conclusion, premise, assumption, and qualifier remain the same. The counterargument presents a reason for *not* having a national college-level test. The reason presented (results could be misused) is counter to the conclusion that we should have a national test. That is why these statements are called counterarguments. Even with the addition of the counterargument, the conclusion remains unchanged. The argument was written in a way that suggests that the counterargument is weaker than the main argument. The point being made is that despite the counterargument, we should still have a national test of college students.

Does this particular example make you uneasy? Can you think of other premises that might support a different conclusion? If so, you have already begun to anticipate the content of the section on how to evaluate arguments.

DIAGRAMMING THE STRUCTURE OF AN ARGUMENT

Arguments are a related series of statements that are made in an attempt to get the reader (or listener) to believe that the conclusion is true. In order to analyze or dissect an argument we need to know not only its component parts, but also how the parts are related to each other. Arguments are made up of parts that are synthesized or put together when an argument is made, and parts that can be disassembled as one way to understand them. The parts that make up an argument are premise(s), conclusion(s), assumption(s), qualifier(s), and counterargument(s). The only restriction on arguments is that each must have at least one premise and one conclusion. Beyond this, any one of a large variety of arrangements is possible. A good way to understand the relationships among the parts of a prose passage is to draw a diagram. Diagrams are used in every chapter of this book because they require the drawer to be specific about the relationships being depicted and to think about underlying relationships. Drawing a diagram is a good general thinking strategy.

Let's consider the simplest argument with only one premise and one conclusion:

> [Be sure to get plenty of exercise][1] because [exercise will help you build a strong cardio-vascular system][2].

This argument is made up of two statements. I have indicated them by putting brackets around each and numbering them "1" and "2." A **statement** is a phrase or sentence for which it makes sense to ask, "Is this true or false?" The answer to this question is not relevant here; that is, it doesn't matter if the statement really is true or false, only whether it makes sense to ask if the phrase is true or false. For example, the following are *not* statements: (a) Rinse the spaghetti. (b) Who lives here? (c) Is that house for sale? (d) Wow! Commands, questions, and exclamations are not statements because it makes no sense to ask if they have a "truth value"; that is, it makes no sense to ask if they are true or false.

Look again at the simple argument in the preceding paragraph. Identify which of the two statements is the conclusion and which is the premise:

Conclusion: [Get plenty of exercise]. (Remember, the conclusion is the statement that indicates what you should believe or what you should do. I started with the conclusion because this is often the easiest part to identify.)

Premise: [Exercise will build a strong cardiovascular system.] (This is the "why" part of the argument that gives a reason for believing the conclusion.)

A diagram of this relationship shows that the conclusion is supported by the premise:

As you can see, the statement that is the conclusion [1] is at the top of the diagram and the premise [2] is holding it up. This is shown with the arrow that points from the premise to the conclusion.

Now let's consider an argument in which two different premises support one conclusion. Again, I have bracketed each statement and numbered each:

[Be sure to get plenty of exercise][1] because [exercise will help you build a strong cardiovascular system][2] and [it will increase the density of your bones].[3]

[1] *Conclusion:* Get plenty of exercise.
[2] *Premise:* Exercise will build a strong cardiovascular system.
[3] *Premise:* Exercise will increase the density of your bones.

A diagram of this argument will look like this:

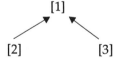

In this diagram, we have two premises supporting one conclusion. Both of the arrows point to the same conclusion. This is called a **convergent structure** because both premises converge onto the same conclusion; that is, they are both reasons why you should get plenty of exercise. Longer arguments will often contain several premises that support a conclusion. Let's compare this argument structure to one in which two premises are linked to each other, so that instead of both premises supporting the same conclusion, the first premise is the reason for the second premise, which in turn becomes the reason for the conclusion:

[It is important that you work through all of the problems in the workbook][1] because [the problems will help you to learn the skills of critical thinking][2]. We can conclude that [working the problems in the workbook will help you to learn the skills]² based on research that shows that [active learning promotes long-term retention]³.

In this example, we really have three different statements. The statement that I labeled [2] appears twice:

[1] Conclusion: It is important to work through all of the problems in the workbook. This is the conclusion—the part that tells you what to do or believe.

[2] Premise for [1]: Working through the problems will help you to learn critical thinking skills. (This is a reason for the conclusion.)

[3] Premise for [2]: Active learning promotes long-term retention. (This is a reason for believing that working the problems will help you to learn critical thinking skills.)

A diagram of this argument will look like this:

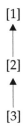

[1]

[2]

[3]

Arguments in which the conclusion of one subargument becomes the premise of a second argument are called **chained (or linked) structures**. Can you see an important distinction between this type of argument in which [3] is a reason for [2] and [2] is a reason for [1] and the previous structure in which both [2] and [3] are reasons for [1]? Remember the old saying that a chain is only as strong as its weakest link? When arguments have a chained structure, the conclusion is only as strong as the weakest subargument. If [3] doesn't provide very much support for [2], then the conclusion [1] is weakened. By contrast, when two or more premises converge onto the same conclusion, we only increase the strength of the conclusion by adding more premises.

Let's consider an example in which there are three premises and two conclusions:

[Taylor was late for school]¹ because [she overslept]² and [she had to stop for gas]³· [Taylor doesn't care much about school]⁴; therefore [she is often late.]⁵

In the chapter on deductive reasoning, I talked about skeleton structures—sort of fill-in-the-blank structures where it doesn't matter what gets filled in. The skeleton is the "bare bones" of an argument, the place where you hang your statements. Let's reduce this argument to its skeleton:

[1] because [2] and [3]. [4] therefore [5].

This is a good way to think about premise and conclusion indicators. Any statement that follows **because** will probably be a premise ([2] and [3]), and any statement that follows **therefore** will probably be a conclusion ([5]).

Can you see how [2] and [3] are premises for [1], and [4] is a premise for [5]?

A diagram of this argument will look like this:

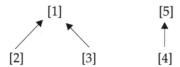

This is an example of two separate arguments in the same paragraph.

Guidelines for Diagramming Arguments

In understanding complex arguments, it is a good idea to identify the conclusions, premises, assumptions, qualifiers, and counterarguments, and then diagram the structure of their relationship. It is often useful to turn the argument into its skeleton form, so that relationships can be seen more clearly apart from the content. This is a useful aid in determining how good a particular argument is. The major difficulty in using this procedure is that complex arguments have complex structures. Sometimes there is more than one possible interpretation and, correspondingly, more than one possible diagram. Sometimes the difficulty lies in deciding if a statement is really part of a subargument or part of the main argument. In longer text, you will often have to restate premises, conclusions, counterarguments, assumptions, and qualifiers in your own words. This can involve reducing whole chapters of books to single statements. Although this can be difficult, it is an excellent strategy for comprehension. Often the process of diagramming will reveal what's wrong or right about a certain argument. If more than one diagram of an argument is possible, then you can consider each separately. Does one diagram provide stronger support for the conclusion? Is one diagram a "truer" representation of the statements being made?

You won't want to diagram every argument you read or hear, but sometimes the issues are troublesome and important and diagramming can be very useful in clarifying the underlying relationships among the statements. Writing and diagramming unstated premises, conclusions, and assumptions can also be very helpful in considering the strength or quality of an argument by making these components explicit and placing them in the argument framework. Like many of the other strategies presented in this book, you will have to work at learning and using the steps in analyzing arguments. But, also like the other strategies, there is good evidence that the work is worth it. Allegretti and Frederick (1995), for example, reported that college students showed significant gains on a standardized test of critical thinking after they learned how to analyze arguments.

Another reason why you should learn how to analyze arguments concerns what Seech (1993) called "points of logical vulnerability." There are some topics about which we have trouble being objective. For example, I know that it would be difficult for me to be objective about the Ku Klux Klan. This is an emotional topic for me, and I would have great difficulty concluding anything positive about this group. If I used argument analysis, especially by reducing an argument to its skeleton and then diagramming its structure, then I could assess the strength of the support for a conclusion more fairly than I could without this sort of analysis. Of course, I could still decide that any belief or action that they are advocating is wrong, but my reasoning becomes less vulnerable to personal biases with these techniques.

Using Argument Structure When Writing and Speaking

In your own writing and speaking, you often need to persuade an audience that your conclusions are correct. Before you write or make an oral presentation, be sure that you can answer the following questions:

1. What is your conclusion? In other words, what is the point (or points) you want to make? Arguments are made, or constructed, from their parts, and there is no argument if there is no conclusion.
2. What are the reasons that support your conclusion?
3. What assumptions are you making? Are they valid assumptions? Should they be explicitly stated?
4. What are the conditions under which the conclusion might not be true? In other words, are qualifiers needed?
5. What are the counterarguments? Why should a reader or listener *not* believe in your conclusion?
6. What's missing? Are other conclusions possible given the reasons? Are there other reasons? Other counterarguments? Other assumptions? This step requires that you step outside of the information that you are using to consider what else might be important.

EVALUATING THE STRENGTH OF AN ARGUMENT

Advertising persuades people to buy things they don't need with money they ain't got.

—Will Rogers (1879–1935)

All arguments are not equally good or equally bad. Think about how your belief about an issue can be swayed or reinforced as each speaker in a debate presents the reasons and conclusions supporting or refuting a position. Some reasons for a particular conclusion are better than others, and sometimes good reasons don't seem to be related to the conclusion. In this section, we consider how to evaluate the strength of an argument.

Arguments are evaluated by how well they meet three criteria. The first criterion concerns the acceptability and consistency of the premises. The second criterion concerns the relationship between the premises and the conclusion. Do they support the conclusion? Does the conclusion follow from them? The third criterion concerns the unseen part of the argument. What's missing that would change your conclusion? Let's consider each of these criteria in turn.

Acceptable and Consistent Premises

No man can think clearly when his fists are clenched.

—George Jean Nathan (quoted in Byrne, 1988, p. 390).

The premises are the "why" part of an argument. The premises must be **acceptable**. A premise is acceptable when it is true or when we can reasonably believe that it is true. Let's consider what this means. If I say that the sun is hot, this is an acceptable premise. I have never touched the sun, but many experts in the field have said that the sun is hot. Much of what we believe to be true comes from experts' statements and personal and common or shared knowledge. Similarly, I have no direct, firsthand knowledge of bacteria, but it is reasonable to believe that they exist. They are commonly acknowledged "truths" of science. I believe that California is larger than New Jersey even though I have never measured them. You could probably give a long list of "facts" that are commonly believed to be true. These are examples of acceptable premises.

Premises that are false are unacceptable. Examples of false premises include: Men can give birth to babies, whales can fly, all mammals are dogs, and Spanish is the

vant to get into the philosophical considerations
Personal or common knowledge and expert
hining acceptability.

either/or proposition in which a premise is either
rt of the job of analyzing an argument involves
s. This may require research on your part. Suppose
about the safety of building a chemical warfare
oration that wants to build the laboratory argues
safe; therefore, you have nothing to worry about.
ility of this premise is to spend some time in the
riments conducted in such laboratories, the kinds
d past accidents at other similar laboratories. You
ts of experts in this area.

are also **consistent**. When several premises are
ey must not contradict each other. For example,
states that we have to reduce unemployment in
another premise states that we have to increase
he economy is an argument that contains incon-
emises are inconsistent, it is possible to eliminate
lty. If you can eliminate the inconsistency among
ge the strength of the argument.

an argument, check for acceptability and consis-
ility and consistency of premises, you will often
he experts who are asserting the premises.

n deciding whom and what to believe you need
tion. Ask yourself the following questions about
an expert who is presenting the reasons for a belief:

1. Is the "expert" a recognized authority in the *same field* in which she is providing
testimony? Why should you believe an expert in computer graphics when the topic
concerns chemical warfare?

2. Is the expert an *independent* party in this issue? If the expert who says the
laboratory is safe was hired by the corporation that owns the laboratory, then her
testimony is suspect. The testimony is not necessarily wrong, but you should be wary
because the motive for personal gain is involved.

3. What are the "expert's" *credentials*? Did she write several journal articles on the
subject that were then published in respected journals, or is her expertise documented
with a single night school course in the topic? Is the expert current in the field? Even
a renowned expert on chemical warfare from World War II will have little knowledge
of advances in the field over the last 40 years.

4. Does the expert have *specific and firsthand knowledge* of the issue? She could
conclude that chemical warfare laboratories are generally safe, but have no direct
knowledge of the one being proposed. Did she check the plans for safety features? Does
she know exactly what sorts of experiments are being planned?

5. What *methods of analysis* were used by the expert? Are there standard safety
assessments for laboratories that contain dangerous chemicals? Were these used?

Reread the advertisement presented at the beginning of this chapter that states that
we can "eat all day and still lose weight." Who are the doctors and what are the

universities that support this claim? (No names are given. You should immediately begin to question the credibility of this information.) Was their expertise in weight loss? What are their credentials? Are they independent or will they make money if you buy this product? What were the methods of analysis that were used to document the statement that it will make you feel stronger and full of pep? (None were mentioned.) Are the claims made in this advertisement credible?

Decisions about the acceptability of premises will often depend on how you evaluate the source of the information. When you have two experts who disagree, which is frequently the case, you need to understand the nature of the disagreement and their relative expertise. Are they disagreeing on research findings or the interpretation of those findings? Try to zero in on the specific points on which they disagree, so that you can scrutinize these points.

In a recent article on credibility, Carlson (1995) distinguished between experts with regard to matters of reality and matters of value. When the topic concerns "reality" (e.g., Do people who live near chemical warfare plants suffer from more illnesses than people who do not live near them?), then the expert can provide evidence, such as the results of studies, that support her conclusion. When the topic concerns values, the identification and role of the expert is more difficult. For example, should euthanasia be allowed? This sort of question involves issues such as whether anyone has the right to terminate his own life, and experimental data will not be useful in formulating a conclusion in this situation. A chemist might be a credible expert for questions concerning chemical warfare, but who is a credible expert for questions of euthanasia? Are the opinions of medical personnel, clergy, or ordinary citizens equally good in making these decisions? There are few guidelines for selecting credible experts in matters of value. Fischhoff (1993) is an expert on expertise. As he wisely noted, by definition, experts know more about some topic than most of us. But, expert knowledge is always incomplete and people can legitimately disagree about a wide range of topics such as which risks are worth taking.

Premises That Support the Conclusion

Consider the following argument:

> It is important that we elect a prime minister from the New Democratic Party (a political party in Canada) because the rain in Spain falls mainly on the plain.

I hope that your response to this was, "huh?" The premise or reason why we should support a candidate from the New Democratic Party had nothing to do with it. The rain in Spain is unrelated to political elections in Canada. In technical terms, the premise does not support the conclusion.

In determining the relevance or relatedness between the premises and the conclusion(s), I like to use an analogy to a table. The conclusion is the top of the table and the premises are the legs. When the premises are unrelated to the conclusion, they are off somewhere in another room and cannot support it. It is easy to detect instances in which the premises are totally unrelated to the conclusion. Other examples are more difficult as relatedness is a matter of degree. Premises can be more or less related to the conclusion.

Premises can deal with the same topic as the conclusion, yet not support the conclusion. For example, suppose I were to argue that you should get plenty of exercise because athletes get plenty of exercise. Both the conclusion and the premise concern exercise, but the premise is not a *reason for* the conclusion. Even if it is true that athletes get plenty of exercise, it may not follow that you should therefore get plenty of exercise.

Maybe you have a "weak" heart and would die from exercise. The conclusion does not follow from the premise. One way of checking for the relatedness of the premise(s) to the conclusion(s) is to ask yourself if the conclusion must be true or extremely likely if the premise is acceptable. If the answer is "no," then you have to question how well the conclusion is being supported by the premise.

Determining the relatedness between the premises and the conclusion can be difficult. This is exactly the sort of determination that judges are required to make all of the time. Consider a rape case in which the defense wants to show that the woman agreed to sexual intercourse. Is her previous sexual behavior related to this issue? Most of the time, the courts have ruled that a woman's past sexual history is unrelated to whether or not she was coerced at the time in question, but under special circumstances, such evidence may be admissible because the judge decides that it may be related to a particular case.

The premises not only have to be related to the conclusion, they also have to be strong enough to support the conclusion. Some authors call this condition **adequate grounds**. When premises provide good support for the conclusion, we say that there are adequate grounds for believing that the conclusion is true or likely to be true.

Let's return to the table analogy. Think of the conclusion as a solid wooden table top. A solid wooden table top will topple over if we try to support it with a few toothpicks. The only way to support it is to use one or more strong legs or many weaker legs that, when used together, will form a strong base of support. These possibilities are depicted in Fig. 5.1.

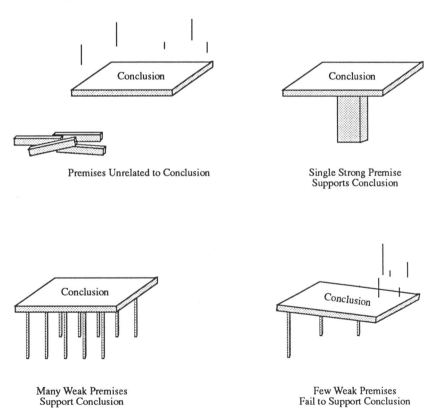

FIG. 5.1. Table analogy for understanding the strength of an argument. The table top is the conclusion and the legs are the premises. Strong arguments have a firm base of support.

Let's consider some examples of strength of support.

1. [Marion and Engelbert have filed for divorce].[1] Therefore, [they plan to get a divorce].[2]

As before, I have bracketed and numbered the statements. In skeleton form, this is [1] therefore [2].

I hope that you can see that statement [1] is a reason for statement [2], the conclusion. Because we have one reason and one conclusion, this is an argument.

The unstated assumption that they are married will be omitted from the diagram because it is not relevant to the point being made, but if it were included, it would point to [1]. Graphically, this becomes:

I have rated the strength of support for the conclusion as strong because I believe that filing for divorce is very strong evidence that they plan to get divorced (although there are other possibilities, which is why it is not absolutely certain).

2. [Marion and Engelbert had eggs for breakfast][1]. Therefore, [they plan to get a divorce][2].

In skeleton form, this is still [1] therefore [2]. Because the premise is unrelated to the conclusion, it provides no support for the conclusion.

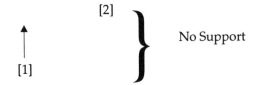

In this example, the reason provides no support for the conclusion. We have no reason to believe that they plan to get a divorce.

3. [Marion and Engelbert had a fight this morning][1.] Therefore, [they plan to get a divorce][2].

The skeleton structure is still [1] therefore [2].

In this example, the premise is related to the conclusion, but the support is weak.

4. [Marion and Engelbert had a fight this morning][1]. In fact, [they fight everyday].[2] [Engelbert is moving out of their apartment and plans to move in with his mother].[3] [Marion made an appointment with a divorce attorney].[4] Therefore, [they plan to get a divorce].[5]

This example contains five statements. Statement [5] is the conclusion. The other four statements are premises for the conclusion. Let's consider each premise and decide how well it supports the conclusion.

[5]: Marion and Engelbert plan to get a divorce. This is the conclusion.
[1]: Marion and Engelbert had a fight this morning. (weak)
[2]: They fight everyday. (weak)
[3]: Engelbert is moving out to live with his mother. (moderate)
[4]: Marion made an appointment with a divorce attorney. (strong)

In this example, there are multiple premises to support the conclusion. Taken together, they provide strong support.

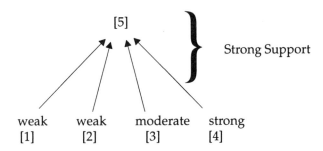

Look at the list of premises. With only the first one, the support for the conclusion was very weak. The addition of the second made the support somewhat stronger because there were now two separate weak premises, which are stronger together than one weak premise. As additional premises were added, support for the conclusion increased. This is another example of a convergent argument structure in which multiple premises point to (converge on) the same conclusion. Additional premises, even weak ones, increase the strength of the argument.

When analyzing the relationship between premises and a conclusion, you need to consider their relevance to the conclusion and the strength of the support that they supply. Using the table analogy, ask yourself if the table top has a sound base of support or if it is shaky and easy to topple over.

You may have been looking for rules or guidelines to determine the strength of support. There really are no firm rules, only guidelines. How you judge the strength of an argument depends on many personal factors including what you already know about the topic and how you make judgments. Thinking, at its heart, is still a very personal action. Although there are many skills that you can learn that will improve how you think, we are in no danger of turning all thinking into a rigid set of steps that will make us all think the same.

Here is a good example in which thoughtful people disagree. How important is a candidate's personal life in determining whether the candidate should be elected? Is it an indication that the candidate will not be honest if you know that he cheats on his spouse? Some people believe that anyone who cheats in marriage will be dishonest in other situations; others believe that the two are unrelated. Similarly, in recent Russian elections, the leading candidate was known to have a problem with alcohol. How important would this be in your decision of whether or not to vote for this candidate? In answering this, you would also want to know about the other candidates running for office and the extent of the alcohol problem, but ultimately, many people disagree over issues such as these.

Missing Components

They will try to tell you to prove you are right; I tell you to prove you are wrong.

—Louis Pasteur (1822-1895)

Most arguments are written to persuade the reader or listener that a conclusion is true or probably true. Good examples of this can be found in advertisements and political rhetoric. When you read or listen to advertisements and political claims it is important to keep in mind the restrictions imposed on these arguments. There are laws that punish false statements by advertisers; similarly, false political statements are likely to be detected by the press or opposition party. Therefore, blatantly false statements are not usually a factor in political and advertising argument analysis, although you should remain wary of them. The bigger problem in attempts to persuade is missing and distorted claims. In other words, it is the missing parts of most arguments that are often the most important parts. In order to evaluate the quality of an argument, you need to consider what's been left out.

When evaluating an argument, consider each component separately and think about ways the statements could have been distorted and what has been omitted. Let's try this with an example that is paraphrased from a newspaper editorial written by Phyllis Schafly, a prominent spokesperson for several conservative issues. The editorial appeared in *The Washington Times* on July 21, 1993:

> In this commentary, Schafly argues against universal mental health care coverage. She provides an anecdote to show that mental health care is too costly and ineffective.

> The story is about a mechanic who "allegedly" injured his wrist. Although he had wrist surgery, he still complained of pain and "claimed" to be unable to work. He then lost his job, and with it, his insurance. During this period, his wife left him because he was beating her. Under universal mental health care coverage, he would be eligible to receive 30 days of psychiatric inpatient treatment and up to 20 sessions of outpatient therapy. Schafly concludes that this would reward his "misbehavior," and create a new welfare.

One of the best ways to think about what's missing is to change your point of view so that you now become an advocate for the "other side." In this case, try to view the argument from the perspective of someone who does not agree with the conclusion that is being advocated. What premises are missing or additional information is needed that would support an opposite conclusion?

First, you should notice the use of certain words that suggest that the mechanic was not really hurt. Schafly does not know if the pain was genuine or not, and neither do we, but the use of terms like "allegedly" and "claims" suggests that, in her opinion, they were not. Second, the surgery would have been performed at the same cost regardless of the mental health care coverage, so it is not relevant to the conclusion that mental health care coverage is too costly. Third, suppose that he had received the mental health care that Schafly opposes and that it helped him to return to work and stop beating his wife. Tremendous amounts of money would be saved because he could go off welfare, and the family might also have been able to survive as a unit. Of course, you can supply other possibilities. When you consider the issues from the perspective of what is not given as information, you often will arrive at a different conclusion.

Although the consideration of missing components could theoretically go on forever, the extent to which we scrutinize an argument depends on its importance. I would spend a great deal of time and effort analyzing an argument in which the conclusion concerns the safety of building a chemical warfare laboratory near my home (or someone else's home). There are many arguments in life that should be carefully evaluated, and this includes seeking and considering missing and misleading statements.

Sound Arguments

A good argument is technically called a **sound argument**. An argument is sound when it meets the following criteria:

1. The premises are acceptable and consistent. (You may have to eliminate some premises so that the others are consistent.)
2. The premises are relevant to the conclusion and provide sufficient support for the conclusion.
3. Missing components have been considered and are judged to be consistent with the conclusion.

Satisfying each of these criteria is a matter of degree. Premises are usually acceptable on some continuum from unacceptable to totally acceptable. The nature of support that they provide for the conclusion also lies on some continuum from no support to complete support. Similarly, the missing components, especially counterarguments, may weaken the argument anywhere from completely to not at all. Because all of these assessments have to be combined to decide if an argument is sound, we usually think of soundness as ranging from unsound to completely sound.

An argument is unsound if its premises are false, or if they are unrelated to the conclusion, or if a critical counterargument is missing. An argument is completely sound if the premises are acceptable and related to the conclusion in a way that guarantees the acceptability of the conclusion. Most real-life arguments fall somewhere between these two extremes. For this reason, conclusions are often preceded with probability terms like, "it is likely that," or "we can probably conclude that." Here are some examples of different degrees of soundness:

Completely Sound Argument (premises are acceptable and related to the conclusion in a way that guarantees the conclusion)
All mothers are women who have (or had) children. Suzi is a woman who has a son. Therefore, Suzi is a mother.

Unsound arguments (either the premises are unacceptable or they are unrelated to the conclusion)
All fathers have given birth to a child. Norbert has a son. Therefore Norbert has given birth to a child. (Premise is unacceptable.)
Norbert has a son; therefore, Norbert also has a daughter. (Premise is unrelated to the conclusion.)

Don't confuse the truth or acceptability of a conclusion with the soundness of an argument. A conclusion can be objectively true, even when the argument is unsound.

The conclusion could be true for reasons that have nothing to do with the information stated in the argument. Here is an example of a conclusion that is objectively true embedded in an unsound argument:

> The structure of the family has been changing rapidly, with more single parents now heading their own households. Consequently, the divorce rate has begun to level off and decline slightly.

The conclusion about the divorce rate is true (according to demographers), but the argument is unsound because the premise does not support the conclusion.

Complex issues rarely have one correct conclusion. More often many conclusions are possible, and the task of analyzing an argument involves deciding which of two or more conclusions has the greater strength or support.

How to Analyze an Argument

1. The first step is to read or listen to the passage to determine if it contains an argument. Is there at least one premise and at least one conclusion? If not, no further analysis is needed.

2. Identify all the stated and unstated component parts: premises, conclusions, assumptions, qualifiers, and counterarguments.

3. Check the premises for acceptability and consistency. If all of the premises are unacceptable, stop here because the argument is unsound. If only some of the premises are unacceptable, eliminate them and continue with the acceptable premises. If the premises are inconsistent with each other, decide if you can justifiably eliminate one or more. An argument cannot be sound if the premises are inconsistent or contradict each other, but you may be able to eliminate the contradiction.

4. Diagram the argument. Consider the strength of the support that each premise provides for the conclusion. Rate the strength of support as nonexistent, weak, medium or strong. Look over the number of supporting premises. A large number of supporting premises can provide strong support for the conclusion in a convergent structure, even when separately each only provides weak support. Recall that in a linked structure a single weak link can destroy an argument.

5. Consider the strength of counterarguments, assumptions, and qualifiers (stated or omitted) and omitted premises. Do they destroy the support provided by the premises or strengthen or weaken it?

6. Finally, come to a global determination of the soundness of the argument. Is it unsound, completely sound, or somewhere in between? If it is somewhere in between, is it weak, medium, or strong?

Here is a completed example. The following passage was edited and abstracted from a syndicated column by Jane E. Brody (1988):

> With 1 in 10 women destined to get breast cancer, the National Cancer Institute had planned to study the possible link between breast cancer and dietary fat. But, as noted in the consumer newsletter *Nutrition Action*, the researchers were worried about the probability of the 16,000 women in the intervention group sticking to a diet as low in fat as the Japanese, with only 20% of the calories coming from fat.
>
> There was also concern about a study by Harvard researchers who found no relationship between fat intake and breast cancer risk. But, other evidence suggests that such a link might exist. A study of diet and breast cancer mortality conducted by the director of the American

Health Foundation showed the higher the daily fat intake, the higher the death rate from breast cancer. Studies of migrants also showed that when women leave a country with one breast-cancer rate, they soon acquire the breast cancer rate of their adopted country.

But, is fat the cause? Might total caloric intake be the answer since calories increase along with fat intake? Some of these difficulties can be resolved with animal studies in which diet and fat intake can be controlled. The animal studies are clear cut: Animals on high-fat diets are far more likely to get mammary cancer and die of it than those consuming a low fat diet.

Few women can afford to wait for definitive evidence.

Let's apply the steps for evaluating arguments using this passage:

1. It contains at least one premise and one conclusion, so it satisfies the minimal requirements for an argument.
2. Identify the components. I have bracketed and numbered the statements so that they would be easy to identify and diagram.

I also had to paraphrase what is being said, which is often necessary with longer and more complex arguments. Assumptions that are acceptable are listed, but not shown on the diagram unless they are essential to the argument.

[1] conclusion: Women should reduce dietary fat. I think that it is fair to represent the author's conclusion this way. The conclusion is found in the last sentence, although these exact words do not appear anywhere in the article.

[2] premise: Low-fat diets reduce the risk of cancer. This is the reason for the conclusion.

[3] counterargument: In the study mentioned, Harvard researchers found no effect of dietary fat on the risk of breast cancer. (They are a credible source of information.)

[4] counterargument: Controlled studies with humans have not been conducted. (These counterarguments work against the conclusion.)

[5] premise for [2]: Cross-cultural research shows a link between dietary fat and breast cancer. This is a reason for believing that low-fat diets reduce the risk of cancer.

[6] premise for [2]: Migration studies show that risk of cancer changes when people move from one country to another. This is another reason why we should believe that low-fat diets reduce the risk of cancer.

[7] assumption for [5]: Immigrants change their eating habits so that their diets become like those in their new country. This is an unstated assumption. Because it seems acceptable, it will not appear in the diagram.

[8] premise for [2]: Controlled animal studies show an association between dietary fat and breast cancer. This is another reason for believing that low-fat diets reduce the risk of cancer.

[9] counterargument for [8]: Results found with other animals may not apply in the same way to humans. (unstated counterargument—it weakens the support from animal studies)

[10] qualifier: Fat levels may have to be reduced to less than 20% of caloric intake in order to get reduced risk of cancer. (unstated, but modifies conclusion)

[11] assumption for [3]: Controlled research with humans may never be possible. This is an assumption that seems acceptable, so it is not shown on the diagram.

[12] missing premise: There are many other health benefits to a low-fat diet (e.g., weight reduction and reduced risk of coronary disease).

Now, go back over the list of component parts, organize them so that premises are listed under conclusions, and rate the premises for acceptability. There are no absolute standards here except for the two extremes of "must be true" and "must be false." Unfortunately few things in life fall into these categories. You are really on your own at this point in how you assign ratings. There are no absolute standards for rating strength of support.

Conclusion [1]: Eat a low-fat diet.
Premise [2]: Low-fat diets reduce the risk of cancer.
    [10]: Qualifier for [2]: needs to be less than 20% fat
    Premises for [2]:
        [5]: results of cross-cultural studies (weak)
        [6]: migration studies (moderate)
        [8]: animal studies (strong)
        but, [9], animal studies may not be relevant, so [9] is counter to [8]
Premise [12]:Other health benefits to low-fat diets (strong)
Counterargument [3] Harvard study did not support conclusion
Counterargument [4] There are no controlled human studies

The diagram of this argument is shown in Fig. 5.2. Look it over very carefully as you read the next paragraph. Do you end up with a firm structure or one that is wobbly and easy to topple over?

Looking over the diagram of the argument, I see that there are three premises that support the belief that low-fat diets reduce the risk of cancer: [5], [6], [8]. Two counterarguments weaken the conclusion: [3], [4]. The strength of support that the premises provide for the statement that low-fat diets reduce the risk of cancer [2] has been rated

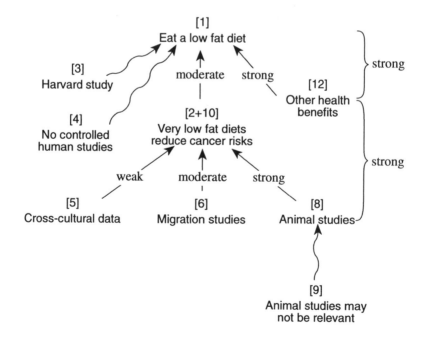

FIG. 5.2. A diagram of the argument made by Brody (1988). Note how the premises "point to" the conclusion that they support. Counterarguments are noted with wavy lines that point to the conclusion that they weaken.

as weak (cross-cultural data), moderate (migration studies), and strong (animal studies). The strongest premise (animal studies) is modified by a weak counterargument (animal studies may not be relevant). With all of these components considered, I rate the support that [2] supplies to the conclusion (eat a low fat diet) as moderate. The counterarguments weaken the support for the conclusion, but don't destroy it. I rate this argument as strong in the strength that it supplies to the conclusion overall.

You may be thinking that this was a lot of work. You are right. Diagramming and evaluating complex arguments can be as demanding as a long proof in mathematics or comprehending a complex novel or a chemical chain reaction. But, before you decide to make lifelong changes in your diet or some other decision concerning an important belief or action, you want to be sure that the decision is based on sound reasoning. In this case, the conclusion is based on acceptable premises that provide strong support for the conclusion.

I realize that few people will formally diagram an argument in real life; however, it is a powerful and useful tool for comprehending complex arguments. Practice with diagramming arguments will aid in the analysis of other arguments even when, for time or other reasons, actual diagramming is not feasible. It will help you distinguish among the components of an argument and make judgments about its strength. When the issue is important and complex, making a diagram of its structure can be well worth the time and effort required.

Reasoning and Rationalizing

People are irrational, short-sighted, destructive, ethnocentric, emotional, and easily misled by demagogues.

—Philip E. Tetlock (1994, p. 3)

It is important to note that when you evaluate arguments you are also evaluating your own knowledge about the subject matter. There may be other counterarguments that are quite strong, but are unknown to you. Similarly, your ratings of the strength of the components may be biased in ways that support a conclusion that you favor. Nickerson (1986) made an important distinction between reasoning and **rationalizing**. When we rationalize, we attend to information that favors a conclusion that is preferred. We may selectively gather information that supports a preferred conclusion or rate counterarguments as weak because they detract from a preferred conclusion. The nature of the missing components that we supply is also affected by a type of bias. When we add to an argument, the information that we supply is information that is readily recalled. If you've already read chapter 2 (Memory), then you are well aware of the many ways that memory can be biased. Rationalizing is usually not a deliberate process to distort the analysis of arguments, which makes it difficult to recognize and guard against. It is easier to recognize rationalizing when someone else is doing it. Perhaps the best we can do is realize that rationalization does occur and try to be especially vigilant for rationalizing when there is a preferred conclusion.

The willingness to invest time and effort into analyzing complex arguments is a hallmark of what Sears and Parsons (1991) described as the "ethic" of a critical thinker. When you analyze an argument, you must identify the main point that the author or speaker wants you to believe. You also have to consider both premises and counterarguments.

It is well documented in the research literature that we tend to weigh evidence that favors a belief more heavily than evidence that disconfirms it. This bias was clearly demonstrated in a study in which college students served as subjects (Lord, Ross, & Lepper, 1979). They were asked to write an essay in which they argued for or against a controversial issue such as abortion or capital punishment. The students were then given the results of experimental studies that supported a "middle of the road" point of view—that is, it was neither for nor against the controversial issue. After reading the balanced review, students who favored the "pro" position of the controversial issue believed that the objectively neutral article supported the "pro" position. Similarly, students who favored the "con" position and then read the same objectively balanced review believed that it favored the "con" position. Instead of bringing the two sides closer together, as might have been expected, the balanced review drove them further apart. Each position focused on the information that supported their own point of view and judged the evidence that ran counter to their favored position to be weak. This same finding has been found with all sorts of subject pools, including NASA scientists who favored evidence and arguments that supported their preferred hypothesis over ones that did not.

Just telling people that we tend to judge information that we favor as stronger than information that we oppose doesn't work to correct this bias. Is it any wonder why it is so difficult to get people to assess controversial issues in a fair-minded manner? Because we are not aware that we judge reasons in a way that supports what we believe to be true, it is very difficult to change the way we evaluate information. One successful attempt was accomplished by Koriat, Lichtenstein, and Fischhoff (1980). They required students to list reasons that support a conclusion and reasons that run counter to a conclusion (counterarguments), and to rate the strength of each. This should be familiar because they are the steps used in analyzing arguments. They found that students became more accurate in their assessments after this training in "giving reasons." These sorts of experimental results show that the giving and assessing of reasons can have beneficial results that improve the thinking process.

A Rubric for Scoring Arguments—Even Your Own

Of course, we also present arguments, and don't just analyze those that are made by other people. In a book that was written for college professors, Norris and Ennis (1989) suggested criteria that can be used to evaluate an argumentative essay. When you write your own essays or plan oral presentations, consider these criteria:

1. Do you clearly state the conclusion and define necessary terms?
2. Is the material that you included relevant to the conclusion?
3. Is the argument sound? Do the premises provide good support for the conclusion?
4. Have you considered the credibility of your experts?
5. Is the essay well-organized with different issues addressed separately?
6. Have you fairly presented alternative points of view and counterarguments?
7. Have you used good grammar and a clear style of writing?

PERSUASION AND PROPAGANDA

Through clever and constant application of propaganda, people can be made to see paradise as hell, and also the other way round, to consider the most wretched sort of life as paradise.

—Adolf Hitler (1889–1944; from *Mein Kampf*)

Whenever we are confronted with an argument, it is important to keep in mind that the material we are reading or hearing has been written to persuade us to do something or to believe something. Much of the communication that we receive is concerned with getting us to act or think in a certain way. Pratkanis and Aronson (1992) defined **propaganda** as "mass suggestion or influence through the manipulation of symbols and the psychology of the individual" (p. 9). This broad definition is applicable to a great variety of situations. Propaganda, like beauty, is often in the eyes of the beholder. It does not require that the information be false or misleading, but it does at least imply less concern for truth or rigorous argument than the sort of arguments found in scholarly journals or presented by independent parties. Frequently, the information provided is charged with appeals to emotion rather than reason.

Humans are very clever in using techniques that aim to influence others' thinking. The cleverest way to influence how someone thinks is with a well-crafted argument. If you were thinking that the work of analyzing an argument is not worth it, you have not considered the agonies of history in which people failed to analyze political arguments. Consider the evil genius of men like Joseph Goebbel, Hitler's minister of propaganda. Have you ever wondered how millions of people could be persuaded to kill millions of other people whose sole crime was believing in another religion? Of course, such evil was rooted in a long history of scapegoating, which is the practice of blaming a minority group for all of the ills in society. In order to kill so many people efficiently, it was necessary to set up "death factories" that operated with the efficiency of an assembly line, much like the factories that produce refrigerators or automobiles. First, Goebbel told lies, false reasons to support the conclusion that genocide was justified. He spread rumors about "secret books" that told about an alleged tradition of drinking the blood of innocent Christian children. Of course, there were no books, and this disgusting practice never occurred, but many people were willing to believe that it was true.

Arguments were most frequently used to persuade Nazis and others that millions of people should be slaughtered, but there were other propaganda techniques that Goebbel used including visual images and threats of violence for anyone who didn't agree. Although other techniques are considered in more detail later in this chapter and in other chapters, I note here the particularly blatant ploy of showing pictures of Jews that were alternated with pictures of rats and roaches, so that viewers would come to associate certain facial features that are common in many Jews with disgusting rodents and bugs. These same sorts of techniques have been used to promote other types of equally horrific genocide. The propaganda used to justify slavery and lynchings in the United States, the slaughter of Cambodians in Asia and Armenians in Europe, and the purges by Mao in China and Stalin in the former Soviet Union, show that propaganda has been used all over the world to encourage prejudice and killing. Why did education fail all these people in so many places around the world? For example, how did millions of Chinese, in this century, believe that Mao was their "loving father," when he was responsible for the death of millions of Chinese? Why didn't they stop to consider if the reasons they were given to support this Chinese holocaust (e.g., the cultural revolution) were not acceptable? Do you understand Hitler's now infamous quote, "What luck for rulers that men do not think" (quoted in Byrne, 1988, p. 359)?

THE PSYCHOLOGY OF REASONS

As you now realize, an argument requires the use of reasons, and we like to have reasons for our beliefs, even when the reasons are not very good and the argument itself is weak. Three psychologists conducted a study in which they examined how people respond to the *appearance* of reasons (Langer, Blank, & Chanowitz, 1978). In this study, they had a confederate (someone working with the experimenters whose identity is not known to the subjects) try various combinations of requests and reasons for barging ahead of people waiting in line to use a copy machine. There were three different conditions: (a) request alone ("Excuse me, I have five pages. May I use the Xerox machine?"), (b) request plus reason ("Excuse me, I have five pages. May I use the Xerox because I'm in a rush?"), and (c) request plus the appearance of a reason ("Excuse me, I have five pages. May I use the Xerox machine because I have to make some copies?").

The results of this study are very interesting. In the request alone condition 60% of the people waiting said that it was okay for the confederate to make the copies. In the request plus reason condition, this figure jumped to 94%. What about the request plus appearance of a reason? In this condition, 93% of the people waiting to use the machine let the confederate go ahead. The use of the word "because" suggested that there was a reason. Remember the section on premise indicators? "Because" was listed as a word that is frequently followed by a reason. The statement "because I have to make some copies" is not a reason to let someone ahead of you in line at the copy machine. Everyone standing in line has to make some copies. It seems that we like to believe that our actions and beliefs are reasonable, that is based on reasons. Unfortunately, even nonreasons, poor reasons, and reasons that are unrelated to the action or belief often will suffice. People who want to change how we think and act often rely on this human tendency and will deliberately use unsound reasoning to convince us that a conclusion is true.

You probably think that irrelevant reasons for a conclusion would have no effect on how people evaluate a conclusion. It seems that this should be true because irrelevant reasons are, well, irrelevant. But, psychologically, irrelevant reasons often influence what we believe and how we act even though logically, they should not. A study of consumer decisions showed that irrelevant reasons in support of a product tend to weaken support for the product, and irrelevant reasons that run counter to a product tend to strengthen support for the product (Simonson, Nowlis, & Simonson, 1993). An example should help here. Suppose that you are a runner who is looking for good running shoes. As a salesperson, I tell you that Adibok brand is well known for their aerobic shoes, but they also make good running shoes. The fact that they are well known for their aerobic shoes should be irrelevant to the selection of running shoes, but it seems to work against this hypothetical brand. Consumers assume that if Adibok is good at making aerobic shoes, then it is less good at making running shoes. Thus, an irrelevant reason in support of this brand is psychologically converted into a reason against this brand.

Similarly, suppose that you have no interest in saunas. If I told you that the Marrotten Hotel chain does not have a sauna, a seemingly irrelevant reason against the Marrotten Hotels, you would likely take this as a reason for selecting Marrotten. Psychologically, this irrelevant reason against Marrotten Hotels is converted into thinking that it may have something else positive that balances this irrelevant negative. In this way, an irrelevant reason for not staying at Marrotten Hotels becomes a reason for staying at Marrotten.

The point of this discussion is that people often do not behave in ways that are logical; irrelevant reasons influence how we think. This is important for you to understand because knowledge of how people assess arguments can help you to improve your own thinking and to persuade others, a topic that I turn to next.

Unsound reasoning techniques used for the purpose of persuasion are called **fallacies**. As you go through the list of fallacies presented in the next section, you can classify each as violating one or more of the criteria for sound arguments—the premises are unacceptable, or the premises are unrelated to the conclusion or inconsistent, or the expert is not credible, or important information is missing.

It is impossible to list every fallacy that has been employed to change how people think. The list would be too long to be useful, with only subtle differences among several of the techniques. Accordingly, only the most common and representative techniques are discussed. If you understand how fallacies work in general, you'll be better prepared to recognize and defend against them. Toulmin, Rieke, and Janik (1979) called the ability to recognize fallacies "a kind of sensitivity training" because they train the reader to be sensitive to common tricks of persuasion.

TWENTY-ONE COMMON FALLACIES

1. Association Effects

One of the oldest principles in psychology is the notion that if two events occur close together in time and/or space the mind will form an association between them. Thereafter, when one occurs, the other is expected to occur. This principle has become widely used in the political arena, especially to create **guilt by association**. Suppose you read in the newspaper that a violent mass murderer endorsed a presidential candidate. This endorsement would be detrimental to the candidate, even if she did not desire it and did nothing to promote it.

An example of the propagandistic use of association came from a political group called "California Tax Reduction Movement." Their 1983 literature stated: "This court, dominated by Jerry Brown appointees, and having radical views close to those of Jane Fonda and Tom Hayden, has twisted the words until we don't even recognize them!" You might be wondering what Jane Fonda and Tom Hayden are doing in a sentence about the California Supreme Court. In the jargon of analyzing arguments, the premise is unrelated to the conclusion. Fonda and Hayden had no connection with the court. This literature was written with the belief that people who favor tax reductions will also be opposed to Jane Fonda and Tom Hayden. The court is being made guilty by association with them. Although it is implied, it does not logically follow that the Supreme Court therefore has views similar to Jane Fonda and Tom Hayden. It may or may not have had such views. (Note also the use of the emotion-laden word "radical.") Whenever you see examples of associations with no justifiable connection like this one, be wary of the rest of the message. It is likely to contain an appeal to your emotions rather than to your cognition.

Just as one can have guilt by association, it is also possible to have **virtue by association**. In this instance, the names or label attached to the person are "good" ones. Perhaps this is why certain political offices tend to run in families. People expected the Kennedy brothers to be similar as politicians because of their obvious association with each other. This expectation is being passed onto their children, many of whom are now involved in or considering political careers. Would you vote for or against an unknown Kennedy simply because he or she is in the Kennedy family?

A wary recipient of messages that rely on association will ask about the nature of the association. If a candidate is a leader of the Ku Klux Klan, then associating the doctrine of the Klan with this individual is reasonable. If, on the other hand, a friend of the candidate's mother is a member of the Klan, the association is ludicrous.

2. Arguments Against the Person

Arguments against the person is the formal term for name calling or, in its Latin form, argumentatum ad hominem. This form of persuasion or propaganda attacks the people who support a cause, and not the cause itself. As an example of this, the Nazis believed that the theory of relativity was wrong because its discoverer was a Jew named Albert Einstein. They never considered the evidence for or against the theory, just the religion of its originator. It is basically another form of the association effect. In this case, the association that is being made is between an idea and a person. The underlying principle is that if you don't like the person who supports an idea, then you should also oppose the idea itself because the idea and the person are associated.

Suppose you were serving on a jury that had to decide which of two witnesses was telling the truth. Would you be swayed if one attorney told you to disregard one man's testimony because he had been divorced twice? Presumably not, because the man's marital status is irrelevant to the issue. Suppose you were told that one of the men had two previous convictions for lying to a jury. Would this argument against the person be relevant? I would think so. In this case, the information provided about the witness is relevant to the question of whether or not he is lying. Consider the strength and relevancy of the argument and the purpose for which it is used, and don't be misled by irrelevant attacks on the supporters or detractors of any position.

3. Appeals to Pity

An **appeal to pity** is easy to spot. "Support this position" or "buy that product" because it needs your help. A rental car agency has made it well known that they're number 2 in their business, and therefore will try harder. They hope that consumers will root for the "underdog" and support the company that is number 2. Does this conclusion logically follow from the fact that they're number 2? No! You could also logically conclude that the number 1 company will try harder to retain their lead or that the number 2 company would have been number 1 if it had tried harder. Appeals to pity are often found in legal pleadings. A defendant's poor background or turbulent home life will often be brought up during a trial. These appeals to pity have nothing to do with the question of whether a defendant is guilty or innocent, although they may be persuasive appeals for leniency in sentencing if the defendant is found guilty.

4. Popularity and Testimonials

The **popularity** technique (also known as the "bandwagon") relies on the need for conformity for its persuasive power. It is persuasive because it explains that everyone supports a position or buys a certain product. It is expected that the message recipients will adopt the belief or buy the product in order to feel as if she or he belongs to the groups mentioned. Implicitly, the message is, "if everyone is doing it, it must be right." This fallacy was presented earlier in this chapter when we considered the advertisement for LaBaroness, the car that more people are buying than any other American car.

A variation of the popularity technique is **testimonials**. Respected politicians or movie stars endorse a belief or product. It is believed that people will want to be similar to the people they respect, so they will choose to use the same deodorant or foot powder or support the same causes. The recipients of testimonials are expected to infer a conclusion from the information stated. It is expected that they will reason along these lines: Christie Brinkley is a gorgeous model. She uses the advertised beauty product. If I use this beauty product, I will look like Christie Brinkley. Of course, this conclusion does not follow from the first two sentences, but many people believe that it does or

Calvin and Hobbes   by Bill Watterson

at least that it might. This fallacy is worsened when the testimonial is not even in the area in which the personality has expertise. Christie Brinkley also endorses a national newspaper. As far as I know, this is an area in which she has no expertise. She is not a credible expert in the area of journalistic quality. Yet, advertisements like these do sell products.

Sometimes, however, the popularity technique and testimonials can be valid persuasive techniques. If, for example, all of the members of an unbiased expert panel established to study the effects of a drug decide that it is unsafe, I would consider this information relevant to the question of the drug's safety because it passes the test of credibility. Similarly, if a leading educator endorses a reading text, this might properly have an impact on your evaluation of the text. Both of these examples presume that the "experts" have no personal motives for their endorsements—that is, they're not being paid for saying these things and their expertise is relevant to the position or product that they're supporting. In this case, they are credible sources of information.

5. False Dichotomy

Don't give him two sides to a question to worry him. Give him one; better yet, give him none!

—Ray Bradbury (*Farenheit 451*, 1950)

There are very few political or social decisions that have simple answers or that can be solved with simple choices. Yet simple slogans are the **prototype** or most common and representative form of persuasive techniques. **False dichotomy** is sometimes called simplification or the *black or white fallacy* because readers are asked to decide between two positions, without allowing other alternatives or "gray areas" that would combine aspects of both choices.

The following question appeared in a questionnaire that was sent by an Assembly-man to his constituents (Assemblyman Montjoy Needs Your Views, 1983):

"Would you prefer that government cut spending or increase taxes?"

             cut spending   increase taxes

Does this question bother you? It should. The answers to our fiscal problems are not this simple. You should ask where and how the cuts would be made and how much taxes would be increased. Perhaps "cuts" could be combined with small or temporary increases in taxes. Can you guess which answer the assemblyman prefers? Given this choice, I believe that most people would prefer to "cut spending," yet, for many, an entirely different response would result from a question that was worded differently.

When you are faced with a false dichotomy or the simplification of a complex issue, don't ask yourself if the ideas are good or bad. Ask instead what is good about the ideas and what is bad about them. Consider other alternatives and combinations of ideas. Remember that one of the steps in analyzing arguments calls for supplying missing components—omitted premises, assumptions, qualifiers, and counterarguments.

6. Appeals to Pride or Snobbery

Speech was given to man to disguise his thoughts.

—Talleyrand (1754–1838; quoted in Macmillan, 1989, p. 544)

An **appeal to pride or snobbery** usually involves praise or flattery. A blatant and humorous example can be found in an advertisement that was mailed to me at home (notice that it begins with my name, a sure attention-getting technique):

Dear Dr. Halpern,

You may just be the solution.

Here is the problem: How do you find the right subscribers for an extraordinary magazine that is about to be published—BUT, a magazine that isn't for everyone? A magazine that is, in fact, for only a handful of bright, literate people, people who still in this world of instant communication love to sit down with a good book.

I'd love to believe that the publishers know me personally, and have written a magazine just for the kind of person I'd like to be. The truth is, this letter went to tens of thousands of people whose names were bought as part of various mailing lists. Clearly, they are attempting to persuade me to purchase their magazine by appealing to my pride or snobbery.

Consider the following question that appeared as part of a "1982 Congressional Questionnaire" (Congressman Carlos J. Moorhead Reports, Summer 1982):

In an attempt to make federal social programs more responsive to citizens' needs, less wasteful and more efficient, the Administration has proposed a New Federalism where the programs and funds—in the form of block grants—are transferred to local government for management and administration. Do you think that you, your neighbors, and your local officials have the ability to handle this new responsibility?

yes   no

Do you think that this question is slanted toward a "yes" response? The appeal to pride and snobbery is less obvious in this question than in the first example, possibly making it even more potent. The question is really, "Are you and your friends smart enough to handle X?" It doesn't matter what X is; most people believe that they are smart. The congressman has also posed the wrong question. You may be able to "handle this new responsibility" without believing that block grants are a good idea. Responses to this question were subsequently used to support the idea of block grants. Be wary of persuasive communications that include flattery. Although flattery is not in and of itself wrong, it may be used to obscure real issues.

7. Card Stacking or Suppressed Information

Card stacking or suppressed information operates as a persuasive technique by omitting information that supports the unfavored view. An automobile company recently compared the car they were advertising on television with a competitor. The advertisers stressed that their car got better mileage and cost less. What about the variables they omitted? Which car needed fewer repairs, had the more comfortable seating, or accelerated better? What about other makes of cars? Did a brand that was not mentioned exceed the advertised one on all of these dimensions? When considering persuasive information, be sure to consider what has not been stated along with the stated claims.

This is another example of the need to consider the missing components in an argument.

8. Circular Reasoning

In **circular reasoning** the premise is simply a restatement of the conclusion. If you were to diagram the structure of this sort of argument, you would get a circle because the support for the conclusion is a restatement of the conclusion. Here is an example of circular reasoning:

We need to raise the speed limit because the current legal speed is too slow.

In this example, the reason given (current speed is too slow) is just another way of saying that we need to raise the speed limit. It does not support the conclusion. The conclusion would be supported with premises such as the assertion that there has been no change in the number or severity of automobile accidents with a lower speed limit or some similar statement that supports this conclusion.

9. Irrelevant Reasons

Arguments that utilize irrelevant reasons are fairly common. The Latin word for this sort of fallacy is *non sequitur*, which literally translates to "it doesn't follow." In other words, the reason or premise is unrelated to the conclusion. Of course, you recognize the importance of having relevant premises as one of the criteria for sound arguments. (If you don't, go back over the section on evaluating the quality of an argument.)

One example that comes to mind is a statement that a faculty member made at a curriculum committee meeting in which we were discussing whether or not we should require every student to take classes in a foreign language. The faculty member in favor of this proposal made this statement: "We should require every student to study a foreign language because it is important that we provide our students with a quality education." Look carefully at the conclusion and the premise. Is the premise related to the conclusion? Everyone on the curriculum committee believed that all students should receive a quality education, but the issue was whether all students should be required to study a foreign language. There were no reasons given as to why studying a foreign language should be a required part of a quality education. The conclusion did not follow from the reason that was given.

10. Slippery Slope or Continuum

The **slippery slope** fallacy is best described by an example. One of the arguments against court-ordered desegregation of the schools was that if we allow the court to determine which public schools our children will attend, the court will also tell us whom we have to allow into our churches, whom we have to invite into our homes, and even whom we should marry. In this example, the action (court-ordered desegregation) lies on a continuum with the court ordering whom we should marry at an extreme end. The argument being made is that if we allow the court to have jurisdiction over events at one end of the continuum, then it will take over the other events on the continuum. For this reason, this fallacy is called either slippery slope (once you start sliding down a slope you can't stop) or the fallacy of **continuum**.

Most life events can be ordered along a continuum. It does not necessarily follow that actions concerning some part of the continuum will also apply to other portions of the continuum. Let's consider a second example. The Irish believe that current U.S. immigration laws are biased against immigrants from Ireland. They have asked the U.S. immigration service to increase the quota for Ireland. Those who have argued against increasing the immigration quotas for Ireland have said that if we increase the quota for Ireland, then we'll have to increase the quota for every other country in the world, an action that they see as disastrous. Increasing the number of immigrants we accept from Ireland does not mean that we would also have to increase the quotas for other countries. The immigration office may or may not decide to alter quotas from other countries, but taking an action on behalf of one country does not mean that the other actions will follow. A more colorful name for this fallacy is "the camel's nose in the tent." It is based on the idea that if we let a camel stick its nose in the tent, the rest of the camel will soon follow (Kahane, 1992).

11. Straw Person

A **straw person** is weak and easy to knock down. With a straw person argument, a very weak form of an opponent's argument is set up and then knocked down. It occurs when an opponent to a particular conclusion distorts the argument in support of the conclusion and substitutes one that is much weaker. Again, an example is probably the best way to describe this sort of fallacy. In a discussion about whether students should be evaluating their professors, one opponent to this idea offered this straw person argument: "You say that students' evaluations of their professors should be included in decisions about which professors we should be promoting. Well, I certainly don't think that the decision as to which professors get promoted should be made by students." Notice how the original argument that "student evaluations should be included in the decision-making process" was changed to "students should not be deciding which professors get promoted." The original argument was for student evaluations to be *part of* the criteria used in the decision-making process. This is not the same as having students make the decisions. In its changed form, the argument is easier to knock down, just like a straw person.

12. Part–Whole

Part–whole fallacies are flip sides of the same error. A part–whole fallacy is made whenever a speaker (or writer) assumes that whatever is true of the whole is also true of all of its parts, and whatever is true of the parts is also true of the whole. Consider some outstanding, prestigious university. (Are you thinking about your own school?) As a whole, the student body is highly intelligent, but it would be wrong to believe that every student who attends that university is therefore highly intelligent. Similarly, think of several brilliant scientists. Just because they are each brilliant doesn't mean that if we put them on a committee together (made a whole out of them), the committee would be brilliant. They might never agree, or perhaps they would spend so much time impressing each other with how smart they are that no work would get done.

13. Appeals to Ignorance

The peculiar thing about **appeals to ignorance** is that they can often be used to support two or more totally different conclusions. This should be a clue to you that the reasoning involved is fallacious. In appeals to ignorance, the premise involves something we don't know. Our ignorance is being used to argue that because there is no evidence to support a conclusion, the conclusion must be wrong. Our ignorance of a topic can also be used to support a conclusion by stating that because there is no evidence that contradicts it, the conclusion must be right. I have heard both sides argue this way in a debate on the existence of God. Believers have argued that because no one can prove that God doesn't exist, He therefore must exist. Nonbelievers have argued that because no one can prove that God exists, He therefore doesn't exist. The absence of evidence doesn't support any conclusion.

14. Weak and Inappropriate Analogies

The topic of analogies was presented in chapter 3. It also appears later in the book in chapters 9 and 10. Analogies are a basic thinking skill. We use analogies whenever we encounter something new and try to understand it by reference to something we already know. Although analogies can be extremely useful aids to comprehension, they can also be misused. Two objects or events are analogous when they share certain properties. When we argue with analogies, we conclude that what is true of one object or event is true of the other.

Consider the mother who decides that her child should not be given piano lessons because the child had dropped out of dance class. The mother formed the analogy that the child dropped out of one type of creative arts lessons and because dance class and piano lessons were similar in some ways, the child would also drop out of piano lessons. The child may or may not have continued with piano lessons, but it was a weak sort of analogy that formed the support for this conclusion. Dance class and piano lessons are similar in certain respects, but they also have many distinct differences. When considering an argument by analogy, it is important to consider the nature and the salience of the similarity relationship. It is possible that the child would have stuck with piano.

15. Appeals to Authority

I already introduced this fallacy in an informal way earlier in this chapter when I discussed expert credibility. Much of what we know and believe is based on what we learn from authorities. The fallacy of **appeals to authority** occurs when the authority we use to support the premises in an argument is the wrong one. If I wanted to sell you a stereo, it would be valid if I quoted from an article on stereos written by a professor of acoustics (who is an independent authority). It would be a fallacious appeal if I told you that Pee Wee Herman called it the best stereo system he had ever seen. Thus, the fallacy is not in appealing to an authority on a topic, but in appealing to someone who is not a credible authority.

16. Incomplete Comparisons

"More doctors agree that Dopeys can give you the fastest pain relief." Advertisements like this one are so common that it's almost impossible to open a magazine without seeing one. Two different comparisons are made in this statement and both are incomplete. Whenever you see comparative terms ask yourself "more than what," "fastest compared to what?" **Incomplete comparisons** are missing the other half of the equation.

Incomplete comparisons often contain evaluative terms like "better," "safest," and, of course, "cleanest." This is a special case of considering missing components in an argument. How was *better* defined? How was it measured? By whom? Compared to what? There is no way to interpret claims like, "Washo will make your whole wash cleaner" without additional information. An ice cream store that I pass on my way to work has a large sign outside that states, "Voted the best ice cream." I presume that I am supposed to infer that their ice cream was voted the best, but by whom, compared to which other ice creams, what criteria were used to decide which was best, and how were the ice creams evaluated with these criteria? Every time you see a comparative claim, you should ask yourself these questions. If the answers aren't provided, then the comparison is incomplete.

17. Knowing the Unknowable

Sometimes we are given information that it is impossible to know. This is the fallacy of **knowing the unknowable**. Suppose you read in the newspapers that we need to increase the size of the police force because the number of unreported rapes has increased dramatically. A little alarm should go off when you read this: How can anyone know about the number of unreported rapes? I don't doubt that many rapes are not reported to the police or that this is an important issue. What is at question is the increase or decrease in the number when the actual number is unknowable. There are numerous times when sources give precise figures when such figures are impossible. Child abuse is another example. This is a tragic and important issue for society to grapple with, but estimates about the number of children involved can never be very accurate because much of it is undetected. Researchers can try to extrapolate from the number of child abuse cases that are treated in the emergency rooms of hospitals or that go to court, but there are no good methods of converting these known figures to unreported cases. An increase in the number of cases of rape or child abuse may be due to increased awareness and education about these crimes. An increase in reported cases could be associated with an increase, decrease, or no change in unreported cases. There is no way we can know the unknowable.

18. False Cause

The fallacy of **false cause** is discussed more completely in chapter 6, but it is also important to discuss in the context of reasoning fallacies. The fallacy of false cause occurs whenever someone argues that because two events occur together, or one follows the other closely in time, that one caused the other to occur. An example of this is an explanation of the finding that as the number of churches increase in a city so does the number of prostitutes. It would be false to conclude that churches cause an increase in prostitution or that prostitutes cause more churches to be built. In fact, as the size of a city increases so does the number of churches and the number of prostitutes, as well as the number of schools, dry cleaners, and volunteer agencies. Neither of them caused any of the others. They all resulted from a third factor —in this case an increase in population. Of course, it is possible that one variable *did* cause the other to occur, but more than co-occurrence is needed to justify a causal claim.

19. Put Downs

Only a fool would endorse this candidate! No patriotic American would disagree! You'd have to be stupid to believe that! These are all examples of **put downs** (also known as belittling the opposition). An opposing viewpoint is belittled so that agreeing with it would put you in the class of people who are fools, or unpatriotic, or stupid. This technique is not so much a reasoning fallacy as it is an emotional appeal or dare.

20. Appeals to Tradition

"That's the way we've always done it." Anyone who has tried to change a policy has heard this sentence or its variant, "If it ain't broke, don't fix it." In **appeals to tradition** the unstated assumption is that what exists is best. It may be true that current policy is better than some suggested change, but it also may not be true. There is nothing inherent in the fact that "that's the way we've always done it" that makes it a good or best way to accomplish an objective. One of the attitudes of a critical thinker that was presented in the first chapter is flexibility. Appeals to tradition deny the possibility that a different way may be an improvement.

21. False Charge of Fallacy

That's a fallacy! It seems that after some people learn to recognize fallacious reasoning, they then label everything that anyone says as a fallacy (Levi, 1991). Not everything is a fallacy. The idea of critical thinking is to develop an amiable skepticism, not a cynical view that everything and everyone is false. It is important to know when to accept some statements as acceptable as it is to know when and what to question.

DISTINGUISHING AMONG OPINION, REASONED JUDGMENT, AND FACT

Compare the following three statements.

- Computereasy is the best personal computer you can buy. I like it.
- Computereasy is the best personal computer you can buy for under $2,000. It is easier to use than the five other leading brands and will run all of the software programs that I use.
- Computereasy comes with a gigantic hard disk drive, a built-in laser printer, and is fully compatible with all software written for the IBM, Apple, and Apple Macintosh.

In the first example, I have expressed an **opinion**. It is a simple assertion of a preference. I like it; I think it's best. No reasons were given to support the evaluation. Opinion reflects how an individual or group has assessed a position or product—for example, "Vote for Max Lake; he's the best man for the job!"

The second example also expresses a preference, but in this example, the preference is supported by reasons. I prefer X because Y. This is an example of **reasoned judgment**. Other examples of reasoned judgment are provided throughout the chapter. Remember the extended argument concerning the relationship between low-fat diets and breast cancer? The premises supported the conclusion, which in this case was a statement about which type of diet is best.

The third statement concerns factual claims. **Facts** have a verifiable truth value—for example, Gravel-Os breakfast cereal has 100% of the recommended daily requirement of iron. Although I can't personally check the truth value of these facts, a credible authority (e.g., the Food and Drug Administration) has verified these claims for me. Often, the distinction among fact, opinion, and reasoned judgment is a fine one. If we say that Gravel-Os is a good cereal because it has 100% of the recommended daily requirement of iron, this is a reasoned judgment based, in part, on the unstated assumption that it is good to eat cereals that contain 100% of the recommended daily requirement of iron. The distinction becomes even more difficult when you recall that opinions can serve as the premises (reasons) in an argument. Thus, when I say that Gravel-Os is a good cereal because I like its nutty taste, I have a reason to support my conclusion. If I were to add that Gravel-Os is a good cereal because I like its nutty taste and it supplies all of my iron needs for the day, this would increase the strength of the argument.

"Pure" facts that are untainted by opinion are often hard to come by. Take, for example, your daily newspaper. Although news reporters are obligated to provide readers with facts, their opinions certainly color what they report and how they report it. Compare the way two different newspapers cover the same story. One newspaper could make it the headline on page 1, thus making it important news that will be read by many; whereas the other could place it in an inside section in smaller print, thus making sure that fewer people will read the story. Look at the words used to convey the same story. A quiet night in Poland during a period of martial law could be described as "Poland Enforces Martial Law" or as "All Is Quiet in Poland." Both of these headlines could be factually correct, yet they clearly convey different ideas about Polish life.

Most news media (news magazines, newspapers, television news) are biased toward providing information that "sells." The news media often treat complex issues in a very simplistic manner with a heavy emphasis on controversies because they are more interesting than agreements. The usual rules of scientific evidence and reasoning often are abandoned in the news media where deadlines determine the news you get and interest value can drive content. The distinction between fact and opinion is becoming increasingly difficult to discern. As King (1994) noted, television programs like *Hard Copy* are supposedly "reenactments" of real events, but we never know how close the story is to reality. Add some "partially fictionalized" accounts of gruesome real-life murders and the filming of actual police arrests for entertainment shows, and the situation gets even messier. The fuzzy distinction between the real and unreal gets even more difficult now that "virtual reality" computer programs are available that rival "real reality." It is a brave, new world that we are entering, one that makes critical thinking more necessary than ever.

You may be thinking that at least one source of honest facts is your textbooks. Although it is usually safe to assume that text authors do not set out deliberately to mislead students, the facts that they report are also subject to interpretation. Easily quantified and verifiable information, such as the number of soldiers sent to a South American country or the size of the national deficit, is probably correct or as close to correct as possible, presuming that there has been no deliberate attempt to lie. Other facts, such as the sequence of events and their importance in causing a war, or strategies at political conventions, or explanations of poverty in America, need to be interpreted by text authors who will decide how to describe them. The words they use, the events included and omitted, and the amount of information given, all contribute to the "factual" information that is printed. Personal bias can, of course, influence the way the ideas are presented.

It has been said that there is never just one war fought. Each side has its own version, and rarely do they agree. Unfortunately, there is always fighting somewhere around the world so that you can verify this statement for yourself. It is not unusual for each side to claim that the other fired first, or for both sides to claim victory in a battle. Obviously, in the absence of verifiable truth there is no way to know which, if either, side is presenting the facts. As before, the best way to assess the quality of the information provided is to consider the credibility of the reporter. I would prefer a report from an independent third party with firsthand and direct knowledge and appropriate credentials to a report from spokespersons from either of the sides involved in a dispute.

Advertisements make extensive use of opinions dressed up as fact. Consider the advertisements for headache remedies. Often they will show an attractive man in a white laboratory coat, obviously selected to portray a physician. He tells you that, "Speedo works fast on headache pain." Although this may seem like a fact, it is an opinion. "Fast" is a vague term, and therefore it is a matter of judgment. If the appropriate tests with a large number of people had shown that, on the average, Speedo brings pain relief in 20 minutes, this information would be a fact. If you are in doubt as to whether information is fact or opinion, check for vague or evaluative terms (fast, better, lovelier, etc.), and ask yourself how the evaluative term was defined and what type of test was conducted to support the claim. This topic is covered in more detail in the next chapter.

VISUAL ARGUMENTS

He who controls images controls everything.

> —Robert Townsend (quoted in Beilensen & Jackson, 1992, p. 15)

We are living in an increasingly visual society where we get more of our information from visual displays than from words. Television is a major source of information and entertainment for many people. The average television viewer will see approximately 30,000 commercials *every* year. The message in each is mostly the same—whatever your problem is (e.g., rough elbows; waxy, yellow buildup on the kitchen floor; overweight), you can buy a product that will solve it (Postman & Powers, 1992). Much of the persuasive message in television commercials is conveyed through the pictures that we see, often with the accompanying dialogue being of secondary importance. Images are also important in magazines, newspapers, video games, and billboards. The effects of visual images are more difficult to gauge because they are often subtle. Consider a sample of cigarette advertisements. Smoking is linked to beauty, glamour, youth, health, and popularity (Kidd, 1991). A popular theme in visual cigarette advertisements is horses and the outdoors. These beautiful, happy people are smoking and enjoying the good life. The horses suggest ruggedness and an unrestrained independence—just the sort of person who won't be swayed with facts that link smoking with many diseases. Careful market research pinpoints specific markets for cigarette smokers and designs images to appeal to market segments; for example, young women, with no more than a high school education, who wear jeans, and work at blue-collar jobs. The images in these ads are very different from those targeted at more educated women, who are shown reading and talking while they smoke.

Visual images are used effectively in political campaigns. Consider this description of the television advertisements that were used in a "race" for the governor in California. Wilson, the Republican incumbent, used ads that made him appear to be a leader who should not be blamed for California's woes, and Brown, the Democratic challenger, used ads in which she appeared to be a bright solution to California's problems. In Brown's television ads, California is shot in black-and-white scenes of urban decay—only Brown appears in color. By contrast, Wilson shows scenes of serial rapists and stealthy bands of illegal immigrants with Wilson's somber face appearing to be taking care of these grave problems.

Visual images can be powerful determinants of public opinion and policy. Who can forget the pictures of starving children in Somalia, which eloquently spoke of the dire need to send U.S. troops to assist with this disaster? And, who can forget the image of a dead U.S. serviceman being dragged through the dusty streets of Somalia, which moved us to promptly leave Somalia? What if the images had been different? Suppose that instead of the dead peacekeeper being dragged through the street, the media had shown pictures of Somalians receiving food and clean water—people who were alive because of the peacekeepers? The images we are shown have profound effects on how we think.

Figure 5.3 shows some old propagandist images that were popular in Russia in the early and mid-20th century. Note the image of the fat, rich capitalist. His piglike face and bloated body are deliberately unattractive, and his sea of gold depicts his solitary concern with material wealth. Compare this poster to the United States poster from World War II that shows the cartoon-like and menacing faces of our enemies. Notice how close they are to the United States. Look also at the Soviet Army recruiter with the outstretched, pointing finger urging Russians to volunteer. Compare him to the military recruiting posters that were popular in the United States during the same time period, a time when we all knew that "Uncle Sam wants you."

HOW TO CHANGE BELIEFS

We are constantly surrounded by people and groups who want to change what we think and how we act. Nearly every social interaction involves persuasion (Siegel, 1991). Advertising agencies want us to buy whatever product they are selling; political candidates want our votes; the beef council wants us to change what we eat. The list is endless. Some of these beliefs and actions are beneficial, but others are not. One of the best ways to understand the dynamics of changing beliefs is to consider the issues from the perspective of someone who wants to change the beliefs of someone else. You can use this knowledge to change beliefs or to resist change. The following list is loosely adapted from a summary of the attitude change literature (Dember, Jenkins, & Teyler, 1984):

1. Provide a credible source for the information you are presenting. The source of information should be a person or agency with the necessary expertise in the field who is independent with respect to the issue. Additional requirements for assessing the credibility of an information source are provided in this chapter.

2. Anticipate counterarguments, raise them, and provide counterexamples. This is a good technique when debating an issue before an audience. It can leave the opposition with few points to make. As you know, counterarguments weaken the support for a conclusion. This technique allows you to weaken the counterarguments.

3. Don't appear one-sided, especially when the audience may be predisposed to the opposite side. The willingness to use qualifiers and to consider counterarguments makes your position appear more credible.

4. Be direct. "Tell them what to believe." By explicitly stating the conclusion, you eliminate the possibility that the audience will arrive at a different conclusion or not "see" the support for the conclusion that you are advocating.

5. Encourage discussion and public commitment. These variables have not been discussed in this chapter, although they appear in other places in the book. The

FIG. 5.3.   Images of persuasion. The piglike man surrounded with his gold was designed to represent the capitalist. It was a common image during the years when Soviet Communists needed to keep the idea that "capitalism is bad" alive. The U.S. war poster from 1942 presents an ugly image of the Japanese and Nazis very close to taking over the United States, even though the United States was never in physical danger. By contrast, the Soviet recuiter has his arms open to welcome all to the great cause. He bears an uncanny similarity in pose and nonverbal gestures to the American recruiting poster where we were told "Uncle Sam Wants You."

discussion allows the audience to generate reasons and to "own" them or view them as reasons that they provided. Public commitment is a powerful motivator. If someone signs a document or speaks in favor of a position, a host of psychological mechanisms are brought into play. It is a kind of a promise to believe or act in a certain way. This technique was used extensively by Caesar Chavez and others in their attempt to get consumers to boycott grapes. (The motivation for the boycott was to protest the use of certain pesticides on the grapes.)

6. Repeat the conclusion and the reasons that support the conclusion several times. People prefer positions that are familiar to them. You can make the same points in several different ways. Repetition is a useful aid in recall. Thus reasons that are easily remembered (i.e., more available in memory) are more readily used to assess the strength of an argument. (The potent effects of repeated exposure are presented in chapter 8.)

7. Provide as many reasons to support the conclusion as is feasible. As you already know, one way to increase the strength of an argument is by increasing the number of reasons that support it.

8. The message should be easy to comprehend. People are negatively affected by messages that they find incomprehensible (Fiske & Taylor, 1984).

9. You could use any of the 21 common fallacies presented in this chapter. But be wary; they are examples of unsound reasoning. If you want to persuade someone, your reasoning should be sound. Shoddy reasoning is detectable, and if detected, it could (and should) destroy your credibility.

10. Use vivid images that will be difficult to forget and be sure that they make your point.

APPLYING THE FRAMEWORK

Let's consider the steps in applying the general framework for thinking to analyzing arguments.

1. What is the goal?   You'll want to use the skills for analyzing arguments anytime you encounter attempts to persuade you or you attempt to persuade someone that a particular conclusion is either true or likely to be true. Once you become accustomed to "looking for arguments" (in its technical meaning, not in its everyday meaning) and looking at reasons, you'll be surprised how frequently you are bombarded by advertisements, political claims, and other attempts to "change your point of view." You will also need to use the information in this chapter when you make your own arguments.

2. What is known?   This question is about starting points in the thinking process. In analyzing arguments, you begin with statements and determine if they contain an argument. The statements are then evaluated to assess the quality of the argument. The process proceeds by identifying the conclusion and premises and systematically applying the steps of argument analysis in order to reach the goal of making a determination about how good the argument is. When you make an argument, begin with the reasons and counterarguments. Assemble the reasoning so that it supports a conclusion.

3. Which thinking skill or skills will get you to your goal?   The skills of analyzing arguments involve the sequential application of "tests of goodness": How acceptable are the premises, how much support do they provide for the conclusion, and which and how many components are missing? At a minimum, you should be able to apply the three criteria for sound arguments to any set of statements. Unlike most of the other chapters, the skills involved in analyzing arguments are ordered, with less emphasis on selecting the correct skill than on the systematic application of the entire set.

It is almost as important to be able to say why an argument is unsound as it is to be able to identify unsound arguments. You should be able to recognize the 21 fallacies presented in this chapter and explain how each of them violates one of the principles of sound arguments.

The following skills for analyzing arguments were presented in this chapter. If you are unsure about how to use any of these skills, be sure to reread the section in which it is discussed.

- Identifying arguments.
- Diagramming the structure of an argument.
- Evaluating premises for their acceptability.
- Examining the credibility of an information source.
- Determining the consistency, relevance to the conclusion, and adequacy in the way premises support a conclusion.
- Remembering to consider missing components by assuming a different perspective.
- Assessing the overall strength of an argument.
- Recognizing, labeling, and explaining what is wrong with each of the 21 fallacies that was presented.
- Recognizing differences among opinion, reasoned judgment, and fact.
- Understanding how visual arguments can be effective.
- Judging your own arguments for their strength.

4. Have you reached your goal? This is a particularly important question in analyzing arguments because one of the steps involves considering components that are not there. Have you consciously tried to restructure the argument using an opposite perspective? Are you able to make an overall judgment about the strength of the argument? Have you arrived at a sound conclusion? It is important to review the way in which you weighted the supporting premises. Often a decision to weigh a premise as either weak or moderate will have very different effects on your overall assessment of the strength of the argument.

CHAPTER SUMMARY

1. An argument is an attempt to convince the reader (or listener) that a particular conclusion is true based on the reasons presented.

2. All arguments must have at least one conclusion and one premise (reason). Arguments may also have assumptions, qualifiers, and counterarguments.

3. Arguments have structures that can be identified and diagrammed.

4. Sound (good) arguments meet three criteria: The premises are acceptable and consistent, the premises provide support for the conclusion by being relevant to the conclusion and sufficiently strong, and missing components of the argument (e.g., assumptions, counterarguments, qualifiers, premises and rival conclusions) have been considered.

5. When analyzing the strength of an argument, the amount of support each premise supplies to the conclusion is weighed along with the negative effects of counterarguments. Missing components are made explicit and are considered along with the stated components.

6. It is often necessary to assess the credibility of a source of information when deciding on the acceptability of a premise. There are important differences between experts for issues of reality and experts for issues of value.

7. People like to believe that their beliefs and actions are "reasoned"; however, most people are not sensitive to poor or weak reasoning.

8. There is a widespread bias to assign greater importance to reasons that support a conclusion that we favor than to reasons that run counter to a conclusion that we favor. This bias can be reduced by listing reasons and consciously deciding how strongly they support or run counter to a conclusion.

9. A critical part of the analysis of arguments is the consideration of missing parts and misleading statements.

10. Arguments of all sorts have been used to justify genocide and other versions of "ethnic cleansing." The techniques presented here could prevent future horrors, if people are willing to invest the time and hard work in analyzing arguments.

11. Twenty-one common techniques of propaganda were presented. Most can be categorized as types of unsound reasoning in which emotional appeals are often substituted for reasons.

12. A distinction was made among the terms "opinion," "reasoned judgment," and "fact." An opinion is an unsupported statement of preference. Reasoned judgment is a belief that is based on the consideration of premises that support that belief. Facts have a verifiable true value. It is often difficult to discern the difference among these terms in real-life settings.

13. Visual images are used to persuade. Strong images that are difficult to forget can support or refute a conclusion.

14. The beliefs of others can be changed with sound and unsound reasoning. Beware of attempts to manipulate your beliefs with shoddy reasoning techniques.

TERMS TO KNOW

Check your understanding of the concepts presented in this chapter by reviewing their definitions. If you find that you're having difficulty with any term, be sure to reread the section where it is discussed.

Argument. An argument consists of one or more statements that are used to provide support for a conclusion.

Conclusion. The belief or statement that the writer or speaker is advocating.

Reasons. The bases for believing that a conclusion is true or probably true. Note: This word may be singular or plural as there may be one or more reasons for a conclusion. When we reason (singular only), we are following rules for determining if an argument is sound.

Premises. The formal term for the statements that support a conclusion.

Premise Indicators. Key words that often (but not always) signal that the statement or statements that follow them are premises.

Conclusion Indicators. Key words that often (but not always) signal that the statement or statements that follow them are conclusions.

Assumptions. In an argument, assumptions are statements for which no proof or evidence is offered. They may be stated or implied.

Subarguments. Arguments that are used to build the main argument in an extended passage.

Main point. The principal argument in an extended passage.

Qualifier. A constraint or restriction on the conclusion.

Counterargument. Statements that refute or weaken a particular conclusion.

Statement. A phrase or sentence for which it makes sense to ask the question, "Is it true or false?" Questions, commands, and exclamations are *not* statements.

Convergent Structures. A type of argument in which two or more premises support the same conclusion.

Chained (or Linked) Structures. Argument types in which the conclusion of one subargument becomes the premise of a second argument.

Acceptable. A standard for assessing the quality of a premise. A premise is acceptable when it is true or when we can reasonably believe that it is true.

Consistent. A standard for assessing the quality of an argument. When the premises that support a conclusion are not contradictory, they are consistent.

Adequate Grounds. A standard for assessing the quality of an argument. Occurs when the premises provide good support for a conclusion.

Sound Argument. Meets three criteria: (a) Premises are acceptable and consistent, (b) premises are relevant and provide sufficient support for the conclusion, and (c) missing components are considered and evaluated.

Rationalizing. A biased analysis of an argument so that a preferred conclusion will be judged as acceptable or a nonpreferred conclusion will be judged as unacceptable. The process of rationalizing is usually not conscious.

Propaganda. Information presented by proselytizers of a doctrine or belief. The objective is to get the reader or listener to endorse the belief.

Fallacies. Unsound reasoning techniques that are used to change how people think.

Guilt by Association. The propaganda technique of associating a position or person with an undesirable position or person in order to create a negative impression.

Virtue by Association. The propaganda technique of associating a position or person with a desirable position or person in order to create a favorable impression. Compare with guilt by association.

Arguments Against the Person. A form of propaganda that attacks the people who support a cause and not the cause itself.

Appeals to Pity. A propaganda technique that asks for your compassion instead of appealing to your reason.

Popularity. A propaganda technique in which the only reason for the conclusion is that it is endorsed by "everyone."

Testimonials. An appeal in which the sole support for a conclusion is someone's unsupported opinion.

False Dichotomy. An argument in which two possible conclusions or courses of action are presented when there are multiple other possibilities. (Also known as *black or white fallacy*.)

Card Stacking. A propaganda technique that omits important information that might support an unfavored view.

Appeals to Pride or Snobbery. The use of praise or flattery to get its recipient to agree with a position.

Circular Reasoning. An argument structure in which the premise is a restatement of the conclusion.

Slippery Slope. Counterargument for a conclusion in which the premise consists of the idea that because certain events lie along some continuum it is not possible to take an action without affecting all the events on the continuum.

Continuum. Fallacy of the continuum is the same as slippery slope.

Straw Person. A type of propaganda in which an opponent to a conclusion distorts the argument that supports the conclusion by substituting a weaker argument.

Appeals to Ignorance. An argument in which the premise involves something that is unknown.

Knowing the Unknowable. Fallacy in which numbers are provided for events that cannot be quantified.

False Cause. Fallacy in which one event is said to have caused the other because they occur together.

Put Downs. Belittling an opposing point of view so that it would be difficult for a listener to agree with it.

Appeals to Tradition. A propaganda technique that utilizes the reason that what exists is best.

SUGGESTED READINGS

Many of the books suggested in chapter 4 also deal with the general topic of analyzing arguments. If you consult some of the recommended books, you will find some differences in the way certain terms are used. One common practice is to label the topics I've included in chapter 4 as "formal reasoning" and to use the label "informal reasoning" for the topics I've included here. Many of the books published within the last few years have taken a more applied and practical approach than the older texts. My favorites among them include Damer's (1987) *Attacking Faulty Reasoning*, Fogelin's (1987) *Understanding Arguments, An Introduction to Informal Logic*, Thomas' (1986) *Practical Reasoning in Natural Language*, and Govier's (1985) *A Practical Study of Argument*. The book by Fogelin has particularly good sections on legal reasoning and scientific arguments.

Although much has been written over the past three decades about persuasion and propaganda, three classic texts that are still contemporary in their content are Flesch's (1951) *The Art of Clear Thinking* and an even older book by Thouless (1939), *Tests of Logical Reasoning: How to Think Straight*. Also recommended is Thouless' earlier book written in 1932, entitled *Straight and Crooked Thinking*. The last chapter in this gem of a book is called "Thirty-Four Dishonest Tricks." It is a list of persuasive techniques that are as current today as the day it was written. Most important, he told us how to defend against them.

A colorful and well-illustrated source of information on persuasion and propaganda is Sparke, Taines, and Sidell's (1975) *Doublespeak: Language for Sale*. Billing itself as "a guide to propaganda for students of propaganda, for citizens generally who are objects of propaganda, and for propagandists" (p. vii), is Lee's (1953) worthwhile book, *How to Understand Propaganda*. Kahane's (1992) text *Logic and Contemporary Rhetoric: The Use of Reason in Everyday Life* also contains numerous examples of political and advertising techniques designed to sell goods and politics to consumers. This popular book is now in its sixth edition, which shows its lasting popularity. I also highly recommend a clever article by Jason (1987) entitled, "Are Fallacies Common? A Look at Two Debates." In this article, he presented and analyzed examples of irrelevant reasons, false cause, arguments against the person, and popularity that he gleaned from presidential debates. This is good reading for anyone who believes that the issues discussed in this chapter are not important. The presidential candidates freely used many of these fallacies to persuade the American public that they were the best candidate for the presidency.

Finally, three excellent books on propaganda and attitude change are *Age of Propaganda: The Everyday Use and Abuse of Persuasion* (Pratkanis & Aronson, 1992), *The Psychology of Attitudes* (Eagly & Chaiken, 1993), and *The Psychology of Attitude Change and Social Influence* (Zimbardo & Leippe, 1991). All three are excellent sources of "food for thought" and highly recommended for everyone who cares about good thinking.

6

Thinking as Hypothesis Testing

Contents

Suppose that the following is true: You are seriously addicted to heroin and you have two choices of treatment programs.

Program 1: This program is run by former heroin addicts. Your therapist will be a recovered addict who is the same age you are. The literature about this program states that among those who stay with the program for at least 1 year, the success rate is very high (80%). One of the biggest advantages of this program is that your therapist knows what it's like to be seriously addicted and can offer you insights from his own recovery.

Program 2: The therapists in this program have studied the psychology and biology of heroin addiction. The success rate that they provide is much lower than that provided for Program 1 (30%), but the percentage of successes is based on everyone who enters treatment. Your therapist has never been addicted to heroin but has studied various treatment options.

This is an important decision for you. Which do you choose?

UNDERSTANDING HYPOTHESIS TESTING

Research is an intellectual approach to an unsolved problem, and its function is to seek the truth.

—Leedy (1981, p. 7)

Much of our thinking is like the scientific method of **hypothesis testing**. A **hypothesis** is a set of beliefs about the nature of the world; it is usually a belief about a relationship between two or more variables. In order to understand the world around us, we accumulate observations, formulate beliefs or hypotheses (singular is hypothesis), and then observe if our hypotheses are confirmed or disconfirmed. Thus, hypothesis testing is one way of finding out the truth about the world. Formulating hypotheses and making systematic observations that could confirm or disconfirm them is the same method that scientists use when they want to understand events in their academic domain; thus, when thinking is done in this manner, it has much in common with the experimental methods used by scientists.

Explanation, Prediction, and Control

All ... by nature desire knowledge.

—Aristotle (cited in J. Bartlett, 1992, p. 77)

There is a basic need to understand events in life. How many times have you asked yourself questions like, "Why did my good friends get divorced when they seemed perfect for each other?" or "How can we understand why the son of the U.S. Surgeon General, the chief doctor in the United States, is addicted to illegal drugs?" When we try to answer questions like these we often function as an "intuitive scientist." Like the scientist, we have our own theories about the causes of social and physical events. It is important to be able to explain why people react in certain ways (e.g., He's a bigot. She's tired and cranky after work.), to predict the results of our actions (e.g., If I don't study, I'll fail. If I wear designer clothes, people will think I'm cool.), and to control some of the events in our environment (e.g., In order to get a good job in business, I'll have to do well in my accounting course.).

The goal of hypothesis testing is to make accurate predictions about the portion of the world we're dealing with (Holland, Holyoak, Nisbett, & Thagard, 1986). In order to survive and function with maximum efficiency, we must reduce the uncertainty in the environment. One way to reduce uncertainty is to observe sequences of events with the goal of determining predictive relationships. Children, for example, may learn that an adult will appear whenever they cry; your dog may learn that when he stands near the kitchen door, you will let him out; and teenagers may learn that their parents will become angry when they come home late. These are important predictive relationships because they reduce the uncertainty in the environment and allow us to exercise some control over our lives. The process that we use in determining these relationships is the same one that is used when medical researchers discover that cancer patients will go into remission following chemotherapy or that longevity is associated with certain lifestyles. Because the processes are the same, some of the technical concepts in scientific methods are applicable to practical everyday thought.

Inductive and Deductive Methods

Inductive reasoning is a major aspect of cognitive development and plays an important role in both the development of a system of logical thought processes and in the acquisition of new information.

—Pellegrino and Goldman (1983, p. 143)

Sometimes a distinction is made between inductive and deductive methods of hypothesis testing (see chapter 4). In the **inductive method** you observe events and then devise a hypothesis about the events you observed. To take a trivial example, you might notice that Armaund, a retired man whom you know, likes to watch wrestling on television. Then you note that Minnie and Sue Ann, who are also retired older adults, also like to watch wrestling on television. On the basis of these observations, you would hypothesize (invent a hypothesis or explanation) that older people like to watch wrestling. In this way, you would work from your observations to your hypothesis. The inductive method is sometimes described as "going from the specific to the general." In an excellent book entitled *Induction* (Holland et al., 1986), the authors argued that the inductive process is the primary way in which we learn about the nature of the world. They stated, "The study of induction, then, is the study of how knowledge is modified through use" (p. 5).

In the **deductive method**, you begin with a hypothesis that you believe to be true and then make systematic observations to see if your hypothesis is correct. You might logically infer that because wrestling is a sport in which the participants are fairly young, older people enjoy watching it on television. After coming up with this hypothesis, you'd look around to find out if older people like to watch televised wrestling. You would also want to compare them to a group of young adults to see if young adults watch wrestling less often than those who are older. When you begin with a hypothesis and then collect evidence that would confirm or disconfirm it, you are using the deductive method. It is very important that you also search for disconfirming evidence. The deductive method is sometimes described as "going from the general to the specific."

Although a distinction is usually made between these two types of reasoning, in real life they are just different phases of the hypothesis-testing method. Often people observe events, formulate hypotheses, observe events again, reformulate hypotheses, and collect even more observations. The question of whether the observations or the hypothesis comes first is moot because our hypotheses determine what we choose to observe, and our observations determine what our hypotheses will be. It's like the perennial question of which came first, the chicken or the egg. Each process is dependent on the other for its existence. In this way, observing and hypothesizing recycle, with the observations changing the hypotheses and the hypotheses changing what gets observed.

If you are a Sherlock Holmes fan, you'll recognize this process as one that was developed into a fine art by this fictional detective. He would astutely note clues about potential suspects. For example, Sherlock Holmes could remember that the butler had a small mustard-yellow stain on his pants when it is well known that you don't serve mustard with wild goose, which was the main course at dinner that evening. He would use these clues to devise hypotheses like, "the butler must have been in the field where wild mustard plants grow." The master sleuth would then check for other clues that would be consistent or inconsistent with this hypothesis. He might check the butler's boots for traces of the red clay soil that surrounds the field in question. After a circuitous route of hypotheses and observations, Sherlock Holmes would announce, "The butler did it." When called upon to explain how he reached his conclusion, he would utter his most famous reply, "It's elementary, my dear Watson."

Many of our beliefs about the world were obtained with the use of inductive and deductive methods, much like those the great Sherlock Holmes used. We use the principles of inductive and deductive reasoning to generate and evaluate beliefs. Arthur Conan Doyle's fictional detective was invariably right in the conclusions he drew. Unfortunately, it is only in the realm of fiction that mistakes are never made. Let's examine the components of the hypothesis-testing process to see where mistakes can occur.

Operational Definitions

Scientific reasoning and everyday reasoning both require evidence-based justification of beliefs, or the coordination of theory and evidence.

—Kuhn (1993, p. 74)

An **operational definition** tells the reader how to recognize and measure the concept that you're interested in. For example, if you believe that successful women are paid high salaries, then you will have to define "successful" and "high salary" in ways that will allow you to identify who is successful and who receives a high salary. If you've already read chapter 3, then you should recognize the need for operational definitions as being the same as the problem of vagueness. You'd need to provide some statement like, "Successful individuals are respected by their peers and are famous in their field of work." You will find that it is frequently difficult to provide good operational definitions for terms. I can think of several people who are not at all famous, but are successful by their own and other definitions. If you used this operational definition, then you would conclude that homemakers, skilled crafts people, teachers, nurses, and others could not be "successful" based on this definition. Thus, this would seem to be an unsatisfactory operational definition. Suppose, for purposes of illustration, that this is our operational definition to classify people into "successful" and "unsuccessful" categories.

How would you operationally define "paid a high salary?" Suppose you decided on, "earns at least $1,000 per week." Once these terms are operationally defined, you could go around finding out whether successful and unsuccessful women differ in how much they are paid. Operational definitions are important. Whenever you hear people talking about "our irresponsible youth," "knee-jerk liberals," "bleeding hearts," "rednecks," "reactionaries," "fascists," or "feminists," ask them to operationally define their terms. You may find that the impact of their argument is diminished when they are required to be precise about their terms.

Many arguments hinge on operational definitions. Consider, for example, the debate over whether homosexuality is a mental disorder. The issue turns on the answer to operational definitions. What defines a "mental disorder?" Who gets to decide how "mental disorder" should be defined? Does homosexuality possess the defining characteristics? The vitriolic arguments about whether abortion is murder can be transformed into calmer arguments over what is the appropriate definition of murder, and again, the more important question, who is the right authority to define what constitutes murder. Thus, with critical thinking, explosive divisions over issues like abortion will not be resolved, but they will be changed in their character as people consider what is really being argued about.

When you use operational definitions, you avoid the problems of ambiguity and vagueness. Try, for example, to write operational definitions for the following terms: love, prejudice, motivation, good grades, sickness, athletic, beautiful, and maturity.

Independent and Dependent Variables

A **variable** is any measurable characteristic that can take on more than one value. Examples of variables are gender (female and male), height, political affiliation (Republican, Democrat, Communist, etc.), handedness (right, left, ambidextrous), and attitudes toward traditional sex roles (could range from extremely negative to extremely positive). When we test hypotheses, we begin by choosing the variables of interest.

In the opening scenario of this chapter, you were asked to determine which of the two programs would more likely help you kick your heroin habit. In this example, there are two variables—type of treatment, which is the **independent variable** or the one that is under your control (Program 1 and Program 2) and recovery, which is the **dependent variable** or the one that you believe will change as a result of the different treatments (you either [a] will recover from the addiction, or [b] won't recover from the addiction). You want to select the program that will help you to recover. In the jargon of hypothesis testing, you want to know which level of the independent variable will have a beneficial effect on the dependent variable.

The next step in the hypothesis-testing process is to define the variables operationally. Suppose we decide to define "recovery" as staying drug-free for at least 2 years and "not recovering" as staying drug-free for less than 2 years, which would include never being drug-free. It is important to think critically about operational definitions for your variables. If they are not stated in satisfactory terms, the conclusions you draw from your study may be wrong.

Measurement Sensitivity

When we measure something, we systematically assign a number to it for the purposes of quantification. Someone who is taller than you are is assigned a higher number of inches of height than you are. If not, the concept of height would be meaningless.

When we think as scientists and collect information in order to understand the world, we need to consider how we measure our variables. For example, suppose you believe that love is like a fever, and that people in love show fever-like symptoms. To find out if this is true, you could conduct an experiment, taking temperatures from people who are in love and comparing your results to the temperatures of people who are not in love. How will you measure temperature? Suppose that you decide to use temperature headbands that register body temperature with a band placed on the forehead. Suppose further that these bands measure temperature to the nearest degree (e.g., 98°, 99°, 100°, etc.). If being in love does raise your body temperature, but only raises it one half of a degree, you might never know this if you used headband thermometers. Headband thermometers just wouldn't be sensitive enough to register the small increment in body temperature. You would incorrectly conclude that love doesn't raise body temperatures, when in fact it may have. As far as I know, this experiment has never been done, but it is illustrative of the need for sensitive measurement in this and other situations.

Populations and Samples

People make innumerable decisions daily about other people that affect their lives and careers. These decisions are inevitably fraught with errors of judgment that reflect ignorance, personal biases, or stereotypes.

—W. Grant Dahlstrom (1993, p. 393)

In deciding which heroin treatment program to enter, or for that matter, which college to attend or which job to accept, you are making a bet about a future event that necessarily involves uncertainty. Hypothesis-testing principles are used to reduce uncertainty. We cannot eliminate uncertainty, but we can use hypothesis-testing principles to help us make the best choice. In the example that I opened the chapter with, you would have to examine and evaluate information about the success rate of both programs. You would then use this information to make your decision.

The group that we want to know about is called a **population**. Because we obviously can't study every heroin addict to determine which program has more successes, we need to study a subset of this population. A subset of a population is called a **sample**. In this example, all of the people who entered each of the programs constitute the sample.

Biased and Unbiased Samples

We want our sample to be representative of our population. To be representative, the addicts in our sample would need to be both women and men, from all socioeconomic levels, all intellectual levels, rural and urban areas, and so on. We need **representative samples** so that we can generalize our results and decide, in general, that one program is more successful than the other. **Generalization** refers to using the results obtained with a sample to infer that similar results would be obtained from the population, if everyone in the population had been measured.

What happens when the sample is not representative of the population? Suppose that one program is very expensive and one is county-run to serve the poor. These are examples of **biased samples**. Because they are not representative or unbiased, you could not use these samples to draw conclusions about the population of all heroin addicts.

The biggest fiasco in sampling history probably occurred in 1936 when the *Literary Digest* mailed over 10 million straw ballots to people's homes in order to predict the winner of the presidential election that was to be held that year (Kimble, 1978). The results from this large sample were clear-cut: The next president would be Alf Landon. What, you don't remember learning about President Landon? I'm sure that you don't because Franklin Delano Roosevelt was elected president of the United States that year. What went wrong? The problem was in how they sampled voters. They mailed ballots to subscribers to their literary magazine, to people listed in the phone book, and to automobile owners. Remember, this was 1936 and only the affluent belonged to the select group of people who subscribed to literary magazines, or had phones, or owned automobiles.

They failed to sample the large number of poorer voters, many of whom voted for Roosevelt instead of Landon. Because of biased sampling, they could not generalize their results to the voting patterns of the population. Even though they sampled a large number of voters, the results were wrong because they sampled in a biased way.

It is often not easy to recognize the profound effect that biased sampling can have on the information that we receive. For example, phone-in polls are very popular, probably because someone makes money from the phone calls. Suppose that a phone-in poll shows that 75% of the people who responded to a question about the death penalty were opposed to it. What can we conclude from this poll? Absolutely nothing! Polls of this sort are called *slops*, which stands for *selected listener opinion polls* and also describes their worth. Only people with extreme views on a topic will take the time and expense to call in their opinions. Even though these polls are usually preceded with warnings like "this is a nonscientific survey," the announcer then goes on to present meaningless results as though they could be used to gauge public opinion.

Another pitfall in sampling is the possibility of **confounding**. Because patients in these two hypothetical heroin treatment programs differ systematically in more than one way—that is, Program 1 provides peer counseling and the addicts in this program are very wealthy, whereas addicts in Program 2 get a different type of treatment and they are very poor—we cannot determine if any differences in recovery rate are due to the type of treatment or income levels of the patients. Because you can't separate the effect of type of treatment and income, you could not use these results to decide which treatment is more successful.

Usually, scientists use **convenience samples**. They study a group of people who are readily available. The most frequent subjects in psychology experiments are college students and rats. The extent to which you can generalize from these samples depends on your research question. If you want to understand how the human visual system works, college students should be useful as subjects, especially if you want to know about young, healthy eyes. If, on the other hand, you want to understand sex role stereotyping in adults, college students would not be a representative sample because college students tend to be less stereotyped than other adults. In this case, you could only generalize about college students.

In a recent election in California, there was much debate over the issue of establishing a voucher system as a means of paying for K–12 education. As you may know, some people believe that education would improve if parents received vouchers in an amount that is equal to what the state pays to educate a child in the public schools. The parents could then use this voucher to select any school that they deemed best for their children. This is a complex issue as proponents argue that the competition would improve all schools, and opponents argue that wealthy parents would supplement the voucher and send their children to private schools, whereas the poor parents would have to use the vouchers at cheaper and inferior schools. I do not want to debate the issue of vouchers here, but I do want to repeat an advertisement that was continually seen during the pre-election period. It went something like this:

> The public schools in California are doing a poor job of educating our children. Did you know that California high school students score much lower than high school students from Mississippi on the college entrance examinations?

There are many ways the thinking in this advertisement could be criticized (including the obvious slur on the state of Mississippi), but for the purpose of this discussion consider only the nature of the samples that are being compared. Only students who are planning to attend college take the college entrance examinations. A much greater proportion of high school students in California take these examinations than those in Mississippi. Although I don't know what the actual figures are, suppose that the top 40% of California high school graduates take these exams but only the top 10% of Mississippi high school graduates take these exams. Can you see why you would expect Mississippi students to score higher because of the bias in sampling? There are other reasons why we might expect that these results do not relate to the quality of education. California has many recent immigrants, which means many students whose English is not as good as that of native English speakers. This fact would also lower statewide averages. Again, this is a sampling problem because comparable groups that differ only on the variable of interest (state in which education was obtained) are not being compared. Of course, it is possible that students in Mississippi are getting a better education than those in California, but we cannot conclude this from these data.

Sample Size

Given a thimbleful of facts, we rush to make generalizations as large as a tub.

—Gordon Allport (1954, p. 8)

The number of subjects you include in your sample is called the **sample size**. Suppose that treatment Program 1 has had 6 patient/subjects and Program 2 has had 10 patient/subjects. Both of these numbers are too small to determine the success rate of the treatments. (A subject is a person, animal, or entity who participates in an experiment.) When scientists conduct experiments, they often use large numbers of subjects. If, for some reason, they cannot use a large number of subjects, they may need to be more cautious or conservative in the conclusions that they derive from their research. Although a discussion of the number of subjects needed in an experiment is beyond the scope of this book, it is important to keep in mind that for most everyday purposes, we cannot generalize about a population by observing how only a few people respond.

Suppose this happened to you: After months of deliberation, you finally decided to buy a Chevrolet Camero. You found that both *Consumer Reports* and *Road and Track* magazines have given the Camaro a good rating. The Camaro is priced within your budget, and you like its racing stripes and "sharp" appearance. On your way out the door to close the deal, you run into a close friend and tell her about your intended purchase. "A Camaro!" she shrieks. "My brother-in-law bought one and it's a tin can. It's constantly breaking down on the freeway. He's had it towed so often that the rear tires need replacing." What do you do?

Most people would have a difficult time completing the purchase because they are insufficiently sensitive to sample size issues. The national magazines presumably tested many cars before they determined their rating. Your friend's brother-in-law is a single subject. You should place greater confidence in results obtained with large samples than in results obtained with small samples (assuming that the "experiments" were equally good). Yet, many people find the testimonial of a single person, especially if it's someone they know, more persuasive than information gathered from a large sample.

We tend to ignore the importance of having an adequately large sample size when we function as intuitive scientists. This is why testimonials are so very powerful in persuading people what to do and believe. But testimonials are based on the experiences of only one person, and often that person is being paid to say that some product or purchase is good. I have an advertisement for a psychic phone line that offers "real cases" as proof that psychics are effective sources for advice on a variety of problems: "A Lansing, Michigan, resident winds up with a more positive outlook in her life after one conversation. ... And a woman from Pittsburgh, Pennsylvania, feels as if the psychic has reached into her soul" (*Cosmopolitan*, January, 1994). The reference to a particular, unnamed person along with the name of a city and state makes these comments more personal and authentic sounding. The more specific the information we receive, the more likely we are to believe that it is true. Give me a break!

I would like to dismiss this sort of "evidence" as hogwash that no one would fall for, but I know differently. A family member spent over $300 in calls to psychics when struggling with decisions regarding her critically ill husband. This was money that she did not have for advice that was, at best, harmless, and, at worst, caused her to ignore the recommendations of the hospital staff. I later was told that psychics are not permitted to predict that anyone will die, so they gave her false hope, which made the death even more difficult to bear. I am telling you this true personal anecdote because I hope that it will be effective in causing you to think about the sort of evidence that you would need to spend hundreds of dollars for advice by a paid stranger who has no credentials or training in psychology or science.

Variability

The term **variability** is used to denote the fact that all people are not the same. Suppose that you know someone who "smoked like a haystack" and lived to be 100 years old. Does this mean that the hype about the negative effects of smoking on health are wrong? Of course not. The effect of smoking on health was determined by numerous separate investigators using large numbers of subjects. Not everyone responds in the same way, or maintains the same opinion, or has the same abilities. It is important to remember the role of variability in understanding results.

Several years ago, there was much excitement over the use of laetrile, an extract from apricot pits, as a cure for cancer. Although the U.S. medical establishment found that it was worthless in the fight against cancer, many people continued to believe that it could be used as a cure. Suppose you read about someone who was diagnosed as having cancer, and this person then took laetrile. Later this lucky individual recovered from her cancer. What can you conclude? Would you be willing to conclude that, at least for some people, laetrile can cure or help to cure cancer? This conclusion is unwarranted. Some people recover from cancer, whereas others do not. Just as people are variable in the beliefs and attitudes that they maintain, they are also variable in the way they respond to disease. With a sample size of one, we cannot conclude that the laetrile contributed to her cure. Large-scale studies are needed that compare the survival rates of groups of people on laetrile with groups of people who used other forms of cancer treatments to decide if laetrile can be beneficial in the treatment of cancer. When these tests were conducted by the U.S. government, laetrile was found to be worthless. It's easy to see how desperate cancer patients can be misled into believing results obtained with a very small number of people.

People's willingness to believe that results obtained from a few subjects can be generalized to the entire population is called the **law of small numbers** (Tversky & Kahneman, 1971). In fact, we should be more confident when predicting to or from large samples than small samples (Kunda & Nisbett, 1986). In an experimental investigation of this phenomenon (Quattrone & Jones, 1980), college students demonstrated their belief that if one member of a group made a particular decision, then the other members of that group would make the same decision. This result was especially strong when the college students were observing the decisions of students from other colleges. Thus, it is easy to see how a belief in the law of small numbers can maintain prejudices and stereotypes. We tend to believe that the actions of a single group member are indicative of the actions of the entire group. Have you ever heard someone say, "_____'s (fill in your group) are all alike?" An acquaintance once told me that all Jamaicans are sneaky thieves. She came to this conclusion after having one bad experience with a person from Jamaica. Expressions like this one are manifestations of the law of small numbers. Can you see how the law of small numbers can also explain the origin of many prejudices like racism? A single memorable event involving a member of a group with which we have little contact can color our beliefs about the other members of that group. Generally, when you collect observations about people and events, it is important to collect a large number of observations before you reach a conclusion.

There is one exception to the general principle that we need large samples in order to make valid generalizations about a population. The one exception occurs when everyone in the population is exactly the same. If, for example, everyone in the population of interest responded exactly the same way to any question (e.g., Do you approve of the death penalty?) or any treatment (e.g., had no "heart attacks" when treated with a single aspirin), then sample size would no longer be an issue. Of course, all people are not the same. You may be thinking that this was a fairly dumb statement because everyone knows that people are different. Unfortunately, research has shown that most of us tend to underestimate the variability of groups with which we are unfamiliar.

Minority members of any group often report that the leader or other group members will turn to them and ask, "What do African Americans (or women or Hispanics, or Asians, or whatever the minority is) think about this issue?" It's as though the rest of the group believe that the few minority members of their group can speak for the minority group as a whole. This is a manifestation of the belief that groups other than the ones to which we belong are much more homogeneous (less variable) than the groups to which we belong.

The ability to make accurate predictions depends, in part, on the ability to make accurate assessments of variability. It is important to keep the concept of variability in mind whenever you're testing hypotheses either formally in a research setting or informally as you try to determine relationships in the everyday environment.

DETERMINING CAUSE

Do you believe that children who are neglected become teenage delinquents?
Does jogging relieve depression?
Will a diet that is low in fat increase longevity?
Do clothes make the man?
Will strong spiritual beliefs give you peace of mind?
Does critical thinking instruction improve how you think outside the classroom?

All of these questions concern a causal relationship in which one variable (e.g., neglect) is believed to cause another variable (e.g., delinquency). What sort of information do we need to determine the truth of causal relationships?

Isolation and Control of Variables

Stop and think for a minute about the way you would go about deciding if neglecting children causes them to become delinquent when they are teenagers. You could decide to conduct a long-term study in which you would divide children into groups—telling some of their parents to cater to their every need, others to neglect them occasionally, and still others to neglect their children totally. You could require everyone to remain in their groups, catering to or neglecting their children as instructed until the children reach their teen years, at which time you could count up the number of children in each group who became delinquents—remembering, of course, that you would have to define operationally the term "delinquent." This would be a good, although totally unrealistic, way to decide if neglect causes delinquency. It's a good way because this method would allow you to control how much neglect each child received and to isolate the cause of delinquency, as this would be the only systematic difference among the people in each group. It's unrealistic to the point of being ludicrous, because very few people would comply with your request to cater to or neglect their children. Furthermore, it would also be unethical to ask people to engage in potentially harmful behaviors.

In some experimental settings it is possible to isolate and control the variables you're interested in. If you wanted to know if grading students for coursework will make college students work harder and therefore learn more, you could randomly assign college students to different grading conditions. Half the students could be graded as pass or fail (no letter grades), whereas the other students would receive traditional letter grades (A, B, C, D, or F). At the end of the semester, all students would take the same final exam. If the average final exam score for the students who received grades was statistically significantly higher than for the students in the pass–fail condition, we'd conclude that grades do result in greater learning. (See chapter 7 for a discussion of significant differences.)

Can you see why it's so important to be able to assign students at random to either the graded or pass–fail conditions instead of just letting them pick the type of grading they want? It is possible that the students who would pick the pass–fail grading are less motivated or less intelligent than the students who would prefer to get grades or vice versa. If the students could pick their own grading condition, we wouldn't know if the differences we found were due to the differences in grading practices or due to differences in motivation or intelligence, or some other variable that differs systematically as a function of which grading condition the students select.

Let's return to the question of whether child neglect causes delinquency. Given the constraint that you cannot tell parents to neglect their children, how would you go about deciding if child neglect causes delinquency? You could decide to find a group of parents and ask each about the amount of care he or she gives to each child. Suppose you found that, in general, the more that children are neglected, the more likely they are to become teenage delinquents. Because you lost the control over your variables by not assigning parents to catering and neglecting groups, it is not possible, on the basis of this experiment alone, to conclude that neglect causes delinquency. It is possible that parents who neglect their children differ from caring parents in other ways. Parents who tend to neglect their children may also encourage drug use, or engage in other lifestyle activities that contribute to the development of teenage delinquency. Because parents couldn't be assigned to groups, it would take many different studies to establish conclusively this relationship. A point that is made in several places in this book is that just because two variables occur together (neglect and delinquency) doesn't necessarily mean that one caused the other to occur.

Three-Stage Experimental Designs

When researchers want to be able to make strong causal claims, they use a three-stage experimental design (Kimble, 1978). An experimental design is a plan for how observations will be made:

1. The first stage involves creating different groups that are going to be studied. In the example about the effect of pass–fail grading on how much is learned, the two

groups would be those who receive a letter grade and those who receive a grade of either "pass" or "fail." It is important that the two groups differ systematically only on this dimension. You wouldn't want all the students in the letter grade group to take classes taught by Professor Longwinded whereas those in the pass–fail group take classes taught by Professor Mumbles. One professor may be a better teacher, and students may learn more in one condition than the other because of this confounding variable. One way to avoid this confound is to assign half of the students in each class to each grading condition with the assignment of students to either group done at random. Strong causal claims will involve equating the groups at the outset of the experiment. *The random assignment of subjects to groups is essential in determining cause.*

2. The second stage involves the application of the "experimental treatment." If we were conducting a drug study, one group would receive the drug and the other group would not receive the drug. Usually, the "nondrug" group would receive a **placebo,** which would look and/or taste like the drug, but would be chemically inert. The reason for a placebo is to avoid any effects of subjects' beliefs or expectancies. The topic of expectancies and the way they can bias results is discussed later in this chapter. As discussed in an earlier section, when these sorts of controls were used to determine the effectiveness of laetrile, it was found to be worthless against cancer. In the grading example, the term "treatment" doesn't fit well, but it corresponds to taking the course under the two different grading conditions.

3. Evaluation is the final phase. Measurements are taken and the two (or more) groups are compared on some outcome measure. If the study involved a new drug for headaches, the two groups would be compared on measures of headache frequency and severity. In the grading example, final examination scores for students in the letter grade group would be compared to the scores for students in the pass–fail group. If students in one group performed significantly better than the students in the other group, then we would have strong support for the claim that one grading method *caused* students to study harder and learn more than the other.

Of course, we are not always able to equate groups at the outset and randomly assign subjects to groups, but when we can, results can be used to make stronger causal claims than in less controlled conditions.

Consider this hypothetical example:

> Researchers at Snooty University have studied the causes of divorce. They found that 33% of recently divorced couples reported that they had serious disagreements over money during the 2-year period that preceded the divorce. The researchers concluded that disagreements over money are a major reason why couples divorce. They go on to suggest that couples should learn to handle money disagreements as a way of reducing the divorce rate.

What, if anything, is wrong with this "line of reasoning"? Plenty. First, we have no data from a comparison group that did not divorce (i.e., no control group). Maybe 33% of all families disagree about money; maybe the number is even higher in families that stay together. Second, there is no reason to believe that disagreements over money *caused* or even contributed to divorce. Maybe families in the process of breaking up disagree more about everything. Third, there is the problem of retrospective review, a topic that is discussed in the next section. Studies like this one are found everywhere, from radio talk shows, news reports, scientific journals, and people's casual examinations of life. If you rely on the principles of hypothesis testing to interpret findings like this one, you are less likely to be bamboozled.

Using the Principles of Isolation and Control

In an earlier chapter, I presented Piaget's notion that people who have attained the highest level of cognitive development can reason about hypothetical situations. Piaget called the highest level of cognitive development the *formal stage of thought*. He developed several different tasks that could be used to identify people who could think at this level. If you already read Chapter 5, then you will recall the "combinatorial reasoning" task devised by Piaget. It required a planful and orderly procedure for combining objects. Another one of Piaget's tasks involved using the principles of isolation and control that are integral to hypothesis testing. Try this task.

Bending Rods. This task is to determine which of several variables affects the flexibility of rods. Imagine that you are given a long vertical bar with 12 rods hanging from it. Each rod is made of either brass, copper, or steel. The rods come in two lengths and two thicknesses. Your task is to find which of the variables (material, length, or thickness) influence how much the rods will bend. You can test this by pressing down on each rod to see how much it bends. You may perform as many comparisons as you like until you can explain what factors are important in determining flexibility. It may help you to visualize the setup as presented in Fig. 6.1. What do you need to do to prove that length, or diameter, or the material rods are constructed from or some combination of these variables is important in determining flexibility? Stop now and write out your answer to this problem. Don't go on until you have finished this problem.

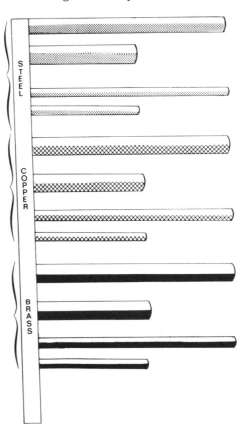

FIG. 6.1. Bending rods. How would you determine whether material, length, or thickness affects rod flexibility?

Solving the Task of Bending Rods. How did you go about exploring the effect of length, diameter, and material on rod flexibility? In order to solve this problem, you had to consider the possible factors that contribute to rod flexibility, and then systematically hold constant all of the variables except one. This is a basic concept in experimental methods. If you wanted to know if material was an important factor, which rods would you test? You would bend a brass rod, a copper rod, and a steel rod of the same length and diameter. This would hold constant the length and diameter variables while testing the material variable. Some possible tests of this would be to compare flexibility among the short and wide brass, copper, and steel rods. Similarly, if you wanted to find out if length is important, you would bend a short and a long rod of the same diameter that was constructed with the same material. An example of this would be to compare the short and wide copper rod with the long and wide copper rod.

How would you decide if diameter influences rod flexibility? By now it should be clear that you would compare two rods of the same material and length and different diameters. You could test this by bending a short and wide steel rod with a short and thin steel rod. Thus, you should be able to recognize that the same principles used in hypothesis testing were needed in this task and be able to apply them correctly in order to solve this seemingly unrelated problem.

Prospective and Retrospective Research

Consider a medical example: Some health psychologists believe that certain stressful experiences can cause people to develop cancer. If this were your hypothesis, how would you determine its validity? One way would be to ask cancer patients if they had anything particularly stressful happen to them just before they were diagnosed as having cancer. If the stress caused the cancer, it would have to precede (come first in time) the development of cancer. When experiments are conducted in this manner, they are called **retrospective experiments**. Retrospective experiments look back in time to understand causes for later events. There are many problems with this sort of research. As discussed in chapter 2, memories are selective and malleable. It is possible that knowledge of one's cancer will change how one's past is remembered. Moderately stressful events like receiving a poor grade in a college course may be remembered as being traumatic. Happier events, like getting a raise, may be forgotten. It's even possible that the early stages of the cancer were causing stress instead of the stress causing the cancer. Thus, it will be difficult to determine if stress causes cancer from retrospective research.

A better method for understanding causative relationships is **prospective research**. In prospective research, you identify possible causative factors when they occur and then look forward in time to see if the hypothesized result occurs. In a prospective study, you would have many people record stressful life events when they occur (e.g., death of a spouse, imprisonment, loss of a job) and then see which people develop cancer. If the people who experience more stressful events are more likely to develop cancer, this result would provide support for your hypothesis.

Most of the research we conduct as intuitive scientists is retrospective. We often seek explanations for events after they have occurred. How many times have you tried to understand why a seemingly angelic child committed a serious crime, or why a star rookie seems to be losing his touch, or why the underdog in a political race won? Our retrospective attempts at explanations are biased by selective memories and lack of systematic observations. (See the section on Hindsight and Forethought in chapter 8 for a related discussion.)

Correlation and Cause

The process by which children turn experience into knowledge is exactly the same, point for point, as the process by which those whom we call scientists make scientific knowledge.

—Holt (1989, p. 93)

What you are about to read is absolutely true: As the weight of children increases, so does the number of items that they are likely to get correct on standardized tests of intelligence. In other words, heavier children answer more questions correctly than lighter ones. Before you start stuffing mashed potatoes into your children in an attempt to make them smarter, stop and think about what this means. Does it mean that gaining weight will make children smarter? Certainly not! Children get heavier as they get older, and older children answer more questions correctly than younger ones.

In the preceding example, the variables weight and number of questions answered correctly are related. An increase in one variable is associated with an increase in the other variable—as weight increases the number of questions answered correctly concomitantly (at the same time) increases. **Correlated variables** are two or more variables that are related. If you've already read chapter 5, then you should recognize this concept as the fallacy of false cause.

People frequently confuse correlation with cause. Consider the following example: Wally and Bob were arguing about the inheritance of intelligence. Wally thought about everyone he knew and concluded that because smart parents tend to have smart children, and dumb parents tend to have dumb children, intelligence is an inherited characteristic. Bob disagreed with Wally's line of reasoning, although he concurred with the facts that Wally presented. He agreed that if the parents score high on intelligence tests, then their children will also tend to score high, and if the parents score low on intelligence tests, then their children will also tend to score low. When two measures are related in this way—that is, they tend to rise and fall together—they have a **positive correlation.** Although parents' intelligence and their children's intelligence are positively correlated, we cannot infer that parents caused their children (through inheritance or any other means) to be intelligent. It is possible that children affect the intelligence of their parents, or that both are being affected by a third variable that hasn't been considered. It is possible that diet, economic class, or other lifestyle variables determine intelligence levels, and because parents and children eat similar diets and have the same economic class, they tend to be similar in intelligence.

Let's consider a somewhat different example. Many people have taken up jogging in the belief that exercise will help them to lose weight. The two variables in this example are *exercise* and *weight.* I've heard people argue that because there are no fat athletes (except perhaps sumo wrestlers), exercise must cause people to be thin. I hope that you can think critically about this claim.

It does seem to be true that exercise and weight are correlated. People who tend to exercise a great deal also tend to be thin. This sort of correlation, in which the tendency to be high on one variable (exercise) is associated with the tendency to be low on the other variable (weight), is called a **negative correlation.** Let's think about the relationship between exercise and weight. There are several possibilities: (a) It is possible that exercise causes people to be thin; or (b) It is possible that people who are thin tend to exercise more because it is more enjoyable to engage in exercise when you are thin; or (c) It is possible that a third variable, like concern for one's health, or some inherited trait, is responsible for both the tendency to exercise and the tendency to be thin.

Perhaps there are inherited body types that naturally stay thin and also are graced with strong muscles that are well suited for exercise.

If you wanted to test the hypothesis that exercise causes people to lose weight, then you would use the three design stages described earlier. If the subjects who were assigned at random to the exercise group were thinner after the treatment period than those in a no-exercise condition, then you could make a strong causal claim for the benefits of exercise in controlling weight.

Actually, the question of causation is usually complex. It is probably more accurate to use the word "influence" instead of cause because there is usually more than a single variable that affects another variable. A colleague (Dr. Richard Block at Montana State University) suggested the following example to clarify this point: When a man is being hanged for having committed a crime, is it because someone gave him money to buy the weapon he used in the crime, or is it because someone saw him commit the crime, or is it because no one stopped him? A single direct cause is rarely identifiable.

In summary, when considering the relationship between variables there are several possible explanations. Of course, it is also possible that they are unrelated or not correlated. Some examples of variables that are not correlated are typing speed and hat size, number of hairs on your head and grade point average, and height and reaction time on a driving test.

Some positive correlations are height and weight, number of churches and number of prostitutes in a city (both increase with increases in population), and the number of ice cream cones sold and number of reported rapes (both increase with increases in temperature). Two negative correlations are amount of fluoride children consume and number of cavities they get, and hours spent studying and number of courses failed. In understanding the relationship between two correlated variables, it is possible that Variable A caused the changes in Variable B (A → B), or that Variable B caused the changes in Variable A (B → A), or both A and B caused changes in each other (A → B and B → A) or that both were caused by a third variable C (C → A and C → B).

Illusory Correlation

An amusing anecdote of attributing cause to events that occur together was presented by Munson (1976):

> A farmer was traveling with his wife on a train when he saw a man across the aisle take something out of a bag and begin eating it. "Say, Mister," he asked, "What's that thing you're eating?"
>
> "It's a banana," the man said. "Here, try one."
>
> The farmer took it, peeled it, and just as he swallowed the first bite, the train roared into a tunnel. "Don't eat any, Maude," he yelled to his wife. "It'll make you go blind!" (p. 277)

Do blondes really have more fun? A popular advertisement for hair dye would like you to believe that having blonde hair will cause you to have more fun. Many people believe that they see many blondes having fun; therefore, blondes have more fun than brunettes, for example. The problem with this sort of observation is that there are many blondes who are not having more fun (a term badly in need of an operational definition) than brunettes, but because they are at home or in other places where you are unlikely to see them, they don't get considered. The term **illusory correlation** has been coined for the erroneous belief that two variables are related when, in fact, they are not (Chapman & Chapman, 1967, 1969).

Professionals and nonprofessionals alike maintain beliefs about relationships in the world. These beliefs guide the kinds of observations they make and how they determine if a relationship exists between two variables.

Let's try another example. Do you believe that you often see fat people overeating? Most people believe that they do; yet, research has shown that overweight adults tend to eat less in public places than normal-weight people. We expect to see overweight people overeating and, therefore, we believe that we see the world according to our beliefs. Beware of illusory correlations when you function as an intuitive scientist. This phenomenon works to maintain stereotypes (e.g., redheads are hot-tempered, Scots are cheap, women can't understand math, etc.). Our beliefs about relationships between variables guide the observations we make and the way we utilize this information to formulate conclusions.

Validity

The **validity** of a measure is usually defined as the extent to which it measures what you want it to measure. If I wanted to measure intelligence and measured the length of your big toe, this would obviously be invalid. Other examples of validity are less obvious. A popular radio commercial, touting the benefits of soup, points out that tomato soup has more vitamin A than do eggs. This is true, but it is not a valid measure of the goodness of tomato soup. Eggs are not a good source of vitamin A. Thus, the wrong comparisons were made, and the measure does not support the notion that soup is an excellent food. If you've already read chapter 5, then you should realize that the claim that tomato soup has more vitamin A than eggs does not support the conclusion that "soup is good food." It may well be true that soup is an excellent source of vitamins, but claims like this one don't support that conclusion.

How would you react to this claim: "The Baroness is a sleek new luxury car that will provide its owner with dependable transportation for many years to come. In fact, in a recent laboratory test, the Baroness went from 0 to 60 miles per hour in 7 seconds flat, beating out the six other cars in the competition." Is the acceleration speed of a car a valid index of its dependability? Probably not. Even if the figure is accurate, it is not a valid measure of dependability. If you want to know about dependability, you'll want to know about the frequency of repairs, average number of miles the car can be expected to be driven before it gets turned into scrap metal, and how it performs on impact.

Convergent Validity

When several different measures all converge onto the same conclusion, the measures are said to have **convergent validity**. If, for example, you wanted to measure charisma—the psychological trait that is something more than charm that people as diverse as Tina Turner, Bill Cosby, and Roseanne Barr are said to possess—you'd need convergent validity for your measure. People who scored high on your charisma test should also be the ones who are selected for leadership positions and have other personality traits that are usually associated with charisma. If the class wallflower scored high on your test of charisma, you'd need to rethink the validity of your test.

People outside the laboratory also need to be mindful of the need for convergent validity. Before you decide that your classmate, Willa Mae, is shy because she hesitates to talk to you, you need to determine if she acts shy with other people in other places. If she frequently speaks up in class, you wouldn't want to conclude that she is a shy person because this inconsistency in her behavior would signal a lack of convergent validity.

The idea of convergent validity is very similar to the topic of convergent argument structures that was presented in chapter 5. If you have already read chapter 5, then you should recall that the strength of an argument is increased when many premises support (or converge on) a conclusion. This is exactly the same situation as when several sources of evidence support the same hypothesis. The language used in these two chapters is different (support for a conclusion vs. support for a hypothesis), but the underlying ideas are the same: The more reasons or evidence we can provide for believing that something is true, the greater the confidence we can have in our belief.

Illusory Validity

Everyone complains of his memory and no one complains of his judgement.

—La Rochefoucauld (1613–1680)

Both professionals and nonprofessionals place great confidence in their conclusions about most life events, even when their confidence is objectively unwarranted. Overconfidence in judgments is called **illusory validity**. In an experimental investigation of this phenomenon, Oskamp (1965) found that as clinicians were given more information about patients, they became more confident in the judgments they made about patients. What is interesting about this result is they were not more accurate in judgment, only more confident that they were right. Why do people place confidence in fallible judgments? There are several reasons why we persist in maintaining confidence in our judgments. A primary factor is the selective nature of memory. Consider this personal vignette: As a child, I would watch Philadelphia Phillies baseball games on television with my father. As each batter would step up to home plate, my father would excitedly yell, "He's going to hit a home run, I just know it!" Of course, he was usually wrong. (Phillies fans had to be tough in the 1950s and 1960s). On the rare occasions when a Phillies batter actually did hit a home run, my father would talk about it for weeks. "Yep, I knew as soon as he stepped up to home plate that he would hit a home run. I can always tell just by looking at the batter." In this instance, and countless others, we selectively remember our successful judgments and forget our unsuccessful ones. This tends to bolster confidence in the judgments we make.

A second reason for the illusion of validity is the failure to seek or consider disconfirming evidence. (See chapter 8 for an additional discussion of this phenomenon.) This is the primary reason people tend to believe that variables are correlated when they are not correlated. Suppose that you have the job of personnel officer in a large corporation. Over a period of a year, you hire 100 new employees for your corporation. How would you go about deciding if you're making good (valid) hiring decisions? Most people would check on the performance of their new employees. Suppose that you did this and found that 92% of the new employees were performing their jobs in a competent, professional manner. Would this bolster your confidence in your judgments? If you answered yes to this question, you forgot to consider disconfirming evidence. What about the people you didn't hire? Have most of them gone on to become vice presidents at General Motors? If you found that 100% of the people you didn't hire are superior employees at your competitor's corporation, you would have to revise your confidence in your judgmental ability.

Part of the reason that we fail to utilize disconfirming evidence is that it is often not available. Personnel officers don't have information about the employees they don't hire. Similarly, we don't know much about the person we chose not to date, or the course we didn't take, or the house we didn't buy. Thus, on the basis of partial information, we may conclude that our judgments are better than they objectively are.

In a scathing review of the Rorschach test (the test that is commonly known as the inkblot test because subjects are asked to tell what they see in amorphous, symmetrical blots of ink), Dawes (1994) concluded that it is not a valid measure of mental functioning. That is, there is no evidence that it is useful in diagnosing or treating mental disorders (although it is possible to determine if someone gives unusual answers). This means that the Rorschach has no validity. Despite these empirical results, Dawes reported that some psychotherapists respond to this fact with, "Yes, I know that it has no validity, but I find it useful." Do you see why this is a ridiculous statement? If it has no validity, then it cannot be useful. If therapists believe that it is useful, they are fooling themselves and demonstrating the phenomenon of illusory validity. It may seem useful because they interpret the responses in ways that they believe make sense, but its only real value is as a clear demonstration of the biases that we maintain.

Reliability

The **reliability** of a measure is the consistency with which it measures what it's supposed to measure. If you used a rubber ruler that could stretch or shrink to measure the top of your desk, you'd probably get a different number each time you measured it. Of course, we want our measurements to be reliable.

Researchers in the social and physical sciences devote a great deal of time to the issue of reliable measurement. We say that an intelligence test, for example, is reliable when the same person obtains scores that are in the same general range whenever she takes the test. Few of us even consider reliability when we function as intuitive scientists. When we decide if a professor or student is prejudiced, we often rely on one or two samples of behavior without considering if the individual is being assessed reliably.

Suppose that you learn that your friend Ricardo failed a college course that all others easily passed. Could you conclude that his teacher is prejudiced? You'd need to collect many other observations of the same teacher to see how consistently or reliably Hispanic men failed his class. If there is an unusually high failure rate among Hispanic men (or whatever group you're interested in) in his class compared to their failure rate in other classes, then you'd have a strong case for the inference that the teacher is prejudiced. Without careful measurement and, in this case, a larger sample size, you cannot infer that the professor is prejudiced.

THINKING ABOUT ERRORS

To a scientist a theory is something to be tested. He seeks not to defend his beliefs, but to improve them. He is, above everything else, an expert at "changing his mind."

—Wendell Johnson

When we try to understand relationships by devising and testing hypotheses, we will sometimes be wrong. This idea is expanded on more fully in chapter 7, which concerns understanding probabilities. For now, consider this possibility: Suppose that you drive into work every day with a friend. Every morning you stop at a drive-up restaurant window and buy coffee. You decide that instead of hassling every morning with who will pay (I'll get it—No, no let me"), he will flip a coin. When the outcome is heads, he will pay; when the outcome is tails you will pay. Sounds fair enough, but on 9 of the last 10 days the coin landed with tails up. Do you think that your friend is cheating?

The truth is that your friend is either cheating or he is not cheating. Unfortunately, you don't know which is true. Nevertheless, you need to make a decision. You will decide either that he is cheating or he is not cheating. Thus, there are four possibilities: (a) He is cheating and you correctly decide that he is cheating; (b) He is not cheating and you correctly decide that he is not cheating; (c) He is cheating and you incorrectly decide that he is not cheating; and (d) He is not cheating and you incorrectly decide that he is cheating. With these four possibilities, there are two ways that you can be right and two ways that you can be wrong. These four combinations are shown in Table 6.1. As you can see from Table 6.1, there are two different ways that we can make errors in any hypothesis-testing situation. These two different errors are not equally "bad." It is far worse to decide that your friend is cheating when he is not (especially if you accuse him of cheating) than it is to decide that he is not cheating when he is. Because of this you would want stronger evidence to decide that he is cheating than you would want to decide that he is not cheating. In other words, you need to consider the relative "badness" of different errors when testing hypotheses.

If you take a course in statistics or experimental design, you'll find that the idea of error "badness" is handled by requiring different levels of confidence for different decisions. The need to consider different types of errors is found in many contexts. A basic principle of our legal system is that we have to be very certain that someone has committed a crime (beyond a reasonable doubt) before we can convict her. By contrast, we don't have to be convinced beyond a reasonable doubt that she is innocent because wrongly deciding that someone is innocent is considered a less severe error than wrongly deciding that someone is guilty. Similarly, when you are testing hypotheses informally, you also need to be aware of the severity of different types of errors. Before you decide, for example, that no matter how hard you study, you'll never pass some course or that the medicine you're taking is or isn't making you better, you need to consider the consequences of right and wrong decisions. Some decisions require that you should be more certain about being correct than others.

Experience Is an Expensive Teacher

Suppose that your friend shares her "secret" for losing weight—she rubs her stomach and other "problem areas" with garlic and the fat seems to melt away. You are dubious, but she persists: "I know it works. I've tried it, and I have seen it work with my own eyes." I am certain that there are many people who would respond to this testimonial

TABLE 6.1
Four Possible Outcomes for the "Who Buys the Coffee" Example

	You Decide	
	He is cheating.	*He is not cheating.*
The Truth is: He is cheating.	He is cheating and you decide that he is cheating. Correct Decision!	He is cheating and you decide that he is not cheating. An Error!
He is not cheating.	He is not cheating and you decide that he is cheating. A Serious Error!	He is not cheating and you decide that he is not cheating. Correct Decision!

Note. The error associated with deciding that he is cheating is more serious than the error associated with deciding that he is not cheating. Because of the difference in the severity of the errors, you will want to be more certain when deciding that he is cheating than when deciding that he is not cheating.

by rubbing garlic over fat areas of their body, just as there are many people who willingly swallow capsules filled with ground rhinoceros penis to increase their sexual potency, megavitamins to feel less tired, and ginseng root for whatever ails them. You may even join the ranks of those who tout these solutions because sometimes you will lose weight after rubbing yourself with garlic—sometimes a desired effect follows some action (like taking capsules of ground rhinoceros penis). But, did the action cause the effect that followed it? This question can only be answered using the principles of hypothesis testing. Personal experience cannot provide the answer.

Dawes (1994) corrected the famous expression that we attribute to Benjamin Franklin. It seems that Franklin did not say that "experience is the best teacher"; instead he said "experience is a dear teacher," with the word *dear* meaning expensive or costly. Sometimes, we are able to use systematic feedback about what works and what doesn't work so that we can use our experience to improve at some task, but it is also possible to do the same thing over and over without learning from experience. We are far better off using information that is generated by many people to determine causal relationships than to rely on personal experience with all of its biases and costs.

SELF-FULFILLING PROPHECIES

Science is not simply a collection of facts; it is a discipline of thinking about rational solutions to problems after establishing the basic facts derived from observations. It is hypothesizing from what is known to what might be, and then attempting to test the hypotheses.

—Rosalyn S. Yalow (distinguished professor, City University of New York, 1988)

Robert Rosenthal, a well-known psychologist, and his colleague (Rosenthal & Fode, 1963) had their students train rats to run through mazes as part of a standard course in experimental psychology. Half of the students were told that they had rats that had been specially bred to be smart at learning their way through mazes, whereas the other half of the students were told that they had rats that had been specially bred to be dumb at this task. As you probably expected, the students with the bright rats had them outperforming the dull rats in a short period of time. These results are especially interesting because there were no real differences between the two groups of rats. Rosenthal and Fode had lied about the rats being specially bred. All of the rats were the usual laboratory variety. They had been assigned at random to each group. If there were no real differences between the groups of rats, how do we explain the fact that students who believed they had been given bright rats had them learn the maze faster than the other group?

The term **self-fulfilling prophecies** has been coined as a label for the tendency to act in ways that will lead us to find what we expected to find. I don't know what the students did to make the rats learn faster in the "bright" group or slower in the "dull" group. Perhaps the bright group was given extra handling or more food in the goal box. (When rats learn to run through mazes, they are given a food reward when they reach the goal box to keep them motivated.) Maybe the students given the "dull" rats dropped them harshly into the maze or were not as accurate in the records that they kept. Whatever they did, somehow, they influenced their experimental results so that the results were in accord with their expectations.

If self-fulfilling prophecies can influence how rats run through mazes, what sort of an effect will it have on everyday thinking and behavior? Earlier in this chapter, illusory correlations were discussed as the tendency to believe that events that you are observing are really correlated because you believe that they should be. Psychologists are becoming increasingly aware of the ways that personal convictions direct our selection and interpretation of facts. When you function as an intuitive scientist, it is important to keep in mind the ways we influence the results we obtain.

One way to eliminate the effects of self-fulfilling prophecies is with **double-blind procedures**. Let's consider a medical example. There are probably 100 home remedies for the common cold. How should we decide which, if any, actually relieve cold symptoms? Probably, somewhere, sometime, someone gave you chicken soup when you had a cold. Undoubtedly, you got better. Almost everyone who gets a cold gets better. The question is, "Did the chicken soup make you better?" This is a difficult question to answer because if you believe that chicken soup makes you better, you may rate the severity of your symptoms as less severe even when there was no real change. This is just another example of self-fulfilling prophecies. The only way to test this hypothesis is to give some people chicken soup and others something that looks and tastes like chicken soup and then have each group rate the severity of their cold symptoms. In this example all of the subjects are blind to the nature of the treatment they are receiving. It is important that the experimenters also be unaware of which subjects received the "real" chicken soup so that they don't inadvertently give subtle clues to the subjects. Experiments in which neither the subjects nor the experimenters know who is receiving the treatment are called double-blind experiments.

Although the chicken soup example may seem a little far-fetched, the need for double-blind procedures is critical in deciding whether any drug or treatment is working. Formal laboratory research on drugs that may be effective against AIDS or cancer always use double-blind procedures. Most people, however, do not apply these same standards when making personal decisions such as which type of psychotherapy is effective or whether massive doses of a vitamin or advice from a palm reader will improve some aspect of their life. Before you decide to see a therapist who claims to be able to improve your diabetes by manipulating your spine or to engage in screaming therapy to improve your self-confidence, look carefully for double-blind studies that support the use of the proposed therapy.

OCCULT BELIEFS AND THE PARANORMAL

Media distortions, social uncertainty, and deficiencies of human reasoning seem to be at the basis of occult beliefs.

—Barry Singer and Victor Benassi (1981, p. 49)

Do you believe in "channeling, clairvoyance, precognition, telepathy, psychic surgery, psychic healing, healing crystals, psychokinesis, astral travel, levitation, the Bermuda triangle mystery, unidentified flying objects (UFOs), plant consciousness, auras, [or] ghosts" (Gray, 1991, p. ix)? If you answered yes to any of these, you are not alone. In a survey of college students, more than 99% expressed belief in at least one of these phenomena (Messer & Griggs, 1989). According to a Gallup Poll of 1,236 Americans, 78% of women and 70% of men read their horoscopes at least occasionally (Lister, 1992).

How can we understand these beliefs when there is *no good evidence* that they have any basis in fact (Shermer, 1992)? In our attempt to make sense out of events in the world, we all seek to impose a meaningful explanation, especially for unusual events. Have you thought about a friend whom you haven't seen in many years and then received a phone call from him? Did you ever change your usual route home from school or work and then learn that there was a tragic accident that you probably would have been in if you had not changed your route? What about stories of people who recover from deadly disease after they use imagery as a means of healing? We are all fascinated by these unusual events and try to understand them. Can you understand how small sample sizes (usually a single example), retrospective review (in hindsight we seek explanations that are available in memory), illusory correlations, self-fulfilling prophecies, difficulty in understanding probabilities, and other cognitive biases contribute to the popularity of paranormal beliefs? The facts are that there is no positive evidence whatsoever for the existence of any psychic abilities. There are many anecdotes, but there has never been a statistically significant finding of psychic power that has been duplicated in another independent laboratory. "Anecdotes do not make a science" (Shermer, 1992, p. 19).

There are many real mysteries in the world and much that we don't understand. It is possible that someone has found a strange herbal cure for cancer, or that the lines on the palms of our hand or pattern of tea leaves in our tea cups are indicators of important life events, but if these are "real" phenomena, then they will hold up under the bright lights of double-blind, controlled laboratory testing. We can all laugh at the predictions made by "psychic" Jeane Dixon who predicted that George Bush would be reelected and that broccoli would become the miracle vegetable of the 1990s or Los Angeles "psychic" Maria Graciette who predicted that a secret UFO base would be found in the Mexican desert, but we need to become much more skeptical when a friend tells us that crystals have healing powers or vitamin E can be used to revive those who have recently died. This topic is also addressed in chapter 7, in which I discuss how to reason with probabilities.

THINKING AS AN INTUITIVE SCIENTIST

One theme that has followed throughout this chapter is that everyday thinking has much in common with the research methods used by scientists when they investigate phenomena in their academic domains. Many of the pitfalls and problems that plague scientific investigations are also common in everyday thought. If you understand and avoid some of these problems, you will be a better consumer of research and a better intuitive scientist.

When you are evaluating the research claims of others or when you are asserting your own claims, there are several questions to keep in mind:

1. What was the nature of the sample? Was it large enough? Was it biased?
2. Are the variables operationally defined? What do the terms mean?
3. Were the measurements sensitive, valid, and reliable? Are the appropriate comparisons being made to support the claims?
4. Were extraneous variables controlled? What are other plausible explanations for the results?
5. Do the conclusions follow from the observations?
6. Are correlations being used to support causative arguments?
7. Is disconfirming evidence being considered?
8. How could the experimenter's expectancies be biasing the result?

Let's apply these guidelines to the choice of treatment programs that was presented at the opening of this chapter. First, what is the evidence for success rates? Although Program 1 cites a much higher success rate than Program 2, these numbers cannot be used to compare the two programs because Program 1 gives the success for those who stayed with the program at least 1 year, and we have no information about how many dropped out before achieving the 1-year mark. Thus, the success rate for Program 1 is not a valid measure of success. We also have no information about how likely someone is to maintain recovery without treatment. In other words, there is no control group against which to measure the efficacy of treatment. Unfortunately, there is no information about the sample size because we are not told how many patients entered each program. If this were a real decision, then you would ask for this information. So far, there is little to go on. I have found that most people like the idea that the therapist is a recovered addict who "has been there himself." The problem with this sort of qualification is that his anecdotes about "what worked for him" may be totally worthless. Dawes (1994) is highly critical of the sort of reasoning that leads people to believe that a former addict is a good choice for a counselor. As Dawes noted, the thinking that goes into this evaluation is something like this:

The therapist was an addict.
He did X and recovered.
If I do X, then I will also recover.

I hope that you can see that this is very weak evidence. If you have already read chapter 4 on reasoning, then you will recognize this as a categorical syllogism—one that is invalid. You have a single individual (sample size of one), all the biases of memory, no independent verification that X is useful, the problem of illusory correlation, and more. Of course, this individual could be an excellent therapist, but with the information that you are given, there is no reason to expect it. On the other hand, the therapist who has studied the psychology and biology of addiction should know about different treatment options, theories of addiction, and most important, the success rates for a variety of different types of treatments. This is an important point. Try posing the question that I used at the opening of this chapter to friends and relatives. You will probably find the bias toward selecting the recovered addict as a therapist.

If you scrutinize your own conclusions and those of others with the principles of hypothesis testing in mind, you should be able to defend yourself against invalid claims and improve your own ability to draw sound conclusions from observations.

APPLYING THE FRAMEWORK

In applying the general thinking skills framework to thinking as hypothesis testing, consider the following questions:

1. What Is the Goal?   You should use the skills developed in this chapter whenever you are devising hypotheses about the relationships among events and then collecting observations to test the validity of your hypotheses. There is a virtually endless number of examples of when these skills are applicable. They should be used when considering social relationships (e.g., She likes it when I compliment her), physical relationships (e.g., The mercury in the tube rises when the temperature increases), treatment effects (e.g., Laughter therapy can improve the recovery rate from some dread diseases), and when functioning as a consumer of research.

2. What Is Known?   This question is about how to plan the thinking process. When thinking like an intuitive scientist, you need to begin by explicitly deciding on the nature of the hypothesis that you're testing and the way you will go about making observations. You also need to consider the relative severity of different kinds of errors. The knowns include how you will operationalize your variables and how confident you want to be before you decide if your hypothesis is correct. In short, this step involves becoming explicit about your starting point in the thinking process. One of the most important pieces of information in determining cause is whether the subjects were assigned at random to different "treatment" groups. If not, it is extremely difficult to make valid causal claims.

3. Which Thinking Skill or Skills Will Get You to Your Goal?   The selection of the appropriate skill depends on how you answered the previous questions. If you decide that the hypothesis that you're testing is important enough to require a formal test, then you'll want to sample subjects in an unbiased manner and be certain that the number of subjects is sufficiently large and that measurement was accurate. Of course, I don't expect you to be testing lethal drugs based on the hypothesis-testing skills presented in this chapter. This sort of testing needs to be conducted by researchers with extensive knowledge of research and experimental design. But, you should know how to be a consumer of this sort of research and look for evidence of good hypothesis-testing methods.

The skills involved when thinking as an intuitive scientist include:

- Recognizing the need for and using operational definitions.
- Understanding the need to isolate and control variables in order to make strong causal claims.
- Checking for adequate sample size and unbiased sampling when a generalization is made.
- Being able to describe the relationship between any two variables as positive, negative, or unrelated.
- Understanding the limits of correlational reasoning.
- Seeking converging validity to increase your confidence in a decision.
- Checking for and understanding the need for control groups.
- Being aware of the bias in most estimates of variability.
- Considering the relative "badness" of different sorts of errors.
- Determining how self-fulfilling prophecies could be responsible for experimental results or everyday observations.
- Knowing when causal claims can and can't be made.

These skills should be used in your own thinking and in critiquing the thinking of others. After reading this chapter, you should be able to use these skills in any context in which they are appropriate.

4. Have You Reached Your Goal?   The final question to consider is whether you have reduced uncertainty: Can you predict the results of certain actions or can you make better decisions because you used the hypothesis-testing skills presented in this chapter? The ubiquitous concern for accuracy is always the final test of the quality of the decision you've arrived at. When you function like an intuitive scientist, you will sometimes make wrong decisions because we never know "truth." But, you can minimize wrong decisions by carefully using the hypothesis-testing skills presented in this chapter.

CHAPTER SUMMARY

1. Much of our everyday thinking is like the scientific method of hypothesis testing. We formulate beliefs about the world and collect observations to decide if our beliefs are correct.

2. In the inductive method we devise hypotheses from our observations. In the deductive method we collect observations that confirm or disconfirm our hypotheses. Most thinking involves an interplay of these two processes so that we devise hypotheses from experience, make observations, and then, on the basis of our observations, we redefine our hypotheses.

3. Operational definitions are precise statements that allow the identification and measurement of variables.

4. Independent variables are used to predict or explain dependent variables. When we formulate hypotheses, we want to know about the effect of the independent variable on the dependent variable(s).

5. When we draw conclusions from observations, it's important to utilize an adequately large sample size because people are variable in the way they respond. Most people are too willing to generalize results obtained from small samples.

6. In determining if one variable (e.g., smoking) causes another variable (e.g., lung cancer) to occur, it is important to be able to isolate and control the causal variables. Strong causal claims require the three-stage experimental design that was described in this chapter.

7. In everyday contexts, we often use retrospective techniques to understand what caused an event to occur. This is not a good technique because our memories tend to be selective and malleable and because we have no objective systematic observations of the cause. Prospective techniques that record events when they occur and then see if the hypothesized result follows are better methods for determining cause–effect relationships.

8. Variables that are related so that changes in one variable are associated with changes in the other variable are called correlated variables. Correlations can be positive as in the relationship between height and weight (taller people tend to weigh more, whereas shorter people tend to weigh less) or negative as in the relationship between exercise and weight (people who exercise a great deal tend to be thin, and those who exercise little tend to be heavy).

9. A common error is to infer a causative relationship from correlated variables. It is possible that Variable A caused Variable B, or that Variable B caused Variable A, or that A and B influenced each other, or that a third variable caused them both.

10. The belief that two variables are correlated when they are not (illusory correlation) is another type of error that is common in human judgment.

11. It is important that you use measurements that are sensitive, valid, and reliable or the conclusions you draw may be incorrect. Few people consider the importance of measurement issues when they draw everyday conclusions about the nature of the world.

12. Although many of our judgments lack validity, people report great confidence in them. This is called illusory validity.

13. Inadvertently, we may act in ways that will lead us to confirm or disconfirm hypotheses according to our expectations. These are called self-fulfilling prophecies.

TERMS TO KNOW

Check your understanding of the concepts presented in this chapter by reviewing their definitions. If you find that you're having difficulty with any term, be sure to reread the section in which it is discussed:

Hypothesis. A set of beliefs about the nature of the world, usually concerning the relationship between two or more variables.

Hypothesis Testing. The scientific method of collecting observations to confirm or disconfirm beliefs about the relationships among variables.

Inductive Method. A method of formulating hypotheses in which you observe events and then devise a hypothesis about the events you observed.

Deductive Method. A method of testing hypotheses in which you formulate a hypothesis that you believe to be true and then infer consequences from it. Systematic observations are then made to verify if your hypothesis is correct.

Operational Definition. An explicit set of procedures that tell the reader how to recognize and measure the concept in which you're interested.

(A) Variable. A quantifiable characteristic that can take on more than one value (e.g., height, gender, age, race).

Independent Variable. The variable that is selected (or manipulated) by the experimenter who is testing a hypothesis to see if changes in the independent variable will result in changes in the dependent variable. For example, if you want to know if people are more readily persuaded by threats or rational appeals, you could present either a threatening message or a rational appeal to two groups of people (message type is the independent variable), and then determine how much their attitudes toward the topic have changed (the dependent variable).

Dependent Variable. The variable that is measured in an experiment to determine if its value depends on the independent variable. Compare with independent variable.

Population. For statistical and hypothesis-testing purposes, a population is the entire group of people (or animals or entities) in which one is interested and to which one wishes to generalize.

Sample. A subset of a population that is studied in order to make inferences about the population.

Representative Sample. A sample that is similar to the population in important characteristics such as the proportion of males and females, socioeconomic status, and age.

Generalization. Using the results obtained in a sample to infer that similar results would have been obtained from the population if everyone in the population had been measured. (When used in the context of problem solving, it is a strategy in which the problem is considered as an example of a larger class of problems.)

Biased Sample. A sample that is not representative of the population from which it was drawn.

Confounding. When experimental groups differ in more than one way, it's not possible to separate the effects due to each variable. For example, if you found that teenage girls scored higher on a test of verbal ability than preteen boys, you wouldn't know if the results were due to sex differences or age differences between the two groups.

Convenience Samples. The use of a group of people who are readily available as participants in an experiment. Such samples may be biased in that they may not be representative of the population from which they were drawn.

Sample Size. The number of people selected for a study.

Subject. A person, animal, or entity who serves as a participant in an experiment.

Variability. Term to denote the fact that people (and animals) differ in the way they respond to experimental stimuli.

Random Sample. A sample in which everyone in a population has an equal chance of being selected.

Law of Small Numbers. The willingness to believe that results obtained from a few subjects can be generalized to the entire population.

Retrospective Research. After an event has occurred, the experimenter looks backward in time to determine its cause.

Prospective Research. A method of conducting research in which possible causative factors of an event are identified before the event occurs. Experimenters then determine if the hypothesized event occurs.

Correlated Variables. Two or more variables that are related. See negative correlation and positive correlation.

Positive Correlation. Two or more variables that are related so that increases in one variable occur concomitantly with increases in the other variable, and decreases in one variable occur with decreases in the other.

Negative Correlation. Two or more variables that are related such that increases in one variable are associated with decreases in the other variable.

Illusory Correlation. The belief that two variables are correlated, when in fact they are uncorrelated.

Sensitive Measures. Measures that are able to detect small changes in the dependent variable.

Validity. The extent to which a measure (e.g., a test) is measuring what you want it to.

Convergent Validity. The use of several different measures or techniques that all suggest the same conclusion.

Illusory Validity. The belief that a measure is valid (measures what you want it to) when, in fact, it is not. This belief causes people to be overconfident in their judgments.

Reliability. The consistency of a measure (e.g., a test) on repeated occasions.

Double-Blind Procedures. An experimental paradigm in which neither the subjects nor the person collecting data know the treatment group to which the subject has been assigned.

Self-Fulfilling Prophecy. The tendency to act in ways that influence experimental results so that we obtain results that are consistent with our expectations.

SUGGESTED READINGS

There are many good books that discuss the basic principles of hypothesis testing. Stanovich's (1992) *How to Think Straight About Psychology* (3rd ed.) is a slim volume that applies many of the concepts presented in this chapter to problems in psychology. Another slim book with a similar title, but different content, is R. A. Smith's (1995) *Challenging Your Preconceptions: Thinking Critically About Psychology*. Smith's book is particularly well written with relevant examples and a good section on psychology and the popular press. A somewhat different approach to the topics in this chapter can be found in *Thinking and Reasoning* by Garnham and Oakhill (1994). The authors assumed a more formal and philosophical view of these topics.

A somewhat strange and iconoclastic book is *Against Method* by Feyerabend (1975). In this classic book, he argued against the use of scientific methods. Although this book is not easy reading, it is interesting. As an example that supports the notion that we don't need scientific methods, he argued that Galileo's views were eventually accepted, not on their scientific merit, but because Galileo "was clever in techniques of persuasion," wrote in Italian instead of Latin, and appealed to people who prefer new ideas to old ones.

The notion that we function as "intuitive" or everyday scientists is developed in *Human Inference: Strategies and Shortcomings of Social Judgment* by Nisbett and Ross (1980). Although it is an older text, it is filled with familiar examples and concisely reviews research on the way people utilize research principles in everyday life. An advanced treatise on the topics discussed in this chapter can be found in Holland, Holyoak, Nisbett, and Thagard's (1986) book entitled *Induction: Processes of Inference, Learning, and Discovery*. They took the position that induction is the primary thinking process by which we learn about the nature of the world. The authors are, by training, two psychologists, a computer scientist with expertise in artificial intelligence, and a philosopher with a common interest in how we think. It is highly recommended for advanced students.

There are some very good books that take a careful look at occult beliefs. Interested readers will want to read an edited book by Frazier (1991) entitled, *The Hundredth Monkey and Other Paradigms of the Paranormal*. It contains a collection of articles on topics ranging from channeling (How can we assess the claim of a woman in Washington who contacts a 35,000-year-old being named "Ramtha" who speaks English with an Indian accent?) to the use of crystals that "amplify spiritual vibrations for the attuned human" (p. 2). There is even a chapter by the prolific science writer, Carl Sagan. A book by Gray (1991), *Thinking Critically About New Age Ideas*, also takes a serious look at New Age beliefs. It provides guidelines for making judgments about paranormal claims like channeling and out-of-body experiences. Another new book that focuses on how to think about the weird is Schick and Vaughn's (1995) *How to Think About Weird Things*. They seem to have covered almost every weird belief that you can imagine—psychic surgery, UFOs, and monkeys with amazing intellect. They even addressed the imponderable question, "Did Adam and Eve have navels?"I also recommend the magazine *Skeptic*, which is sold on newsstands and does a great job of asking tough questions and providing interesting exchanges among readers and experts.

Finally, many of the topics discussed in this chapter are applied to an analysis of psychotherapy by Dawes (1994) in his book *House of Cards: Psychology and Psychotherapy Built on Myth*. In case you're wondering, he concluded that psychotherapy is often effective, but he made strong arguments against the use of some projective tests (e.g., the Rorschach) and the credential program for psychologists.

7

Likelihood and Uncertainty: Understanding Probabilities

Contents

The jury was facing a difficult decision in the case of *People v. Collins*, 1968 (cited in Arkes & Hammond, 1986). The robbery victim could not identify his assailant. All he could recall was that the robber was a woman with a blonde pony tail who, after the robbery, rode off in a yellow convertible driven by a Black man with a moustache and a beard. The suspect fit this description, but could the jury be certain "beyond a reasonable doubt" that the woman who was on trial was the robber? She was blonde and often wore her hair in a pony tail. Her codefendant "friend" was a Black man with a moustache, beard, and yellow convertible. If you were the attorney for the defense, you would stress the fact that the victim could not identify this woman as the robber. What strategy would you use if you were the attorney for the prosecution?

The prosecutor produced an expert in probability theory who testified that the probability of these conditions "co-occurring (being blonde *plus* having a pony tail *plus* having a Black male friend *plus* his owning a yellow convertible and so on, when these characteristics are independent) was 1 in 12 million. The expert testified that this combination of characteristics was so unusual that the jury could be certain "beyond a reasonable doubt" that she was the robber.

The jury returned a verdict of "guilty."

PROBABILISTIC NATURE OF THE WORLD

The theory of probabilities is nothing but common sense confirmed by calculation.

—La Place (1749–1827)

As seen in the preceding example, the legal system recognizes that we can never have absolute certainty in legal matters. Instead, we operate with various degrees of uncertainty. Juries are instructed to decide that someone is guilty of a crime when they are certain "beyond a reasonable doubt." This standard was adopted because there is always some small amount of doubt that the accused may be innocent. Jurors are instructed to operate under a different level of doubt when they are deciding about guilt or innocence in a civil case. In civil cases, they are told to deliver a verdict of guilty when the "preponderance of evidence" supports this decision. Thus, jurors are instructed to operate under two different levels of uncertainty when the case before them is either criminal or civil. They need to be more certain when deciding that an accused party is guilty in a criminal case than in a civil case.

Probability is the study of likelihood and uncertainty. It plays a critical role in all of the professions and in most everyday decisions. All medical diagnoses and treatment decisions are inherently probabilistic, as are decisions made in business, college admissions, advertising, and research. Probability is the cornerstone of science; the laws of probability guide the interpretation of all research findings. Many of our leisure activities also rely on the principles of probability, most notably horse racing and card games. Every time you decide to take an umbrella, invest in the stock market, buy an insurance policy, or bet on a long shot in the Kentucky Derby, you are making a probability judgment. Other than the proverbial death and taxes, there is very little in life that is known with certainty. Because we live in a probabilistic world, critical thinking will require an understanding of probability.

There is good evidence that training in the use of probability will improve your ability to utilize probability values in an appropriate manner. In an investigation of the use of statistical thinking in everyday reasoning tasks, researchers concluded that, "This study indicated clearly that statistical training can enhance the use of statistical rules in reasoning about everyday life and can do so completely outside the context of training" (Fong et al., 1986, p. 280). In other words, although the thinking skills presented in this chapter will require the use of basic arithmetic and probably some concentrated effort, it's likely that you'll be a better thinker for having worked through the problems.

Likelihood and Uncertainty

If your facts are wrong but your logic is perfect, then your conclusions are inevitably false. Therefore, by making mistakes in your logic, you have at least a random chance of coming to a correct conclusion.

—Christie-Davies' Theorem (reference unknown, taken from a calendar)

If I flip a "fair" coin (i.e., one that is not biased, which means that either a head or tail is equally likely) into the air and ask you to guess the probability that it will land heads up, you would say that the probability of a head is 50% (or .50). This means that the coin is expected to land heads up half of the time. Although the word *probability* is used in several different ways, the definition of **probability** that is most useful in the present context is the number of ways a particular outcome (what we call a success) can occur divided by the number of possible outcomes (when each possible outcome is equally likely). It is a measure of how often we expect an event to occur in the long run. Success may seem like a strange word in this context, but you can think of it as the outcome you're interested in. In this case, a success is getting the coin to land heads up. There is only one way for a coin to land heads up, so the number of ways a success can occur in this example is 1. What are all the possible outcomes of flipping a coin in the air? The coin can either land heads up or tails up. (I've never seen a coin land on its edge, nor have I ever seen a bird come along and carry it off while it's flipped in the air, so I'm not considering these as possible outcomes.) Thus, there are two possible outcomes, each of which is as likely to happen as the other. To calculate the probability of getting a coin to land heads up, compute the number of ways a head can occur (1), divided by the number of possible outcomes (2), or ½, an answer you already knew. Because many people find it easier to think in percentages than in fractions, ½ is sometimes changed to 50%. Thus, you can expect the coin to land heads up 50% of the time, *in the long run.*

Let's try another example. How likely are you to roll a 5 in one roll of a die? As there is only one way for a 5 to occur, the numerator of the probability fraction is 1. A die is a six-sided (cube) figure; thus there are six possible outcomes in one roll. If the die is not "loaded"—that is, when each side of the die is equally likely to land facing up—the probability of rolling a 5 is ⅙, or approximately 17%.

What is the probability of rolling an even number in one roll of a fair die? To find this probability, consider the number of ways a success can occur. You could roll a 2, 4, or 6, all possible even numbers. Thus, there are three ways a success can occur out of six equally likely outcomes, so the probability of rolling an even number is ³⁄₆ = ½.

What is the probability of rolling a whole number less than 7? If someone asked me to bet on this happening, I'd put up my house, my children, and my meager savings account to make this bet. In other words, I'd bet that this *will* happen. Let's see why. The number of ways a whole number less than 7 can occur in one roll of a die is six (1, 2, 3, 4, 5, or 6), and the number of possible outcomes is six. Thus, the probability is ⁶⁄₆, or 1. When a probability is equal to 1 (or 100%), it must happen; it is certain to occur.

What is the probability of rolling an 8 in one roll of a die? Again, I'd put up everything I own, but this time I'd bet against this occurrence. The number of ways an 8 can occur is zero. Thus, the probability of this occurring is 0; it cannot occur. This situation also reflects absolute certainty. Probabilities range from 0 (can never happen) to 1 (must happen). Probability values close to 0 or 1 represent events that are almost certain not to occur or almost certain to occur, whereas probabilities near .5 (50%) represent maximum uncertainty, because either outcome is equally likely, and thus there is no basis for predicting either one. This relationship is depicted in Fig. 7.1.

Odds

It is often convenient to discuss probabilities in terms of **odds**. If a friend gives you 3-to-1 odds that his school's championship tiddly-winks team will beat your school's tiddly-winks team, this means that if four games were played, he would expect his team to win three of them. Authorities on organized sports (announcers, sports page editors, and almost everyone else) usually express their degree of belief in the outcome of a sporting event in terms of odds. (Betting odds like those posted at race tracks and boxing matches refer to the amount of money that has been bet on each contender and, thus, have a slightly different meaning from the one described here.)

To convert odds to a probability, add the two numbers that are given (e.g., 3:1 = 4), use the first number as the numerator and the sum as the denominator (¾), and this is the equivalent probability.

The Laws of Chance

The most important phrase in the last section was "in the long run." Except for those special cases when the probability of an outcome is either 0% or 100%, we cannot know

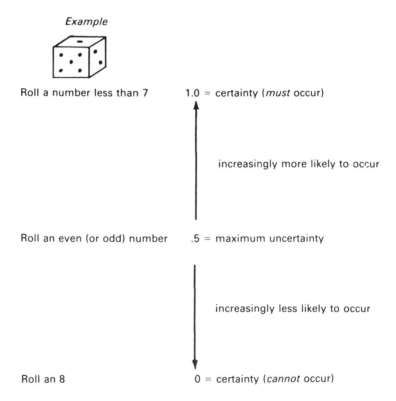

Example

Roll a number less than 7   1.0 = certainty (*must* occur)

increasingly more likely to occur

Roll an even (or odd) number   .5 = maximum uncertainty

increasingly less likely to occur

Roll an 8   0 = certainty (*cannot* occur)

FIG. 7.1. Probability and likelihood.

with certainty what will happen. I cannot know when I roll a die whether I will roll a 5, but, if I keep rolling a fair die for many, many trials, I do know that about 17% of the time I will roll a 5. I cannot know which trials will produce a 5, but I do know approximately how many trials will land with a 5 showing, if I keep rolling for a long time. This is an important point. When we speak of the **laws of chance** (or laws of probability), we are referring to the ability to predict the number or percentage of trials on which a particular outcome will occur. With a large number of trials, I can be very accurate about the number of times a particular outcome will occur, but I cannot know which trials will yield a particular outcome. This means that I can make good "long-run" predictions and poor "short-run" predictions.

Let's consider insurance as an applied example of this distinction. When you buy a life insurance policy (or any other type of insurance policy), you are making a bet with the insurance company. You agree to pay a certain amount of money to the insurance company each year. They agree to pay your beneficiary a certain amount of money when you die. There are many different types of life insurance policies available, but for the purposes of this chapter, we consider the simplest. I use some simple numbers to demonstrate the statistical point that I want to make—in real life, the actual costs and payoffs are different from those used in this example. Suppose that you are 30 years old and that you agree to pay the insurance company $1,000 per year. When you die, your beneficiary will receive $20,000. You are betting with the insurance company that you will die at a fairly young age (a bet that you hope to lose) so that you will have paid them only a small amount of money and your beneficiary will receive a larger amount of money. If you die before the age of 50, you win the bet. Ignoring complications like inflation and interest, you will have paid less than the $20,000 your beneficiary will receive if you die at a young age. The insurance company, on the other hand, will win the bet if you live to a ripe old age. If you die when you are 70 years old, you will have paid them $40,000 and your dearly beloved will receive only $20,000.

Insurance companies can make money because of the laws of chance. No one knows when you or anyone else will die, but insurance companies do know how many people aged 30 (the age at which you bought your policy) will die before they reach their 50th birthday. Thus, although no one can predict accurately the age at death for any single individual, we can use the laws of chance to predict how many people will live to be any particular age.

Degrees of Belief

Probability is sometimes used to express the strength of a belief about the likelihood of an outcome. This is a second definition for the term **probability**. For example, if you apply for a job and believe that the interview went well, you might assess the probability that you will be offered the job as 80%. This probability value was not mathematically derived by calculating the number of ways a success could occur divided by the number of possible outcomes. Instead, it indicates your degree of belief that the job will be offered. It suggests a moderate to high likelihood. If someone else interviewed for the same job and believed that his chance of being offered the job was 50%, it would be obvious that he was less confident about getting the job than you were.

The use of probability to express one's degree of belief in the likelihood of an outcome is particularly prevalent at election time. Political analysts will often attach probability values to the likelihood of a candidate's election. If a political analyst gives a candidate a 30% chance of winning, she is predicting that although the candidate might win, she believes that the candidate is more likely to lose. Probability values are handy ways of quantifying confidence in an outcome.

FACTORS AFFECTING JUDGMENTS ABOUT LIKELIHOOD
AND UNCERTAINTY

The odds against there being a bomb on a plane are a million to one, and against two bombs a million times a million to one. Next time you fly, cut the odds and take a bomb.

—Benny Hill (quoted in Byrne, 1988, p. 349)

There is a large research literature documenting the fact that most people are biased in their assessment of probabilities. We fail to appreciate the nature of randomness and, because of this, have strong misconceptions about likelihood and uncertainty (Garfield & Ahlgren, 1988). This is not a surprising finding given that we can only use probabilities to understand events "in the long run" and most of our everyday experiences are based on short-run observations. For example, there is a large body of data that show that, on the average, people who smoke die at a younger age than those who don't (Paulos, 1994). Most of us can't discover this relationship because we don't know the age at death for large numbers of people, but we may know one or two people who smoked two packs a day and lived into their 90s. This sort of personal experience would lead us to doubt the statistics that were collected from many people. A point that is made in several chapters is that personal experience is not a good way to make many judgments about the world. Recall from the last chapter that experience is an expensive teacher, not a good one.

The Search for Meaning

To live, it seems is to explain, to justify, and to find coherence among diverse outcomes, characteristics, and causes.

—Gilovich (1991, p. 22)

We seek causes for events that happen to us and others, but most of us rarely consider the randomness of many events. We look for patterns and meaning, a quest that can often be helpful, but also can lead to beliefs that are groundless. For example, consider this true story: A student stopped in my office to talk with me. He told about an "amazing thing" that just happened to him. He was a student in a class of 15 students. Each student had to make an oral presentation, and the order in which they were to present was determined by drawing numbers from a box. "Guess who picked number 1?" he asked excitedly. I guessed that he did. "Exactly, and do you know the probability of that!" I did, it was 1/15 or approximately 7%. "Isn't that amazing? Out of 15 people in the class, I picked number 1. How can you explain that?" I attributed this not-so-amazing outcome to chance; after all someone had to pick number 1. He was certain that was a sign of something; maybe the "gods" had intervened or his karma had gone berserk (whatever that means). He was looking for a cause that could explain this event, and he never considered just plain "chance."

Overconfidence

By definition, there is always some uncertainty in probabilistic events. Yet, research has shown that people tend to be more confident in their decisions about probabilistic events than they should be. Consider an example that Daniel Kahneman, a researcher in this area, likes to use. When he and his coauthors began working on a text on decision making, they were fairly confident that they would have it completed within a year, despite the fact that they knew that most books like the one they were writing take many years to complete. They believed that they would beat these "odds." In fact, it took them several years to complete the text.

A similar phenomenon is at work whenever we consult investment advisors. The probability of making money by investing in high-risk stocks is such that we would often make more money if we left our money in a low-interest passbook account. Yet, most people believe that they will defy the odds and make a winning investment.

In an experimental investigation of the **overconfidence phenomenon**, people were asked to provide answers with a specified degree of confidence to factual questions (Kahneman & Tversky, 1979). Try it with this question: "I feel 98% certain that the number of nuclear plants operating in the world in 1980 was more than _____ and less than _____." Fill in the blanks with numbers that reflect 98% confidence. The researchers investigating this effect found that nearly one third of the time, the correct answer did not lie between the two values that reflected a 98% level of confidence. (The correct answer to this question is 189.) This result demonstrates that people are often highly confident when their high degree of confidence is unwarranted.

Have you ever bought a lottery ticket? Do you know what the odds are against your hitting the jackpot? The laws of probability dictate that you should expect to lose, yet countless numbers of people expect to win. In fact, a recent and disturbing poll published in Money magazine revealed that almost as many people are planning for their retirement by buying lottery tickets (39%) as are investing in stocks (43%) (Wang, 1994).

People tend to be most confident in uncertain situations when they believe that they have control over the uncertain events. Many state lottery advisors are familiar with this principle of human nature and now have a lottery plan that allows the buyer to select his own number. People prefer to select their own numbers over being given a number at random because it gives them an illusion of control. The winning number is still selected randomly, but people believe they are more likely to win in the self-selection lottery.

USING PROBABILITY

Without giving it much thought, we utilize probabilities many times each day. Let's start with one of the few examples where probability values are made explicit. Many people begin each day by reading the weather forecast in the morning paper. What do you do when you read that the probability of rain is 80% today? Most people will head off to school or work toting an umbrella. But, what if it does not rain? Can we conclude that the forecaster was wrong? The forecast of an 80% probability of rain means that out of every 100 days when the weather conditions are like those on this particular day, there will be rain on 80 of them. Thus, a probability of rain is, like all probability values, based on what we would expect in the long run. Weather experts know that 80 out of 100 days will have rain, but the forecasters cannot know which days it will rain.

Suppose that you are to be married on this hypothetical day, and a magnificent outdoor ceremony is planned. Suppose that an 80% probability of rain was forecast, and it did not rain. Would you believe that something other than chance was responsible for the good weather or that the absence of rain is a good (or bad) sign for your marriage? If you would interpret the good weather as a sign from the heavens or some other astral body, then you have demonstrated the point that was just made—we seek meaning in events, even events as seemingly uncontrollable as the weather, and rarely consider plain old chance.

The number of instances in which we are given explicit probability values that have been computed for us is relatively small. One area where this practice is growing is in the use of medical information sheets that are designed to help patients understand the risks and benefits of taking a particular drug. The Food and Drug Administration requires that all oral contraceptive medications (birth control pills) be packaged with statistical information about the health risks associated with them. In order to arrive at an intelligent decision based on the information provided, potential oral contraceptive users must be able to understand the statistical summaries that are presented in the medical information sheets.

The following excerpt from an oral contraceptive packaged insert provides an example: "For women aged 20 to 44, it is estimated that about 1 in 2,000 using oral contraceptives will be hospitalized each year because of abnormal clotting. Among nonusers in the same age group, about 1 in 20,000 would be hospitalized each year" (Ortho Pharmaceutical Corp., 1979, p. 16). Although consumers can readily assess that clotting is more likely for pill users, this information is of little practical value unless an oral contraceptive consumer can decide if 1 in 2,000 is a large or small number; that is, "Is it a danger to me if I am taking the pill?" Two related experiments (Halpern & Blackman, 1985; Halpern et al., 1989) have shown that most people find information like this to be relatively meaningless.

Consider the following: Suppose you read that the risk of developing heart disease is 10.5 times more likely for oral contraceptive users than for nonusers. Most people will conclude from this information that oral contraceptives present a substantial risk of heart disease. Suppose now that you are told that only 3.5 women out of 100,000 users will develop heart disease. You probably would interpret this sentence as meaning that there is little risk associated with oral contraceptive use. Consider the "flip side" of this information and think about how you would assess safety if you read that 99,996.5 women out of 100,000 users will not develop heart disease. Does it seem even safer? Another way of presenting the same information is to convert it to a percentage. There is only a .0035% chance that oral contraceptive users will develop heart disease. Most people would now consider the risk associated with oral contraceptive use to be minuscule.

Which of these statements is correct? They all are. The only way they differ is the way in which the statistical information is presented, and different ways of presenting the same statistical information lead to very different assessments of safety (Halpern et al., 1989). It is important to keep this in mind when interpreting statistical information. There is a trend to provide consumers with statistical risk information so that they can make informed safety judgments about a diverse assortment of topics including how to treat a particular type of cancer and the safety of nuclear energy. Although the topic of risk is considered in more detail later in this chapter, keep in mind that the best way to convert risk probabilities to a meaningful value is to write out all of the mathematically equivalent values (i.e., X out of Y occurrences, number of times greater risk than a meaningful comparison event, number that will die, number that will not die). Graphic representations of relative risks can also be helpful when there are many values that need to be compared simultaneously. The use of spatial arrays is touted throughout this book (e.g., circle diagrams when interpreting syllogisms, graphic organizers to comprehend complex prose, tree diagrams for use in making sound decisions). One advantage that they confer in this situation is that they reduce the memory load in working memory and allow us to consider several different alternatives "at a glance."

Games of Chance

We are a country of people who love to play games. From Las Vegas to Atlantic City, and in all of the small towns in between, people spend countless hours and dollars playing games of chance, skill, and semiskill. For many people, the only serious consideration they have ever given to probability is when playing games of chance.

Cards

Card playing is a ubiquitous pastime, with small children playing "fish" and "old maid," and their older counterparts playing canasta, bridge, poker, pinochle, blackjack, hearts, and too many others to mention. The uncertainty inherent in card games adds to the pleasure of playing (although the camaradarie and pretzels and beer also help).

Good card players, regardless of the game, understand and utilize the rules of probability. Let's apply the definitional formula for probability to card games. For example, how likely are you to draw an ace of spades from a deck of 52 cards? The probability of this happening is 1/52, or approximately 2%, because there is only one ace of spades and 52 possible outcomes. How likely are you to draw an ace of any suit from a full deck of cards? If you've been following the probability discussion so far, you'll realize that the answer is 4/52, or approximately 8%, because there are four aces in a 52-card deck.

Although some professional card players claim to have worked out careful plans that will help them to change the odds of winning in their favor, it is not possible to "beat the house" for most card games, no matter how good a player one is. It is always difficult to tell the extent to which these stories of successful gamblers are hype. Professional gamblers often enjoy bragging about their winnings and conveniently forget about the times when they lost. Furthermore, most of the self-proclaimed expert gamblers are selling their "winning system." I hope that you recall from the chapters on reasoning and analyzing arguments that when an "expert" stands to gain from the sale of a product, the expert's opinion becomes suspect.

According to Gunther (1977), Vera Nettick (who is a real person) is a lucky lady. While playing a game of bridge, she was dealt a hand that contained all 13 diamonds. Breathlessly, she won a grand slam with the once-in-a-lifetime card hand. Any statistician will be quick to point out that every possible combination of cards will be dealt to somebody sooner or later. Thus, Vera Nettick's hand was no more unusual than any other card hand, although it certainly is more memorable. Can you guess how often such a hand would occur? Gunther (1977) figured this out as follows:

> There are roughly 635 billion possible bridge hands. Of these, eight might be called "perfect" hands, though some are more perfect than others. To begin with, there are four perfect no-trump hands. Such a hand would contain all four aces, all four kings, all four queens, and one of the four jacks. Any of these four hands would be unequivocally perfect, because no bid could top it. Slightly less perfect, in descending order, are hands containing all the spades, all the hearts, all the diamonds, and all the clubs. If there are eight of these perfect hands in a possible 635 billion, the statistical probability is that such a hand will be dealt one in every 79 billion tries, give or take a few.

> Now all we have to do is estimate how many games of bridge are played every year and how many hands are dealt in each game. Using fairly conservative estimates, it turns out that a perfect hand should be dealt to some lucky bridge player, somewhere in the United States, roughly once every three or four years. (p. 30)

Actually, Gunther's figures are too low, because new decks of cards are organized in ascending order by suits so that one or two "perfect" shuffles will produce "perfect" bridge hands (Alcock, 1981). (A perfect shuffle occurs when, following a "cut," there is a one-to-one interleaving of cards from each half of the deck.) And, of course, none of these calculations addresses the possibility of cheating, which would change the probabilities because each possible combination of cards would no longer be equally likely. Consider the two card hands shown in Fig. 7.2. Every possible combination of cards is equally likely when the cards are dealt at random. This topic is also discussed in chapter 8.

Roulette

Roulette is often thought of as an aristocratic game. It is strange that it has gained this reputation, because it is a game of pure chance. Unlike most card games, there is no skillful way to play roulette. As you probably know, roulette is played by spinning a small ball inside a circular array of numbered and colored pockets. Eighteen of the pockets are red; 18 are black; and 2 are green. Players can make a variety of bets. One possible bet is that the ball will land in a red pocket. What is the probability of this event when the ball is equally likely to land in any pocket? There are 18 red pockets out of 38 pockets (possible outcomes); therefore, the probability of the ball landing in a red pocket is 18/38. Because this is a number less than .5, we know that it will land in a red pocket slightly less than half of the time. Thus, if you kept betting on red, you would lose slightly more often than you would win. Suppose now you bet on black pockets. Again, the probability would be 18/38; and again, if you continue to bet on black pockets, you will lose more often than you win. Of course, sometimes you will win, and at other times you will lose, but after many spins—in the long run—you will lose at roulette.

The odds or probability of winning at any casino game are always favorable to the "house," otherwise, casinos could not stay in business. Actually, there is one person

FIG. 7.2. Which of these two card hands are you more likely to be dealt from a well shuffled deck of cards?

who has been able to "beat" the roulette odds. One of my heros is Al Hibbs, a scientist who gained fame for his work at the Jet Propulsion Laboratory in Pasadena, California, where much of the work on the U.S. space program is done. When he was a student, he used his knowledge of probability to run his original stake of $125 up to $6,300 at the Pioneer Club in Reno. Here's how he did it: Hibbs knows that although every number in a roulette wheel should be equally likely to occur, all manufactured devices have imperfections. These imperfections make some numbers more likely to occur than others. Hibbs and a friend recorded the results of 100,000 spins of a roulette wheel to find the numbers that occurred most often. Accordingly, they bet on these numbers. Unfortunately, none of us can duplicate his success, because the wheels are now taken apart and reassembled with different parts each day. Thus, although each wheel is still imperfect, the imperfections differ from day to day.

Computing Probabilities in Multiple-Outcome Situations

We are often concerned with the probability of two or more events occurring, such as getting two heads in two flips of a coin or rolling a 6 at least once in two rolls of a die. These sorts of situations are called **multiple outcomes**.

Using Tree Diagrams

Although it is relatively easy to understand that the probability of getting a head on one flip of a fair coin is ½, it is somewhat more difficult to know intuitively the probability of getting four heads in four flips of a fair coin. Although an example of flipping a coin may seem artificial, it is a good way of showing how probabilities combine over many trials. Let's figure it out. (Follow along with me, even if you are math-phobic. The calculations and mathematical thinking are relatively easy, if you work along with the examples. Do *not* look at the next several figures and exclaim, "no way, I'll just skip it." It is important to be able to think with and about numbers.)

On the first flip, only one of two possible outcomes can occur; a head (H) or tail (T). What can happen if a coin is flipped twice? There are four possible outcomes: a head on the first flip and a head on the second (HH), a head on the first flip and a tail on the second (HT), a tail on the first flip and a head on the second (TH), and a tail on the first flip and a tail on the second (TT). Because there are four possible outcomes and only one way to get two heads, the probability of this event is ¼ (again assuming that the coin is fair, that is, that getting a head is as likely as getting a tail). There is a general rule, the "and rule," for calculating this value in any situation. When you want to find the probability of one event *and* another event (a head on the first and second flip), you multiply their separate probabilities. By applying the "and rule," we find that the probability of obtaining two tails when a coin is flipped twice is equal to ½ x ½, which is ¼. Intuitively, the probability of both events occurring should be less likely than either event alone, and it is.

A simple way to compute this probability is to represent all possible events with **tree diagrams**. Tree diagrams were used in chapter 4 when we figured the validity of "if, then" statements. In this chapter, we add probability values to the "branches" of the tree to determine the probability of different combinations of outcomes. Later in this book, I return to tree diagrams once again as a way of generating creative solutions to problems.

On the first flip, either an H or T will land facing up. For a fair coin, the probability of a head is equal to the probability of a tail, which is equal to .5. Let's depict this as follows:

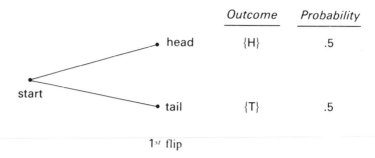

When you flip a second time, either an H on the first flip will be followed by an H or T, or a T on the first flip will be followed by an H or T. The probability of a head or tail on the second flip is still .5. Outcomes from a second flip are added as "branches" on a tree diagram.

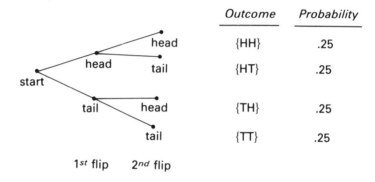

As you can see from this tree, there are four possible outcomes. You can use this tree to find out the probability of other events. What is the probability of getting exactly one H in two flips of a coin? Because there are two ways for this to occur (HT) or (TH), the answer is 2/4 or ½. When you want to find the probability of two or more different outcomes, add the probability of each outcome. This is called the "or rule." Another way to ask the same question is, "What is the probability of getting either a head followed by a tail (¼) or a tail followed by a head (¼)?" The correct procedure is to add these values, which equals ½. Intuitively, the probability of two or more events occurring should be higher (more likely) than the probability of any one of them occurring, and it is.

We can only use the "or rule" and the "and rule" when the events we're interested in are **independent**. Two events are independent when the occurrence of one of them does not influence the occurrence of the other. In this example, what you get on the first flip of a coin does not influence what you get on the second flip. In addition, the "or" rule requires that the outcomes be mutually exclusive, which means that if one occurs, the other cannot occur. In this example, the outcomes are mutually exclusive because we cannot obtain both a head and a tail on any single trial.

Tree diagrams are general ways of representing events that are useful in many situations. Let's extend this example. Suppose a man with a long handlebar moustache, shifty, beady eyes, and pinstripe suit stopped you on the street and asked you to bet on a coin-flipping game. He always calls heads. On the first flip, the coin lands heads up. On the second flip, the coin lands head up. On the third flip, the coin lands heads up. When would you begin to suspect that he wasn't using a fair coin? Most people would start to get suspicious by the third or fourth flip. Calculate the probability of a fair coin (probability of heads = .5) landing heads up in three and four tosses.

To calculate the probability of three heads in three flips, you would draw a probability tree with three sets of "nodes" with two "branches" coming off each node.

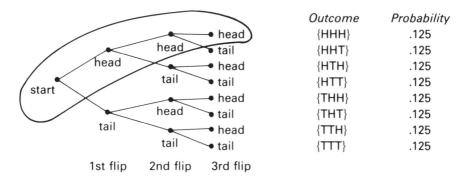

Outcome	Probability
{HHH}	.125
{HHT}	.125
{HTH}	.125
{HTT}	.125
{THH}	.125
{THT}	.125
{TTH}	.125
{TTT}	.125

1st flip   2nd flip   3rd flip

In this example, we are interested in finding the probability of getting three heads in a row when the coin is fair. Look at the column labeled "outcome" and find the outcome that shows {HHH}. Because this is the only outcome with 3 Hs, multiply the probabilities along the HHH branch (circled in the previous diagram), which are .5 x .5 x .5 = .125. A probability of .125 means that if the coin is fair, it would, on the average, land heads up three times in a row or 12.5% of the time. Because this is unlikely to happen, most people would begin to suspect that the coin is not fair if it landed heads up three times in a row.

To calculate the probability of four heads in four flips, add another branch to the tree.

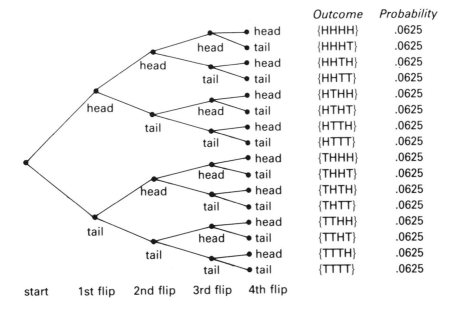

Outcome	Probability
{HHHH}	.0625
{HHHT}	.0625
{HHTH}	.0625
{HHTT}	.0625
{HTHH}	.0625
{HTHT}	.0625
{HTTH}	.0625
{HTTT}	.0625
{THHH}	.0625
{THHT}	.0625
{THTH}	.0625
{THTT}	.0625
{TTHH}	.0625
{TTHT}	.0625
{TTTH}	.0625
{TTTT}	.0625

start   1st flip   2nd flip   3rd flip   4th flip

The probability of 4 Hs is .5 x .5 x .5 x .5 = .0625, or about 6.25% of the time. As most of you already know, this is mathematically equal to $(.5)^4$; that is, multiplying a number by itself four times is the same as raising it to the fourth power. If you work this on a calculator with the ability to raise numbers to the fourth power, you'll get the same answer, .0625. Although this is a possible outcome, one that will sometimes occur, it is an unlikely outcome. In fact, it is so unlikely or unusual that many people would be willing to say that the shifty-eyed man is probably cheating. Certainly, by the fifth head in a row, it would seem reasonable to conclude that the man is cheating. For most scientific purposes, an event is considered "unusual" if it would be expected to occur by chance less than 5% of the time. (In probability jargon, this is $p < .05$.)

Let's get away from the artificial example of coin fliping, and apply the same logic in a more useful context. I'm sure that every student has, at some time or other, taken a multiple-choice test. (Some students like to call them multiple-guess tests.) Most of these tests have five alternative answers for each question. Only one of these is correct. Suppose also that the questions are so difficult that all you can do is guess randomly at the correct answer. What is the probability of guessing correctly on the first question? If you have no idea which alternative is the correct answer, then you are equally likely to choose any of the five alternatives, assuming that each alternative is equally likely to be correct. Because the sum of all possible alternatives must be 1.0, the probability of selecting each alternative, when they are equally likely, is .20. One alternative is correct, and four are incorrect, so the probability of selecting the correct alternative is .20. A tree diagram of this situation is shown here.

	Outcome	Probability
Correct	{C}	.2
Incorrect	{I}	.2
Incorrect	{I}	.2
Incorrect	{I}	.2
Incorrect	{I}	.2

Probability of being incorrect on the first question = .8.

start   1st Question

What is the probability of getting the first two multiple-choice questions correct by guessing? We'll have to add a second branch to a tree that will soon be very crowded. To save space and to simplify the calculations, all of the incorrect alternatives can be represented by one branch labeled "incorrect." The probability of being incorrect on any single question is .8:

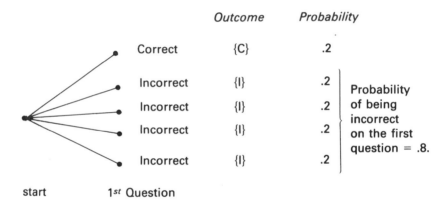

Outcome	Probability
{CC}	.04
{CI}	.16
{IC}	.16
{II}	.64

The probability of two correct questions by guessing is .2 x .2, which equals .04. That means that this would happen by chance only 4% of the time. Suppose we extend our example to three questions. I won't draw a tree, but you should be able to see by now that the probability is .2 x .2 x .2 = .008. This is so unusual that it would occur less than 1% of the time by chance. What would you conclude about someone who got all three of these questions correct? Most people (professors are people, too) would conclude that the student wasn't guessing, and that she really knew something. Of course, it is possible that the student was just lucky, but it is so unlikely that we would conclude that something other than luck was responsible for the outcome we obtained.

Let me point out a curious side to this kind of reasoning. Consider the plight of Sara. She took a 15-question multiple-choice test in which every question had five alternatives. Sara got all 15 questions wrong. Can you determine the probability of this happening by chance? I won't draw the tree diagram to depict this situation, but it is easy to see that the probability of being wrong on one question is .80; therefore the probability of being wrong on all 15 questions is $(.80)^{15}$. This is .80 times itself 15 times, which equals .0352. Because this would happen by chance only 3.52% of the time, can Sara present the argument to her professor that something other than chance determined this unusual result? Of course, Sara can make this argument, but would you be willing to believe her if you were her professor? Suppose she argued that she must have known the correct answer to every question. How else could she have avoided selecting it in all 15 consecutive questions? I don't know how many professors would buy her assertion that getting all 15 questions wrong demonstrates her knowledge, even though identical reasoning is used as proof of knowing correct answers when the probability of getting all the questions correct is about the same. (In this example, the probability of getting all 15 questions correct just by guessing is $[.20]^{15}$, which is a number far less than .0001.) Personally, if I were the professor, I'd give Sara high marks for creativity and for her understanding of statistical principles. It is possible that Sara did know "something" about the topic, but that "something" was systematically wrong. I'd also point out to her that it is possible that she was both unprepared and unlucky enough to guess wrong 15 times. After all, unusual events do happen sometimes.

Before going on to the next section, be sure that you understand how tree diagrams are used to compute probabilities and to consider all possible outcomes. I return to these diagrams later in this chapter. Once you learn how to use them, you'll be surprised at how many possible applications there are for tree diagrams.

Conjunction Error—Applying the "And Rule"

The following problem was posed by Tversky and Kahneman (1983):

> Linda is 31 years old, outspoken and very bright. She majored in philosophy. As a student, she was deeply concerned with issues of discrimination and social justice, and also participated in anti-nuclear demonstrations.
>
> For the following list of statements, estimate the probability that it is descriptive of Linda.
>
> A. Linda is a teacher in elementary school.
> B. Linda works in a bookstore and takes yoga classes.
> C. Linda is active in the feminist movement.
> D. Linda is a psychiatric social worker.
> E. Linda is a member of the League of Women voters.
> F. Linda is a bank teller.
> G. Linda is an insurance salesperson.
> H. Linda is a bank teller and is active in the feminist movement.
>
> Stop now and estimate the probability for each statement. (p. 297)

The short paragraph about Linda was written to be representative of an active feminist, which is Statement C. Thus, if we rely on common stereotypes of the "typical feminist," C would seem to be a likely description. Look at statements F (bank teller) and H (feminist *and* a bank teller). How did you rank these two sentences? Most people believe that H is more probably true than F. Can you see why F *must be* more likely than H when being a bank teller and being a feminist are independent of each other? There are some bank tellers who are not active in the feminist movement. When determining the probability of both of two events occurring, you multiply the probabilities of each one occurring (the "and" rule). Thus, the probability of two events *both* occurring must be less likely than the probability of one of these events occurring. In Tversky and Kahneman's (1983) study, 85% of the subjects judged Statement H to be more probable than Statement F. The error of believing that the occurrence of two events is more likely than the occurrence of one of them is called the **conjunction error**.

For those of you who think better with spatial arrays, let's represent this problem with circle diagrams, a form of representation that was used with syllogisms in the chapter on reasoning. Draw one circle to represent every bank teller in the world, and a second circle to represent every feminist. The two circles have to overlap somewhat because there are some bank tellers who are feminists. This area of overlap is shaded in Fig. 7.3. As you can see in Fig. 7.3, the shaded area that represents all people who are *both* bank tellers and feminists must be smaller than the circle that represents all bank tellers because there are bank tellers who are not feminists.

Now that you understand the conjunctive error, try the next question (also taken from Tversky and Kahneman, 1983):

A health survey was conducted in a sample of adult males in British Columbia, of all ages and occupations.

Please give your best estimate of the following values:

What percentage of the men surveyed have had one or more heart attacks? _____

What percentage of the men surveyed both are over 55 years old and have had one or more heart attacks? _____ (p. 308)

Stop now and fill in the blanks with your best estimate of these values.

Over 65% of the respondents believed that a higher percentage of the men would be both over 55 and have had a heart attack than the percentage of men who reported that they had a heart attack. Do you recognize this as another example of a conjunction error? The probability of two uncertain events both occurring cannot be greater than the probability of just one of them occurring.

FIG. 7.3. The two circles represent "All Feminists" and "All Bank Tellers." The intersection of these two circles shows those individuals who are both feminist and bank tellers. Because there are feminists who are not bank tellers and bank tellers who are not feminists, the area of their overlap must be smaller than either set alone.

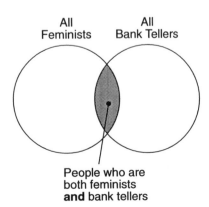

All
Feminists

All
Bank Tellers

People who are
both feminists
and bank tellers

Cumulative Risks—Applying the "Or Rule"

It should be obvious that the probability of getting three questions correct by chance when there are five alternatives will be much smaller than the probability of getting just one question correct by chance and that the probability of getting at least one question correct by chance out of three questions will be higher than the probability of getting one question correct when there is only one question. The kinds of examples presented so far were deliberately simple. Let's see how this principle applies in real-world settings.

Most real-life risks involve repeated exposure to a risky situation. Consider driving. The probability of having an accident in one car ride is very low. But what happens to this probability when you take hundreds or thousands of car rides? According to the "or rule," this is the probability of an accident on the first *or* second *or* ... nth car ride. In an interesting study of how people understand the concept of cumulative risk, Shaklee (1987) gave subjects different probability values that supposedly corresponded to the yearly risk of a flood. Subjects then had to estimate the likelihood of a flood in 1 month, 5 years, 10 years, and 15 years. Only 74% of her subjects knew that the likelihood of a flood increased with intervals over 1 year. Among those who gave higher probability values for intervals over 1 year, most seriously underestimated the **cumulative probability**.

Let's consider a similar example. In the case of contraception, a method that is 96% effective per year will result in an average of four pregnancies per 100 couples per year. Assuming a constant failure rate over time, we would expect even more women would become pregnant when using this method for a period of 5 years, and an even greater number when using this method over 15 years (Shaklee, 1987). In a study with college students, only 52% realized that the number of expected pregnancies would increase over time, and most of them significantly underestimated the number of pregnancies.

The message here should be clear: When you are determining risk, it is important to understand whether the value you are being given is per some unit of time (e.g., 1 year) and how cumulative risks increase with repeated exposure. It seems that many people do not understand the concept that cumulative risks are greater than one-time risks.

EXPECTED VALUES

Which of the following bets would you take if you could only choose one of them?

1. The Big 12: It will cost you $1 to play. If you roll a pair of dice and get a 12, you'll get your $1 back, plus another $24. If you roll any other number, you'll lose your $1.
2. Lucky 7: It will cost you $1 to play (same cost as above). If you roll a "lucky 7" with a pair of dice, you'll get your $1 back, plus another $6. If you roll any other number, you'll lose your $1.

Stop now and select either Item 1 or 2.

Most people choose Item 1, reasoning that $24 if a 12 is rolled is four times more than they can win if a 7 is rolled, and the cost is the same for each bet. Let's see if this thinking is correct.

In order to decide which is the better bet, we need to consider the probability of winning and losing and the corresponding value of each. There is a formula that will take these variables into account and yield the **expected value** (EV) for each gamble.

An expected value is the amount of money you would expect to win on each bet if you continued playing over and over. The formula for computing an expected value (EV) is:

EV = (probability of a win) x (value of a win) + (probability of a loss) x (value of a loss)

Let's consider the EV for Choice 1. We'll begin by computing the probability of rolling a 12 with a pair of dice. There is only one way to roll a 12, and that is with a 6 on each die. The probability of this happening when the dice are fair is $1/6 \times 1/6 = 1/36 = .028$. (Because we are interested in finding the probability of a 6 on the first *and* the second die, we use the "and rule," and multiply.) Thus, we'd expect to roll a 12 about 2.8% of the time. What is the probability of not rolling a 12? Because we are certain that you will either roll a 12 or not roll a 12 (this covers all possible events), you can subtract .028 from 1.00. The probability of not rolling a 12 is .972. (You could also arrive at this figure, with some small rounding differences, by calculating the probability of each of the 35 other possible outcomes—each will be 1/36—and adding them together.) All possible outcomes from rolling a pair of dice are shown in Fig. 7.4.

Using these probability values, the EV formula for Choice 1 becomes:

EV   =   (Probability of a 12) x (Value of a 12) + (Probability of
(Choice 1)   *not* getting a 12) x (Value of *not* getting a 12)

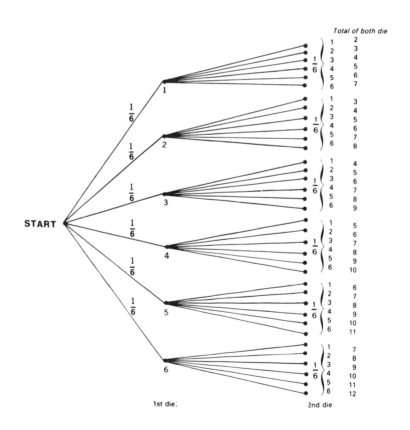

FIG. 7.4.   A tree diagram depicting all possible outcomes of rolling a pair of dice.

EV	=	[(.028) x ($24)] + [(.972) x (-$1)]
(Choice 1)		

EV	=	$.672 - $.97
(Choice 1)		

EV	=	-$.30
(Choice 1)		

Let's review what happened in this formula. If you rolled a 12, you'd win $24, which is the value associated with this win. If you rolled a number other than a 12, you'd lose the $1 you paid to play this game, thus -$1 is the value associated with this loss. The probability of a win was multiplied by the value of a win. The probability of a loss was multiplied by the value of a loss. Then, these two products were added together. The EV of this bet is -$.30. This means that in the long run, if you continue playing this game many times, you could expect to lose, on the average, $.30 for every game played. Of course, on any single game, you'd either lose $1 or win $24, but after many, many games you would have lost an average of $.30 per game. If you played 1,000 games, making the same bet each time, you'd be $300 poorer.

How does this compare with Choice 2? To calculate the EV of Choice 2, we'll begin by computing the probability of rolling a 7. How many ways is it possible to roll a 7 with a pair of fair dice? You could get a 1 on the first die and a 6 on the second, a 2 and a 5, a 3 and a 4, a 4 and a 3, a 5 and a 2, or a 6 and a 1. Thus, there are 6 possible ways to roll a 7 out of 36 possible outcomes. The probability of any one of these outcomes is 1/6 x 1/6, which equals 1/36. (This is the probability of rolling, e.g., a 1 on the first die and a 6 on the second die.) Thus to determine the probability of one number followed by a second number you would apply the "and" rule. Because you are now concerned with the probability of a 1 followed by a 6 *or* a 2 followed by a 5 *or* a 3 followed by a 4 *or* a 4 followed by a 3 *or* a 5 followed by a 2 *or* a 6 followed by a 1, you should recognize the second step as a case where the "or rule" is needed. Because there are six possible combinations, you would add 1/36 six times (which is, of course, the same as multiplying it by 6). Thus, the probability of rolling a 7 with a pair of dice is 6/36 (1/6 or .167). The probability of not rolling a 7 is 1 - .167, which equals .833. Now we calculate the EV of Choice 2:

EV	=	(Probability of a 7) x (Value of a 7) + (Probability of not
(Choice 2)		getting a 7) x (Value of not getting a 7)

EV	=	[(.167) x ($6)] + [(.833) x (-$1)]
(Choice 2)		
	=	($1.002 - .833)
	=	$.169, or approximately $.17

This means that if you continued to gamble on Choice 2, you would win an average of $.17 for every game played. Thus, after 1,000 games, you could expect to be $170 richer. Of course, as in Choice 1, you would never actually win this amount on any single game; this is what would result if you continued playing many, many games. This is what would happen in the long run.

Even though you might have originally thought otherwise, Choice 2 is the better choice because of the relatively high probability associated with rolling a 7. Seven has a high probability because there were six possible combinations that would add up to a 7.

There is a party game that is based on the principle that the more ways an event can occur, the more likely it is to occur. Suppose you get a random sample of 40 people together in a room. Estimate the probability that two of them share the same birthday. You may be surprised to learn that the probability is approximately .90. Can you figure out why it is so high? There are many, many ways that 40 people can share the same birthday. To figure out the exact probability, you would take all combinations of 40 people, 2 at a time. Thus, we'd have to start with the combination of Person 1 with Person 2, then Person 1 with Person 3, and so on until Person 1 is matched with Person 40, then we'd begin again matching Person 2 with Person 3, 2 with 4, on until 2 is matched with 40. This whole process would have to be repeated until everyone of the 40 people is matched with every other one. Because there are so many possible combinations of any two people sharing any birthday in the year, this "coincidence" is more probable than it may have seemed at first. The probability of 2 people sharing a common birthday is over .50, when there are 23 people and over .75 when there are 32 people (Loftus & Loftus, 1982). You can use this knowledge to make wagers at parties or at any gathering of people. It's a fairly good bet when the number of people is close to 40. Most people find it hard to believe that the probability is so high.

You can also use your knowledge of probability to improve your chances in other situations. Take, for example, Aaron and Jill, who have been arguing over who should take out the garbage. Their mother agrees to help them settle this matter by picking a number from 1 to 10. The one whose number comes closer to the one selected by their mother will win the dispute. Aaron goes first and picks 3. What number should Jill select to maximize her chances of winning? Stop now and decide what number she should select.

The best number for Jill to pick is 4. If her mother was thinking of any number greater than 3, Jill would win with this strategy. Thus, she can change the probability of winning in what seems like a chance situation.

SUBJECTIVE PROBABILITY

We usually do not deal directly with known or objective probabilities, such as the probability of rain on a given day or the probability of developing heart disease if oral contraceptives are taken. Yet, every day we make decisions using our best estimate of the likelihood of events. **Subjective probability** refers to personal estimates of the likelihood of events. This term is in distinction from **objective probability**, which is a mathematically determined statement of likelihood about known frequencies. Psychologists who have studied subjective probability have found that human judgments of probability are often fallible, yet we rely on them to guide our decisions in countless situations.

Gambler's Fallacy

The "Wheel of Fortune" is a popular game at fairs, casinos, amusement parks, and on television game shows. It consists of a large wheel that can be spun. The wheel is divided into many numbered sections, much like a roulette wheel. A rubber marker indicates the winning number.

Suppose that your friend, Vanna, decides to approach the Wheel of Fortune in a scientific manner. She sits at the Wheel of Fortune and records when each number comes up as the winning number. Suppose Vanna has recorded the following series of winning numbers: 3, 6, 10, 19, 18, 4, 1, 7, 7, 5, 20, 17, 2, 14, 19, 13, 8, 11, 13, 16, 12, 15, 19, 3, 8. After examining these numbers very carefully, she proclaims that a 9 has not appeared in the last 25 spins; therefore, she plans to bet heavily on number 9, because it is now much more likely to occur. Would you agree with her that this is a good bet?

If you responded, "Yes," you have committed a very common error in understanding probability. The Wheel of Fortune has no memory for which numbers have previously appeared. If the wheel had been built so that each number is equally likely to win, then a 9 is equally likely on each spin, regardless of how frequently or infrequently it appeared in the past. People believe that chance processes like spinning a Wheel of Fortune should be self-correcting so that if an event has not occurred in a while it is now more likely to occur. This misconception is called **gambler's fallacy**.

Gambler's fallacy can be found in many settings. Consider a sports example. A "slumping" batter who hasn't had a hit in a long while is sometimes believed to be more likely to have a hit because he is "due" one. A sports enthusiast, who is a friend of mine, told me the following story about Don Sutton, a former pitcher for the Dodgers. One season, Sutton gave up a great many runs. He predicted that this "slump" would be followed by a "correction" so that he would end up the season at his usual average. Unfortunately, there is no correction for chance factors and, because he had such a poor start to the season, he ended the season below his usual average.

Often, people will continue to believe in gambler's fallacy even after it has been explained to them. Students have told me that although they can understand on an intellectual level why gambler's fallacy must be wrong, on an intuitive or "gut" level, it seems that it ought to be right. Understanding probability often requires that we go against our intuitive hunches because they are often wrong. Let's try another example.

Wayne and Marsha have four sons. Although they really don't want to have five children, both have always wanted a daughter. Should they plan to have another child, because they are now more likely to have a daughter, given that their first four children were boys? If you understand gambler's fallacy, you'll recognize that a daughter is as likely as a son on the fifth try, just as it was on each of the first four. (Actually, because slightly more boys than girls are born, the probability of having a boy baby is slightly higher than the probability of having a girl baby.)

Gambler's fallacy also has a flip side, that is the belief that random events run in streaks. Consider the following two scenarios:

A. A basketball player has just *missed* 2 or 3 of the last shots in a row. She is about to shoot again.
B. A basketball player has just *made* 2 or 3 of the last shots in a row. She is about to shoot again.

Is she more likely to make the basket in A or B?

Gilovich (1991) asked questions like this one to knowledgeable basketball fans and found that 91% believed that the player was more likely to be successful in B than in A. In other words, they believed that players shoot in streaks. In order to determine whether there is any evidence to support the "belief in streaks," Gilovich analyzed data from the Philadelphia 76ers. He found:

- If a player just made a shot, 51% of the next shots were successful.
- If a player just missed a shot, 54% of the next shots were successful.
- If a player made two shots in a row, 50% of the next shots were successful.
- If a player missed two shots in a row, 53% of the next shots were successful.

These data show no evidence that players shoot in streaks. Yet, interviews with the 76ers players themselves showed that they *believe* that they shot in streaks. It is very difficult to convince people that chance is exactly that—it doesn't self-correct or run in nonrandom streaks.

Base-Rate Neglect

Charlie is anxious to experience his first kiss. If he asks Louise to go to the movies with him, he's only 10% sure that she'll accept his invitation, but if she does, he's 95% sure that she'll kiss him goodnight. What are Charlie's chances for romance?

Initial or a priori probabilities are called the **base rate**. In this problem, the first hurdle that Charlie has to "get over" is getting Louise to go out with him. The probability of this occurring is 10%. It is important to think about this figure—the base rate. Ten percent is a fairly low value, so it is likely that she will not go out with him. He wants to know the probability of two uncertain events occurring—she both goes out with him *and* she kisses him. Before we start to solve this problem think about the kind of answer you would expect. Will it be greater than 95%, between 95% and 10%, or less than 10%?

To solve this problem, we'll use a tree diagram to depict the possible outcomes and the probability associated with each. Of course, it is not likely that Charlie or any other Romeo-wanna-be will actually compute the probability values or draw a tree diagram for determining the probability of this momentous event, but this example demonstrates how likelihoods combine. Maybe he'll decide that the probability of a kiss from Louise is so small that he'll opt for Brunhilda, who is both more likely to accept his offer of a date and succumb to his romantic charms. Besides, anyone who has actually estimated probability values for romance might also want to be more precise in his estimates of two or more events.

We'll start with a tree diagram that first branches into Louise accepts his date and Louise declines. A second branch will be drawn from the Louise accepts his date node indicating whether he gets kissed or not. Each branch should have the appropriate probability labels. Of course, if Louise declines his invitation, Charlie definitely won't get kissed. The branch from the "Louise declines" node is thus labeled 1.00 for "Charlie doesn't get kissed."

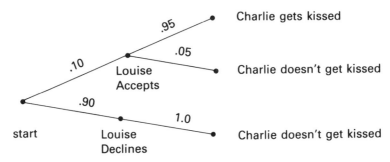

According to the "and rule" for finding the probability of two (or more) events, the probability that Louise will kiss Charlie goodnight is:

$$.10 \times .95 = .095$$

Are you surprised to find that the objective probability is less than the low base rate of 10% and much less than the higher secondary or subsequent rate of 95%? Most people are. I hope that you recognized that any value greater than 10% would have been indicative of a conjunction error. Recall from the earlier section on conjunction errors that the probability of two uncertain events both occurring (Louise accepts *and* kisses Charlie) must be less than the probability of either event alone. Most people ignore (or underestimate) the low base rate and estimate their answer as closer to the higher secondary rate. In general, people tend to overestimate the probability of two or more uncertain events occurring. This type of error is known as **base-rate neglect**.

MAKING PROBABILISTIC DECISIONS

Most of the important decisions that we make in life involve probabilities. Although decision making is discussed more fully in chapter 8, let's consider how tree diagrams can be an aid for decision making.

Edith is trying to decide on a college major. She attends a very selective university that has independent admissions for each of its majors. She is seriously thinking about becoming an accountant. She knows that the accounting department accepts 25% of the students who apply for that major. Of those accepted, 70% graduate and 90% of those who graduate pass the national accounting examination and become accountants. She would like to know what her chances are of becoming an accountant if she pursues the accounting major.

To answer this question, draw a tree diagram with branches that represent the "path" for success in accounting.

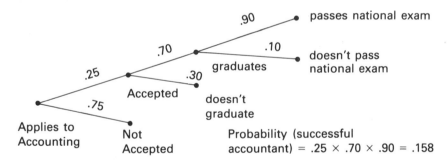

From the preceding diagram, you can see that the probability of becoming a successful accountant is equal to .25 x .70 x .90, which is .158. At this point, Edith should consider other options. For example, she could consider applying to both the accounting major and to the education major. She could recalculate her chances for success in one of these majors, both of these majors (if this is a possible option for her), and neither of these majors.

This example assumes that we have no additional information on which to base Edith's chances of success. Suppose instead that we know that Edith has excellent math skills. Shouldn't this sort of information change the probabilities involved and make it more likely that Edith be admitted, graduate, and succeed in a math-related occupation? Intuitively, the answer is "yes." Let's see how the problem changes by considering José's probability for success in the following example.

Combining Information to Make Predictions

José has always wanted to be an actor. Accordingly, he plans to sell his worldly possessions and head for a career in the "Big Apple" (the loving nickname for New

York). Suppose that you and José both know that only about 4% of all aspiring actors ever "make it" professionally in New York. This value is the base rate; it is based on information that is known before we have any specific information about José. Stop and think about this figure—the base rate. It tells us that very few aspiring actors become professionals in this field. In other words, the chance of success in low. Suppose that you had no additional information about José. What value would you predict as his chance of success? If you said 4%, right on! In the absence of any other information, use the base rate.

José tells you not to worry, because 75% of those who are successful have curly hair and can sing and tell jokes well. Because he has curly hair, is a good singer, and a hilarious comedian, he feels confident that he will soon be sending 8 x 10 glossy pictures of himself to his fan club members. This second value is called the secondary; it is the probability value that relates specific information about characteristics that are associated with José and with an outcome. We'll use these two probability values to decide if José's optimism is warranted. Exactly how likely is he to succeed? Before you continue, make a probability estimate for his chance of success. Remember, probabilities range from 0 to 1, with 0 meaning he will definitely fail and have to return to Peoria, and 1 meaning he will definitely succeed on Broadway. Stop now and make a subjective probability judgment of his chance for success.

Can you think of a way of objectively finding his chance of success? In order to arrive at an objective probability, you'll need to know another number, one that is often ignored—the percentage of those who fail and have the attributes that are associated with success (in this case, curly hair and the ability to sing, dance, and joke). Few people realize that they need to consider this value in assessing the probability of success. For ease of reference, I'll call the attributes that are associated with success (curly hair, ability to sing and tell jokes) "curly hair," and the absence of these attributes, I'll call "not curly hair." Suppose that 50% of those who fail have these attributes. Once again, tree diagrams can be used to determine probabilities in this context. Let's begin at a starting point and consider all possible outcomes. In this case, he will either succeed or fail, so we'll label the first branches "succeed" and "fail." As before, we'll put the probability of each event along the appropriate branch:

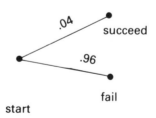

Notice that these two probabilities (.04 and .96) sum to 1.0, because they include all possibilities. One of these two possibilities must occur, so they will add up to 1.0 to indicate absolute certainty.

José knows that 75% of those who succeed have curly hair. In this example, what we are trying to find is the probability of a certain outcome (success) *given that* we already have information that is relevant to the probability of that outcome. Let's add a second branch to the tree diagram, branching off from the succeed node and the fail node. There are four different probabilities involved in this example: the probability of succeeding and having curly hair, the probability of succeeding and not having curly hair, the probability of failing and having curly hair, and the probability of failing and not having curly hair. These four possibilities are shown in the next tree diagram:

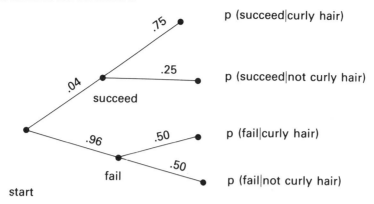

p (succeed|curly hair)

p (succeed|not curly hair)

p (fail|curly hair)

p (fail|not curly hair)

Note that because 75% (.75) of those who succeed have curly hair, and 25% (.25) do not have this attribute, the sum of all probabilities from a tree node must sum to 1.0. Similarly, 50% of those who fail have curly hair, whereas 50% of those who fail do not possess this attribute. Because we are considering everyone who fails, these values must also sum to 1.0.

Once the tree diagram is drawn, it is a simple matter to compute José's objective probability of success. As before, multiply along each branch to find the probabilities. In this case, we would multiply the values along each branch of the tree diagram and compile the information in a chart:

P[Succeed & Curly Hair]	= .04 x .75 =	.03
P[Succeed & Not Curly Hair]	= .04 x .25 =	.01
P[Fail & Curly Hair]	= .96 x .50 =	.48
P[Fail & Not Curly Hair]	= .96 x .50 =	.48
		1.00

From this table, we can see that the total proportion of people with curly hair is .03 + .48 = .51.

To determine José's true chance of success, we need to divide the proportion who succeed and have curly hair (.03) by the total proportion who have curly hair (.48 + .03 = .51). We are trying to *predict* José's success based on the knowledge that he has curly hair and that some proportion of all people with curly hair are successful. Of all of those with curly hair (.51), what proportion of them succeed (.03)?

$$\frac{\text{Proportion who succeed \& curly hair}}{\text{Total proportion of people with curly hair}} = \frac{.03}{.03 + .48} \approx .06$$

Thus, José's chances for success are 50% higher (6% vs. 3%) than they are for any unknown, aspiring actor, but they are still very low. Knowing that he has certain attributes that are associated with success improved his probability of success above the base rate, but the improvement was very small.

You may find it easier to follow the logic of these calculations by putting the information in a table format.

Success⟍ Hair, etc.	Succeed	Fail	Row Totals
Curly hair, etc.	.03	.48	.51
No curly hair, etc.	.01	.48	.49
Column totals	.04	.96	1.00

Are you surprised to find that his chance of success is so low given that the posterior or secondary probability value was so high (75%)? Most people are. The reason that José has such a slim chance of becoming an actor is because so few people, in general, succeed. The probability value José obtained was close to the a priori, or base rate, of success among all aspiring actors. Because so few actors, in general, succeed, José, and any other would-be thespian, has a low chance for success. Research has shown that, in general, most people overestimate success when base rates are low and underestimate success when base rates are high. In the earlier example concerning Edith, we had only base-rate information to use in predicting success. By contrast, we had additional information about José that allowed us to improve upon the base rate when predicting his success, although because of the low rate of success for actors in general, the improvement was slight.

For those of you who prefer to think spatially, think about a large group of people, 4% of whom are successful actors and 96% are not. This group is shown in Fig. 7.5. Four of the 100 "people" depicted are smiling—these represent the successful actors. If you had no other information to use to predict success for José, you would use this base-rate information and give him a 4% probability for success.

Now let's consider the additional information. Seventy-five percent of those who are successful have curly hair, whereas 50% of those who are not successful have curly hair. This information is combined with the base-rate information. It is depicted in Fig. 7.6 with the addition of curly hair to the successful and unsuccessful actors. Of the 4

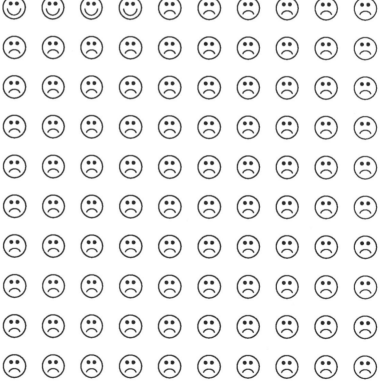

FIG. 7.5. Pictorial representation of a 4% success rate. Note that 4% of the faces are smiling.

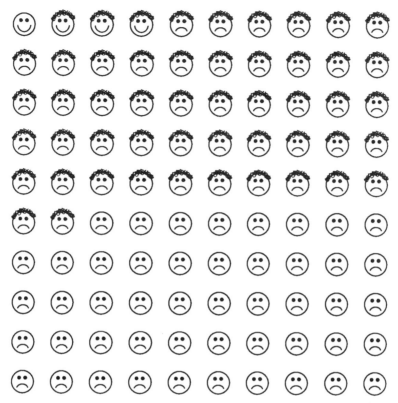

FIG. 7.6. Pictorial representation of the relative proportion of successful and unsuccessful actors who have the same attributes as José. These are depicted by the addition of curly hair.

smiling faces, 3 have curly hair (75%), and of the 96 frowning faces, 48 (50%) have curly hair.

By examining these figures, it should be easy to see that what we are doing mathematically is finding the proportion of smiling faces with curly hair relative to all of the faces with curly hair in order to use this information about José to predict his success. Graphically, this is 3 smiling faces with curly hair as a proportion (or fraction) of the 51 faces that have curly hair:

$$\frac{3}{51} \approx .06$$

To review, when you are calculating the probability of an outcome, given that you have information that is relevant to its probability, you will:

1. Draw a complete tree diagram, with the base-rate information (e.g., succeed or fail) as the first set of nodes. Use the secondary information to draw the second set of nodes.

2. Make a chart with all combinations of the base-rate information and secondary information as the rows in the chart.

3. Multiply probabilities across each of the branches of the tree diagram and fill in each row of the chart with these values.

4. Form a ratio (fraction) with the probability value from the branch that you are interested in (e.g., succeed given that he has curly hair) as the numerator and the sum of this value and the other branch that contains the same conditional statement (e.g., fail given that he has curly hair).

5. Check your answer. Does it make sense? Would you expect, as in this example, that the probability of success is higher than the base rate because we know something about the individual that is associated with success? (If we knew that José had some trait that was associated with failure, we would predict that his chance of success would be less than the base rate, but with low base rates, it probably won't be much less.)

There are many diseases that occur with low base rates in the population. Medical test results must be interpreted in light of the relevant base rates for each disease. Medicine, like most other disciplines, is a probabilistic science, yet few physicians receive training in understanding probabilities. Failure to utilize base-rate information can lead to improper diagnoses. Base-rate neglect is a pervasive error in thinking about probabilistic outcomes. Consider Dreman's (1979) summary of a large body of research on this effect: "The tendency to underestimate or altogether ignore past probabilities in making a decision is undoubtedly the most significant problem of intuitive predictions" (cited in Myers, 1995, p. 331). The implications of such consistent errors and cognitive biases are enormous, not only in economics, management, and investments, but in virtually every area where such decision-making comes into play.

Nonregressive Judgments

Harris is a new student at Rah-Rah State University. The average grade point average (GPA) for all students at Rah-Rah is 2.8. Harris is new to this college and has not yet taken any exams. Although we have no information about Harris specifically, what would be your best guess that his grade point average will be? Stop here and make your best guess for his grade point average.

After his first set of midterm exams, Harris has a midterm GPA of 3.8. Given this new information, what would you now predict for Harris' GPA at the end of the school year? Most people readily answer the first question with 2.8, the average GPA for all students at Rah-Rah. This is a correct answer, as in the absence of any specific information, the average for all students, the population at Rah-Rah, is the best estimate for anyone. Most people answer the second question with 3.8. Unfortunately, this is not the best answer. Although it is true that someone who scores high on midterms will also tend to score high on finals, the relationship is not a one-to-one or perfect relationship. In general, when someone scores extremely high on some scale, she or he will score closer to the average the second time. Thus, the best prediction for Harris' GPA at the end of the school year will be less than 3.8 and greater than 2.8. (The actual value can be mathematically determined, but the calculations are beyond the scope of this book.) This is a difficult concept to understand, because most people find it to be counterintuitive. Yet, it is true.

It may be useful to think about a sports example. Consider your favorite athletes. Although they may have a truly exceptional performance one day, most often they will perform closer to average, but still above average on other days. After all, no one bowls all perfect games or bats 1.000. Sports enthusiasts will recognize this principle as the "sophomore slump." After an outstanding first year at a sport, the star will usually perform closer to average during her second year. Another example that may help to clarify the concept is an often used one about fathers' and sons' heights. In general, very tall fathers will have sons that are closer to average height (although still above average) than the fathers are. This phenomenon is called **regression toward the mean**. (Mean is just another term for average—it is computed by adding up all the values you're interested in and dividing by the number of values.)

Earlier in this chapter, I talked about the laws of chance. No one can predict accurately the height of any particular individual. But, in the long run—that is with many, many extremely tall fathers—most of their son's heights will show regression toward the mean. Thus, as before, we can make better predictions by knowing about the laws of chance, but we won't always be accurate. It is important to understand this concept whenever dealing with probabilistic events.

Kahneman and Tversky (1973) studied what can happen when regression toward the mean is not understood by professionals. Israeli flight instructors were told that they should praise their students when they successfully performed difficult flight patterns and maneuvers and that they should criticize exceptionally poor performance. Based on what you've just learned about regression toward the mean, what, in general, should happen after a pilot performs extremely well? Subsequent maneuvers should be closer to average, or less than exceptional, because the performance moved or regressed toward the mean (average). Conversely, what should you expect to happen following very poor performance? Again, subsequent maneuvers should tend to be more average, or in this case, they would improve, although they may still be less than average. The Israeli flight instructors did not understand regression toward the mean and errone-ously concluded that praise led to poorer performance and criticism improved it.

Let's consider another example of regression to the mean. Regression to the mean is ubiquitous, yet few people ever recognize it. Suppose that you learn of a self-help group for people with children who seriously misbehave. (There really are such groups.) Most parents will enter these groups when their child's behavior is at its worst because most parents will seek help only when the behavior is extremely bad. After a few weeks in the program, many parents report an improvement in their child's behavior. Can we conclude that the program probably worked to help parents control their children's behavior? Think regression to the mean! If parents entered the program when the behavior is extremely bad, then no matter what they do, including nothing at all, the child's behavior will most likely regress toward the mean. In other words, if a child is extremely misbehaved, it is statistically true that the child will move toward the average on measures of behavior. We would not predict angelic or even average behavior, just some improvement or movement toward the mean. Because this is a statistical predic-tion, sometimes, we will be wrong, but on the average (in the long run), we will be right with this prediction. Thus, we cannot conclude anything about the effectiveness of this program unless we conduct a true experiment of the sort that was described in chapter 6. We would need to randomly assign children and families to these groups and to "no-treatment control groups" and then determine if the children in the self-help group were significantly better behaved than those who received no treatment. We must be able to randomly assign families to groups before we can conclude that the self-help group was helpful in improving the child's behavior. Once you start looking for regression to the mean, you will be surprised how many events in life are best explained by "moving toward the average" and not to other causes.

RISK

If we examine data from hundreds of communities around the United States or around the world, we will find that some communities have exceptionally high rates of some sorts of cancers, birth defects, brain tumors, unexplained deaths, and other maladies. How can we know if there are links between these high rates of illness and toxic substances such as pesticides in the water, magnetic fields from electrical power lines, or whether they are due to chance?

The notion of frequency, or how often an event occurs, is inherent in the definition of probability. If an event is frequent, then its occurrence is highly probable. In order to determine the risk involved with a disastrous event, we need to first determine the frequency with which it occurs. Because most disastrous events are rare (e.g., plane crashes, leaks from nuclear plants) and, in some cases, take years before they are evident (e.g., cancers from environmental hazards), determining their frequency is a very difficult task. In order to understand how people make judgments involving risks, we need to understand how they determine the frequency of real-life risky events. Several researchers (Lichtenstein et al., 1978) focused on the way people judge the frequency of lethal (deadly) events. They studied this by asking college students and members of the League of Women Voters to decide which of two possible causes of death is more probable for several pairs of lethal events. In order to understand their experiment and their results, let's try a few examples. For the following pairs of items, indicate which is the more likely cause of death, and then estimate how much more likely your choice is than the other event. (Actual frequencies are presented at the end of this section.)

A. Asthma   or   Tornado
B. Excess Cold   or   Syphilis
C. Diabetes   or   Suicide
D. Heart Disease   or   Lung Cancer
E. Flood   or   Homicide
F. Syphilis   or   Diabetes
G. Asthma   or   Botulism
H. Poisoning by Vitamins   or   Lightning
I. Tuberculosis   or   Homicide
J. All Accidents   or   Stomach Cancer

Researchers found that although, in general, people were more accurate as the differences in the true frequencies of occurrence between the events increased, they made a large number of errors in estimating the relative frequencies of the events. Their subjects overestimated the frequencies of events that occurred very rarely and underestimated the frequencies of those events that occurred very often. In addition, lethal events that had received a great deal of publicity (e.g., airplane crashes, flood, homicide, tornado, botulism) were overestimated, whereas those that were undramatic, silent killers (e.g., diabetes, stroke, asthma, tuberculosis) were underestimated. It seems that publicized events were more easily brought to mind and this biased judgments of their frequency. Hazards that are unusually memorable, such as a recent disaster or an event depicted in a sensationalized way on the news like a major plane crash or botulism in undercooked hamburgers, distort our perceptions of risk. In chapter 2, I made the point that memory is an integral component of all thinking processes. What we remember is a major influence on how we think. The importance of being mindful of possible biases in memory when evaluating thought processes is seen in this quote:

...[O]ur society most often makes judgments about hazardous activities for which adequate statistical data is lacking, such as recombinant DNA research or nuclear waste disposal. We suspect that the biases found here (overestimation of rare events, underestimation of likely events, and an undue influence of drama or vividness) may be operating, indeed, may even be amplified in such situations. (Lichtenstein et al., 1978, p. 577)

It is not surprising that we tend to overestimate the probability of events that receive excessive coverage in the media. We rely on the information that is available to us to make decisions, and we are usually not aware when that information is biased or sensationalized (Fischoff, 1993). Homicides are routinely part of every news broadcast and every newspaper; deaths from heart disease are rarely mentioned in these contexts. Not surprisingly, many people believe that they are more likely to be murdered than to die of heart disease (a fact that, sadly, is true for adolescents and young adults in some of America's large cities, but untrue for almost everyone else).

Assessing Risks

Every day we take risks and avoid others. It starts as soon as we wake up.

—Wilson and Crouch (1987)

How do the experts make decisions that involve potentially disastrous outcomes? How can we as informed citizens and voters make risky decisions? Questions like these are timely, but not easy to answer.

The goal of risk assessment is to find ways to avoid, reduce, or manage risks (Wilson & Crouch, 1987). Risk is associated with every aspect of life. For example, approximately 200 people are electrocuted each year in accidents involving home wiring or appliances, and 7,000 people die each year in U.S. homes as a result of falls (most of them are over 65 years old). Yet, few of us would interpret these risks as great enough to either forgo electricity or stop walking in our homes. Other risks are clearly too large to take. Few of us, for example, would decide to cross a busy freeway wearing a blindfold. And still other risks are largely unknown, such as the release of a new chemical into the environment or the development of a new technology. Wilson and Crouch (1987) suggested several ways of estimating risks that voters and consumers should consider when deciding if an action or a technology is safe enough:

1. One method of risk assessment involves *examining historical data*. For example, to understand the risk of cancer due to exposure to medical X-rays, there are data that indicate that for a given dose per year (40 mrem) there is an expected number of cancers (1,100). This sort of risk information can be compared to other known risks so that consumers can decide if the benefits of medical X-rays outweigh the risks.

2. The risk of a new technology for which there are no historical data can be computed when the occurrence of the events are independent by *calculating the risk of separate components and multiplying along the branches of a decision tree*. This method of calculating probabilities was presented in an earlier section of this chapter. A well-known example is the probability of a severe accident at a chemical plant.

3. Risks can also be calculated by analogy. (The use of analogies as an aid to problem solving is discussed more fully in the following two chapters.) When animals are used to test drugs, the experimenter is really using an analogy to extrapolate the risk to humans.

Biases in Risk Assessment

Psychologists and others who study the way people determine if something is "too risky" know that most of us fall prey to common biases when we assess the "murky psychometrical stew" (Paulos, 1994, p. 34) that constitutes the numerical information and misinformation that we need to interpret. Here are some common biases (Wandersman & Hallman, 1993):

1. When a risk is voluntary, it is perceived to be less risky than one that is not voluntary. For example, cosmetic surgery is often believed to be safer than a nonelective surgery. After all, patients choose to undergo cosmetic surgery, so they must rationalize that it is "safe enough."

2. Natural risks are believed to be less hazardous than artificial ones. For example, many people believe that naturally occurring toxins in our food are less dangerous than ones that are caused by pesticides or preservatives that are added.

3. Memorial events in which many people are harmed at once are perceived as riskier than more mundane and less vivid events. An example of this effect is the large number of people who are terrified of plane crashes, but give little thought to automobile safety.

4. Events over which we have some perceived control are believed to be safer than those over which we don't have control. Most people tend to feel safer when they are driving an automobile than when others are driving because most of us believe that we are better-than-average drivers.

5. Phenomena that are not observable and are associated with spectacular dreaded outcomes (DNA technology, radioactive waste, AIDS, and nuclear reactors) are believed to be riskier than phenomena that involve known risks or less dreaded outcomes (smoking, auto accidents, dynamite, and handguns; Slovic, 1987).

It is clear that personal risk perceptions are not the same as scientific risk estimates. Experts in risk assessment perceive risks based on annual mortality so that the event that results in the greater number of deaths is judged to be the greater risk. Experts, for example, ranked motor vehicles as riskier than nuclear power (because more people are expected to die from motor vehicle accidents), whereas samples of college students and members of the League of Women Voters ranked nuclear power as the greater risk (because it is an example of a spectacular dreaded outcome).

A major difficulty in interpreting low-probability risks like flood or a nuclear accident is that the figures involved are not readily meaningful. Knowing that a particular risky event occurs in 1 in 10,000 individuals is difficult to interpret. We need to be able to convert this information into an answer to the question, "Is this likely to happen to me?" One suggestion for making this sort of information more meaningful is to convert all such risks to a standard "risk per hour" metric (Slovic, Fischoff, & Lichtenstein, 1986). For example, suppose you learned that the risk involved in taking a motorcycle trip is the same as the risk of being 75 years old for 1 hour. Would this type of information be helpful in interpreting the risk of a motorcycle trip in a meaningful way? Although information of this sort might be useful for judging comparative risk (motorcycle trip compared to hang gliding), it may not be useful by itself because it is still difficult to understand what is meant by the risk of being 75 years old for 1 hour.

As voters and as consumers we face countless decisions about a large and diverse array of topics, which include nuclear energy, food irradiation, surgical procedures, air and water quality, and drug use. An informed decision will always require a careful consideration of the information that is relevant to risk assessment (e.g., historical data, risk by analogy, and risks of separate components) as well as an understanding of the way subjective estimates of risk are biased.

Here are the answers to the questions about the probability of lethal events along with the true frequency of each event (rate per 100,000,000). Check your answer and see if you made the common errors of overestimating events that are more memorable and likely to affect many people at one time (like a plane crash) and understimating those risks over which we believe have some control (like driving an automobile).

	More Likely	*Rate*	*Less Likely*	*Rate*
A.	Asthma	920	Tornado	44
B.	Syphilis	200	Excess Cold	163
C.	Diabetes	19,000	Suicide	12,000
D.	Heart Disease	360,000	Lung Cancer	37,000
E.	Homicide	9,200	Flood	100
F.	Diabetes	19,000	Syphilis	200
G.	Asthma	920	Botulism	1
H.	Lightning	52	Poisoning/Vitamins	.5
I.	Homicide	9,200	Tuberculosis	1,800
J.	All accidents	55,000	Stomach Cancer	46,600

STATISTICAL USE AND ABUSE

There are three kinds of lies: lies, damned lies, and statistics.

—Disraeli (1804–1881)

When we want to find out something about a group of people, it is often impossible or inconvenient to ask everyone in the group. Suppose you want to know if people who donate blood to the Red Cross are, in general, kind and generous people. Because you can't examine everyone who donates blood to determine how kind and considerate she or he is, you would examine a portion of the population, which is called a **sample**. A number calculated on a sample of people is called a **statistic**. ("Statistics" is also the branch of mathematics that utilizes probability theory to make decisions about populations.)

Statistics are found everywhere, from baseball earned run averages to the number of war casualties. Many people are rightfully suspicious of statistics. A small book by Huff (1954) humorously illustrates many of the possible pitfalls of statistics. The book is entitled *How to Lie With Statistics*. In it, he rhymed the following message: "Like the 'little dash of powder, little pot of paint,' statistics are making many an important fact look like what she ain't" (p. 9).

On the Average

What does it mean to say that the average American family has 2.1 children? This number was computed by finding a sample of American families, adding up the number of children they have, and dividing by the total number of families in the sample. This number could provide an accurate picture of American families, as most may have about two children, with some having more and others less, or it could be very misleading. It is possible that half of the families had no children and half had four or more children, thus misleading the reader into believing that most families had "about" two children, when in fact none did. This is like the man who has his head in the oven and feet in the freezer and reports that, on the average, he's quite comfortable. It is also possible that the sample used to calculate this statistic was not representative of the population—in this case, all American families. If the sample consisted of college students or residents in Manhattan, the number obtained would be too low. On the other hand, if the sample was taken in rural farm areas, the number obtained may be too high. When samples are not representative of the population, they are called **biased samples**. The statistics calculated on biased samples will not yield accurate information about the population.

Averages can also be misleading, because there are three different kinds of averages. Consider Mrs. Wang's five children. The oldest is a successful corporate executive. She earns $500,000 a year. The second is a teacher who earns $25,000 a year. Child 3 is a waiter who earns $15,000 a year. The other two are starving artists, each earning $5,000 a year. If Mrs. Wang wants to brag about how well her children turned out, she could compute an arithmetic average, which is called the **mean**. The mean is what most people have in mind when they think about averages. It is the sum of all of the values divided by the total number of values. The mean income for Mrs. Wang's children is $550,000/5 = $110,000. Certainly, anyone who is told this figure would conclude that Mrs. Wang has very successful and wealthy children.

The reason that the mean income for Mrs. Wang's children was so high is because there is one extreme score that inflated this type of average. Averages are also called **measures of central tendency**. A second kind of measure of central tendency is the **median**. It is not affected by a few extreme scores. To compute the median, the values are lined up in ascending or descending order. The middle value is the median. For Mrs. Wang's children, this would be:

$5,000; $5,000; $15,000; $25,000; $500,000.

The middle value, or median, is the third value of $15,000. Thus, she could also claim that her children earn, on the average, $15,000. (When there is an even number of values, the median is equal to the mean of the middle two values.)

Mrs. Wang can honestly claim that her children earn, on the average, $110,000 or $15,000. The point of this discussion is that you should be wary of average figures. To understand them, you need to know whether the average is a mean or median as well as something about the variability of the data and the "shape" of the distribution (the way the numbers "stack up.").

Precision

Suppose I tell you that a scientific survey was conducted on the length of work days for office workers. Furthermore, this study found that the mean work day is 8.167 hours long. Does this sound impressive and scientific? What if I told you that most office workers work about 8 hours a day? Most of you would say, "I know that. Why did they bother?" The point is that we are often impressed with precise statistics, even when the precision is unwarranted.

Let me give you an example from a prestigious weekly news magazine. It is important that the magazine readers accept the articles as truthful and authoritative. A few years ago, a news magazine ran an article about the health hazards associated with dog droppings in New York City. To give the reader an idea of the magnitude of the problem, they presented the daily weight of New York City dog droppings in pounds, accurate to two decimal places (the nearest .01 pound!). I have no idea how they arrived at that figure, nor do I even want to think about how they collected their data. I do know that they could not measure it that accurately. Of course, the impression that is created with such precise statistics is that the news magazine is a carefully researched journal that can be trusted for the information it provides.

A more humorous example of overprecision comes from one of America's most famous authors, Mark Twain. He once reported that the Mississippi River was 100 million and 3 years old. It seems that 3 years earlier, he learned that it was 100 million years old.

Significant Differences

If you wanted to know the mean height of all women, you could select a sample of 100 women, measure their height, and compute the mean. Suppose you took another sample of 100 women and computed their mean height. Would you expect the means of these two samples to be exactly the same? No, of course not, because there could be expected to be small differences or fluctuations between these values. Each value was computed on different women, and each will yield a slightly different mean value.

If someone measured a sample of women who belong to sororities and found that their mean height is 5'5" and then measured women who don't belong to sororities and found their mean height to be 5'4½", would you conclude that sorority sisters are taller than nonsorority women? I hope not, because small differences between groups can be expected to occur just by chance, especially when the **sample size**, or number of people in the sample, is small. There are statistical procedures to determine if a difference computed on two or more samples is likely to have happened by chance. If it is very unlikely to be a chance occurrence, it is called a **significant difference**.

The question of whether a change is meaningful also applies to populations as well. If your college enrollment went from 15,862 to 15,879, would the administrators be justified in concluding that the increase in enrollment is meaningful? The answer to this question depends on many other variables. If the enrollment figure has been edging up slowly every year for the last 5 years, then these figures may represent a slight, but steady, trend. On the other hand, the relatively small increase could be due to chance fluctuations and may not represent a meaningful trend. Because of chance factors, it could just as easily have gone down. Similarly, a change in the unemployment rate from 10.0% to 9.9% may be nothing more than random fluctuation, or it may be signaling the end of an economic quagmire. You can expect that Democrats and Republicans will interpret these figures differently depending on who is in office at the time.

Extrapolation

Extrapolation occurs when a value is estimated by extending some known values. If the number of psychology majors over the last 5 years at Podunck University was approximately 150, 175, 200, 225, and 250, respectively, then most people would feel comfortable about the prediction that the number of psychology majors next year will be approximately 275.

Extrapolation can be wrong, and sometimes even ridiculous. For example, suppose we were to examine the drop in the size of American families between 1900 and 1950. By extrapolation, we would predict that the averge family size will soon be zero, and then become a negative number. This is, of course, an inconceivable idea! This is like saying that if the times for the 100-meter dash keep decreasing, eventually someone will run it in 0 seconds and then in negative time.

Bamboozled by Statistics

How can you turn pure fat into a concoction that is 96% fat-free? No, it's not magic; in fact, it's easy. If you take two pats of butter and eat them, 100% of the calories are from fat. But, if you drop the same two pats of butter into a glass of water and drink this revolting concoction, then you have created a 96% fat-free drink (i.e., 96% water)! You would ingest the same number of calories, all of them from fat, but the 96% fat-free drink sounds healthier. This is why products that are labeled "percentage fat-free" are bogus health foods labeled in a way that is intended to misinform (Nutrition Action Healthletter, 1991).

Many of the statistics that we routinely rely on are woefully wrong. Bozell (1993) questioned the accuracy of the data that we are given by the media. For example, he cites a CBS reporter who warned that heterosexual AIDS increased by 30% in 1992 alone. But, according to Bozell, the Centers for Disease Control reported that heterosexual AIDS increased 17% in 1992, down from an increase of 21% in 1991. Similarly, he quotes an NBC news anchor who claimed that right now in the United States there are 5 million people who are believed to be homeless, yet the Census Bureau in 1990 counted 220,000 homeless. These are big differences, but how can we determine which of these statistics is closer to the truth?

First, it is important to develop the habit of questioning the statistics that we are given. How were they collected and who collected them? It is difficult, for example, to count accurately the number of homeless because they don't have convenient addresses or phones. How were the two estimates of this number derived? Did the data collectors sample from downtown New York or from Salt Lake City? Do you have any reason to believe that the data are being deliberately misused? For example, a conservative political group with an obvious agenda, Concerned Women for America, ran an advertisement in national newspapers in which they advocated a ban on gays and lesbians in the military. In support of their position, they reported a study that found "homosexual behavior to be promiscuous, compulsive, and uncontrollable" (quoted in Boxall, 1993, p. A18). The ad went on to claim that the "typical homosexual" had at least 68 sex partners each year! Are you wondering where and how this statistic was obtained? I hope so. The "study" was over a decade old and it deliberately sought highly promiscuous gay males and therefore is not representative of gays in general. If you question the statistics that you routinely are exposed to, you are less likely to be misled by crooked statistics.

APPLYING THE FRAMEWORK

Let's consider the steps in applying the general framework for thinking to understanding and using probabilities.

1. What Is the Goal?   Whenever you are making decisions about uncertain events, you will need to consider the skills developed in this chapter. This is particularly true whenever you are given probability values or when degrees of belief are presented or implied. This situation exists in most of the problems that we solve and decisions that we make because they often involve future events, which can never be known with certainty.

2. What Is Known?   In setting up the problem, you need to know if the probability values you are being given were derived objectively or subjectively. You need to look for ways that these values could be biased. Has the desirability of an outcome influenced the probability values assigned to it? Although the topic of considering the credibility of a source of information was presented in chapter 5, it is also relevant in this context. Before you begin the process of using probabilities, you need to assess the quality of the information that you have. Because we frequently persuade others with probability values, you need to consider how the numbers that are being presented relate to the argument that is being offered.

When determining what is known, look for information that can be used in computing probability estimates. For example, if a probability of a risk is given, is it per year, per exposure (e.g., X-ray), or per lifetime? Is there additional information available that can be combined with base rates so that a more accurate prediction can be made?

3. Which Thinking Skill or Skills Will Get You to Your Goal?   Numerous thinking skills have been presented for use when working with probabilistic events. One of the most useful is drawing a tree diagram complete with probability values on each branch. This method allows you to "see" and objectively compute the likelihood of multiple outcomes. When you are combining information with base-rate information, it is important to form the appropriate ratios so as to avoid the problem of base-rate neglect. Other skills require recognition of the type of error that frequently occurs (e.g., conjunction error, failure to consider cumulative risks) and use of the "or" and "and" rules to improve probabilistic decision making.

Because there are so few things in life that are known with certainty, the skills for understanding and using probabilities should be used frequently. After reading this chapter, you should be able to:

- Compute expected values in situations with known probabilities.
- Recognize when regression to the mean is operating and adjust predictions to take this phenomenon into account.
- Use the "and rule" to avoid conjunction errors.
- Use the "or rule" to calculate cumulative probabilities.
- Recognize and avoid gambler's fallacy.
- Utilize base rates when making predictions.
- Use tree diagrams as a decision-making aid in probabilistic situations.
- Adjust risk assessments to account for the cumulative nature of probabilistic events.
- Understand the differences between mean and median.
- Avoid overconfidence in uncertain situations.
- Understand the limits of extrapolation.
- Use probability judgments to improve decision making.
- Consider indicators like historical data, risks associated with different parts of a decision, and analogies when dealing with unknown risks.

4. Have You Reached Your Goal?   The reason for considering probabilities is to quantify and reduce uncertainty. You will have reached your goal when you can attach more accurate probability values to uncertain events.

CHAPTER SUMMARY

1. Because few things are known with certainty, probability plays a crucial role in many aspects of our lives.

2. Probability is defined as the number of ways a particular outcome (what we call a success) can occur divided by the number of possible outcomes (when all outcomes are equally likely). It is also used to indicated degrees of belief in the likelihood of events with unknown frequencies and previous frequency of occurrence.

3. In general, people tend to be more confident about uncertain events than the objective probability values allow.

4. Mathematically equivalent changes in the way probability information is presented can lead to dramatic changes in the way it is interpreted.

5. Tree diagrams can be used to compute probabilities when there are multiple events (e.g., two or more flips of a coin). When the events are independent, the

probability of any combination of outcomes can be determined by multiplying the probability values along the tree "branches."

6. Expected values can be computed that will take into account the probabilities and values associated with a loss and a win in betting situations.

7. Subjective probabilities are our personal estimates of how often events with unknown frequencies will occur. These values are distorted systematically when people believe that they have some control over probabilistic events.

8. Most people fail to consider the cumulative nature of the likelihood of risky events.

9. People judge events that are dramatic and more publicized to be more likely than events that are less dramatic or less well known. In general, people overestimate frequent events and underestimate infrequent ones.

10. There is a tendency to ignore base-rate information especially when making predictions that involve combining information.

11. Few people realize that if a person scores extremely high or low on one measure, she or he will tend to score closer to average on the second measure.

12. There are two measures of central tendency that are frequently used—the mean and median. Each is computed with a different mathematical formula.

13. There are several systematic biases that operate when most people assess risks. These include downgrading the probability of voluntary risks and those over which we have some perceived control and overestimating risks that are artificial, memorial, and unobservable.

14. Many people erroneously believe that statistics expressed in precise numbers (e.g., many decimal places) are highly credible.

15. Extrapolation occurs when a value is estimated by extending a trend from known values.

TERMS TO KNOW

Check your understanding of the concepts presented in this chapter by reviewing their definitions. If you find that you're having difficulty with any term, be sure to reread the section where it is discussed:

Probability. The number of ways a particular event can occur divided by the number of possible outcomes (when all outcomes are equally likely). It is a measure of how often we expect an event to occur *in the long run*. The term is also used to express degrees of belief and previous frequency of occurrence.

In the Long Run. Refers to the need for numerous trials in order to derive estimates of the proportion of outcomes that will be a "success."

Odds. A mathematical method for indicating probability that is commonly used in sporting events.

Laws of Chance (or Probability). The ability to predict the number or percentage of trials on which a particular outcome will occur.

Overconfidence Phenomenon. The tendency for people to be more confident in their judgments of probability than the objective probability values allow.

Multiple Outcomes. Refers to the probability of an event occurring in two or more trials such as getting two heads in two flips of a coin.

Tree Diagrams. Branching diagrams that may be used to compute probabilities by considering all possible outcomes in a sequence of events.

Independent Events. Two or more events are independent when the occurrence of one event does not affect the occurrence of the other events.

Cumulative Probabilities. The probability of an event occurring over many trials.

Conjunctive Error. Mistaken belief that the co-occurrence of two or more events is more likely than the occurrence of one of the events.

Expected Value. The amount of money you would expect to win in the long run in a betting situation. The mathematical formula for determining expected values is the probability of winning times the value of winning plus the probability of losing times the value of losing.

Subjective Probability. Personal estimates of the probability or likelihood of uncertain events.

Objective Probability. Mathematically determined statements about the likelihood of events with known frequencies.

Gambler's Fallacy. The mistaken belief that chance events are self-correcting. Many people erroneously believe that if a random event has not occurred recently, it becomes more likely.

Relative Frequency. How often an event occurs relative to the size of the population of events at the time of its occurrence.

Base Rate. Initial or a priori probability that an event will occur.

Base-Rate Neglect. Pervasive bias to ignore or underestimate the effect of initial probabilities (base rates) and to emphasize secondary probability values when deciding on the likelihood of an outcome.

Regression Toward the Mean. In general, when someone scores extremely high or low on some measure, she or he will tend to score closer toward the mean (average) on a second measurement.

Sample. A subset of a population that is studied in order to make inferences about the population.

Statistic. A number that has been calculated to describe a sample. (In its plural form it is the branch of mathematics that is concerned with probabilities and mathematical characteristics of distributions of numbers.)

Biased Sample. A sample that is not representative of the population from which it was drawn.

Measures of Central Tendency. Numbers calculated on samples or populations that give a single-number summary of all of the values. Two measures of central tendency are the mean and median.

Mean. A measure of central tendency that is calculated by taking the sum of all the values divided by the total number of values.

Median. A measure of central tendency that is calculated by finding the middle value in a set of scores.

Sample Size. The number of people selected for a study.

Significant Difference. A difference between two groups or observations that is so large that it probably didn't occur by chance.

Extrapolation. The estimation of a value from a trend suggested by known values.

SUGGESTED READINGS

The classic in the misuse of probability and statistics is Huff's *How to Lie with Statistics* (1954). You'll find this small paperback both entertaining and instructive, despite the fact that it is older than most of the people who are reading this text. Two other "oldie, but goodie" books on this topic that also maintain an informal style are Campbell's

Flaws and Fallacies in Statistic Thinking (1974) and Kimble's *How to Use (and Misuse) Statistics* (1978). For those of you who are interested in the design and rationale of college courses that attempt to improve thinking skills with everyday examples of statistics, you'll enjoy Derry, Levin, and Schauble's (1995) article, "Stimulating Statistical Thinking Through Situated Simulations."

If you found the section on the ways people judge the frequency of lethal events interesting, you'll enjoy reading *Acceptable Risk* by Fischhoff, Lichtenstein, Slovic, Derby, and Keeney (1981). In their book, the authors described the variables that people consider when deciding whether the risk associated with an event (e.g., X-rays, nuclear accident, motorcycle riding) is low enough to be considered acceptable. A readable and up-to-date article on this topic is written by Wandersman and Hallman (1993) entitled, "Are People Acting Rationally? Understanding Public Concerns About Environmental Threats," which appeared in the *American Psychologist* (Vol. 48, pp. 681–686).

Summaries of the literature on subjective probabilities can be found in the following sources: Hogarth's (1988) *Judgment and Choice: The Psychology of Decision* (2nd ed.), Dawes' (1988) *Rational Choice in an Uncertain World*, and Nisbett and Ross' older classic (1980) *Human Inferences: Strategies and Shortcomings of Social Judgment*. The Nisbett and Ross work interprets much of the literature on subjective probability in a social psychology framework. An excellent collection of articles on real-world applications of these principles appears in an edited book by Arkes and Hammond (1986) *Judgment and Decision Making: An Interdisciplinary Reader*.

An interesting new addition to the literature is Spirer and Spirer's (1994) *Data Analysis for Monitoring Human Rights*. This husband and wife team used statistics to demonstrate the extent and seriousness of human rights abuses around the world. It is extremely difficult to obtain reliable data from repressive regimes, so the Spirers used whatever data are available to estimate the numbers involved in human atrocities. For example, estimating the number of rapes in the former Yugoslavia is a complex task, in part because the women who were raped often would not report these crimes out of shame and fear of reprisals. To arrive at an estimate, the Spirers found that a hospital in the small town of Zenica had performed 632 abortions in the first half of 1992, prior to the "ethnic cleansing campaign" that spurred the massive number of rapes of Muslim women. In the second half of 1992, 1,474 abortions were performed in the same hospital. They reasoned that abortions would more likely be sought for pregnancies that resulted from rape. They also obtained data that, on the average, one pregnancy results from every 100 rapes, and were able to estimate the number of rapes that had probably occurred. Without data of this sort, it is difficult to convince the rest of the world that a true human rights crisis of massive proportions is occurring (D. L. Wheeler, 1994).

8

Decision Making

Contents

Six doctors in white hospital coats approach your bed. No one is smiling. The results of the biopsy are in. One doctor explains that the cells were irregular in shape; they appeared abnormal. It seems that the tumor was not clearly malignant, but not clearly normal either. They probably removed the entire tumor. It's hard to be certain about these things. You have some choices. You could leave the hospital this afternoon and forget about this unpleasant episode, except for semiannual checkups. There is an above-average chance, however, that some abnormal cells remain and will spread and grow. On the other hand, you could choose to have the entire area surgically removed. Although this would be major surgery, it would clearly reduce the risk of cancer.

How do you decide what to do? Your first response is probably to ask the doctors what they recommend. But if you do, it's likely that you won't receive a consensus of opinion. Often physicians disagree about the best way to treat a disease, especially when there are many options as in the case of complicated diseases like cancer or AIDS. It is possible that some will believe that the risk of cancer is small enough to warrant the wait-and-see decision (Why rush to operate?), whereas others will believe that immediate surgery is the best decision (Better safe than sorry). Ultimately the decision is yours.

Of course, not all decisions are a matter of life and death. We are constantly making minor decisions without much thought, such as what to wear, what to eat for breakfast, which pen to buy, and when to go to sleep. Everyone is faced with a lifetime of decisions, and some of them have major and far-reaching consequences. In this chapter we are concerned with life's major decisions. Major decisions include medical decisions like the one at the beginning of this chapter, whether to marry, whom to marry, if and when to have children, what kind of occupation to choose, how to spend your hard-earned dollars, and so forth. These are all personal decisions that virtually everyone has to make. We also must decide on a host of political and business issues like whether to support off-shore drilling for oil, when to increase a company's inventory, which stock to invest in, how to negotiate a contract, which party to support during political upheaval, and how to increase profits. In this chapter, you will learn skills designed to help you make sound decisions. To accomplish this, we look at the way psychologists and others study decision making, examine common pitfalls and fallacies in the decision-making process, consider the risks involved, and develop a general strategy or plan that you can use when faced with a major decision.

Decision making always involves making a choice among a set of possible alternatives. If you've read the previous chapters in this book, then you've already encountered several sections on how to make intelligent choices. In the chapter on analyzing arguments, for example, you considered the way in which reasons support or refute a conclusion. When analyzing arguments, you make many decisions about the relevance and accuracy of information and how well the reasons that are provided support an action or a belief. In the chapters on hypothesis testing and using probabilistic information, there were sections on drawing tree diagrams, collecting information, and computing likelihoods to make decisions. Because decision making is a central theme in critical thinking, different aspects of it are presented throughout this book.

MAKING SOUND DECISIONS

Decisions per se, *take place when a goal is specified, when information is gathered and judged, when values are used to choose the best solution, and when detailed plans are made and evaluated.*

—Wales & Nardi (1984, p. 1)

The decision-making process is frequently stressful. Ask anyone you know who has recently made an important decision and you will most likely be told about sleepless nights, loss of appetite (or excessive eating), irritability, and generalized feelings of anxiety. Autobiographical and biographical accounts of decision-making stress can be found in the books written by and about several past presidents and many key figures in history. Theodore C. Sorensen (1965) in his book, *Kennedy*, told of the stress John Kennedy faced during the Berlin blockade crisis, and a book written by Richard M. Nixon before his presidency, appropriately titled *Six Crises* (1962), told about the stress caused by his early political decisions. Of course, all world leaders face crises that can make our own personal crises look insignificant by comparison. Most of us can only imagine the pressures involved when military or large-scale economic decisions have to be made.

One way to cope with the stress of decision making is to avoid making decisions whenever possible. Although avoidance is one way of handling stressful decisions, it is seldom a good way. Every time you find yourself avoiding a decision, remember that, in most cases, avoiding a decision is, in fact, making one without any of the benefits of a carefully thought out consideration of the problem.

A Framework for Decision Making

Results from past research have indicated that poor decisions with regard to drugs, alcohol, and other issues involving personal risks often stem from poor decision-making strategies.

—Knight & Dansereau (1992, p. 1)

There is a common model or framework that can be used to organize our thinking about decision making. It is extended in chapters 9 and 10, which are concerned with solving problems and thinking creatively. The three topics that are discussed in these chapters—decision making, problem solving, and creative thinking—have a great deal of overlap in the way they are conceptualized. Sometimes, the term "decision making" is used when the task requires the decision maker to select the best alternative from among several possibilities, and the term "problem solving" is used when the task requires the problem solver to generate alternatives. This sort of distinction is arbitrary, and in real life, it is often difficult to decide if the task requires the generation of alternatives or the selection of alternatives. This sort of distinction is not used here because I do not believe that it is useful.

Take the time to examine Fig. 8.1 carefully. It contains the essential components of a framework for understanding and improving decision making, problem solving, and creative thinking. In Fig. 8.1, the process of making a decision is depicted as a series of boxes, each of which represents a different component, and several arrows that show the recursive nature of the process. These boxes are set in a large oval, which represents the context in which the decision is being made. The first stage in making a decision is the identification or realization that a decision is needed. This is followed by the generation of two or more alternatives that would satisfy a goal or desired outcome that is implied by the decision. Usually each alternative has several pros and cons associated with it. The task for the decision maker is to choose the "best" alternative. The consideration of what is "best" requires an evaluation phase in which "best" often turns out to be multidimensional—best for whom? best by what criteria? best in the immediate future or long term?

Decisions also involve uncertainty because we cannot know in advance the consequences of our actions. Much of the difficulty when making decisions lies in judging

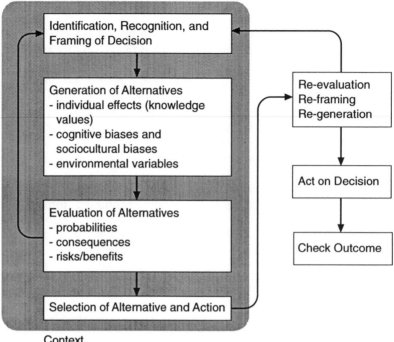

FIG. 8.1.   A multiprocess model of decision making. Each of the boxes represents a stage in the decision-making process. The arrows show that the process
is recursive with frequent recycling through the stages (e.g., generating alternatives may be followed by reframing the decision). The rectangular boundary
represents the effects of context.

which alternative is best. Usually decisions have to be made with missing information
and involve guesses and predictions about future events. It is also a recursive or
recycling process because the nature of the decision may change as more alternatives
are generated and evaluated. The decision also requires an action, although it may not
be an overt movement—you could decide whom or what to believe, or to do nothing
at all. All of these processes occur in a context that influences what happens and relies
heavily on the information you bring with you to the decision and the information that
you obtain during the decision-making process. For example, you may make a different decision if you are being observed by your friends than if you were alone (context
effect), and an expert in a field may reach a different decision than a novice (effect of
prior knowledge). Personal values are also a strong influence on the way the decision
is phrased, the alternatives that are generated, and the way they are evaluated.

In the medical scenario at the beginning of this chapter, the best decision must take
into account the likelihood of developing cancer at some time in the future, the risks
and pain of surgery, the pros and cons of various treatment regimens, and personal
factors such as your personal feelings about quality of life issues. When you decide
which stock to invest in, you must consider what the economy will be like in the years

to come. Similarly the decision whether or not to have children requires that you think about what your life will be like with children who don't even exist yet.

Decision making is an active process. The decision maker takes responsibility for her or his own future. After all, you are in the best position for determining how you want to spend your life and how you should make the business and professional decisions that will ultimately reflect on you. Good decision makers are more likely to get the good jobs and make favorable decisions about their personal lives as well. Although many famous instances of good decisions (profitable investments, successful army maneuvers) and bad decisions (Watergate, the U.S. attempt to rescue American hostages in Iran, NASA's decision to launch the Challenger in bad weather) come to mind, it is important to realize that a decision is judged to be good or bad after the fact. For example, most Americans would have agreed that President Carter made a wise decision to rescue American hostages in Iran, if it had been successful and no lives were lost. However, because it failed and eight Americans were killed, it is now seen as a bad decision. Thus, there is an important distinction between how good a decision is when it is being made and its outcome. Decisions are made using the information available at the time, and because much of the information that is available when the decision is being made is probabilistic in nature, sometimes good decisions will have bad outcomes. Conversely, bad decisions will sometimes have good outcomes. For example, you could decide to bet your life savings on a horse race (a bad decision), and "get lucky." Of course, good decisions will result in desirable outcomes much more frequently than poor decisions will.

Often, we will never know if the best decision was made. If you are a college senior who must decide between a lucrative career in accounting or a more personally rewarding career as a high school English teacher, you may never be sure if you picked the better option because you can only speculate about the career you didn't select. Robert Frost, the famous American poet, captured this feeling in his poem about a traveler who comes to a fork in the road. The traveler can never know about "the road not taken."

Before a decision can be made, the individual must realize that a decision is needed and that there are several possible alternatives. Let's consider an example with which many of you will be able to identify. Monica is taking several demanding college courses. She needs to supplement her income by working part time and has family obligations as well. Her free time is virtually nonexistent. Monica needs to consider alternatives to her current lifestyle. She must decide how to juggle all of these commitments while still having some time left for herself. Monica has to realize that she can change her life. Too often this first step is missed and inertia sets in. People will continue doing what they have been doing without contemplating ways to improve a difficult situation. A clear definition of the problem is the first step in successful decision making. Simply stated, the problem is that Monica has too many responsibilities and this is making her feel anxious and stressed. The best solution will give her more time for herself while still allowing her to fulfill her responsibilities. As these are essentially conflicting goals, the best decision will probably involve a compromise that will only partially satisfy each. It is not likely that she will find a course of action that will allow her to fill her days with leisure activities while maintaining high grades, earning money, and caring for her family.

The objective criteria for a good decision are that it is feasible and that it will, at least, help to alleviate the problem. Some possible good decisions for Monica include finding a higher paying job or reducing her expenses so she would need to work fewer hours, beginning a more efficient study program, taking a lighter course load, and visiting her family less frequently. You may be surprised to find that with a little effort, several possibilities occur to you that you might otherwise never have considered.

Devoted "Trekkies" (fans of the television and movie series called *Star Trek*) can recall many stories in which the plot involved particularly clever decision making. Consider, for example, the Trekkie-classic movie *Star Trek II: The Wrath of Khan*. In the opening scene, an attractive pointy-eared Vulcan is facing a serious problem. A sister spaceship has wandered into enemy territory and has sent a distress signal. If she does not go in to save them they will perish; if she does, she risks enemy attack. She nervously decides to follow them into enemy territory and is immediately apprised that her starship is under attack. We soon learn that this is a computer-simulated drill designed to test the decision-making skills of future starship commanders and that only one person has made the correct decision in this drill. Of course, it is Captain Kirk, the hero of this series. The question of interest is whether he decided to attempt to save the sister ship by entering enemy territory and thus risk attack of his own spaceship or whether he decided to sacrifice the crew of the sister ship to save lives on his own spaceship. It seems that Captain Kirk did neither. Later we find out that he redesigned the computer problem so that he would have additional choices with more favorable outcomes. For him, the problem was "how to change contingencies in a mock drill." For others, the problem had been "how to save the sister starship without being attacked." Captain Kirk made a superior decision because he defined the problem in a unique way. His unusual and excellent alternative made this decision very creative, a topic that is discussed in a later chapter. Some may say that he cheated or "copped out" by redesigning the simulation, but perhaps, he would use his ability to define problems in a unique way if he were out in space and that's what makes him an outstanding starship commander. The point being made here is that often there are alternative ways of formulating what the decision requires, and some will result in more favorable outcomes than others. Different formulations will lead to different solutions.

DESCRIPTIVE AND PRESCRIPTIVE PROCESSES

Whenever there is a simple error that most laymen fall for, there is always a slightly more sophisticated version of the same problem that experts fall for.

—Amos Tversky (quoted in Gardner, 1985, p. 360)

Researchers who study decision making look at what people do when they are making a decision, often contrasting what people actually do with what they should do in order to maximize the probability of a good decision. This is the difference between a descriptive and a prescriptive account of the process. Any program that is designed to help people make better decisions will have to take into account what typically is right and wrong with most decisions, and then provide a systematic way of eliminating or reducing common errors while increasing those processes that underlie good decisions. With so many processes involved and so many decisions that need to be made, it is easy to find ways that decision making goes wrong.

Baron (1990) analyzed all thinking into "search" and "inference" stages. The search occurs when we have to generate alternatives, and to a lesser extent when we decide what constitutes a good decision. The inference relates to the kinds of judgments that are made and the way information is used. Thinking goes wrong when the search process misses some good alternatives or when the inference is incorrect (e.g., selecting an alternative that really will not solve the problem or will create other problems).

The alternatives that people generate are tied to the way memory is structured and accessed (Payne, Bettman, & Johnson, 1993). An oft-repeated theme throughout this book is the pervasive influence of memory on all aspects of thinking. The sort of alternatives that are generated will depend on what we can recall in the particular situation. It is also constrained by the amount of cognitive effort that is invested in the processes of generation and evaluation. We don't want to spend huge amounts of time and energy in making most decisions, so we rely on shortcuts that sometimes lead to poor decisions. The idea is to be flexible so that the cognitive effort is proportional to the importance of the decision.

It seems logical that one way to understand how good decisions are made is by studying professional decision makers—doctors, judges, research scientists, and others who routinely make important decisions that affect society. In recent years, a comprehensive series of experiments by several leading psychologists has revealed an interesting fact about the decisions made by trained professionals. They are often wrong. Moreover, they are wrong in predictable ways. This finding is of great concern because it is the professional decision makers in our society who determine, for example, whether a tissue sample is malignant, whether an individual has committed a crime, and whether a certain level of radiation is harmful. Because the unfortunate consequences of wrong decisions by professional decision makers are painfully obvious, an examination of the types of errors they make is an important initial step toward correcting them.

It seems that despite the many years of education they receive, professionals make the same kinds of mistakes that are made by people without their specialized education. Although physicians learn medicine and lawyers learn jurisprudence, few are being trained in the essential skills of decision making. Not even those trained in formal disciplines such as logic and probability theory are free from certain flaws in thinking.

A **fallacy** is an error or mistake in the thinking process. An example of common thinking fallacies among trained professionals can be found in research with nurses conducted by Smedslund (1963) and recently reconfirmed by Berger (1994) with a sample of physicians. Smedslund presented trained nurses with a deck of cards that supposedly contained information gleaned from the files of 100 patients. Each card indicated whether a patient had a particular disease and whether a particular symptom was present or absent in the patient. Thus, there were four possible combinations for each patient. The patient (a) has the disease and has the symptom, (b) does not have the disease and does not have the symptom, (c) does not have the disease but has the symptom, (d) has the disease but does not have the symptom. The task for the nurses was to determine if there is a relationship between the symptom and the disease. The number of cases in each of these four categories is shown in Fig. 8.2. Stop now and look over the data presented in Fig. 8.2. Do you think that there is a relationship between the symptom and the disease?

Overwhelmingly, the nurses concluded that there was a symptom–disease relationship, basing their decisions on the fact that 37 patients had both the disease and the symptom and 13 had neither the disease nor the symptom. They tended to ignore the 33 cases in which the symptom was present without the disease and the 17 cases in which patients had the disease, but not the symptom. These trained nurses and, more recently, a sample of physicians, routinely ignored half of the available information. The correct decision should have been that there was no relationship because there was a high probability of the disease without the symptom and the symptom without the disease. You can see this by looking at the marginals, that is the numbers at the end of the rows and columns. Think about the meaning of these probability values and see how they support the conclusion that there is no relationship. If you just finished reading chapter 7, you should be able to see how the probability data that are used to make decisions in this context rely on the same thinking principles that were discussed in that chapter. Decisions very often involve probabilistic information, and decision-

	Has the Disease	Doesn't Have the Disease	Marginals for Rows
Has the Symptoms	37/100 = 37%	33/100 = 33%	70/100 = 70 % have the symptoms
Don't Have the Symptoms	17/100 = 17%	13/100 = 13%	30/100 = 30% don't have the symptoms
Marginals for columns	54/100 = 54% have the disease	46/100 = 46% doesn't have the disease	100% in both directions

a. of everyone with the symptoms, 52% (37/70) have the disease. This means that if you have the symptoms, you are about as likely to have the disease as to not have the disease.
b. of everyone with the disease, 68% (37/54) have the symptoms. This means that if you have the disease, you have about a 2/3 probability of having the symptoms.
c. of everyone who does *not* have the disease, 72% (33/46) have the symptoms. This means that if you do *not* have the disease, there is over a 2/3 probability of having the symptoms.
d. of everyone who does *not* have the symptoms, 56% (17/30) have the disease. This means that if you do *not* have the symptoms, there is a greater than 50% probability that you have the disease.

FIG. 8.2.   Number of patients within each disease/symptom category. Is there a relationship between the disease and the symptoms? Look carefully at the numbers in the marginals and think about the kind of information that they provide about the possibility of a disease–symptom relationship.

making errors using probabilities, like the one described here, are prevalent in the everyday thinking of people from all walks of life. We need to examine common decision-making fallacies because a skilled decision maker will need to know what to avoid as well as what to do.

PITFALLS AND PRATFALLS IN DECISION MAKING

… great moments in history all turned on someone's judgment as to what should be done and someone's decision to do it.

—Arkes and Hammond (1986, pp. 211–212)

A pitfall is a danger or difficulty that is not easily avoided. If you've ever spent long afternoons at the beach, you've probably seen bratty kids creating pitfalls. They dig holes in the sand and cover them with newspaper so that unsuspecting sun lovers will fall into them. The word *pratfall* needs no formal definition for fans of comedians who are famous for their frequent pratfalls. The American Heritage dictionary defines a pratfall as "a fall on the buttocks." Put these terms together and you will realize that unless common pitfalls in decision making are avoided, the decision maker will slip and fall on the part of the anatomy that is featured on blue jeans commercials without reaching the best decision. Let's examine some of the common fallacies or pitfalls in decision making.

Failure to Seek Disconfirming Evidence

Some of the worst disasters nations have known are traceable to faulty judgments or distorted perceptions of their political leaders.

—Kruglanski (1992, p. 455)

Suppose you have a friend who is always working on crossword puzzles, anagrams, mazes, and other similar problems from puzzle books. He corners you one day with the following problem:

> I'm going to give you a series of numbers. This series conforms to a simple rule. You have to figure out what the rule is. The way to do this is by coming up with your own series of numbers. I'll tell you whether or not your own series conforms to this rule. You can give me as many series of numbers as necessary to discover the rule. When you believe that you know the rule, tell it to me and I'll let you know if you're right.

Reluctantly you agree to participate. You are given the following number series:

2 4 6

Stop right now and think how you would go about generating other number series that conform to the same rule as this one.

This problem was actually presented to many subjects in an experiment conducted by Wason (1960, 1968). He found that most people had difficulty with this task. Suppose that you believe that the rule is "any continuous series of even numbers." To test this rule most subjects would try series like "14, 16, 18." The experimenter would respond that this series conforms to the rule. To be certain most subjects would try again with another series, "182, 184, 186." Again the experimenter would respond affirmatively. Confidently, the subject would announce the rule, "Any continuous even series of numbers." The experimenter then informs the subject that this is not the correct rule.

Typically, subjects will try again, this time thinking up a new rule that will describe the correct number series. Suppose, this time the subject decides to try out the rule "the middle number is halfway between the other two." Now the subject asks about the series "50, 100, 150." The experimenter answers that this series is correct. The subject tries again "1006, 1007, 1008" and is told that this also conforms to the rule. Even more confident this time, the subject announces that the correct rule is "the middle number is halfway between the other two." The experimenter tells him that this is not the correct rule.

Have you discovered the correct rule by now? It is "increasing whole numbers." After almost an hour of working on this problem one of Wason's subjects came up with this rule: "The rule is that either the first number equals the second minus two, and the third is random but greater than the second, or the third number equals the second plus two, and the first is random but less than the second." You can imagine how this poor subject felt when he was told that this rule was incorrect.

Why is this problem so difficult? In all of the sample number series I've given and most of the ones people actually try, the number series conform to the rule they have in mind. There is an infinite number of possible number series that conform to the correct rule, "numbers in increasing order of magnitude." What subjects should have done is try out series that would disconfirm the rule they were trying out. For example, if you believed that the correct rule is "any continuous series of even numbers" you should try the series "1, 2, 4. If the experimenter tells you that you are correct, then you know that the rule "any continuous series of even numbers" must be wrong.

The tendency to seek information that agrees with the ideas we have is called **confirmation bias**. We have a bias or predilection to look for confirming information. Another interesting example of the confirmation bias or failure to seek disconfirming evidence is discussed chapter 4. This is the same error that was described in the previous section in which the nurses failed to consider evidence that disconfirmed the hypothesis that the symptoms and disease were related. This bias is pervasive; examples can probably be found in every applied setting. For example, a recent study of how jurors reach decisions about the guilt or innocence of a defendant shows that they construct a likely story about what probably happened at the scene of the crime. They then look for information that was revealed during the trial that is consistent with the story (Kuhn, Weinstock, & Flaton, 1994). Thus, jurors also rely heavily on evidence that confirms their beliefs.

What can we infer from the bias to seek confirming evidence? Suppose someone confronts your best friend with "the opportunity of a lifetime." A dynamic saleswoman offers him the chance to invest in a new corporation that will manufacture and sell computers that are so small they will fit in your wallet. It sounds good, but he's unsure. Prudently he decides to do some investigating. He checks out 10 computer companies that are listed on the New York Stock Exchange. He finds that IBM is a large profitable corporation. If he only had invested in IBM when it was just being formed, he'd be a rich man today. He can already imagine himself lighting cigars with $10 bills. What advice would you give your friend?

Hopefully, you would point out to him that he only looked for evidence that supports the decision to invest in the corporation as only substantial corporations are listed on the stock exchange. He also needs to seek evidence that would disconfirm this decision. He should find out how many new computer corporations with big dreams have gone bankrupt and how many have not gone bankrupt in the last 10 years. He also should attempt to estimate the future market for wallet-sized computers.

Another real-life (nonlaboratory) example can be drawn from medical decision making. Imagine a young physician examining a sick patient. The patient is complaining of a high fever and sore throat. The physician must decide on a diagnosis from among myriad possible diseases. The physician decided that it may be the flu. She asks the patient if he feels "achy all over." The answer is "yes." The physician asks if the symptoms began a few days ago. Again, the response is "yes." It should be clear to the reader that the physician should also be seeking evidence that would disconfirm the flu diagnosis. She should also ask about patterns of symptoms that are not usually associated with the flu, like a rash or swollen joints or flesh-eating bacteria.

The confirmation bias is a pitfall in decision making. Wason claims that it is prevalent in the thoughts and research of scientists. In fact, a large-scale study of NASA scientists showed a strong confirmation bias (Mynatt, Doherty, & Tweney, 1978). We all need to be trained to seek and examine data that are inconsistent with the ideas we are considering. There is good evidence that when people are required to consider counterevidence, they make better decisions (Koriat et al., 1980).

Overconfidence

Overconfidence is a decision-making pitfall that is related to the bias to seek confirming evidence. In general, most people do not see the need to improve the way they make decisions because they believe that they are already making excellent decisions. The unwarranted belief that we are usually correct is a major, real-life barrier to critical thinking. After all, if most people are very confident that they are making the correct decision, why should they exert the time and effort to learn and apply the skills of critical thinking?

Why do we tend to believe that we are good decision makers? In part because we cannot remember other alternatives that might have led to better decisions (e.g., I can't think of any reasons why I might not be right) and because we can never know about the outcomes that would have resulted from other decisions. In a discussion of political decision making, Kruglanski (1992) listed ambition, status seeking, delusions, and prejudice as some of the reasons for bad decisions. If these less-than-ideal motives are added to politicians' overly-confident belief that the decisions they make are usually right, it is easy to explain some very bad political decisions.

Availability Heuristic

A **heuristic** is any "rule of thumb" that we use to solve problems. It won't always give us the right answer, but it is a helpful aid. Psychologists usually distinguish between heuristics and algorithms. An **algorithm** is a procedure that will always yield the correct answer if you follow it exactly. Let's try a simple example from mathematics to clarify these terms. Remember the procedures you learned in solving long-division problems. Given a problem like $176\overline{)7019}$, you were first told to estimate about how often 176 would "go into" 701, as it is unlikely that you ever learned the 176 tables. You might estimate it to be about 4 times. The problem thus far would look like this:

$$\frac{4}{176\overline{)7019}}$$

You would check out this estimate with the appropriate multiplication.

$$\begin{array}{r} 4 \\ 176\overline{)7019} \\ \underline{704} \end{array}$$

Oops, too large!

You would soon realize that 4 was too large and would probably try 3. This procedure is a heuristic. It is a guide or aid to help you find the correct answer, but it doesn't always work perfectly as seen in the preceding example. On the other hand, an algorithm always leads to the correct answer. If you want to find the area of a rectangle that is 3 feet long and 2 feet wide you will always get the correct answer if you use the formula: length x width, or in this case, 3 feet x 2 feet = 6 square feet. The use of an appropriate algorithm is an example of cognitive economy, a topic that was introduced earlier in this book. We don't need to use mental effort and "reinvent" ways to find the area of a rectangle when there is a ready-to-use algorithm that we can call upon for the correct answer.

There are many situations in which we use both heuristics and algorithms. In cooking, for example, a recipe is an algorithm. If the recipe is followed exactly, the result should always be the same dish that is described in the cookbook. When cooks ad lib by adding additional seasoning or when they create a new recipe, they are using their general knowledge about the types of flavors that go together. This is an example of a heuristic. Heuristics or "rules of thumb" are frequently used by a decision maker without the realization by the decision maker that they're being used.

Availability is a commonly used heuristic. The term "availability heuristic" was coined by two prominent psychologists, Daniel Kahneman and Amos Tversky (1973; Tversky & Kahneman, 1974), who have conducted numerous experiments on decision making. In order to understand the availability heuristic, consider the following questions:

1. Are there more words in the English language that begin with the letter *r* or have the *r* in the third position?

2. Would you expect the 1990 census to show that there are more librarians or farmers in the United States?
3. Are there more deaths due to homicide or due to diabetes-related diseases?

If you answer the first question like most people, you believe that there are more words that start with the letter *r* than there are words with *r* in the third position. In answering this question most people find that they can think of more words that start with *r* (rice, root, room, roam, religion, rhinoceros, rye) than have *r* in the third position (bird, torrid, horror, hero). In the jargon of psychology, words starting with the letter *r* are more available than words with *r* in the third position. That is, they come to mind more easily. If you answered "words that start with *r*," you were wrong. According to Berger (1995), the English language contains many more words with *r* in the third position than in the first position. It is just more difficult to think of them because it is easier to retrieve words from memory by the first letter than by the third. Earlier in this chapter, I talked about the pervasive influence of memory in every aspect of critical thinking. This is another example of the way in which the kinds of memories we retrieve can determine how decisions are made.

Your answer to the second question probably depends on whether you live in an urban or rural area. Most city dwellers believe that there are more librarians than farmers in the United States. After all, few city dwellers have ever met a farmer whereas they probably know, or at least know of, several librarians. Actually, there are many more farmers in the United States than there are librarians, a fact that was more likely to be answered correctly by readers from rural farm regions. This is another example of how the use of the availability heuristic can lead to the wrong decision.

Most residents of large cities probably believe incorrectly that there are more deaths due to homicide than to diabetes. The reason for this is not difficult to understand. Pick up any newspaper or watch television news on any day and there is likely to be a report of one or more homicides. Although you may know only a few people who have diabetes and may not know personally anyone who has been murdered, you've heard or read about many homicide victims, so there seem to be more of them. A study of people who watch many violent television shows has found that these people believe that they are more likely to be a victim of a violent crime than those who don't watch these shows (Gerbner, Grass, Morgan, & Signorielli, 1980). Presumably, they maintain this belief because examples of violent crimes are more readily available in their memory. This finding has important implications because it would be expected to affect how frequent viewers of televised violence vote on crime-related propositions and how they make decisions like buying a home burglary alarm, keeping a gun in the house, or going out at night.

The availability heuristic can be found in many applied settings. Its influence can best be understood with an example: In a medical text written by Gifford-Jones (1977), the author discussed the difficult medical decision concerning whether women in their late 30s or early 40s should have their ovaries removed when they are having a hysterectomy. Like all difficult decisions, there are pros and cons associated with each alternative. In discussing how this decision is often made, Gifford-Jones (1977) wrote:

> I recall operating some time ago with a former professor of gynecology at Harvard. He was in a rather philosophical mood and was pondering the pros and cons of what to do with the ovaries. "Sometimes whether or not I remove the ovaries depends on what has happened to me in the last few weeks," he said. "If I've watched a patient die from cancer of the ovary, I often remove them. But if I've been free of this experience for a while, I'm more inclined to leave them in." (pp. 174–175)

The availability heuristic is frequently seen in other medical examples. It is not unusual for a pediatrician whose own children suffer from severe allergies to be especially vigilant about possible allergic reactions in his patients. This may or may not be a good thing. The best physician is one who has a broad scope of experience with a large variety of illnesses so that he has a large number of medical diagnoses available to him.

Prejudice and stereotypes may also exist, at least in part, because of the human tendency to utilize readily available information. Although prejudice and stereotypes were discussed more fully in chapter 2, it is easy to see how availability plays a role in establishing and maintaining them. If a minority person is convicted of a heinous crime, many people will distrust other members of the same minority. The thousands of honest hard-working minority persons are forgotten or overlooked. Their existence is overshadowed by the salient criminal.

Availability has been carefully studied in the laboratory by research psychologists because it plays a role in decisions that are made in a wide range of settings. In another experiment by Tversky and Kahneman (1974), groups of college students were given one of the two following arithmetic problems:

$$8 \times 7 \times 6 \times 5 \times 4 \times 3 \times 2 \times 1 = ?$$

or

$$1 \times 2 \times 3 \times 4 \times 5 \times 6 \times 7 \times 8 = ?$$

The college students examined either the first or second row of numbers for 5 seconds. Their task was to estimate the product because 5 seconds was not enough time to solve the problem. Students who were given the first problem, the one beginning with large numbers, gave an average estimate of the product to be 2,250. Students who were given the second problem, the one beginning with small numbers, gave an average estimate of the product to be 512. The correct answer is 40,320. Thus, when the problem began with large numbers the estimated answer was large compared to the problem that began with small numbers. The estimate differences between the ascending and descending series demonstrates that judgments were systematically biased toward the most readily available information.

Representativeness Heuristic

Suppose that a young man in a pinstripe suit, black shirt, and white tie comes up to you and asks if you'd like to make some money by betting on whether a coin lands on "heads" or "tails." (If you have already read Chapter 7, you may recall a similar sneaky character.) You look at him dubiously. He explains that it's really quite simple. He'll flip one coin six times. All you have to do is bet on the pattern of heads and tails that will result from six tosses of a coin. Although there are many sequences possible, you decide to concentrate on three of them. Using the letter "H" to represent heads and "T" to represent tails, which of the following three outcomes would you bet on?

H-T-H-T-T-H
H-H-H-T-T-T
H-T-H-T-H-T

If you responded like most other people, then you selected the first series of heads and tails, probably because it seemed more similar to a random or chance pattern of heads and tails. In fact all three series are equally likely. Any series of heads and tails taken six at a time is as likely to occur as any other. The preceding example demonstrates the belief that an outcome of a random process should look like or be representative of randomness. Because our common-sense notion of randomness is that of a process without a pattern, we tend to think that H-T-H-T-H-T is not as likely to occur from six tosses of a coin as a more random-looking series. This, however, is not true. (What some people find even more surprising is that H-H-H-H-H-H is as likely as H-T-H-T-H-T.)

Of course, you're more likely to get approximately equal numbers of heads and tails after many coin flips than you are to get mostly or all heads or mostly or all tails because there are more possible patterns that yield these outcomes. For example, there is only one pattern of outcomes that will correspond to six heads (H-H-H-H-H-H), whereas there are many ways to get three heads and three tails in six flips of a coin (e.g., H-H-H-T-T-T; H-T-H-T-H-T; T-T-T-H-H-H; H-T-H-T-H-T; etc.). Each series or pattern of heads and tails is equally likely. This concept is also discussed in chapter 7.

To clarify the **representativeness heuristic**, let's try another example. Suppose you get a letter from an old friend from whom you haven't heard in many years. He tells you that he is the proud father of six children—three girls and three boys. After trying to consider what life is like with six children, you then wonder about their birth order. Which of the following orders do you think is more likely (with "G" standing for girls and "B" standing for boy):

B-B-B-G-G-G
or
B-G-G-B-G-B

If you've followed the discussion so far, you will realize that although the second series appears to be more representative of a random process, they are, in fact, equally likely.

Wishful Thinking (Pollyanna Principle)

Quite often people will overestimate their chances for success or the likelihood of a desired outcome. Halpern and Irwin (1973) found that when participants in an experiment wanted an event to occur (they would win money), they believed that it was more likely to occur than when its occurrence would have been unfavorable (they would lose money). It seems that humans are an optimistic species. The tendency to believe that pleasant events are more likely than unpleasant ones is a manifestation of **wishful thinking**, the idea that if we want something to happen it will. This has also been called the Pollyanna Principle in honor of the protagonist of a 1913 novel who always found something to be happy about, no matter how bleak the situation.

A large fast-food hamburger chain is basing a promotional gimmick on wishful thinking. The corporation that made golden arches an integral part of American life is offering a game that pays off with large sums of money. Some lucky Big Mac hamburger consumer will match up small game coupons for the grand prize. A blitz of television advertising shows lucky burger eaters exclaiming over the money they've won. Apparently, the lure of winning must sell more hamburgers, or it would have been discontinued. It must be assumed that people grossly overestimate their chance of winning the prizes. The actual estimated probability of winning the grand prize is less than a million to one. As required by law, these odds are posted (in fine print) on the posters that announce the game, yet they are routinely ignored and thought to be more favorable than they actually are. Few of us can appreciate astronomical odds like this one. You're probably more likely to find a needle in a haystack. Yet, because of wishful thinking, many people will line up for hamburgers and a chance to win.

Optimism is a potent human trait that often directs how we think and act. Seligman (1991) identified optimism as a critical element in political elections. It seems that candidates who are optimistic about the future are more likely to garner winning votes than those who are pessimistic. He found that in 9 out of 10 presidential elections in the United States, the candidate who gave the more optimistic speeches won the election. Optimism may be a wonderful human trait, but not when it distorts the decision-making process. Good decisions rely on realistic assessments of likelihood, not optimistic ones. Failure to consider seriously unpleasant outcomes can lead to disastrous consequences.

Currently, seismologists (people who study earthquakes) are predicting that a major earthquake will occur in Southern California within the next 50 years. Few people will be prepared, however, if an earthquake occurs because they are duped by wishful thinking. Most believe that a major earthquake won't occur, or alternatively, if it does, it will be "somewhere else." Random "person on the street" interviews shown on television reveal that the Pollyanna Principle is alive and well and living in Southern California. Similar reactions have been found with people living in other regions that are plagued with floods, hurricanes, and other natural disasters.

Entrapment

Suppose you were offered the opportunity to bid on a $1 bill. You and some friends can make bids, and the highest bidder will pay the amount bid and get $1 in return. The only hitch is that both the highest bidder and second highest bidder must pay the amount they bid, but only the highest bidder will receive the dollar in return. Suppose that you agree to play and that you continue to raise your bid until you have offered 80¢. Now a friend bids $1. What do you do? You will probably decide to bid $1.05 for the $1 because you'll certainly lose 80¢ unless you continue to increase your bid. Shubik (1971) found that people will continue to bid amounts over $1 to win the dollar bill in an attempt to keep their losses at a minimum in this game.

What has happened in this game is **entrapment**, a situation in which an individual has already invested money, time, or effort and decides to continue in this situation because of the initial investment. Entrapment is also called **sunk costs** because of the importance that we attach to the costs we have already "sunk" into a course of action. People commonly fall prey to entrapment. Consider Fred's decision about his automobile. He has already replaced the muffler, brakes, and ignition system when he finds out that his car needs a new transmission. Because he has already invested so much money into his car, he feels "trapped" into replacing the transmission instead of buying a new car. Or consider another common example. Everyone has had the frustrating experience of calling on the phone for some information and being put on "hold." After listening to the irritating strains of "elevator music" for several minutes, you need to decide whether to hang up or continue waiting. Many people continue to wait because of the time they've already invested.

Making decisions in light of previous investments requires that the individual consider *why* the investment has been so high either in terms of money or time, and whether, at this point in time, the car is worth the additional sum of money or the phone call is worth an additional 10 minutes on "hold." Examples of entrapment are commonly found in government budget hearings (Fischer & Johnson, 1986). One argument in favor of continuing to support the development of the MX missile is that the millions of dollars that have already been spent on it would be lost if we decided to discontinue the project.

In a study of how people respond in sunk-costs situations, researchers asked subjects open-ended questions about common decisions (Larrick, Morgan, & Nisbett, 1990). Consider this one:

> You and a friend just spent $7 each to see a movie. About a half hour into the movie, you both realize that it is "two thumbs down"—a really bad movie. What do you do? List some good reasons for staying until the end of the movie, then list some good reasons for leaving after a half hour.

> Stop now and try this demonstration.

Look over your reasons. Of course, you just read about entrapment, so you are not a naïve subject, but review the answers that you gave anyway. If you listed the fact that you spent $7 as a good reason for staying, you are demonstrating the fallacy of entrapment. If you listed as a good reason for leaving the fact that the movie is a waste of time, then you receive partial credit for recognizing the cost of staying. If you also listed the fact that you could be doing something better with your time, then you would get credit for recognizing that by staying you would also be losing out on doing some better activity. Let's go over the reasoning again because I have found that many students have difficulty with this concept:

You already spent the $7 for the movie. No matter what you decide to do at this point in time, the money is gone, and you are down by $7. So it should not be relevant to your decision. You lost $7, no matter what you decide to do. At a half-hour into the movie, you have a decision. If you stay, you will not only have to endure a bad movie, but you will also miss out on some more pleasurable activity that you could be doing. Thus, there is a dual cost to staying—seeing a bad movie and missing out on some better activity. Try out this example with some friends or family. Explain to them the fallacy of entrapment.

Psychological Reactance

Our emotional states have a major impact on the kinds of decisions that we make (Kavanaugh & Bower, 1985). We select alternatives that seem "best" to us, and our determination of what's best is not always based on sound rational criteria. One example of the effect of emotional states on the kinds of decisions people make has been labeled **psychological reactance,** which is resistance arising from restrictions of freedom. Consider this example of psychological reactance (Shaver, 1981): It's been a bitterly cold winter and you can hardly wait for a much deserved spring break. One of your close friends is planning on basking in the Fort Lauderdale sun. Another friend can't wait to hit the slopes in Vail. Both friends have asked you to join them in their spring break revelry. As you consider the options, you begin to favor the bikini-clad vacation when your Florida-bound friend tells you that you *must* go to Florida with him. How does this loss of freedom affect your decision?

Logically, it would seem that being told that you must do what you want to do would have no effect on your decision, but many people do not react in this manner. Some people would react to this loss of freedom by deciding to go skiing instead. The extent to which psychological reactance affects a decision depends on the number of freedoms that are being threatened and the source of the threat. There are also large differences among individuals in the extent to which they are prone to reactance. Consider how you will probably respond when you are told what to do in different situations. If you are likely to do the opposite, no matter you are told to do, then you are demonstrating reactance and will sometimes make poor decisions because of this tendency. Whether you're dealing with your parents, an employer, or a foreign government, psychological reactance can interfere with the decision-making process by causing you to select a less desirable alternative.

Liking

It should seem obvious that people select alternatives that have been evaluated positively along some dimension. This point is made more explicitly later in this chapter; however, it is important to consider here some of the factors that influence positive evaluations. In other words, what are some factors that determine liking?

Reciprocity. When assessing the pros and cons of various alternatives, our subjective feelings about the alternatives play a large role in decision making. Simply put, we choose people and actions that we like. Reciprocity is one determinant of what and whom we like. We tend to like people who like us. In Cialdini's (1993) delightful book about myriad influences that affect our thoughts and actions, he tells about the "World's Greatest Car Salesman." The super salesman seems to differ from other more mundane sellers in several ways, but the most interesting is his strange habit of correspondence. Super salesman sends a card to each of his more than 13,000 former customers each month. Can you guess the message on this card? No, it's not a list of maintenance tips or repair coupons. In fact, every card every month contains the same message: "I like you." Twelve times a year, every former customer receives the same obviously impersonal message. It seems to work. When the time comes to decide where to purchase another car, these former customers are reminded of their "friend" who likes them. Reciprocity of liking apparently has a powerful effect on decision making in this context.

The psychological literature is full of other examples of the influence of reciprocity on decisions. For example, you are much more likely to buy a product if I give you a free sample than if I don't. The next time you are in the supermarket when samples are being given away, watch how people respond to the covert pressure to buy the product they have just tasted. You'll find that a surprisingly high number will buy the product. People seem to feel that they owe something in exchange for the "free" sample. Political favors are blatant examples of reciprocity-induced liking as are charitable requests that are accompanied by "gifts" like address labels, key rings, and stamped return envelopes.

Mere Exposure Effect. Suppose that you walked into a voting booth on a primary election day and were faced with the following choice:

County Solicitor (Choose One)
Myron Jones
John Adams
Victor Light

Unfortunately, you have not kept up with local politics, and are unfamiliar with the record of any of these candidates. Which candidate would you vote for? Studies indicate that you probably chose John Adams.

In an election in New Hampshire about 10 years ago, John Adams, an unemployed cab driver who did not campaign, won the Republican nomination for the State's First Congressional District. Why did John Adams, a man who spent no money on his campaign and who never gave a speech, win his party's nomination? Psychologists believe that when voters were confronted with three names they didn't recognize, they picked the one linked in history with a political figure. Hence, prior exposure creates a sense of familiarity, which in turn can enhance your liking for the stimulus, a phenomenon known as the **mere exposure effect**.

Political commercials often operate on this principle. They repeatedly hark, "Vote for Brandon Lee, He's the One!" Such commercials give absolutely no information about the candidate. They rely on the well-documented effect that familiarity will enhance liking. Based on this principle, repetition was commonly used in Nazi Germany and North Korean prison camps during World War II in an attempt to make their political ideologies more palatable to the prisoners.

What should you do if you face unknown candidates' names in a voting booth? If you can't vote intelligently for an office, skip that section and vote for the offices that you're familiar with. Intelligent voters ask themselves, "What do I know about these candidates?" and do not fall prey to a familiar-sounding name.

Emotional States

Like many cognitive psychologists, I often forget the critical role that emotions play in the thinking process. (Astute readers will probably recognize this as due to the availability heuristic.) Intuitively, we all know that emotions are important. For example, would you ask your boss for a raise if you knew that he just had a fight with his wife? Of course, your boss' relationship with his wife should be irrelevant to whether you get a raise, but a bad mood tends to spill over and affect unrelated decisions. So does a good mood. In an investigation of the way mood influences the way decisions are made, Bower (1994) found that interviewees for a job were rated higher when the interviewers were given good news prior to the interview than when they were given bad news. In a laboratory study of the way negative events affect the decisions people make, subjects were required to keep their hand in a bucket of ice water—a condition that is known to be stressful. They were then asked to provide their opinions of various people. The researchers found that the decisions these subjects made were much more hostile than in a control condition in which they did not have the physical stressor caused by keeping a hand in ice water (Berkowitz & Thome, 1987).

It is easier to recognize the effect of emotions on the way we think than it is to correct for it. It is important that we all consider how our own moods may be affecting the quality of the decisions that we make, and we may also try to influence the mood of others who will be making decisions that affect us.

Mindlessness

People often think they are making carefully calculated decisions when they are not. Cost-benefit analyses usually take place after the fact.

—Langer (quoted in Coughlin, 1993, p. A9)

Although we may believe that we are rational, thoughtful people, Langer (1989, 1994) found that many of the decisions that we make are **mindless**, that is without conscious thought about what we are doing. For example, she told about a time when she presented a credit card to a store clerk. The clerk looked at the card and then told her that she had not yet signed it. (It was a new card.) Langer then signed the card and signed the charge slip. The clerk mindlessly checked the two signatures to see if they matched. (She had just seen her sign both.) This simple example serves to show that many of the actions that we take are done without conscious thought. Langer argued that mindlessness is a bad habit, and that with effort, we can and should be more consciously aware of what we are doing and why we are doing it.

In fact, Langer (1994) argued that the conscious awareness of being able to make decisions is important to our health. Her research has documented several examples in which residents in a nursing home showed physical and mental improvement when they were involved in the day-to-day decision making that most of us take for granted.

EVALUATING CONSEQUENCES

Murphy's Law: Anything that can go wrong, will.
Comment on Murphy's Law: Murphy was an optimist.

If you return to Fig. 8.1, you'll see that evaluation is done repeatedly as new alternatives are generated, the decision is phrased differently, and the consequences of alternatives are considered. Decision making always involves uncertainty because we are thinking about the way different actions will have some future effect. The decisions that we make have implications for the future, and the future inherently involves unknowns. For this reason, the principles involved in assessing likelihood and uncertainty that were presented in chapter 7 are an integral part of the decision-making process.

Research on how people typically deal with uncertainty has shown that the usual response is to ignore it (Hogarth, 1988). Although this may reduce the immediate complexity of a decision, it is obviously a maladaptive procedure that could lead to catastrophic results. It is possible to reduce the number of unknowns in any situation. This will almost always involve some work by the decision maker, but if the decision is an important one, it will be time well spent. Let's consider a common example. Most of us will purchase several automobiles in our lifetimes. For a majority of Americans, this will represent the second largest expenditure that they will make, exceeded only by a home purchase. The quality of this decision can be improved with a little research. You can determine which automobile variables are important to you and gather relevant data about each car you are considering for possible purchase.

Almost any decision can be improved with a little research that would reduce the uncertainty. For example, if you are uncertain about the safety of nuclear plants, an afternoon at the library reading both pro and con materials should allow you to make a much more informed decision about this important issue.

Assessing Desirable and Undesirable Consequences

We can understand judgment as the quality of analysis, reflection, and ultimately insight that informs the making of politically consequential framing decisions.

—Renshon (1992, pp. 481–482)

The decision maker must always be aware of the risks and benefits associated with taking or not taking a particular course of action. The way consequences are evaluated will depend on the context. For example, the consequences of not taking an umbrella will be greater if you are heading off for a business meeting where showing up dry is important than if you are taking the dog for a walk and then returning home.

If you live in an apartment near a college campus, you are well aware of the "joys" associated with apartment hunting. Rental units are often in short supply in college communities and are priced in a range that strains the typical student's budget. Students may find themselves considering an apartment that lacks the amenities they were hoping for at a price that is really above their income. The risk associated with turning the apartment down is that they might not find another apartment within walking distance to the college campus. The risks associated with renting the apartment must also be considered. What if they find that they really can't afford to keep up the monthly rental payments? The decision maker has to decide which risk is greater and the likelihood of each occurring. Obviously, both risks need to be assessed very carefully and additional alternatives considered. Perhaps a cheaper apartment can be found in another section of town with good public transportation to campus, or perhaps a roommate can be found to share the rent.

A poignant example of failure to assess risks adequately can be found in an analysis of the United States' military actions just prior to the attack on Pearl Harbor. Admiral Kimmel, Commander in Chief of Naval Operations in the Pacific, had received several warnings from Washington that a Japanese attack in the Southwest was possible. He decided to downplay the probability of an attack on Pearl Harbor because he believed that other naval sites were more likely targets. Quite by accident, and almost an hour before the attack, two army privates spotted on a radar screen large unidentified aircraft flying toward Pearl Harbor. Realizing that these could be Japanese bomber planes, they reported the presence of the unidentified aircraft to the Army's radar center.

Let's consider the plight of the officer on duty at the radar center. The United States was not at war with Japan. He had never received the recent warning that a Japanese attack was imminent. He had to decide whether the unidentified objects on the radar screen belonged to the United States or Japan. There were costs and risks associated with either choice. If he had erroneously decided that they were Japanese planes, he would have been responsible for recalling personal "leaves" for large numbers of servicemen and women and creating havoc and panic on the military base. There were also large financial costs involved in preparing for antiaircraft maneuvers. Because he assessed the possibility of a Japanese attack to be low, he told the two privates to forget about the objects detected by radar. He decided that they were probably the Army B-17s that were expected to arrive some time that day. With the unfortunate benefit of hindsight, it is clear that he failed to assess adequately the risks associated with each decision. The result was the worst naval disaster in U.S. history with over 2,000 lives lost. Even though he believed that an attack was unlikely (wishful thinking), he should have realized that the risks were too great to justify his decision. Decisions made under extreme risks need careful scrutiny and not an off-hand dismissal. In this case the risks associated with deciding that the planes belonged to the United States were many times greater than those associated with the decision that they were Japanese bombers.

Research has shown that the Pearl Harbor scenario is not unusual. Whenever extreme risk is associated with a course of action, there is a tendency to minimize the unfavorable consequences (Janis & Mann, 1977). This is sometimes called **biased discounting**. It is the bias or predilection to discount or reduce perceived risk or its probability. It often operates along with wishful thinking, which causes the decision maker to assess the probability of a desirable outcome too high, the failure to seek disconfirming evidence, which is the tendency to ignore evidence that would not support your favored hypothesis, and overconfidence in the quality of the decision that was made. These tendencies, taken together, allowed the radar officer to bolster his decision to ignore the unidentified objects by rationalizing either that even if they were Japanese bomber planes they probably would not do much damage or it was extremely unlikely that they were Japanese aircraft. A more recent example in which the failure to consider the consequences of certain decision alternatives can be seen is in an analysis of the Gulf War that involved the United States, Iraq, and Kuwait. The researcher who conducted the Gulf War analysis found many similarities to the decisions that were made at Pearl Harbor (Renshon, 1992).

ELIMINATION BY ASPECTS

Let's return to the earlier problem of deciding which automobile to buy because it is a decision that most of us will make several times. With so many automobiles on the market, where do you begin? Most people begin decision-making processes of this sort with a strategy known as **elimination by aspects**, although few people know it by this name (Tversky, 1972). An individual who is concerned about unemployment in the U.S. car industry would begin by eliminating cars that are not manufactured in the United States. In this instance, the aspect under consideration is the place in which the automobile is manufactured. At this point, most people will decide which features (or aspects) of automobiles are important to them. Suppose that you are on a limited budget so that cost is an important feature to you. You would probably determine the cost of various models of Fords, Plymouths, Chevrolets, and other U.S. autos. Models that cost more than your price ceiling would be eliminated.

Let's suppose further that frequency of repair is another important variable. Of course, no one can tell you how frequently the car you choose will need repair, but you can reduce some of the uncertainty associated with this variable by finding out how often other models similar to the ones you are considering have needed repair in the past. This information is available in consumer periodicals in every library. If some of the models that you are still considering are judged as "worse than average" on the frequency of repairs, then presumably these would be eliminated from further consideration. The elimination by aspects strategy would be recycled repeatedly until the decision maker is left with a few possible models from which to choose. Typically, small and seemingly insignificant differences will come into play to complete the process—for example, "I'm tired of shopping," or "Let's just take this one," or "The dealer will include at no extra cost fuzzy dice to hang from the rear view mirror if I buy this model," or "I can drive this one home today." The use of small and relatively inconsequential factors to close the decision is an example of mindlessness, a topic that was discussed earlier in this chapter. Most consumers are not aware that something as "small" as free fuzzy dice tilts the balance of what had been a prudent process.

The method of elimination by aspects can be used in many contexts. Political candidates, for example, can be thought of as choices that vary along several criteria. If you decide that the issues that are important to you include a strong military defense, reduction of taxes, and school prayer, then you could rank each of these candidates along these aspects and eliminate the candidates who don't share these views with you. You would have to determine which of these aspects is most important if you find that none of the candidates shares all of your views about these important issues.

PREPARING A WORKSHEET

The time is ripe for a major national and international effort to include thinking and decision-making in school curricula.

—Baron and Brown (1991, p. 6)

We have clear evidence that decision-making biases do not go away just by telling people not to make them, but decision making can be improved with effective training programs (e.g., Payne et al., 1993; Shanteau, Grier, Johnson, & Berner, 1991). Researchers have found that the best way to make an important decision involves the preparation and utilization of a decision worksheet. The purpose of a worksheet is to optimize decision making. Psychologists who study **optimization** compare the actual decision made by a person to a theoretical "ideal" decision to see how similar they are. Proponents of the worksheet procedure believe that it will yield optimal (best) decisions. Although there are several variations on the exact format that a worksheet can take, they are similar in their essential aspects. Worksheets require framing the decision in a clear and concise way, listing many possible alternatives that would achieve a desired goal, listing the relevant considerations that will be affected by the decision, determining the relative importance of each consideration, and mathematically calculating a decision. The end product of the worksheet procedure is a single numerical summary of each possible solution or alternative. The alternative with the highest number of points emerges as the best decision.

Most important problems are multifaceted with several different ways of framing the decision, and many alternatives to choose from, each with unique advantages and disadvantages. One of the benefits of a pencil-and-paper decision-making procedure is that it permits us to deal with more variables than our immediate processing ability would allow. If you've already read chapter 2, you'll recall (I hope) that working memory is limited in the number of pieces of information it can deal with at one time. A worksheet can be especially useful when the decision involves a large number of variables with complex relationships.

Let's consider the worksheet procedure with a realistic example for most college students: "What will I do after graduation?" A hypothetical student, Evan, has several postgraduation opportunities. He is contemplating the following: (a) a job in a large fashionable department store where he will train to be a buyer, (b) a teaching position in an inner-city school, probably a fifth or sixth grade class, (c) a graduate school degree in business administration, (d) a law school degree, and (e) a year off to "bum around" Europe. A decision-making worksheet will be very important in helping him choose the best alternative.

Framing the Decision

The first step is the realization that a decision needs to be made. A decision-making worksheet begins with a succinct statement of the problem that will also help to narrow it. Thus, the problem for Evan becomes "What will I do after graduation that will lead to a successful career?" If Evan words his decision this way, he has already decided that his decision will involve long-range goals and not immediate ones. It is important to be clear about this distinction because most often long-range goals will involve a different decision than short-range ones. Thus the options of attending graduate or law school are really statements about working in business or as a lawyer and not decisions about school per se.

The importance of this first step cannot be overemphasized. The entire decision-making process depends on the way the problem is defined. If Evan had posed the problem as "How can I best earn a good living?" he would find that the process would focus on monetary considerations. Similarly, the process would change if he posed the problem as "Should I go to graduate school?" Research with business managers has shown that the ability to redefine business problems is an important characteristic of good decision making in management (Merron, Fisher, & Torbert, 1987). The way the decision is framed will determine the alternatives that are generated and the way they are evaluated. This is an important point. If you are worried about world hunger, you could frame the decision about what to do about it several ways: How can we produce enough food to feed all the people in the world? How can we adjust the world population so that it does not exceed the food supply? How can we move food from wealthy countries to poor ones? How can we develop nonfood alternatives that are nutritious? Each of these decisions will suggest different alternatives.

A worksheet procedure can have many important applications for social problems. Consider the contemporary problem of violence, which is filled with numerous decision points. It seems that it should be possible to teach aggressive children and adults to reframe their problems in ways that suggest nonviolent alternatives. For example, instead of asking "How can I get even with a classmate?" the child could be trained to ask "How can I improve a bad situation?" Perhaps a thoughtful, creative reader will devise an educational program that teaches children, and perhaps even politicians, to reframe decisions so that nonaggressive alternatives are generated.

Generating the Alternatives

The next step is to write out in separate columns across the top of the worksheet all possible alternatives that could solve the problem. You'll need a large sheet of ruled paper because it would make no sense to cut the worksheet process short because you run out of space on your paper. It is important that you don't evaluate the alternatives at this stage; however, this is not the place for fiction either. If you are tone deaf, this is not the time to fantasize about a career in the opera. Allow room for two columns under each alterative, which will be used later for calculations. Thus far, Evan's worksheet would look something like Table 8.1.

Evan notices while drawing up his worksheet that these alternatives are not all mutually exclusive. There's no reason why he can't decide to travel around Europe for a year and then select a career goal; besides, a vacation in Europe is not a long-range plan and the decision currently being made is for life career goals. He decides at this point to erase the fifth alternative because it seems to require a separate decision from the other four. He also remembers at this point that his father always hoped that Evan would want to run the family-owned lumber business after his graduation from college. Although this is not an appealing idea to Evan, he substitutes it as an additional choice because the rules for this step of the process do not allow for evaluation.

Listing the Considerations

The decision Evan makes will have multiple effects. His feelings about making a personal contribution to society, his income and his future lifestyle, his parents' and friends' opinions of him, the quality of his workday, and many other variables are at stake. If Evan were married with children, the impact of each decision on his spouse and children would also need to be considered. At this point Evan should cover the alternatives and list on the left-hand side of his worksheet the considerations or

TABLE 8.1
What Will I Do After College That Will Lead to a Successful Career?

Alternatives	Dept. Store buyer	Teacher—inner city school	Graduate School—Business	Law School	"Bum" in Europe for a year

TABLE 8.2
What Will I Do After College That Will Lead to a Successful Career?

Alternatives	Dept. Store Buyer	Teacher— Inner City School	Graduate School— Business	Law School	Run Family Lumber Business
Considerations					
Desire to Help Society					
Income					
Parents' Opinions					
Friends' Opinions					
Interest in the Work					

variables that will be affected by his decision. The worksheet would now look like Table 8.2.

Before proceeding, Evan should now put the worksheet away and mull over the way the decision was framed and the alternatives and the considerations that he listed. Often people find that in the course of worksheet preparation they think of new alternatives and discover which considerations are important to them. It is also a good idea to ask other people you trust if they can think of additional alternatives and considerations. Considerations and alternatives that are not listed on the worksheet will not be considered, so it is extremely important to list all the relevant alternatives and considerations. This is another vulnerable point in the decision-making process—failure to consider possible alternatives. Don't cut this part of the decision-making process short. It is important.

Be sure, however, that you don't let other people make the decision for you. Suppose that Evan's friend suggests that Evan seriously pursues his interest in music and becomes a jazz musician. In addition, Evan thinks up several additional considerations that he lists on his worksheet. He also decides that as he is planning for his future, he should realistically consider his chances for success at each alternative. (See Table 8.3.)

Listing all relevant considerations is an important part of the worksheet process. Janis and Mann (1977) believe that poor decisions often result from failures to think through all of the relevant considerations. They suggested that considerations be listed under four categories—gains and losses for self, gains and losses for significant others, self-approval and disapproval, and social approval and disapproval—to avoid overlooking important considerations.

Weighing the Considerations

It is almost always true that the considerations are not equally important to the decision maker and therefore need to be weighed accordingly. A 5-point scale, in which 1 = of slight importance, 5 = of great importance, and the numbers 2, 3, and 4 reflect gradations of importance between these end points, can be used to quantify the relative importance of each consideration. Weighing considerations is a personal matter. It is likely that each of us would assign weights somewhat differently. If Evan felt that his desire to help society was moderately important to him he would rate it a 3. Similarly, if he believed that income was more than moderately important to him, but less than "of great importance" he would rate it a 4. The appropriate weights are placed alongside each consideration.

Weighing the considerations is an another important part of the worksheet process. After assigning numbers (the weights) to each consideration you should stop to survey the weights. If Evan rated "friends' opinions" with a larger number than "parents' opinions," this reflects how he feels about their relative opinions. This is a good way to clarify which considerations are most important to you. It is a good way to consider your own values.

Weighing the Alternatives

Now is the time to think carefully about each alternative and determine how well each satisfies the considerations listed. The alternatives will be weighed using the numbers -2, -1, 0, +1, and +2. A positive number indicates that it is favorable or "pro" the consideration with +2 indicating that it is highly favorable and +1 indicating that it is somewhat favorable. A negative number will be used if an alternative is incompatible with or "con" a consideration, with -2 indicating that it is highly incompatible and -1 indicating that it is somewhat incompatible. Zero will be used when an alternative is neither favorable nor unfavorable to a consideration.

We use Evan's worksheet to demonstrate how to weigh alternatives. First, Evan has to contemplate how becoming a department store buyer will satisfy his desire to help society. Certainly it won't hurt society, but it probably won't help it either. Evan believes that although it may create additional jobs in related industries (fashion, sewing, etc.), this is not really what he had in mind when he thought about helping society; therefore, he rates it a zero on this consideration. This number is placed under "Department Store Buyer" in the left-hand column on the first row. Subsequent ratings will be placed directly below this number. If he does eventually become a buyer for a large department store, he probably will earn a satisfactory income. He certainly won't be rich, but it will be enough money to allow him to live comfortably; therefore, he gives it a +1. Both his parents and friends will consider it to be a moderately good job, so he rates it a +1 on both these considerations. He believes that it should be very interesting work and rates it a +2 on "Interest in the Work." It should be a moderately prestigious occupation and thus rates a +1 in this category. Unfortunately, it probably won't offer much employment security because department store sales are tied to the economy, which seems to fluctuate erratically; he therefore rates it -1 on "Employment Security."

TABLE 8.3
What Will I Do After Graduation That Will Lead to a Successful Career?

Alternatives	Dept. Store Buyer	Teacher— Inner City School	Graduate School— Business	Law School	Run Family Lumber Business	Jazz Musician
Considerations						
Desire to Help Society						
Income						
Parents' Opinions						
Friends' Opinions						
Interest in the Work						
Prestige of Occupation						
Employment Security						
Amount of Vacation and Free Time						
Likelihood of Success						

TABLE 8.4
What Will I Do After College That Will Lead to a Successful Career?

TABLE 8.4
What Will I Do After College That Will Lead to a Successful Career?

Alternatives		Dept. Store Buyer	Teacher— Inner City School	Graduate School— Business	Law School	Run Family Lumber Business	Jazz Musician
Considerations							
Desire to Help Society	(3)	0	+2	0	+1	0	0
Income	(4)	+1	−1	+2	+2	0	−1
Parents' Opinions	(2)	+1	0	+1	+2	+2	−1
Friends' Opinions	(3)	+1	+2	0	+1	−1	+2
Interest in the Work	(5)	+2	+2	+1	0	−1	+1
Prestige of Occupation	(1)	+1	−1	+2	+2	−2	+1
Employment Security	(3)	−1	−2	0	+1	+2	−2
Amount of Vacation and Free Time	(2)	−2	+2	−2	−2	+1	+2
Likelihood of Success	(5)	+1	+1	−1	−1	+2	−2

A department store buyer is required to work a 40-hour or more work week with only a few weeks a year for vacation, thus rating a -2 on vacation and free time. He notes that he is moderately likely to succeed as a department store buyer, so he rates it +1 on this consideration.

It is usually necessary to gather more information at this stage of the decision-making process. Evan may need to phone the local school district to find out what the median salary is for school teachers. He also might seek the advice of his college advisor to determine if he has the math skills needed to succeed in business administration.

Each alternative is rated in a similar manner by thinking how well it satisfies the objectives of each consideration. When he completed weighing the alternatives, Evan's worksheet looked like this (Table 8.4).

Calculating a Decision

If you have carefully followed the worksheet procedure this far, you've realized that it requires numerous decisions before even coming close to yielding the one you want to make. By now Evan has decided what type of decision he's making (long range), listed all the alternatives and all the considerations that he believes to be necessary, decided how important each consideration is to him and how well each alternative satisfies the objectives of each consideration.

There are three different strategies for calculating a decision at this point. They are overall assessment, dimensional comparison, and the "⅔ Ideal Rule." Each utilizes a different criterion for selecting the best decision from a worksheet.

Overall Assessment

An **overall assessment** is obtained by determining how well each alternative satisfies the considerations taken as a whole or overall. This is calculated by multiplying the weight previously assigned for each consideration by the value assigned to how well an alternative satisfies that consideration. For example, Evan has rated his desire to help society a 3 and the department store buyer alternative a 0 on this consideration. The first cell of the worksheet is 3 x 0 = 0. This result, 0, is placed in the right-hand column under "Department Store Buyer." Continuing down to the next consideration, we see that Evan rated income as 4 and the department store buyer alternative +1 on income. Because 4 x 1 = 4 he would place a 4 in the right-hand column below Department Store Buyer and next to "Income." This procedure is repeated for each alternative. The right-hand column for each alternative is then added, yielding a total score for each alternative. This is demonstrated in Table 8.5.

Perusal of the worksheet now shows that based on an overall assessment, the alternative with the highest total score is "Teacher—Inner-City School." You will also notice that the alternative to become a department store buyer obtained a fairly high score that was close to a winning alternative. Thus far, it seems that Evan should seriously be thinking about a career as a teacher.

Dimensional Comparison

In a **dimensional comparison** strategy, each consideration (the "dimensions") is examined to find which alternative has the highest score. For example, if "Desire to Help Society" is examined, you will see that "Teacher—Inner-City School" had the highest rating among all the other alternatives; therefore, it would "win" on this consideration and get one point. Looking at "Income" you will see that both "Graduate School—Business" and "Law School" were assigned +2 on this dimension. In the event of ties each of the winning tied alternatives is awarded one point. If each consideration is examined in a similar manner, the following number of considerations won for each alternative will result:

Number of Considerations Won

Dept. Store Buyer	Teacher—Inner-City School	Graduate School—Business	Law School	Run Family Lumber Business	Jazz Musician
1	4	2	3	3	2

As seen here, the alternative "Teacher—Inner-City School" scored highest among the alternatives on four considerations. Thus, the results of the dimensional comparison strategy agree with the overall assessment results. Notice that both "Law School" and "Run Family Lumber Business" won three considerations each, yet scored fairly low on the overall assessment.

TABLE 8.5
What Will I Do After College That Will Lead to a Successful Career?

Alternatives		Dept. Store Buyer		Teacher— Inner City School		Graduate School— Business		Law School		Run Family Lumber Business		Jazz Musician	
Considerations													
Desire to Help Society	(3)	0	0	+2	6	0	0	+1	3	0	0	0	0
Income	(4)	+1	4	−1	−4	+2	8	+2	8	0	0	−1	−4
Parents' Opinions	(2)	+1	2	0	0	+1	2	+2	4	+2	4	−1	−2
Friends' Opinions	(3)	+1	3	+2	6	0	0	+1	3	−1	−3	+2	6
Interest in the Work	(5)	+2	10	+2	10	+1	5	0	0	−1	−5	+1	5
Prestige of Occupation	(1)	+1	1	−1	−1	+2	2	+2	2	−2	−2	+1	1
Employment Security	(3)	−1	−3	−2	−6	0	0	1	3	+2	6	−2	−6
Amount of Vacation and Free Time	(2)	−2	−4	+2	4	−2	−4	−2	−4	+1	2	+2	4
Likelihood of Success	(5)	+1	5	+1	5	−1	−5	−1	−5	+2	10	−2	−10
			18		20		8		14		12		−6

2/3 Ideal Rule

The **2/3 Ideal Rule** was suggested by Carkhuff (1973). It requires the decision maker to calculate an overall assessment total for a perfect or ideal alternative. If an ideal alternative were added to Evan's worksheet, it would rate +2 on each consideration because it would be highly favorable to each consideration. A total overall score for an ideal alternative can be arrived at by adding all of the consideration weights and multiplying the total by 2 as seen here:

$$3 + 4 + 2 + 3 + 5 + 1 + 3 + 2 + 5 = 28$$

$$28 \times 2 = 56$$

The reasoning behind the 2/3 Ideal Rule is that a best alternative may not be good enough if it fails to measure up to 2/3 of an ideal solution. Thus, according to this rule a minimally acceptable alternative would score an overall 37.5 (2/3 x 56 = 37.5). If you turn back to the completed worksheet you'll see that the highest total was for the teacher alternative and it rated, by the overall assessment method, a 20 (considerably less than the 37.5 required by this rule). Evan has several choices at this point. He can disregard the 2/3 Ideal Rule (which is likely if he is pleased with the decision to become a teacher), or he can expand and recycle the process by generating additional considerations and alternatives until he reaches a consensus with all three calculating procedures.

The 2/3 Ideal Rule is based on the idea that some alternatives are "good enough" whereas others are not. Searching for alternatives that are good enough is called **satisficing** (Marsh & Shapira, 1982; Tversky & Kahneman, 1981). Satisficing refers to terminating the decision-making process when an alternative that is "good enough" to satisfy most of the important considerations is found. The decision-making process cannot go on forever, so at some point, the decision maker will have to decide that one alternative is "good enough." The problem really is *when* to terminate the process, and there are no simple answers to this question. Important decisions like the one considered in this example should be given the time and effort they deserve. Often, better decisions are possible if the decision maker would invest more time and effort into generating alternatives and listing considerations.

Dilemmas in Decision Making

The decision maker will often encounter dilemmas in calculating a decision. It is not unusual for two or more alternatives to have exactly the same high score or for one alternative to obtain the highest total with the overall assessment and a different one with the dimensional comparison. This can always be remedied by generating additional considerations and repeating the process until an alternative emerges as best. It is also possible to combine two or more alternatives. For example, Evan could become a buyer in a department store and volunteer to tutor children on weekends. This would allow him to realize his desire to help society while maintaining the benefits of the buyer alternative. Sometimes the decision maker will abandon the worksheet before it's completed because the process helped to clarify the issues and led directly to a decision without the calculations.

Certainly, the worksheet procedure requires a great deal of work, as its name implies. You might be wondering if there is any evidence to suggest that it's worth the extra effort—that it actually leads to better decisions. Yes, there is. In a study by Mann (1972), he randomly selected 30 high school seniors (15 females and 15 males) from a college preparatory program to participate in an experimental investigation of the worksheet procedure. He taught them how to prepare a worksheet that would help them make decisions about college. The procedure he used was similar to the one presented here, but not identical to it. He also employed a "control group" of 20 students who were not taught the worksheet procedure. Mann contacted the students approximately 6 weeks after they notified the colleges about their decision concerning which college they planned to attend. The group that had received worksheet training (the experimental group) had less postdecision stress and anxiety and were happier about the decisions they made than the control group. Mann also reported that they had considered possible unfavorable consequences of their decision more carefully than the control group. Thus, if something does go wrong they will more likely be prepared for it than those in the group without worksheet training.

Additional evidence that supports the validity of the worksheet procedure comes from a study by Wanous (1973). He conducted an experiment to study the employment decisions of telephone operators. One group of prospective telephone operators was shown a film that portrayed both the positive and negative aspects of the job whereas a control group was shown the standard training film that stressed only the positive aspects. All subjects in both groups decided to accept the employment offer to become telephone operators. One month later, subjects who had viewed the "balanced" presentation reported that they were happier with their decision than were the other telephone operators who had viewed the standard one-sided film. In addition, significantly fewer subjects from the experimental group were thinking about quitting their job than those from the control group. In a similar vein, Janis and Mann (1977) reported several studies in which the worksheet procedure has been utilized in health decisions (e.g., elective surgery) with beneficial outcomes.

More recently, Knight and Dansereau (1992) used a decision-making worksheet with college students who were presented with a story about "Chris," a student who had to make decisions about alcohol and other drug use. The students who were required to complete a worksheet showed evidence of better decisions regarding alcohol and drug use than a control group that did not receive training with worksheets. I don't know if these college students will actually make better real-life decisions about alcohol and other drug use, but other studies with decision-making worksheets suggest that they will. One of the benefits of the worksheet procedure is that it allows people to feel more confident about difficult decisions and better prepared for decision-making situations because they are required to evaluate alternatives in a systematic manner.

POSTDECISION COMMITMENT AND EVALUATION

To begin with it was only tentatively that I put forward the views that I have developed ...
but in the course of time they have gained such a hold upon me that I can no longer think in
any other way.

—Sigmund Freud (1856–1939)

The decision-making process doesn't end with the decision. Once a course of action has been selected, the decision maker must make detailed plans to carry it out and needs to remain committed to the decision. However, if a major change occurs in the evaluation of the consideration, then the process should be repeated. For example, if Evan were unexpectedly offered a lucrative contract to become a jazz musician, he would be wise to reconsider this alternative. Success at this alternative would now seem much more likely and a large income would be assured. Decision making is not a static process. Our major life decisions will have to be reconsidered whenever a major variable changes.

Cognitive Dissonance

Most of the time, people find that they are pleased with their decisions. This finding has been of considerable interest to research psychologists. Leon Festinger (1964), a famous research psychologist, proposed a theory to explain this phenomenon. It is called the theory of **cognitive dissonance**. It is based on the idea that people like their beliefs, attitudes, and actions to be consistent, and when they are not consistent an unpleasant internal state arises—dissonance. Dissonance needs to be reduced. If you believe that it is wrong to smoke marijuana and you attend a party where you smoke marijuana, you will feel uncomfortable because your actions and beliefs are not in agreement. They are not consistent with each other. In order to reduce the discomfort of cognitive dissonance, the unpleasant internal state, you will generally change your beliefs and conclude that you did the right thing because "marijuana probably isn't so bad after all." In general, the theory of cognitive dissonance has received considerable experimental support. In one study (Brehm, 1956) subjects rated the desirability of several gifts (e.g., toaster, coffee maker). They were then asked to choose between two gifts that they had rated as equally desirable. After a decision had been made, subjects rated the rejected gift as being much less desirable than the one they chose. The theory of cognitive dissonance would have predicted this result because subjects would now believe that they must like the selected object much more than the rejected one in order to maintain consistency. It seems that once a decision is made the alternatives that were not selected will seem much less attractive than the one that was.

The theory of cognitive dissonance can be applied in a number of situations. It can be used to explain the famous fable The Fox and the Sour Grapes. The story goes something like this: A hungry fox spies grapes hanging high overhead. After repeated unsuccessful attempts to reach them, he decides that they were probably sour and walks away. Like the human subjects described in this section, he downplayed the desirability of the object he didn't obtain.

The theory of cognitive dissonance only applies when a conscious decision has been made. If you were coerced in some way, there would be no dissonance. Suppose that you were required to write an essay on some topic that you are opposed to, like the inferiority of a racial or ethnic group, or why drugs should be available to elementary school children. If you were coerced into doing this, there would be no need to change your attitudes to keep them consistent with this behavior. However, if you voluntarily decided to write such an essay, then cognitive dissonance theory would predict a change in your attitude toward the position you took in the essay. This is a major theory in social psychology that explains why people are usually satisfied with the decisions they make. It is easy to see how it contributes to the unwarranted confidences that most people have in their decisions.

Hindsight and Forethought

The term **hindsight** is probably not a new one for you. After a decision has been made and the relevant events occur, well-meaning friends will often tell you they could have predicted the consequences of your decision. If you have ever been divorced (or have exchanged confidences with someone who has), there were probably several acquaintances who claimed to have known all along that, "he (or she) was no good for you."

Events appear different with the benefit of hindsight. Forethought is the opposite of hindsight. There should be fewer unfortunate consequences if decisions are carefully thought out before they are made.

In experimental investigations of hindsight, most participants erroneously believed that they could have predicted the consequences of historical and personal decisions before they occurred. In our earlier analysis of the Pearl Harbor disaster, it seemed obvious that the only possible decision was to assume that the aircraft belonged to the Japanese. It should be remembered that we analyzed the disaster with the full knowledge of the ensuing events. Hindsight occurs only when poor or wrong decisions have been made. It is seldom that good decisions are analyzed after the fact. Forethought and hindsight are qualitatively different. At the time of the decision (forethought) there is doubt and deliberation, but following the unfavorable consequences of the decision (hindsight) there is often a great sense of certainty that the future should have been predicted more accurately.

An example of the power of hindsight occurred in 1974 when an editorial in a Eugene, Oregon, newspaper called upon the local prison warden to resign. A "convicted murderer, bank robber, and all-around bad actor" had been given a 4-hour pass to leave the state penitentiary (Fischhoff, 1975). Instead of returning, he kidnapped and murdered an Oregon couple. With the benefit of hindsight, that is with the full knowledge of the result, does it seem that the warden should have known that this would happen? Given the disastrous outcome it was a wrong decision, but was the result obvious or even likely before the pass was granted? The convict had been a model prisoner before the pass was granted. Do you think that the warden should have been required to resign?

Hindsight is of little value in the decision-making process. It distorts our memory for events that occurred at the time of the decision so that the actual consequence seems to have been a "forgone conclusion." Thus, it may be difficult to learn from our mistakes. Retrospective (after the fact) review, on the other hand, can be a valuable aid in improving future decisions. Unlike hindsight, it does not involve a faulty reconstruction of the information available at the time of the decision so that the consequence appears obvious.

There are plenty of examples of the hindsight bias whenever a political decision results in a disastrous outcome. For example, you may recall the tragic end to the Branch Davidians in Waco, Texas, in 1993. Attorney General Janet Reno ordered that federal agents take over the compound following a lengthy siege and the shooting of several federal agents by the members of this religious cult. At least 15 children in the Davidian compound were killed by their parents during an apparent murder/suicide frenzy that occurred when the Davidians were attacked by the federal agents. Did Reno make a bad decision? It is clear that the decision had a bad outcome, but given what was known at the time the decision was made, should she have reasonably expected that the Davidians would kill each other if the agents stormed the compound? Federal agents are involved in many activities, with very, very few ever resulting in disaster. There were no good reasons to have predicted that these religious parents would kill their children and then each other. Dawes (1993) pointed out how the news media used their knowledge of this salient, improbable, and painful outcome to cloud their understanding of the factors that were available at the time the decision was made. The next time a major disaster follows from a decision, look at the way the decision is analyzed by the news media and the political party that is likely to gain from this tragedy. Ask yourself if the outcome could have reasonably been predicted prior to the decision.

It is a good idea to determine what went wrong if a poor decision has been made or if a good decision had a negative consequence, as long as we do not fall prey to hindsight. Immediately after the tragic bombing of a federal building in Oklahoma in 1995, numerous political pundits proclaimed that they knew that a disgruntled militia was a serious threat to society. *After* it happened, we all "could see it coming."

APPLYING THE FRAMEWORK

In applying the general thinking skills framework to decision making, consider the following questions:

1. What Is the Goal?   The skills involved in decision making should be used whenever you are faced with selecting the best alternative among a set of alternatives. Examples of situations that require the use of these skills include personal, professional, and political decisions. The process starts with the recognition that a decision is needed and then a careful consideration of how it should be framed. Because a common failure occurs in the generation of a limited number or limited scope of alternatives, exert time and effort on this stage of the process. Additional alternatives and new kinds of alternatives can be generated when the decision maker invests the time and the effort. The time and effort should be proportional to the importance of the decision. Think through positive and negative consequences of various alternatives.

2. What Is Known?   The entire decision-making process is predicated on the belief that you are selecting from among a set of alternatives. If you have no alternatives, then there is no decision. Similarly, the process requires that you frame the decision in several ways so that you can generate a range of alternatives. A decision can only be as good as the information that it is based on. If you do not know much about a problem, then you cannot select intelligently from a set of solutions. Probably, the greatest difficulty with making decisions is the failure to consider alternatives that aren't listed on a worksheet or aren't made conscious in some other way. Good decisions will require information gathering and assessment *before* the selection of alternatives begins.

3. Which Thinking Skill or Skills Will Get You to Your Goal?   The kind of skill you select when you are confronted with an important decision depends on the nature of the problem. Some of the skills involve avoiding common fallacies like the failure to seek disconfirming evidence or the reliance on available information to assess the likelihood of an outcome. If the decision has potentially negative consequences, then the positive and negative results of a course of action have to be compared to each other and to those associated with other alternatives. The weighing of considerations to calculate relative importance and likelihood is helpful whenever there are multiple alternatives and the decision is an important one.
The following decision-making skills were developed in this chapter:

- Listing alternatives and considering the pros and cons of each.
- Reframing the decision so as to consider different types of alternatives.
- Recognizing the need to seek disconfirming evidence and deliberately seeking disconfirming evidence.
- Understanding the way that information that is readily recalled or information that appears representative of a random process can influence how decisions are made.

- Considering how overly optimistic assessments bias the selection of alternatives.
- Recognizing arguments that are based on entrapment and considering why the costs have been high.
- Being mindful of the way liking can affect the evaluation of alternatives.
- Evaluating positive assessments of alternatives that are based on reciprocity or familiarity.
- Seeking information to reduce uncertainty when making risky decisions.
- Preparing a decision-making worksheet for important decisions.
- Understanding the distinction between the quality of a decision and its outcome.
- Understanding the way emotional states like reactance and anger can affect the way we evaluate alternatives and behaving in ways that minimize their effects.
- Recognizing that hindsight analysis of a decision is usually biased and of limited value.

4. Have You Reached Your Goal?   The process of making a decision could, theoretically, go on forever. Most decisions, however, have deadlines. After you have carefully considered various outcomes, you need to take an overview of your decision and then follow through and act on it. Does the decision seem right? Are you satisfied with the process and outcome? As stated in the chapter, because of the uncertainty inherent in decisions, sometimes good decisions will have poor outcomes. When this happens, scrutinize the nature of the outcome. Was there a consideration that you failed to consider at the time the decision was made? Can you learn from the negative outcome? Can you imagine the consequences of an alternative you rejected?

CHAPTER SUMMARY

1. Decision making is an active process that begins with a clear definition of the decision and a set of alternative solutions from which to choose.

2. One way to improve on the way in which decisions are made is to frame the decision in several ways. Additional alternatives can emerge by changing the focus of what is being decided on.

3. Because few people have ever received formal instruction in thinking skills, even trained professionals commit common decision-making fallacies.

4. A common error in decision making is the failure to seek disconfirming evidence.

5. People often rely on heuristics or "rules of thumb" to help them make decisions. The availability heuristic or reliance on events that are readily recalled is a common decision-making heuristic.

6. Because of the widespread but erroneous belief that the laws of chance are self-correcting, many people believe that "random-looking" sequences of outcomes are more probable outcomes of a random process than orderly sequences of outcomes.

7. Unwarranted optimism can also lead to poor decisions because it prevents realistic assessment of both desirable and undesirable consequences of a decision.

8. People often fall prey to entrapment. They find it difficult to reverse their decision after having invested large amounts of time or money.

9. Decisions are often biased by emotional states like psychological reactance (the resistance to a loss of freedom), mood, and liking induced by reciprocity and familiarity.

10. Risky decisions require special care. There is often a tendency to downplay the likelihood of a disastrous outcome.

11. When the alternatives vary along several dimensions, decisions are sometimes made by eliminating alternatives until only one or two choices remain.

12. Important decisions can be optimized by preparing a worksheet in which alternatives and considerations are listed and weighed in a table format.

13. People are most often satisfied with the decisions that they make, possibly because cognitive dissonance works to maintain consistency between actions and beliefs and because they cannot think of any reason why they might be wrong. Thus, we reason that if we decided on a course of action it must have been the best one.

14. After the consequences of a decision have occurred, there is a great sense of certainty that the consequences should have been obvious. Hindsight is a ubiquitous phenomenon that distorts how we perceive the information that was available before the decision was made.

15. There is an important distinction between a good decision that is based on the information that is available when the decision is being made and its outcomes. Sometimes, good decisions will have undesirable outcomes because of the inherent uncertainty in most important decisions.

TERMS TO KNOW

Check your understanding of the concepts presented in this chapter by reviewing their definitions. If you find that you're having difficulty with any term, be sure to reread the section in which it is discussed:

Fallacy. An error or mistake in the thinking process.

Confirmation Bias. The predilection to seek and utilize information that supports or confirms one's hypothesis or beliefs while ignoring disconfirming information.

Overconfidence. An unwarranted confidence in the quality of decisions that are being made.

Heuristic. A general "rule of thumb" or strategy that we use to solve problems and make decisions. Although it doesn't always produce a correct answer, it is usually a helpful aid. Compare with algorithm.

Algorithm. A problem- solving or decision- making procedure that will always yield the solution to a particular problem if it is followed exactly. Compare with heuristic.

Availability Heuristic. A decision-making "rule of thumb" that is used when estimates of frequency or probability are made based on the ease with which instances come to mind; for example, many college students believe that there are more professors in America than farmers because they can think of more professors whom they know than farmers.

Representativeness Heuristic. A decision-making "rule of thumb" in which the determination of a sample's likelihood is made by noting its similarity to a random process. If it "looks like" a random process, it is judged to be more probable than if it appears orderly or patterned.

Wishful Thinking. People tend to overestimate their chances of success or the likelihood of a desirable outcome.

Entrapment. A situation in which an individual has already invested much money, time, or effort and therefore decides to continue in this situation because of the money, time, or effort that has already been invested.

Psychological Reactance. Resistance arising from restrictions of freedom. Some people will select a less preferred alternative if they are told that they must select the preferred alternative.

Mere Exposure Effect. Very often, repeated exposure to a stimulus will enhance your liking for it.

Mindlessness. Making decisions with little or no conscious effort.

Biased Discounting. Predilection to discount or reduce the magnitude or probability of risk.

Elimination by Aspects. A decision-making strategy in which choices are sequentially eliminated if they fail to meet one or more considerations.

Optimization. In decision making, it refers to making the best possible decision in any situation.

Overall Assessment. A method of calculating a decision from a worksheet. The alternative with the highest worksheet total would be selected. Compare with dimensional comparison and 2/3 Ideal Rule.

Dimensional Comparison. A method for calculating a decision from a worksheet. The alternative that has "won" the greatest number of considerations would be selected. Compare with overall assessment and 2/3 Ideal Rule.

2/3 Ideal Rule. A method for calculating a decision from a worksheet. Only alternatives whose worksheet totals are at least 2/3 as large as the ideal choice would be chosen. Compare with dimensional comparison and overall assessment.

Satisficing. Terminating the decision-making process when an alternative that is "good enough" to satisfy most of the important considerations is found.

Cognitive Dissonance. A theory based on the notion that people want their beliefs, attitudes, and actions to be consistent. When they are not consistent an unpleasant internal state arises—dissonance—which needs to be reduced. We reduce dissonance by changing our beliefs and attitudes so that they are in accord with our actions.

Hindsight. Reevaluation of a decision after it has been made and its consequences have occurred with the belief that the consequences should have been known before the decision was made.

SUGGESTED READINGS

A wealth of new books have appeared in the last several years that are designed to help readers become better decision makers. One of the gurus of this area is Irving Janis, who is recently deceased. The author of many books on decision making, his last one was *Crucial Decisions: Leadership in Policy Making and Crisis Management* (1989). Janis suggested that leaders become vigilant and use good decision-making strategies even though the managers may work in incompetent organizations, receive incomplete information, and must operate under unresolvable uncertainties. Janis urged that managers adopt the habit of reconsidering alternatives that were rejected earlier in the decision-making process and that additional emphasis be given to major risks that could result from a decision. Of course, it is not only top managers who have to make tough decisions. In an edited text by Baron and Brown (1991), the authors considered the whys and how-tos of *Teaching Decision Making to Adolescents*. They convinced me that this should be a national priority.

J. F. Yates' (1990) book, *Judgment and Decision Making*, addresses a more advanced audience. Yates was more concerned with probability issues in making judgments than the other authors. He used a mathematical and philosophical approach to many of the same issues that are addressed in other books. Plous' (1993) award-winning book *The*

Psychology of Judgment and Decision Making is written for a general audience. It is an excellent text for anyone who wants a general introduction to this area.

Decision making is a very applied area of research because decisions are an integral part of real life. An interesting article by Heller, Saltzstein, and Caspe (1992) shows how many of the principles that are discussed in this chapter operate in medical decision making. I also recommend an edited text that deals specifically with the way experts make decisions. It is *Expertise and Decision Support* by Wright and Bolger (1992).

There are several "oldies but goodies" that still make excellent reading, such as a book appropriately named *Decision Making* by Janis and Mann (1977) and *A Practical Guide for Making Decisions* by D. D. Wheeler and Janis (1980). Both have an extensive section on the worksheet procedure. Several excellent articles on heuristics and biases appear in a volume edited by Johnson-Laird and Wason (1977) entitled *Thinking: Readings in Cognitive Science*. A book that is fun to read because the examples of decision strategies are humorous and current is *Decisions Decisions: Game Theory and You* by Bell and Caplans (1976). An interesting multidisciplinary approach can be found in *Making Decisions: A Multidisciplinary Introduction* by Hill et al. (1979). This book begins with the problem of "What to do with dear Aunt Sarah?" It discusses the ethical, economic, psychological, and philosophical problems that a family is faced with in planning the future of an aging aunt. A collection of interdisciplinary articles appears in Arkes and Hammond (Eds.) (1986a) book entitled *Judgment and Decision Making: An Interdisciplinary Reader*.

An excellent text on decision making that is highly recommended is Baron's (1988) *Thinking and Deciding*. Fischhoff tackled some of the most difficult issues in decision making in a volume edited by Sternberg and Smith (1988), entitled *The Psychology of Human Thought*. Fischhoff discussed how certain safety decisions reflect inherent beliefs about the worth of a human life. It is fascinating reading no matter what your level of expertise in this area is.

If you're interested in learning more about the theory of cognitive dissonance, you can consult the classic in this area in a volume edited by Festinger (1964) called *Conflict, Decision and Dissonance*. An interesting study of dissonance with a group of people who believed that the world would end on a given day and their reactions when it didn't appears in *When Prophecy Fails* by Festinger, Riecken, and Schacter (1956). Although this book is quite old, the topic is likely to be particularly timely as it is expected that more groups will be predicting the end of the world as we approach and pass the year 2000. For a contemporary update on these issues see Cialdini's (1993) book, *Influence*. This book is so well written that it's the sort of book you would read even if you didn't have to. It's one of my very favorites. Finally, an award-winning book by Neustadt and May (1986), *Thinking in Time: The Uses of History for Decision Makers*, is highly recommended. These authors proposed that political leaders use lessons from the past to tackle current problems.

9

Development of Problem-Solving Skills

Contents

Suppose you're driving alone at night on a long, dark stretch of freeway that is infrequently traveled when you suddenly hear the familiar "thump-thump" of a very flat tire. You pull onto the shoulder of the road and begin the unpleasant task of changing a tire, illuminated only with the light of the moon and a small flashlight. Carefully, you remove the lug nuts and place them in the hubcap by the roadside. A speeding motorist whizzes past you, hitting the hubcap and scattering the lug nuts across the dark freeway and out of sight. Here you sit, a spare tire in one hand, a flat tire propped against the car, and no lug nuts, on a dark night on a lonely stretch of freeway. To make matters worse, a cold rain is beginning to fall. What would you do?

One of my students told me that this incident actually happened. He went on to elaborate that the flat tire occurred alongside a large mental institution near our college. While the hapless motorist sat pondering his problem, he attracted the attention of several "residents" of the institution, who gathered near the motorist along the chain link fence that separated them. One resident offered this solution to the motorist's problem: Remove one lug nut from each of the other three tires and use them to attach the spare. Each tire should hold securely with three lug nuts until the motorist reaches a gas station. The grateful motorist thanked the institution resident and then asked, "How'd you think of such a good solution to this problem?" The resident replied, "I'm not dumb, I'm just crazy!"

I doubt if this exchange ever really occurred. After this problem appeared in the first and second editions of this book, students from all over the country wrote to tell me that they heard the same story, but with the poor motorist breaking down near their school. In any case, virtually everyone agrees that the resident offered a good solution to the motorist's predicament. Why was it so difficult for the motorist to solve the problem? Why did the solution seem so easy and obvious after it was revealed? How did the resident come up with such a good solution?

ANATOMY OF A PROBLEM

Finding the right answer is important, of course. But more important is developing the ability to see that problems have multiple solutions, that getting from X to Y demands basic skills and mental agility, imagination, persistence, patience.

—Mary Hatwood Futrell, President, NEA (cited in Heiman & Slomianko, 1986, p. 18)

Consider this more mundane problem that differs in several important ways from the "lug nut" problem: Keith has to catch a 9:00 a.m. plane for Philadelphia, and he's already behind schedule. The freeway route to the airport is the quickest, except when the traffic is heavy. The traffic is almost always heavy with commuters during the morning rush hour. There is a back-roads route that might be a good one, if the road along the river isn't flooded. The road is frequently closed because of flooding after heavy rains. As you can probably guess by now, it rained last night. The surface-street route is the longest. If Keith chooses this route, he may miss his plane. Of course, if he spends too much time pondering this problem, he'll surely miss his plane. Which route should he take?

In order to understand any complex phenomenon, like problem solving, we need a model or theoretical framework that we can use to study and understand how people solve all sorts of problems. A model is an "as, if" statement. This means, let's examine the phenomenon that we want to know about "as if" it were something else. In an earlier chapter, I suggested that you think about memory as if it consisted of stages in a computer program and to think of different kinds of memory as different ways of slicing a pizza. Theoretical models of this sort are useful for organizing what we know about thinking and for suggesting new types of research and ways to improve the process we are trying to understand.

In their classic book, Newell and Simon (1972) conceptualized all problems as being composed of the same basic parts or structures. Their idea is that problems can be understood by reducing them to their anatomical parts. According to this view, the **anatomy of a problem** can be thought of as having a starting or **initial state** (Keith's home) and a final or **goal state** (the airport). Hayes (1978) used this framework when he asked: "What is a problem? ... The problem is the gap which separates where you are from where you want to be" (p. 177). All of the possible **solution paths** from the initial state to the goal state comprise the **problem space**. In solving a problem, people search through the problem space to find the best path from the initial state to the goal; that is, they consider the alternatives that would lead to the goal and select the best one.

In addition to an initial state, a goal state, and the paths connecting them, there are givens or information and rules that place constraints on the problem. The givens include the knowledge needed to reach the goal and the need to select the best route. The given information can be explicitly stated or implicitly assumed. Two implicit givens in the problem presented earlier were the knowledge that Keith would drive a car to the airport and that he would take either the freeway route, back-roads route, or surface-street route. This anatomy or framework for conceptualizing problems has proven useful in understanding the process of problem solving. We are all faced with countless problems, and surely know one when we see one. Yet, like most of the topics in this book, the word problem remains a difficult one to define. Polya (1962), a pioneer in this area, offered the following definition: "Solving a problem means finding a way out of a difficulty, a way around an obstacle, attaining an aim that was not immediately understandable." The anatomy of the airport problem is schematically shown in Fig. 9.1. We return to the airport problem later in the chapter as different problem-solving strategies are considered.

Problems differ in many ways, including difficulty and where, in the problem space, the gap occurs. In the airport problem, the difficulty lies in choosing which of the three paths (routes) would get Keith to the goal in the shortest time. In the lug nut problem the difficulty was in generating any solution path. The initial state was a spare tire with

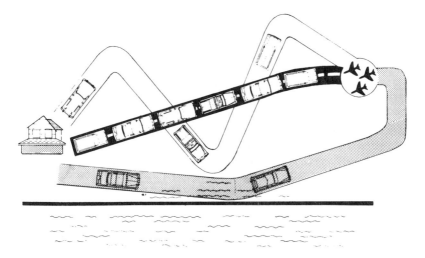

FIG. 9.1.   The anatomy of the airport problem. Givens: Keith will drive to the airport. He will take one of these routes. He must take the fastest route.

no lug nuts; the goal was a spare tire attached to the car securely enough to drive the car. The problem was the apparent absence of paths to the goal.

Consider Rubik's cube as a difficult problem. The goal for a Rubik's cube is to align each small colored square so that each of the six sides of the cube will be a uniform color. This is a prohibitive problem because there are millions of combinations of possible moves (paths to the goal). The "trick" is to determine which combination of moves will lead to the goal. In this sort of problem, the difficulty lies in reducing the number of possible paths so that only potentially correct ones will be chosen. Newell and Simon (1972) calculated that the average 40-move chess game has 10^{120} paths. This is a number hugely greater than the national debt! Perhaps this is why we view great chess masters with such awe. They have the knowledge to avoid blind paths (bad moves) that won't lead to the goal (winning) and to select the best combination of moves.

Although problem solving, decision making, and creativity are discussed in separate chapters in this book, there is considerable overlap among these topics. Many decisions are involved in solving a problem, and generating satisfactory solution paths often requires considerable creativity. The division among these topics is for ease of presentation. All of the chapters in this text are interrelated in that they represent somewhat arbitrary ways of "cutting up the thinking pie." The information presented in the other chapters will also contribute to your understanding of problem solving.

STAGES IN PROBLEM SOLVING

The aim of heuristics is to study the methods and rules of discovery and invention. ... Heuristic, as an adjective, means "serving to discover."

—Polya (1945, pp. 112–113)

In 1926 Graham Wallas examined anecdotal accounts of creative scientists and concluded that problem solving progresses in a series of stages. Although there is disagreement among psychologists as to whether all problem solving is done in qualitatively different stages, a brief review of the hypothesized stages may prove useful to problem solvers.

The first stage is **preparation or familiarization**. This includes the time spent in understanding the nature of the problem, the desired goal, and the givens. This is a crucial part in problem solving because a correct solution cannot be generated without an adequate understanding of the problem. The second stage is the **production stage**. During this stage, the problem solver produces the solution paths that define the problem space. **Judgment or evaluation** is the third stage. During this stage, individuals evaluate the solution paths in order to select the best one. The fourth stage is a strange one that may or may not occur, depending on the problem. Sometimes when we can't find a solution path, we stop working on the problem. The period when we're not actively considering the problem is called the **incubation stage**. There are many reports from famous scientists that a solution came to them during the incubation phase—seemingly "out of the blue." Because of the fascination incubation holds for most people, it deserves separate consideration.

Incubation

The idea of an incubation phase is attractive to most people. It represents one of the few instances in which we may get something for nothing. An oft-cited example of incubation comes from the writings of the famous French mathematician Poincare (1929):

Then I turned my attention to the study of some arithmetical questions apparently without much success and without a suspicion of any connection with my preceding researches. Disgusted with my failure, I went to spend a few days at the seaside, and thought of something else. One morning, walking on the bluff, the idea came to me, with just the same characteristics of brevity, suddenness and immediate certainty, that the arithmetic transformations of indeterminate ternary quadratic forms were identical with those of non-Euclidean geometry. (p. 388)

Have you ever had the experience of working unsuccessfully on a problem, then having the solution come to you sometime later when you were not consciously thinking about it? If so, then you have experienced incubation effects firsthand. The term *incubation* suggests a mother hen sitting on great ideas that are about to hatch.

Incubation is a poorly understood phenomenon. If your employer found you sitting with your feet propped on your desk, gazing out the window, she probably would not be pleased to learn that you were "incubating" on company time. A familiar experience is having a correct answer come to someone immediately after turning in an exam or paper. This is most likely the result of incubation. It's a good idea to work well ahead of deadlines to allow ample time for incubation effects to occur. We don't know how people are able to produce solutions during time-outs. There is no evidence that people continue to work on the problem at an unconscious level, although some people have suggested that this is how incubation effects occur. Most likely, the time-out period serves to dissipate fatigue and allows individuals to get out of sets or ruts in their thinking processes so that they can view the problem from a different perspective.

Herbert A. Simon (1977), the Nobel Prize-winning psychologist, has attempted to explain incubation as due, in part, to selective forgetting. He suggested that when we are working on a problem we rely on a relatively small number of concepts held in a limited-capacity short-term or working memory. (See chapter 2 for a detailed discussion of this concept.) When we're not working on a problem, the information held in short-term memory is quickly forgotten. If this information was not productive for discovering a solution, then having forgotten it will be beneficial to finding a good solution. There is good evidence that when we are trying to recall a name or word that we know we know, but can't recall (that frustrating tip-of-the-tongue feeling), successful retrieval will often occur sometime later, when we are not actively trying to remember the name or word (e.g., Burke, MacKay, Worthley, & Wade, 1991).

It's a good idea to put aside a problem that you're having difficulty solving and return to it at a later time (S. M. Smith & Blankenship, 1991). This is especially good advice during an exam. At least you'll be sure of getting credit for the easier problems, but watch your time limits carefully so that you can correctly finish as many problems as possible in the allotted time. (Of course, it's also a good idea to work on the problems worth the most points first to maximize your exam score.)

Insight

Did you ever have the solution to a problem come to you "in a flash?" Sudden knowledge of the solution is called **insight** or the Aha! experience. Insightful solutions can occur during periods of incubation or while actively working on a problem. It is metaphorically referred to as a light bulb in the head that is suddenly switched on. Interestingly, the earliest studies of insight were conducted with chimpanzees, not humans (Kohler, 1925). It seems that when chimpanzees are confronted with problems, such as reaching food that can only be obtained by putting two sticks together to form

Reprinted with special permission of NAS, INC.

a rake, a period of seemingly random behavior is followed by what appears to be sudden insight into the problem.

Insight experiences are common. I have found them to occur frequently in the statistics classes that I teach. Often students will ponder over a problem or listen attentively to a lecture, then suddenly they'll break into a broad grin and exclaim, "Now I understand." A law school student once told me that she spent the first three fourths of her first year in law school in an intellectual fog. She really felt that she understood very little about the basic concepts. Then, something "clicked" and she suddenly understood the reasoning that went into legal principles. It's as if a little light went on that illuminated the concepts. Her insight paid off into a successful legal career.

It should be noted that insight follows a period of concentrated effort. It occurs after the problem solver has become familiar with the problem and has considered possible solutions. A review of the problem-solving strategies presented later in this chapter provides some thinking guides that serve to direct the thinking processes in ways that will increase the likelihood of insightful solutions.

Persistence

I have a bias which leads me to believe that no problem of human relations is ever insolvable.

—Ralph Bunche (quoted in Beilensen & Jackson, 1992, p. 31)

Although persistence doesn't usually appear as a stage in problem solving, it is probably the most important variable in determining success. An individual who persists at a problem is much more likely to solve it than an individual who gives up. Persistence is close to Levine's (1994) idea of "intimate engagement" (p. 3). Intimate engagement is the willingness to work on a problem in an involved and concentrated way. For example, suppose that you are given a problem to solve in mathematics. It should be obvious that if you give up as soon as you find that the solution isn't immediately apparent, you will not perform as well in mathematics as someone who continues to work on difficult problems.

Think about the anatomy of the problems that were just described. Suppose that you cannot find a path from the initial state to the goal. Giving up will assure failure. Several studies have shown that terminating the search through the problem space too early in the problem-solving process is a leading reason for failure in problem solving.

Heller et al. (1992) compared the way experienced physicians go about solving the problem of making an accurate diagnosis with the way novice physicians make a diagnosis. When you visit a physician, you are there because you have a problem. You need to find the cause for your symptoms, so that the symptoms and the underlying cause can be treated. Novice physicians terminated their search for a cause as soon as they found a plausible alternative. By contrast, the senior physicians persisted in their search through the problem space even after they found a possible cause. Similar results were found when students who were successful in solving problems in a genetics class were compared to unsuccessful students. The most salient difference between the successful and unsuccessful problem solvers was the tendency to consider more options; that is, the good problem solvers persisted longer than the poor problem solvers when searching for solutions (M. U. Smith, 1988). This is an important point: In order to become a good problem solver, you must be willing to work at the problem and to search the problem space for solution paths even when none are obvious or a plausible one has been found.

WELL-DEFINED AND ILL-DEFINED PROBLEMS

Here is Edward Bear, coming downstairs. Now, bump, bump, bump, on the back of his head, behind Christopher Robin. It is, as far as he knows, the only way of coming downstairs, but sometimes he feels that there really is another way, if only he could stop bumping for a moment and think of it.

—A. A. Milne (*Winnie the Pooh*, 1926, p. 3)

Problems come in all shapes and sizes. Consider the following two problems:

1. The parallelogram problem (after Wertheimer, 1959). Some time back in fifth or sixth grade, you learned that in order to find the area of a rectangle you should multiply the height by the length. Now you are given the following parallelogram that is 4" long and 2" high. What is its area?

2. Write a poem expressing the joy you feel when spring flowers bloom.

Do these problems seem qualitatively different to you? The parallelogram problem has a single correct answer. Have you figured it out? Wertheimer (1959) suggested that the correct answer lies in **perceptual reorganization**, or seeing the problem in a new way. The new way consists of seeing the parallelogram in terms of a rectangle and two triangles. Thus, the parallelogram becomes:

Once the problem is restructured this way, it is only a short leap to figure out that the area of the parallelogram can be found with the same formula for the area of a rectangle because the two triangles can be fit together so that a new rectangular figure is formed with a 4" length and a 2" height. In the present example, the area of the parallelogram is 2" x 4" = 8 square inches. There is no other correct answer. The goal (correct answer) is **well defined,** as is the path to the goal.

Writing a poem is a different sort of problem. The goal (a beautiful poem) is **ill defined,** as there are many forms a poem can take. There are countless ways to write a poem. The greatest difficulty in this case lies in evaluating the quality of the end product. The goal is uncertain in ill-defined problems, thus part of the difficulty lies in determining if the problem has been solved (Dorner, 1983).

Most of the problems that confront people outside of school are ill defined; the problem solver must decide how to define the goal and then evaluate how well the goal has been attained. By contrast, many of the problems that students are asked to solve in school are well defined; that is, there is a single correct answer. Other examples of ill-defined problems are: creating a way to increase sales for a business, finding more effective ways to study, writing a clear easy-to-read textbook, saving money for college tuition, building a better mousetrap, de-escalating the nuclear arms race, getting a date with the attractive newcomer at your school, and improving the environment. In ill-defined problems, the goal may be vague or incomplete, which makes the generation of solution paths difficult and their evaluation even more difficult.

One of the best ways to approach ill-defined problems is to make the goal explicit. It is usually possible to state the goal in several different ways for ill-defined problems. For example, the problem of increasing sales can be reidentified as the problem of increasing profits because the real goal is to find ways to make more money. When asked in this form, the problem changes from its initial conceptualization. Solution paths can now include ways to cut losses, reduce inventories, or collect bad debts. The best way to approach ill-defined problems is to specify multiple goals in objective terms so that a variety of solution paths can be considered. Whenever you are faced with an ill-defined problem, state the goal in at least four ways. This sort of exercise will suggest additional solutions and can improve the way you search for solutions.

Sometimes the distinction between well-defined and ill-defined problems blurs. Consider again the problem of getting Keith to the airport on time. If the problem is selecting among the three routes to the airport, it is well defined, but if other solution paths and goals are possible—for example, fly to the airport, take a different plane from a nearer airport, take the subway—then the problem becomes somewhat more difficult to define. Even when a problem seems to be well defined, it is useful to consider whether other goal states would solve the problem, and, if so, what sorts of solution paths are possible with different goals.

PROBLEM PLANNING AND REPRESENTATION

In the mathematics and science courses I took in college, I was enormously irritated by the hundreds of hours that I wasted staring at problems without any good idea about what approach to try next in attempting to solve them. I thought at the time that there was no educational value in those "blank" minutes and I see no value in them today.

—Wickelgren (1974, p. ix)

Recent research in problem solving has focused on the importance of devising a plan for finding and selecting solutions (Friedman, Scholnick, & Cocking, 1987). Planning is a higher order thinking skill that is used to direct and regulate behavior (Pea & Hawkins, 1987; Scholnick & Friedman, 1987). A plan provides a structure that problem solvers can use in a step-by step manner to help them reach the desired goal. Stating the goal in at least four different ways, which results in multiple goal states, even when the problem appears to be well defined, is an example of a planful approach to problem solving. The generation of multiple goal states will increase the size of the problem space and provide more opportunities for finding a good solution. This sort of plan is **transcontextual**, which means that it can be used in any context with any sort of problem (Ceci & Ruiz, 1993). Here is an example to illustrate this approach:

Various opinion polls have identified "fear of crime" as the number 1 concern of most Americans. Not too surprisingly, politicians have made crime a major part of their campaign pledges. Fear of crime is an important and ill-defined problem. Suppose we turn this problem into a clearly articulated goal.

Goal #1: Reduce crime. Given this goal, what are some possible solutions, that is paths of action, that will move our society from its present start state of "fear of crime" toward the goal of reducing crime? Here are two possible solutions for this goal:

- Make capital punishment a national law
- Incarcerate criminals for life if they are convicted of three major crimes

Now, let's state the goal at least four different ways, and see how each restatement of the goal suggests different solutions. One approach for restating the goal state is to view the problem from different perspectives. What is a goal state for those citizens who are potential victims of crime?

Goal #2: Make life safer for honest citizens. This sort of goal shifts solutions from the criminals to the potential victims of crime. Some possible solutions that come to mind for attaining this goal:

- Provide better security for honest citizens
- Teach everyone self-defense
- Organize anticrime groups in every neighborhood

Goal #3: Reduce the number of criminals. Given this goal, solutions now focus on numbers rather than methods. For example:

- Send criminals to Siberia
- Return to gallows and public floggings to send a strong anticrime message to would-be criminals
- Begin community programs that act as a deterrent to a life of crime (e.g., improve education and sports programs)

Goal #4: Change people's perceptions so that they no longer fear crime. This sort of goal will not affect the actual crime rate, rather it will change how people think about crime. Some possible solutions for this goal:

- Give everyone drugs that reduce anxiety (so they no longer fear crime)
- Provide information that shows that the crime rate is really very low (this could be true or false; either would satisfy this goal, although lying is obviously unethical)

Goal #5: Reduce violent crimes. This goal also shifts how we think about the problem because it concerns the degree of violence instead of the number of crimes, number of criminals, or how people feel about crime. Some possible solutions:

- Make it illegal to own a gun
- Legalize drug use

Another way to generate goal states is to view the problem from the perspective of the criminals. What would it take to get them to not engage in crime? It soon becomes clear that crime is not a homogeneous category, and different sorts of actions are needed for different sorts of crimes. Suppose that you were a car-jacker. What would prevent you from hijacking cars? Would having a job make a difference? What if you abused your spouse? What would work to stop this sort of crime?

Of course, some of these possible solutions are ludicrous, such as sending criminals to Siberia or giving everyone antianxiety drugs, and others are unethical. The idea behind this example is that new perspectives on a difficult problem emerge when we are forced to state an ill-defined goal in several ways. It is likely that several solutions can be used together so that America's number 1 fear is alleviated. Try this sort of exercise with other difficult problems. You may be surprised to find that you can think of different categories of solutions by specifying qualitatively different sorts of goals and by viewing the problem from different perspectives.

Most programs designed to improve problem-solving skills stress the importance of a "planful approach" (Covington, 1987). Numerous computer programs are now available that offer a plan for approaching problems. The software explosion has resulted in many new programs that claim to improve the problem-solving skills of users, but most are too new to provide evidence of their effectiveness.

Although plans for solving problems can vary in complexity, most will consist of five basic steps: (a) recognition that a problem exists (This is an important stage that often is the mark of creativity, a topic that is addressed in chapter 10. Consider any change such as the change from horse and buggy to motorized vehicles. For most of the world, horses worked very well, and the proposition that they could be replaced by a box on wheels that constantly broke down and needed fuel to run was ludicrous. Few people had any problem with travel by horse), (b) construction of a representation of the problem that includes the initial and goal states, (c) generation and evaluation of possible solutions, (d) selection of a possible solution, and (e) execution of the possible solution to determine if it solves the problem.

Unfortunately, some or all of the steps will have to be repeated if the goal is not attained. This could include changing the representation or redefining the goal as well as generating additional possible solutions and reevaluating the possible solutions.

Bransford and Stein (1993) used the acronym IDEAL to stand for these five steps: I (Identify the problem); D (Define and represent the problem); E (Explore possible strategies); A (Act on the strategies); L (Look back and evaluate the effects of your activities).

A major goal of The Productive Thinking Program (Covington, Crutchfield, Davies, & Olton, 1974), one of the oldest and most popular programs designed to help children "learn to think," is to develop the habit of planning a solution strategy. Figure 9.2 shows a few sample frames from this program that emphasize the need to approach problems in an orderly manner.

The best way to solve a problem is to devise the best representation. This forces the problem solver to be explicit about the desired goal and to plan carefully the steps necessary to reach the goal. Mayer (1992) found that good visual representations can help readers comprehend difficult text. One principle of good thinking that appears in almost every chapter is to use multiple representational systems—that is using diagrams along with printed text and using verbal descriptors with spatial information.

Work on the problem in a planful way.

FIG. 9.2.   Advice for children on how to devise a problem solving plan. (From *The Productive Thinking Program* by Covington, Crutchfield, Davies, & Olton, 1974, Lesson 6, p. 17).

The representation of a problem is a good index of how well it is understood (Greeno, 1973, 1992). A good representation will contain all of the relevant information and display the relationships among the givens (rules and constraints) in a way that will facilitate progress toward the goal. A good problem representation is a critical element in finding a solution.

In discussing the way good representations are constructed, Newell (1983) said that "Memory must be tickled," a phrase that I have often used because I believe that it is a critical consideration in how we think. What he meant by this remark is that the individual's knowledge about the problem must be accessed and utilized. The problem solver must be able to make inferences from problem statements in order to build an adequate problem representation—one in which missing and conflicting information is made obvious and critical relationships are easy to grasp.

Try this example:

Draw a representation and write an algebraic formula that corresponds to the following statement: There are six times as many students as professors at this university.

If you are like many college students, you drew a diagram like this one:

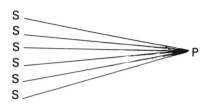

This translates into 6S = P.

If I gave you the number of students, you could use this formula to find the number of professors and vice versa. Can you see why the formula derived from this representation is wrong? The formula states that there are more professors than there are students, rather than the reverse! The reason that so many students have difficulty with this problem and others like it lies in the way in which the words are translated into a diagram. The juxtaposition of the words "six times the number of students" seems to automatically suggest that the number of students should be multiplied by six. Mayer found a significant improvement in the mathematical problem-solving skills of college students after only 3 hours of training on how to devise correct representations (Lewis & Mayer, 1987). It is difficult to overstate the importance of a good representation when solving problems.

The following sections contain suggestions for devising good representations and demonstrate the intimate relationship between the representation and the solution to the problem. Good representations share certain characteristics. They take advantage of spatial locations to group information in a visual format; they also act as a check on how well you understand the problem. Let's try some examples of ways to represent problems.

Write It Down

All problems are initially represented in your head. It is a good idea to get the paths and goals on paper or into some other concrete form. This will reduce the memory load and allow you to view the problem visually. The simplest example of the aid provided by a pencil and paper is a straightforward multiplication problem. Solve the following problem without writing anything:

$$\begin{array}{r} 976 \\ \times\, 893 \\ \hline \end{array}$$

Of course, you would consider this a ridiculous request because it is a simple problem with paper and pencil and a difficult one to perform in your head because of the memory demands. Whenever there are several facts or different options to keep track of, it is a good idea to use paper and pencil.

Draw a Graph or Diagram

"A bear, starting at point P, walked one mile due south. Then he changed direction and walked one mile due east. Then he turned again to the left and walked one mile due north, and arrived exactly at the point P he started from. What was the color of the bear?" (Polya, 1957, p. 234).

Does this problem seem strange or even impossible to you? If you draw a simple "map" of the bear's route, it will be a pie-shaped wedge. Where on earth is this possible? Think about a globe. Did you just say "Why, of course, point P must be the

North Pole" to yourself? Once you realize that you're at the North Pole, this problem becomes easy to solve. The bear must be white, because only polar bears live at the North Pole.

Consider the following problem: A venerable old monk leaves the monastery at exactly 6:00 a.m. to climb a winding mountain trail to the solitude of the mountain peak. He arrives at exactly 4:00 p.m. After spending the night in sleep and prayer, he leaves the mountain peak at exactly 6:00 a.m. and arrives at the monastery at exactly 4:00 p.m. There are no constraints on the speed at which he walks. In fact, he stops several times along the way to rest. Is there some point on the mountain trail that he passes at exactly the same time each day?

Stop and think about this problem for a moment. Does it seem like a difficult one? There are two ways to consider this problem that will make the answer seem simple, but before you go on, decide how you would go about solving this problem, then solve it. As you can probably guess, a good representation will be an important determinant of the solution.

One solution is to draw a graph of the monk's ascent and descent. The graph can take any shape because you know nothing about his hourly progress. The graphs of the ascent and descent should appear as in Fig. 9.3.

Now, superimpose the two graphs and see if there must be some point where the graphs intersect. If there is, then there is some time when the monk passed the same

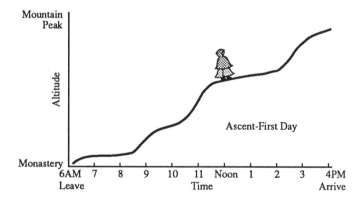

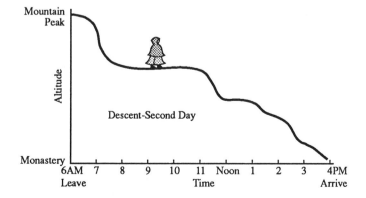

FIG. 9.3. Graphs of the monk's ascent and descent. The graphs can take any shape because the monk can rest as often as he wishes when he climbs the hill and when he descends.

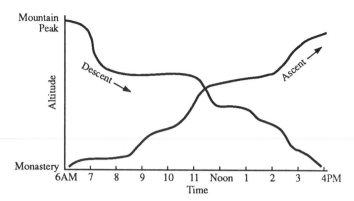

FIG.   9.4. By superimposing the ascent and descent graphs, it is easy to see that
there must be some place at which the graphs intersect. Thus, there must be a
place on the mountain trail that the monk crosses at the same time each day.

point at the same time on each day. This is shown in Fig. 9.4. Drawing a graph provides
a clear picture of the results. Actually, an easier way of solving this problem involves
changing the representation and restating the facts in the problem in an equivalent,
but different, form. Assume two people traverse the same mountain path at the same
time on the same morning. If one starts at the monastery and the other starts at the
mountain peak, both leaving at 6:00 a.m. and both arriving at their opposite destina-
tions at 4:00 p.m., it is obvious they must meet somewhere along the path no matter
how often each chooses to rest and reflect. Thus, with a change in representation, a
difficult problem can become trivial.

Drawing a graph is often an excellent strategy for solving problems. Several years
ago, I taught a laboratory course in experimental psychology. In that course, college
students were required to conduct experiments, gather data, and interpret their data
in a meaningful way. Although the students were taught the statistical methods needed
for data analysis, I found that when they graphed their results they obtained a much
better understanding of the phenomenon they were investigating. They were able to
use their experimental results to formulate sound conclusions because they understood the nature of their findings. The students found that a simple graph was a more
valuable tool for comprehension than the elaborate statistical procedures that they
were required to use.

Graphs and other kinds of diagrams are especially useful comprehension strategies
in mathematical and scientific problem solving. For example, a common problem in
undergraduate statistics courses requires finding the area between two points under a
certain kind of curve called a "normal" or "bell-shaped" curve. This can be a difficult
or confusing problem for students, but it becomes easy if they draw the curve and
shade in the area they want to find. In fact, I don't give my statistics students the
algebraic rules for finding the appropriate area. Students find it easier to figure it out
for themselves from the diagrams they draw.

Consider the geometry problem that was posed by Kohler (1969). You are given only
information in Fig. 9.5, shown on the following page, and the fact that the radius of the
circle is 5". Can you find the length of line L in inches?

One of the reasons that this is a difficult problem is that in the pictorial representation
line L appears most saliently as the hypotenuse of two right triangles, the triangle with
sides LDX, and the triangle with the other two sides defined by the intersecting
horizontal and vertical radii. How can you change this diagram so that the solution
can be obtained?

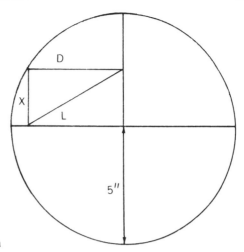

FIG. 9.5. Using only the information given in this figure, can you determine the length of line L? (Problem adapted from Köhler, 1969)

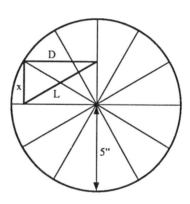

FIG. 9.6. Additional radii have been drawn over Fig. 9.5 as an intermediate step toward a solution. Can you use the additional radii to find the length of the line L?

Consider the information given. Because the only length given in this diagram is the radius of the circle, it is likely that this will be needed in solving the problem. Try drawing in additional radii around the circle as shown in Fig. 9.6. Does this help to suggest the solution?

Look carefully at the quadrant containing L. Can you find another line equal in length to L? If you think of L as the diagonal inside a rectangle with sides D, X, and the unlabeled sides formed by the intersection of the horizontal and vertical radii, the other diagonal in the rectangle must be the same length as L. The other diagonal must be the radius; thus line L, like the radius, is also 5" long. Although the initial representation of the problem was somewhat misleading, a solution was found with the appropriate operations.

Of course, there was no way of knowing at the outset that moving the radii around the circle would lead to the answer. It was obvious, however, that the answer would depend on the radius in some way, because it was the only measurement given, and the goal was to find the length of line L. The operations used to transform the givens into solution paths involved the knowledge you brought with you to the problem. If you did not know that the two diagonals in a rectangle must be equal, then you could not have solved the problem. Good problem solvers utilize a solid knowledge base that is built up over a lifetime of educational experiences—ones that are accumulated both inside and outside of the classroom. The best strategy for solving problems is to know a great deal about a great many topics.

Let's try another example in which graphs or diagrams will simplify the search for a solution path.

In order to save money and their sanity, Melvin, Brock, Marc, and Claire decide to form a baby-sitting cooperative. They agree to baby-sit for each other's children with the understanding that when one of them stays with another's children, the recipient will repay the sitter with an equal number of baby-sitting hours. They decide to tally baby-sitting hours at the end of the month. During the month, Melvin sat with Brock's children 9 hours, Marc sat with Melvin's children 3 hours, and Claire stayed with Melvin's children 6 hours. Marc baby-sat 9 hours with Claire's children and Brock baby-sat 5 hours with Claire's children. Which of these people has 12 hours of baby-sitting time due to him or her?

A good diagram of the relationship among these four people is clearly needed. The relevant givens will involve the four people and the number of hours owed to each. Let's start with the first sentence, "Melvin sat with Brock's children 9 hours." Thus, Brock owes Melvin 9 hours of baby-sitting at the end of the month. The operation being used is the transformation of number of hours spent baby-sitting into number of hours owed to each sitter. A simple diagram of this relationship is:

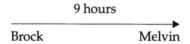

The next sentence translates into "Melvin owes Marc 3 hours and Melvin owes Claire 6 hours."

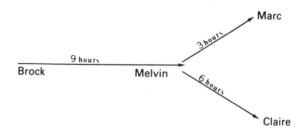

Then, changing the third sentence so that it reflects what is owed, Claire owes Marc 9 hours and Claire owes Brock 5 hours.

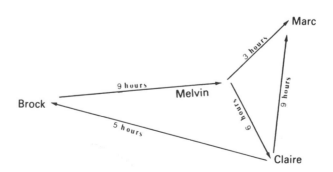

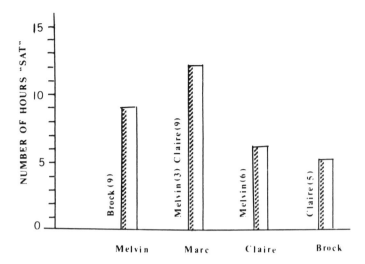

FIG. 9.7.   Alternative form of representation for solving the co-op problem.

It is easy to see from this diagram that only Marc is owed 12 hours of baby-sitting, 3 hours from Melvin and 9 hours from Claire. A diagram of the hours owed is essential in finding the solution to this problem.

There are several other ways of representing the information in the baby-sitting co-op problem that will display all of the essential relationships, and thus also give the correct answer. When a colleague (Dr. Susan Nummedal at California State University, Long Beach) posed this problem to her students, she found that they devised a variety of representations to solve the problem. One student used a simple bar graph to keep track of the number of hours sat by each participant. This representation is shown in Fig. 9.7.

Other students used a variety of table formats. One listed the number of hours "gave" as a positive number and "received" as a negative number because it was owed. Another student split the information into "sitter" and "sat for" categories, then filled in a table of information summing across the columns for the total number of "sat for" hours for each participant, and summing down the rows for the total number of "sitter" hours for each participant. These representations are offered in Tables 9.1 and 9.2, respectively.

As the baby-sitting co-op problem demonstrates, there are often many ways of representing a given problem. As you work through the problems in this chapter, try a variety of representations. A good representation will present all of the relevant information in a way that it can be readily understood and assimilated. Good representations provide the necessary solution paths to the goal.

Try a Hierarchical Tree

Hierarchical trees are branching diagrams. They are most frequently used to assess mathematically the probability or likelihood of uncertain outcomes. (See chapter 4 for the use of tree diagrams in solving "if, then" problems and chapter 7 for the use of decision trees in calculating probabilities.) Hierarchical trees or tree diagrams can be useful aids in decision making and problem solving. In this context, they are called decision trees. (As stated earlier in this chapter, the distinction between problem solving and decision making is somewhat artificial because they are closely related concepts.)

TABLE 9.1
A Table Format for Representing the
Information in the Babysitting Co-op Problem

	Gave	Received	Total Due
Melvin	+9	−3, −6	0
Marc	+3, +9		12
Claire	+6	−9, −15	−8
Brock	+5	−9	−4

TABLE 9.2
An Alternative Table Format That Can Be Used to Represent the
Information in the Babysitting Co-op Program

	Sitter				Total Number of Hours Sat For
	Melvin	Marc	Claire	Brock	
Sat For — Melvin		3	6		9
Sat For — Marc					0
Sat For — Claire		9		5	14
Sat For — Brock	9				9
Total Number of Hours Sat	9	12	6	5	

If the problem you're working on is fairly complex, with each possible solution path requiring subsequent additional paths, a hierarchical tree or tree diagram should be considered.

Here is a classic problem first presented by Duncker (1945). Although the problem is a medical one, no specialized knowledge is needed to solve it:

A patient has an inoperable tumor deep within her stomach. The problem is to devise a way of treating the tumor with X-rays without damaging the healthy tissue that surrounds the tumor on all sides. Stop and think for a few minutes how you would go about solving this problem.

Most of Duncker's (1945) subjects went about reaching a solution in several steps. Although a variety of solutions were attempted, the best solution is to use several weak rays, each coming from different places outside the body focused so that they would meet and summate at the tumor site. In this manner, the healthy tissue won't be hurt by the weak rays and the tumor will receive a high level of radiation. This solution was formulated from a broader category of solutions that included having each ray grow stronger as it reached the tumor.

One subject's search for solution paths is shown in Fig. 9.8 in a hierarchical tree diagram. Note that the goal is explicitly stated at the top of the tree. General broad strategies are listed one level below the goal, with more specific ways of satisfying each strategy on lower levels.

Tree diagrams are particularly useful when the given information has a natural hierarchical organization. For example, all living things are classified into a hierarchical organization by biologists. If you ask a child if a bee is an animal, he will probably respond that it isn't an animal because it is an insect. The problem can be made clear to him by drawing a biological classification tree like the one shown in Fig. 9.9.

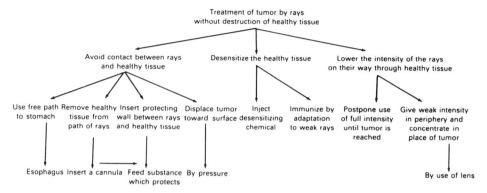

FIG. 9.8. A hierarchical tree diagram of one subject's attempted solutions to Duncker's X-ray problem. (After Duncker, 1945)

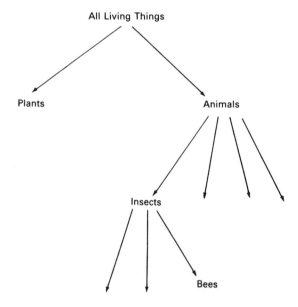

FIG. 9.9. A hierarchical tree diagram that can be used to answer the question, "Are bees animals?"

Another example of using trees to solve problems is the familiar use of family trees. Estate lawyers, who often face a tangled web of family relationships, need to be able to determine the relations among family members in order to handle wills and estate taxes. Multiple spouses, cohabitation, stepchildren, half-siblings, and out-of-wedlock births can make the difficult matter of inheritance a legal nightmare. A carefully drawn family tree that places each member on the appropriate generation branch is an invaluable aid in solving tangled inheritance claims.

Make a Matrix

A **matrix** is a rectangular array of facts or numbers. It is really just a fancy word for a chart. When the givens in a problem can be broken down into categories, a matrix may be a good method of representation. Consider the problem posed by Whimbey and Lochhead (1982):

Three men—Fred, Ed, and Ted—are married to Joan, Sally, and Vickie, but not necessarily in that order. Joan, who is Ed's sister, lives in Detroit. Fred dislikes animals. Ed weighs more than the man who is married to Vickie. The man married to Sally breeds Siamese cats as a hobby. Fred commutes over 200 hours a year from his home in Ann Arbor to his job in Detroit. Match up the men with the women they married. (p. 67)

What are the categories of information given in this problem? The givens concern husbands and wives. Set up a three-by-three matrix and fill in as much of it as you can with the information:

	Joan	Sally	Vickie
Fred			
Ed			
Ted			

Because Joan is Ed's sister, she cannot be his wife, so fill in a "NO" in the Joan–Ed cell of the matrix. Skip the next two statements for the time being and go on to the statement that Ed weighs more than the man married to Vickie; therefore, Ed is not married to Vickie. Ed must be married to Sally. So far the matrix appears as below:

	Joan	Sally	Vickie
Fred		NO	
Ed	NO	YES	NO
Ted		NO	

Peruse the problem for more clues. Have you found the important one? Fred lives in Ann Arbor and Joan lives in Detroit; therefore, we would conclude that they're probably not married. Because Fred is not married to Joan or Sally, he must be married to Vickie. Who's left for Ted? Joan must be married to Ted.

	Joan	Sally	Vickie
Fred	NO	NO	YES
Ed	NO	YES	NO
Ted	YES	NO	NO

The completed matrix:

Let's try another example. This problem is from a delightful book by Phillips (1961) called *My Best Puzzles in Logic and Reasoning*. This one should seem easier because you are now familiar with the technique:

"My four granddaughters are all accomplished girls." Canon Chasuble was speaking with evident self-satisfaction. "Each of them," he went on, "plays a different musical instrument and each speaks one European language as well as—if not better than—a native."

"What does Mary play?" asked someone.

"The cello."

"Who plays the violin?"

"D'you know," said Chasuble, "I've temporarily forgotten. Anno Domini, alas! But I know it's the girl who speaks French."

The remainder of the facts which I elicited were of a somewhat negative character. I learned that the organist is not Valerie; that the girl who speaks German is not Lorna; and that Mary knows no Italian. Anthea doesn't play the violin, nor is she the girl who speaks Spanish. Valerie knows no French; Lorna doesn't play the harp; and the organist can't speak Italian.

What are Valerie's accomplishments?

Stop now and work on solving this problem. Don't go on until you've actually worked through this problem.

You'd begin by realizing that because the relevant information is categorical, a matrix is a good form of representation. There are four granddaughters, musical instruments, and languages. Thus, the matrix can be set up as:

Granddaughter	Musical Instrument	Language
Mary	Cello	
Valerie		
Lorna		
Anthea		

Because most of the information we have is negative, let's list the possible combinations of granddaughters, instruments, and languages.

Granddaughter	Musical Instrument	Language
Mary	Cello	Spanish or French or German
Valerie	Violin or Harp	Spanish or Italian or German
Lorna	Violin or Organ	French or Italian or Spanish
Anthea	Harp or Organ	Italian or German or French

Because the girl who plays the violin speaks French, this must be Lorna. Anthea is the organist who speaks German. This means that only Mary can speak Spanish. The only combination left for Valerie is the harp and Italian.

Admittedly, these are artificial problems, not much like the ones we encounter in real life. Let's consider a more practical application of the matrix form of problem representation.

There is considerable controversy over the issue of vitamin C as a deterrent for the common cold. How would you decide if vitamin C prevents colds? Most probably, you'd give vitamin C to some people and not others and count the number of colds in each group. Suppose you found the following results: 10 people who took vitamin C did not catch a cold, 4 people who took vitamin C caught a cold, 8 people who didn't take vitamin C didn't catch a cold, and 6 people who didn't take vitamin C caught a cold. What would you conclude?

Because we have categories of information (took or didn't take vitamin C and caught or didn't catch a cold) a matrix displaying the appropriate values will help us understand the givens:

		Vitamin C		
		Took Vitamin C	Didn't Take Vitamin C	
	Caught a Cold	4	6	Total number who caught a cold 10
Cold				
	Didn't Catch a Cold	10	8	Total number who didn't catch a cold 18

By examining every cell of the matrix, you can determine if vitamin C prevented colds. To see if vitamin C worked, you need to consider how many of those who caught a cold had taken vitamin C. The answer is 4 out of 10, or 40%. You also need to consider how many of those who didn't catch a cold had taken vitamin C. The answer is 10 out of 18, or 55.5%. Few would be willing to conclude from these data that vitamin C helped to prevent colds. (Research concepts are discussed more fully in chapters 6 and 7.) The point being made here is that by representing the information in a matrix, the results can be more easily understood. This is essentially the same problem that was discussed in chapter 8 when the nurses and physicians had to decide if there was a relationship between a disease and a set of symptoms. Given the overlap among the topics, you would expect that techniques that are useful in one context will also be useful in related contexts.

Manipulate Models

It is often a good idea to make a concrete representation for abstract problems. I'm sure that you've seen an architect's model for a planned complex like a shopping center, office building, or college campus. The miniature buildings and walkways are not made because architects love doll-sized buildings. Although they are often made to communicate architectural plans to others who are not skilled at reading blueprints, the miniature models also help the architect solve problems. With the movable parts, she or he can move the buildings to find the best way to place them before construction begins.

Let's try a problem where making a model will help in finding a solution. There are two groups of beings on a mythical planet in a far-away galaxy: They are Hobbits and Orcs. One day three Hobbits got lost while exploring the homeland of the Orcs. The Hobbits could get home safely if they could cross the river that separates their two homelands. Three Orcs agreed to help the Hobbits cross the river, but the only boat they had could hold only two beings at a time, and the Hobbits could not let themselves ever be outnumbered by the Orcs or the Orcs would eat them.

Your problem is to figure out a sequence of moves that will carry all three hobbits to the other side of the river and return all three Orcs to their own side. The constraints are that only two beings can fit in the boat at one time, and if at any time the Orcs on one shore outnumber the Hobbits, you'll have to start over.

This would be an impossible problem to solve without some external form of representation. Use some small objects to represent the Hobbits and Orcs and move them across an imaginary river. Three large paper clips for the hobbits and three small paper clips for the Orcs will work well. You'll have to imagine that you are transporting them in a boat. Be sure to write down all of your moves. Plan to take as long as 10–15 minutes to solve this problem. As you work toward the solution, be aware of how

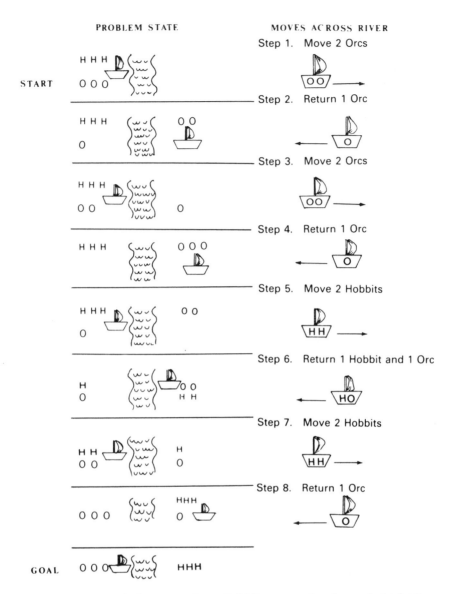

FIG. 9.10. Steps needed to move three Hobbits across the river using a boat that will hold only two beings without allowing the Orcs to ever outnumber the Hobbits.

you're thinking about the moves. Don't go on until you've worked through the problem.

The complete sequence of moves needed to move the Hobbits is shown in Fig. 9.10. One of the greatest difficulties with this problem is the need to move all three Orcs across the river, a situation that is not desired, in order to move the Hobbits without allowing them to become outnumbered. Problems of this sort have come to be known as **detour problems** because the path to the goal is not a direct linear one. Intermediate steps are required that seem directly opposite to the goal—in this case moving all three Orcs to the opposite side of the river when the desired goal is to have all of them on the side from which they originated. It is important to recognize that the route to a goal will often involve detours. As a more realistic example, consider Leon's goal to become very wealthy. One solution path to the goal may involve going deeply into debt in order to finance his education. Although going deeply into debt is seemingly antagonistic to becoming wealthy, it may be a necessary detour. Be sure to consider solution paths that involve detours when faced with difficult problems.

Select the Best Representation

It's a good idea to utilize an external form of representation (e.g., paper and pencil) whenever there are more than a few givens that need to be manipulated. The immediate or working memory span can quickly become overloaded. If you have already read chapter 8, you will recognize the importance of writing down alternatives and considerations so that you can reduce the load on working memory. Experimental results or almost any other pattern of numbers should always be graphed. If your problem is mathematical or spatial, a diagram is likely to be helpful. Diagrams can help to disentangle any situation in which the givens have many complex interrelationships. Diagrams can make important relationships explicit, a fact that can often lead directly to the goal. Hierarchical trees are a natural form of representation when the material itself forms a hierarchically arranged structure. Matrices are likely to be useful when the givens can be grouped into categories for meaningful comparisons. "Mock-ups" or miniature models can aid in problem solving when movement and placement of the givens determine the solution. Often the way a problem is represented can mean the difference between a solution or nonsolution (Posner, 1973). If you find that one form of representation isn't fruitful, try a different one.

PROBLEM-SOLVING STRATEGIES

Solving problems can be regarded as the most characteristically human activity.

—Polya (1962)

It does no good to tell someone who is faced with a problem that he should plan a solution, if he has no idea how to plan. The steps look deceptively simple—generate and evaluate possible solutions. But, what if you can't think of any solutions? There are several strategies that can be used in a systematic manner to help you generate solutions. Although no single strategy can guarantee perfect solutions every time, learning how to use several different strategies can give you direction and confidence when presented with a new problem.

Schoenfeld (1979) found that many mathematicians and scientists claimed to use specific strategies and rules when solving problems in their academic disciplines. Many of the scientists and mathematicians believed that their students would solve problems better if they learned some basic skills for attacking problems. In addition, several researchers have found that instruction in general problem-solving skills can improve problem-solving ability (e.g., Klein & Weizenfeld, 1978; Wickelgren, 1974). You can think of the following strategies or problem-solving aids as ways to plan a solution.

Means–Ends Analysis

Most often progress toward the goal is not made along a single well-paved road. When the goal is not immediately attainable, we often need to take detours or break the problem down into smaller problems, called **subproblems**, each with its own goal, called a **subgoal**.

Like all of the strategies for solving problems, selecting and utilizing subgoals requires planning. The procedure by which people select subgoals and use them to progress toward the goal is called **means–ends analysis**. This is a general, often powerful method for problem solving. The problem is first broken down into subgoals. Operations that will reduce the distance between the problem solver's current state and the subgoal are then used. In this manner, the problem solver will move closer and closer to the goal. Work through the following examples in order to clarify this concept.

The first step in means–ends analysis is to enumerate appropriate subgoals and to select the most promising one. Suppose that during a game of chess you decide that a good subgoal is to put the opposing king in check. The goal, of course, is to win the game, but it will be necessary to work toward subgoals to attain the goal. Putting the opposing king in check is the immediate "end" toward which you're working. You now need to select the "means" for obtaining that end, hence the term *means–ends analysis*. In order to achieve your subgoal, determine the current state (i.e., the current position of your pieces). Then, identify any difference between where your pieces are and where you want them to be. Operations would be selected that would reduce this difference, and place the opposing king in check. Suppose no single move can achieve this subgoal. The means–ends analysis procedure would recycle, this time selecting a smaller subgoal, perhaps moving another piece out of the way. The constant recycling of these two processes—setting subgoals and reducing distances—will allow you to make progress toward the goal.

A favorite problem of psychologists that can be used to demonstrate means–ends analysis is the Tower of Hanoi problem. The name of this puzzle is derived from an interesting legend. Suppose that there are three pegs and 64 disks, each one a different size, stacked on one of the pegs in size order. It may help to think of the disks as 64 different size doughnuts that can stack one on top of each other on the pegs. The task is to transfer all of the disks from the first peg to the third peg using the middle peg as an intermediary. The rules for moving disks include moving only one disk at a time and never placing a disk on top of a smaller one. The legend around this task is that there are monks in a monastery near Hanoi who are working on this puzzle, and when they complete it the world will come to an end. Even if this legend were true, you would have little cause for worry because if they were to make perfect moves at the rate of one per second, it would take close to a trillion years to complete this task (Raphael, 1976).

Because you probably don't want to spend quite that much time solving the Tower of Hanoi, you can try a simplified version of it using only three disks. You can easily work this problem using any three coins of different sizes (a quarter, penny, and dime will work well) and three small sheets of paper. Stack the coins with the smallest on top and largest on the bottom on one sheet of paper. The task is to move the coins from the first piece of paper to the third so that they will be in the same size order. You may move only one coin at a time. All three pieces of paper may be used in solving the problem. Write down all of the moves you make in solving this problem. The initial and goal states are shown in Fig. 9.11.

In a means–end analysis of the Tower of Hanoi problem, one obvious subgoal is to get the quarter on the third piece of paper. This cannot be done immediately because the dime and penny are on it; therefore, a second subgoal needs to be considered. A second subgoal is to end up with the penny on the quarter. This can be accomplished when the penny is on the second paper and the quarter is on the third paper. This subgoal cannot yet be pursued because the dime must be moved first. In this manner, subgoals or ends are considered along with the means to accomplish them. A complete

FIG. 9. 11.   Start state and goal for the Tower of Hanoi problem. Use the strategy of means–ends analysis to solve this problem.

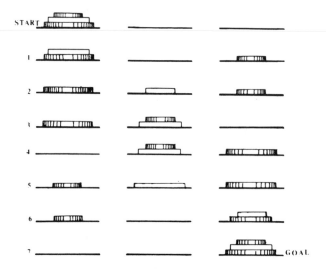

FIG. 9.12.   Solution to the Tower of Hanoi problem. Notice how subgoals are planned and obtained in reaching the goal.

solution with all of the moves is shown in Fig. 9.12. If you try the problem with four or five coins instead of three, you'll find that it gets much more complicated, although the strategy remains the same.

Working Backward

Means–ends analysis is a **forward-looking strategy**, which means that all of the planning is done by considering operations that move you closer to subgoals and, ultimately, the final goal. Sometimes, it is a better strategy to plan operations by **working backward** from the goal to your present or initial state. The simplest example of this can be found in the paper-and-pencil mazes that many children love to solve.

Some of these mazes have several possible paths leading away from the start box and only one correct path ending in the goal box. Even young children realize that they can solve the maze more quickly if they work the maze backward, beginning from the goal and drawing their path to the start box. An example of this type of maze is shown in Fig. 9.13.

Working backward is a good strategy to use whenever there are fewer paths leading from the goal than there are leading from the start. Of course, mazes aren't the only situation when working backward is a good strategy. Consider the following problem: "Water lilies on a certain lake double in area every twenty-four hours. From the time the first water lily appears until the lake is completely covered takes sixty days. On what day is it half covered?" (Fixx, 1978, p. 50).

The only way to solve this problem is to work backward. Can you solve it with this hint? If the lake is covered on the 60th day and the area covered by the lilies doubles every day, how much of the lake is covered on the 59th day? The answer is half. Thus, by working backward, the problem is easy to solve. A forward-looking strategy with this problem will ensure insanity.

It is often a good idea to combine forward and backward strategies. If you are faced with the task of solving proofs in geometry and trigonometry, a combination of forward and backward strategies may often prove most useful. You can start from the goal, transforming expressions on each line, and then alternate operations between the start state and the goal until the solution path meets somewhere between the two.

Simplification

You turn the problem over and over in your mind; try to turn it so it appears simpler. ... Is the problem as simply, as clearly, as suggestively expressed as possible?

—Polya (1962)

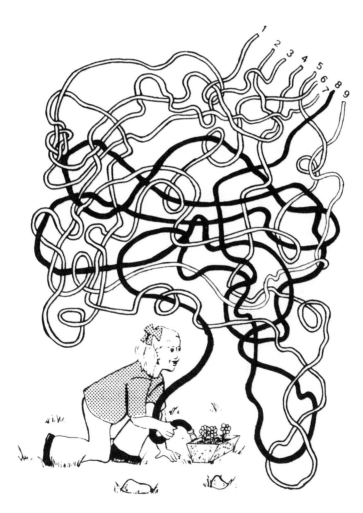

FIG. 9.13. Working backward is a good strategy when there are fewer paths from the goal than from the start.

Problems that are difficult to solve are often complex in nature. A good way to approach such problems is to strip away as much of the complexity as possible in order to reduce them to a simple form. Often, the best form of representation can perform the task of **simplification** because it will allow you to "see" the solution in an efficient way.

Suppose you are faced with the classic cat-in-the-tree problem. According to common folklore, cats can climb up trees, but not down. (There is no more truth to this than to the notion that elephants are afraid of mice.) Suppose that you are faced with the task of retrieving a cat from the top branch of a 10-foot-tall tree. The only ladder you have is 6 feet long. You'll need to place the base of the ladder 3 feet from the trunk of the tree to steady it. Will you be able to reach the cat?

Like most problems, a good way to approach this problem is to diagram the given facts. A diagram of this problem has been drawn in Fig. 9.14. Once the information is presented in a diagram format, it is easy to perceive the problem as a simple geometry problem: What is the hypotenuse of a triangle whose two other sides are 10 feet and 3 feet long? At this point, you'd need to rely on previously acquired knowledge about triangles to recognize and solve this problem. When the topic is thinking, there is no substitute for a good education to provide the foundation and raw materials for thought.

The formula for finding the hypotenuse of a right triangle is:

$$a^2 + b^2 = c^2$$

Substituting the appropriate values in the previous equation:

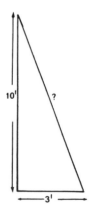

FIG. 9.14. The cat-in-the-tree problem. Once the information is drawn in a diagram form, it is easy to see that it is a simple geometry problem.

FIG. 9.15. If the cat-in-the-tree problem is changed so that the unknown value is how high a 6-foot ladder will reach if it is placed 3 feet from the trunk, a different answer is obtained.

$$10^2 + 3^2 = c^2$$
$$100 + 9 = c^2$$
$$109 = c^2$$
$$\sqrt{109} = c$$
$$10.4 = c$$

Thus, the ladder would need to be 10.4 feet long to reach the top. But wait, could you redraw the problem using the information given to find out if you could still use the 6-foot ladder to reach the cat? See Fig. 9.15 for a slightly different diagram of the problem.

The same formula can be used, but now the unknown is not the hypotenuse, but another one of the sides of the right triangle.

Rearranging the terms will yield:

$$a^2 + b^2 = c^2$$
$$a^2 = c^2 - b^2$$
$$a^2 = 6^2 - 3^2$$
$$a^2 = 36 - 9$$

$$a^2 = 27$$
$$a = \sqrt{27}$$
$$a = 5.2$$

Thus, the top rung of the ladder will touch the tree 5.2 feet above the ground. Will you be able to reach the cat? Draw yourself near the top rung of the ladder. If you are over 5 feet tall you should have no trouble reaching the cat if you are standing on the top or second rung. In fact, you won't even have to reach up.

Simplification is a good strategy when the problem is abstract or complex or contains information that is irrelevant to finding a solution. Often, simplification will work hand in hand with selecting the optimal form of representation because a good representation will often simplify a problem.

Generalization and Specialization

When confronted with a problem, it is sometimes helpful to consider it as an example of a larger class of problems (**generalization**); or to consider it as a special case (**specialization**).

The form of problem representation that is most compatible with the generalization and specialization strategy is the tree diagram. Most goals can be classified as both a subset of a larger category and as a heading for a smaller one. Let's work an example to clarify what this means. As a furniture designer, you are given the problem of designing a chair that will be especially well suited for reading. How would you go about solving this problem?

As you probably realized, this is an ill-defined problem. The difficulty is largely centered on evaluating which of several possible chairs will best satisfy the goal. Use a tree diagram to classify chairs in general, and "chairs for reading" in particular. Although there are many possible diagrams, one example is presented in Fig. 9.16.

I hope that you worked through this problem and drew your own tree diagram. As you can see in Fig. 9.16, thinking about "chairs for reading" as a subset of the category "chairs" can help you to incorporate other features of chairs in your design while

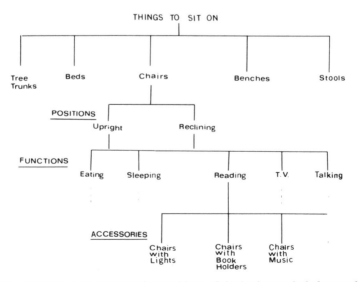

FIG. 9.16. Possible tree diagram for problem of designing a chair for reading.

custom tailoring the chair with some of the possibilities that are unique to "chairs for reading." Thus, the process of generalization and/or specialization can help you to consider your problem from both broad and narrow perspectives.

Random Search and Trial-and-Error

Recall that the anatomy of a problem consists of a start or initial state, a goal, and solution paths leading from the start state to the goal. One strategy for searching among possible solution paths is **random search**. Although this probably seems like a non-strategy or "un-strategy," in some cases it will work quite well. When there are very few possible solution paths, random search will lead to the goal in a short time. A truly random search would mean that there is no systematic order in which the possible paths are explored and no memory for paths already tried. A systematic **trial-and-error** search through the problem space (contains the paths, goal, and start state) is preferable. Trial-and-error search is best applied to well-defined problems with few possible solution paths. Simple, short anagrams are good candidates for these search methods. Unscramble the following letters to form an English word:

THA

Because there are only six possible orders for these three letters (THA, TAH, HTA, HAT, ATH, AHT), trying each one until a solution is found is fairly straightforward and simple strategy. If you used a truly random search, you would not keep track of which letter orderings you used and would repeat some until the correct order was found. Systematic trial-and-error is almost always superior to random search, although only slightly better when there are very few possibilities.

Both trial-and-error and random search are poor strategies when the number of possible paths increases, because of the sheer number of possible combinations. Often, in larger problems, it is helpful to eliminate some of the paths and then search among a smaller subset with a trial-and-error strategy.

Rules

Some kinds of problems, like series problems, depend on **rules**. Once the underlying principles are established, the problem is solved. Most problems in mathematics and the physical sciences follow rules. A good way to discover rules is to look for patterns in the givens or subgoals. Problems requiring rule discovery are often used on tests of intelligence.

Complete the following pattern:

ABBACCCADDDDA

This is a fairly simple series problem. The next six letters are EEEEEA. Certain patterns are common in problems of this sort. To detect them, count the number of repeating symbols, look across the series for repetitions at long intervals, try simple additions and subtractions, and so forth. This is not a trivial problem. The decoding of enemy war messages during World War II was a major factor contributing to our victory. The United States and British governments employed many professional decoders whose job it was to find rules that could be used to decipher German and Japanese military messages.

Suppose for a minute that there is intelligent life in outer space, and that they are also wondering about us. How would they let us know that they exist? Some scientists, science fiction authors, and members of the general public believe that they would make their presence known by sending messages. No one believes that these messages would be in English, or Chinese, or Samoan, or any other Earth language. They would send messages in their own native tongue or native whatever if they don't have tongues. How would we on Earth recognize such messages? The U. S. military has decided that if we are being sent messages from outer space the one distinguishing characteristic of these messages would be a rule-governed "grammar" or patterned repetition. As strange as this may seem, the military does monitor outer space for anything that seems like a patterned communication. So far, they haven't received any and we can continue to believe, for the time being at least, that we are the most intelligent beings in space (or that the more intelligent beings do not want us to know they are out there, or that they can't reach us, or they don't want to reach us).

Hints

Hints are additional information that is given after an individual has begun to work on a problem. Often the hint provides additional information that is important to your solution. Sometimes a hint will require that you change the way you have been approaching the problem. A common example of the use of hints is the "hot–cold" game played by children. An object is hidden in a room. The child who is "it" wanders around the room while the other children yell "hotter" if she is moving closer to the hidden object and "colder" if she is moving away from the hidden object. In this problem, the child who is "it" should take one small step at a time continuing in the same direction when the hint is "hotter" and trying a slight change in direction when the hint is "colder." Research on the way people use hints has shown that general hints like "think of new ways of using objects" don't facilitate the problem solution (Duncan, 1961). The more specific the hint, the greater the benefit derived from it.

One of psychology's favorite problems is the two-string problem. Imagine walking into a room with two strings hanging from the ceiling. The strings are too far apart for you to reach both at the same time, yet your task is to do exactly that. This situation is depicted in Fig. 9.17.

The best solution to the two-string problem involves setting one string in a swinging motion, usually by tying a heavy object to the end of one string to serve as a weight, so that the problem solver can reach the string as it swings toward him. When researchers provided hints for the problem solver by pretending to accidentally bump against one string to get it swinging, most of the problem solvers hit upon this solution, but few were consciously aware that they utilized this hint (Maier, 1931).

In one experimental investigation of how people use hints, researchers had subjects learn pairs of words so that if the experimenter said one word, the subject would respond with its pair. (This is called paired-associates learning.) One of the pairs that the subjects learned was "candle–box." After learning the list of paired associates, subjects were given Duncker's (1945) candle problem, which involved affixing a candle to a wall by using a box as the candle holder (see Fig. 1.1 in chapter 1). Did this hint help them to solve this problem? In general, their performance on this task was improved only if they were told by the experimenter to think about the pairs of words they had learned as a problem-solving aid (Weisberg, DiCamillo, & Phillips, 1978). They did not spontaneously use this hint to solve the problem, most likely because they were unaware that it was a hint. Recent research has confirmed these results with other types of problems (Perfetto, Bransford, & Franks, 1983). In general, it seems that hints are helpful only when the problem solver perceives the hint as a possible solution aid.

FIG. 9.17. The two-string problem.
How could you reach both strings at
the same time? (After Maier, 1930)

Good problem solvers will seek out hints. Gathering additional information can be thought of as hint-seeking behavior. It is almost always a good strategy to get all of the information that you can about your problem. The additional givens will help to restructure the problem space and provide direction so that solution paths may be found more easily.

Split-Half Method

The **split-half method** is an excellent search strategy when there is no a priori reason for selecting among a sequentially organized set of possible solution paths. Suppose, for example, that there is a stoppage in the plumbing system that prevents water from coming out of your kitchen sink. The stoppage is somewhere between the place where your pipes connect with the other pipes on your street and your kitchen faucet. How would you search for the pipe stoppage while making as few holes as possible in the pipe?

In this example, the solution (the place where the pipe is stopped) lies somewhere along a linear route. The best way to search in this problem is the split-half method. Because this problem requires that you break the pipe each place you search, you want to search as efficiently as possible. Begin halfway between the street connection and your kitchen sink. If you find that water can still run freely at this point, you know that the stoppage is between this point and your sink. If this happens, look again halfway between this point and your kitchen sink. If the water is still running freely at this point, then you'll know that the stoppage is closer still to the sink and you'll look again midway between that point and your sink.

Suppose that on your first attempt you find that the water is not running at this point. Then the stoppage must be between the street and this midpoint. Your next search would be midway between the current search point and the street connection. In this manner, you would continue searching until the stoppage is found. This is a good method anytime you have a similar problem, such as trying to locate a break in the electrical wiring in your home or auto.

You can use the split-half method to play a party game called "Guess Your Age." (I made this game up.) Your friends can pretend to be any age. You can guess the age of anyone between 0 and 100 with no more than seven guesses. How would you do it? Begin with the age that is midway between 0 and 100, which, of course, is 50. The player would have to respond by telling you if the age she is thinking of is older or younger than 50. Thus, she would respond with "younger" or "older." Suppose that she responds "younger." What age should you guess next? You'd pick the age midway between 0 and 50, which is 25. Suppose she now responds "older." Your third guess should be halfway between 25 and 50. Because we're only concerned with whole numbers, your next guess would be 38. If she now responds younger, you'd guess 32, as this number is midway between 25 and 38. If the next response is older, you'd guess 35 (midway between 32 and 38). If the response is younger, you'd guess 33. At this point you know that she is pretending to be either 33 or 34. Thus, any age can be guessed with at most seven guesses. Try this method out with some friends. It will be good practice in using the split-half strategy. Consider this strategy whenever there are several possible equally likely solutions.

Brainstorming

The best way to have good ideas is to have lots of ideas.

—Linus Pauling

Brainstorming is fun. It was originally proposed by Osborn (1963) as a method for group problem solving, but it's also useful for individuals working alone. Brainstorming is useful in generating additional solution paths and thus should be considered whenever the difficulty involves finding solution paths. The goal of brainstorming is to produce a large number of possible solutions. Problem solvers are encouraged to think up wild, unusual, imaginative ideas and to write them all down, no matter how silly they seem. The underlying principle is that the greater the quantity of ideas, the greater the likelihood that at least one of them will be good. In order to foster creative use of imagination, rules include no criticism or ridicule, even when the ideas may appear ridiculous. Judgments about the worth of the ideas are deferred until a later evaluation phase. Sometimes parts of the various ideas are combined or refined to improve upon them.Brainstorming can be done in large or small groups or alone. After the brainstorming session, the list of possible solutions can be perused to find ones that will solve the problem in light of the problem constraints, which often include financial and time limitations and/or ethical considerations.

Brainstorming was used effectively by a food manufacturer faced with the problem of finding a better way to bag potato chips. The problem solvers (corporate executives) were asked to think up the best packaging solution they had ever seen. Someone said that bagging wet leaves was the best packaging solution he had ever seen. If you attempt to bag dry leaves they crumble and don't fit into trash bags well, but if you hose them down before bagging them you can use fewer bags and fill them more easily with less empty space in each bag. Following this lead, they tried wetting potato chips and then putting them into bags. The result was disastrous—the potato chips dried into tasteless crumbs. But, this idea ultimately led to the popular potato chip that comes stacked in a can. The identical chips are formed from a liquid potato mixture that is cooked into chip-shaped molds. In this manner, a wild and not-too-good solution (wetting potato chips) was parlayed into a highly successful solution.

Contradiction

The best solution to many problems often involves contradictory properties. For example, consider the problem of the perfect pizza box—one that keeps the pizza hot, but doesn't allow steam to collect inside the box so that the crust doesn't get wet and soggy. These are contradictory properties—keep the pizza covered so it stays hot *and* don't let the steam condense and turn the crust soggy. The next time you send out for a pizza, examine the box. Most pizza boxes represent a compromise between these two properties—the lid is closed to keep it hot, but it also has small vents to allow some of the steam to escape. The result is a compromise solution. The pizza gets cold sooner because the vents let cold air in, and the pizza gets only a little soggy because the amount of condensed moisture is limited.

One suggestion for solving any problem that involves contradictions is to never compromise; instead, devise a solution that satisfies all of the desirable properties of a good solution. Sure, but how? In the pizza box problem, Valdman and Tsourikov (cited in Raia, 1994) designed a box with "dimples" (raised dots) on the bottom so that the moisture would condense below the crust and not on it, while trapping hot air below the pizza to serve as additional insulation.

Valdman and Tsourikov have designed a computer-assisted program that suggests ways to satisfy contradictions in any problem without compromising. They culled the files of the U. S. Patent Office and discovered over 200 general principles that can be used alone or in combination to solve a wide range of problems. The program begins by asking for a clear definition of the type of problem that is being solved. It is looking for general principles (e.g., the need for insulation and eliminating condensation, without regard to pizza). Solutions are suggested from its computerized bank of solutions based on other problems that involve similar sorts of contradictions. They call their algorithm (steps used to solve a problem) the theory of inventive problem solving. Although their advertisements for this commercially available software program make fantastic claims of success, additional studies by unbiased researchers are needed before we can evaluate its efficacy. Using their basic ideas, we can all imagine an optimal solution to any problem and then find ways to satisfy seemingly contradictory properties of the optimal solution.

Here is another example of a problem involving contradictions. Consider the problem of picking tomatoes. Mechanical tomato pickers are cheap and fast, but they bruise the tomato. A compromise would be to pad the arms of the mechanical picker or slow down the process so that fewer tomatoes are bruised. But, the cardinal rule of the theory of inventive problem solving is to never compromise. An even better idea, one that won't require the picker to slow down or bruise the tomatoes, is to develop a tomato with a thicker skin so that it won't bruise when it is picked by the clumsy and fast-moving machine (The Cognition and Technology Group at Vanderbilt, 1993). Thus, the apparent contradiction (pick tomatoes fast with a machine and do not allow bruising) was resolved without compromise.

Restate the Problem

Restating the problem is a most useful strategy for ill-defined problems. In well-defined problems the goal is usually explicitly stated in unambiguous terms that leave little room for restatement, although, as suggested earlier, a seemingly well-defined problem could in fact have multiple possibilities if we are able to restate the problem and the goal. This general strategy was introduced earlier in this chapter.

Consider the problem that faces virtually every adult I've ever met: "How can I save money?" Countless families around the world shop in discount markets, eat peanut butter sandwiches, and spend their Saturday evenings at home in an attempt to solve this problem. Suppose you restate this problem so that it becomes, "How can I have more money?" Additional solutions would now include finding a better paying job, moving to a less expensive apartment, marrying a rich man or woman, investing in high-paying stocks, winning the Irish Sweepstakes, and so forth. Whenever you are faced with an ill-defined problem, try to restate the goal. This is often a very good strategy because a different goal will have different solution paths. The greater the number of solution paths you have to consider, the more likely you are to obtain the goal.

Analogies and Metaphors

We can scarcely imagine a problem absolutely new, unlike and unrelated to any formerly solved problem; but if such a problem could exist, it would be unsolvable. In fact, when solving a problem, we should always profit from previously solved problems, using their result or their method, or the experience acquired in solving them.

—Polya (1945, p. 92)

Gick and Holyoak (1980) asked, "Where do new ideas come from?" Many scientists and mathematicians respond that their ideas or solutions to problems come from recognizing **analogies** and **metaphors** drawn from different academic disciplines (Hadamard, 1954). In fact, it seems that the most common form of inference is made by noting similarities (analogies and metaphors) between two or more situations. Like hints, the analogy must be recognized as relevant in the problem being considered and then modified for the particular situation.

Consider the following problem:

A small country fell under the iron rule of a dictator. The dictator ruled the country from a strong fortress. The fortress was situated in the middle of the country, surrounded by farms and villages. Many roads radiated outward from the fortress like spokes on a wheel. A great general arose who raised a large army at the border and vowed to capture the fortress and free the country of the dictator. The general knew that if his entire army could attack the fortress at once it could be captured. His troops were poised at the head of one of the roads leading to the fortress, ready to attack. However, a spy brought the general a disturbing report. The ruthless dictator had planted mines on each of the roads. The mines were set so that small bodies of men could pass over them safely, since the dictator needed to be able to move troops and workers to and from the fortress. However, any large force would detonate the mines. Not only would this blow up the road and render it impassable, but the dictator would then destroy many villages in retaliation. A full-scale direct attack on the fortress therefore appeared impossible. (Gick & Holyoak, 1980, p. 351)

To help you solve this problem, I'll also give you a hint. The solution is analogous to one discussed earlier in this chapter, although the context is entirely different. Stop for a few minutes and attempt to work on this problem. Think about the problems presented earlier. It should help if you draw a diagram.

The solution to this problem is analogous to the one used in the inoperable stomach tumor problem. In that problem (Duncker, 1945), the best solution involved sending weak rays through the body simultaneously from several different points so that they would converge on the tumor. Similarly, the army could be divided into small groups that would attack the fortress from all sides. Did you recognize that these problems were essentially similar in form and could be solved with the same solution?

Gordon (1961), originator of a group called "Synectics," presented guidelines for the use of analogies in solving problems. The term "Synectics" was taken from the Greek. It means joining together of different and apparently unrelated elements. Gordon suggested that we consider four different types of analogies when faced with a problem:

1. Personal Analogy

If you want to understand a complex phenomenon, think of yourself as a participant in the phenomenon. For example, if you want to understand the molecular structure of a compound, think of yourself as a molecule. How would you behave? What other molecules would you want to attach yourself to? Get away from reliance on scientific notations and actually pretend to be a molecule bouncing in a compound. You may see relationships from this perspective that you were blind to when acting as a scientist.

The use of personal analogies is especially well-suited for solving a wide range of conflict problems. If each side of a conflict can imagine how the problem appears to the other side, including acceptable goals, new solutions can become apparent. Both sides can identify common interests and use them to invent options that they both find acceptable (Bernstein, 1995; Fisher & Ury, 1991).

2. Direct Analogy

Compare the problems you're working on with several problems in other domains. According to Gordon (1961), this method was used by Alexander Graham Bell: "It struck me that the bones of the human ear were very massive indeed, as compared with the delicate thin membrane that operated them, and the thought occurred that if a membrane so delicate could move bones relatively so massive, why should not a thicker and stouter piece of membrane move my piece of steel. And the telephone was conceived."

A particularly fertile area for analogies is biology, where many solutions to biological problems have been evolving since the first life form appeared on Earth. When a Synectics group was faced with the problem of devising a bottle closure that could be used with glue or nail polish, the analogy they used was the biological closure of the anus (rectum). Apparently, this solution worked quite well. (You can think about this the next time you use a bottle of LePage's mucilage.)

CROCK   by **Bill Rechin & Don Wilder**

Reprinted with special permission of King Features Syndicate.

3. **Symbolic Analogy**

This solution strategy utilizes visual imagery. Its goal is to get away from the constraints of words or mathematical symbols. Students who utilized imagery to visualize the tumor problem and the fortress problem were most likely to notice spontaneously that the two problems were analogous. If you work on generating a clear image of a problem, you may "see" a solution that had been overlooked.

4. **Fantasy Analogy**

In your wildest dreams, what would you want of a solution? An example of this is to imagine two small insects that would automatically zip your jacket or a silk worm that would spin silk rapidly to keep you warm when the temperature drops. These are fantasy analogies. Like brainstorming, a fantasy analogy can result in wild, impractical solutions that can later be modified to practical, workable ones.

Although it is clear that analogies are important aids in problem solving, it is rare for most people to spontaneously notice a potential analogy (VanLehn, 1989). If you are able to diagram the underlying relationships, as in the preceding problem, or to state the general rules, as in the contradictions problem, you are more likely to notice structural relationships and find useful analogies.

Consult an Expert

If at first you don't succeed, try, try, again. Then quit. No use being a damned fool about it.

—W. C. Fields (quoted in Teger, 1979, p. XIV)

Often in life, we don't have to solve problems alone. Sometimes, the best way to solve a problem is to let experts do it for us. People seek accountants for help with their tax problems, attorneys for their legal problems, physicians for their health problems. We elect officials to handle the problems of running our country and rely on military experts to wage wars. These people became experts in their field by obtaining the appropriate knowledge in their subject area and through repeated applications of this knowledge to real-world problems. Consulting an expert is often an excellent solution strategy. Their greater experience and knowledge will allow them to solve many problems in their area of expertise much more efficiently than a novice. If you decide to consult an expert, the problem becomes: (a) how to know somebody who is an expert, and (b) how to select which "expert" to use. Once you've passed these hurdles, your problems still aren't over. You need to be sure that the expert has all of the facts and has considered all of the relevant alternatives. Listen carefully to the expert's analysis of the risks and alternatives, but make the decision yourself. An expert is a problem-solving aid, not the solution. For some guidelines in recognizing an appropriate expert, consult Carlson (1995) and review the section on authorities in chapter 4.

Select the Best Strategy

Thirteen different strategies have been presented as aids in problem solving. When confronted with a problem, how do you know which to use? It is important to keep in mind that these strategies are not mutually exclusive. It will often be best to use them in combinations. The best strategy or strategies depends on the nature of the problem. After all, if you are taking an exam, you could be expelled if you consult the paper of an "expert" student sitting next to you.

Along with each strategy, I presented some guidelines for its appropriate use. In general, a few higher level "strategies for selecting strategies" include:

1. If the problem is ill defined, restate the goal or the problem in several different ways.

2. When there are very few possible solutions, a trial-and-error approach will work well.

3. If a problem is complex, try simplification, means–ends analysis, and generalization and specialization.

4. When there are fewer paths leading away from the goal than there are from the start state, work backward.

5. If you can gather additional information, do it. Look for and utilize hints, and consult experts with specialized knowledge.

6. If there is an ordered array of equally likely alternatives, try the split-half method and seek rules.

7. If the problem is a lack of possible solution paths, brainstorm to generate alternative solution paths.

8. Problems in design and engineering are good candidates for devising solutions that seem, at first, to require contradictions in their solution.

9. Using analogies and metaphors and consulting an expert are widely applicable to all sorts of problems, but be prepared to use visualization and to deliberately seek analogies in order to recall an analogous solution.

10. Remember that these are only guidelines to solving problems. The best way to be an expert problem solver is to solve lots of problems.

PROBLEM-SOLVING PROBLEMS

Problems are our most important product.

—Beardsley

Functional Fixedness and Mental Set

Recall the two-string problem presented earlier in this chapter. The task was to grasp simultaneously two strings that hung from the ceiling. The correct solution involved setting one string into motion, perhaps by tying a heavy object like a pair of pliers to its end to serve as a weight. One reason why this was such a difficult problem is **functional fixedness**. Subjects were fixated or "stuck" on the usual function of a pair of pliers and have difficulty thinking of them as having a different function.

Another example of functional fixedness was presented in the Introduction (chapter 1). In a classic problem, subjects were asked to attach a candle to the wall so that it could be burned, using only a box of thumbtacks and some matches. Subjects had difficulty thinking of the box as a candle holder because they saw it in terms of its usual function—a container for thumbtacks.

Functional fixedness is one kind of **mental set**. I think of these terms as "ruts in one's thinking." They are predispositions to think and respond in certain ways. To demonstrate how powerful some sets can be, work on the nine-dot problem in Fig. 9.18. Stop now and work on this problem.

The difficulty posed by the nine-dot problem comes from a perceptual set imposed by the square arrangement. Most people attempt to solve the problem by staying within the imaginary boundary formed by the outer dots. If you extend your lines

FIG. 9.18.   The nine-dot problem. Using no more than four straight lines and without lifting your pencil from the paper, draw a line through all nine dots.

beyond this imaginary boundary, you'll find that the problem is easy to solve. In addition, most people attempt solutions in which the line goes through the center of each dot. One solution to the nine-dot problem is shown in Fig. 9.19.

There are several other solutions to the nine-dot problem. Each of them involves set-breaking in some way. Two solutions are presented in Fig. 9.20. A few other more exotic solutions, including one submitted by a 10-year-old girl, which consists of one very fat line drawn through all nine dots, can be found in J. L. Adams' (1979) gem of a book, *Conceptual Blockbusting*. The set of staying within the rectangular area is pervasive and difficult to break. Strategies that get you to view problems in novel ways, like the personal analogy strategy, are good ways to work on set-breaking solutions.

Misleading and Irrelevant Information

My father used to love this riddle:

> Suppose you are a bus driver. On the first stop you pick up 6 men and 2 women. At the second stop 2 men leave and 1 woman boards the bus. At the third stop 1 man leaves and 2 women enter the bus. At the fourth stop 3 men get on and 3 women get off. At the fifth stop 2 men get off, 3 men get on, 1 woman gets off, and 2 women get on. What is the bus driver's name?

Could you answer this question without rereading the problem? The bus driver's name is, of course, your name because the riddle began, "Suppose you are a bus driver." All of the information about the rest of the passengers was irrelevant. Often information that is irrelevant to the problem serves to mislead problem solvers down dead-end paths.

Real-life problems often involve deciding what information is relevant. To avoid being misled by information, be clear about the goal state. Simplification will sometimes help in separating the relevant from the irrelevant givens.

Let's try another example:

> If you have black socks and brown socks in your drawer mixed in the ratio of 4 to 5, how many socks will you have to take out to make sure of having a pair of the same color? (Fixx, 1978)

Think about this problem. What is relevant? What is irrelevant? The answer is three socks because any two must match if there are only brown and black socks. The information about the ratio of socks is irrelevant and misleading. Imagine yourself actually picking socks from a drawer and this problem will be easier to solve.

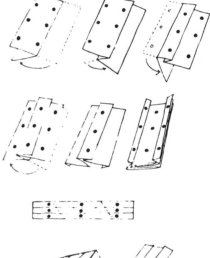

FIG. 9.19. One possible solution to
the nine-dot problem. Note that the
solution involves breaking "set."
Most people assume that the lines
must form a square and that each line
must pass through the center of each
dot.

Another possible solution is to
fold the paper as indicated so
that the dots line up in a straight
line.

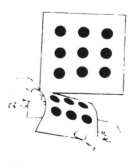

It is also possible to roll up the
puzzle and draw a spiral through
the dots, and otherwise violate
the two-dimensional format.

FIG. 9.20. Other possible solutions to
the nine-dot problem. (From Adams,
1979; Reprinted by permission from W.
W. Norton.)

A common attribute of ill-defined problems is that they potentially involve a huge amount of information. Consider the very real-world problems in international relations, such as "How can we influence Russia so that it cleans up its environmental hazards?" or "How can we provide food for the countless numbers of people who go hungry in the United States and the rest of the world?" The "problem," with broad problems such as these, requires the selection of information that could lead to the desired goal. Unlike the motorist problem that I presented at the opening of this chapter, the difficulty is not in the absence of paths to the goal, but in too many possible paths. Which is most likely to be the best? How can we choose among the better options? There are no simple answers for these questions, which is why we continue to have environmental threats and hunger.

Worldview Constraints

Often we fail to solve problems because of the **worldview constraints** placed on us by our social class, nationality, or political views. Consider the following problem:

> A ping pong ball 1" in diameter falls into a 3" length of pipe that is 1 1/8" in diameter. The pipe is firmly affixed to the concrete pavement. It is extremely important to remove the ball. You and some friends are faced with this task. All you have is some fine wire and your collective abilities to solve this problem. What do you do?

Most people approach this task by attempting to bend fine wire into tweezers to pluck it up. A better solution is to urinate into the pipe so that the ball will float to the top. This probably never occurred to you because it is not an acceptable thought for most people in our society. Although this has never been verified, it would probably be an easier task for people in other societies where urination is not considered as private an act as it is in our society.

I received a firsthand lesson in the ways in which worldviews influence problem solving during the semester that I spent at Moscow State University in Russia. Russia is a country emerging from communism, and a communist solution to a problem is very different from a capitalist solution. Under communism, the state is expected to solve problems like inflation, unemployment, and the supply of consumer goods, whereas, under capitalism these sorts of problems are handled largely by the private sector. It is difficult to imagine the tremendous effect that culture has on the way we think without an extended experience in a culture other than the one you know best. It is for this reason that I tout the educational benefits of extended foreign travel. It can change your own worldview and help you to appreciate the extent to which the problems we identify and the solutions we generate are influenced by cultural factors.

Mechanization

Using jars with the following capacities, measure the amount of water desired. (After Luchins, 1942):

	Jug A	Jug B	Jug C	Desired
1	14	163	25	99
2	18	43	10	5
3	9	42	6	21
4	20	59	4	31
5	23	49	3	20

STOP NOW and solve these five problems. Keep a record of how you went about solving them.

The first four problems can be solved by filling Jug B, then filling Jug A from it once and then filling Jug C from it twice. The water left in Jug C will be the desired amount. In algebraic terms, it's B-A-2C.

Look at how you solved the fifth problem. Did you use this formula? Most people do although it's much simpler to fill Jug A, then pour from it into C to get the answer. People overlook the simpler solution because their approach to the problem has become mechanized. You can guard against this by rethinking occasionally the way you are solving a problem. **Mechanization** can be helpful in that it saves solution times when we don't have to stop and rethink each problem, but it can also blind us to better solutions.

APPLYING THE FRAMEWORK

The general thinking skills framework that we've been using throughout the book is particularly applicable to problem solving.

1. What Is the Goal?   One of the first steps in solving a problem is to be explicit about the goal. This is relatively easy for well-defined problems (e.g., How many ounces are in a pound?). Most problems, however, are ill defined and can have multiple goals. Being explicit about the goal and considering alternative goals will force you to cast the problem in the thinking skills framework and to begin goal-directed thinking.

2. What Is Known?   This is part of the preparation or familiarization process. The knowns or "givens" determine the nature of the problem. It is often possible to improve on what is known by gathering additional information. Once you have a clear determination of the knowns, you can use that information as a guide to selecting the best representation and best problem-solving strategy.

3. Which Thinking Skill or Skills Will Get You to Your Goal?   Thirteen different kinds of strategies or skills were presented in this chapter. You need to select the ones most likely to solve the problem. A trial-and-error approach to selecting a strategy is, itself, a poor strategy. Guidelines were presented for evaluating strategies depending on the nature of the problem.

The skills for planning and solving problems that were presented in this chapter are applicable to almost any problem. After reading this chapter you should be able to:

- Plan and monitor a strategy for finding a solution.
- Identify any problem as either well defined or ill defined and adjust your solution plan according to the type of problem.
- Use graphs, diagrams, hierarchical trees, matrices, and models as solution aids.
- Devise a quality representation of a problem.
- Select the problem-solving strategies that are appropriate for the problem.
- Use all of the following strategies: mean–ends analysis, working backward, simplification, generalization and specialization, random search and trial-and-error, rules, hints, split-half method, brainstorming, contradiction, restate the problem, analogies and metaphors, and consulting an expert.
- Be aware of functional fixedness so as to avoid it.
- Distinguish between relevant and irrelevant information.
- Understand how worldviews can constrain the problem solving process.

4. Have You Reached Your Goal?   The final step in problem solving is an assessment of the quality of the solution. In well-defined problems, this question becomes: Is your solution the correct one? In ill-defined problems, the solution has to be evaluated qualitatively both in an absolute sense (Does it alleviate or reduce the problem?) and in a relative sense (Is it the best alternative?).

CHAPTER SUMMARY

1. All problems can be conceptualized as being composed of "anatomical" parts that include a start state, a goal state, and paths leading from the start to the goal. This entire structure is called the problem space.

2. It is common to divide the problem-solving process into four stages: preparation or familiarization, production, judgment or evaluation, and incubation. Incubation is an optional stage that does not always occur. Persistence is a critical trait of good problem solvers.

3. Problems can be classified along a continuum ranging from well defined to ill defined. Well-defined problems have explicit paths and goals. Ill-defined problems are subject to multiple interpretations. Most of the problems encountered in life are ill defined.

4. Solution strategies need to be planned. A plan for solving a problem will include the construction of a representation and the generation and evaluation of possible solutions.

5. An invaluable aid in solving problems is to devise an external form of representation. The best representation to choose will depend on the type of problem.

6. Thirteen different strategies for generating and evaluating solutions were presented. Often several will be used together in solving a problem. General guidelines were offered for the appropriate use of each.

7. There are four common sources of difficulty that problem solvers encounter. Functional fixedness refers to the failure to utilize items in unusual ways. Mental set, which is closely related to functional fixedness, refers to the predisposition to respond to any situation in a fixed way. Misleading and irrelevant information can "derail one's trail of thought" and can lead you down blind paths. The constraints imposed upon us by our society cause us to view problems from our own narrow frames of reference. Mechanization refers to the rote, unthinking applications of previous solutions without stopping to think about improving our strategies.

TERMS TO KNOW

You should be able to define or describe the following terms or concepts. If you find that you're having difficulty with any term, be sure to reread the section in which it is discussed:

Anatomy of a Problem.   Newell and Simon (1972) conceptualized all problems as consisting of parts or components—an initial state, a goal state, and solution paths that link the initial state to the goal state.

Initial State.   The starting or beginning place in a problem. A problem is solved when the problem solver can find "paths" from the initial state to the goal.

Goal State.   The desired end state in a problem. When a problem solver finds "paths" to the goal, the problem is solved.

Solution Paths. Methods or means for solving problems. Routes that lead from the initial state to the goal state in a problem.

Problem Space. All possible paths from the initial state to the goal state in a problem.

Preparation or Familiarization Stage. The first stage in problem solving, which includes the time spent in understanding the nature of the problem, the desired goal, and the givens.

Production Stage. The second stage in problem solving. During this state, the problem solver produces the solution paths that define the problem space.

Judgment or Evaluation Stage. The third stage in problem solving during which time the problem solver evaluates the solution paths in order to select the best one.

Incubation. A period in problem solving when the problem solver is not actively working on the problem. Sometimes people report that a solution comes to them during this "time-out" period.

Insight. Sudden knowledge of a solution to a problem. Also known as the Aha! experience.

Well-Defined Problems. Problems with a single correct answer.

Ill-Defined Problems. Problems with many possible correct answers. The difficulty with these problems lies in evaluating possible solutions to decide which is best. Often the goal in these problems is vague or incomplete.

Transcontextual. A problem-solving strategy that is useful in any context with any sort of problem. An example of a transcontextual strategy is to state the goal four different ways whenever a problem is encountered.

Perceptual Reorganization. Seeing or restructuring a problem in a new way so that attempts to find a solution will be facilitated. Perceptual reorganization is one way to break mental sets or predispositions to respond in fixed ways.

Hierarchical Trees. Branching diagrams that serve as a representational aid in solving problems. Instances of categories provide the "nodes" of the trees.

Matrix. A rectangular array of numbers that is used as a means of representing problems that contain categories of information.

Detour Problems. Problems in which the path to the goal is not a direct linear one. Intermediate steps are required that seem directly opposite the goal.

Subproblems. When difficulty is encountered in solving a problem, it can be broken down into several smaller problems or "subproblems."

Subgoal. When difficulty is encountered in solving a problem, it can be broken down into several smaller problems called "subproblems." Each subproblem has its own goal, called a "subgoal."

Means–Ends Analysis. A general problem-solving strategy in which operations are used to reduce the distance between the problem solver's current state and the nearest possible subgoal or goal.

Working Backward. A problem-solving strategy in which operations are planned that move from the goal to the present or initial state. This method is usually contrasted with the forward-looking strategy.

Forward-Looking Strategy. A problem-solving strategy in which all of the planning is done by considering operations that move the problem solver closer to subgoals and the goal. This method is usually contrasted with working backward from the goal.

Simplification. A problem-solving strategy in which as much of the complexity as possible is removed from the problem in order to facilitate a solution.

Generalization. A problem-solving strategy in which the problem is considered as an example of a larger class of problems.

Specialization. A problem-solving strategy in which the problem is considered as a special case drawn from a larger set of problems.

Random Search. A problem-solving strategy in which all possible solution paths from the initial state to the goal are considered in an unsystematic (random) manner. This method is usually contrasted with trial-and-error search.

Trial-and-Error. A problem-solving strategy in which all solution paths from the initial state to the goal are searched systematically. This method is usually contrasted with random search.

Rules. The principles that underlie some problems. For example, solutions to problems that require a prediction of the next element in a series depend on the discovery of their rules.

Hints. Additional information that is given after an individual has begun to work on a problem.

Split-Half Method. A problem-solving strategy that is useful when there is no a priori reason for selecting among a sequentially organized set of possible solution paths. The method consists of continually selecting a point that is halfway between the present state and the goal as a systematic means for "guessing" at the solution.

Brainstorming. A group or individual method for generating solution paths for problems. Problem solvers are encouraged to think up wild, imaginative solutions and to defer judgment on these solutions until a later time when they may be modified or combined. The goal is to produce a large number of possible solutions.

Restating the Problem. A problem-solving strategy that is best suited for ill-defined problems. It is sometimes easier to find a solution to a problem when it is expressed in different words.

Analogies (in problem solving). Problem-solving strategies in which similarities are noted between two or more situations, while simultaneously discerning that there are also differences; for example, by noting similarities between two different problems, the problem solver may discover that similar solutions are applicable.

Personal Analogy. A problem-solving strategy suggested by Gordon (1961) in which you think of yourself as a participant in the phenomenon that you want to understand.

Direct Analogy. A problem-solving strategy suggested by Gordon (1961) in which you note similarities between your problem and related problems in other domains.

Symbolic Analogy. The deliberate use of visual imagery or other symbolic representation as a problem-solving aid.

Fantasy Analogy. A problem-solving strategy suggested by Gordon (1961) in which problem solvers utilize their imagination to conceptualize ideal solutions.

Functional Fixedness. A type of mental set in which individuals only consider the usual use (function) of objects.

Mental Set. Predispositions to think and respond in a certain way.

Worldview Constraints. Limitations on the way we approach problems placed upon us by our social class, nationality, or political views.

Mechanization. A routinized approach to solving commonly encountered problems.

SUGGESTED READINGS

There are many excellent books and articles on problem solving. My personal favorites are Sternberg's (1986) *Intelligence Applied*, which presents a problem-solving view of intelligence, Bransford and Stein's (1993) *The Ideal Problem Solver* (2nd ed.), a book that emphasizes problem finding, J. L. Adams' (1979) *Conceptual Blockbusting: A Guide to Better Ideas* (3rd ed.), which has many clever examples of how to approach problems, and Levine's (1994) *Effective Problem Solving* (2nd ed.), a relatively slim book with good examples. They all provide many examples of clever solutions to problems as well as helpful guidelines for those who want to be better problem solvers.

An older classic in the field of problem solving is Rubinstein's (1975) text *Patterns of Problem Solving*. This text is heavily mathematical and requires serious concentration. His coauthored undergraduate text (Rubinstein & Pfeiffer, 1980), *Concepts in Problem Solving*, is highly recommended, although readers may find that it is somewhat dated. A more scholarly approach to this area can be found in an edited volume by Sinnott (1989) entitled *Everyday Problem Solving: Theory and Applications*. Its 19 chapters contain a review of theory and research. A similar approach is taken by Sternberg and Frensch's (Eds.) (1991) book *Complex Problem Solving: Principles and Mechanisms*.

Polya's (1957) book *How to Solve It* gives helpful advice about understanding problems, devising plans, carrying them out, and then looking back. I am a great fan of Polya's work, even though it is now several decades old. He was the first to offer explicit advice on what to do when you're staring at a problem that you can't solve. If you'd like some empirical evidence that people can, in fact, improve the way they solve problems by learning general strategies, see Schoenfeld and Herrmann's (1982) journal article "Problem Perception and Knowledge Structure in Expert and Novice Mathematical Problem Solvers." Schoenfeld and Herrmann found that after college students took a general problem solving course they demonstrated a marked improvement in their problem-solving performance. An interesting investigation was reported by Hains and Hains (1987). They taught problem-solving skills to a group of delinquent teenagers, using common social dilemmas as their problems. They found all of the delinquents improved in their ability to solve difficult social problems and that these gains were observable in their behavior (when rated by staff who were unaware that the delinquents had received this specialized training). Good problem-solving skills are useful in many aspects of life and offer hope for solving many real-world intractable social problems.

A thought-provoking article by Dawes (1989) shows that successful problem solving in clinical settings depends on how well clinicians understand the diagnostic categories and how well they utilize systematic feedback about their diagnoses. He provided evidence that having a great deal of experience as a clinician does not necessarily imply that the clinician has developed expertise and that experience per se does not mean that the individual learned from that experience.

The literature on problem solving for children has been proliferating in recent years. Much of the advice given in children's books is useful for adults as well, and often it is better written and easier to understand than the adult counterparts. *The Productive Thinking Program* (Covington et al., 1974) is a delightful series designed for children in the upper elementary school years. Although it is over 20 years old, it is still delightful. Also recommended among the children's books are Walberg's (1980) *Puzzle Thinking* and Kohl's (1981) *A Book of Puzzlement*.

10

Creative Thinking

Contents

364

The history of civilization is essentially the record of man's [and woman's] creative ability.

—Osborn (1963, p. ix)

I spent a morning at a special summer program for "mentally gifted kids," the ones who score within the top one or two percent of all children in their age group on intelligence tests. Every morning, the 2nd- to 10th-graders gather in a small auditorium to contemplate a "thought for the day," work on a puzzle, plan activities, and gripe about the usual things all kids gripe about. The puzzle for the day was "How can you take one away from 9 and get 10?" The kid sitting next to me whispered, "Do you know the answer?" After a few seconds thought, I gloated with a "Yes" response, pleased as punch that I could keep up with this elite group of short people.

Many hands shot up in response to the puzzle. The first child to answer was a tiny, redheaded girl, reminiscent of Charlie Brown's heartthrob. "It's easy," she said as she walked confidently to the chalkboard. "If you take away a negative one, the effect will be the same as addition." As she spoke, she wrote the following on the board:

$$9 - (-1) = 9 + 1 = 10$$

I was amazed. Why hadn't I thought of that? A second hand went up and a young boy on the verge of adolescence explained another answer: "In Roman numerals, nine is written 'IX,' so if you take 'I' (one) away, you'll end up with 'X,' the Roman numeral for 10."

Another child responded with a sheepish grin, saying that, "This is a little silly, but, if you write '9' and take the one, or vertical line, away and place it in front of the changed number, you'll have '10.'" I don't know why this was a silly answer—it was the one I had been thinking of.

Still more hands were up, anxious to demonstrate more ways to answer the puzzle. One child wrote out the word "NINE," then erased the second letter (the i that looked like a one), which left her with a "N NE." If you count the number of straight lines left in these letters, there are 10 (three in each "N" and four in the "E").

Actually there were even more answers, but I lost track as I sat with my mouth gaping open, trying to follow each explanation. The director of this summer program for gifted children was Dr. Barbara Clark from California State University, Los Angeles. Their usual summer curriculum included activities designed to encourage creative thinking. Watching the children work on their daily puzzle made me keenly aware of the great creative potential in this small group of children.

DEFINING CREATIVITY

A psychology of man is impossible without understanding man's ability to create.

—Arasteh & Arasteh (1976, p. 3)

Creativity is a difficult word to define. We say that someone "is creative" when she has produced an outcome or a product that is both unusual and appropriate (or meaningful or useful or particularly good). Thus, creativity is defined by two aspects of its consequence and not the process that led to the consequence.

Both the unusualness and appropriateness criteria require judgments: How unusual is the idea and how well does it meet some objective? Because both of these criteria vary along quantitative dimensions, creativity exists in degrees. This means that any action can be more or less creative. Creativity is not a single trait that people either have or don't have. It is a set of processes that occurs in a context. These processes involve novelty in one or more of the processes that lead to creative outcomes—ways of identifying that a problem exists, defining a problem, generating and evaluating possible solutions, and judging how uniquely and how well the problem is solved.

Suppose that you are invited to supper at your friend Hazel's house. You know that she is an adventuresome cook and therefore you look forward to the meal with relish. The main dish is an original concoction of hot dogs and fruit salad in a cold mustard sauce. (This part is a true story. I was once served this at a friend's house.) The coup de grace is a dessert that she made with her new ice cream maker—liver-and brussel sprout-flavored ice cream. Although these are unusual dishes, few people would willingly eat them. Most of us would not judge these culinary delights as creative because they do not satisfy the criterion that the idea or product be good or useful.

One problem with our working definition of creativity concerns the terms "unusual" and "good" or "useful" because satisfaction of these criteria is a matter of judgment, and people will often disagree. This means that creativity exists in the eyes of the observer. It's easy to see why creativity has been an elusive topic. Someone or some group must judge an act or idea as unusual and good or useful before it can be labeled creative, and there will often be disagreement on the way these attributes are judged. Judgments of creativity also change over time so that a "zany" idea at one time in history (e.g., the earth revolves around the sun and not the reverse) may come to be viewed as "monumental" at some time later.

Prince (1970) offered a somewhat poetic definition of creativity, which, I believe, is itself creative. Consider his definition:

> CREATIVITY: an arbitrary harmony, an expected astonishment, a habitual revelation, a familiar surprise, a generous selfishness, an unexpected certainty, a formidable stubbornness, a vital triviality, a disciplined freedom, an intoxicating steadiness, a repeated initiation, a difficult delight, a predictable gamble, an ephemeral solidity, a unifying difference, a demanding satisfier, a miraculous expectation, an accustomed amazement. (p. 1)

Gardner (1989) added an additional requirement to his personal definition of creativity. Gardner wanted creativity to include the idea that the creative individual *regularly* solves problems or fashions products that are creative. This additional requirement would remove "luck" from the creative process because luck or random actions cannot account for regular results. However we choose to define creativity, we need it, and we all possess it to some extent. Our everyday life is more pleasurable because of our creative actions; the arts depend on it for their existence; the sciences and mathematics could not progress without it. Every time we express a complex thought or fill a blank piece of paper with our words, we are creating; when we do it particularly well in an unusual way, then we are creative.

Lateral and Vertical Thinking

Vertical thinking is concerned with digging the same hole deeper. Lateral thinking is concerned with digging the hole somewhere else.

—DeBono (1977, p. 195)

The distinction between lateral and vertical thinking was first made by DeBono (1968). It is best illustrated with a short story that is probably an old fable that has been told for many generations:

Many years ago when a person who owed money could be thrown into jail, a merchant in London had the misfortune to owe a huge sum to a money-lender. The money-lender, who was old and ugly, fancied the merchant's beautiful teenage daughter. He proposed a bargain. He said he would cancel the merchant's debt if he could have the girl instead.

Both the merchant and his daughter were horrified at the proposal. So the cunning money-lender proposed that they let Providence decide the matter. He told them that he would put a black pebble and a white pebble into an empty money-bag and then the girl would have to pick out one of the pebbles. If she chose the black pebble she would become his wife and her father's debt would be cancelled. If she chose the white pebble she would stay with her father and the debt would still be cancelled. But if she refused to pick out a pebble her father would be thrown into jail and she would starve.

Reluctantly the merchant agreed. They were standing on a pebble-strewn path in the merchant's garden as they talked and the money-lender stooped down to pick up the two pebbles. As he picked up the pebbles the girl, sharp-eyed with fright, noticed that he picked up two black pebbles and put them into the money-bag. He then asked the girl to pick out the pebble that was to decide her fate and that of her father.

What would you do if you had been the girl? If you think about this problem in a careful, logical, straightforward way, you're using **vertical thinking**, a type of thinking that will not be much help in this situation. Typical "vertical thinking" answers are: Let the girl sacrifice herself or expose him for the crook he is. Consider DeBono's suggested solution: The girl should fumble when she draws the pebble from the bag, dropping it onto the pebble-strewn path. She should then tell the villain that they can determine the color of the pebble she took by seeing the color of the one left in the bag. Because the remaining pebble must be black, the money-lender will be forced to admit that she had chosen the white pebble or expose himself as a crook.

Virtually everyone agrees that this is both a good and unusual answer to the girl's dilemma. **Lateral thinking** is a way of thinking "around" a problem. "Lateral thinking generates the ideas and vertical thinking develops them" (DeBono, 1968, p. 6). Lateral thinking, then, is sometimes used as a synonym for creative thinking or idea discovery, whereas vertical thinking is the refinement and improvement of existing ideas.

The world's most famous fictional detective, Sherlock Holmes, often exhibited lateral thinking. One of my favorite examples was Holmes' response to an idea by his faithful assistant, the good Dr. Watson. Watson pointed out that a certain dog would not be at all helpful in solving a mystery because the dog had done nothing on the night of the murder. Sherlock cleverly noted that the dog was extremely important in solving the mystery precisely because he had done nothing on the night of the murder because dogs would be expected to bark or become excited at the sight of strangers or of violent struggles.

Creative Genius or Pedestrian Process?

The human mind treats a new idea the way the body treats a strange protein; it rejects it.

—P. B. Medawar (quoted in Byrne, 1988, p. 16)

Are creative individuals qualitatively different from the rest of us, or do we all have what it takes to create something great? Increasingly, psychologists have come to believe that there is "nothing special" about creative giants like Einstein, Madame Curie, and Mozart and that the creative process can be understood as an extension of common, everyday thinking processes. Weisberg (1988, 1993) championed the every-day view of creativity in his analysis of the antecedents of creative thinking. For example, he presented a brief biography of Alexander Calder (1898–1976), a popular artist who is best known for his brightly colored mobiles. Calder invented the mobile as an art form. As a child, Calder used wire to make jewelry for his sister. His parents were artists who made certain that he had art lessons and was surrounded with both sculpture (his father's profession) and drawings (his mother's profession). He visited the studios of Piet Mondrian, an abstract artist who used strong, primary colors and abstract designs in his work. It is easy to see how these life experiences led to an art form in which brightly colored abstract patterns were strung together and hung in space. The creative act was the assimilation of these diverse forms and influences—one that, at least in hindsight, could have been predicted from Calder's life experiences.

The view that even great creative products can be produced by almost anyone with at least slightly above-average intelligence and expertise in a discipline, is gaining in popularity. For example, Hayes (1989) noted that there are no cognitive abilities that separate creative and noncreative people. According to this view, most of us have "what it takes" to be highly creative. From a cognitive perspective, creative thinking uses thought processes that are quite ordinary. We can all come up with "novel products of value" (Weisberg, 1993, p. 4). All we need to do is learn how.

Sensitivity, Synergy, and Serendipity

Creative thought is innovative, exploratory, venturesome.

—Kneller (1965, p. 6)

Creativity has been described as the three Ss: sensitivity, synergy, and serendipity (Parnes, Noller, & Biondi, 1977). **Sensitivity** is the use of our senses, our "windows to the world" that we use to touch, smell, taste, and see. It has been suggested that highly creative people may experience the physical world with greater intensity than the rest of us, although I don't know of any data to support this possibility. It does seem that creative thinking involves the "noticing" or remembering of some critical aspect of the environment or a problem that the rest of us overlooked. One of the benchmarks of a creative person is the ability to find problems and not just solutions to them. Look at Fig. 10.1. This is called "Boring's Wife-and-Mother-In-Law." Can you guess why? Look closely. Can you see both an old woman and a young woman in the picture? Count the prongs on Fig. 10.2. Do they disappear as you count them? This is an impossible figure—impossible because it can't ever exist, except in the artist's mind. In creating each of these figures, the artists displayed a sensitivity to details that is both unusual and appropriate. Perhaps these are examples of heightened sensitivity to visual stimuli.

Synergy is the bringing together of seemingly disparate parts into a useful and functioning whole. It is close to Koestler's (1964) notion of **bisociative thinking** in which two previously unconnected "frames of reference" are amalgamated. If you can take ideas from different domains and bring them together so that they work successfully in a new context, you have demonstrated synergy. Examples of synergy can be found in the brief biography of Calder that was presented earlier, who brought together his experiences with wire objects, bright colors, and abstract drawing to create his wildly popular mobiles.

Gordon (1961) suggested that one way to promote creativity is to bring people from diverse fields together to find problems and to create solutions, the two mainstreams of the creative process. In order to bring together diverse ideas, you need to have a broad range of experiences and knowledge. One argument for a liberal arts education is that it provides the breadth of knowledge needed to view the world from different perspectives and to permit the combination of ideas across domains of knowledge.

FIG. 10.1. Boring's Wife-and-Mother-In-Law. Can you see both an old woman and a young woman in this picture?

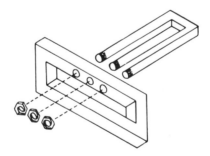

FIG. 10.2. An impossible figure. Try to count the prongs.

According to von Oech (1983), Johannes Gutenberg conceived of the printing press by combining two previously unconnected ideas—the wine press and the coin punch. The purpose of the coin punch was to leave an impression on a small area such as a coin. By contrast, the wine press applied pressure over a large area in order to squeeze the juice out of grapes. One day Gutenberg put the coin punch under the wine press and found that he could get images on paper. This simple, but original, combination resulted in the printing press and literally changed the world by making books widely available.

Serendipity is an unexpected discovery that is unplanned. Biographies of great scientists often contain accounts of serendipitous events, some of them seemingly preposterous. I have often felt that focusing on serendipity did the scientist a great injustice. A new miracle drug may have been the result of an accidental spill, but it was the prepared scientist who could appreciate the results of the accident that created the drug. The scientist was able to select the relevant information from the accident so that it could be used in a novel way instead of simply labeling it a mistake and forgetting about it. Although serendipity may have contributed to a creative act, the persistence, motivation, and hard work on the part of the creator allowed the serendipitous event to occur. Serendipity may play a role in great scientific discoveries, but such fortuitive "accidents" seem most likely to occur in the laboratory at 2 a.m.

Consider how an artist friend of mine combined sensitivity, synergy, and serendipity to create a new form of art. Robert Perine, a San Diego artist (who also created the beautiful and novel depiction of "The Thinker" on the cover of this book), decided to incorporate the glass that is used to cover pictures into the pictures themselves. He cut odd-shaped glass coverings and placed them over his water color paintings to see how the beveled edges in the glass would refract the paint beneath it and give it a glossy, shimmering appearance. It was a simple idea that brought together the framing process and the picture itself in a new art form that incorporates the picture and the glass used to protect it. Creative ideas often seem simple and surprising.

Jokes, puns, and witticisms could also be considered as a form of creative expression. A joke brings together two ideas that are not usually combined.

Did you hear the one about the two former schoolmates who meet unexpectedly for the first time in 25 years? As they caught up on the details of their lives, one asked the other if he had any children. Sorrowfully he replied, "Yes, one living and one married." The listener was expecting the phrase "one living and one dead" and the surprise juxtaposition of "living and married" is the humorous element in this joke. Laughter is often the response to original ideas also. The surprising combination of elements (synergy) makes for good jokes and creative ideas.

CREATIVITY AS A COGNITIVE PROCESS

The man [or woman] with a new idea is a crank until the idea succeeds.

—Mark Twain

If the creative act is "nothing special," then we should be able to understand it and predict when it will occur using a common cognitive framework. Several different psychologists have suggested that creativity is as "simple" as problem solving, except that the problem or the solution are novel and appropriate (Sternberg, 1988). According to this view, creative thinking is a multistage process that consists of identifying a problem, deciding what is important about the problem, and arriving at a novel way of solving it. Perkins (1988) stressed the processes of searching and selecting as integral to creative acts, but these are the same processes that were used to understand more mundane problem solving and decision making. "Creativity" brings together many topics that have been addressed in earlier chapters; yet, it is also more elusive and mysterious because, by definition, we cannot tell anyone how to create the "unusual." What makes the processes of identifying problems, searching for solutions, selecting the most promising ones, and conveying the outcome, creative?

Redefining the Problem and Selecting Relevant Information

It is useful to conceptualize creative thinking within the framework that was developed in chapter 9. A problem exists when there is a discrepancy between where the problem solver is and the desired end state or goal. A solution is a plan for attaining the goal. Guilford (1977) described the relationship between problem solving and creativity this way:

> [P]roblem-solving and creative thinking are closely related. The very definitions of those two activities show logical connections. Creative thinking produces novel outcomes, and problem-solving produces a new response to a new situation which is a novel outcome. Thus, we can say that problem-solving has creative aspects.

The Problem of Problem Definition

All of our great inventors were problem finders. They recognized problems that the rest of the world never saw. For example, why did people need electric lights when gas worked well, or why should we even want to travel in a metal box propelled with a new-fangled engine when horses were more reliable (at that time)? We all studied the great inventors of the past, people like Benjamin Franklin, George Washington Carver, and Thomas Edison. Present-day inventors also find problems. An "Invention Convention" is held annually in the United States to highlight the creative talents of current inventors. Some of the items first displayed at this convention are a double-headed toothbrush that can brush both sides of the teeth at the same time, a portable hot water shower that can be used for camping because it is lightweight and relies on the sun to heat the water, bedroom slippers with headlights, and an electric box that makes and bakes a loaf of bread—all you do is pour in the ingredients. These have all become commercial successes, which means that the general public believes that they are good solutions to a problem that most of us never knew existed.

Consider this "problem": One sure sign of a fancy restaurant is the large pepper mill that is dragged around by an obsequious waiter who offers to grind it over your meal. As restauarants compete for the upscale crowd, the pepper mills have gotten bigger and flashier. I just came across an ad for an electric pepper mill that grinds pepper in various grades of coarseness. It is gold-plated and sells for an unbelievable $170. I suppose that this is a good example of problem finding. I certainly didn't know that there was a problem with hand-turned pepper grinders or that degree of pepper coarseness was an important consideration. Perhaps I am misinterpreting the problem. This "solution" can also be conceptualized as one solution to the problem of getting the wealthy to give you some of their money. No matter how you conceptualize the problem, this seems to be a creative solution.

Selecting Relevant Information

Virtually every creative act involves a novel way of defining a problem and selecting information that is relevant to reaching the goal. We usually think of creativity in the arts and sciences, but it can and should exist in a host of everyday settings that range from planning your finances so that your money lasts until the end of the month to getting your teacher to accept a late paper.

Consider a couple seeking marriage counseling. The wife complains that her husband spends too much time at work, and if he really loved her he would spend more time at home. The husband complains that he has a great deal of pressure at the office and that he has to work long hours to "get ahead." If his wife loved him more, she would understand. There are multiple possible ways to define their problem. They could pose the problem as: "Should we get a divorce?" But, other possible problem definitions include: (a) How can we find ways to spend more time together? (b) How can we assure each other that we are still in love? (c) How can the husband "get ahead" while spending less time at work? (d) How can they learn to adjust to the present situation? (e) Is "getting ahead" an important goal? and (f) What can the wife do so that she doesn't feel lonely and resentful when her husband is at work?

If you consider the problem for a few more minutes, you can come up with many other problem definitions. The nature of the solution will change every time the problem is redefined. The selection of relevant information to help you reach a goal is related to your knowledge of the problem space (topic). In this example, you would need to know more about the couple to help them find a good solution. Suppose that you know that the wife is an aspiring artist. You could suggest that she pursue her art interests so that she would feel less lonely and deserted. Alternatively, if you know about the availability of other jobs for the husband, you could suggest that he change jobs.

Lateral thinking or "thinking around a problem" is really just another term for "redefining the problem." In the story about the clever girl who knew she was being offered two black pebbles, she didn't conceptualize the problem as "What should I do when I pick the black pebble?" Instead, she redefined the problem as "How can I avoid the appearance that I picked up the black pebble?" It's not so much "thinking around the problem" as it is redefining the problem so that it can be solved in a favorable way. This point was also made in the previous chapter on problem solving. In a review article of research and theory on creativity, Mumford and Gustafson (1988) noted that creativity is related to "information that is seemingly irrelevant to the solution of the problem at hand" (p. 30). By focusing on the fact that the pebbles on the path were black and white and therefore she could drop one without its being identified, the heroine of this short story was able to generate a novel solution.

Generation, Exploration, and Evaluation

Creativity is a puzzle, a paradox, some say a mystery.

—Margaret A. Boden (1990, p. vii)

If creative thinking is just a variant of everyday problem solving, then there should be general principles that can be applied across domains of knowledge. Are the creative dancer, scientist, teacher, and writer all using the same sorts of processes in their creation despite the fact that they are using different modes of expression with very different problems? Although there are obvious differences, they all have to generate possible solutions to their problem and explore the "problem space," a term that was defined in chapter 9 as all of the possible goals and ways of getting from the start point to the goal. Finke, Ward, and Smith (1992) posited a two-phase model that they called **geneplore**, named for the repeated cycles of generation and exploration that are part of every problem-solving process. Creative individuals need to be involved and committed so that they continue the processes long enough to allow a creative solution to emerge. Levine (1994) called the willingness to work on a problem "intimate engagement," a term that connotes the close links among motivation, hard work, time on task, and willingness to explore possibilities.

Evaluation is also a creative act because the problem solver must be able to recognize when a good solution has been obtained (Doolittle, 1995). Effective evaluation is needed to terminate the process or the problem solver can be caught in unending loops of exploration and generation. Notice that a problem-solving view of creativity also entails all of the other stages of cognition. A successful exploration of the problem space requires that the problem solver be able to notice and remember critical aspects of the problem. Thus, as in all of thinking "memory must be tickled."

Insight and Incubation

Not surprisingly, both the terms "insight" and "incubation" were discussed in chapter 9. Insight was described as the sudden awareness of a solution; incubation was described as period of time when an individual is not actively working on a problem that is followed by a successful solution. These two stages in the problem-solving process are often associated with creative solutions. Although these are both "hidden" processes that are seemingly mysterious, it is possible to examine them within the framework of a general cognitive model.

I hope that you can recall from chapter 2 the idea that the information people store in memory is connected in weblike networks. For example, your information about flowers is connected such that what you know about roses is (metaphorically) stored close to your information about petunias, azaleas, and other flowers. If you know a great deal about flowers, then you have an extensive and highly interconnected network of information. If you grew up in the tropics, then your knowledge of flowers is probably very different from that of someone who grew up in Antarctica because you probably would have very different information about flowers.

The interconnectedness of knowledge is important here. All of your knowledge about flowers is also connected to your knowledge of water and sun, which in turn are connected to many different types of information. Theoretically, if you start at any point in this giant interconnected web, you could trace your way to any other place in the web. A hypothetical schematic of a section of someone's knowledge network is shown in Fig. 10.3.

FIG. 10.3. An example of the way information in memory is interconnected in a giant weblike knowledge structure. Creativity involves "noticing" or making unusual connections.

When a new idea suddenly comes to someone, it means that he has successfully traveled his personal knowledge network from one place to another—the new idea representing the connection between two previously unconnected nodes. Think about someone you love. What sorts of ideas and images come to mind? Does the image of a rose seem appropriate? If so, it may be because I brought your knowledge of roses to mind in the last paragraph and the path from your love to that of roses was "activated." Does the phrase, "My love is like a red, red rose" have any meaning for you? Does the sudden association of your love and roses seem insightful?

Psychologists call the "thinking about" or the "reminding" process **spread of activation** to denote the idea that the activity that was begun when I told you to think about a loved one spread to your knowledge of roses. People with large knowledge nets will have more places for the activation to spread, and the best way to have a large knowledge net is to have a large number of interconnected knowledge structures. There is no substitute for knowledge about a topic. If you want to be more creative in the sciences, for example, you would need to acquire knowledge about the field so that relevant information will be available for solving problems about science. We use our large knowledge nets for new ideas, and skimpy nets can yield few ideas (Tardiff & Sternberg, 1988). It is the ability to use the information stored in memory that allows us to create by going beyond what we have learned.

Let's consider what else is happening when you solve a problem. Suppose that you are reading a murder mystery in which the prime suspect is the hero, and hence, unlikely to be the murderer. You are focusing on another character who, you believe, "did it." Dutifully, you generate possible solutions and explore the problem space, but to no avail. You cannot connect your prime suspect to the murder scene, so you "forget" about the problem and resume other activities. In other words, you create a period of incubation. Then, when you return to the book, you "see" that it was not your prime suspect, but some other character. Using the jargon of the problem-solving literature, you were fixated on one solution type (finding a way to link your suspect to the crime) and the incubation period allowed you to "forget" this type of solution so that other more profitable paths could be pursued—sort of a release from fixation.

Good problem solvers know how to search through a large problem space, so as to make it an efficient process. When there are a large number of possible paths to a goal, good problem solvers use heuristics, or search plans, to "prune the search tree" (Boden, 1990, p. 78). If you have an extensive knowledge net concerning some topic, then you have more potential paths or links among concepts and more retrieval cues that can help you remember and select relevant information when it is needed.

Analogical Thinking

Analogy is inevitable in human thought.

—Oppenheimer (1956, p. 129)

Analogies underlie much of our everyday thinking, our artistic expressions, and scientific achievements. Sternberg (1977) noted, "reasoning by analogy is pervasive in everyday experience. We reason analogically whenever we make a decision about something new in our experience by drawing a parallel to something old. When we buy a new goldfish because we liked our old one, or when we listen to a friend's advice because it was correct once before, we are reasoning analogically" (p. 353). Thinking involves the ability to note resemblances or correspondence between two objects, while simultaneously discerning that there are also differences. When you use analogies you observe that two entities are similar with respect to some property, and dissimilar with respect to others. You'll find that analogies are discussed in several chapters in this book because they are pervasive in human thought.

We utilize analogies to make sense out of the world. They help us to understand new events by relating them to ones already known; they allow us to communicate our thoughts; they are the foundations of creative thinking. Analogies are one way of making the unfamiliar known. Analogies are always imperfect because they imply a similarity between objects and events that are not identical. In evaluating and creating analogies, carefully consider the nature of the comparison. If I say that you are like your brother because you both have two eyes, you would certainly object because the number of eyes one has is not a relevant dimension for comparison. However, if I say that you are like your brother because you are both passive and stingy, you might still object, but the nature of the comparison is a relevant one.

A **metaphor** is an analogy that notes similarities between things that are basically dissimilar. (The English grammatical distinction between metaphor and simile is not being considered here because it is irrelevant to this discussion.) When Shakespeare wrote, "My love is like a red, red rose," he was speaking metaphorically because roses and love are basically dissimilar. Analogies enhance the creative process by encouraging the problem solver to recombine elements from two concepts that are initially perceived as dissimilar (Gilhooly, 1987; Halpern, 1987a, 1987b). For example, if I tell you that the atom is like a miniature solar system, you can use your knowledge of the solar system to infer information about the atom. To use analogies and metaphors creatively, practice forming them, extending familiar ones, changing common ones, or reversing the process and seeking differences instead of similarities.

One of the most famous creative uses of analogy is seen in the story of Archimedes. He was given the task of determining if the King's crown was pure gold—the only kind of crown worthy of a king. According to the legend, Archimedes did not know how to solve this problem because of the irregular shape of the crown. One day, while lowering himself into a bathtub full of water, the tub overflowed. The answer was immediately obvious. Like his body, a solid gold crown would display a volume of water identical to that displaced by a bar of gold that was equal in weight to that of the crown. The story goes on to say that in his excitement he ran naked through the street yelling, "Eureka, I have found it!" He had a true creative insight mediated by the analogy of his body displacing his bathtub water and the knowledge that a gold crown would displace a predetermined volume of water. In case you're interested, the crown was pure gold and the king was very happy.

Although the use of analogies from distant domains is a common theme in discussions of creativity, in fact, the spontaneous noting of similarities in very different contexts is not a common occurrence. Perhaps it is because it is unusual that it figures prominently in our belief about creativity—which requires an unusual outcome or process.

Making the Familiar Strange

Although the usual function of analogies is to make the unfamiliar familiar, Gordon (1961, 1976), the founder of a creative technique known as synectics, suggested that we reverse the process for creative results. Gordon (1976) suggested that we use analogies and metaphors by trying "strange new contexts in which to view a familiar problem" (p. 251). Gordon posited, as an example, that we consider a naive student examining a fish's heart for the first time. Because the student knows nothing about anatomy, the context is strange, yet the flow of blood through the heart may remind him of a filter system for a local swimming pool. The student's analogy is a creative contribution to his understanding of anatomy.

Gordon (1976) suggested four specific types of analogies for use when attempting to solve a problem creatively. They are personal analogy, direct analogy, symbolic analogy, and fantasy analogy. Each is described in chapter 9. Analogies can also be used creatively to find problems. For example, executives at Bradford Associates (Westport, Connecticut) spent an afternoon sipping martinis and brainstorming about possible new products that would be marketable. As they were enjoying their own liquid refreshments, they decided that the time had come "for a six-pack that a dog could ask for by name." They are now marketing a chicken-flavored soft drink for dogs known as "Arf 'n'Arf." Here is a clear example of the use of analogies to find problems (the need for a doggie soft drink). Similarly, a popular dog product is now being developed for people. Many dogs enjoy munching on bone shaped biscuits that help to keep their teeth and gums healthy. A similar biscuit that will help humans to keep their gums and teeth healthy will soon appear on market shelves. (I don't know what shape it will be.)

Bionics

Bionics is a special type of analogy. It relies on analogies from nature that can be adapted to human problems. For example, special properties of the eyes of beetles have suggested a new type of ground-speed indicator for airplanes, and the principles of adhesion used by cockleburs have served as the prototype for Velcro-type closures. Bionics is also concerned that the broad impact of solutions be considered because, borrowing another analogy from nature, small changes in our ecological system can result in disastrous consequences to other life forms in the food chain. Papanek (1977) called this the "total-chain-of-design idea." It requires the creative consideration of entire systems and interrelationships of parts.

Weber and Perkins (1992) conceptualized the creative process as finding ways to bridge different problem spaces, so that solutions can be applied and modified across domains of knowledge. Consider modern surgery to unclog clogged arteries. A thin tube is threaded into the artery. When the clog is reached, a small "balloon" is inflated in the artery to open the clogged area. This is the same technique that has been used by plumbers to open clogged pipes. Thus, a common problem-solving technique in plumbing is being used by surgeons to save lives. Many creative acts involve adapting solutions from one field for use in an unrelated field.

Remote Associations Test

There is a test of creativity that rests on the notion that creative people can form connections between seemingly very different topics. Mednick and Mednick (1967) created a test to tap this dimension of creativity. It is called the Remote Associations Test or RAT for short. Test takers are given three words and are asked to come up with a fourth word that relates to all three. As an example, what word relates to:

RIVER   NOTE   BLOOD

Can you come up with the relational word? (The answer is *bank*—river bank; bank note; blood bank.) Try some other remote associations similar to the ones on the RAT:

1. BOARD   DUCK   DOLLAR
2. FILE   HEAD   TOE
3. BOILED   LID   FLOWER

4. BALL   MALARIA   BUTTER
5. CLASS   STAGE   SOCCER

(The answers are on p. 392.)

Do creative people come up with remote associations when they think creatively? It seems that some do. An invention by Michael Reynolds of Taos, New Mexico, seems to epitomize this type of thinking. He combined his knowledge of the high cost of housing with the problem of soda cans littering the countryside and the proverbial light bulb went on. He made these remote associations and constructed a house of aluminum soda cans. For his second house, he is filling the cans with water so that the solar-heated cans of water can supplement his home energy needs.

ENCOURAGING CREATIVITY

One of the objections I hear to setting forth creativity as a goal for higher education is, "We can't all be Einsteins." This is undeniable; it is also irrelevant.

—Hutchings (1986, p. 14)

There has been considerable debate over the question of whether it is possible to make people more creative by providing them with special experiences that are designed to enhance creativity. There is a sizable research literature that shows that it is possible. This is not really a surprising conclusion given that creative thinking shares many features with everyday sorts of problem solving, and the evidence reviewed in the first chapter, and in several places throughout this book, showed that improved thinking is a possible outcome of education. In a review of the research literature on creativity, Baer (1993) cautiously concluded that there are many variables that are involved in the enhancement of creative thinking, and, in conclusion, "an interpretation of the results as providing modest support for the hypotheses that divergent thinking training improves creative performance seems warranted" (p. 74).

What are the many variables that are important in determining when and how much creativity can be enhanced?

The Person, the Problem, the Process

Discovery consists of looking at the same thing as everyone else and thinking something different.

—Albert Szent-Gjorgyi (Nobel Prize Winner in Medicine; in von Oech, 1983, p. 7)

It is clear that creativity is not something that exists in an all-or-none fashion. People are more or less creative, just as they are more or less athletic or good-looking or prejudiced. The question of whether there is some inborn or inherited trait that is associated with high creativity has been difficult to answer. Most of the research has centered on the relationship between creativity and intelligence. Are intelligent people the most creative ones?

In general, people with above-average scores on intelligence tests tend to be creative, whereas those with low IQ scores tend not to be; but the relationship is not a perfect one. It is not true that the very smartest people are always the most creative. It seems best to conclude that there is a certain minimum intelligence that is needed to be creative, but beyond the minimal level, IQ doesn't seem to matter much. Even if you're not a particularly intelligent person, you may have great creative potential. In addition, we all have different abilities. A person with a broad knowledge net about football strategies and skill in running and throwing is more likely to be a creative football player than an individual who has little knowledge of the field and is clumsy with a football, but the second individual may be more creative in an unrelated domain of knowledge such as poetry or ballet.

Environmental Factors

People will be most creative when they feel motivated primarily by the interest, enjoyment, satisfaction, and challenge of the work itself—not by external pressures.

—Hennessey and Amabile (1988, p. 11)

Creative thinking, like all activities, takes place in a social context—a fact that is often overlooked in the cognitive literature. Amabile and her colleagues (Amabile, 1983, 1989; Hennessey & Amabile 1987, 1988) have studied the environmental/social factors that can encourage or discourage creativity. Unfortunately, they concluded that much of what happens in school and work settings is not conducive to the development of creativity. They found that creative individuals view their work as a labor of love. They work long hours because they are impelled by their curiosity and their own desire to achieve a goal. Hard work is a repeated theme among those who study the creative process. This sort of motivation is called **intrinsic motivation** because it comes from within the individual. By contrast, much of the motivation provided at school and work is **extrinsic motivation**, that is motivation that comes from others such as promises of a good grade or money. According to Amabile and her colleagues, the best way to promote creativity is to arrange the environment so as to maximize intrinsic motivation. Six conditions that tend to kill intrinsic motivation are (a) constant evaluation, (b) surveillance, (c) reward, (d) competition, (e) restricted choice (e.g., limited choice of materials to use), and (f) an extrinsic orientation towards work.

Schank and Childers (1988) agreed that the academic environment is often hostile to innovative ideas. They suggested that the tendency to discourage new ideas is best seen in the grant review process that is part of academic life for university researchers. Colleagues often turn down funding requests for ideas that haven't been proven. Thus, risk taking, an essential component of creativity because of its reliance on the unusual, is punished even in those institutions that are supposed to encourage creative efforts.

Most school and work environments tend to be heavily weighted toward extrinsic motivators; teachers and supervisors watch while students and employees work, and the workers receive grades or payment for their efforts. It is impossible to avoid extrinsic motivators completely as there will always be deadlines, competition, and choice restrictions, for example. Despite these realities, it is possible to design school and work environments to foster creativity by reducing the focus on extrinsic motivators and emphasizing the intrinsic rewards of the creative process. Of course, in addition to these changes in the environment, creativity training also needs a skills component. No one can become a creative scientist or great author or talented artist without the factual knowledge and technical skills that are relevant to their chosen field. If you want to promote creativity, there is no substitute for subject matter knowledge (Langley, Simon, Bradshaw, & Zytkow, 1987; Snow, 1986).

Environmental factors are important. A quality education (both inside and outside of school) will give you the basis for the remote associations or divergent thoughts or novel ideas. You need a head filled with thoughts and facts in order to create with them. The inferences from Amabile's work are clear: Cultivate a love of learning; reward your own creative efforts; take the college courses that will fill your mind with new thoughts (and not just the easiest courses offered). Creative endeavors result from hard, intellectual work that is self-motivated and self-monitored. Don't be afraid to engage in it.

Personality Factors

There are certain personality factors that are consonant with creativity. Because creativity (as we have defined it) requires an unusual or novel act, the creative individual must not be swayed by a need for conformity nor be resistant to change. Perhaps there is some validity to the notion of the "eccentric" artist or scholar.

The creative person must be self-motivated. Sometimes, school experiences tend to favor the noncreative students, as many traditional assignments don't call for creative responses. Creative people may have to create their own rewards for their actions and find satisfaction in the creative process itself.

The ability and willingness to take risks and to tolerate ambiguity is also needed for creative acts. When we try to do things differently, we sometimes fail. Most of the great discoveries in modern times were initially met with ridicule and repeated failure (a horseless carriage, a machine that could fly, etc.). We need to teach children and learn ourselves that failure is an important part of life and that every great success was built upon previous failures.

In a study of creative people (Barron, 1958), writers, artists, musicians, and mathematicians were given a battery of tests to determine if they had any personality traits in common. In general, these highly creative individuals were nonconforming, unconventional, and generally less concerned with "making a good impression." One contemporary American hero is the recently deceased Richard Feynman. Feynman was the Nobel Prize-winning physicist who investigated the tragic explosion of the Challenger. He demonstrated that "O" rings, rubber circular gaskets used on the Challenger, get brittle when they get cold. His simple test consisted of dunking an "O" ring in ice water and showing that it could crack when cold. The attitude of risk taking and nonconformity is exemplified by the title of an autobiographical book about his life entitled *What Do You Care What Other People Think?* (1989). Of course, this does not mean that if you become nonconforming and unconventional, you'll then become highly creative, but it suggests that a more open-minded and less self-conscious approach to life's problems can pay off. Feynman also demonstrated a natural curiosity and immense breadth of knowledge. His interests weren't limited to physics and extended to many domains. I recall with great clarity a time when I sat next to him at an informal dinner party. He remarked to my daughter, who was young at that time, that growing old was a peculiar thing. When he was my daughter's age, he could never get enough dessert, and now that is older and can have all the dessert he wishes, he no longer wants it! At the time, I thought that this was an odd discussion between a child and older man; now I think it was just part of the eccentricity that marked his genius.

The ability to tolerate uncertainty is also an important characteristic of creative people. Langer (1989) showed the need to see the world in terms of probabilities rather than categorical certainties. She also emphasized the necessity to create conceptual bridges across domains of knowledge: "The ability to transcend context is the essence of mindfulness and central to creativity in any field" (p. 31).

STRATEGIES FOR CREATIVE THINKING

The nation that neglects creative thought today will assuredly have its nose ground into the dust of tomorrow.

—Fred Hoyle

Creativity has never been given the attention it deserved in standard educational settings. Over three decades ago, Lowenfeld (1962) called creativity "education's stepchild," a fact that remains true today. There seems to be no place in the traditional school curriculum for creativity training. There have been many programs developed with the specific goal of training people to be creative in order to fill this gap.

Basic Principles

Although there are considerable differences among creativity-training programs, they all share some basic common principles:

1. Teach students to think of different ways to accomplish an objective and then how to select the best one.
2. Provide plenty of examples and exercises to model and practice creative skills.
3. Teach students how to ask relevant questions and how to discover when a problem exists.
4. Evaluate the quality of an idea by its consequences.
5. Reward original and relevant ideas, but be certain to keep the reward secondary to the enjoyment of the creative process. Let students know that their ideas are valuable.
6. Provide unstructured situations. Teach them the value of persistence when they fail.
7. Provide students with a tangible plan for finding solutions. This means that they should be trained in ways that will help them to make relevant information that they have stored in memory accessible and to find ways to bridge areas of knowledge. Plans include recognizing puzzling facts, seeking information, generating possible solutions, changing perspectives, and restating the goal.
8. Restrain from labeling or categorizing problems or solutions too quickly in the problem-solving process because labeling tends to encourage fixation, the opposite sort of set that is needed for flexible thinking.

You may be thinking that there is no such thing as "strategies for creative thinking" because creativity involves breaking rules, not following them—a sort of a free activity. Bailin (1987) argued against this notion of creativity. As she noted, most creative actions take place within a framework of rules. Even the most beautiful sonnet contains 14 lines of specified meter and rhyme, all great ballets are performed with the principles and techniques of dance, and all scientific discoveries are made by experts who are knowledgeable in their field. In order to depart from a framework or to bend the usual rules, the creative individual must have some knowledge of convention as well as some guidelines for unconventional thinking.

Productive Thinking Program

The most famous creative training program was developed by Covington et al. in 1974 for fifth- and sixth-graders. The program consisted of a workbook in which the brother-and-sister team of Jim and Lila had to solve a series of detective stories. The reader, along with Jim and Lila, had to formulate hypotheses, gather evidence, and ask questions in order to solve the crime. If you've already read chapter 6, you'll recognize this sequence as the steps used in experimental methods of discovery. All along Jim and Lila were guided by a wise "Uncle John" who would provide hints and explain their mistakes. This program was discussed briefly in chapter 9.

One of my favorite stories concerned a missing jewel. As guests arrived at a party, they brought wrapped gifts for the wealthy hostess. Suddenly, the lights went out, and when they went on again a valuable jewel was missing. Lila and Jim had to determine what had happened to the jewel. No one could have left or entered the room as the door had remained locked. The window was opened, but there were no footsteps in the fresh snow that covered the ground. Later we learn that there is a feather on the floor and that one of the boxes has a hole in the bottom. Have you solved the crime by now? A trained pigeon was taken from a wrapped box and used to transport the jewel to an accomplice.

It takes Lila and Jim a while to find and put together the clues in order to solve this crime. Crutchfield (1966) asserted that with direct training with stories like this one, children can learn to think more creatively. The reader engages in the discovery process along with the protagonists, and may even solve the problem before Lila and Jim. A modern version of this sort of student involvement in using clues and solving problems that are embedded in realistic situations is now on interactive computer discs. For example, *The Adventures of Jasper Woodbury*, an interactive educational program that teaches mathematics and other sorts of problem-solving skills, was developed by the Technology Group at Vanderbilt University (Van Haneghan, Barron, Young, Williams, Vye, & Bransford, 1992). It includes many of the principles that are discussed in this chapter. Several other programs have recently arrived on the market or are scheduled for release in the near future. Although many of these programs are promising, potential users are urged to ask for the evidence that they actually work as promised. It is very difficult to find solid evidence that children trained with these methods actually grow up to be more creative adults or that they ever apply these skills in real-life settings. This is, of course, the real goal of any thinking skills program—use of the skills in unrelated situations. The teacher is an important variable in any program's success because it is what students are asked to do with information that is important in determining the outcome.

Other creativity-training programs have offered evidence of success. One of the more spectacular successes is attributed to a creativity-training program at Sylvania Electric Company that resulted in "double profit; 2,100 new products; increased patent applications five-fold; saved $22 million" (Edwards, 1968). Although these claims seem fantastic, we really have no idea what these figures should be compared to and therefore a more restrained enthusiasm is probably prudent.

Although any single study or method may have its limitations and qualifications, numerous experimental programs indicate that creativity can be stimulated under proper conditions. It is not an inborn gift for a lucky few. We all can become more creative. Instead of attempting to review each of the training programs, let's examine some of the strategies and methods they've used so that you can apply them in your own life in an attempt to increase your creativity.

Quantity Breeds Quality

The notion that if you have lots of ideas, some of them will be good is the major thrust of **brainstorming**. Brainstorming was discussed in chapter 9 as a way to find solution paths that solve problems. It is a creative way to generate solution paths and is often used in creative problem solving. Brainstorming is a way of producing a list of ideas that can subsequently be evaluated. Although brainstorming can be done individually, it is more commonly considered a group activity. The only rule of brainstorming is that all judgment be deferred until some later time so that no one hesitates to offer unusual or off-beat ideas. Osborn (1963) offered many examples in his book, *Applied Imagination*. For example, Osborn reported that a 15-minute brainstorming session at American Cyanamid Corporation produced 92 ideas, or more than six ideas per minute. This was an average of eight ideas per participant. Simonton (referenced in Begley, 1993) found that creative people had many more bad ideas and many more good ideas than their less creative peers because they had many more ideas overall.

The quantitative advantages of brainstorming are without question. But do more ideas necessarily imply better ones? Often, the best ideas result from the combination (synergy) and alteration of the ideas listed. The atmosphere of deferred judgment is clearly consistent with the discussion on environment presented earlier in the chapter. It encourages risk taking and unconventionality, both of which are prerequisites to creative thinking. At the very least, brainstorming is fun. It is a recommended strategy for enhancing creative thought.

Osborn had a group of parents brainstorm on how to get their children to watch less television and read more books. Read carefully through the list of ideas the parents came up with. It seems to me that some combination of these ideas would surely be effective.

1. Pull plug in TV set.
2. Break up the set.
3. Set a definite time for looking at TV.
4. Arouse interest in books.
5. Acquire a bad horizontal tube.
6. Reorient antenna in order to get bad reception.
7. Select a book that has been seen on TV.
8. Set example by reading yourself.
9. Buy a portable radio for children.
10. Evaluate TV programs.
11. Encourage visits to library.
12. Have the children write book reports.
13. Give money for movies.
14. Donate a TV to library.
15. Provide more outdoor companionship with parents.
16. As a result of seeing TV story (say Robinson Crusoe) children given same book to read and do research on.
17. Start reading aloud to them when young.
18. Read them good books.
19. Make reading as convenient as TV.
20. Give them their own bookcase in room.
21. Give records for hi-fi.
22. Give subscriptions to children's magazines.
23. Select books suitable to age.
24. Get them interested in daily newspapers, even if only the comics.
25. Help them with their homework.
26. Select type of news they read.
27. Discuss with them the books they have read.

28. Have them read to you.
29. At PTA meeting, have subject discussed with teachers; get teachers to recommend books.
30. Encourage group reading.
31. Buy them a good dictionary.
32. Always answer questions if you can.
33. Buy a good children's encyclopedia.
34. Institute games requiring the use of words and general knowledge.
35. Get local schools to have course in fast reading and good reading.
36. Have children checked physically—there may be some reason why they are unable to read.
37. In addition to their allowance, give them a fee for each good book that they read.

Creative Ideas Checklist

Another method for producing creative ideas is to present people with a checklist of diverse categories or adjectives or questions that could conceivably apply to the question or problem at hand. These lists are called **creative ideas checklists**. By forcing people to change the type of answer that they are considering, flexibility in thinking is encouraged. Doolittle (1995) found that the use of many different types of solutions is more important in creative problem solving than just having many different solutions that all involve the same category of response. In order to understand this distinction, consider a problem that involves moving A to B. There may be many different ways to move A (car, boat, roller skates), but a flexible list would include other categories of responses such as having them meet in the middle or moving B or moving both to Point C, or solving the problem without moving either A or B.

In one study of the use of lists to stimulate creative ideas, Davis and Roweton (1968) gave students the following list which was labeled "Aids in Thinking of Physical Changes":

a.   Add or Subtract Something
b.   Change Color
c.   Change the Materials
d.   Change by Rearranging the Parts
e.   Change Shape
f.   Change Size
g.   Change Design or Style

Students who were given this list were told to "List as many physical changes as you can for a thumbtack." Davis and Roweton (1968) reported that the group that had received the checklist produced a greater number of ideas and more creative ideas than a control group that had not been given the checklist. Recently, a cookie manufacturer began making "reverse" chocolate chip cookies —chocolate cookies with white chocolate chips. They have become an overnight financial and taste success. You should recognize this simply as (d) in the preceding list—a change by rearranging the parts. This simple creative act has paid well for its innovator.

Perhaps the most famous checklist is a generalized one that can be applied in a variety of situations. Whiting (1958) attributed this list to Osborn:

Put to Other Uses? New ways to use as is? Other uses if modified?

Adapt? What else is like this? What other idea does this suggest? Does past offer parallel? What could I copy? Whom could I emulate?

Modify? New twist? Change meaning, color, motion, odor, form, shape? Other changes?

Magnify? What to add? More time? Greater frequency? Stronger? Larger? Thicker? Extra value? Plus ingredient? Duplicate? Multiply? Exaggerate?

Minify? What to substitute? Smaller? Condensed? Miniature? Lower? Shorter? Lighter? Omit? Streamline? Split up? Understate?

Substitute? Who else instead? What else instead? Other ingredient? Other material? Other process? Other power? Other place? Other approach? Other tone of voice?

Rearrange? Interchange components? Other pattern? Other layout? Other sequence? Transpose cause and effect? Change pace? Change schedule?

Reverse? Transpose positive and negative? How about opponents? Turn it backward? Turn it upside down? Reverse roles? Change shoes? Turn tables? Turn other cheek?

Combine? How about a blend, an alloy, an assortment, an ensemble? Combine units? Combine purposes? Combine appeals? Combine ideas? (p. 62)

Although there are many such lists, a third one worth considering is from Parnes (1967) who suggested that you ask yourself these idea-spurring questions when you're looking for new ideas:

1. Effects on objective?
2. Individuals and/or groups affected?
3. Costs involved?
4. Tangibles involved (material, equipment, etc.)?
5. Moral or legal implications?
6. Intangibles involved (opinions, attitudes, feelings, aesthetic values, etc.)?
7. New problems caused?
8. Difficulties or implementation and follow-up?
9. Repercussions of failure?
10. Timeliness?, etc. (p. 231)

Although the purpose of creative ideas checklists is to create novel ideas, it is also possible that they could have an inhibiting effect. If you only considered the possibilities on a small checklist, you could miss other ideas by narrowing your search to ones that are suggested by the list.

We've all had the experience at one time or another of being "stuck," when ideas don't seem to flow. If you go through these checklists, pondering each item, you're bound to get your thoughts flowing again. Using the cognitive framework introduced earlier, they all provide probes for searching knowledge networks so that different sorts of information can become available for use.

Attribute Listing

In **attribute listing**, every characteristic or quality of the item or situation is listed and then examined for possible modification or recombination. Let's try an example.

Suppose you want to make something really different for dinner tonight. In fact, you want to make a food that no one else in the world has ever tasted before. How would you go about doing this? First, you could list many different foods:

which is applicable at all levels, should help to eliminate writer's block because it is a way of activating one's knowledge of the topic so that it can be used. I have used it in several college classes that I teach with good results.

Browsing

In our society we have great institutions that function as repositories for ideas. They are called libraries. Wicker (1981) suggested that we "probe library sources" to generate new ideas. Pick up newspapers and magazines, case histories and biographies, scholarly journals, joke books, and even children's literature. Use a broad range of sources. You can't make "remote associations" or borrow ideas from other fields if your own knowledge is confined to a narrow discipline.

Use qualitative and quantitative information. Census reports can suggest new problems because they succinctly state what people are doing, where they are doing it, what they are eating, how they are living, and how they are dying. Learn something new every day. If you pick up a journal at random and read one new article a day, you'll be surprised at how the newly acquired information crops up in everyday contexts. Libraries are a great source for new ideas. You can also browse with quality television shows like *Nova, 60 Minutes, and National Geographic.* They contain a wealth of fascinating information on almost any topic of interest. Don't forget to go to museums, art galleries, theater, and the opera. If you feel that you can't afford these outings, remember that many have a "free day" once a month and offer reduced rates for students, the elderly, and groups.

Visual Thinking

When Mozart was asked where he got his ideas he said, "Whence and how they come I know not; nor can I force them."

—(quoted in Vernon, 1970, p. 53)

Creative thinking often calls for images. The musician must first "hear" the sounds before she places the notes on paper; the poet must hear the rhyme before it is written; the painter must see the forms before his first brush stroke; and the chef must "taste" the combination of ingredients before the new recipe is created. It does seem that there are certain creative acts for which words are inadequate. Most people report that, at least some of the time, they think in images. An **image** is a picturelike representation in the mind. (See chapter 2 for a discussion of imagery.)

Shaw and de Mers (1986–1987) examined the relationship between imagery and creativity. They gave children three tests of creativity—the Remote Associations Test, which was described earlier, the Circles Test, which requires the individual to draw unique figures from circles, and the Just Suppose Test, in which children describe the consequences of improbable circumstances (e.g., suppose a great fog fell over the earth so that all we could see of people were their feet)—and three tests of visual imagery. They found a stronger relationship between imagery and creativity for children with high IQs than for children who score within the average range on intelligence tests. A relationship between creativity and imagery has been suggested by other researchers. The rationale behind this proposed relationship is that good imagers should be able to "see" problems in ways that should help them to generate solutions that are different from their peers who are low in the ability to create images. A suggested method for solving problems is to draw a diagram, thus transforming a verbal problem into a visual one. J. L. Adams (1979) called visual thinking an "alternative thinking language." It is an alternative to verbal-based thought. Adams suggested that we each take a drawing course to improve our ability to see and, in turn, to think creatively. He claimed that we can improve our visual thinking with practice.

Imagine the following (J. L. Adams, 1979):

1. A pot of water coming to a boil and boiling over;
2. Your Boeing 747 being towed from the terminal, taxiing to the runway, waiting for a couple of other planes, and then taking off;
3. Your running cow changing slowly into a galloping racehorse;
4. An old person you know well changing back into a teenager;
5. A speeding car colliding with a giant feather pillow;
6. The image in (5) in reverse.

It seems that how well we visualize a problem may depend on the medium in which it is presented. In a study reported in a newspaper article ("TV Linked to Memory," 1988), both imagery and memory were enhanced when children listened to stories on the radio compared to when they saw the same stories on television. Greenfield and Beagles-Roos, the psychologists who conducted this study, believe that the audio version helped students to create dynamic visual images, a process that was not enhanced in the video condition in which the children are presented with the images. It may be that Marshall McLuhan was right when he said, "The medium is the message."

Putting It All Together

Several different strategies or methods to produce creative thoughts have been presented. It would be naive to believe that if you can recite each of these methods, you will automatically have creative thoughts. They are merely guidelines for hard work, and some of us will have to work harder than others.

It is clear that creative thinking is a skill that can be cultivated (Edwards & Baldauf, 1987). The strategies presented in this chapter are the plans for developing that skill. You may be wondering, "Where do I begin?" You begin with a problem or a need. For some, creative ideas will immediately seem to flow; for others it will be more like pulling teeth. If you find yourself "out of fresh new ideas," try the techniques listed. Visualize the situation, use analogies and metaphors, consider relations, list attributes, mull checklists, and brainstorm. The creative process within you should ignite with some help from these strategies.

APPLYING THE FRAMEWORK

In applying the general thinking skills framework to decision making, consider the following questions:

1. What Is the Goal?   The creative process is defined by its outcome. The goal in thinking creatively is the production of a novel and appropriate response. Often it also involves the identification of a novel problem. The creative problem solver knows which problems are solvable and worth solving.

2. What Is Known?   A point that was made in this chapter is that one cannot be creative in a vacuum. You need the knowledge and skills of a domain to be creative.

There is no substitute for information about the problem. You may have the potential to become a truly great architect or writer, but without knowledge of these fields, it is unlikely that you will design an innovative structure or write a truly great novel. In the problem about the merchant's daughter that was told in this chapter, there would have been no creative answer if she had not used her knowledge about the dishonest money lender to watch closely when he picked up the pebbles. Similarly, a careful consideration of the particular aspects of any problem is needed for finding problems and for finding solutions. Begin the creative process by listing the "givens."

3. Which Thinking Skill or Skills Will Get You to Your Goal? This is really the question of how we can be creative. Numerous skills were suggested to guide the creative thinking process. The skill you select will depend on the nature of the problem. For example, visualizing the problem is more likely to be helpful with problems that have a spatial aspect to them, such as geometry problems or terrain problems. The skill of generating a list of topic-relevant words can be helpful in a variety of situations, but seems particularly well suited for writing and composing. Creative thinking checklists are useful in design problems; whereas "plus, minus, interesting" can be used anytime you find that you don't know how to begin finding a solution.

The following creative thinking skills were developed in this chapter. Review each skill and be sure that you understand how to use each one:

- Defining a problem in multiple ways.
- Brainstorming to increase the number of ideas produced.
- Working with people from different backgrounds in order to increase the probability of bisociative thinking.
- Considering the physical changes listed in the creative ideas checklist.
- Arranging the environment to maximize intrinsic motivation.
- Encouraging an attitude of risk taking.
- Evaluating possible solutions using the questions suggested by Parnes (1967).
- Listing and combining attributes to devise a novel product.
- Forming sentences about the problem using relational words.
- Evaluating solutions and other aspects of the problem along the dimensions of plus, minus, interesting.
- Listing terms that are related to the problem before you attempt a solution.
- Gathering additional information.
- Using analogies to make the unfamiliar known and distorting analogies to make the familiar unknown.
- Visualizing the problem.

4. Have You Reached Your Goal? Because the creative process is judged by its outcome, the solution or product will need to be evaluated along the twin dimensions of originality and appropriateness. The evaluation is also a component in the creative process. If it fails on either of these dimensions, then the thinking process will have to begin again until a creative outcome is produced.

CHAPTER SUMMARY

1. Creativity involves the dual notion of unusual or unique and good or useful. It always involves judgment, and people may not agree on which actions or outcomes deserve to be labeled "creative."

2.   DeBono has made a distinction between vertical thinking and lateral thinking. Vertical thinking is logical and straightforward, whereas lateral thinking is a creative way to think "around" a problem.

3.   An increasingly popular view in psychology is that creative individuals are not qualitatively different from the rest of us. We all have the ability to be creative.

4.   Virtually all creative acts will involve novel ways of defining a problem and the selection of relevant information.

5.   Creativity has been described as a blend of sensitivity, synergy, and serendipity. It is as if a fortuitous event brings together remote ideas in a person who is sensitive to their combination.

6.   Creativity can be understood as a cognitive process that involves using the information stored in memory to go beyond what is learned from experience. Cognitive psychologists describe the process as a spread of activation through a knowlege network with repeated cycles of generation and exploration.

7.   Although it is true that, in general, intelligent people are more creative than less intelligent people, it seems that a minimal level of intelligence is all that is needed for creative expression.

8.   Analogies are often part of the creative process in which solutions are adapted from different domains of knowledge.

9.   Creative people tend to be self-motivated, tolerant of ambiguity, and willing to take risks.

10.   Intrinsic motivation seems to be one of the best predictors of creative behavior. In order to encourage the production of creative outputs, the environment needs to support intrinsic motivation.

11.   Several strategies to foster creative thinking were presented. Brainstorming is based on the supposition that if you have many ideas some of them will be good. Each item on a checklist of creative ideas can be applied to a problem to see if a creative spark is struck. Crovitz's relational algorithm relies on changing the relations among the parts of a problem to arrive at a solution. The PMI strategy encourages novel solutions by requiring the problem solver to evaluate various aspects of the problem. Analogies and metaphors tune us in to similarities and differences that can be valuable in creating novel solutions. Visual thinking seems to be involved in many sorts of creative endeavors—especially the arts and sciences.

12.   All of the strategies to enhance creativity involve searching an individual's knowledge net so that remote ideas can be associated, analogies applied across domains of knowledge, and information that is stored in memory can become available.

TERMS TO KNOW

You should be able to define or describe the following terms and concepts. If you find that you're having difficulty with any term, be sure to reread the section in which it is discussed:

Creativity.   The act of producing something that is original and useful.
Lateral Thinking.   Thinking "around" a problem. Used to generate new ideas. Sometimes used as a synonym for creative thinking. Compare with vertical thinking.
Vertical Thinking.   Thinking that is logical and straightforward. Used in the refinement and development of ideas. Compare with lateral thinking.

Sensitivity. Responsiveness to the information we perceive through our senses, which includes "noticing" stimuli that may be critical to a creative solution.

Synergy. The bringing together of seemingly disparate parts into a useful and functioning whole. Creative thinking often seems to involve such combinations.

Bisociative Thinking. Bringing together two previously unassociated ideas or "frames of reference."

Serendipity. A happy, unexpected discovery that occurs when you don't expect it.

Geneplore. Term coined by Finke et al. (1992) to denote the cycles of generation and exploration that are part of the creative process.

Metaphor. An analogy or comparison that notes similarities between two things that are basically dissimilar.

Intrinsic Motivation. Inherent desire to engage in a task for its own sake and without regard for reward or punishment.

Extrinsic Motivation. Engaging in a task in order to receive reward or to avoid punishment.

Brainstorming. A group or individual method for generating solution paths for problems. Problem solvers are encouraged to think up wild, imaginative solutions and to defer judgment on these solutions until a later time when they may be modified or combined. The goal is to produce a large number of possible solutions.

Creative Ideas Checklists. Lists that suggest ways to generate creative ideas by varying a problem's components and relationships among the components.

Attribute Listing. A method of generating creative solutions in which every characteristic or quality of the item or situation is listed and then examined for possible modification or recombination.

Relational Algorithm. A method for generating creative ideas that relies on changing the relations among items using relational words such as *on, between, under,* and *through.*

Plus, Minus, Interesting. DeBono's (1976) plan for searching for a solution by noting positive, negative, and other interesting aspects of the solutions being considered.

Ideational Fluency. The process of generating many ideas in order to solve problems.

Bionics. The use of analogies from nature that can be adapted to human problems.

Image. A picturelike representation in the mind.

SUGGESTED READINGS

The psychological literature on creativity seems to divide into two distinct time periods. Several decades ago, there was a great deal of interest in this topic. The older literature, although dated in many ways, is still interesting to anyone who finds himself fascinated with the topic. If you're seriously interested in increasing your creative potential, Parnes et al.'s (1977) *Guide to Creative Action: Revised Edition of Creative Behavior Guidebook* contains detailed instructions for 225 hours of creativity training, complete with practice exercises, an annotated bibliography, and articles on other creativity programs. In another decades-old text, Osborn (1963) outlined the concept of brainstorming and other creativity strategies in *Applied Imagination: Principles and Procedures of Creative Problem Solving.* Another book that is filled with very good "self-help" creativity ideas is Davis and Scott's (Eds.) (1971) *Training Creative Thinking.*

The concepts of vertical and lateral thinking are developed in three books by DeBono: *The Use of Lateral Thinking* (1967), *New Think* (1968), and *Teaching Thinking*

(1991). Stein (1974, 1975) has a two-book series that comprises an excellent overall review of the topic. They are appropriately titled *Stimulating Creativity: Individual Procedures (Vol. I)* and *Stimulating Creativity: Group Procedures (Vol. II)*.

J. L. Adams' (1979) *Conceptual Blockbusting* is a very good little book on a big topic. Even if you find the area dull, you'll find this book entertaining. I also recommend J. L. Adams' (1986) book *The Care and Feeding of Ideas: A Guide to Encouraging Creativity*. If you're interested in the life-span development of creativity, Arasteh and Arasteh's (1976) *Creativity in Human Development* will fit your needs. It is divided into three sections that mirror human development—the young child, adolescence, and adult. The relevant literature for each portion of the life span is reviewed. Regretfully, old age is missing, possibly because we don't know much about creativity in old age.

There are several newer looks at creativity. For example, see Sternberg's (1988) edited book *The Nature of Creativity* and Finke et al.'s (1992) *Creative Cognition: Theory, Research, and Applications,* which take a contemporary and scholarly look at the multi-faceted creature we call creativity.

Amabile's (1989) *Growing Up Creative: Nurturing a Lifetime of Creativity* contains a wealth of information on the environmental influences that can either promote or discourage the development of creativity. One of the most recent books about creativity is Weisberg's (1993) *Creativity: Beyond the Myth of Genius*. This is his second book on the topic of creativity. It is a novel and appropriate look at creativity. The serious student of creativity will want to consult any of several books by Gardner, a psychologist who has spent much of his lifetime studying the creative process. I particularly suggest his (1982) *Art, Mind, and Brain* and his (1993) *Creating Minds: An Anatomy of Creativity Seen Through the Lives of Freud, Einstein, Picasso, Stravinsky, Eliot, Graham, and Gandhi.* (Is there a prize for longest title?) Sternberg and Lubart's (1995) *Defying the Crowd: Cultivating Creativity in a Culture of Conformity* is likely to become a classic. Among the topics it addresses are environment, motivation, and thinking styles.

A short paperback that was produced as a companion to the PBS televison series is entitled *The Creative Spirit* by Goleman, Kaufman, and Ray (1993). It has beautiful color pictures and engrossing text, but it is intended for general (i.e., not college-level) audiences. It would make a great gift for a junior or senior high school student. Finally, there is a journal that is dedicated to research and theory concerning creativity called *The Journal of Creative Behavior*.

Answers to remote associations presented earlier in the chapter: 1. Bill 2. Nail 3. Pot 4. Fly 5. Coach.

11

The Last Word

Thinking is like loving and dying: Each must do it for him (her) self.

—Anonymous

You may find that this is your favorite chapter because it is essentially a blank chapter. As you worked your way through this book, you learned information that should help you to become a better thinker. This is especially true if you also worked your way through the exercises, questions, and reviews in the Exercise Book that accompanies this text. Each chapter dealt primarily with one type of thinking category. This was necessary because a large block of information needed to be broken down so that it could be presented in manageable units. Unfortunately, thinking doesn't break into neat and separate categories and mixed sorts of skills are needed in most situations. Memory must always be accessed, the type of representation and the words we use will affect how we think, evidence always needs to be considered, thinking must be logical, and so on. As you go through life, you will need to use all of the skills that you practiced and improved upon in each of the chapters. But, most important, you need to adopt the attitudes and dispositions of a critical thinker. You need to find problems that others have missed, support conclusions with good evidence, and work persistently on a host of problems. I hope that your encounters with this book will help you become a better thinker.

This is also a good time to step back and reflect on the definition of critical thinking that was presented in the first chapter and the broad categories of information and strategies in the following chapters. Does the working definition of critical thinking seem like it captured the multiple dimensions of complexity that are inherent in critical thinking? Can you and will you use some of the information presented? Are you more likely to have a desirable outcome because of something that you learned? Have you adopted at least some of the attitudes of a critical thinker?

Although this is a nonchapter, there is a corresponding chapter in the Exercise Book that requires you to select and integrate thinking skills as you think through a variety of problems. As you work on these problems, try to put the entire text together in some way that is useful and meaningful to you. You are what and how you think. Be sure to act on your thoughts and to use them to advance yourself and to improve even a small corner of the world. Think well and with great wisdom. The future depends on it.

Reprinted with special permission of King Features Syndicate.

References

Adams, A., Carnine, D., & Gersten, R. (1982). Instructional strategies for studying content area texts in the intermediate grades. *Reading Research Quarterly, 18,* 27–55.

Adams, J. L. (1979). *Conceptual blockbusting: A guide to better ideas* (2nd ed.). New York: Norton.

Adams, J. L. (1986). *The care and feeding of ideas: A guide to encourage creativity.* Reading, MA: Addison-Wesley.

Adler, R. B., Rosenfeld, L. B., & Towne, N. (1980). *Interplay: The process of interpersonal communication.* New York: Holt, Rinehart & Winston.

Alcock, J. E. (1981). *Parapsychology: Science or magic?* Oxford, England: Pergamon.

Allegretti, C. L., & Frederick, J. N. (1995). A model for thinking critically about ethical issues. In D. F. Halpern & S. G. Nummedal (Eds.), Psychologists teach critical thinking [Special issue]. Teaching of Psychology, 22, 46–48.

Allport, G. W. (1954). *The nature of prejudice.* Cambridge, MA: Addison-Wesley.

Amabile, T. M. (1983). *The social psychology of creativity.* New York: Springer-Verlag.

Amabile, T. M. (1989). *Growing up creative: Nurturing a lifetime of creativity.* New York: Crown.

American Association of Medical Colleges. (1984). Report of the working group on fundamental skills. *Journal of Medical Education, 59,* 1.

American Psychiatric Association. (1994). *Diagnostic and statistical manual of mental disorders* (4th ed.). Washington, DC: Author.

American Psychological Association. (1992). Learner-centered psychological principles: Guidelines for school redesign and reform [Draft]. *The Psychology Teacher Network, 2,* 5–12.

Anderson, B. F. (1980). *The complete thinker: A handbook of techniques for creative and critical problem solving.* Englewood Cliffs, NJ: Prentice-Hall.

Arasteh, A. R., & Arasteh, J. D. (1976). *Creativity in human development.* New York: Schenkman.

Arkes, H. R., & Hammond, K. R. (Eds.). (1986a). *Judgment and decision making: An interdisciplinary reader.* Cambridge, MA: Cambridge University Press.

Arkes, H. R., & Hammond, K. R. (1986b). Law. In H. R. Arkes & K. R. Hammond (Eds.), *Judgment and decision making: An interdisciplinary reader* (pp. 211–212). Cambridge, MA: Cambridge University Press.

Arnheim, R. (1971). *Visual thinking.* Berkeley: University of California Press.

Asimov, I. (1989, March 31). Combatting US scientific illiteracy. *Los Angeles Times,* Part V, p. 8.

Atkinson, R. C. (1975). Mnemotechnics in second-language learning. *American Psychologist, 30,* 821–828.

Baddeley, A. D. (1986). *Working memory.* London: Oxford University Press.

Baddeley, A. D. (1992). Working memory. *Science, 255,* 556–559.

Baer, J. (1993). *Creativity and divergent thinking.* Hillsdale, NJ: Lawrence Erlbaum Associates.

Bailin, S. (1987). Creativity and skill. In D. N. Perkins, J. Lochhead, & J. Bishop (Eds.), *Thinking: The second international conference* (pp. 323–332). Hillsdale, NJ: Lawrence Erlbaum Associates.

Baron, J. (1987). An hypothesis about the training of intelligence. In D. N. Perkins, J. Lochhead, & J. Bishop (Eds.), *Thinking: The second internal conference* (pp. 60–67). Hillsdale, NJ: Lawrence Erlbaum Associates.

Baron, J. (1988). *Thinking and deciding.* New York: Cambridge University Press.

Baron, J. (1990). Harmful heuristics and the improvement of thinking. In D. Kuhn (Ed.), *Developmental perspectives on teaching and learning thinking skills* (pp. 28–47). New York: Basel, Karger.

Baron, J., & Brown, R. V. (Eds.). (1991). *Teaching decision making to adolescents.* Hillsdale, NJ: Lawrence Erlbaum Associates.

Baron, J. B., & Sternberg, R. J. (Eds.) (1987). *Teaching thinking skills: Theory and practice.* New York: Freeman.

Barron, F. (1958). The psychology of imagination. *Scientific American, 199,* 151–166.

Bartlett, F. C. (1932). *Remembering: A study in experimental and social psychology.* Cambridge, England: Cambridge University Press.

Bartlett, J. (1980). *Familiar quotations* (15th and 125th anniversary eds.). Boston: Little, Brown.

Bartlett, J. (1992) *Familiar quotations.* (17th ed.). Boston: Little, Brown.

Bauer, M. I., & Johnson-Laird, P. N. (1993). How diagrams can improve reasoning. *Psychological Science, 4,* 372–378.

Begley, S. (1993, June 28). The puzzle of genius. *Newsweek,* pp. 46–49.

Beilensen, J., & Jackson, H. (Eds.). (1992). *Voices of struggle, voices of pride.* White Plains, NY: Peter Pauper Press, Inc.

Bell, R., & Caplans, J. (1976). *Decisions, decisions: Game theory and you.* New York: Norton.

Berger, D. (1994). *Critical thinking.* Paper presented at Loma Linda Medical Center. Available from author at Claremont Graduate School, Claremont, CA.

Berger, D. (1995). Errors in judgments and decisions: Understanding our cognitive fallibilities. In P. Foster (Ed.), *Critical Thinking: Views and values in college teaching* (pp. 48–68). Riverside, CA: La Sierra University Press.

Berkowitz, L., & Thome, P. R. (1987). Pain expectation, negative affect, and angry aggression. *Motivation and Emotion, 11,* 183–193.

Berlin, B., & Kay, P. (1969). *Basic color terms: Their universality and evolution.* Berkeley: University of California Press.

Berliner, H. J. (1977). Some necessary conditions for a master chess program. In P. N. Johnson-Laird & P. C. Wason (Eds.), *Thinking: Readings in cognitive science.* Cambridge, England: Cambridge University Press.

Bernstein, D. A. (1995). A negotiation model for teaching critical thinking. In D. F. Halpern & S. G. Nummedal (Eds.), Psychologists teach critical thinking. [Special Issue]. *Teaching of Psychology, 22,* 22–24.

Beyth-Marom, R., Dekel, S., Gombo, R., & Shaked, M. (1985). *An elementary aproach to thinking under uncertainty.* Hillsdale, NJ: Lawrence Erlbaum Associates.

Block, R. A. (1985). Education and thinking skills reconsidered. *American Psychologist, 40,* 574–575.

Bloom, B. S., & Broder, L. J. (1950). *Problem solving processes of college students.* Chicago: The University of Chicago Press.

Boden, M. A. (1990). *The creative mind: Myths & mechanisms.* New York: Basic Books.

Boring, E. G. (1932). Intelligence as the tests test it. *New Republic, 35,* 35–37.

Bousfield, W. A. (1953). The occurrence of clustering in the recall of randomly arranged associates. *Journal of General Psychology, 49,* 229–240.

Bower, G. H. (1970). Organizational factors in memory. *Cognitive Psychology, 1,* 18–46.

Bower, G. H. (1972). Mental imagery and associative learning. In L. Gregg (Ed.), *Cognition in learning and memory.* New York: Wiley.

Bower, G. (1994, May 25). *Electronic communication from Marina Volkov at the Federation of Behavioral, Psychological, and Cognitive Sciences.* federation@apa.org.

Bower, G. H., & Cirilo, R. K. (1985). Cognitive psychology and text processing. In *Handbook of Discourse Analysis,* (Vol. 1, pp. 71–105). New York: Academic Press.

Bower, G. H., & Clapper, J. P. (1989). Experimental methods in cognitive science. In M. I. Posner (Ed.), *Foundations of cognitive science* (pp. 245–301). Cambridge, MA: MIT Press.

Bower, G. H., & Clark, M. C. (1969). Narrative stories as mediators for serial learning. *Psychonomic Science, 14,* 181–182.

Boxall, B. (1993, October 12). Statistics and science can be twisted to suit debate. *The Los Angeles Times,* p. A18.

Bozzell, L. B., III. (1993, July 21). Exposing statistical myths. *The Washington Times,* p. 64.

Bradbury, R. (1950). *Fahrenheit 451.* New York: Simon & Schuster.

Braine, M. D. S. (1978). On the relation between the natural logic of reasoning and standard logic. *Psychological Review, 85,* 1–21.

Bransford, D. (1979). *Human cognition: Learning, understanding and remembering.* Belmont, CA: Wadsworth.

Bransford, J. D., Arbitman-Smith, R., Stein, B. S., & Vye, N. J. (1985). Improving thinking and learning skills: An analysis of three approaches. In J. W. Segal & S. F. Chipman (Eds.), *Thinking and learning skills: Volume 1. Relating instruction to research* (pp. 133–206). Hillsdale, NJ: Lawrence Erlbaum Associates.

Bransford, J. D., & Johnson, M. K. (1972). Contextual prerequisites for understanding: Some investigations of comprehension and recall. *Journal of Verbal Learning and Verbal Behavior, 11,* 717–726.

Bransford, J. D., Sherwood, R., Vye, N., & Rieser, J. (1986). Teaching thinking and problem solving: Research foundations. *American Psychologist, 41,* 1078–1089.

Bransford, J. D., & Stein, B. S. (1993). *The ideal problem solver: A guide for improving thinking, learning, and creativity* (2nd ed.). New York: Freeman.

Brehm, J. W. (1956). Postdecision changes in the desirability of alternatives. *Journal of Abnormal and Social Psychology, 52,* 384–389.

Brennan, J. (1993b, May 20). Why polls can be poles apart. *The Los Angeles Times,* p. A5.

Brim, O. G., Jr. (1966). High and low self-estimates of intelligence. In O. G. Brim, Jr., R. S. Crutchfield, & W. H. Holtzman (Eds.), *Intelligence: Perspectives 1965.* New York: Harcourt, Brace & World.

Brody, J. E. (1988, March 30). Unresolved relationship: Breast cancer, dietary fat. *San Francisco Chronicle,* pp. 2–3.

Brooks, L. W., Simutis, Z. M., & O'Neil, H. F., Jr. (1985). The role of individual differences in learning strategies research. In R. F. Dillon (Ed.), *Individual differences in cognition* (Vol. 2, pp 219–251). New York: Academic Press.

Bross, I. D. J. (1973). Languages in cancer research. In G. P. Murphy, D. Pressman, & E. A. Mirand (Eds.), *Perspectives in cancer research and treatment* (pp. 213–221), New York: Alan R. Liss.

Brown, R. (1958). *Words and things.* New York: The Free Press.

Brown, A. L., & Campione, J. C. (1990). Communities of learning and thinking or a context by any other name. In D. Kuhn (Ed.), *Developmental perspectives on teaching and learning thinking skills. Contributions to human development* (Vol. 21, pp. 108–126). Basel, Switzerland: Karger.

Brown, S., & Walter, M. (1993). *Problem posing: Reflections and applications.* Hillsdale, NJ: Lawrence Erlbaum Associates.

Bruer, J. T. (1993). *Schools for thought.* Cambridge, MA: MIT Press.

Bruner, J. S. (1957). On going beyond the information given. In *Contemporary approaches to cognition* (pp. 41–69). Cambridge, MA: Harvard University Press.

Bruner, J. S., Goodnow, J. J., & Austin, G. A. (1956). *A study of thinking.* New York: Wiley.

Bugliosi, V. (1978). *Till death do us part.* New York: Bantam Books.

Burke, D. M., MacKay, D. G., Worthley, J. S., & Wade, E. (1991). On the tip of the tongue: What causes word finding failures in young and older adults? *Journal of Memory and Language, 30,* 542–579.

Byrne, R. (1988). *One thousand nine hundred eleven best things anybody ever said.* New York: Fawcett.

Campbell, S. K. (1974). *Flaws and fallacies in statistical thinking.* Englewood Cliffs, NJ: Prentice-Hall.

Carey, J., Foltz, K., & Allan, R. A. (1983, February 7). The mind of the machine. *Newsweek.*

Carkhuff, R. R. (1973). *The art of problem solving.* Amherst, MA: Human Resource Development Press.

Carlson, E. (1995). Evaluating the credibility of sources: A missing link in the teaching of critical thinking. In D. F. Halpern & S. G. Nummedal (Eds.), Psychologists teach critical thinking [Special issue]. *Teaching of Psychology, 22,* 39–41.

Carpenter, E. J. (1981). Piagetian interviews of college students. In R. G. Fuller et al. (Eds.), *Piagetian programs in higher education* (pp. 15–22). Lincoln: University of Nebraska Press.

Carroll, D. W. (1986). *Psychology of language.* Belmont, CA: Brooks/Cole.

Carroll, L. (1971). *Through the looking glass.* London: Oxford University Press. (Original work published 1872)

Cassel, J. F., & Congleton, R. J. (1993). *Critical thinking: An annotated bibliography.* Metuchen, NJ: Scarecrow Press.

Ceci, S. J., & Ruiz, A. I. (1993). Inserting context into our thinking about thinking: Implications for a theory of everyday intelligent behavior. In M. Rabinowitz (Ed.), *Cognitive science foundations of instruction* (pp. 173–188). Hillsdale, NJ: Lawrence Erlbaum Associates.

Ceraso, J., & Protivera, A. (1971). Sources of error in syllogistic reasoning. *Cognitive Psychology, 2,* 400–410.

Champagne, A. B. (1992). Cognitive research on thinking in academic science and mathematics: Implications for practice and policy. In D. F. Halpern (Ed.), *Enhancing thinking skills in the sciences and mathematics* (pp. 117–134). Hillsdale, NJ: Lawrence Erlbaum Associates.

Chance, P. (1986). *Thinking in the classroom: A survey of programs.* New York: Teachers College Press.

Chang, J. (1993). *Wild swans: Three daughters of China.* New York: HarperCollins.

Chapman, L. J., & Chapman, J. P. (1959). Atmosphere effect reexamined. *Journal of Experimental Psychology, 58,* 220–226.

Chapman, L. J., & Chapman, J. P. (1967). The genesis of popular but erroneous psychodiagnostic observations. *Journal of Abnormal Psychology, 72,* 193–204.

Chapman, L. J., & Chapman, J. P. (1969). Illusory correlation as an obstacle to the use of valid psychodiagnostic signs. *Journal of Abnormal Psychology, 74,* 271–280.

Cheng, P. W., & Holyoak, K. J. (1985). Pragmatic reasoning schemas. *Cognitive Psychology, 17,* 391–416.

Chesler, P. (1972). *Women and madness.* New York: Doubleday.

Chi, M. T. H., Glaser, R., & Farr, M. J. (Eds.). (1988). *The nature of expertise.* Hillsdale, NJ: Lawrence Erlbaum Associates.

Cialdini, R. B. (1993). *Influence: Science and practice* (3rd ed.). Glenview, IL: Scott, Foresman.

Clark, H. H., & Clark, E. V. (1977). *Psychology and language: An introduction to psycholinguistics.* New York: Harcourt Brace.

Clark, H. H., & Haviland, S. E. (1977). Comprehension and the given-new contract. In R. O. Freedle (Ed.), *Discourse production and comprehension.* Norwood, NJ: Ablex.

Clarkson-Smith, L., & Halpern, D. F. (1983). Can age related deficits in spatial memory be attenuated through the use of verbal coding? *Experimental Aging Research, 9,* 179–184.

Clinton's message to USA's students: Learn to earn. (1994, February 24). USA Today International Edition, p. 6A.

The Cognition and Technology Group at Vanderbilt. (1993). Toward integrated curricula: Possibilities from anchored instruction. In M. Rabinowitz (Ed.), *Cognitive science foundations of instruction* (pp. 33–56). Hillsdale, NJ: Lawrence Erlbaum Associates.

Cohen, G. (1989). *Memory in the real world.* Hillsdale, NJ: Lawrence Erlbaum Associates.

Collins, A. F., Gathercole, S. E., Conway, M. A., & Morris, P. E. (Eds.). (1993). *Theories of memory.* Hillsdale, NJ: Lawrence Erlbaum Associates.

Collins, C., & Mangieri, J. N. (Eds.). (1992). *Teaching thinking: An agenda for the 21st century.* Hillsdale, NJ: Lawrence Erlbaum Associates.

Copi, I. M. (1986). *Informal logic.* New York: Macmillan.

Cordes, C. (1983, April). Search goes on for "best" ways to learn science. *American Psychological Association Monitor,* pp. 7–8.

Coughlin, E. K. (1993, November 10). When people make up their minds, psychologist says, they often do not really make up their minds at all. *The Chronicle of Higher Education,* pp. A9, A15.

Covington, M. V. (1987). Instruction in problem solving and planning. In S. L. Friedman, E. K. Scholnick, & R. R. Cocking (Eds.), *Blueprints for thinking: The role of planning in cognitive development* (pp. 469–511). Cambridge, MA: Cambridge University Press.

Covington, M. V., Crutchfield, R. S., Davies, L. B., & Olton, R. M., Jr. (1974). *The productive thinking program.* Columbus, OH: Charles E. Merrill.

Craik, F. I. M., & Salthouse, T. A. (Eds.). (1992). *The handbook of aging and cognition.* Hillsdale, NJ: Lawrence Erlbaum Associates.

Crovitz, H. F. (1970). *Galton's walk: Methods for the analysis of thinking, intelligence and creativity.* New York: Harper & Row.

Crutchfield, R. S. (1966). Creative thinking in children: Its teaching and testing. In O. G. Brim, Jr., R. S. Crutchfield, & W. H. Holtzman (Eds.), *Intelligence: Perspectives 1965, The Terman-Otis Memorial Lectures.* New York: Harcourt, Brace & World.

Dahlstrom, G. W. (1993). Tests: Small samples, large consequences. *American Psychologist, 48*(4), 393–399.

Damer, T. E. (1987). *Attacking faulty reasoning* (2nd ed.). Belmont, CA: Wadsworth.

d'Angelo, E. (1971). *The teaching of critical thinking.* Amsterdam: Gruner.

Davis, G. A., & Roweton, W. (1968). Using idea checklists with college students: Overcoming resistance. *Journal of Psychology, 70,* 221–226.

Davis, G. A., & Scott, J. A. (Eds.). (1971). *Training creative thinking.* New York: Holt, Rinehart & Winston.

Dawes, R. M. (1979). The robust beauty of improper linear models in decision making. *American Psychologist, 34,* 571–582.

Dawes, R. M. (1988). *Rational choice in an uncertain world.* New York: Harcourt, Brace, Jovanovich.

Dawes, R. M. (1989). Experience and validity of clinical judgment: The illusory correlation. *Behavioral Sciences and the Law, 7,* 457–467.

Dawes, R. M. (1993, June 9). Finding guidelines for tough decisions. *The Chronicle of Higher Education,* p. A40.

Dawes, R. M. (1994). *House of cards: Psychology and psychotherapy built on myth.* New York: The Free Press.

Day, R. S., Rodin, G. C., & Stoltzfus, E. R. (1990, March 31). *Alternative representations for medication instructions: Effects on young and old adults.* Paper presented at the 3rd Cognitive Aging Conference, Atlanta.

DeBono, E. (1967). *The use of lateral thinking.* London: Ebenezer Bayles and Son, Limited.

DeBono, E. (1968). *New think: The use of lateral thinking in the generation of new ideas.* New York: Basic Books.

DeBono, E. (1976). *Teaching thinking.* London: Temple Smith.

DeBono, E. (1977). Information processing and new ideas—lateral and vertical thinking. In S. J. Parnes, R. B. Noller, & A. M. Biondi (Eds.), *Guide to creative action: Revised edition of creative behavior guidebook.* New York: Scribner's.

DeBono, E. (1991). *Teaching thinking.* London: Penguin.

Decyk, B. N. (1994). Using examples to teach concepts. In D. F. Halpern (Ed.), *Changing college classrooms: New teaching and learning strategies for an increasingly complex world* (pp. 39–63). San Francisco: Jossey-Bass.

deGroot, A. A. (1983). Heuristics, mental programs, and intelligence. In R. Groner, M. Groner, & W. F. Bischof (Eds.), *Methods of heuristics* (pp. 109–129). Hillsdale, NJ: Lawrence Erlbaum Associates.

deGroot, A. D. (1966). Perception and memory versus thought: Some old ideas and recent findings. In B. Kleinmuntz (Ed.), *Problem solving: Research, method and theory.* New York: Wiley.

De Lopez, R. S. (1992, June 16). Promote thinking, say university leaders. *The News,* Mexico City, p. B4.

Dember, W. N., Jenkins, J. J., & Teyler, T. (1984). *General psychology* (2nd ed.). Hillsdale, NJ: Lawrence Erlbaum Associates.

Derry, S., Levin, J. R., & Schauble, L. (1995). Stimulating statistical thinking through situated simulations. In D. F. Halpern & S. G. Nummedal (Eds.), *Psychologists teach critical thinking* [Special issue]. *Teaching of Psychology, 22,* 51–57.

Dewey, J. (1933). *How we think: A restatement of the relation of reflective thinking to the educative process.* Boston: Heath.

Doolittle, J. H. (1995). Using riddles and interactive computer games to teach problem solving. In D. F. Halpern & S. G. Nummedal (Eds.), *Psychologists teach critical thinking* [Special Issue]. *Teaching of Psychology, 22,* 33–36.

Dorner, D. (1983). Heuristics and cognition in complex systems. In R. Groner, M. Groner, & W. F. Bischof (Eds.), *Methods of heuristics* (pp. 89–107). Hillsdale, NJ: Lawrence Erlbaum Associates.

Dreman, D. (1979). *Contrarian investment strategy: The psychology of the stock market success.* New York: Random House.

Duncan, C. P. (1961). Attempts to influence performance on an insight problem. *Psychological Reports, 9,* 35–42.

Duncker, K. (1945). On problem solving. *Psychological Monographs* (Whole No. 270).

Eagly, A., & Chaiken, S. (1993). *The psychology of attitudes.* New York: Harcourt Brace.

Edwards, J., & Baldauf, B., Jr. (1987). The effects of the CORT-1 thinking skills program on students. In D. N. Perkins, J. Lockhead, & J. Bishop (Eds.), *Thinking: The second international conference* (pp. 453–473). Hillsdale, NJ: Lawrence Erlbaum Associates.

Ekman, P. (1992). *Telling lies: Clues to deceit in the marketplace, politics and marriage.* New York: Norton.

Evans, J. St. B. T. (1989). *Bias in human reasoning: Causes and consequences.* Hillsdale, NJ: Lawrence Erlbaum Associates.

Evans, J. St. B. T., & Newstead, S. E. (1993). *Human reasoning: The psychology of deduction.* Hillsdale, NJ: Lawrence Erlbaum Associates.

Eylon, B., & Linn, M. C. (1988, Fall). Learning and instruction: An examination of four research perspectives in science education. *Review of Educational Research*, pp. 251–301.

Facione, P. (1991, August). *Teaching college-level critical thinking skills.* Paper presented at the 11th Annual International Conference on Critical Thinking and Educational Reform, Sonoma, CA.

Ferguson, G. (1981). Architecture. In N. L. Smith (Ed.), *Metaphors for evaluation: Sources of new methods.* Beverly Hills, CA: Sage.

Festinger, L. (Ed.). (1964). *Conflict, decision and dissonance.* Palo Alto, CA: Stanford University Press.

Festinger, L., Riecken, H. W., & Schacter, S. (1956). *When prophecy fails.* Minneapolis: University of Minnesota Press.

Feyerabend, P. (1975). *Against method.* London: Verso.

Feynman, R. (1989). *What do you care what other people think?* New York: Bantam.

Finke, R. A., Ward, T. B., & Smith, S. M. (1992). *Creative cognition: Theory, research, and applications.* Cambridge, MA: Bradford.

Fischer, G. W., & Johnson, E. J. (1986). Behavioral decision theory and political decision making. In R. R. Lau & D. O. Sears (Eds.), *The 19th Annual Carnegie Symposium on Cognition: Political Cognition* (pp. 55–65). Hillsdale, NJ: Lawrence Erlbaum Associates.

Fischoff, B. (1975). Hindsight ≠ foresight: The effect of outcome knowledge on judgment under uncertainty. *Journal of Experimental Psychology: Human Perception and Performance, 1,* 288–299.

Fischhoff, B. (1993, March/April). Controversies over risk: Psychological perspective on competence. *Psychological Science Agenda, 6,* 8–9.

Fischoff, B., Lichtenstein, S., Slovic, P., Derby, S. L., & Keeney, R. L. (1981). *Acceptable risk.* Cambridge, England: Cambridge University Press.

Fisher, R., & Ury, W. (1991). *Getting to "yes": Negotiating agreement without giving in (2nd ed.).* New York: Penguin.

Fiske, S. T. (1993). Controlling other people: The impact of power on stereotyping. *American Psychologist, 48,* 621–628.

Fiske, S. T., & Taylor, S. E. (1984). *Social cognition.* New York: Random House.

Fixx, J. F. (1978). *Solve it.* New York: Doubleday.

Flesch, R. (1951). *The art of clear thinking.* New York: Harper & Row.

Fogelin, R. J. (1987). *Understanding arguments, an introduction to informal logic* (3rd ed.). New York: Harcourt Brace.

Fong, G. T., Krantz, D., & Nisbett, R. E. (1986). The effects of statistical training on thinking about everyday problems. *Cognitive Psychology, 18,* 253–292.

Fong, G. T., & Nisbett, R. E. (1991). Immediate and delayed transfer of training effects in statistical reasoning. *Journal of Experimental Psychology: Human Learning and Cognition, 120,* 34–45.

Footnotes. (1994, April 20). *The Chronicle of Higher Education.*

Fox, L. S., Marsh, G., & Crandall, Jr., J. C. (1983, April 30). *The effect of college classroom experiences on formal operational thinking.* Paper presented at the 1983 Annual Convention of the Western Psychological Association, San Francisco.

Frammolino, R. (1993, December 17). Most college GEDs fail simple tests, study finds. *The Los Angeles Times,* pp. A41, A43.

Frazier, K. (Ed.). (1991). *The hundredth monkey and other paradigms of the paranormal.* Buffalo, NY: Prometheus.

Friedman, S. L., Scholnick, E. K., & Cocking, R. R. (Eds.). (1987). *Blueprints for thinking: The role of planning in cognitive development.* Cambridge, MA: Cambridge University Press.

Fruzzetti, A. E., Toland, K., Teller, S. A., & Loftus, E. A. (1992). Memory and eyewitness testimony. In M. M. Gruneberg and P. E. Morris (Eds.), *Aspects of memory: The practical aspects (Vol. 1)* 2nd ed. New York: Routledge.

Gardner, H. (1982). *Art, mind and brain: A cognitive approach to creativity.* New York: Basic Books.

Gardner, H. (1983). *Frames of mind: The theory of multiple intelligences.* New York: Basic Books.

Gardner, H. (1985). *The mind's new science: A history of the cognitive revolution.* New York: Basic Books.

Gardner, H. (1989). *To open minds.* New York: Basic Books.

Gardner, H. (1993). *Creating minds: An anatomy of creativity seen through the lives of Freud, Einstein, Picasso, Stravinsky, Eliot, Graham, and Gandhi.* New York: Basic Books.

Garfield, J., & Ahlgren, A. (1988). Difficulties in learning basic concepts in probability and statistics: Implications for research. *Journal for Research in Mathematics Education, 19*(1), 44–63.

Garnham, A., & Oakhill, J. (1994). *Thinking and reasoning.* Oxford, England: Blackwell.

Geiselman, R. E., & Fisher, R. P. (1985, December). Interviewing victims and witnesses of crime. *Research in Brief, National Institute of Justice,* 1–4.

Gentner, D., & Gentner, D. R. (1983). Flowing water or teeming crowds: Mental models of electricity. In D. Gentner & A. L. Stevens (Eds.), *Mental models.* Hillsdale, NJ: Lawrence Erlbaum Associates.

Gerbner, G., Grass, L., Morgan, M., & Signorielli, N. (1980). *Violence profile No. 11: Trends in network television drama and viewer conceptions of social reality.* Philadelphia: Annennberg School of Communication.

Gick, M. L., & Holyoak, K. J. (1980). Analogical problem solving. *Cognitive Psychology, 12,* 306–355.

Gifford-Jones, W. (1977). *What every woman should know about hysterectomy.* New York: Funk & Wagnalls.

Gilbreth, F. B. (1963). *Cheaper by the dozen.* New York: Crowell.

Gilhooly, K. J. (1987). Mental modeling: A framework for the study of thinking. In D. N. Perkins, J. Lochhead, & J. Bishop (Eds.), *Thinking: The second international conference* (pp. 19–32). Hillsdale, NJ: Lawrence Erlbaum Associates.

Gillette, R. (1987, December 4). Exotic ways to learn doubted by U.S. study. *The Wall Street Journal,* pp. 1, 32.

Gilovich, T. (1991). *How we know what isn't so: The fallibility of human reason in everyday life.* New York: Macmillan.

Glaser, R. (1984). Education and thinking: The role of knowledge. *American Psychologist, 39,* 93–104.

Glaser, R. (1992). Expert knowledge and processes of thinking. In D. F. Halpern (Ed.), *Enhancing thinking skills in the sciences and mathematics* (pp. 63–76). Hillsdale, NJ: Lawrence Erlbaum Associates.

Glucksberg, S., & Weisberg, R. W. (1966). Verbal behavior and problem solving: Some effects of labeling in a functional fixedness problem. *Journal of Experimental Psychology, 71,* 659–664.

Goleman, D., Kaufman, P., & Ray, M. (1993). *The creative spirit.* New York: Penguin.

Gordon, W. J. J. (1961). *Synectics.* New York: Harper & Row.

Gordon, W. J. J. (1976). Metaphor and invention. In A. Rothenberg & C. R. Hausman (Eds.), *The creativity question.* Durham, NC: Duke University Press.

Govier, T. (1985). *A practical study of argument.* Belmont, CA: Wadsworth.

Gray, W. (1991). *Thinking critically about new age ideas.* Belmont, CA: Wadsworth.

Greeno, J. G. (1973). The structure of memory and the process of solving problems. In R. L. Solso (Ed.), *Contemporary issues in cognitive psychology.* Washington DC: Winston.

Greeno, J. G. (1992). Mathematical and scientific thinking in classrooms and other situations. In D. F. Halpern (Ed.), *Enhancing thinking skills in the sciences and mathematics* (pp. 39–62). Hillsdale, NJ: Lawrence Erlbaum Associates.

Griffiths, D. H. (1976). Physics teaching: Does it hinder intellectual development? *American Journal of Physics, 44,* 81–85.

Gruneberg, M., & Morris, P. (Eds.), (1992). *Aspects of memory; The practical aspects. (Vol. 1)* 2nd. ed. New York: Routledge.

Guilford, J. P. (1977). *Way beyond the IQ.* Buffalo, NY: Creative Education Foundation.

Gunther, M. (1977). *The luck factor.* New York: Macmillan.

Hadamard, J. (1954). *The psychology of invention in the mathematical field.* Princeton, NJ: Princeton University Press.

Hains, A. A., & Hains, A. H. (1987). The effects of a cognitive strategy intervention on the problem solving abilities of delinquent youths. *Journal of Adolescence, 10,* 399–413.

Halpern, D. F. (1985). The influence of sex role stereotypes on prose recall. *Sex Roles, 12,* 363–375.

Halpern, D. F. (1987a). Analogies as a critical thinking skill. In D. Berger, K. Peydek, & W. Banks (Eds.), *Applications of cognitive psychology: Computing and education* (pp. 75–86). Hillsdale, NJ: Lawrence Erlbaum Associates.

Halpern, D. F. (1987b). Thinking across the disciplines: Methods and strategies to promote higher-order thinking in every classroom. In M. Heiman & J. Slomianko (Eds.), *Thinking skills instruction: Concepts and techniques* (pp. 69–76). Washington, DC: National Education Association.

Halpern, D. F. (1992). *Sex differences in cognitive abilities* (2nd ed.). Hillsdale, NJ: Lawrence Erlbaum Associates.

Halpern, D. F. (Ed.). (1994). *Changing college classrooms: New teaching and learning strategies for an increasingly complex world.* San Francisco: Jossey-Bass.

Halpern, D. F. (in press). The skewed logic of *The Bell Curve. Skeptic.*

Halpern, D. F., & Blackman, S. (1985). Magazines vs. physicians. The influence of information source on intentions to use oral contraceptives. *Women and Health, 10,* 9–23.

Halpern, D. F., Blackman, S., & Salzman, B. (1989). Using statistical risk information to assess oral contraceptive safety. *Applied Cognitive Psychology, 3,* 251–260.

Halpern, D. F., Hansen, C., & Riefer, D. (1990). Analogies as an aid to comprehension and memory. *Journal of Educational Psychology, 82,* 298–305.

Halpern, D. F., & Irwin, F. W. (1973). Selection of hypotheses as affected by their preference values. *Journal of Experimental Psychology, 101,* 105–108.

Halpern, D. F., & Nummedal, S. G. (Eds.). (1995). Psychologists teach critical thinking [Special Issue]. *Teaching of Psychology, 22.*

Hanson, N. R. (1958). *Patterns of discovery.* Cambridge, England: Cambridge University Press.

Harman, G. (1986). *Change in view: Principles of reasoning.* Cambridge, MA: MIT Press.

Harris, R. J. (1977). Comprehension and pragmatic implications in advertising. *Journal of Applied Psychology, 62,* 603–608.

Harris, S. B. (1993). The resurrection myth in religion, science, and science fiction. *Skeptic, 2,* 50–59.

Hasher, L., & Zacks, R. T. (1984). Automatic processing of fundamental information. *American Psychologist, 39,* 1372–1388.

Hayes, J. R. (1978). *Cognitive psychology.* Homewood, IL: Dorsey.

Hayes, J. R. (1982). Issues in protocol analysis. In G. R. Ungson & D. N. Braunstein (Eds.), *Decision making: An interdisciplinary approach.* Boston: Kent.

Hayes, J. R. (1989). Cognitive processes in creativity. In J. A. Glover, R. R. Ronning, & C. R. Reynolds (Eds.), *Handbook of creativity* (pp. 135–145). New York: Plenum.

Heiman, M., & Slomianko, J. (1986). *Critical thinking skills.* Washington, DC: National Education Association.

Heller, R., Saltzstein, H. D., & Caspe, W. (1992). Heuristics in medical and non-medical decision-making. *The Quarterly Journal of Experimental Psychology*, pp. 211–235.

Henle, M. (1962). On the relation between logic and thinking. *Psychological Review, 69*, 366–378.

Hennessey, B. A., & Amabile, T. M. (1987). *Creativity and learning*. Washington, DC: National Education Association.

Hennessey, B. A. & Amabile, T. M. (1988). The conditions of creativity. In R. J. Sternberg (Ed.), *The nature of creativity: Contemporary psychological perspectives* (pp. 11–38). Cambridge, MA: Cambridge University Press.

Herrmann, D. J. (1991). *Super memory*. Emmaus, PA: Rodale.

Herrmann, D. J., Weingartner, H., Searleman, A., & McEvoy, C. L. (Eds.). (1992). *Memory improvement: Implications for memory theory*. New York: Springer-Verlag.

Herrnstein, R. J., & Murray, C. (1994). *The bell curve: Intelligence and class structure in American life*. New York: The Free Press.

Herrnstein, R. J., Nickerson, R. S., de Sanchez, M., & Swets, J. A. (1986). Teaching thinking skills. *American Psychologist, 41*, 1279–1289.

Hill, P., Bedau, H., Checile, R., Crochetiere, W., Kellerman, B., Dunjian, D., Pauker, S., & Rubin, J. (1979). *Making decisions: A multidisciplinary introduction*. Reading, MA: Addison-Wesley.

Hitchcock, D. (1983). *Critical thinking: A guide to evaluating information*. Toronto: Methuen.

Hogarth, R. M. (1988). *Judgment and choice: The psychology of decision* (2nd ed.). Chichester, England: Wiley.

Holland, J. H., Holyoak, K. J., Nisbett, R. E., & Thagard, P. R. (1986). *Induction: Processes of inference, learning, and discovery*. Cambridge, MA: MIT Press.

Holley, C. D., & Dansereau, D. F. (1984). Networking: The technique and the empirical evidence. In C. D. Holley & D. F. Dansereau (Eds.), *Spatial learning strategies: Techniques, applications, and related issues* (pp. 81–108). New York: Academic Press.

Holley, C. D., Dansereau, D. F., McDonald, B. A., Garland, J. D., & Collins, K. W. (1979). Evaluation of a hierarchical mapping technique as an aid to prose processing. *Contemporary Educational Psychology, 4*, 227–237.

Holt, J. (1964). *How children fail*. New York: Dell.

Holt, J. (1989). *Learning all the time*. Reading, MA: Addison-Wesley.

Hostetler, A. J. (1988, January). Army eyes novel learning methods. *The American Psychological Association Monitor, 19*, 7.

Huff, D. (1954). *How to lie with statistics*. New York: Norton.

Hunt, E. (1989). Cognitive science: Definition, status, and questions. In M. R. Rosenzweig & L. W. Porter (Eds.), *Annual review of psychology, 40*, 603–630.

Hunt, M. (1982). *The universe within: A new science explores the human mind*. New York: Simon & Schuster.

Hutchings, P. (1986). Some late night thoughts on teaching creativity. *American Association for Higher Educaion, 39*, 9–14.

Izawa, C. (1993). Efficient learning: The total time, exposure duration, frequency, and programming of the study phase. In C. Izawa (Ed.), *Cognitive psychology applied* (pp. 43–78). Hillsdale, NJ: Lawrence Erlbaum Associates.

Izawa, C., & Hayden, R. G. (1993). Race against time: Toward the principle of optimization in learning and retention. In C. Izawa (Ed.), *Cognitive psychology applied* (pp. 15–42). Hillsdale, NJ: Lawrence Erlbaum Associates.

Jacoby, L. L., Kelley, C. M., & Dywan, J. (1989). Memory attributions. In H. L. Roedinger III & F. I. M. Craik (Eds.), *Varietes of memory and consciousness: Essays in honor of Endel Tulving* (pp. 391–422). Hillsdale, NJ: Lawrence Erlbaum Associates.

James, W. (1890). *The principles of psychology*. New York: Holt.

Janis, I. L. (1989). *Crucial decisions: Leadership in policymaking and crisis management*. New York: The Free Press.

Janis, I. L., & Mann, L. (1977). *Decision making: A psychological analysis of conflict, choice and commitment*. New York: The Free Press.

Jason, G. (1987). Are fallacies common? A look at two debates. *Informal Logic, 8*, 81–92.

Jensen, A. R. (1980). *Bias in mental testing*. New York: The Free Press.

Jensen, A. R. (1981). *Straight talk about mental tests*. New York: The Free Press.

Johnson, M. K., & Raye, C. L. (1981). Reality monitoring. *Psychological Review, 88*, 67–85.

Johnson-Laird, P. N., & Byrne, R. M. J. (1991). *Deduction*. Hillsdale, NJ: Lawrence Erlbaum Associates.

Johnson-Laird, P. N., Legrenzi, P., & Legrenzi, M. (1972). Reasoning and a sense of reality. *British Journal of Psychology, 63*, 395–400.

Johnson-Laird, P. N., & Wason, P. C. (1970). A theoretical analysis of insight into a reasoning task. *Cognitive Psychology, 1*, 134–148.

Johnson-Laird, P. N., & Wason, P. C. (Eds.). (1977). *Thinking: Readings in cognitive science*. Cambridge, England: Cambridge University Press.

Kahane, H. (1980). *Logic and contemporary rhetoric: The use of reason in everyday life* (2nd ed.). Belmont, CA: Wadsworth.

Kahane, H. (1992). *Logic and contemporary rhetoric: The use of reason in everyday life* (6th ed.). Belmont, CA: Wadsworth.

Kahneman, D., & Tversky, A. (1973). On the psychology of prediction. *Psychological Review, 80*, 237–251.

Kahneman, D., & Tversky, A. (1979). Prospect theory: An analysis of decision under risk. *Econometrica, 47,* 263–291.

Kamin, L. J. (1974). *The science and politics of I.Q.* New York: Wiley.

Kavanaugh, D. J., & Bower, G. H. (1985). Mood and self-efficacy: Impact of joy and sadness on perceived capabilities. *Cognitive Therapy & Research, 9,* 507–525.

Kelley, D. (1988). *The art of reasoning.* New York: Norton.

Kellogg, R. T. (1990, Fall). Effectiveness of prewriting strategies as a function of task demands. *American Journal of Psychology,* pp. 327–342.

Kidd, V. (1991, Fall). An analysis of the California tobacco education campaign's visual anti-smoking messages. *Feedback, 32,* 14–18.

Kimble, G. A. (1978). *How to use (and misuse) statistics.* Englewood Cliffs, NJ: Prentice-Hall.

King, A. (1989). Effects of self-questioning training on college students' comprehension of lectures. *Contemporary Educational Psychology, 14,* 1–16.

King, A. (1992). Facilitating elaborative learning through guided student-generated questioning. *Educational Psychologist,* pp. 111–126.

King, A. (1994). Inquiry as a tool in critical thinking. In D. F. Halpern (Ed.), *Changing college classrooms: New teaching and learning stratagies in an increasingly complex world* (pp. 13–38). San Francisco: Jossey-Bass.

King, A. (1995). Inquiring minds really do want to know: Using questioning to teach critical thinking. In D. F. Halpern & S. G. Nummedal (Eds.), Psychologists teach critical thinking [Special issue]. *Teaching of Psychology, 22,* 13–17.

Klaczynski, P. A. (1993). Reasoning schema effects on adolescent rule acquisition and transfer. *Journal of Educational Psychology, 85,* 679–692.

Klein, G. A., & Weizenfeld, J. (1978). Improvement of skills for solving ill-defined problems. *Educational Psychologist, 13,* 31–41.

Kneller, G. F. (1965). *The art and science of creativity.* New York: Holt, Rinehart & Winston.

Knight, K., & Dansereau, D. F. (1992). Tools for drug and alcohol education: Using decision worksheets in personal problem solving. *Journal of Drug Education, 22*(3), 261–271.

Koestler, A. (1964). *The act of creation.* London: Hutchinson.

Kohl, H. (1981). *A book of puzzlements: Play and invention with language.* New York: Schocken Books.

Kohler, W. (1925). *The mentality of apes.* New York: Harcourt, Brace.

Kohler, W. (1969). *The task of Gestalt psychology.* Princeton, NJ: Princeton University Press.

Koriat, A., Lichtenstein, S., & Fischhoff, B. (1980). Reasons for confidence. *Journal of Experimental Psychology. Human Learning and Memory, 6,* 107–118.

Kruglanski, A. W. (1992). On methods of good judgment and good methods of judgment: Political decisions and the art of the possible. *Political Psychology, 13,* 455–475.

Kuhn, D. (1993, January). Connecting scientific and informal reasoning. *Merrill–Palmer Quarterly,* pp. 74–103.

Kuhn, D., Weinstock, M., & Flaton, R. (1994). How well do jurors reason? Competence dimensions of individual variation in a juror reasoning task. *Psychological Science, 5,* 289–296.

Kunda, Z., & Nisbett, R. E. (1986). The psychometrics of everyday life. *Cognitive Psychology, 18,* 195–224.

Langer, E. J. (1989). *Mindfulness.* Reading, MA: Addison-Wesley.

Langer, E. (1994, July). *Improving the quality of thinking in a changing world.* Paper presented at the Sixth International Conference on Thinking, Cambridge, MA.

Langer, E. J., Blank, A., & Chanowitz, B. (1978). The mindlessness of ostensibly thoughtful action: The role of "placebic" information in interpersonal interaction. *Journal of Personality and Social Psychology, 36,* 635–642.

Langley, P., Simon, H. A., Bradshaw, G. L., & Zytkow, J. M. (1987). *Scientific discovery: Computational explorations of the creative process.* Cambridge, MA: MIT Press.

Langrehr, S. (1990) *Sharing thinking strategies.* Bloomington, IN: National Educational Service.

Larrick, R. P., Morgan, J. N., & Nisbett, R. E. (1990). Teaching the use of cost-benefit reasoning in everyday life. *Psychological Science, 1,* 362–370.

Lee, A. M. (1953). *How to understand propaganda.* New York: Holt, Rinehart & Company.

Leedy, P. D. (1981). *How to read research and understand it.* New York: Macmillan.

Lehman, D. R., Lempert, R. O., & Nisbett, R. E. (1988). The effects of graduate training on reasoning: Formal discipline and thinking about everyday-life events. *American Psychologist,* pp. 431–442.

Lehman, D. R., & Nisbett, R. E. (1990). A longitudinal study of the effects of undergraduate training on reasoning. *Developmental Psychology, 26,* 431–442.

Leive, C. (1994, April). Miss America. *Glamour,* pp. 234–237, 275–281.

Levi, D. S. (1991). *Critical thinking and logic.* Salem, WI: Sheffield.

Levine, M. (1994). *Effective problem solving* (2nd ed.) Englewood Cliffs, NJ: Prentice-Hall.

Lewis, A. B., & Mayer, R. E. (1987). Students' miscomprehension of relational statements in arithmetic word problems. *Journal of Educational Psychology, 79,* 363–371.

Lichtenstein, S., Slovic, P., Fischoff, B., Layman, M., & Combs, B. (1978). Judged frequency of lethal events. *Journal of Experimental Psychology: Human Learning and Memory, 4,* 551–578.

Lister, P. (1992, July). A skeptics guide to psychics. *Redbook,* pp. 103–105, 112–113.

Little, L. W., & Greenberg, I. (1991) *Problem solving, critical thinking, and communication skills.* New York: Longman.

Lochhead, J. & Clement, J. (Eds.). (1979). *Cognitive process instruction: Research on teaching thinking skills.* Philadelphia: Franklin Institute Press.

Lockhart, R. S., Lamon, M., & Gick, M. L. (1988). Conceptual transfer in simple insight problems. *Memory and Cognition, 16,* 36–44.

Loftus, E. F. (1979). *Eyewitness testimony.* Cambridge, MA: Harvard University Press.

Loftus, E. F. (1980). *Memory: Surprising new insights into how we remember and why we forget.* Reading, MA: Addison-Wesley.

Loftus, E. F. (1993). The reality of repressed memories. *American Psychologist, 44,* 518–537.

Loftus, E. F., & Ketchum, K. (1994). *The myth of repressed memory: False memories and the accusations of sexual abuse.* New York: St. Martin's Press.

Loftus, G. R., & Loftus, E. F. (1982). *Essence of statistics.* Monterey, CA: Brooks/Cole.

The Long Term View. (1994, Summer). Has American education forsaken critical thinking? [Special issue]. (Vol. 2, No. 3). Andover: Massachusetts School of Law.

Lopes, L. L. (1982). Doing the impossible: A note on induction and the experience of randomness. *Journal of Experimental Psychology: Learning, Memory & Cognition, 8,* 626–636.

Lorayne, H. (1975). *Remembering people.* New York: Stein & Day.

Lorayne, H., & Lucas, J. (1974). *The memory book.* New York: Stein & Day. (Also published in paperback by Ballantine Books, 1975)

Lord, C., Ross, L., & Lepper, M. (1979). Biased assimilation and attitude polarization: The effects of prior theories on subsequently considered evidence. *Journal of Personality and Social Psychology, 37,* 2098–2109.

Lowenfeld, V. (1962). Creativity: Education's stepchild. In S. J. Parnes & H. F. Harding (Eds.), *A source book for creative thinking.* New York: Scribner's.

Luchins, A. S. (1942). Mechanization in problem solving: The effect of Einstellung. *Psychological Monographs, 54*(6, Whole No. 248).

Macmillan Publishers (1989). *Macmillan dictionary of quotations.* New York: Author.

Maier, N. R. F. (1931). Reasoning in humans II: The solution of a problem and its appearance in consciousness. *Journal of Comparative Psychology, 12,* 181–194.

Mann, L. (1972). Use of a "balance sheet" procedure to improve the quality of personal decision making: A field experiment with college applicants. *Journal of Vocational Behavior, 2,* 291–300.

Marsh, J. G., & Shapira, Z. (1982). Behavioral decision theory and organizational decision theory. In G. R. Ungson, & D. N. Braunstein (Eds.), *Decision making: An interdisciplinary inquiry.* Boston, MA: Kent.

Matlin, M. (1994). *Cognition* (3rd. ed.). Orlando, FL: Harcourt Brace.

Mayer, R. E. (1987). *Educational psychology A cognitive approach.* Boston: Little, Brown.

Mayer, R. E. (1992). Teaching of thinking skills in the sciences and mathematics. In D. F. Halpern (Ed.), *Enhancing thinking skills in the sciences and mathematics* (pp. 95–116). Hillsdale, NJ: Lawrence Erlbaum Associates.

McCormick, C. B., & Levin, J. R. (1987). Mnemonic prose-learning strategies. In M. A. McDaniel & M. Pressley (Eds.), *Imagery and related mnemonic processes* (pp. 392–406). New York: Springer-Verlag.

McGuire, W. J. (1981). The probabilogical model of cognitive structure and attitude change. In R. E. Petty, T. M. Ostrom, & T. C. Brock (Eds.), *Cognitive responses in persuasion.* Hillsdale, NJ: Lawrence Erlbaum Associates.

McKeachie, W. J. (1992). Update: Teaching thinking. In D. J. Stroup and R. Allen (Eds.), *Critical thinking: A collection of readings* (p. 3). Dubuque, IA: Brown.

McKim, R. H. (1980). *Thinking visually: A strategy manual for problem solving.* Belmont, CA: Wadsworth.

McKinnon, J. W., & Renner, J. W. (1971). Are colleges concerned with intellectual development? *American Journal of Psychology, 39,* 1047–1052.

McTighe, J. (1986). Thinking about adolescent thinking. *The early adolescence magazine, 1,* 7–13.

Mednick, S. A., & Mednick, M. T. (1967). *Remote associates test: Examiners manual.* Boston: Houghton Mifflin.

Meirovitz, M. (1985). *ThinkAbility.* Hillsdale, NJ: Lawrence Erlbaum Associates.

Merron, K., Fisher, D., & Torbert, W. R. (1987). Meaning making and management action. *Group & Organization Studies, 12,* 274–286.

Messer, W. S., & Griggs, R. A. (1989). Student belief and involvement in the paranormal and performance in introductory psychology. *Teaching of Psychology, 16*(4), 187–191.

Miller, J. E., Jr. (1972). *Words, self, reality: The rhetoric of imagination.* New York: Dodd, Mead.

Milne, A. A. (1926). *Winnie the Pooh.* New York: Dutton.

Moore, B. N., & Parker, R. (1994). *Critical thinking* (4th ed.). Mountain View, CA: Mayfield.

Morgan, J. J. B., & Morton, J. T. (1944). The distortion of syllogistic reasoning produced by personal convictions. *Journal of Social Psychology, 20,* 39–59.

Moss, J. (1950). *How to win at poker.* Garden City, NY: Garden City Books.

Mumford, M. D., & Gustafson, S. B. (1988). Creativity syndrome: Integration, application, and innovation. *Psychological Bulletin, 103,* 27–43.

Munby, H. (1982). *Science in the schools.* Toronto: University of Toronto.

Munson, R. (1976). *The way of words.* Boston: Houghton Mifflin.

Myers, D. G. (1995). *Psychology.* New York: Worth.

Mynatt, C. R., Doherty, M. E., & Tweney, R. D. (1978). Consequences of confirmation and disconfirmation in a simulated research environment. *Quarterly Journal of Experimental Psychology, 30,* 395–406.

Narode, R., Heiman, M., Lochhead, J., & Slomianko, J. (1987). *Teaching thinking skills: Science*. Washington, DC: National Education Association.

National Commission on Excellence in Education. (1983). *A nation at risk: The imperative for educational reform*. Washington, DC: Author.

National Education Goals Panel. (1991). *The national education goals report: Building a nation of learners*. Washington, DC: U.S. Government Printing Office.

National Research Council. (1994). *Learning, remembering, believing: Enhancing human performance*. Washington, DC: National Academy Press.

Neisser, U. (1982). *Memory observed: Remembering in natural contexts*. San Francisco: Freeman.

Nelson, T. O. (Ed.). (1992). *Metacognition: Core readings*. Boston: Allyn & Bacon.

Nelson, T. O., & Narens, L. (1990). Metamemory: A theoretical framework and new findings. *The psychology of learning and motivation, 26*, 125–141.

Neubert, G. A., & Binko, J. B. (1992). *Inductive reasoning in the secondary classroom*. Washington, DC: National Education Association.

Neustadt, R. E., & May, E. R. (1986). *Thinking in time: The uses of history for decision makers*. New York: The Free Press.

Newell, A. (1983). The heuristic of George Polya and its relation to artificial intelligence. In R. Groner, M. Groner, & W. F. Bischof (Eds.), *Methods of heuristics* (pp. 195–243). Hillsdale, NJ: Lawrence Erlbaum Associates.

Newell, A., & Simon, H. A. (1972). *Human problem solving*. Englewood Cliffs, NJ: Prentice-Hall.

Nickerson, R. S. (1986). *Reflections on reasoning*. Hillsdale, NJ: Lawrence Erlbaum Associates.

Nickerson, R. S., (1987). Why teach thinking? In J. B. Baron & R. J. Sternberg (Eds.), *Teaching thinking skills: Theory and practice* (pp. 27–37). New York: Freeman.

Nickerson, R. S., & Adams, M. J. (1979). Long-term memory for a common object. *Cognitive Psychology, 11*, 287–307.

The nightly crime news. (1994, March 21). *Newsweek*, p. 71.

Nisbett, R. E. (Ed.). (1993). *Rules for reasoning*. Hillsdale, NJ: Lawrence Erlbaum Associates.

Nisbett, R. E., & Ross, L. (1980). *Human inference: Strategies and shortcomings of social judgment*. Englewood Cliffs, NJ: Prentice-Hall.

Nisbett, R. E., & Wilson, T. D. (1977). Telling more than we can know: Verbal reports on mental processes. *Psychological Review, 7*, 231–259.

Nixon, R. M. (1962). *Six crises*. Garden City, NY: Doubleday.

Norman, D. A. (1976). *Memory and attention: An introduction to human information processing*. New York: Wiley.

Norman, D. A. (1988). *The psychology of everyday things*. New York: Basic Books.

Norris, S. P. (1992). Introduction: The generalizability question. In S. P. Norris (Ed.), *The generalizability of critical thinking* (pp. 1–15). New York: Teachers College Press.

Norris, S. P., & Ennis, R. H. (1989). *Evaluating critical thinking*. Pacific Grove, CA: Critical Thinking Press & Software.

Nutrition Action Health Letter. (1991, July/Aug). *Eater's Digest*, p. 13.

Oppenheimer, J. R. (1956). Analogy in science. *American Psychologist, 11*, 127–135.

Ortho Pharmaceutical Corp. (1979). *The pill—After your doctor prescribes*. ... Raritan, NJ: Author.

Orwell, G. (1949). *1984*. New York: Harcourt, Brace.

Osborn, A. F. (1963). *Applied imagination: Principles and procedures of creative problem solving* (3rd rev. ed.). New York: Scribner's.

Osgood, C. E. (1953). *Method and theory in experimental psychology*. New York: Oxford University Press.

Oskamp, S. (1965). Overconfidence in case-study judgments. *Journal of Consulting Psychology, 29*, 261–265.

Palincsar, A. S., & Brown, A. L. (1984). Reciprocal-teaching of comprehension-monitoring activities. *Cognition and Instruction, 1*, 117–175.

Papanek, V. J. (1977). Tree of life: Bionics. In S. J. Parnes, R. B. Noller, & A. M. Biondi (Eds.), *Guide to creative action: Revised edition of creative behavior guidebook*. New York: Scribner's.

Parducci, A. (1968). The relativism of absolute judgments. *Scientific American, 219*, 84–90.

Park, D. C. (1992). Applied cognitive aging research. In F. I. M. Craik, & T. A. Salthouse (Eds.), *The handbook of aging and cognition* (pp. 449–494). Hillsdale, NJ: Lawrence Erlbaum Associates.

Parnes, S. J. (1967). *Creative behavior workbook*. New York: Scribner's.

Parnes, S. J., Noller, R. B., & Biondi, A. M. (1977). *Guide to creative action: Revised edition of creative behavior guidebook*. New York: Scribner's.

Patterson, M. E., Dansereau, D. F., & Wiegmann, D. A. (1993). Receiving information during a cooperative episode: Effects of communication aids and verbal ability. *Learning and Individual differences, 5*, 1–11.

Paulos, J. A. (1994, March). Commentary: Counting on dyscalculia. *Discover*, p. 30–36.

Payne, J. W., Bettman, J. R., & Johnson, E. J. (1993). *The adaptive decision maker*, Cambridge, England: Cambridge University Press.

Pea, R. D., & Hawkins, J. (1987). Planning in a chore-scheduling task. In S. L. Friedman, E. K. Scholnick, & R. R. Cocking (Eds.), *Blueprints for thinking: The role of planning in cognitive development* (pp. 273–302). Cambridge, MA: Cambridge University Press.

Peck, J. (1986). Not killing is a crime? In B. Lown & E. Chazov (Eds.), *Peace: A dream unfolding* (p. 146). Ontario, Canada: Somerville House Books Ltd.

Pellegrino, J. W., & Goldman, S. R. (1983). Developmental and individual differences in verbal and spatial reasoning. In R. F. Dillon & R. R. Schmeck (Eds.), *Individual differences in cognition* (pp. 137–180). New York: Academic.

Perfetto, G. A., Bransford, J. D., & Franks, J. J. (1983). Constraints on access in a problem solving context. *Memory & Cognition, 11*, 24–31.

Perkins, D. N. (1981). *The mind's best work: A new psychology of creative thinking.* Cambridge, MA: Harvard University Press.

Perkins, D. N. (1985). Postprimary education has little impact on informal reasoning. *Journal of Educational Psychology, 77*, 562–571.

Perkins, D. N. (1986). *Knowledge as design.* Hillsdale, NJ: Lawrence Erlbaum Associates.

Perkins, D. N. (1988). Creativity and the quest for mechanism. In R. J. Sternberg & E. E. Smith (Eds.), *Psychology of human thought.* New York: Cambridge.

Perkins, D. N., Lochhead, J., & Bishop, J. C. (Eds.). (1987). *Thinking. The second international conference.* Hillsdale, NJ: Lawrence Erlbaum Associates.

Pestel, B. C. (1993). Teaching problem solving without modeling through "Thinking Aloud Pair Problem Solving." *Science Education, 77*(1), 83–94.

Phillips, H. (1961). *My best puzzles in logic and reasoning.* New York: Dover.

Piper, D. (1985). Syllogistic reasoning in varied narrative contexts: Aspects of logical and linguistic development. *Journal of Psycholinguistic Research, 14*, 19–43.

Pitt, J., & Leavenworth, R. (1968). *Logic for argument.* New York: Random House.

Plous, S. (1993). *The psychology of judgment and decision making.* New York: McGraw-Hill.

Pogrow, S. (1992). A validated approach to thinking development for at-risk populations. In C. Collins & J. N. Mangieri (Eds.), *Teaching thinking: An agenda for the 21st century* (pp. 87–101). Hillsdale, NJ: Lawrence Erlbaum Associates.

Poincare, H. (1929). *The foundations of science.* New York: Science House.

Polya, G. (1945). *How to solve it: A new aspect of mathematical method.* New York: Doubleday.

Polya, G. (1957). *How to solve it: A new aspect of mathematical method* (2nd ed.). Garden City, NY: Doubleday.

Polya, G. (1962). *Mathematical discovery* (Volume 1). New York: Wiley.

Posner, M. I. (1973). *Cognition: An introduction.* Glenview, IL: Scott, Foresman.

Postman, N., & Powers, S. (1992). *How to watch TV news.* New York: Penguin.

Potts, G. R. (1972). Information processing strategies used in the encoding of linear orderings. *Journal of Verbal Learning and Verbal Behavior, 11*, 727–740.

Powell, D. (1985). *The wisdom of the novel: A dictionary of quotations.* New York: Garland.

Pratkanis, A., & Aronson, E. (1992). *Age of propaganda: The everyday use and abuse of persuasion.* New York: Freeman.

Prince, G. M. (1970). *The practice of creativity.* New York: Harper.

Quattrone, G. A., & Jones, E. E. (1980). The perception of variability within in-groups and out-groups: Implications for the law of small numbers. *Journal of Personality and Social Psychology, 38*, 141–152.

Raia, E. (1994, June 2) Russian style. *Purchasing,* pp. 28–29.

RAND Corporation. (1992, Fall). Health care and the uninsured: Who will pay? *RAND Research Review, XVI*, 6–8.

Raphael, B. (1976). *The thinking computer: Mind inside matter.* San Francisco: Freeman.

Renshon, S. A. (1992). The psychology of good judgment: A preliminary model with some applications to the Gulf War. *Political Psychology, 13*, 477–495.

Resnick, L. B. (1985). Cognition and instruction. In B. L. Hammonds (Ed.), *Psychology and learning: The master lecture series* (pp. 127–186). Washington, DC: American Psychological Association.

Restak, R. M. (1988). *The mind.* Toronto: Bantam.

Reyes, R. M., Thompson, W. C., & Bower, G. H. (1980). Judgmental biases resulting from differing availabilities of arguments. *Journal of Personality and Social Psychology, 39*, 2–12.

Rips, L. J. (1988). Deduction. In R. J. Sternberg & E. E. Smith (Eds.), *The psychology of human thought.* (pp. 116–152). New York: Cambridge University Press.

Roediger, H. L. III (1990). Implicit memory: Retention without remembering. *American Psychologist, 45*, 1043–1056.

Rokeach, M. (1960). *The open and closed mind.* New York: Basic Books.

Rosch, E. (1977). Human categorization. In N. Warren (Ed.), *Studies in cross-cultural psychology (Vol. 1).* New York: Academic Press.

Rosenthal, R., & Fode, K. L. (1963). The effect of experimental bias on the performance of the albino rat. *Behavioral Science, 8*, 183–187.

Ross, J., & Laurence, K. A. (1968). Some observations on memory artifice. *Psychonomic Science, 13*, 107–108.

Rothenberg, A. (1979). *The emerging goddess.* Chicago: University of Chicago Press.

Rubinstein, J., & Slife, B. D. (1982). *Taking sides: Clashing views on controversial psychological issues.* Guilford, CT: Dushkin.

Rubinstein, M. F. (1975). *Patterns of problem solving.* Englewood Cliffs, NJ: Prentice-Hall.

Rubinstein, M. F. (1980). A decade of experience in teaching an interdisciplinary problem-solving course. In D. J. Tuma & F. Reif (Eds.), *Problem solving and education: Issues in teaching and research.* Hillsdale, NJ: Lawrence Erlbaum Associates.

Rubinstein, M. F., & Pfeiffer, K. R. (1980). *Concepts in problem solving.* Englewood Cliffs, NJ: Prentice-Hall.

Ruggiero, V. R. (1995). *Beyond feelings: A guide to critical thinking* (4th ed.). Mountain View, CA: Mayfield.

Sadler, W. A., Jr., & Whimbey, A. (November, 1985). A holistic approach to improving thinking skills. *Phi Delta Kappan, 67,* 199–202.

Sapir, E. (1960). *Culture, language and personality.* Berkeley: University of California Press.

Schafly, P. (1993, July 21). A mental health care nightmare. *The Washington Times,* (p. G4).

Schank, R. C., & Childers, R. C. (1988). *The creative attitude: Learning to ask and answer the right questions.* New York: Macmillan.

Schauble, L., & Glaser, R. (1990). Scientific thinking in children and adults. In D. Kuhn (Series Ed., Vol. Ed), *Contributions to Human Development: Vol. 21. Devlopmental perspectives on teaching and learning thinking skills* (pp. 9–27). New York: Basel, Karger.

Schick, T., Jr., & Vaughn, L. (1995). *How to think about weird things.* Mountain View, CA: Mayfield.

Schoenfeld, A. H. (1979). Can heuristics be taught? In J. Lochhead & J. Clement (Eds.), *Cognitive process instruction: Research on teaching skills.* Philadelphia: Franklin Institute Press.

Schoenfeld, A. H. (1985). *Mathematical problem solving.* New York: Academic Press.

Schoenfeld, A. H., & Herrmann, D. J. (1982). Problem perception and knowledge structure in expert and novice mathematical problem solvers. *Journal of Experimental Psychology: Learning, Memory, and Cognition, 8,* 484–494.

Scholnick, E. K., & Friedman, S. L. (1987). The planning construct in the psychological literature. In S. L. Friedman, E. K. Scholnick, & R. R. Cocking (Eds.), *Blueprints for thinking: The role of planning in cognitive development* (pp. 3–38). Cambridge, MA: Cambridge University Press.

Scriven, M. (1976). *Reasoning.* New York: McGraw-Hill.

Searleman, A., & Herrmann, D. (1994). *Memory from a broader perspective.* New York: McGraw-Hill.

Sears, A., & Parsons, J. (1991). Towards critical thinking as an ethic. *Theory and Research in Social Education, 19*(1), 45–68.

Seech, Z. (1993). *Open minds and everyday reasoning.* Belmont, CA: Wadsworth.

Segal, J. W., Chipman, S. F., & Glaser, R. (Eds.). (1985). *Thinking and learning skills: Vol. 1. Relating instruction to research.* Hillsdale, NJ: Lawrence Erlbaum Associates.

Seligman, M. (1991). *Learned optimism.* New York: Knopf.

Shaklee, H. (1987, November). *Estimating cumulative risk: Flood and contraceptive failure.* Paper presented at the Twenty-Eighth Annual Meeting of the Psychonomic Society, Seattle, WA.

Shanteau, J., Grier, M., Johnson, J., & Berner, E. (1991). Teaching decision-making skills to student nurses. In J. Baron & R. V. Brown (Eds.), *Teaching decision making to adolescents* (pp. 185–206). Hillsdale, NJ: Lawrence Erlbaum Associates.

Shaver, K. G. (1981). *Principles of social psychology.* Cambridge, MA: Winthrop.

Shaw, G. A., & de Mers, S. T. (1986–1987). Relationships between imagery and creativity in high-IQ children. *Imagination, Cognition & Personality, 6*(3), 247–262.

Shermer, M. (1992). Anecdotes do not make a science: The skeptics reply. *Skeptic, 1,* 18–19.

Shubik, M. (1971). The dollar auction game: A paradox in noncooperative behavior and escalation. *Journal of Conflict Resolution, 15,* 109–111.

Siegel, E. (1991, May). Persuasion and decision-making. *APS Observer,* p. 8.

Simon, H. A. (1977). The psychology of scientific problem solving. In H. A. Simon (Ed.), *Models of discovery.* Dordrecht, Netherlands: D. Reidel.

Simon, H. A., & Kaplan, C. A. (1989). In M. I. Posner (Ed.), *Foundations of cognitive sciences* (pp. 1–47). Cambridge, MA: MIT Press.

Simonson, I., Nowlis, S. M., & Simonson, Y. (1993). The effect of irrelevant preference arguments on consumer choice. *Journal of Consumer Psychology, 2,* 287–306.

Singer, B., & Benassi, V. A. (1981). Occult beliefs. *American Scientist, 69,* 49–55.

Sinnott, J. D. (Ed.). (1989). *Everyday problem solving: Theory and applications.* New York: Praeger.

Skeptic. (1995). Race and IQ. 3.

Slovic, P. (1987). Perception of risk. *Science, 236,* 280–285.

Slovic, P., Fischhoff, & Lichtenstein, S. (1986). In H. Arkes & K. R. Hammond (Eds.), *Judgment and decision making: An interdisciplinary reader.* Cambridge, MA: Cambridge University Press.

Smedslund, J. (1963). The concept of correlation in adults. *Scandinavian Journal of Psychology, 44,* 165–173.

Smith, L. (1992, June 2). Rick's place revisited. *The Los Angeles Times,* p. A1.

Smith, M. U. (1992). Expertise and the organization of knowledge: Unexpected differences among genetic counselors faculty, and students on problem categorization tasks. *Journal of Research in Science Teaching, 29*(2), 179–205.

Smith, M. U. (1988). Successful and unsuccessful problem solving in classical genetic pedigrees. *Journal of Research in Science Teaching, 25*(6), 411–433.

Smith, R. A. (1995). *Challenging your perceptions: Thinking critically about psychology.* Pacific Grove, CA: Brooks/Cole.

Smith, S. M., & Blankenship, S. E. (1991). Incubation and the persistence of fixation in problem solving. *American Journal of Psychology, 104*(1), 61–87.

Snow, R. E. (1986). Individual differences and the design of educational programs. *American Psychologist, 41,* 1029–1034.

Snyder, M., & Uranowitz, S. W. (1978). Reconstructing the past: Some cognitive consequences of person perception. *Journal of Personality and Social Psychology, 36*, 941–950.

Solorzano, L. (1985, January 14). Think! Now schools are teaching how. *U.S. News & World Report.*

Sorensen, T. C. (1965). *Kennedy.* New York: Harper & Row.

Sparke, W., Taines, B., & Sidell, S. (1975). *Doublespeak: Language for sale.* New York: Harper's College Press.

Spirer, L., & Spirer, L. (1994). *Data analysis for monitoring human rights.* Annapolis Junction, MD: AAAS Distrubution Center.

Stahl, N. N., & Stahl, R. J. (1991). We can agree after all! Achieving consensus for a critical thinking component of a gifted program using the Delphi Technique. *Roeper Review, 14*(2), 79–88.

Stanovich, K. E. (1992). *How to think straight about psychology* (3nd ed.). New York: HarperCollins.

Steen, L. A. (1987). Mathematics education: A predictor of scientific competitiveness. *Science, 237*, 251–252.

Stein, M. I. (1974). *Stimulating creativity: Individual procedures* (Vol. I). New York: Academic Press.

Stein, M. I. (1975). *Stimulating creativity: Group procedures* (Vol. II). New York: Academic Press.

Sternberg, R. J. (1977). Component processes in analogical reasoning. *Psychological Review, 84*, 353–373.

Sternberg, R. J. (1981). Intelligence and nonentrenchment. *Journal of Educational Psychology, 73*, 1–16.

Sternberg, R. J. (1982). Who's intelligent? *Psychology Today, 16*, 30–33, 35–39.

Sternberg, R. J. (1985). Instrumental and componential approaches to the nature and training of intelligence. In S. F. Chipman, J. W. Segal, & R. Glaser (Eds.), *Thinking and learning skills: Vol. 2. Research and open questions.* Hillsdale, NJ: Lawrence Erlbaum Associates.

Sternberg, R. J. (1986). *Intelligence applied: Understanding and increasing your intellectual skills.* New York: Harcourt Brace.

Sternberg, R. J. (Ed.). (1988). *The nature of creativity.* New York: Cambridge University Press.

Sternberg, R. J., & Frensch, P. A. (Eds.). (1991). *Complex problem solving: Principles and mechanisms.* Hillsdale, NJ: Lawrence Erlbaum Associates.

Sternberg, R. J., & Lubart, T. (1995). *Defying the crowd: Cultivating creativity in a culture of conformity.* New York: The Free Press.

Sternberg, R. J., & Smith, E. E. (1988). (Eds.). *The psychology of human thought.* New York: Cambridge University Press.

Sternberg, R. J. & Wagner, R. K. (Eds.). (1986). *Practical intelligence: Nature and origins of competence in the everyday world.* New York: Cambridge University Press.

Sternberg, R. J., & Weil, E. M. (1980). An aptitude-strategy interaction in linear syllogistic reasoning. *Journal of Educational Psychology, 72*, 226–234.

Stewart, J. K. (1985). From the director. *National Institute of Justice: Research in brief.* Washington, DC: U.S. Department of Justice.

Stroup, D. J., & Allen, R. D. (Eds.). (1992). *Critical thinking: A collection of readings.* Dubuque, IA: Brown.

Summers, G. J. (1968). *New puzzles in logical deduction.* New York: Dover.

Summers, G. J. (1972). *Test your logic: 50 puzzles in deductive reasoning.* New York: Dover.

Swartz, R. J., & Parks, S. (1994). *Infusing the teaching of critical and creative thinking into elementary instruction.* Pacific Grove, CA: Critical Thinking Press.

Taplin, J. E., & Staudenmayer, H. (1973). Interpretation of abstract conditional sentences in deductive reasoning. *Journal of Verbal Learning and Verbal Behavior, 12*, 530–542.

Tardif, T. Z., & Sternberg, R. J. (1988). What do we know about creativity? In R. J. Sternberg (Ed.), *The nature of creativity: Contemporary psychological perspectives* (pp 429–440). New York: Cambridge University Press.

Teger, A. I. (1979). *Too much invested to quit: The psychology of escalation of conflict.* New York: Pergamon.

Tetlock, P. E. (1994). The psychology of futurology and the future of psychology. *Psychological Science, 5*, 1–4.

Thomas, S. N. (1986). *Practical reasoning in natural language* (3rd ed.). Englewood Cliffs, NJ: Prentice-Hall.

Thouless, R. H. (1932). *Straight and crooked thinking.* New York: Simon & Schuster.

Thouless, R. H. (1939). *Tests of logical reasoning: How to think straight.* New York: Simon & Schuster.

Tinzman, M., Jones, B. F., & Pierce, J. (1992). Changing societal needs: Changing how we think about curriculum and instruction. In C. Collins and J. N. Mangeri (Eds.), *Teaching thinking: An agenda for the 21st century* (pp. 185–220). Hillsdale, NJ: Lawrence Erlbaum Associates.

Toulmin, S., Rieke, R., & Janik, A. (1979). *An introduction to reasoning.* New York: Macmillan.

Tulving, E. (1972). Episodic and semantic memory. In E. Tulving & W. Donaldson (Eds.), *Organization of memory.* NY: Academic Press.

Tuma, D. J., & Reif, F. (Eds.). (1980). *Problem solving and education: Issues in teaching and research.* Hillsdale, NJ: Lawrence Erlbaum Associates.

Turing, A. (1950). Computing machinery and intelligence. *Mind, 59*, 433–460.

Tutu, D. (1986). How to eat an elephant. In B. Lown & E. Chazov (Eds.), *Peace: A dream unfolding* (p. 216). Ontario: Somerville House Books Ltd.

Tversky, A. (1972). Elimination by aspects. A theory of choice. *Psychological Review, 79*, 281–299.

Tversky, A., & Kahneman, D. (1971). Belief in the law of small numbers. *Psychological Bulletin, 76*, 104–110.

Tversky, A., & Kahneman, D. (1974). Judgment under uncertainty: Heuristics and biases. *Science, 185*, 1124–1131.

TV linked to memory, radio to imagination. (1988, July 25). *The Los Angeles Times*, Part II, p. 3

Tversky, A., & Kahneman, D. (1981). The framing of decisions and the psychology of choice. *Science, 211*, 453–458.

Tversky, A., & Kahneman, D. (1983). Extensional versus intuitive reasoning: The conjunction fallacy in probability judgment. *Psychological Review, 90,* 293–315.

Vancouver Community Business Directory. (1987). *Pink Pages.* Advertising, Ltd.

Van Haneghan, J., Barron, L., Young, M., Williams, S., Vye, N., & Bransford, J. (1992). The Jasper series: An experiment with new ways to enhance mathematical thinking. In D. F. Halpern (Ed.), *Enhancing thinking skills in the sciences and mathematics* (pp. 15–38). Hillsdale, NJ: Lawrence Erlbaum Associates.

VanLehn, K. (1989). Problem solving and cognitive skill acquisition. In M. Posner (Ed.), *The foundations of cognitive science* (pp. 527–580). Cambridge, MA: MIT Press.

Vaughan, J. L. (1984). Concept structuring: The technique and empirical evidence. In C. D. Holley & D. F. Dansereau (Eds.), *Spatial learning strategies: Techniques, applications, and related issues* (pp. 127–147). New York: Academic Press.

Vernon, P. (1970). *Creativity: Selected readings.* Harmondsworth, England: Penguin.

von Oech, R. (1983). *A whack on the side of the head.* New York: Warner Books.

Vosniadou, S., & Orotony, A. (Eds.). (1989). *Similarity and analogical reasoning.* Cambridge, England: Cambridge University Press.

Walberg, F. (1980). *Puzzle thinking.* Philadelphia: Franklin Institute Press.

Wales, C. E., & Nardi, A. (1984). *Successful Decision-Making.* Morgantown, WV: Center for Guided Design.

Wallas, G. (1926). *The art of thought.* New York: Harcourt Brace.

Walsh, J. (1981). A plenipotentiary for human intelligence. *Science, 214,* 640–641.

Wandersman, A. H., & Hallman, W. K. (1993). Are people acting irrationally? Understanding public concerns about environmental threats. *American Psychologist, 48,* 681–686.

Wang, P. (1994, October). How to retire with twice as much money. *Money,* pp. 77–84.

Wanous, J. P. (1973). Effects of a realistic job preview on job acceptance, job attitudes, and job survival. *Journal of Applied Psychology, 58,* 327–332.

Wason, P. C. (1960). On the failure to eliminate hypotheses in a conceptual task. *Quarterly Journal of Experimental Psychology, 12,* 129–140.

Wason, P. C. (1968). On the failure to eliminate hypotheses: A second look. In P. C. Wason & P. N. Johnson-Laird (Eds.), *Thinking and reasoning.* Baltimore: Penguin.

Wason, P. C. (1969). Structure simplicity and psychological complexity. *Bulletin of the British Psychological Society, 22,* 281–284.

Wason, P. C., & Johnson-Laird, P. N. (Eds.). (1968). *Thinking and reasoning.* Harmondsworth, England: Penguin.

Wason, P. C., & Johnson-Laird, P. N. (1972). *Psychology of reasoning.* Cambridge, MA: Harvard University Press.

Weber, R. J., & Perkins, D. N. (Eds.). (1992). *Inventive minds: Creativity in technology.* New York: Oxford University Press.

Weisberg, R. W. (1988). Problem solving and creativity. In R. J. Sternberg (Ed.), *The nature of creativity: Contemporary psychological perspectives* (pp. 148–177). New York: Cambridge University Press.

Weisberg, R. W. (1993). *Creativity: Beyond the myth of genius.* New York: Freeman.

Weisberg, R., DiCamillo, M., & Phillips, D. (1978). Transferring old associations to new situations: A nonautomatic process. *Journal of Verbal Learning and Verbal Behavior, 17,* 219–228.

Wertheimer, M. (1959). *Productive thinking* (2nd Ed.). New York: Harper.

Wheeler, D. D., & Janis, I. L. (1980). *A practical guide for making decisions.* New York: The Free Press.

Wheeler, D. L. (1994, March 16). *Chronicle of Higher Education,* pp. A41–A43.

Whimbey, A. (1976). *Intelligence can be taught.* New York: Bantam.

Whimbey, A., & Lochhead, J. (1982). *Problem solving and comprehension: A short course in analytic reasoning.* Philadelphia: Franklin Institute Press.

Whitehead, A. N., & Russell, B. (1927). *Principa mathematica* (2nd. ed.). New York: Cambridge University Press.

Whiting, C. S. (1958). *Creative thinking.* New York: Reinhold.

Whorf, B. (1956). *Language, thought, and reality.* Cambridge, MA: MIT Press.

Wickelgren, W. (1974). *How to solve problems.* San Francisco: Freeman.

Wicker, A. W. (1981). *Getting out of our conceptual ruts: Strategies for generating new perspectives on familiar research problems.* Paper presented at the 1981 annual convention of the Western Psychological Association, Los Angeles.

Wilson, R., & Crouch, E. A. C. (1987). Risk assessment and comparisons: An introduction. *Science, 286,* 267–270.

Wilson, T. D., & Nisbett, R. E. (1978). The accuracy of verbal reports about the effects of stimuli on evaluations and behavior. *Social Psychology, 41,* 118–131.

Wright, G., & Bolger, F. (1992). *Expertise and decision support.* New York: Plenum.

Yates, J. F. (1990). *Judgment and decision making.* Englewood Cliffs, NJ: Prentice-Hall.

Zimbardo, P. G., & Leippe, M. R. (1991). *The psychology of attitude change and social influence.* New York: McGraw-Hill.

Author Index

Subject Index

Numbers in **bold** indicate pages with definitions from the end of chapters.

first letters, 65–66
keywords and images, 62–64
methods of places, 64–65
overview, 61–62
principles, 66–67
remembering events, 67–68
rhymes, 64
Model manipulation, problem solving, 338–340
Modeling techniques, thought protocol analysis, 18–19
Mood, syllogistic reasoning, 137, 138–140, 151–154, **165**, *see also* Reasoning
Motivation, performance testing, 24
Motor memory, acquisition, 41, **71**
Motor skills, memory comparison with history, 40
Mr. Spock, rational thought, 20
Multiple intelligences, concept, 17
Multiple outcomes, computing probabilities, 251–255, **278**
Multiple-choice tests
answer selection and probabilities, 254–255
thinking skills programs, 9
Mutually exclusive outcomes, probabilities, 252

N

Name calling, meaning effect on readers and listeners, 93
Names of people, attention and recall, 44
National Education Goals Panel, goals for college graduates, 3
Natural language
arguments, 169, 171–172
syllogistic reasoning, 153–154
Negation, **116**
framing of responses, 98
if, then statements, 130–131
terms in linear ordering, 124–125
Negative correlation, hypothesis testing, 226–227, **239**
Nerds, characterization, 20
Networks, **117**, *see also* Language
comprehension, 106–109
learning writing, 113
New information, presenting to listeners, 80–81, *see also* Information; Language
News media, distinguishing between opinion, fact, and reasoned judgment, 202
Nine-dot problem, solving, 355–356, 357, *see also* Problem solving
Nodes, if, then statements, 127
Noncognitive factors, awareness, 50–51
Nonconformity, creativity, 379
Nondirected thinking, daily routinized habits, 6, **34**
Nonregressive judgments, probability, 268–269
Novel tasks, approach and intelligence, 22

O

Objective criteria, decision making, 285
Objective probability, estimates of likelihood, 260, 264, **279**
Obligation schemata, if, then statements, 133–135, **164**, *see also* Reasoning

Observations, hypothesis testing, 214–215
Occult beliefs, hypothesis testing, 233–234
Odds, probabilities, 245, *see also* Games of chance
Operating principles, memory, 40
Operational definition, hypothesis testing, 215–216, **238**
Opinion
distinguishing among reasoned judgment and fact, 201–203
individual right, 6–7
Optimism, decision making, 295
Optimization, decision making, 302, **315**
"Or" rule, probabilities, 252, 257
Oral contraceptives, probabilities, 248
Organization, memory, 48–49
Outcomes, probabilities, 243
Overall assessment, decision-making worksheets, 306–307, **315**
Overconfidence, **278, 314**
decision making, 290–291, 299
probabilities, 246–247
remembering, 53, 55
Overestimating, probability, 266, 270
Overlearning, **116**
comprehension, 103
recall, 50

P

Paired-associate learning, problem solving, 348
Paper and pencil
maze solving, 342
problem solving, 328
Paraphrase, comprehension, 102, **116**
Particular affirmative, mood in syllogistic reasoning, 137, 139–141, 145, 151–154, **165**, *see also* Reasoning
Particular negative, mood in syllogistic reasoning, 137, 139–140, 151–154, **165**, *see also* Reasoning
Part–whole, fallacies in arguments, 198
Pearl Harbor, assessing consequences, 300, *see also* Decision making
Penny, paying attention to details, 45
Perceptions of risk, 270–271
personal vs. scientific, 272
Perceptual reorganization, problem solving, 323, **361**
Perfect relationship, probability, 268
Performance-competence, distinction, 25–28, *see also* Thinking
Performance components, Triarchic Theory of Intelligence, 25
Performance test items, Wechsler Adult Intelligence Test, 23, 24
Permission schemata, if, then statements, 133–135, **164**, *see also* Reasoning
Persistence
critical thinking, 26
problem solving, 322–323
Personal analogy, problem solving, 353, **362**
Personal beliefs, logical/illogical conclusions, 120–121, 122, *see also* Reasoning
Personal bias, textbooks, 202

Retention interval, recall association, 40, 41, **71**, *see also* Memory
Retrieval, *see also* Memory
    cues, 56–57, 66
    definition, 71
    forgetting, 54–55
    generation of multiple cues, 49–50
    recalling errors, 55–56
    thinking and forgetting, 55
Retrieval goal, memory, 69, **72**
Retrospective research, hypothesis testing, 225, **239**
Retrospective review, decisions, 311
Reviewing, comprehension, 103
Rhymes, mnemonic device, 64
Risk
    assessment methods, 271
    creativity, 378, 379
    perceptions, memory relation, 37–38
    probability, 269–271
Risk averse, situation and rejection, 97, **116**, *see also* Language
Risk per hour metric, risk assessment, 272
Robust effect, if, then statements, 132, *see also* Reasoning
Rorschach test, validity, 230
Roulette, probabilities, 250–251
Rubrik's cube, problem solving, 320
Rules, **362**
    constraints on problems, 319
    problem solving, 347–348

S

Sample, **238, 279**
    hypothesis testing, 217–220
    statistics, 273
Sample size, hypothesis testing, 219–220, **238, 279**
Sapir–Whorf hypothesis, language–thought relationships, 91, **116**
Satisficing, decision-making worksheets, 308, **315**
Scapegoating, propaganda, 191
Schemata, internal representations, 5, **33**, *see also* Thinking
Search
    creativity, 374
    decision making, 286
Secondary information, probability, 264, 267, *see also* Information
Segments, thought protocol analysis, 18
Selective forgetting, incubation stage of problem solving, 321
Self-correction, willingness and critical thinking, 26
Self-fulfilling prophecies, hypothesis testing, 232–233, **239**
Self-motivation, creativity, 379
Self-reflective tasks, monitoring remembering, 60–61
Semantic memory, acquisition, 41, **71**
Semantic slanting, emotional response, 93, **116**
Sensitive measures, **239**
Sensitivity, creativity, 368, **391**
Serendipity, creativity, 369–370, **391**
Set theory, Venn diagrams, 138
Settings, cigarette advertising, 7

Sex role stereotypes, errors in memory, 52, *see also* Stereotypes
Short-range goals, decision making, 302
Significant difference, statistics, 275, **279**
Silent speech, thinking as, 12–17
Simplification, problem solving, 343–346, **361**
Skeletonal form, argument, 176, 177, 182
Sleep, lack of and ability to learn, 50
Sleep learning, no evidence to support claims, 11
Slippery slope, fallacies in arguments, 197–198, **210**
Slips of the tongue, retrieval of information, 55, *see also* Memory
Slops, biased sampling, 218
Smoking
    thinking critically about, 7
    variability and hypothesis testing, 220
Solution paths, **361**
    anatomy of a problem, 319, 320
    ill-defined problems, 324, 334
    random search and problem solving, 347
Sophomore slump, sports, 268
Sound argument, criteria, 185–186, **209**
Spare tire, problem solving, 318, 319–320
Spatial methods
    comprehension, 104–106, 113
    decision making, 266, 267
    linear ordering, 124, 125
    risk situations, 248
    syllogistic reasoning, 138–150
Specialist, defining, 87
Specialization, problem solving, 346–347, **362**
Specialized terms, communication between professionals, 15, *see also* Thinking
Speed, performance testing, 24
Spin masters, political debates, 20
Split-half method, problem solving, 349–350, **362**
Spontaneous transfer, thinking skills programs, 10
Spread of activation, creativity, 374
SQ3R, comprehension, 102, **116**, *see also* Language
Standardized tests of intelligence, thinking skills programs, 9, *see also* Intelligence; Thinking
Stanford–Binet test, measuring intelligence, 23, *see also* Intelligence; Thinking
Start point, if, then statements, 127, *see also* Reasoning
Stated assumptions, arguments, 172
Statement, argument, 174, **209**
Statistical information, assessing, 248
Statistical training, probabilities, 242–243
Statistics, use and abuse, 273–276, **279**, *see also* Probability
Stereotypes
    availability heuristics, 293
    biases in memory, 68
    categorization, 88
    illusory correlations, 228
    law of small numbers, 221
    negative, 20
    retention, 51–53
Strategies
    comprehension
        flow charts, 111–112
        graphic organizers, 103–106